15.80

# A COMPANION TO THE
# ROYAL NAVY

# A COMPANION TO THE
# ROYAL NAVY

## DAVID A. THOMAS

LONDON

*First published in Great Britain* 1988
by HARRAP LIMITED
19-23 Ludgate Hill, London EC4M 7PD

ISBN 0 245-54572-7

Designed by Michael R. Carter

Type set in Palatino by
The Design Team,
Ascot, Berkshire.

Printed and Bound by
Richard Clay Limited
Chichester, Surrey

# CONTENTS

# ILLUSTRATIONS

**SECTION III**

# MAPS

# ACKNOWLEDGMENTS

A Companion such as this can only be compiled with the help of a great number of people who were generous with their patience and time in answering a multitude of questions over a long period. I am indebted to them all, and am pleased to acknowledge their contribution. Others kindly pointed the direction for further research and suggested improvements; to them too I record my gratitude. But I readily declare my own responsibility for the selections I have made and for my errors of omission or commission.

Expressions of gratitude are due in full measure to the staff of the Naval Historical Library, Ministry of Defence, and in particular I mention David Ashby and Alan Francis: they were specially tolerant and helpful over a very long period in providing the mass of information relating to ships' names, histories and badges, and to naval battles; and in steering a course through the rough waters of battle honours.

Similar thanks are due to the managing director at HM Dock Yard, Devonport, and still more specifically to his cheerful and helpful staff, for information regarding ships' badges. Particular thanks are due to Dominic Frost for the excellence of his drawings of badges, which make a significant contribution to Section 2.

To the Trustees and in particular the staff of the Reading Room at the National Maritime Museum at Greenwich must go my personal thanks for their customary professional help; also to other members of staff from other Rooms and Sections, including the Photographic department.

The staff of several libraries are deserving of thanks; the British Library and the Cambridge University Library reaped a rich harvest of information; the staffs of the reference sections of several Essex libraries — Chelmsford and Harlow, particularly — gave unstinting help as did the staff at Redbridge, Ilford.

The splendid track charts in Section 4 are reproduced by kind permission of the artist Helmut Pemsel and Messrs Arms and Armour Press.

Other acknowledgments to authors and publishers where relevant are made in each Section of the Companion. Every effort has been made to trace copyright-holders, but one or two have slipped the net: any omissions will be gladly rectified in future editions. In Section 1 I specifically commend the scholarship and style of Dr N. A. M. Rodger's *The Admiralty* (1979) whose work I found indispensable.

Finally I record my gratitude for the guidance of my publisher, Derek Johns; for the meticulous care of my editor, Roy Minton, who deserves a dedication from Horace for his work on this Companion: *Exegi monumentum aere perennius* — I have set up a monument more enduring than brass.

**Picture credits**

I am grateful to BBC Hulton Picture Library for supplying the pictures of Robert Dundas, George Eden, John Poyntz and Reginald McKenna. All the other illustrations are by courtesy of the National Maritime Museum with the exception of HMS *Resolution* and *Invincible* which were kindly supplied by Vickers Shipbuilding & Engineering Co Ltd. Gieves & Hawkes Ltd provided the officer's cap badge reproduced on the front cover.

# INTRODUCTION

This Companion tells the story of the Royal Navy in a unique way. The cross-reference feature of the Sections enables the reader to follow the fortunes of individual ships throughout four centuries of naval history. Almost every modern ship of any significance or size in living memory is included, and her ancestry can be traced. Each Section is compiled carefully to present as concisely yet as comprehensively as possible within the limitations of space stories of the ships of the Royal Navy, their battles and battle honours.

The honour of founding the Royal Navy has known many claimants. Historians have dubbed King Alfred 'Father of the Navy' for his first seaborne engagement in the Stour estuary in 882. Alfred's grandson Edgar, and Edward the Confessor (1004−66), founder of Westminster Abbey as well as of the ancient maritime institution of the Confederation of the Cinque Ports, have their supporters. Even Richard I set some basic disciplines for the proper maintenance of the fleet in 1190; and though he was better known for his crusading, it was he who also laid the foundations of the port and dockyard of Portsmouth.

Early in the thirteenth century the much maligned King John commandeered ships for his use: 'We command you ... to hasten immediately on receipt of these letters without let or delay to the ports of Southampton, Kilhaven, Christchurch and Yarmouth ... and detail all vessels fit for passage ...' In the brief span of three years he had more than fifty ships built, a new mole constructed at Portsmouth, new warehouses for stowing ships' tackle and stores. Oars were ordered by the thousands, and cloth for sails by the thousand ells. By 1212 Britannia was beginning to rule the waves.

Edward III was a colossus among sovereigns. He became known as 'King of the Seas' for the victory his longbowmen gave him at the battle of Sluys in 1340. But his ships were mainly commandeered merchant vessels with fore- and after-castles rapidly erected to give the bowmen their advantage.

It is the Tudor age which contributed much to the foundation of the Royal Navy, and credit is due in some measure to Henry VII, but it was his son, Henry VIII, who won the title 'Father of the English Navy'. Certainly he emerges as a leading claimant: he had ships of a new design built, with improved seaworthiness and armaments. He established an Office of Admiralty, with a Navy Office, introduced rates of pay, encouraged recruitment and deserves credit for setting up the administrative machinery of control of a fleet. Henceforward England was to produce eminent naval officers in a never-ending stream. Henry's daughter, Elizabeth I, reaped the harvest; Drake, Raleigh,

Howard, Grenville, Hawkins, Frobisher all mastered the maritime scene and set the seal on their superiority in the Armada campaign.

The Navy's fortunes declined in the early Stuart period, reaching its nadir about 1620. By the Interregnum such generals-at-sea as Robert Blake, George Monck and William Penn began to re-establish some command of the sea. However, it was with the restoration of Charles II that a claim to have founded the Royal Navy finds most support, for it was Charles who granted the Royal prefix in 1660.

He had returned to the throne of England to the enthusiasm of the general populace and the relief of naval commanders who were prompt in expressing their support of the monarchy. Monck, Penn, Lawson, Montagu pledged their services and Charles dispensed his privileges and kingly rewards. Three individuals emerged to play a prominent part in the restoration of the Navy's fortunes: firstly came the zealous Duke of York, brother of the King, with the newly reinstated rank of Lord High Admiral;[1] secondly came Sir William Penn, on whose discretion and broad experience James was to draw heavily; third of the trio came the enterprising and devoted administrator Samuel Pepys.

It was in 1661 that the Naval Discipline Act which established the foundation of the Royal Navy by permanent Statute bore the splendid preamble: 'His Majesty's Navies, ships of War, and forces by Sea, wherein under the good Providence and Protection of God, the Wealth, Safety and Strength of this Kingdom is so much concerned.'[2] In 1749 the Act received minor amendments, and in 1866 the phrase was modified to '... wealth, safety and strength of the kingdom chiefly depend'. In 1955 the Naval Discipline Act diluted this to '...wealth, safety and strength of the kingdom so much depend'. The significance, of course, is that the phrase, with only a change in emphasis, has survived in essence for more than 570 years.

It may seem a discordant note to the purists, therefore, to read in this Companion about the Armada (1588), Cadiz (1596), Kentish Knock (1652) and Santa Cruz (1657); to read of Drake, Howard and Frobisher; for none of these, be they battles or seamen, represented a Navy that was Royal or even British: simply English. For the dates all preceded 1660.

But even the Admiralty has displayed an inconsistency here. Royal Navy battle honours, judiciously defined and awarded by an Admiralty Committee, predate the 1660 datum line to include these very battles and implicitly the seamen as far back as the Armada. This Companion sensibly conforms by following in the wake.

The battle honours recorded here will find a useful cross-reference to descriptions of the battles themselves, though most single-ship actions and most campaigns cannot be covered because of space considerations.

The bibliography of the Royal Navy is vast. Rather than presenting a comprehensive, general bibliography of only moderate worth, care has been taken to provide a balanced section of titles as follows: Section 1 dealing with the Admiralty has its own bibliography. Section 2 contains references to sources only. Section 3 covering Battles has a Further Reading listing. Sections 4 and 5 are not thought to require a bibliograph

Section 5, on chronology, has been included in order to set all the above

1  James had borne the title since he was a child, but Charles II bestowed the title afresh upon his younger brother on 21 May 1660.

2  The Commons in 1415 had first expressed this view: *'La dit Naveye est la griendre substance du bien, profit et prosperitée du vostre dit Rioalme.'*

information into its proper time scale: events need a datum point or line, a true time comparative to allow sensible judgment and perspective. How else can Nelson and Trafalgar be fairly considered and judged than by the barbarous standards of 1805 ? Certainly not by the comfort of today's standards with its push-button micro-chip technology, by its computerized, electronic, missile-orientated weaponry and equipment.

John Masefield wrote of the Trafalgar era:[3]

> Our naval glory was built up by the blood and agony of thousands of barbarously maltreated men ... sea life in ... our navy was brutalising, cruel, and horrible ... a kind of life which no man today would think good enough for a criminal. There was barbarous discipline, bad pay, bad food, bad hours of work, bad company, bad prospects. There was no going ashore until the ship paid off, or a peace was declared...The sailor was bled by the purser for slops and tobacco; by the surgeon for ointment and pills; and by those who cashed his pay-ticket...It was the long, monotonous imprisonment aboard which made the life so intolerable.

Since time began and gave Britain the geographic benefit of being an offshore island, the sea has ruled the destiny of our island race. For centuries the British Isles have commanded the exits from the Baltic, the North Sea, the whole of North-West European ports to the open Atlantic and the world's oceans beyond. This was so in the bitterly fought Dutch Wars of the seventeenth century, and equally so when the *Tirpitz* and *Bismarck* were blockaded and contained in the twentieth century. Providence — in geographic terms — had smiled benevolently on Britain.

Britain was not slow to capitalize on this good fortune: the British recognized early that the sea was an active ally as well as a defensive moat. It was a highway to wealth and power. The lessons of the power of command of the seas were soon learnt. As early as 31 December 1600 there was founded a joint-stock company (the East India Company) under a Royal Charter to promote trading interests in India. From these early stirrings there developed the British trading centres in Bombay, Madras and Calcutta that later spread to the whole of the sub-continent of India.

Command of the seas enabled the British to transport not only traders and their merchandise, but also armies of soldiers and marines to far-flung outposts, and it was only because command of the seas had been grasped and retained that these outposts were conquered. General Wolfe could not have captured Quebec without the navigational skills and seamanship of Admiral Saunders, his ships and men.[4] The victory was won on the dangerous waters of the St Lawrence just as surely as by scaling the Heights.

Trafalgar (1805), it can be argued, helped frame the victory at Waterloo ten years later. Many of the great battles of WW II on land were won by command of the seas. This Companion will help to show how this power, this admiralty, was acquired by the hard-fought endeavours of the ships and men of the Royal Navy.

A word or two of definition may be helpful in respect of the term 'Post Captain'. During the eighteenth century when an officer was 'made post', or

---

3  *Sea Life in Nelson's Time*, by John Masefield (1905).

4  One of these was James Cook, later Captain and one of the world's finest navigators.

appointed to a captain's command, his name was placed at the bottom of a list which was headed by the Admiral of the Fleet. Promotion up the list thereafter became automatic so long as one remained alive and was not court martialled. Clearly, it became desirable to be 'made post' as early as possible, but even this could not guarantee reaching the top: Nelson, for example, although made post at twenty only became a Vice Admiral — as did Collingwood.

An explanation, too, is needed for the designation of an admiral's rank by use of the colours Red, White and Blue. By definition an admiral is the commander of the fleet or of one of the fleet's divisions or squadrons. The post of Lord Admiral dates from 1485 and became established in Tudor times, but Blake — and before him Frobisher and Drake — bore the title 'Generals-at-Sea'. The ancient office of Lord High Admiral was revived by Charles II at his Restoration, and the present holder of the title is Queen Elizabeth II, who adopted it in 1964.

An elaborate hierarchy of ranks developed, based on the three main squadrons — the Red, White and Blue — into which fleets were organized. These squadrons were themselves further divided into the front (van), the middle (or centre) and rear divisions. An admiral commanded each squadron with junior-ranking admirals — rear and vice — also wearing their flags in each squadron. The most senior officer was the Admiral of the Red.

By the eighteenth century these squadronal colours and the promotional ladder had become well established:

Rear Admiral of the Blue
Rear Admiral of the White
Rear Admiral of the Red

Vice Admiral of the Blue
Vice Admiral of the White
Vice Admiral of the Red

Admiral of the Blue
Admiral of the White
Admiral of the Red

Admiral of the Fleet

Abolition of these squadronal colours came in 1864, but the principle survives to this day in the allocation of different ensigns to the three main branches of the maritime services: to the Royal Navy went the St George's red cross on a white field with the Union flag in the upper canton — the White Ensign. To the naval reserves went the Blue Ensign, and to the merchant service the Red Ensign.

# SECTION 1
# ADMIRALTY

# ADMIRALTY

Nothing, nothing in the world, nothing that you may think of or dream of, or anyone else may tell you: no argument however seductive, must lead you to abandon that naval supremacy on which the life of our country depends.

Winston S. Churchill, *26 November 1918.*

**If blood be the price of admiralty,**
**Lord God, we ha' paid in full !**

Rudyard Kipling, *'The Song of the Dead.'*

## INTRODUCTION

When the office of Lord High Admiral — effectively the First Lord of the Admiralty — was re-established in favour of James, Duke of York at the Restoration in 1660, the Navy had already experienced nearly two centuries of parliamentary or monarchical involvement.

We must be allowed to cast a glance over our shoulder to the Tudor days of Henry VII who shared in the cautious development of the Navy. At his death in 1509 'the Navy Royal was no nearer possessing a permanent administration than it had ever been',[1] even though he had created a Clerk of the Ships and John de Vere the first Lord Admiral.

Henry VIII's justification to be awarded the title 'Father of the Navy' lies not only in his establishing the climate and the opportunity for the Navy to embark upon the route to sea power but in the establishment of the first permanent administration of the Navy, and therefore the foundation for a lasting existence.[2]

William Gunson became Henry's 'Keeper of the Storehouses' at Erith, Deptford and Portsmouth, and effectively paymaster of the Navy. In March 1539 he was entrusted with £500 to spend on naval administration.[3]

When Gunson committed suicide in 1544 the loosely defined responsibilities

1  *The Admiralty*, by N.A.M.Rodger (1979), p.4, quoting *History of the Administration of the Royal Navy and of Merchant Shipping in Relation to the Navy 1509-1660*, by M.Oppenheim (1896), pp 32-6.

2  Notwithstanding his increasing the Navy tenfold, the mounting of heavy guns in warships, the construction of the *Henri Grace à Dieu* and the acquisition of dockyard establishments.

3  '...to be by him employed aboute his highnes affaires upon the Sea.' Rodger, p 5.

ADMIRALTY BOARD ROOM 1808

of offices of the naval administration, still without formal unity of action and channels of communication to the ennobled Lord Admirals, the process of naval reform received further impetus. By Letters Patent of 20 April 1546[4] the Principal Officers of the Navy were increased in number and formed into a body to be called the 'Council of the Marine', the 'Chief Officers of the Admiralty' or even more simply 'the Admiralty'. In fact, the body later became known as The Navy Board. And for the very first time a permanent chart of command and communication was provided between the political direction (King and Council), the high command (the Lord Admiral) and the effective administration of the fleet (the Navy Board).

During Queen Elizabeth I's reign the Treasurer was accorded an 'ordinary' — that is, a regular annual sum[5] to cover the cost of standing charges such as the 320 shipwrights employed in the three naval dockyards of Deptford, Woolwich and Portsmouth. Chatham too became well established and victualling of the fleet taken under the wing of a General Surveyor of Victuals for the Seas.

By now significant changes had affected the Board: firstly, as naval

4  Applied retrospectively to the previous Christmas.

5  It was £14,000 in 1557 and £10,000 in 1560.

administrators they became the natural advisers on naval affairs, but they were ill fitted and inexpert in that field. Further, the Treasurer of the Navy presided at the Board and this secured control of one of the largest departments of government as well as one of the biggest industrial enterprises in the country.

The Navy grew more politically dependent, and by the time of the Armada with John Hawkins as Treasurer, the Navy Royal had as effective an administration as was possible within the limitations provided or imposed by the logistics 'of building, maintaining, arming, manning and above all victualling a fleet at sea'.[6] The outlook of officials, of members of the Navy Board, differed totally from today's concept of government and office-holding. The Lord Admiral, for example, was one of the great officers of state, his 'position and prestige derived from antiquity',[7] enjoying an office of honour from commanding the Queen's forces in action and of profit from the Court of Admiralty.

Charles, Lord Howard of Effingham, later Earl of Nottingham, was Lord Admiral from 1585 to 1619: he was the last of the medieval admirals. He commanded the English fleet at the Armada despite having no sea experience — it was not expected of a nobleman — but he and most members of the Navy Board exercised their rightful place at sea as advisers to the Admiral during that eventful year of 1588.

In 1618 when Howard's influence waned and the young Buckingham's soared a Royal Commission comprising members of influence and knowledge of naval affairs enquired into corruption, maladministration and 'the present institutions of the Navy — and how it might be improved'. Such was the corruption that one Board member, Lionel Cranfield, ironically commented that rather than bring ships up to Woolwich or Deptford for repair 'it had been better for his Majesty to have given them away at Chatham and £300 or £400 in money to any who would have taken them'. Non-existent ships were even perpetuated to the profit of officials.

During this same year young Buckingham had bought out — i.e., actually purchased — Nottingham's post of Lord Admiral:[8] in due time he became the first to adopt the title of Lord High Admiral. The Navy Board was disbanded for ten years and Buckingham headed a permanent commission, effectively heading naval administration just as Henry VIII had envisaged years before.[9]

Buckingham was no mean administrator and he took a good deal of interest in his duties. In doing so he radically changed the status of Lord Admiral from an officer of state to something more like a responsible Minister.

One curious consequence of Buckingham's assassination in 1628 arose not from the gap left in the administration system but from his personal debts. Edward Nicholas, who was Buckingham's private secretary for Admiralty affairs, presented to the King a scheme whereby the Duke's purely naval functions should be put into commission (i.e., into abeyance), reserving the profits to pay off his debts — and to provide for the Duchess. Charles I accepted the scheme and instituted the Commission of Admiralty or Board of Admiralty.

---

6  Rodger, p.7.

7  Ibid. p.8.

8  Offices were bought, sold and mortgaged like property in those days.

9  Buckingham was a 'pluralist' on a grand scale. He was also Master of the Horse, Lord Warden of the Cinque Ports, Chief Justice in Eyre South of the Trent, Gentleman of the Bedchamber and Chief Clerk of King's Bench. Nicholas himself enjoyed several secretaryships. The situation is analogous to city directorships. Rodger p 13, quoting Oppenheim pp.279–82 and others.

Detailed administration of the Navy remained in the hands of the members of the Navy Board, but it was the Admiralty Board — comprising individuals with many outside interests — which was responsible for the central direction of the Navy.

The period from 1628 to 1660 was of administrative experiment and expediency, while the size of the Navy increased substantially. For many of these years the land lay in the grip of civil war and the Interregnum. After Pride's Purge in the House in December 1648 the office of Lord Admiral was abolished and the Navy Board replaced by a Navy Commission, and the Council of State delegated naval affairs to an Admiralty Committee. In 1653 an Admiralty Commission was formed, and it continued to direct naval affairs until the Restoration.

The years of the Commonwealth and the Protectorate saw naval administration, accompanied by fleets of a size and efficiency unmatched in decades, reach a peak largely due to the ability and prodigious industry of Sir Henry Vane who dominated the post of Treasurer of the Navy (lining his own pockets with corrupt wealth at the same time) and the various Boards and Committees on which he served.

By 1660 three successive Secretaries of the Admiralty — Jessop, Coytmore and Blackburne — had set the germ-seed of the Admiralty as a permanent, professional, incorruptible and non-political department of state, even though another fifty years were to pass before the Board of Admiralty became stabilized and accepted as a routine means of directing the Navy's affairs.

The Navy which Charles II inherited in 1660 was the most powerful in Europe, comprising 109 ships costing £40,000 a month to run: a cost which the Treasurer was unable to control and which had created an accumulated cash flow deficit of £670,000. The inheritance was a fragile one.[10]

A Privy Council Committee was set up by an Order in Council, with the result that in the July of that heady summer the office of Lord High Admiral was restored and the Navy Board reconstituted: the powers and functions of the Admiralty were vested in this office — and with variations it was to continue in this manner for the next three centuries.

The organization was largely the work of that naval veteran and administrator Sir William Penn. The new Board comprised men of experience and ability to advise the Lord High Admiral, and all seemed to be going well. 'This day,'[11] wrote William Coventry, Clerk of the Acts (in effect the Navy Board's Secretary), 'Sir G. Carteret[12] did tell us... that the Navy (excepting what is due to the yards... and what few bills he hath not heard of) is quite out of debt which is extraordinary good news.'

It was too good to last. The work-load strained the Board structure. Two years after 'the extraordinary good news' the naval suppliers were going bankrupt and starving seamen were besieging the Navy offices demanding their pay.

James, the Lord High Admiral, gradually lost control, due in part to the King's own genuine interest in the Navy.[13] Sir William Coventry's dismissal further undermined James's authority, defeats in the Second Dutch War and the King's

10  *Samuel Pepys and the Royal Navy*, by J.R. Tanner (1920).

11  3 December 1663.

12  Treasurer of the Navy.

13  His interest continued for years: he attended 195 out of 305 recorded meetings of the Board, at which he presided.

JAMES, DUKE OF YORK

political difficulties added to his burden. His papal commitments contributed to the Test Act of 1673 which led directly to his resignation in June of that year.

Charles II turned to the new Clerk of the Acts — now styled the Secretary to the Admiralty — the redoubtable Samuel Pepys, for resolution of the problems. Pepys, confidant of the Lord Admiral, with many years' experience on the Board and an incredible organizational ability, devised an ingenious scheme.

5

SAMUEL PEPYS

By an Order in Council of 13 June 1673 the King reserved to himself the profits of the Admiralty Court and the issuing of orders to the Navy and the Navy Board. He thus reduced the office of Lord High Admiral to insignificance, and it was placed in abeyance.

A month later the existing members of the Committee of the Navy, now designated Lord Commissioners (for executing the office of Lord Admiral) received their Patent.

Pepys directed the naval organization of the Second Dutch War and became responsible for many important developments after the war: he set out on a comprehensive programme of radical reform. He enjoyed the complete trust of the King, who gave him orders directly, often circumventing the Board, who received their instructions from Pepys — 'more like an admiral than a secretary.'[14] He held a powerful sway over the Navy and its administration.

---

14   Rodger p.26, quoting *The Significance of the Political Career of Samuel Pepys*, Journal of Modern History, Vol XXIV, by B.McL. Ranft.

Power had passed from Prince Rupert, the First Lord, to the Secretary.

Those days were dangerously volatile. Soon Pepys suffered an unwarranted eclipse and he found himself in the Tower under suspicion of treason, his very life in jeopardy. The Whigs dissolved the Admiralty Board and set up in its place a Board of Admiralty chosen more democratically from the majority party in parliament under Sir Henry Capel, whose first official duty was to dismiss Pepys, the only man who could provide the experience and the continuity that the rest of the Board lacked. Five years of decline ensued. The morale and efficiency of the Navy flagged.

When Charles was able to exert his influence again in 1684 a new Board found itself with a reinstated Samuel Pepys complete with Letters Patent under the Great Seal giving him the office of Secretary for the Affairs of the Admiralty (not as private secretary to the First Lord), with greater power, akin to that of a Secretary of State, and within a few years[15] he was wielding all the power of an influential minister.

Pepys himself wrote *The State of the Royal Navy of England at the Dissolution of the late Commissioners of the Admiralty*[16] immediately on reappointment, and he deplored the neglect and squandering of the money voted for the great construction programme of 1677. The Secretary himself had seen 'toad-stools... as big as my fists' in the damp, neglected 'tween decks of a once-powerful warship.

Less than two years after publication of this booklet Pepys proposed yet another replacement of the Board by a Commission headed by Admiral Arthur Herbert, and after this suggestion was adopted the benefits to the Navy and the nation began to flow almost immediately. The Special Commission of 1686 was Pepysian in conception, execution and style. He drafted the terms, chose the members and kept 'my daily eye and hand upon them'. His vast ship-repair programme was impressive. In the period under review 69 ships were repaired and 20 rebuilt. Three 4th-rates were built plus a hoy and two lighters. Only four ships still remained with repairs uncompleted and four more not started. In addition to all this, another 29 ships had been repaired though not included on the original programme. It was a crowning achievement.

Pepys overcame almost insuperable obstacles during his term of office: he infused the Navy with a stability and permanence and incorruptibility it had never known. Even his severest Whig opponents conceded he was 'a man of extraordinary knowledge... of great talents and the most indefatigable industry.'[17]

In 1687 the total staff Pepys employed amounted to six: four clerks, a manager and a doorkeeper — plus himself. But that great department of state the Admiralty can be said to have had its foundations laid by this powerful Secretary whose allegiance lay not with master, patron, king nor parliament, but to the Navy and its well-being.

His talents and friendships brought him a seat in parliament: he had found a platform. He was virtually Minister for the Navy, and an influential one at that. Historian Richard Ollard is clear in his conclusions: Pepys was one of the greatest civil servants that England ever had... 'but had the misfortune to live

---

15   Upon the death of Charles on 6 February 1685 James had succeeded to the throne, followed in under four years by his abdication and the accession of William and Mary.

16   Published in May 1684, the slim book, elaborately bound in black morocco leather with hand-tooled gilt, graces his library at Cambridge.

17   *The Navy in the War of William III 1689–97* by John Ehrman (1953) p. 196.

before the civil service was invented'.[18] He was saviour not only of the Navy, but of the nation: in particular, he put his hallmark on the administration of the Navy.

The principal prize William of Orange secured for himself — apart from the kingdom itself — was the Royal Navy: a weapon of incalculable power which he could wield with ferocity against his arch-enemy, France. It was too valuable to be entrusted to the hands of Stuart men: it must be commanded by men he could trust — and the Lord Admiral's post should be reserved for himself. The Admiralty was placed in commission and Arthur Herbert (created Earl of Torrington in 1689) was appointed First Lord and C-in-C at sea.

William's governance was principally through Secretaries of State and this channel of command gradually usurped the authority of the Admiralty, whose power dwindled till the members of the Board were quite often ignorant of the whereabouts of the fleet.

The survival of the Admiralty during William's reign was a close-run thing. Politically, the Admiralty Board was manipulated, consistently ignored, so that it became of no service to the Navy and precious little to the government. Just how abused it was is exemplified by Russell's action: he was the victor of Barfleur (1692), brought from retirement to become First Lord, C-in-C, Treasurer of the Navy and a member of the cabinet. He sailed with the fleet for the Mediterrranean leaving his colleagues in total ignorance of his plans for several months. He communicated to and fro with secretaries of state, by-passing the Admiralty. The Admiralty had no bite at all.

The Navy Office, though, grew in size and stature. By 1704 it had 63 clerks, had men of weight and experience in principal positions and its work became indispensable to the fleet. Political strife, the battling of Whigs and Tories, the heavy losses of English shipping in the War of Spanish Succession and the wrangling in the House of Commons was humiliating. The weakness of the Admiralty Board led to naval strategy being dictated by Act of Parliament. The Cruizers and Convoys Act of 1708 effectively removed 43 ships from the Lord Admiral's strategic control to be employed as the Commons saw fit.

In the twenty years since William of Orange had ascended the throne and been succeeded by Queen Anne the authority and importance of the Admiralty had declined drastically. The fact that it survived is due in large measure to the Secretaries, the successors of Pepys. James Southerne was followed by William Bridgeman in 1694 — 'a seasoned administrator'. He set out the Admiralty's first establishment: two chief clerks, six clerks, a messenger, two servants, a porter, a watchman and the necessary woman (housekeeper).They were all paid by the state, Bridgeman himself receiving £800 a year. Their work was principally 'a matter of co-ordination of naval policy and administration' — in an apt phrase by Dr Rodger — 'filling the gap between grand strategy and administration'.

Soon after Russell sent home to the Admiralty office his personal secretary Josiah Burchett to share Bridgeman's job. He was to serve the office for half a century and became one of the great Secretaries to the Admiralty. Although he sat in the House of Commons most of his career, he was the first Secretary to be recognized as a permanent official, a senior civil servant, unaffected by political changes in ministries.

---

18  *Pepys: A Biography*, by Richard Ollard (1974), p.285.

Robert Walpole's appearance on the political scene subordinated the Admiralty quite ruthlessly to political expediency. Party government had arrived, and had come to stay; the Whigs with their inherent belief in the right to govern were fiercely opposed by the Tories; the opposition was as powerful as today's between Socialism and Conservatism. Appointments to sea command and to the Admiralty began to follow strict party lines. Further, Walpole's choice of Admiralty Board members comprised all civilians, advised by a single naval member, thus turning an already political Board into a predominantly civilian one — but one now at the mercy of turbulent party-political considerations.

Understandably, it was the cabinet that began to handle the real decision-making process regarding naval operations, sometimes even ignoring the Admiralty Board. Unbelievably, Anson's voyage round the world in 1744 was planned without reference to the Admiralty.

Later, Pitt, in an apocryphal but celebrated anecdote, when he required the Admiralty's signature wrote the instructions himself 'and sent them to their Lordships to be signed, always ordering his secretary to put a sheet of white paper over the writing, thus keeping their Lordships in perfect ignorance of what they signed'.

The middle years of the eighteenth century — from 1744 to 1762, with one year's exception — brought change when three young and able men were appointed to the Admiralty Board to give support to a strong ministry: the First Lord, the Duke of Bedford (thirty-five); his close friend the Earl of Sandwich (twenty-seven); and the public hero, Captain George Anson (forty-eight), fresh from a world voyage.

These three led the Admiralty Board, and Anson in particular displayed courage and resolve in challenging (probably for the first time in history) the right of the Navy Board to administer the Navy with only meagre supervision. At last the Admiralty Board began to *govern*. Indeed, it was Anson who emerged as the authoritative titan, the Board member and later First Lord and C-in-C, who dominated the naval policy of his day with a political, moral and physical courage rarely seen.[19] He could reject patronage requests from as great a person as the Duke of Newcastle — and demand an apology from him. He was not a man to be trifled with, and certainly not one to sign a document with a secretary hiding the writing with a sheet of paper!

By his strong will — he treated all alike, leaving a Minister who ran foul of Anson's sharp brusqueness complaining that the Admiralty 'does not like to be controlled or even advised';[20] he endowed the office of First Lord with an authority it was never to lose.

The Navy employed as many staff as the rest of the government services put together, and the Admiralty controlled all patronage and responsibility for this great enterprise. And Anson controlled the Admiralty. The Admiralty had in its dispensation ten boroughs with influence in many more. Most flag officers sat as MPs. In 1761, of thirty admirals, twenty were MPs and one a Scots peer — and many others were junior officers.

At this time the small Admiralty office employed less than forty people, but the Navy Board now employed many thousands. The Victualling Board alone had seventy-four London officials in 1747.

It was the Secretaries to the Admiralty in the eighteenth century who

19  Incidentally, in 1761 he had the unique distinction of wearing the Union Flag at the main topmast as an Admiral of the Fleet and C-in-C at sea, and First Lord, effectively First Sea Lord.

20  Rodger, p.61.

exercised power and control not enjoyed by other departmental secretaries. It was they with their long years of service (which gave a continuity to the daily routine of running their department and the Navy) that set them apart from their colleagues in other departments. Josiah Burchett served forty-eight years: Thomas Corbett eleven years at sea, ten as Secretary and seventeen as Deputy Secretary; John Cleveland twelve years at the Admiralty and twenty-nine as Secretary and Second Secretary; Philip Stephens twelve years in the Navy Office and thirty as Secretary. These four spanned more than a century of service. In the same period there had been seventeen Secretaries to the Treasury and seventy-six Secretaries of State.

The last quarter of the 1700s and the introductory years of the nineteenth century were dominated by two admirals acting as administrators, and these years are possibly the most momentous in the Royal Navy's history. They spanned the great revolutionary war and the Napoleonic War, the first resulting in a decisive defeat and the loss of an empire; the second in a war that changed the face of Europe and left unhealing scars. The two men who administered naval affairs during these dramatic years were the fourth Earl of Sandwich[21] and the first Lord Barham.

At fifty-four John Montagu understood more about the Navy and its administration than any civilian who had presided at the Board in a century. He excelled at controlling stores, victuals, in the logistics of running dockyards and a fleet at sea. 'He rose early and till a late dinner dedicated his whole time to business,' a contemporary recorded, and he gave his name to the small snacks obtained by sandwiching slices of cold meat between bread. He gave orders and replies 'with despatch'. 'If any man will draw up his case and put his name at [the] foot of the first page,' he once recorded, 'I will give him an immediate reply. Where he compels me to turn over the sheet, he must wait my leisure.'

He 'became the Master of the Admiralty and the Navy as no civilian First Lord had ever been before, or was ever to be again.'[22] He learned from his years on boards with Admiral Anson how to exploit the power lying in the office of First Lord, and ended more than outmatching his mentor.

Reform was needed and undertaken. In 1778 the Admiralty, the Navy Board, the Treasury and Secretary of State took seven months to transport two hundred butts of vinegar from Deptford to New York. It was a routine and proper procedure, but hopeless. The financial affairs of the Navy were also absurdly confused. In 1780 the Navy Pay Office had brought the annual accounts down to 1758. At this time too the principal function of the Admiralty was to try to co-ordinate cabinet policy and the activities of the numerous bodies involved in naval administration and operations.[23] Sandwich proposed new responsibilities at top level:

> Every expedition... is planned by the cabinet, and is the result of the collective wisdom of all HM's confidential ministers. The First Lord of the Admiralty is only the executive servant... and if he is not personally a

21  Great-grandson of Pepys's patron.

22  Rodger, p.75. But see also *The Private Papers of John, Earl of Sandwich*, by G.R. Barnes and O.J.H. Edwards (Navy Records Society; 4 vols 1932−8).

23  As well as the Admiralty and the cabinet itself, there were the Navy Board, the Transport Service, the Victualling Board, the Colonial Secretary, the Treasury, the Ordnance Board — and more.

JOHN MONTAGU, EARL OF SANDWICH

cabinet minister he is not responsible for the wisdom, the policy and the propriety of any naval expedition...

Overhaul of the whole administrative system followed progressively year by year. Captain Sir Charles Middleton (later Lord Barham) was appointed by Sandwich as Comptroller, head of the Navy Board and by definition was '... the main spring belonging to everything that is naval: no price can purchase a man fit for this extensive office: he must... know everything that is going on, in and out of it.'

Middleton believed in God as much as in himself: he believed himself to be the Navy's best administrator, as he probably was. Devout, narrow-minded, he despised Sandwich for living in sin with a mistress and family,[24] criticized the First Lord, the Admiralty and corruption at every occasion. He was ambitious, devious in his aims and a bore of the first water. But his contributions to the Navy were of the highest order, and it is true to say that he stamped his

24  His Countess was insane.

11

ROBERT DUNDAS, VISCOUNT MELVILLE

hallmark on the office of Comptroller, as Lord Commissioner and later as First Lord of the Admiralty.

Middleton rooted out corruption. In 1785 a second Commission — on Fees in Public Offices — denied deputies, sinecures, fees and perquisites, and no public monies or papers kept for private advantage. But to his disappointment he did not attain appointment to a seat at the Admiralty. In 1790 he resigned, but war brought him back in 1794 as Lord Commissioner with a 'junior' lord's seat on the Board. It irked him to serve firstly under Chatham,[25] then under the scholarly Earl Spencer.[26]

Spencer spelled out his explicit ideas on collective responsibility:

25  The laziest man ever to have held office: hundreds of unopened letters were found at his home when he left office.

26  The 36-year-old wealthy aristocrat Whig with a library the envy of Europe. An ancestor of the Princess of Wales.

The idea I entertain of the constitution of this Board, and of the manner in which the business of it should be carried on, is that in every measure determined upon and officially proposed to the Board by the First Lord, every member of the Board is considered to take an active part by his signature: and though the responsibility unquestionably rests with the First Lord, the other members are always understood to concur in his measures.

The individualistic Middleton could not stomach this. Within a year he had resigned.

In 1801 Lord St Vincent succeeded Spencer, whose ideas on collective responsibility made nonsense to him. Autocratic, totally inexperienced in politics, he side-stepped consultations; uncompromising and a very great sea commander, he tackled problems as he would the enemy with broadsides and raking shots. He even dismissed the Navy Board as 'fit for Scotch pack-horses'. He suffered mud-slinging from dockyard workers and helped set up a Commission of Enquiry when he found corruption in the Navy Board.

Renewed war brought Sir Charles Middleton back into office as unofficial adviser to the First Lord and Chairman of the Commission for Revising and Digesting the Civil Affairs of the Navy. Publication in February 1805 of the Tenth Report of the Commission of Enquiry revealed that the current First Lord (Lord Melville) had speculated with naval funds when he was Treasurer of the Navy. He resigned in haste.

Middleton, now ennobled as Barham and aged seventy-nine, assumed the office of supreme command of the Navy. The traffic and logistics of naval and merchant ships world-wide had become huge and complex.[27]

The scale of war at sea was beyond the capabilities of any single Whitehall man to handle. The Admiralty became the only operational centre of not only the grand strategy of the naval war but the day-to-day handling of intelligence, messages, signals, orders.[28]

Barham introduced Sea Lords, delegating to them the day-to-day Admiralty affairs, reserving to himself the governance of the whole, including the concept of grand strategy. He 'lived over the shop' in the new residence at the Admiralty, allowing him to remain in contact with the office at all times, even at night. He was aroused from sleep in the early hours of 6 November 1805 when the Second Secretary, on night duty, announced 'Sir, we have won a great victory, but we have lost Lord Nelson.'

These statements alone testify to the fact that the Admiralty by now was a sophisticated, well-organized, hard-working and relatively efficient administrative base for the world's largest and most powerful Navy, effectively run by Secretaries every bit as worthy as their famous predecessors of the seventeenth and eighteenth centuries. Barham had written: 'If the public officers, on whose orders every preparation and movement depends, are not diligent, regular and

---

27  Rodger quotes on his p.87 a figure of more than 13,000 British ships entered and cleared home ports in 1792, most requiring escort under the Convoy Act. By the new century, with cargoes of timber, hemp and pitch, Baltic convoys of 1,000 sail left fortnightly. Rodger gives as sources *The Defence of British Trade 1689–1815*, by Patrick Crowhurst (1977) and *Britain at Bay: Defence Against Bonaparte 1803–14*, by Richard Glover (1973).

28  From a semaphore telegraph on the Admiralty roof and repeaters en route a signal could be transmitted to Spithead within minutes, and other repeaters ran as far as Plymouth.

GEORGE EDEN, EARL OF AUCKLAND

punctual, it is of little consequence when your admirals and generals are.'[29]

According to Barham, Sir Evan Nepean displayed 'unremitting diligence and integrity'. He and his successor, William Marsden, met Barham's highest standards: they opened and read every letter to the Admiralty and ensured it was answered that day.

At the end of the Great War — for a century the Napoleonic War was so called until a worse conflict fell upon Europe — the Royal Navy had in commission a powerful fleet of over 500 warships manned by nearly 100,000 men.

29  *Letters and Papers of Charles, Lord Barham*, by Sir J.K. Laughton, 3 vols, 1906–10 (Navy Records Society). See Vol II, p.66.

But for nearly a century the Navy was to lose all direction. What ensued with astonishing rapidity can only be described by even the most cautious critics as reckless. Throughout the Victorian age the Navy squandered its energies in chasing Algerine pirates and supporting mini-conflicts throughout what we would now call the Third World. Yet, curiously, in so doing it helped build an empire.

Within a few years of Napoleon's defeat only 20,000 officers and men manned the few ships of the Navy to remain in service: only 13 ships of the line compared with the 98 of a few years previously.

The shrinking of the Navy was reflected in political standing. Gone were the Ansons and Barhams. There followed a long succession of second-raters. Canning's government of 1827 introduced a Gilbertian touch, appointing the Duke of Clarence Lord High Admiral; he promptly invoked the ancient privilege and hoisted his flag at sea, the last Lord High Admiral to do so. (He became William IV and delighted in the nickname 'Sailor Bill'.)

Palmerston found little to occupy himself on the Admiralty Board except 'passing a couple of hours in the Board Room doing little or nothing.'

In addition to the Great Reform Bill of 1832 Lord Grey's Liberal administration passed the Admiralty Act of the same year, framed by the First Lord, Sir James Graham (the naval Beeching of his day) and Sir John Barrow, Second Secretary (the archetypal Permanent Secretary). It effectively brought about the demise of the Navy Board, and the Admiralty became the supreme governor and director of the Navy. Its policies were to be carried out by five Principal Officers: Accountant-General; Storekeeper-General; Comptroller of Victualling; Physician; Surveyor.

These officers were responsible for their Branches direct to a Lord Commissioner. Graham's new structure got off to a good start: the redundancies, cuts and economies effected gave him the reduced budget he sought, but it would be years before the system became overloaded and each Lord swamped with departmental business.

The cabinet cared little for the Navy, and the Admiralty had become something approaching a parochial organization deserving of minimum attention. The Secretary, First Lord and other Lords of the Board had become overwhelmed with the minutiae of administration. Auckland[30] told the story of entering the Board Room of the Admiralty to find Sir William Parker, the First Naval Lord, and Admiral Dundas, his junior colleague, themselves altering the Surveyor's drawings of a ship's draught.

Graham himself later confessed that the system that developed was something to be avoided. Writing of this period, C.C. Lloyd underlined the problem:[31] 'The departmental duties were so arduous and multifarious that it was with difficulty that he [First Lord] could get through the daily routine of office work, much less find time for the careful consideration of those grave and important questions of national defence.'

Sir Thomas Masterman Hardy brought a breath of fresh air to the Board as First Naval Lord and he emerged as an intelligent and sensible reformer. And at a time when the batch of First Lords of the early nineteenth century were a mediocre lot, it took another professional sailor, Sir George Cockburn — as a

---

30   Auckland was an acute and intellectual observer; Earl and First Lord of the Admiralty, he once wrote: 'The mode of transacting business is such as to induce the belief that no mind can have been employed about it since the time of Pepys and James Duke of York,'

31   *Mr Barrow of the Admiralty*, by C.C. Lloyd (1970).

HUGH CHILDERS

First Naval Lord[32] — to excel, as one might expect of the man who put the White House to flame.

When Graham returned to the Admiralty as First Lord just before the Crimean War even he was unable to arrest the confusion and decline. A House of Lords Select Committee was formed following an MP's proposal in 1861 to replace the Admiralty with a Ministry of Marine. But the Committee never reported.

By general consensus it was agreed that the Admiralty — a large and expensive government department — needed radical reform and greater Treasury control, but (again by general agreement) it rated little priority, and reform was left behind in the search for greater Civil Service efficiency.

32  He was another pluralist: he sat on fifteen boards as well as the Lord Admiral's Council.

16

GEORGE GOSCHEN

When Hugh C. E. Childers took office as First Lord in Gladstone's Liberal administration in December 1868 the Admiralty entered a brief three-year period that was nothing short of disaster.

Childers was a ruthless politician with a brutal, offensive manner which endeared him to no one. In effect he abolished the Admiralty Board. By an Order in Council in January 1869 — less than a month after taking office — he set out his reforms. Each Lord was executive chief of his branch, and he was directly responsible for it to the First Lord. All communication between Board members was to be in writing. The First Lord would make the decisions and take the responsibility. The result of this was that co-operation between branches lapsed, co-ordination was lost and the naval lords became dominated by this ruthless politico who rarely seemed to seek their advice.

Rodger records[33] that in 1866 no less than 249 Board meetings were held but in 1879 only 33 — and none of these exceeded half an hour. At least Childers left no one in doubt: he was the decision-maker on behalf of the Navy. It was his decision to proceed with the construction of HMS *Captain*, the revolutionary new turret battleship: designed, constructed and backed by Childers's political affiliates, she displayed the merits of latest technology in warship-construction, but she also displayed instability. She foundered in a storm on her maiden voyage, taking 481 lives with her, including Childers's own son. There was no doubt where the responsibility lay, but Childers wrote a Minute in the name of the whole Board exonerating himself.[34] In the ensuing fierce political row he left office in disgrace, broken in health and spirit.

The inheritance for G. J. Goschen was awesome; his wise and tolerant administrative skills remedied the worst of Childers's excesses. Weekly Board meetings were instituted and daily meetings improved co-ordination. Significantly he also re-appointed Sir Alexander Milne, a well-known Tory, as his First Naval Lord: his was the first senior naval lord appointment by a Ministry of the opposing party, and the first purely professional as opposed to party appointment.

Goschen was later described as the real author of the modern Admiralty, an assessment which is probably too fulsome because he brought only change where reform was needed; first aid when surgery was required.

Neither G. W. Hunt nor W. H. Smith[35] provided that surgery. Ward Hunt was an excessively large gentleman. He had, Disraeli confided to the Queen, 'the sagacity of an elephant as well as its form'. So gross was he that the table in the Board room had a semi-circular section cut from it. It may have been his weight alone, or possibly his lack of friends, which impelled the rest of the Board to decline to act as pall-bearers at his funeral in 1877.

It was the 1880s before a weakened Admiralty Board, so long submerged in administrative trivia and subjected to strong outside influences,[36] began to gain strength and determine its own destiny. This coincided with a time of technological change which was influencing design and performance of ships and their armaments.

By the end of the decade a new spirit had given birth to the Naval Defence Act of 1889 and the adoption of a two-power standard. Old-fashioned ideas and old-fashioned men — Gladstone and all — were swept aside by others who carefully kept a weather eye on Prussian moves and who sought greater naval strength. A Naval Intelligence Division was founded in 1886. Lord George Hamilton (First Lord 1886–92) and Sir Frederick Richards (First Naval Lord 1893–9) gave some quality to a period of political control marred by another five years of Goschen.

By the dawn of the new century the Navy was changing with a swiftness not seen in its whole existence. New ideas, new technology, new ships, new guns helped infuse both Navy and Admiralty with a new pioneering and enterprising spirit.

33  Rodger p. 110, quoting Murray vol. VII, pp.471–3.

34  Some Board members first learnt of this when they read about it in the daily papers.

35  He was a better stationer and bookseller than First Lord. It is said that he was caricatured in Gilbert and Sullivan's HMS *Pinafore*, as Sir Joseph Porter KBE.

36  While many examples of the Board's loss of control abound, this one example will suffice: the War Office had inherited the Ordnance Board and supplied the Navy with its guns and shells.

LORD GEORGE HAMILTON

Despite being an ancient and in some ways peculiar organization, the Admiralty was surprisingly efficient: it coped with the rapid changes, adapted to new and more efficient methods of management and accounting, employed intelligent graduates on the Secretary's staff, yet curiously retained an olde-worlde style of office routine. Correspondence was by handwritten letter rather than by typewriter or telegram; and on the lawn beneath the Board-room tennis was still played.

The Admiralty, with the Navy and its civil establishment, had grown into the largest single industrial complex in the country, like an autonomous state within a state. It controlled a quarter of a million men and women, a fifth of the Exchequer's expenditure. So respected in governmental circles had the Admiralty become that Viscount Esher was impelled to report in 1903 on being asked to reconstruct the War Office in the image of the Admiralty:

> We are directed by the terms of our Reference to take the Admiralty system of higher administration as the basis of our action, and we are convinced that, while there may be imperfections in the working of that system, it is

19

JOHN POYNTZ, EARL SPENCER

absolutely sound in principle. It has been handed down without material change from the period of the great naval wars... it has smoothly and successfully met new demands as they have arisen, including an enormous increase of personnel and material ... Finally, it has retained the confidence of the Navy and of the Nation.[37]

Somehow it seems appropriate that Sir John Fisher was appointed First Sea Lord on the 99th anniversary of Trafalgar in 1904. For ten years he was to dominate the Navy and Admiralty: it is not too great to say that with his brutal and

37 *The Admiralty*, Sir Oswyn Murray, published in Parts I–X in *Mariner's Mirror*, VII p. 478.

domineering personality his achievements changed naval and perhaps world history. To coin a modern cliché, he was a man people loved to hate. He allowed of no neutrality; one either loved him or hated him. But his achievements are undeniable, exemplified by the construction in one year and one day of HMS *Dreadnought*, rendering at the drop of an anchor all other battleships obsolete: scores of warships were scrapped. The world looked on in astonishment.

At last, in 1907, the control of guns (their design and manufacture) was wrested from the War Office and naval gunnery improved out of all recognition.

For all his manifest blessings, Fisher had many failings, perhaps the most blatant of which was his consistent refusal to appoint a naval staff. By 1911, when a worried cabinet wanted to present to his Committee of Imperial Defence a naval and military War Plan, the Army (having modelled its War Office on the Admiralty) presented[38] a comprehensive and coherent War Plan. The naval presentation by Sir Arthur Wilson, the First Sea Lord, was rambling and pathetic.

The upshot was electric. Prime Minister Asquith appointed the youthful Winston Churchill First Lord. And he tackled the job with characteristic zeal. He created a Naval War Staff in 1912 — full of promise, but with imperfections, too. And within a couple of years the imperfect administrative machine was called upon for its most fearsome testing.[39] To Battenberg and Churchill must go much credit for the fact that when war came, the Navy was prepared.

The war wrought casualties ashore as well as at sea. Battenberg's ancestry forced a resignation. Fisher, recalled as First Sea Lord, failed to such a degree that colleagues questioned his sanity. Churchill's lordship foundered on the rocks of the Dardanelles. Three great names of the Navy and the Admiralty became serious casualties.

July 1917 saw Sir Eric Geddes appointed First Lord. On appointment he demanded the honorary rank of Vice Admiral — and got it. He was by training a railway engineer, a blunt north countryman who aroused great enmity in the Navy, not least because he sacked the country's greatest living naval hero, Sir John Jellicoe. Great sea commander though he was, Jellicoe, like many of the First Sea Lords, was unable to delegate easily, and dealt with the trivia of administration personally.

Sir Rosslyn Wemyss, friend of kings, was by contrast with Jellicoe an excellent administrator of the new system, and became an immediate success as First Sea Lord. Three and a half years of war had helped evolve an administrative organization which had been first established about two hundred years previously.

Geddes was instrumental in forming the Admiralty Board into two divisions:

| Operations Committee | Maintenance Committee |
|---|---|
| First Sea Lord | Second Sea Lord |
| Deputy First Sea Lord | Third Sea Lord |
| Deputy and Assistant CNS | Fourth Sea Lord |
| Fifth Sea Lord for the Naval | Controller |
| Air Service | Civil Lord |
| | Financial Secretary |
| | Fifth Sea Lord (if necessary) |

38   In the shape of General Sir Henry Wilson, Director of Military Operations.

39   Winston Churchill wrote: 'Robed in the august authority of naval tradition and armed with the fullest authority available, the Board of Admiralty wielded unchallenged power.'

REGINALD McKENNA

This, in effect, was a modern version of the old Admiralty (the Operations Committee responsible for policy and operational control) and the Navy Board (Maintenance Committee responsible for supply and sustenance of the Navy).

These 1917 reforms marked the end of the Admiralty's centuries-long autonomy. The First Sea Lord and the Chief of the Imperial General Staff (backed by their susbstantial staffs) virtually became Commanders-in-Chief responsible to the cabinet and allowing of a co-ordinated policy of national defence. By the end of World War I the Admiralty had become enormously increased in size and scope, but it was to enter an era of economies while other nations began to look towards aggrandizement.

For eight years, from 1919 till his retirement in 1927, Earl Beatty commanded the Admiralty and the Navy with his intellectual talents and his impressive personality — and matched cabinet ministers in debating skills.[40] He coped with the Washington Disarmament Conference (1921–2) and the 'Axe' of Geddes's Committee on National Expenditure of 1921, with precious little political

40 *Naval Policy Between The Wars*, Vol I 1919–1929, by Stephen Roskill (1968), pp. 44-6.

WINSTON CHURCHILL IN 1912

backing.[41] He coped, too, with five mediocre First Lords in five years, the creation of a Chiefs of Staff Committee in 1923, encouraged the cabinet (when it needed advice) to turn to the Chiefs of Staff (the professionals) rather than to its service Ministers (the politicians).[42]

The 1920s and 1930s were a period of lamentably weak political leadership, reaching a nadir with A.V. Alexander as Labour's first First Lord: to such an extent that Ramsay MacDonald excluded the First Lord from the cabinet, for the first time since the days of Queen Anne. The Admiralty was fortunate, therefore, in having a steady hand on its tiller in the form of Sir Oswyn Murray, a Permanent Secretary of the highest calibre, from 1917 till his death in 1936.

Almost as a direct consequence of the wide-ranging weakness of political leadership — and, it must be said, the Admiralty's inept handling of the May Committee Report — there occurred the Invergordon Mutiny of 1931. Other

41   Between 1920 and 1925 there were five First Lords, seven Parliamentary Secretaries, six Civil Lords and eighteen Sea Lords. See Rodger, p.147.

42   Roskill, ibid, pp.30-3.

than Beatty's and Chatfield's in the later 1930s, the quality of naval leadership also left much to be desired.

Chatfield's firm grasp in office until 1938 had helped considerably to re-establish stability, while Sir William James, a former head of Room 40 and then DCNS, had established the Operational Intelligence Centre.

Firm political leadership returned at the outbreak of World War II and the re-appointment of Churchill as First Lord. But when Churchill became prime minister in 1940 he also assumed the post of Minister of Defence. The cabinet, dominated by Churchill, dealt directly with the Chiefs of Staff, relegating the service ministers to purely administrative duties outside the inner councils of war. The status of the First Lord suffered as a consequence, as did that of the Board of Admiralty.

By the war's end the Admiralty had grown in size and complexity almost beyond imagination, but it maintained an efficiency envied by the other service ministries. Some of the lessons of war taught that there was a need for a high degree of co-ordination between services, and it became increasingly apparent reorganization was necessary to weld together three individualistic service Ministries. It was nevertheless nearly twenty years before Mountbatten published the proposal to abolish the service Ministries and combine them into a unified Ministry of Defence.[43] Angry, shocked debate preceded the amalgamation into a joint Defence Council with a single responsible Minister and a Chief of the Defence Staff appointed in rotation from the three services.

'On 31 March 1964 after 336 years the Board of Admiralty met for the last time, its patent was surrendered and flag hauled down'.[44] On the following day the MOD assumed charge of HM ships and the members of the Board reassumed their seats as The Admiralty Board of the Defence Council, no longer Lords Commissioners. Her Majesty the Queen assumed the office of Lord High Admiral.

43  Cmd. 2097. *Central Organisation for Defence.*

44  *The Central Organisation of Defence,* Michael Howard, 1970.

# PARLIAMENTARY AND NAVAL CONTROL

## LORD ADMIRAL
## LORD HIGH ADMIRAL *and*
## FIRST LORD OF THE ADMIRALTY

### LORD ADMIRAL

1485   John de Vere, Earl of Oxford
1513   Sir Edward Howard[45]
1513   Thomas, Lord Howard, later Earl of Surrey and Duke of Norfolk
1525   Henry Fitzroy, Duke of Richmond
1536   William Fitzwilliam, Earl of Southampton
1540   John, Lord Russell
1542   Edward Seymour, Earl of Hertford
1543   John Dudley, Viscount Lisle, later Duke of Northumberland
1547   Thomas, Lord Seymour
1549   John Dudley, Earl of Warwick (formerly Viscount Lisle)
1550   William, Lord Clinton
1554   William, Lord Howard of Effingham
1558   William, Lord Clinton, later Earl of Lincoln
1585   Charles, Lord Howard of Effingham, Earl of Nottingham
1619   George Villiers, Marquess and Duke of Buckingham.

*There followed a period of more than thirty years from 1628 to 1660 of often fragmented and indecisive parliamentary control of the Navy, often with overlapping functions, including the following:*

1628–38   COMMISSION OF ADMIRALTY
1642–9     COMMISSION OF ADMIRALTY
1645–8     PARLIAMENTARY ADMIRALTY COMMITTEE
1649–52    COUNCIL OF STATE'S COMMITTEE ON THE ADMIRALTY AND NAVY
1652–3     COMMITTEE OF ADMIRALTY AFFAIRS
1653–60    ADMIRALTY COMMISSION

Interspersed with these were:

---

45   Only Lord Admiral of England to have been recorded as killed in action.

# LORD ADMIRAL

1638–42 Algernon Percy, Earl of Northumberland
1643–5 Robert Rich, Earl of Warwick
1648–9 Robert Rich, Earl of Warwick

# FIRST LORD OF THE ADMIRALTY

*This office effectively dates from 1660, although Percy was described thus in 1642, and some later office-holders specifically served as Lord High Admiral — as indicated in parentheses.*

1660 Duke of York (Lord High Admiral)[46]
1673 Prince Rupert
1679 Sir Henry Capel
1681 Daniel Finch, later Earl of Nottingham
1684 Charles II (Lord High Admiral)
1685 James II (Lord High Admiral)
1689 Admiral Arthur Herbert, Earl of Torrington
1690 Thomas Herbert, Earl of Pembroke & Montgomery
1692 Charles, Lord Cornwallis
1693 Anthony Carey, Viscount Falkland
1694 Admiral Edward Russell, later Earl of Orford
1699 John Egerton, Earl of Bridgewater
1701 Earl of Pembroke & Montgomery (Lord High Admiral)
1709 Edward Russell, Earl of Orford
1710 Sir John Leake
1712 Thomas Wentworth, Earl of Strafford
1714 Earl of Orford
1717 James Berkeley, Earl of Berkeley
1727 George Byng, Viscount Torrington
1733 Sir Charles Wager
1742 Daniel Finch, Earl of Winchilsea & Nottingham
1744 John Russell, Duke of Bedford
1748 John Montagu, Earl of Sandwich
1751 George, Lord Anson
1756 Richard Temple, Earl Temple
1757 Earl of Winchilsea & Nottingham
1757 George, Lord Anson
1762 George Dunk, Earl of Halifax
1763 Hon George Grenville
1763 Earl of Sandwich
1763 John Perceval, Earl of Egmont
1766 Sir Charles Saunders
1766 Sir Edward Hawke
1771 Earl of Sandwich
1782 Augustus, Viscount Keppel
1783 Richard, Viscount Howe
1788 John Pitt, Earl of Chatham
1794 George, Earl Spencer (formerly Lord Althorp)

---

46 Nominally Lord High Admiral since 1649.

| 1801 | John Jervis, Earl of St Vincent |
| 1804 | Henry Dundas, Viscount Melville |
| 1805 | Charles Middleton, Lord Barham |
| 1806 | Charles Grey, Viscount Howick |
| 1806 | Thomas Grenville |
| 1807 | Henry Phipps, Lord Mulgrove |
| 1810 | Charles Yorke |
| 1812 | Robert Dundas, Viscount Melville |
| 1827 | Duke of Clarence (Lord High Admiral) |
| 1828 | Robert Dundas, Viscount Melville |
| 1830 | Sir James Graham |
| 1834 | George Eden, Lord Auckland |
| 1834 | Thomas, Earl de Grey |
| 1835 | George, Lord Auckland |
| 1835 | Eliott Gilbert, Earl of Minto |
| 1841 | Thomas Hamilton, Earl of Haddington |
| 1846 | Edward Law, Earl of Ellenborough |
| 1846 | George Eden, Earl of (formerly Baron) Auckland |
| 1849 | Sir Francis Thornhill Baring |
| 1852 | Duke of Northumberland |
| 1853 | Sir James Graham |
| 1855 | Sir Charles Wood |
| 1858 | Sir John S. Pakington |
| 1859 | Edward Seymour, Duke of Somerset |
| 1866 | Sir John S. Pakington |
| 1867 | Henry T. Lowry Corry |
| 1868 | Hugh C. E. Childers |
| 1871 | George J. Goschen |
| 1874 | George Ward Hunt |
| 1877 | William Henry Smith |
| 1880 | Thomas Baring, Earl of Northbrook |
| 1885 | Lord George Hamilton |
| 1886 | George Robinson, Marquess of Ripon |
| 1886 | Lord George Hamilton |
| 1892 | John, Earl Spencer |
| 1895 | George J. Goschen |
| 1900 | William Palmer, Earl of Selborne |
| 1905 | Frederick Campbell, Earl Cawdor |
| 1905 | Edward Marjoribanks, Lord Tweedmouth |
| 1908 | Reginald McKenna |
| 1911 | Winston S. Churchill |
| 1915 | Arthur Balfour |
| 1916 | Sir Edward Carson |
| 1917 | Sir Eric Geddes |
| 1919 | Walter Long |
| 1921 | Arthur, Viscount Lee |
| 1922 | Leopold S. Amery |
| 1924 | Frederic Thesiger, Viscount Chelmsford |
| 1924 | William Bridgeman, later Viscount Bridgeman |
| 1929 | A.V. Alexander, later Earl of Hillsborough |
| 1931 | Sir Austen Chamberlain |
| 1931 | Sir Bolton Eyres-Monsell, later Viscount Monsell |

1936 Sir Samuel Hoare
1937 Alfred Duff Cooper
1938 James, Earl Stanhope
1939 Winston S. Churchill
1940 A.V. Alexander
1945 Brendan Bracken
1945 A.V. Alexander
1946 George, Viscount Hall
1951 Francis, Lord Pakenham
1951 James P.L. Thomas, later Viscount Cilcennin
1956 Quintin Hogg, Viscount Hailsham
1957 Earl of Selkirk
1959 Peter, Lord Carrington
1963 George, Earl Jellicoe
*This office was abolished in 1964.*

# MINISTER OF DEFENCE (1940–64)
## SECRETARY OF STATE FOR DEFENCE (from 1964)
## MINISTER OF DEFENCE FOR THE NAVY (1964–7)
## MINISTER OF STATE FOR DEFENCE
## UNDER SECRETARY OF STATE FOR DEFENCE FOR THE NAVY
## (1964–81)

### MINISTER OF DEFENCE

1940 Winston S. Churchill
1945 Clement Attlee
1946 A.V. Alexander
1950 E. Shinwell
1951 Winston S. Churchill
1952 Earl Alexander of Tunis
1954 Harold Macmillan
1955 Selwyn Lloyd
1955 Sir Walter Monckton
1956 Antony Head
1957 Duncan Sandys
1958 Harold Watkinson
1959 G.E.P. (Peter) Thorneycroft

# SECRETARY OF STATE FOR DEFENCE

*(Unified Ministry of Defence established 1 April 1964 under Peter Thorneycroft)*

1964   Denis Healey
1970   Lord Carrington
1974   Ian Gilmour
1974   Roy Mason
1976   Frederick Mulley
1979   Francis Pym
1981   John Nott
1983   Michael Heseltine
1986   George Younger

## MINISTER OF DEFENCE FOR THE NAVY (1964—7)

1964   Earl Jellicoe
1964   Christopher P. Mayhew
1966   J.P.W. Mallalieu

## MINISTER OF STATE FOR DEFENCE

1970   Lord Balniel
1972   Ian Gilmour
1974   George Younger
1974   William Rodgers
1976   John Gilbert
1979   Lord Strathcona and Mount Royal
1981   Lord Trenchard
1981   Peter Blaker

## UNDER SECRETARY OF STATE FOR DEFENCE FOR THE NAVY (1964—81)

1964   John Hall
1964   J.P.W. Mallalieu
1966   Lord Winterbottom
1967   Maurice Foley
1968   David Owen
1970   Peter Kirk
1972   Anthony Buck
1974   Frank Judd
1976   Patrick Duffy
1979   Keith Speed
*This office was abolished.*

# SENIOR NAVAL LORD
# LORD ADMIRAL
# FIRST NAVAL LORD *and*
# FIRST SEA LORD

## SENIOR NAVAL LORD[47]

| | | |
|---|---|---|
| March | 1689 | Admiral Arthur Herbert |
| January | 1690 | Sir John Chicheley |
| June | 1690 | Admiral Edward Russell (Earl of Orford) |
| January | 1691 | Captain Henry Priestman |
| May | 1694 | Admiral Edward Pellew |
| May | 1699 | Admiral Sir George Rooke |

## LORD ADMIRAL

| | | |
|---|---|---|
| January | 1702 | Thomas Herbert, Earl of Pembroke |
| May | 1702 | Prince George of Denmark |
| November | 1708 | Thomas Herbert, Earl of Pembroke |

## SENIOR NAVAL LORD

| | | |
|---|---|---|
| November | 1709 | Sir John Leake |
| October | 1710 | Sir George Byng |
| September | 1712 | Sir John Leake |
| October | 1714 | Sir George Byng |
| April | 1717 | Matthew Aylmer |
| March | 1718 | Sir George Byng |
| September | 1721 | Sir John Jennings |
| June | 1727 | Sir John Norris |
| May | 1730 | Sir Charles Wager |
| June | 1733 | Lord Archibald Hamilton |
| March | 1738 | Lord Harry Powlett |
| March | 1742 | Lord Archibald Hamilton |
| February | 1746 | Lord Vere Beauclerk |
| November | 1749 | George, Lord Anson |
| June | 1751 | Sir William Rowley |
| November | 1756 | Hon. Edward Boscawen |
| April | 1757 | Sir William Rowley |
| July | 1757 | Hon. Edward Boscawen |
| March | 1761 | Hon. John Forbes |
| April | 1763 | Richard, Admiral Lord Howe |
| July | 1765 | Sir Charles Saunders |
| September | 1766 | Hon. Augustus Keppel |
| December | 1766 | Sir Piercy Brett |
| February | 1770 | Francis Holburne |

47  This position was never formalized. The senior naval member was often the First Lord (q.v.)

# FIRST NAVAL LORD

| | | |
|---|---|---|
| February | 1771 | Augustus Hervey, later Earl of Bristol |
| April | 1775 | Sir Hugh Palliser |
| April | 1779 | Robert Man |
| September | 1780 | George Darby |
| April | 1782 | Sir Robert Harland |
| January | 1783 | Hugh Pigot |
| December | 1783 | John Leveson Gower |
| August | 1789 | Samuel, Lord Hood |
| March | 1795 | Sir Charles Middleton |
| November | 1795 | James Gambier |
| February | 1801 | Sir Thomas Troubridge |
| May | 1804 | James Gambier, later Lord Gambier |
| February | 1806 | John Markham |
| April | 1807 | Lord Gambier |
| May | 1808 | Sir Richard Bickerton |
| March | 1812 | William Domett |
| October | 1813 | Sir Joseph Yorke |
| April | 1818 | Sir Graham Moore |
| March | 1820 | Sir William Johnstone Hope |
| September | 1828 | Sir George Cockburn |
| November | 1830 | Sir Thomas Hardy |
| August | 1834 | George Dundas |
| November | 1834 | Charles Adam |
| December | 1834 | Sir George Cockburn |
| April | 1835 | Sir Charles Adam |
| September | 1841 | Sir George Cockburn |
| July | 1846 | Sir William Parker |
| July | 1846 | Sir Charles Adam |
| July | 1847 | James Deans Dundas |
| February | 1852 | Maurice Berkeley |
| March | 1852 | Hyde Parker |
| June | 1854 | Maurice Berkeley |
| November | 1857 | Sir Richard Saunders Dundas |
| March | 1858 | William Martin |
| June | 1859 | Sir Richard Saunders Dundas |
| June | 1861 | Sir Frederick Grey |
| July | 1866 | Sir Alexander Milne |
| December | 1868 | Sir Sydney Dacres |
| November | 1872 | Sir Alexander Milne |
| September | 1876 | Sir Hastings Yelverton |
| November | 1877 | George Wellesley |
| September | 1879 | Sir Astley Cooper Key |
| July | 1885 | Sir Arthur Hood |
| October | 1889 | Sir Richard Vesey Hamilton |
| September | 1891 | Sir Anthony Hoskins |
| November | 1893 | Sir Frederick Richards |

# FIRST SEA LORD

| | | |
|---|---|---|
| August | 1899 | Lord Walter Kerr |
| October | 1904 | Sir John Fisher |
| January | 1910 | Sir Arthur K. Wilson |
| December | 1911 | Sir Francis Bridgeman |
| December | 1912 | Prince Louis of Battenberg |
| October | 1914 | John, Lord Fisher |
| May | 1915 | Sir Henry Jackson |
| December | 1916 | Sir John Jellicoe |
| January | 1918 | Sir Rosslyn Wemyss |
| November | 1919 | David, Earl Beatty |
| July | 1927 | Sir Charles Madden |
| July | 1930 | Sir Frederick Field |
| January | 1933 | Sir Ernle (later Baron) Chatfield |
| November | 1938 | Sir Roger Backhouse |
| June | 1939 | Sir Dudley Pound |
| October | 1943 | Sir Andrew B. Cunningham |
| June | 1946 | Sir John Cunningham |
| September | 1948 | Bruce, Lord Fraser |
| December | 1951 | Sir Rhoderick McGrigor |
| April | 1955 | Earl Mountbatten |
| May | 1959 | Sir Charles Lambe |
| May | 1960 | Sir Caspar John |
| August | 1963 | Sir J.D. (David) Luce |
| February | 1966 | Sir Varyl C. Begg |
| | 1969 | Sir Michael Le Fanu |
| | 1971 | Sir Michael Pollock |
| | 1974 | Sir Edward Ashmore |
| | 1977 | Sir Terence Lewin |
| | 1980 | Sir Henry Leach |
| | 1983 | Sir John Fieldhouse |
| | 1985 | Sir William Staveley |

## CIVIL LORD OF THE ADMIRALTY

*From 1830 it was fixed in principle — but with minor variations later — that in addition to the First Lord there should be four naval lords. Two years later a Civil Lord of the Admiralty was added.*

| | |
|---|---|
| 1832 | Henry Labouchere |
| 1834 | Lord Ashley |
| 1835 | Lord Dalmeny |
| 1841 | H.T.Lowry Corry |
| 1845 | Henry Fitzroy |
| 1846 | William Francis Cowper |
| 1852 | Arthur Duncombe |
| 1852 | William Francis Cowper |
| 1855 | Sir Robert Peel |
| 1857 | Thomas George Baring |

| 1858 | Lord Lovaine |
| 1859 | Frederick Lygon |
| 1859 | Samuel Whitbread |
| 1863 | Marquess of Hartington |
| 1863 | James Stansfeld |
| 1864 | H.C.E.Childers |
| 1866 | Henry Fenwick |
| 1866 | Lord John Hay |
| 1866 | G.J. Shaw-Lefevre |
| 1866 | Charles du Cane |
| 1868 | Frederick Stanley |
| 1868 | G.O.Trevelyan |
| 1870 | Earl of Camperdown |
| 1874 | Sir Massey Lopes |
| 1880 | Thomas Brassey |
| 1882 | George Wightwick Rendel |
| 1885 | Ellis Ashmead-Bartlett |
| 1886 | Robert William Duff |
| 1886 | Ellis Ashmead-Bartlett |
| 1892 | Edmund Robertson |
| 1895 | Austen Chamberlain |
| 1900 | Ernest Pretyman |
| 1903 | Arthur Lee |
| 1905 | George Lambert |
| 1915 | Duke of Devonshire |
| 1916 | Earl of Lytton |
| 1916 | Ernest Pretyman |
| 1919 | Earl of Lytton |
| 1920 | Earl of Onslow |
| 1921 | Bolton Eyres-Monsell |
| 1922 | Marquess of Linlithgow |
| 1924 | Frank Hodges |
| 1924 | Earl Stanhope |
| 1929 | George Hall |
| 1931 | Euan Wallace |
| 1935 | Kenneth Lindsay |
| 1937 | J. J. Llewellin |
| 1937 | Austin Hudson |
| 1942 | Richard Pilkington |
| 1945 | Walter Edwards |
| 1951 | Simon Wingfield Digby |
| 1957 | Thomas Galbraith |
| 1959 | Ian Orr-Ewing |
| 1963 | John Hay |

## TREASURER OF THE NAVY

| 1660 | Sir George Carteret |
| 1667 | Earl of Anglesey |
| 1672 | Sir Thomas Osborne |

| | |
|---|---|
| 1673 | Sir Edward Seymour |
| 1681 | Viscount Falkland |
| 1689 | Edward Russell |
| 1699 | Sir Thomas Littleton |
| 1710 | Robert Walpole |
| 1711 | Charles Caesar |
| 1714 | John Aislabie |
| 1718 | Richard Hampden |
| 1720 | Sir George Byng |
| 1724 | Pattee Byng |
| 1734 | Arthur Onslow |
| 1742 | Thomas Clutterbuck |
| 1742 | Sir Charles Wager |
| 1743 | Sir John Rushout |
| 1744 | George Bubb Dodington |
| 1749 | Henry Bilson Legge |
| 1754 | George Grenville |
| 1756 | George Bubb Dodington |
| 1756 | George Grenville |
| 1762 | Viscount Barrington |
| 1765 | Viscount Howe |
| 1770 | Sir Gilbert Elliot |
| 1777 | Welbore Ellis |
| 1782 | Isaac Barré |
| 1782 | Henry Dundas |
| 1783 | Charles Townshend |
| 1784 | Henry Dundas |
| 1800 | Dudley Ryder |
| 1801 | Charles Bragge |
| 1803 | George Tierney |
| 1804 | George Canning |
| 1806 | Richard Brinsley Sheridan |
| 1807 | George Rose |
| 1818 | Frederick Robinson |
| 1823 | William Huskisson |
| 1827 | Charles Grant |
| 1828 | William Vesey Fitzgerald |
| 1830 | Thomas Frankland Lewis |
| 1830 | Charles Poulett Thomson |
| 1834 | Viscount Lowther |
| 1835 | Sir Henry Parnell |

*Office combined with that of Paymaster General of the Forces in 1836 to become Paymaster General.*

## SECRETARY TO THE ADMIRALTY
## FIRST SECRETARY TO THE ADMIRALTY

| | |
|---|---|
| 1660 | William Coventry |
| 1667 | Matthew Wren |
| 1672 | Sir John Werden |

| 1673 | Samuel Pepys |
|------|--------------|
| 1679 | Thomas Hayter |
| 1680 | John Brisbane |
| 1684 | Samuel Pepys |
| 1689 | Phineas Bowles |
| 1690 | James Southerne |
| 1694 | William Bridgeman |
| 1694 | William Bridgeman and Josiah Burchett |
| 1698 | Josiah Burchett |
| 1702 | Josiah Burchett and George Clarke |
| 1705 | Josiah Burchett |
| 1741 | Josiah Burchett and Thomas Corbett |
| 1742 | Thomas Corbett |
| 1751 | John Cleveland |
| 1763 | Philip Stephens |
| 1795 | Evan Nepean |
| 1804 | William Marsden |
| 1807 | William Wellesley Pole |
| 1809 | John Wilson Croker |
| 1830 | George Elliot |
| 1834 | George Robert Dawson |
| 1835 | Charles Wood |
| 1839 | Richard More O'Ferrall |
| 1841 | John Parker |
| 1841 | Sidney Herbert |
| 1845 | H.T.Lowry Corry |
| 1846 | Henry George Ward |
| 1849 | John Parker |
| 1852 | Augustus O'Brien Stafford |
| 1853 | Ralph Bernal Osborne |
| 1858 | H.T.Lowry-Corry |
| 1859 | Lord Clarence Paget |
| 1866 | Thomas George Baring |
| 1866 | Lord Henry Gordon-Lennox |
| 1868 | William Edward Baxter |
| 1871 | G.J.Shaw-Lefevre |
| 1874 | Algernon Egerton |
| 1880 | G.J.Shaw-Lefevre |
| 1880 | G.O.Trevelyan |
| 1882 | Henry Campbell-Bannerman |
| 1884 | Thomas Brassey |
| 1885 | C.T.Ritchie |
| 1886 | John Tomlinson Hibbert |
| 1886 | Arthur Bower Forwood |
| 1892 | Sir Ughtred James Kay-Shuttleworth |
| 1895 | William Grey Macartney |
| 1900 | Hugh Arnold-Foster |
| 1903 | Ernest Pretyman |
| 1905 | Edmund Robertson |
| 1908 | Thomas Macnamara |
| 1920 | Sir James Craig |
| 1921 | L.S.Amery |

1922   Bolton Eyres-Monsell
1923   Archibald Boyd-Carpenter, later Lord Boyd-Carpenter
1924   Charles Ammon
1924   J.C.C.Davidson
1926   Cuthbert Morley Headlam
1929   Charles Ammon
1931   Earl Stanhope
1931   Lord Stanley
1935   Sir Victor Warrender
1935   Lord Stanley
1937   Geoffrey Shakespeare
1940   Sir Victor Warrender (Lord Bruntisfield from 1942)
1945   John Dugdale
1950   James Callaghan
1951   Allan Noble
1955   George Ward
1957   Christopher Soames, later Lord Soames
1958   Robert Allan
1959   Ian Orr-Ewing

# PARLIAMENTARY CONTROL: BIBLIOGRAPHY

Ayling, Stanley, *The Elder Pitt, Earl of Chatham* (1976)

Aylmer, G.E., *The King's Servants: The Civil Service of Charles I* (1961)

Barnes, G.R. and O.J.H. Edwards, *The Private Papers of John, Earl of Sandwich*, Navy Records Society, 4 vols, 1932–8.

Bartlett, C.J., *Great Britain and Sea Power 1815–1853* (1963).

Baugh, Daniel, *Naval Administration 1715–1750*, Navy Records Society, 1977.

Chatfield, Lord, *The Navy and Defence* (1942).

Collinge, J.M., *Navy Board Officials 1660–1832*, Institute of Historical Research, 1978, Vol VII of 'Office Holders in Modern Britain'.

Corbett, Julian S. (Ed.) *The Private Papers of George, Second Earl Spencer*, Navy Records Society, 2 vols, 1913–14.

Crowhurst, Patrick, *The Defence of British Trade 1689–1815* (1977).

Davies, C.S.L., *The Origin of The Navy Board Under Henry VIII*, English Historical Review, LXXX.

Erhman, John, *The Navy in The War of William III, 1689–97* (1953).

Erhman, John, *Cabinet Government and War 1890–1940* (1958).

Geddes, Lord, *The Forging of a Family* (1952).

Glover, Richard, *Britain at Bay: Defence Against Bonaparte, 1803–14* (1973).

Howard, Michael, *The Central Organisation of Defence* (1970).

Johnson, F.A., *Defence By Committee: The Committee of Imperial Defence 1880–1959* (1960).

Laughton, Sir J.K., *Letters and Papers of Charles, Lord Barham, 1758–1813*, Navy Records Society, 3 vols, 1906–10.

Lloyd, C.C., *Mr Barrow of the Admiralty* (1970).

Murray, Lady, *The Making of a Civil Servant, Sir Oswyn Murray* (1940).

Murray, Sir Oswyn, *The Admiralty, The Mariner's Mirror*, Parts I–X in Vols XXXIII (1937) to XXXV (1939).

Ollard, Richard, *Pepys: A Biography* (1974).

Oppenheim, M., *History of the Administration of the Royal Navy and of Merchant Shipping in Relation to the Navy, 1509–1660* (1896).

Pack, S.W.C., *Admiral Lord Anson* (1960).

Pepys, Samuel, *Memories Relating to the State of the Royal Navy of England, for Ten Years, Determin'd December 1688*, London, 1690. (Ed. J. Tanner, 1906).

Ranft, B. McL., *The Significance of the Political Career of Samuel Pepys, Journal of Modern History*, Vol XXIV.

Richmond, H.W., *Papers Relating to the Loss of Gibraltar in 1756*, Navy Records Society (1911).

Rodger, N.A.M., *The Admiralty* (1979).

Roskill, S.W., *Naval Policy Between The Wars, 1919–1929*, Vol I (1968).

Roskill, S.W., *The Dismissal of Admiral Jellicoe, Journal of Contemporary History*, Vol I, No. 4, October 1966.

Rowe, Violet A., *Sir Henry Vane, The Younger* (1970).

Sainty, J.C. (Ed), *Admiralty Officials 1660–1870*, Institute of Historical Research, London, 1975, No IV of 'Office Holders in Modern Britain' Series.

Smith, David Bonner (Ed), *The Letters of Lord St Vincent, 1801–1804*, Navy Records Society, 2 Vols, 1921–6.

Tanner, J.R., *Samuel Pepys and the Royal Navy* (1920).

Walker, Sir C., *Thirty-Four Years at the Admiralty*, (1934).

Ward, J.T., *Sir James Graham* (1967).

## COMMAND PAPERS

1921   Cmd 1343   Navy: Distribution of the Duties of the Naval Staff at the Admiralty.

1922   Cmd   1581, 1582 & 1589: First Interim, Second and Third Report of the Committee on National Expenditure (the Geddes Committee).
    Cmd 1587   Remarks of the Admiralty on the Interim Report of the Committee on National Expenditure.

1926   Cmd 2649   Report of the Committee on the Amalgamation of the Common Services of the Navy, Army and Air Force (The Mond-Weir Committee).

1963   Cmd 2097   The Central Organisation For Defence.

# SECTION 2
# SHIPS' NAMES AND BADGES

# SHIPS' NAMES AND BADGES

**I have a Fleet now at Sea, worthy of the English Nation.**
Charles II *to Parliament.*

**It is seamen, not ships, that constitute a Navy.**
Admiral Sir Charles Napier.

**Taken all in all, a ship of the line is the most honourable thing that man, as a gregarious animal, has ever produced.**
Robert Leslie *to John Ruskin, 1884.*

**I hate your pen and ink men; a fleet of British ships of war are the best negotiators in Europe.**
Vice Admiral Nelson *to Lady Hamilton, 1801.*

## INTRODUCTION

THIS section presents well over sixteen hundred ships' names selected from the many thousands which have been used for Royal Navy ships over the past three or more centuries. A number of points call for comment. In order to qualify for selection, the ship must have served during or after World War II. The ship is then given a list of predecessors which have borne the same name, but this list has been pruned to include what can loosely be termed major ships — i.e., sloops or 6th rates and larger in the case of sailing-ships, while all the modern vessels are included down to WW II corvettes, and sometimes smaller vessels too. In addition, each ship entry includes battle honours and motto (if any) while some 230 of the entries have had their ship's badges reproduced. In the case of the mottoes and their translations, my source has been the Naval Historical Library.

As well as the considerable resources of the Admiralty Library, I have consulted the Design Division of the Planning Department at HM Dockyard Devonport. Both sources were most helpful and productive. I have also called upon other, secondary, sources. *British Warship Names* by Captain T.D. Manning and Commander C.F. Walker (1959), and *Crests and Badges of HM Ships* by Alfred E. Weightman (also 1959), are both splendid source documents, and I am grateful to the publishers' successors for allowing me to quote from their works. Another most useful source has been *Ships of the Royal Navy: An Historical Index*, two vols, by J. J. Colledge (1969). John Young's *A Dictionary of Ships of the Royal Navy of the Second World War*, published in 1975, was also useful. In the case of Manning and Walker considerable updating and editing of their listings, and correction of errors, has entailed major editing — in particular of the battle honours awarded to each ship. Weightman's book is more reliable for its battle-honours listings, but it is far less comprehensive than Manning and Walker.

It is a fact that many ships' commanding officers have perpetuated — if not initiated — battle honours on their quarterdeck history scrolls quite unofficially. Manning and Walker allow numerous honours which the Admiralty definitive list excluded. Many ships 'claim' South Africa 1899–1901, when the Admiralty states quite clearly that they are entitled to the medal only; to earn the battle honour the ship must have landed a naval brigade. Toulon 1744 and 1793 are not recognized as battle honours, nor are the two battles at Cuddalore in 1758 and 1783; Dover Patrol 1914–18 is disallowed; Calder's Action and Strachan's Action, both of 1805, are not allowed, but Cornwallis's Retreat of ten years earlier is permitted. The oft-quoted Black Sea 1854–55 is more correctly Crimea, while a host of Far Eastern battles simply are not official battle honours.[1]

Single-ship actions which resulted in battle honours — usually in the form of the name of the enemy ship and the year of the action — appear at the end of each battle-honour entry, except for a few Single-ship Actions which have been given a geographical location such as *Revenge* and Azores 1591.

Displacement figures in this section have been taken from *Jane's Fighting Ships* rather than *British Warships 1914–19* by F.J. Dittmar and J.J. Colledge (1972), and *Warships of World War II* by H.T. Lenton and J.J. Colledge (1973) although all of these have served as sources. Even *Jane's* gives conflicting figures, modifying entries as ships emerge from refits or modernization with increased displacements. Thus it is not necessarily wrong to see a reference to an early 'Battle' class destroyer having a displacement of 2,315 tons when later the reference is to 3,361 tons. The recent adoption of a full load-displacement figure is often given here in addition to the standard tonnage. Submarines, of course, are shown with two figures, for surface and dived displacements, but *Jane's* have recently added a third to indicate light/standard/dived displacements.[2]

The 'Algerine' class of minesweepers (the largest and most efficient in the Navy at the time) are defined as such without a displacement. Lenton and Colledge quote a figure of 850 tons. Early entries in *Jane's* (1944–5) classified these vessels as 950–990 tons. By 1955–6 these had increased to 950–1,040 tons, with 1,245–1,335 full load. The 1958–9 entry gave them 1,040 standard and 1,335 full load.

Dates for each ship listing are generally the date of launching unless otherwise stated.

A sailing-ship's strength was best indicated by the number of guns carried,

---

1  Among many others, the following honours have often been displayed in the past but are not officially accepted: Smyrna Convoy 1693; Fatshan Creek 1857; Pei-Ho Forts 1859; Satsuma 1862; Simonoseki 1864; Suakin 1885–5 and Tsing Tao 1914.

2  Tonnage is probably derived from the fifteenth-century calculation of the nuber of *tuns* or casks of wine a ship could carry.

and this figure is given in parentheses. The 'rating' of ships calls for some explanation. The following table of rates is a typical example of a system that was subject to many changes. Anson, for example, when appointed First Lord of the Admiralty in 1751 raised the line status to exclude 50-gun ships.

At that time 4th-rates of 60 guns were virtually obsolete, so that for practical purposes the British line of battle comprised only ships of the first three rates. In the event the line consisted mainly of 3rd rates, the majority of which were the splendid 'seventy-fours'.

The most numerous ships were the frigates — the 5th and 6th rates — mounting from 28 to 38 guns on a single deck. The smaller 6th rates of 20 to 24 guns were also known as frigates for a time, but they became classified as post-ships, the smallest ships commanded by post captains. The French classified their small vessels of this class as corvettes, a name adopted by the Royal Navy nearly two centuries later.

## RATES OF SHIPS*

| Rate | No. of Guns | Wt of Broadside (lb) | Complement | Tonnage | Length of lower gun-deck (ft) |
|------|-------------|----------------------|------------|---------|-------------------------------|
| 1st | 100 + | 2,500 | 850–950 | 2,000–2,600 | 180 |
| 2nd | 98 | 2,300 | 750 | 2,000 | 180 |
|  | 90 | 2,050 | 750 | 2,000 | 170 |
| 3rd | 80 | 1,974 | 720 | 2,000 | 170–160 |
|  | 74 | 1,764 | 640 | 1,700 |  |
|  | 60 | 1,200 | 490 | 1,300 |  |
| 4th | 50 | 800 | 350 | 1,100 | 150 |

Division between ships of the line or line-of-battle ships

| Rate | No. of Guns | Wt of Broadside (lb) | Complement | Tonnage | Length of lower gun-deck (ft) |
|------|-------------|----------------------|------------|---------|-------------------------------|
| 5th | 44 |  |  |  |  |
|  | 40 |  |  |  |  |
|  | 38 | 636–350 | 320–215 | 900–700 | 150–130 |
|  | 36 |  |  |  |  |
|  | 32 |  |  |  |  |
| 6th | 28 |  |  |  |  |
|  | 24 | 250–180 | 200–160 | 650–550 | 130–120 |
|  | 20 |  |  |  |  |

*It is not possible to give any precise date for these figures, but they are obviously prior to Anson's re-rating of 1751*

The naming of ships in the Royal Navy has developed over more than 750 years from a simple haphazard arrangement where the monarch was directly involved in the actual naming of a ship to the much more studied and formalized business of modern times. The naming of the first *Queen*, for example, dates back to a great ship in King Henry III's reign in 1232, but it was not till two centuries later that a trend began to develop that can be detected: the adoption of names with a distinct religious significance — perhaps not inappropriate when the success or otherwise of a maritime venture would rely more heavily on Divine assistance than navigational accuracy.

It was during the reigns of the two Henrys VII and VIII that warships armed with cannon (as distinct from merchant ships) began to emerge, and some of their names have lasted till this century: *Lion, Dragon, Greyhound* and *Bonaventure* are examples.

The reign of Elizabeth with its long years of war with Spain harvested a rich crop of ships' names, some capturing the warlike attitude of the times: *Triumph, Revenge, Defiance, Repulse*, good, solid names of twentieth-century renown too. This was the time also of the adoption of double-barrelled or compound names: *Warspite, Swiftsure, Dreadnought* and *Vanguard. Warspite* was a compound of 'War — Despite' (but see the *Warspite* ship entry.) *Swiftsure* combines 'Swift' and 'Pursuer': while *Dreadnought* meant fear nothing.

The Commonwealth period only produced one 1st rate, the *Naseby*, but the Roundheads commemorated many of their smaller ships with names of their victories — *Marston Moor, Worcester* and *Taunton* — while ships with a royalist name were rechristened: 'saint ships' had their 'St' prefix lopped off. This period also produced those excellent names the first *London, Hercules, Renown, Drake* and *Pembroke*.

Even before his Restoration, Charles II and his supporters were name-changing. Witness Pepys:[3]

> May 7th 1660: My Lord [Montagu] went this morning about the flag ships, in a boat to see what alterations there must be to the arms and flags.
> May 11th: We began to pull down all the State's arms in the fleet...
> May 23rd: [the day of embarkation aboard *Naseby* in Holland.] After dinner the King and the Duke [of York] altered the name of some ships. The *Naseby* became *Royal Charles*.[4]

Just how deeply involved in ship-naming was Charles II is exemplified in the story of the *London*, which was accidentally burnt in the Thames in 1665. A fund produced £16,000 from the citizens of the city towards the cost of a new ship. A delighted King proclaimed the ship should be named *Loyal London*. After burning in the Medway, she was salved, towed to Deptford and rebuilt. An impoverished citizenry declined to contribute towards the ship again, and in a display of pique Charles struck through the *Loyal* prefix — and plain *London* the ships have remained ever since.

It was in the second half of the seventeenth century that the line of battle was introduced, demonstrating the influence of the Generals-at-sea who brought to naval tactics an orderliness to replace the haphazard Tudor mêlée. This important development impinged upon the rating system, as we have seen

3  Pepys's *Diary*.

4  And thus began the custom of naming the first battleship in a new reign after the sovereign. Unhappily many of the renamed ships found a disastrous end: *Royal Charles* was taken by De Ruyter from the Medway: *Royal James* burnt in the Medway: *Roal Prince* was taken and burnt in the Four Day's Battle: *Royal Sovereign* was destroyed by fire at Chatham.

elsewhere,[5] and this rating of ships by the number of guns they carried was for centuries the best-known method of assessing a ship's fighting strength: it has been adopted throughout this Companion by inserting where known the ship's guns in parentheses.[6]

The naming of captured enemy ships, or prizes, posed a problem. When a prize was ready for RN service her name was often unchanged, unless it was unpronounceable for an Englishman or unless it was already in use. Once the name became added it was used for succeeding ships. France followed the same policy. In some instances enemy names became anglicized, such as *Gloire* to *Glory* and *Renommée* to *Renown*. It was all quite reasonable, and when put to the test it worked. Still, it led to the curious situation at Trafalgar of the *Berwick* fighting for the French, while a *Swiftsure* and an *Achille* served in both fleets, and a *Téméraire* and a *Belleile* fought under the British flag.

In the war-torn eighteenth century more than a thousand names[7] had to be found for ships added to the Navy. Names of Admirals and their victories replaced those of peers and place-names. Birds, animals and fishes were adopted for smaller vessels. One interesting innovation of this period was the introduction of names from Greek and Latin mythology, reflecting the fashionable interest during this classical period. The names of gods (*Jupiter*), kings (*Agamemnon*), heroes (*Bellerophon*) and monsters (*Minotaur*), became the names of battleships, while smaller ships were given the names of goddesses (*Minerva*), nymphs (*Arethusa*) and princesses (*Dido*).

The nineteenth century was a period of relative barrenness in this field except for one important innovation. It was the decision — indefinite at first, but firm at the end of the century — to adopt names for *classes* of ships. In the past ships had been built more or less singly, or at most in pairs. There were exceptions, of course: there was a class of five frigates in 1780 all with classical names, and at the end of the Napoleonic War a class of corvettes was named after rivers, while later in the 1870s there came the 'C' class corvettes and 'River' class gunboats. In the 1880s there was the Admiral class of battleships, and later still the 'R' class. But as a matter of defined policy, ships were not named in classes — even when *Dreadnought* was launched and battleships came off the slipways at the rate of four a year for ten years. Almost without exception they were given splendid names of old line-of-battle ships, names reading like a Trafalgar roll-call.

At the end of the century cruisers became grouped into armoured and light categories, the former generally being given the names of old 3rd rate line-of-battle ships, and the light cruisers those of the frigates from which they were directly descended.

The naming of small ships at this time was a jungle: destroyers, gunboats, sloops, torpedo-gunboats and corvettes were given names from the abundance of post-ships, gun-brigs and cutters of the past. Torpedo-boats were not given names; letters and numbers sufficed for them.

Torpedo-boat destroyers made their appearance in 1893, specifically to

---

5  A list of 1546 refers to 'Shyppes, galleases, pynnaces and roo-baerges' but gives no indication whatsoever of strength. Guns mounted, or 'rating', gave an immediate indication of strength. Manning and Walker, p.21.

6  See Colledge's *Ships of the Royal Navy: An Historical Index* for a historical chronology of rating ships.

7  Manning and Walker, p.32.

counter the torpedo-gunboats of foreign navies. By 1895 forty-two boats of 27 knots known as '27-knotters', had been launched, followed by seventy-two 30-knot boats over the next seven years. Most of them were designed by their builders with little regard for grouping into classes. In 1913 Winston Churchill formed a committee[8] to investigate the names and classification of destroyers.

The Committee recommended primarily that each class of destroyer should have a distinguishing letter, forming the initial letter of all the ships of that class, and secondarily that all existing destroyers should be renamed to conform.[9]

The Admiralty rejected the second recommendation, believing it to be inconvenient and improper to rename ships going back probably twenty years. However, in September 1913 all these surviving destroyers were designated as 'A', 'B', 'C' and 'D' classes: the 27-knotters became the 'A' class and the 30-knotters the 'B', 'C' and 'D' classes, with four, three and two funnels respectively. Other classes were redesignated 'E' through to 'K' (inexplicably, there was no 'J')[10] while the classes then under construction had their names changed to new ones beginning with the letter 'L'.

It was a sensible form of classification, soon to exhaust the alphabet with the need to meet the demands of WWI. The most formidable task, on an unprecedented scale, for the naming committee was presented by the vast flotilla of small ships programmed in the early years of the war. The huge programme of destroyer-construction was absorbing names by the score; now hundreds more were needed. The Admiralty adopted names of flowers, racehorses, racecourses, hunts, dances and small towns, despite the fact there was little historical relevance and that some barely met the Destroyer Committee's criterion of 'not absurd'.

After the wholesale scrapping of warships in the early 1920s the next new programme of any significance was put before parliament in the summer of 1925. Because Great Britain was barred by the Washington Treaty from building any more capital ships (battleships and battlecruisers) before 1931, the largest ships in the programme were cruisers. The Royal Navy was to be allowed seventy of them as against only thirty capital ships (later reduced to fifteen), and the question arose as to whether regular cruiser names should be allocated or whether to 'promote' those projected ships to the names of previous battleships.[11]

The First Sea Lord, Lord Beatty, suggested the following principles:

(a) That the Battleships and Battle Cruisers should be named after great Admirals or have other names of outstanding historical interest.
(b) That for Cruisers after the County and Town classes historical names should be chosen, using possibly for the bigger cruisers, names which have hitherto been borne by ships of the line.
(c) That each year's programme of Destroyers should begin with the same

8 The Destroyer Committee comprised Captain H.Lynes (chairman), Mr E.Marsh and Mr W.G.Perrin (Admiralty Librarian.)

9 In an apt phrase the Committee recommended names should be 'historic, appropriate, harmonious and not absurd'.

10 'E' (River), 'F' (Tribal), 'G' (Beagle), 'H' (Acorn), 'I' (Acheron), 'K' (Acasta).

11 Manning and Walker, p.41.

letter, using the names borne by smaller frigates etc and old destroyer names.

(d) That the practice should now be adopted of naming our Submarines...

The decision-making process began with the Controller (the Third Sea Lord responsible for new construction and the submission of names) consulting with the Admiralty Library and then recommending names to the Secretary of the Admiralty, the First Sea Lord and the First Lord before they were finally laid before the monarch.

The Admiralty adopted much of this recommendation. Destroyer classification on the alphabetical system was continued, starting the alphabet again with 'A', 'B' and 'C' classes for 1925.[12] Submarines were given names for the first time[13] and the twenty-three new boats were designated 'O', 'P', 'R' and 'S' classes to keep their letters well clear of the destroyers.

After the 'Counties' of the late 1920s and 1930s there came the 'Leander' class of light cruisers bearing classical names such as *Orion* and *Ajax*. The following class perpetuated the names of past frigates such as *Penelope* and *Galatea*, and they were succeeded by the heavy 'Town' class of ships like *Sheffield*, *Gloucester* and *Belfast*. The choice of the colonial names for the 'Fiji' class seems to have been a political decision, while the earlier 'Dido' class carried a splendid mixed bag of names from old cruisers and frigates.

For the first time in the Navy's history a capital ship of quite new conception, the aircraft carrier, seemed to have no precedent with regard to a name. Someone at the Admiralty suggested *Ark Royal*, the name of the flagship opposing the Armada, which gave it a historical significance, and the seaplane carrier of WWI gave it an association with naval flying. It was altogether a 'harmonious' naming, and the ship became a legend in her short wartime career.

For future carriers the Admiralty turned to three old ships converted from former light battlecruisers, all with names ending in −*ous*: *Furious*, *Courageous* and *Glorious*. But the naming of carriers lost course with the wide variety of names for the 'Illustrious', 'Audacious' and 'Gibraltar' classes, though it recovered it in 1942 with the introduction of a new class of 24 small fleet carriers for which names of old 3rd rates were revived — names borne by battleships and carriers of a generation earlier. Further, a large number of merchant ships — about two dozen of them — were converted to carriers, and for these smaller vessels a series of small-ship names ending in −*er* was revived, dating from 1797 (e.g., *Battler*, *Stalker*, *Searcher*). A second class was given the names of rulers, such as *Shah*, *Queen* and so on.

These carrier names were the product of the first Standing Ships Names Committee set up at the very end of 1940.[14] Its terms of reference were:

(a) To ... consider the naming of ships of the Annual and Supplementary building programmes and to forward their deliberations to the First Sea Lord and First Lord for approval by HM the King.

---

12  Except flotilla leaders, named after admirals.

13  Except previous experimental boats *Swordfish* and *Nautilus*.

14  The Committee consisted of Vice Admiral Sir Geoffrey Blake, L.G.Carr Laughton (Acting Admiralty Librarian), Captain Manning and Commander Walker.

(b) To ... make recommendations ... on any other name problems which may arise.

The alphabetical system for naming destroyers carried through to 'Z' ('O' to 'Z' were virtually ships of the same design). Then two classes of ships came along which upset the alphabetical system. First, there was a 'C' class of 32 ships, the four flotillas being distinguished by the second letter of their names. Second, there came the 'Battle' class named after land and sea battles — 42 were ordered, but only 24 completed.

Wartime also saw the birth of the 'Weapons' class, but only four were completed and one of these was the *Scorpion*. Now, a scorpion may be a small creature, but a weapon? Cunningham was First Sea Lord at the time, and requested a destroyer named after his *Scorpion*, which he commanded from 1911 to 1918. *Scorpion*, unbelievably, is also a scourge, armed with metal points: and an ancient siege machine. In short, a weapon!

Eight 'D' class ships became known as 'Daring' class ships instead of destroyers.

The USA planned over 500 escort destroyers for the Royal Navy, so a long-running list of names of Captains was allotted, to last for ages. But the first batch of these proved so successful that the USA kept them for themselves and built for us instead small escorts to which we gave the names of rivers and colonies.

Submarines, curiously, reverted to numbers and the prefix 'P' until Winston Churchill instructed otherwise.[15]

The end of WWII brought an end to many of the problems for the Committee. There were so few ships to name. Frigates were of five types at the end of the 1950s: named after naval officers (e.g., *Duncan*, *Keppel*); after seaside towns (*Yarmouth*, *Whitby*); cathedral cities (*Chichester*, *Lincoln*); warlike tribes (*Ashanti*, *Mohawk*) and wild animals of the cat family (*Lynx*, *Jaguar*). The guided-missile destroyers became a new 'County' class. Some submarines took on the names of sea mammals (*Grampus*, *Cachalot*), except nuclear-powered submarines, which assumed more noble names of ships of the line — *Dreadnought*, *Valiant*, *Warspite*.

A final comment on the adoption of names: some of the following listings of ships will give the name's derivation. It was considered unnecessary and repetitive to say that a ship's name derived from a river, a flower or a geographical location, especially when this was self-evident, so these dedications have not earnt a mention. Others with a more interesting source — such as those named after an admiral or mythological creatures — have been given an explanatory note to this effect.

## SHIPS' BADGES

Alfred Weightman in his *Crests and Badges of H.M. Ships*, published in 1957, states that there have been more than 2,000 official and unofficial badges for naval warships. Some ships sported more than one, and unofficial ones often created at the whim of a commanding officer proliferated. In a similar fashion, a ship's 'History Scroll' carved in teak would display quite unofficially battles

---

15 *The Second World War*, Vol IV, Winston S.Churchill, See Appendix C, PM's Minutes to First Sea Lord 5 Nov, 19 and 27 Dec 1942.

attended by the ship, regardless of whether the battle was designated an official Battle Honour or not.

Ships have carried banners, shields, figureheads and a variety of other decorative devices from the very earliest times, and all of them could justifiably be declared the forerunners of the ship's badge. Symbols have been adopted from early history as means of identification[16] — flags were rallying points, the Romans had their eagle, the Athenian owl is familiar, the Scottish clans adopted sprigs of oak and wild myrtle.

The unofficial naval badges survived for years and centuries. Some were crude, many humorous, most based on past exploits of ships of the name. *Swiftsure* is a good example; her badge derives from the figurehead of the first *Swiftsure* of 1573. The lion of the *Vanguard* comes from the most common figurehead in the Navy. Many badges carried initial letters.[17]

It was not till the end of 1918 that the badge became the subject of official acknowledgment when a Major ffoulkes[18] offered to supply ships' badges. Predictably a Ships' Badges Committee was formed in December 1918 and trials were carried out on the Thames before determining that badge shapes, all superscribed with a naval crown, should follow the ruling:

| | |
|---|---|
| circular | battleships |
| pentagonal | cruisers |
| shield-shaped | destroyers |
| diamond-shaped | auxiliary ships: carriers, submarines, depot ships and sloops. |

The design of ships' badges passed to the College of Heralds in 1935. For many years the manufacture of the badges was carried out at Chatham Dock Yard, but nowadays this is done at Devonport Dock Yard. In 1976 the MOD standardized ships' badges following the recommendations of the Ships' Names and Badges Committee (comprising representatives from the Naval Historical Branch, the Naval Staff, Naval Signals and the Secretariat: Commodore Naval Acceptance is the chairman and the Admiralty Adviser of Heraldry also attends.) Today there are more than 1,700 badges listed in the Admiralty files. The shapes are now:

| | |
|---|---|
| circular | HM Ships, submarines, RN Air Squadrons |
| diamond | Shore establishments |
| pentagonal | RFA, RMAS, PAS vessels |

We have adopted this new system throughout this Section, depicting all HM ships in the circular border, although many will be remembered in their older pentagonal, diamond- or shield-shaped badges.

---

16   The Scriptures tell of standards or symbols of the Jewish tribes.

17   In seeking a design for *Bulwark*, Captain Scott thought 'a plain B is rather hackneyed'. Weightman, p.3. Scott continued: 'The design must convey an idea (quaintly or otherwise) ... simple, so it can be distinguished at a considerable distance'.

18   Major Charles ffoulkes CB, OBE, OStJ, Hon DLitt, Oxon, FSA, onetime Master of the Tower Armouries, Director of the Imperial War Museum. He produced a total of 556 designs for badges and became the Admiralty Adviser on Heraldry.

# WARSHIP BUILDERS AND BREAKERS

Listed below are the major warship-builders and shipbreakers of this century. This check-list is not intended to be exhaustive, or to identify in detail each change reflected in a company's story. A notable example is the Armstrong, Whitworth and Vickers association. Armstrong started as Armstrong, Litchell & Co of Elswick. Early in this century Sir W.G. Armstrong, of Whitworth & Co Ltd, operated at Walker-on-Tyne. Vickers Ltd of Barrow-in-Furness linked up with Armstrong, and today this combine is one of the world's greatest builders of modern nuclear-powered submarines.

The decline in shipbuilding is nowhere more apparent than in the Clyde. Formerly the Thames had been a traditional shipbuilding centre, but with the increase in iron and steel in the construction of warships this centre of gravity shifted to the Clyde. By 1914 the Thames shipbuilding activity had declined almost to extinction, while the Clyde could claim more than thirty companies.

WWI gave all British yards — the Tyne and Wear, the Royal Dock Yards at Portsmouth, Chatham, Devonport and Pembroke; yards on the Clyde, Birkenhead and elsewhere — a tremendous boost, only for them to suffer a decline in the post-war years.

WWII saw a repetition of the cyclical trend. Warships were constructed with a speed never before thought possible. Smith's Dock Company of South Bank-on-Tees are believed to have been the originators and designers of the WWII corvettes. These ships had the great wartime merit of speed and easiness of production, though their barrel-like movement at sea was not an endearing feature. Nor were bridge personnel much comforted by the designer's claim that the bridge armour-plating would withstand machine-gun bullets. Twenty-four such craft were ordered in the first batch, two each from Blyth DD; Cook, Welton & Gemmell; Fleming & Ferguson; Henry Robb; William Simons, and Smith's Dock themselves. Three each were ordered from George Brown & Co; Grangemouth Dockyard; Charles Hill and John Lewis.

Ailsa Shipbuilding Co Ltd, Troon
Ardrossan Dockyard Co Ltd, Ardrossan
Armstrong-Whitworth, Newcastle
Sir W.G. Armstrong, Whitworth & Co Ltd, Walker-on-Tyne
S.P. Austin & Son Ltd, Sunderland

Barclay Curle & Co Ltd, Whiteinch, Glasgow
William Beardmore & Co Ltd, Dalmuir, Glasgow
Blyth Shipbuilding Dry Docks & Co Ltd
Blythswood Shipbuilding Co Ltd, Glasgow
Bow McLachlan & Co Ltd, Paisley
J.W. Brooke & Co Ltd, Lowestoft
Brooke Marine, Lowestoft
George Brown & Co (Marine) Ltd, Greenock
John Brown & Co (Clydebank) Ltd, Glasgow
Burntisland Ship Building Co Ltd
Burrard Dry Dock Co Ltd, North Vancouver

Cammell Laird & Co Ltd and (Shipbuilders) Ltd, Birkenhead and Tranmere
Camper & Nicholson Ltd, Gosport, Hants
Caledon Shipbuilding & Engineering Co Ltd, Dundee
HM Dock Yard Chatham
Cochrane & Sons Ltd, Selby
Cook, Welton & Gemmell, Beverley
John Crown & Sons Ltd, Sunderland

William Denny & Bros Ltd, Dumbarton
HM Dock Yard Devonport
J.S. Doig (Grimsby) Ltd
W. Doxford & Sons Ltd, Sunderland
Dunlop, Bremner & Co Ltd, Port Glasgow
R. Dunston Ltd, Thorne, nr Doncaster

Joseph T. Eltringham & Co, South Shields

Fairfield Shipbuilding & Engineering Co Ltd, Govan, Glasgow
Ferguson Bros Ltd, Port Glasgow
Fleetlands Shipyards Ltd
Fleming & Ferguson Ltd, Paisley
Furness Shipbuilding Co Ltd, Haverton Hill-on-Tees

Goole Shipbuilding & Repair Co Ltd
Grangemouth Dockyard Co Ltd
William Gray & Co Ltd, West Hartlepool
Greenock & Grangemouth Dock Yard Co Ltd, Greenock

Alexander Hall & Co Ltd, Aberdeen
Hall, Russell & Co Ltd, Aberdeen
William Hamilton & Co Ltd, Port Glasgow
Harland & Wolff Ltd, Govan, Glasgow
R & W Hawthorn Leslie & Co Ltd, Hebburn-on-Tyne
Charles Hill & Sons Ltd, Bristol

A. & J. Inglis Ltd, Glasgow

James & Stone, Brightlingsea, Essex
Sir James Laing & Sons Ltd, Aberdeen
John Lewis & Sons Ltd, Aberdeen
Lobnitz & Co Ltd, Renfrew
Lytham Shipbuilding Co Ltd, Lytham

A. McMillan & Co Ltd, Dumbarton
Murdoch and Murray Ltd, Port Glasgow

Napier & Miller Ltd, Old Kirkpatrick, Glasgow
North Vancouver Ship Repairs Ltd, Vancouver

Palmers Hebburn Co Ltd
Palmers Shipbuilding & Iron Co Ltd, Hebburn-on-Tyne
Philip & Son Ltd, Dartmouth

William Pickersgill & Sons Ltd, Sunderland
James Pollock Sons & Co Ltd, Faversham
Port Arthur Shipyards
HM Dock Yard Portsmouth

Redfern Construction Co Ltd
Richards Ltd, Great Yarmouth and Lowestoft
Richardson Duck & Co Ltd, Stockton-on-Tees
Henry Robb Ltd, Leith

Scotts Shipbuilding & Engineering Co Ltd, Greenock
William Simons & Co Ltd, Renfrew
Smith's Dock Co Ltd, South Bank-on-Tees
Alex Stephen & Sons Ltd, Govan, Glasgow
Sunderland Shipbuilding Co Ltd, Sunderland
Swan Hunter & Wigham Richardson, Ltd, Wallsend-on-Tyne
Swan Hunter (Shipbuilders) Ltd, Wallsend-on-Tyne

Thames Iron Works, Blackwall
John I. Thornycroft & Co Ltd, Woolston, Southampton

Vickers Ltd, Barrow-in-Furness
Vickers Armstrong Ltd, Newcastle-upon-Tyne
Vickers (Shipbuilders) Ltd, Barrow-in-Furness
Vickers Shipbuilding & Engineering Co Ltd, Barrow-in-Furness
Vosper Ltd, Portsmouth
Vosper Thornycroft Ltd, Woolston, Southampton

Samuel White & Co Ltd, Cowes, Isle of Wight
White's Shipyard, Southampton
Wood, Skinner & Co Ltd, Newcastle-upon-Tyne
Workman, Clark & Co Ltd, Belfast

Yarrow & Co, Poplar and Scotstoun
Yarrow (Shipbuilders) Ltd, Scotstoun, Glasgow.

# SHIP-BREAKERS

The surge in business in the post-war years of WWI and WWII contrasted interestingly. After WWI the ship-breakers (some of whom only acted as agents, purchasing the ships on commission for breakers both at home and abroad) bought the ships on competitive tendering. During WWII the British Iron and Steel Corporation was formed, and after the war the government sold most of its unwanted warships to this corporation, which allocated the ships to various yards for scrapping.

Alloa Ship Breaking Co (later Metal Industries), Rosyth and Charlestown
Arnott, Young, Dalmuir.

Barking Ship Breaking Co Ltd, Barking, Essex
C.A.Beard, Upnor and Teignmouth

Cashmore, Newport
S.Castle, Plymouth
Clarkson, Whitby
Cohen, Briton Ferry, Felixstowe and Swansea
Cox and Danks (Metal Industries in 1949), Upnor and Queenborough

Ellis, Newcastle

Forth Ship Breaking Co (later McLellan)

Granton Ship Breaking Co

Hayes, Porthcawl

A.O.Hill, Dover
J.W.Houston, Montrose
Hughes, Bolckow, Tyne and Blyth

King, Garston
J.J.King, Troon

Metal Industries Ltd, Rosyth and Charlestown
Multiocular Ship Breaking Co, Stranraer

Plymouth and Devon Ship Breaking Co, Plymouth
Pounds, Portsmouth

Rees, Llanelly
Richardson, Westgarth, Saltash
Rosyth Ship Breaking Co

Ship Breaking Co, Swansea
Slouth Trading Co (agent for German company)
Stanlee, Dover

J.E.Thomas, Newport
J.W.Towers, Milford Haven

Unity Ship Breaking Co, Plymouth
Upnor Ship Breaking Co, Upnor

Ward, Barrow, Briton Ferry, Grays, Hayle, Inverkeithing, Lelant, Milford Haven, Morecambe, New Holland, Pembroke Dock, Portishead, Rainham, Swansea

West of Scotland Ship Breaking Co, Troon

Young, Sunderland

# THE NAMES AND BADGES

## ABDIEL

Jutland 1916
Biscay 1941
Crete 1941
Libya 1941
Sicily 1943
Always faithful
Named after the loyal seraph who opposed Satan.
1   1915 minelaying flotilla leader. Sold 1936.
2   1940 minelayer. Mined and sunk 1943.
3   1967 minelayer of 1,375/1,500 tons built by Thornycroft.

## ABELIA

Atlantic 1941−5
Normandy 1944
English Channel 1944
1   1940 corvette of 925 tons built by Harland & Wolff. Sold 1947.

## ABERCROMBIE

Guadeloupe 1810
Dardanelles 1915−16
Sicily 1943
Salerno 1943

Mediterranean 1943
Named after the British Expedition commander in Egypt 1801, General Sir Ralph Abercromby, who died aboard *Foudroyant*. His arms are used on the badge. The Navy has consistently spelt his name wrongly ever since.
1   1809 3rd rate (74). Originally the French *Hautpoult* taken off Puerto Rico. Commanded by Charles Napier. Sold 1817 for £3,810.
2   1915 monitor of 6,150 tons. Originally *Farragut*, then *Admiral Farragut*, then *M1*. Sold 1921.
3   1942 monitor of 7,850 tons. Scrapped 1954.

## ABERDEEN

Atlantic 1939−45
North Africa 1942
*Bon accord* = Good fellowship.
1   1914 trawler.
2   1936 sloop built by Thornycroft. 990 tons. Scrapped 1949.

## ACASTA

San Domingo 1806
Martinique 1809
Jutland 1916
Atlantic 1939−40
Norway 1940
*Scharnhorst* 1940
*Memores majorum* = Mindful of our ancestors.
Named after a mythological Greek ocean nymph.
1   1797 5th rate. Broken up 1821.
2   1912 destroyer built by John Brown. 950 tons.
3   1929 destroyer built at Clydebank. 1,350 tons. Sunk by German battlecruisers west of Narvik 1940.

## ACHATES

Armada 1588
Guadeloupe 1810
Jutland 1916
Atlantic 1940−2
*Bismarck* Action 1941
North Africa 1942
Arctic 1942
Barents Sea 1942
*Fidus Achates* = Faithful Achates.
Named after the faithful friend of Aeneas.
1   1573 vessel of 13 guns. Condemned 1604.
4   1912 destroyer of 950 tons built by John Brown. Sold 1921.
5   1929 destroyer of 1,350 tons built at Clydebank. Sunk after damage from German heavy cruiser *Admiral Hipper* in Barents Sea battle, 1942.

## ACHERON

Cape Tenez 1805
Heligoland 1914
Dogger Bank 1915
Jutland 1916
Norway 1940
*Post tenebras lux* = After darkness, light.
Name taken from a river of Hades.
1   1803 vessel.
2   1838 sloop. Sold 1855.
3   1904: broadside ironclad renamed from *Northumberland*.
4   1911 destroyer built by Thornycroft. Served with 1st Destroyer Flotilla of the Grand Fleet 1914−16. Sold 1921.
5   1930 destroyer built by Thornycroft. 1,350 tons. Lost by mine 1940.
6   1947 submarine built at Chatham. 1,120/1,620 tons. Too late for WWII

service. Scrapped 1972. Disposal
List 1974.

## ACHILLES (Achille)

Belleisle 1761
Trafalgar 1805
River Plate 1939
Guadalcanal 1942−3
Okinawa 1945
*Leopard* 1917
*Fortiter in re* = Bravely in action.
Named after the Greek chieftain hero
of Homer's *Iliad* in the Trojan War. He
was supposed to have been plunged
into the Styx by Thetis, his mother.
1   1744 vessel.
2   1757 ship of 60 guns. Sold 1784.
4   1794 3rd rate prize but broken up
    within two years.
5   1798 4th rate of 74 guns. Fought in
    Lee Division at Trafalgar. Sold
    1864.
6   1863 armoured ship. Renamed
    *Hibernia* 1902.
7   1905 cruiser built by Armstrong.
    13,350 tons. Single-ship action
    1917. Sold 1921.
8   1932 cruiser of 7,030 tons built by
    Cammell Laird. RNZN 1937−43.
    Damaged in *Graf Spee* action, 1939.
    Won Pacific battle honours in
    WWII. Sold to RIN 1948 and
    renamed *Delhi*.
9   1968 general purpose frigate of
    2,500/2,962 tons built by Yarrow.
    Fitted with Seacat missiles.

## ACTAEON

Belleisle 1761
China 1856−60
Name taken from Greek mythology.
The huntsman Actaeon watched
Artemis bathing. When the goddess
saw him she turned him into a stag,
and he was torn to pieces by his own
hounds.
1   1757 frigate (28) of 585 tons built at
    Chatham. Sold 1766.
2   1775 frigate built at Woolwich. Lost
    at Charlestown 1776.
3   1778 5th rate (44) of 887 tons. Sold
    1802.
4   1805 prize taken off Rochefort.
    Broken up 1815.
5   1831 6th rate (26) of 620 tons built
    at Portsmouth. Served in Chinese
    waters. Sold 1889.
6   Frigate (50), ex-*Vernon*, 2,388 tons.
8   1945 sloop of 1,350 tons built by
    Thornycroft. Sold to the Federal
    Republic of Germany 1958 and
    renamed *Hipper*.

## ACTIVE

Lagos 1759
Trincomalee 1782
Camperdown 1797
Egypt 1801
Lissa 1811
Pelagosa 1811
Ashantee 1873−4
Jutland 1916

Atlantic 1939−45
*Bismarck* Action 1941
Diego Suarez 1942
Arctic 1944
Falkland Islands 1982
*Festina lente* = Hasten slowly.
1   1758 frigate. Surrendered 1778.
4   1780 frigate. Wrecked 1796.
8   1797 cutter with Duncan at the
    Nore Mutiny and at
    Camperdown.
13  1799 5th rate. Renamed *Argo*
    1833.
15  1845 5th rate. Renamed *Durham*
    1867.
18  1869 corvette. Sold 1906.
19  1911 cruiser of 3,440 tons built at
    Pembroke Dock Yard. Served
    with Harwich Force and Grand
    Fleet WWI. Sold 1920 for breaking
    up in Norway.
23  1929 destroyer of 1,350 tons built
    at Hawthorn Leslie. Mainly based
    at Gibraltar during WWII. Broken
    up 1948.
24  1972 frigate Type 21, 2,750/3,250
    tons built by Vosper Thornycroft.

## ACTIVITY

Atlantic 1944
Arctic 1944
1   1942 escort carrier of 11,800 tons,
    ex-*Telemachus*, built by Caledon,
    Kincaid. Sold 1946 and became
    *Breconshire*.

## ACUTE

North Sea 1942
North Africa 1942−3
Sicily 1943
Salerno 1943
Atlantic 1943
1   1797 vessel.
3   1942 minesweeper of the 'Algerine'
    class built by Harland & Wolff with
    a distinguished WWII career.

## ADAMANT

Chesapeake 1781
Camperdown 1797
Dardanelles 1915
Lead on. The motto and badge are
from the crest of Lord Hotham.
1   1779 4th rate. Broken up 1814.
2   1911 depot ship for submarines.
    935 tons. Based at Harwich
    1914−15 for 8th submarine flotilla,
    then Mediterranean. Sold 1932.
3   1940 depot ship built by Harland &
    Wolff, 12,700/16,000 tons. In
    Eastern Fleet and Pacific in WWII.
    Scrapped 1970.

# ADVENTURE

Dover 1652
Portland 1653
Gabbard 1653
Lowestoft 1665
Orfordness 1666
Solebay 1672
Barfleur 1692
Belleisle 1761
China 1856−60
Normandy 1944
*Golden Horse* 1681
*Two Lions* 1681
Dare all.
The badge is derived from the
*Adventure* medal awarded to Captain
Wyard, 1650.
1   1594 vessel. Broken up 1645.
2   1646 vessel. Sold 1688.
4   1691 5th rate. Surrendered 1709.
6   1709 5th rate. Broken up 1741.
8   5th rate 1741. Sold 1770.
11  1771 vessel sailed with Cook's
    second voyage 1772−4.
12  1784 5th rate. Broken up 1816.
18  1904 cruiser of 2,670 tons built by
    Armstrong. Sold 1920.
20  1924 cruiser/minelayer of 6,740
    tons built at Devonport.
    Converted to repair ship.
    Scrapped 1947.

# AENEAS

*Audentis fortuna juvat* = Fortune helps
the daring.
Named after one of the great heroes of
Troy and the subject of Virgil's epic
poem.
1   1945 submarine of 1,120/1,620 tons
    built by Cammell Laird. Designed
    for extended-range patrolling in
    Pacific, but too late for hostilities in
    WWII.

# AFFLECK

Atlantic 1943−4
Normandy 1944
English Channel 1944

Named after Admiral Sir Edmund
Affleck, a distinguished flag officer of
the American War of Independence.
1   1943 frigate of 1,300 tons, ex-US
    destroyer *Escort*, built by
    Bethlehem Steel. Constructive
    total loss 1944 but returned to
    USN.

# AFFRAY

Strong in battle.
1   1945 submarine of 1,120/1,620 tons
    built by Cammell Laird. Lost by
    accident off south coast, April
    1951.

# AFRIDI

Belgian Coast 1916−17
Zeebrugge 1918
Norway 1940
1   1907 destroyer built by Armstrong.
    Served throughout WWI at Dover.
    Scrapped 1919.
2   1937 destroyer of 1,870 'Tribal'
    class built by Vickers Armstrong.
    Bombed and sunk off Norway
    1940.

# AGAMEMNON

Ushant 1781
The Saintes 1782
Genoa 1795
Copenhagen 1801
Trafalgar 1805
San Domingo 1806
Crimea 1854−5
Dardanelles 1915−16
*Multa tuli fecique* = I have endured and
done much.
Named after the king of Mycenae who
commanded the besieging Greek
army at Troy.
1   1781 3rd rate. Nelson commanded
    her 1793−7. Wrecked 1809.
2   1852 screw ship. Sold 1870.
3   1879 turret ship. Sold 1903.
4   1906 battleship of 16,500 tons built
    by Beardmore. Served with
    famous 5th Battle Squadron.
    Radio-controlled target ship
    1919−21. Sold 1927.
5   1929 ship of 7,593 tons,
    requisitioned as a minelayer for the
    Navy in 1940. Carried 400 mines.
    Amenities ship 1944. Returned to
    owners 1947.

# AGINCOURT

Camperdown 1797
Egypt 1801
Jutland 1916
*Nestroque* = Now strike.
Commemorates Henry V's victory
over the French in 1415. The badge is
taken from one of Henry's.
1   1796 3rd rate (64) of 1,416 tons.
    Originally an East Indies Company
    ship. Served ingloriously at
    Camperdown and her
    commanding officer lost seniority,
    being displaced to the bottom of
    the Captain's List. Renamed *Bristol*
    1812.
2   1817 3rd rate of 1,747 tons built at
    Plymouth. Admiral Sir Thomas
    Cochrane's flagship off China
    1842−7. Renamed *Vigo* 1895.
3   Ironclad battleship of 10,600 tons
    built by Cammell Laird.
4   1913 dreadnought battleship of
    27,500 tons built by Armstrong.
    Ordered by Brazil as *Rio de Janeiro*,
    sold by them to Turkey as *Sultan
    Osman I*, then requisitioned by the
    Admiralty. Longest battleship of
    her time, and carried the heaviest
    guns.
5   1945 destroyer of 2,780/3,430 tons
    built by Hawthorn Leslie as one of
    the later 'Battle' class. Designed for
    long range and heavy AA
    armament for the Pacific war, but
    was too late for hostilities. Broken
    up in Sunderland in 1974.

# AIRE

Atlantic 1943−5
1   1943 frigate built by Fleming &
    Ferguson. 1,370 tons. Renamed
    *Tamar* 1946. Wrecked on Bombay
    Reefs 1946.

# AIREDALE

Libya 1942
Arctic 1942
1   1941 destroyer of the 'Hunt' class,

1,087 tons, built at Clydebank.[19]
Sunk by enemy aircraft in 1942.

## AISNE

Armed I seek no enmity.
Commemorates a land battle of WWI.
Badge taken from the arms of Sir John French.
1  1915 fishery trawler.
2  1945 destroyer of the later 'Battle' class built by Vickers Armstrong on the Tyne. 2,780/3,430 tons. Disposal List 1974−5.

## AJAX

St Vincent 1780
St Kitts 1782
The Saintes 1782
Egypt 1801
Trafalgar 1805
San Sebastian 1813
Baltic 1854−5
Jutland 1916
River Plate 1939
Mediterranean 1940−1
Matapan 1941
Greece 1941
Crete 1941
Malta Convoys 1941
Aegean 1944

Normandy 1944
South France 1944
*Nec quis quam nisi Ajax* = None but Ajax can overcome Ajax.
The name is taken from Greek mythology. Two Ajaxes played prominent parts in the Trojan War.
1  1767 3rd rate. Sold in 1785.
2  1798 3rd rate. Burnt in 1807.
3  1809 3rd rate. Became a blockship in 1860.
4  1867 ship ex-*Vanguard*. Broken up 1875.
5  1880 turret ship. Sold 1904.
6  1912 battleship of 23,000 tons built by Scotts. Served in 2nd Battle Squadron in WWI. Sold 1926.
8  1931 cruiser of 6,985 tons built by Vickers Armstrong at Barrow. Awarded nine battle honours during WWII.
9  1959 frigate, Improved Type 12, 2,300,/2,800 tons built by Cammell Laird. Fitted with Ikara missiles. Disposal List 1986−7.

## ALACRITY

*Adjuvare propero* = I hasten to help.
China 1900
Korea 1950−2
Falkland Islands 1982
1  1806 vessel.
2  1944 sloop of Modified 'Black Swan' class built by Denny. 1,350 tons. Scrapped 1956.
3  1974 frigate Type 21, 2,750/3,250 tons built by Yarrow.

## ALAMEIN

*Gardez bien* = Guard well.
Commemorates General Montgomery's victory in the Desert Campaign of 1942.
1  1945 destroyer of the later 'Battle' class of 2,780/3,430

tons built by Hawthorn Leslie. Scrapped 1962−3.

## ALARIC

The thicker the hay, the easier mowed.[20]
Name taken from a king of the Visigoths.
1  1807 vessel taken as a prize.
2  1946 submarine of 1,120/1,620 tons built by Cammell Laird. Scrapped 1971.

## ALARM

Havana 1762
The Saintes 1782
North Sea 1942
North Africa 1942−3
1  1758 5th rate. Broken up 1816.
6  1845 6th rate. Coal hulk 1861.
8  1910 destroyer built by John Brown. Sold 1921.
9  1919 minesweeper/tug of 452 tons, requisitioned 1941. Returned to the owners 1946.
10  1942 minesweeper of the 'Algerine' class built by Harland and Wolff. Bombed in Bone harbour and became CTL 1943. Scrapped 1944.

## ALBION

Algiers 1816
Navarino 1827
Crimea 1854−5
Dardanelles 1915
*Fortiter, fedeliter, feliciter* = Boldly, faithfully, happily.
Taken from the Latin word *albus*, meaning white. The white cliffs of Dover gave rise to this old name for England.

19  The 'Hunt' group of fast escort vessels were rated as destroyers till 1947, then reclassified as AA frigates.

20  Attributed to Alaric at the capture of Rome, AD 410.

1 1763 3rd rate (74) built at Deptford. Commanded by Samuel Barrington. Lost 1797.
3 1802 3rd rate (74) built on the Thames. Served at Algiers and Navarino. Served as a lazaretto at Leith. Broken up 1835.
6 1842 2nd rate. Broken up 1884.
7 1898 battleship built by the Thames Ironworks. 12,950 tons. Sold 1919.
10 1947 aircraft carrier of 27,300 tons built by Swan Hunter. Converted to commando carrier 1962. Disposal List 1974−5.

## ALBRIGHTON

English Channel 1942−4
Dieppe 1942
Biscay 1944
Normandy 1944
North Sea 1945
Name taken from the hunt in Shropshire.
1 1941 'Hunt' class destroyer built at Clydebank. 1,050 tons. Sold to the Federal Republic of Germany 1958. Renamed *Raule*.

## ALCIDE

Quebec 1759
Martinique 1762
Havana 1762
St Vincent 1780
St Kitts 1782
The Saintes 1782
*Fortiter ad pacem* = (Work) bravely for peace. (Taken from the arms of Boscawen.)
Derives from Alcides, a name for Hercules.
1 1755 3rd rate prize. Sold 1772.
2 1779 3rd rate. Scrapped 1817.
3 1945 submarine of 1,120/1,620 tons built by Vickers Armstrong at Barrow.

## ALDENHAM

Atlantic 1942
Libya 1942
Sicily 1943
Aegean 1943
Adriatic 1944
South France 1944
Named after the hunt in Hertfordshire.
1 1941 destroyer of the 'Hunt' class of 1,087 tons built by Cammell Laird. Mined and sunk 1944.

## ALDERNEY

1 1735 vessel.
2 1742 6th rate. Sold 1749.
3 1757 sloop. Sold 1783.
4 1945 submarine of 1,120/1,620 tons built by Vickers Armstrong. Designed for extended patrolling in the Pacific but completed too late for hostilities. Disposal List 1974−5.
5 1979 'Island' class OPV (Offshore Patrol Vessel) of 925/1,260 tons built by Hall Russell & Co.

## ALECTO

The Saintes 1782
Benin 1897
*Cave prolem* = Beware of my brood.
1 1781 vessel.
2 1839 sloop. Scrapped in 1865.
3 1910 depot ship for submarines. Scrapped in 1949.

## ALERT

The Saintes 1782
Korea 1950−3
*Lexington* 1777
1 1754 vessel.
7 1793 sloop which surrendered in 1794.
15 1813 sloop. Sold 1832.
18 1856 sloop. Presented to USN 1884.
25 1942 frigate of 850 tons built by Harland & Wolff. Sold 1964 for scrapping at Spezia. Disposal List 1974−5.

## ALGERINE

China 1841−2
China 1856−60
China 1900
North Africa 1942
1 1810 vessel.
6 1895 sloop. Sold in 1919.
7 1941 minesweeper of the 'Algerine' class built by Harland & Wolff. Sunk in 1942 by Italian submarine *Ascianghi* off Bougie.

## ALISMA

Atlantic 1941−5
English Channel 1945
1 1940 corvette of 925 tons built by Harland & Wolff. Sold after WWII. Became *Laconia*, 1949; *Constantine S*, 1950; *Parnon*, 1952. Lost 1954.

## ALLIANCE

Acre 1799
1 1795 6th rate prize. Sold 1802.
2 1945 submarine of 1,120/1,620 tons built by Vickers Armstrong at Barrow.

## ALLINGTON CASTLE

Atlantic 1944−5
Arctic 1944−5
1 1944 corvette/frigate of 1,100 tons built by Fleming & Ferguson. Ex-*Amaryllis*. Sold 1958 for scrapping in Sunderland.

## ALNWICK CASTLE

Arctic 1945
Atlantic 1945
1 1944 corvette/frigate of 1,100 tons built by Brown, Kincaid 1944. Scrapped Gateshead 1958.

## AMARANTHE (Amaranthus)

Martinique 1809
Guadeloupe 1810
Atlantic 1941−5
1 1796 prize. Lost 1800.
2 1797 6th rate prize named *Venus*. Broken up 1804.
3 1803 sloop. Sold 1815.
4 1940 corvette built by Fleming & Ferguson. 925 tons. Sold to the merchant navy 1946. Scrapped at Hong Kong 1953.

## AMAZON

*Audaciter* = Boldly.
Martinique 1762
Copenhagen 1801
Belgian Coast 1914−16
Atlantic 1939−43
Norway 1940
Arctic 1942
Malta Convoys 1942

North Africa 1942–3
*Droits de L'Homme* 1797
*Belle Poule* 1806
Name is derived from a mythological tribe of warlike women.
1   1745 prize named *Panthère*. Sold 1763.
2   1746 prize named *Subtile*.
3   1773 frigate. Broken up 1794.
4   1795 frigate. Wrecked 1797.
5   1799 frigate. Sold 1812.
6   1821 5th rate. Sold 1863.
7   1865 sloop. Sunk in collision 1866.
8   1908 destroyer built by Thornycroft. Sold 1919.
9   1926 destroyer built by Thornycroft. 1,350 tons. Won several battle honours in WWII. Scrapped at Troon 1948.
10  1971 frigate Type 21, 2,750/3,250 tons built by Vosper Thornycroft.

## AMBERLEY CASTLE

Atlantic 1945
1   1943 corvette/frigate of 1,010 tons built by Austin: Clark 1941. Became a weather ship 1960.

## AMBUSCADE

Finisterre I 1747
Lagos 1759
Jutland 1916
Atlantic 1940–4
Arctic 1942
Falkland Islands 1982
*Tempori insidior* = I bide my time.
1   1746 5th rate named *Embuscade* taken as prize. Sold 1762.
2   1773 5th rate. Broken up 1810.
3   1798 5th rate prize named *Embuscade*. Renamed *Seine* 1804.
4   1811 5th rate prize named *Pomone*. Broken up 1812.
5   1913 destroyer built by John Brown. Sold 1921 for scrapping in Denmark.
9   1926 destroyer of 1,173 tons built by Yarrow. Scrapped 1947.
10  1973 frigate Type 21, 2,750/3,250 tons built by Yarrow.

## AMBUSH

1   1945 submarine built by Vickers Armstrong at Barrow. Scrapped 1971. Disposal List 1974–5.

## AMEER

Burma 1944–5
Title of the ruler of Afghanistan.
1   1908 trawler.

2   1942 escort carrier, ex-USN *Baffin's Bay*, built by Seattle-Tacoma. Returned to USN 1946.

## AMETHYST

China 1856–60
Ashantee 1873–4
Heligoland 1914
Dardanelles 1915
Atlantic 1945
Korea 1951–2
*Cerbère* 1800
*Thetis* 1808
*Niemen* 1809
Badge arms are derived from the arms of Seymour: Sir Michael commanded the *Amethyst* of 1808 with distinction.
1   1793 frigate prize named *Perle*. Wrecked 1795.
2   1799 5th rate. Captain Michael Seymour knighted for capture of *Thetis* (40). Later captured *Niemen* (40) in 1809 in Biscay. Created baronet. Wrecked 1811 in Plymouth Sound.
3   1844 6th rate (26) of 923 tons built at Plymouth for Pacific service. Sold 1869.
4   1873 6th rate screw corvette of 1,405 tons built at Devonport. Sold 1887.
5   1903 cruiser of 9,000 tons built by Armstrong. Sold 1920.
9   1943 sloop, later frigate, of Modified 'Black Swan' class, of 1,350 tons built by Stephen. Helped sink *U-482* and *U-1208*. Ran gauntlet of Communist Chinese guns in Yangtse 1949. Broken up 1957.

## AMPHION

Lissa 1811
Baltic 1854–5
Fear none.
Named after a king of Thebes.
1   1780 5th rate. Blown up 1796.
2   1798 5th rate. Sold 1823.

3   1846 5th rate. Sold 1863.
4   1883 cruiser. Sold 1906.
5   1911 cruiser of 3,350 tons built at Pembroke Dockyard. Mined and sunk in the North Sea 1914.
6   1934 cruiser of 6,980 tons built by Beardmore at Portsmouth. Transferred to RAN as *Perth*. Lost in Sunda Strait 1942.
7   1944 submarine of 1,120/1,620 tons built by Vickers Armstrong. Scrapped 1971.

## ANCHORITE

1   1944 submarine of 1,120/1,620 tons built by Vickers Armstrong. Scrapped at Troon 1970. Disposal List 1974–5.

## ANCHUSA

Atlantic 1941–5
English Channel 1945
1   1917 sloop of 1,290 tons built by Armstrong. Torpedoed and sunk by *U-54* off west coast of Ireland 1918.

## ANDREW

Dover 1652
Kentish Knock 1652
Gabbard 1653
Scheveningen 1653
Porto Farina 1655
1   1417 carrack.
2   1650 ex-*St Andrew*. Wrecked 1666. Won all the battle honours.
3   1670 1st rate. Rebuilt 1704 and renamed *Royal Anne*.
4   1946 submarine of 1,120/1,620 tons built by Vickers Armstrong. Broken up in 1977.

## ANDROMEDA

St. Vincent 1780
Unfettered.
Perseus unchained Andromeda from a rock.
1   1967 frigate, general purpose, 2,450/2,860 tons built by Portsmouth Dock Yard. 'Leander' class, armed with Exocet missiles.

## ANEMONE

Dardanelles 1915–16
Atlantic 1940–3
1   1915 sloop of 1,200 tons built by Swan Hunter. Sold 1922.
2   1940 corvette of 925 tons built at

Blyth by Clark. Was still at sea as
*Pelikan* in 1950.

# ANGUILLA

Atlantic 1944
Arctic 1945
1   1943 frigate of 1,318 tons, built by
    Walsh Kaiser in USA 1943. Ex-
    *Hallowell*, and ex-*PF.72*. Returned
    to USN 1946.

# ANNAN

Atlantic 1944
North Sea 1945
1   1943 frigate of 1,370 tons: served
    with RCN 1944–5. Sold to Royal
    Danish Navy 1945 as *Niels Ebbesen*.

# ANSON

The Saintes 1782
Donegal 1798
Curaçoa 1807
Arctic 1942–3
*Nil desperandum* = Never despair.
Named after Admiral of the Fleet
George, Lord Anson, First Lord of the
Admiralty. Badge derived from crest
of Earl of Lichfield.
1   1736 4th rate (60) of 1,197 tons,
    built at Burlesdon.
2   1747 4th rate (64). Sold 1773.
4   1781 3rd rate (64) built at
    Plymouth. Fought at The Saintes.
    Guns reduced to 44. Saw great
    deal of action with French and
    Spanish. Assisted at capture of
    Curaçoa. Ran aground and
    wrecked, killing 60, 1807.
5   1812 3rd rate (74) built at Hull.
    Broken up 1851.
6   1860 3rd rate (91) built at
    Woolwich. Renamed *Algiers* and

became guardship at Chatham
1883.
7   1886 battleship of 10,300 tons
    built at Pembroke. Sold 1909.
10  1940 battleship of 35,000 tons
    built by Swan Hunter. Broken up
    at Faslane 1958.

# ANTELOPE

Armada 1588
Lowestoft 1665
Four Days' Battle 1666
Orfordness 1666
Solebay 1672
Marbella 1705
Atlantic 1939–44
*Bismarck* Action 1941
Malta Convoys 1942
North Africa 1942–3
Falkland Islands 1982
*Aquilon* 1757
*Audax et vigilans* = Daring and
watchful.
1   1546 vessel.
2   1558 vessel, rebuilt in 1618 and
    burnt 1649.
3   1651 vessel. Wrecked 1652.
5   1703 4th rate. Broken up 1783.
6   1802 4th rate. Convict ship.
10  1848 sloop. Sold 1883.
12  1929 destroyer of 1,350 tons built
    by Hawthorn Leslie. Scrapped at
    Blyth 1946.
13  1972 destroyer, Type 21, 2,750/
    3,250 tons built by Vosper
    Thornycroft. Sunk in the
    Falklands in 1982.

# ANTHONY

Armada 1588[21]
Dunkirk 1940
*Bismarck* Action 1941
Diego Suarez 1942
Atlantic 1940–4
English Channel 1944–5
*Fortis in arduis* = Brave under
difficulties.
1   *c*.1417 vessel.
2   1929 destroyer of 1,350 tons built
    by Scotts. Broken up at Troon
    1948.

# ANTIGUA

Martinique 1762
Atlantic 1944
1   1757 vessel.
3   1804 5th rate prize named
    *L'Egyptienne*.

4   1943 frigate of 1,318 tons built by
    Walsh Kaiser. Ex-*Hammond*, ex-
    *PF.73*. Returned to USN 1946.

# ANTRIM

Falkland Islands 1982
*Toujours prest* = Always ready.
1   *c*.1645 vessel, possibly named
    *Mary Antrim*.
2   1903 cruiser of 10,850 tons built by
    John Brown. Sold 1922.
3   1941–4 Belfast trawler base.
4   1967 'County' class destroyer of
    5,440/6,200 tons. Sold to Chile
    1984.

HMS ANTRIM (No. 4)

---

21   The Armada honour more properly belongs to the City of London, for it was a merchant ship rather than a Navy
vessel which was awarded the honour.

## APOLLO

St Vincent 1780
China 1842
Crimea 1854
Normandy 1944
*Fortis et benignus* = Strong and kindly, or merciful.[22]
Named after the sun god, one of the principal gods in the Greek pantheon: the source of inspiration, art, poetry amd medicine.

1 1747 prize named *Apollon* taken from the French by Anson at Finisterre. Hospital ship of 744 tons and 20 guns. Wrecked in a hurricane off Madras 1749.
2 1774 ex-*Glory* (38) of 679 tons. She captured French *Oiseau* (32) in 1780. Broken up 1786.
3 1794 5th rate (38) of 994 tons built on the Thames by Perry & Sons Wrecked off Holland 1799.
4 1805 5th rate. Broken up 1856.[23]
6 1891 cruiser of 3,400 tons built at Chatham. RNR drillship at Southampton 1901–4, then Sheerness, then Devonport.
7 1934 cruiser of 7,000 tons built at Devonport. Transferred to RAN as *Hobart*.
8 1944 minelayer of 4,000 tons, built by Hawthorn Leslie. Scrapped at Blyth 1962.
9 1970 frigate, general purpose, 2,500/2,962 tons built by Yarrow.

## ARAB

Atlantic 1940–3
Norway 1940
Arctic 1942
North Sea 1943–5

1 1795 6th rate prize, *Jean Bart*, renamed *Arab*, but wrecked the following year.
3 1798 6th rate named *Arabe* taken as a prize. Sold 1810.
8 1901 destroyer built by Thomson, served mainly at Scapa. Sold 1919 for scrapping in Sunderland.
9 1936 trawler of 531 tons, requisitioned by RN as A/S trawler 1939. Returned 1945.

## ARABIS

Atlantic 1940–2

1 1915 sloop of 1,250 tons built by Henderson. Sunk by German TBs 1916 off Dogger Bank.

2 1940 corvette of 925 tons built by Harland & Wolff. Lent to USN and renamed *Saucy*. Taken back into RN service as HMS *Snapdragon*. Sold and became *Katina*, 1947 then *Tewfik*, 1950.

## ARBITER

Atlantic 1944
Justice from the skies.

1 1943 escort carrier of 11,420 tons built by Seattle-Tacoma. Returned to USN 1946 and became merchantman *Coracero*, 1948.

## ARBUTUS

Atlantic 1940–2

1 1917 sloop of 1,290 tons built by Armstrong. Torpedoed and sunk by *U-65* in St George's Channel 1917.
2 1940 corvette of 925 tons built by Clark. Torpedoed and sunk 1942.
3 1943 corvette of 980 tons built by Brown, Kincaid. Served with RNZN 1944–8. Scrapped at Grays 1951.

## ARCHER

Baltic 1854–5
Heligoland 1914
Atlantic 1943–5
Biscay 1943

1 1801 vessel.
2 1849 sloop. Sold about twenty years later.
3 1885 cruiser. Sold 1905.
4 1911 destroyer built by Yarrow. War service with Grand Fleet. Sold 1921 and scrapped following year.
5 1941 escort carrier of 8,000 tons: originally 1939 merchantman *Mormacland* built by Sun

Shipbuilding. Returned to USN 1946. Saw merchant service till scrapped New Orleans 1962.
6 1986 coastal patrol craft of 43 tons.

## ARDENT

Camperdown 1797
Copenhagen 1801
Crimea 1854–5
Jutland 1916
Atlantic 1939–40
Norway 1940
Falkland Islands 1982
*Scharnhorst* 1940
Through fire and water.

1 1764 3rd rate. Sold 1784.
2 1782 3rd rate prize at the Saintes. Blown up 1794.
3 1796 3rd rate. Broken up 1824.
4 1841 sloop. Broken up 1864.
5 1894 destroyer. Sold 1911.
6 1913 destroyer built by Denny. Sunk at Jutland 1916.
7 1929 destroyer of 1,350 tons built by Scotts. Sunk by German battlecruisers west of Narvik 1940.
8 1975 Type 21 frigate of 2,750/3,250 tons built by Yarrow. Sunk in the Falklands 1982.

## ARETHUSA

Ushant 1781
St Lucia 1796
Curaçoa 1807
Crimea 1854
Heligoland 1914
Dogger Bank 1915
Norway 1940–1
Malta Convoys 1941–2
Normandy 1944
*Celeriter audax* = Swiftly audacious, or daring.
Name taken from Greek mythology. A sea nymph changed by Artemis into a fountain.

1 1759 prize *L'Arethuse* (38) captured by *Venus* (36). Lost 1779.
2 1781 5th rate (38) known as 'The Saucy *Arethusa*'. Saw action in France and West Indies. Captain knighted for help in capturing Curacoa. Broken up 1814.
3 1817 5th rate (46) of 1,085 tons. built at Pembroke. Renamed *Bacchus* 1844. Became a lazaretto at Liverpool.
4 1849 4th rate (50) built at Pembroke. Last sailing-ship to be in action. Training ship 1874.

22  Some sources quote *Arcu semper intento* = With bow always bent.

23  Sources disagree about Nos. 4 and 5, with regard to displacements, guns — in fact most significant points.

Moored in Thames at Greenhithe till 1932.
5  1882 cruiser. Served at Boxer Rising in China. Sold 1905.
6  1913 cruiser of 3,500 tons built by Chatham Dock Yard. Wrecked by mine near Harwich 1916.
7  1934 cruiser of 5,220 tons built by Parsons at Chatham. Atomic test ship. Broken up at Troon 1950.
8  1963 Type 12 anti-submarine general-purpose frigate, 2,300/2,800 tons built by White. Armed with Ikara missiles.

## ARGONAUT

Arctic 1942
North Africa 1942
Mediterranean 1942
Normandy 1944
South France 1944
Aegean 1944
Okinawa 1945
Falkland Islands 1982
*Audax omnia perpeti* = Bold to endure.
An Argonaut was a member of the ship's crew of *Argo*, in which Jason sailed to find the Golden Fleece.
1  1782 3rd rate prize named *Jason* (64) of 1,452 tons. Captained by Sir Samuel Hood. Hospital ship in the Medway 1797–1802 then at Chatham. Scrapped 1831.
2  1898 cruiser of 11,000 tons built by Fairfields. Singularly uneventful career. Sold 1920.
3  1941 cruiser of 5,450 tons built by Cammell Laird. Extensively damaged by torpedo. Broken up at Newport 1955.
4  1966 anti-submarine general-purpose frigate 2,450/3,200 tons built by Hawthorn Leslie. Armed with Exocet missiles.

## ARGUS

Groix 1795
Ashantee 1873–4
Atlantic 1941–2
Arctic 1941

Malta Convoys 1942
North Africa 1942
*Oculi omnium* = The eyes of all (*cf.* Psalm 145).
Named after the hundred-eyed messenger killed by Hermes. Hera was so angered by the death of her friend Argus that she took his eyes to adorn her favourite bird, the peacock.
1  1792 vessel.
6  1849 sloop. Broken up 1881.
11  1917 aircraft carrier of 14,450 tons built by Beardmore. Purchased when building as the Italian liner *Conte Rosso*. Later modified for WWII service. Sold 1946 and scrapped the following year at Inverkeithing.

## ARIADNE

St Lucia 1778
Leyte Gulf 1944
*Celer et audax* = Quick and bold *or* Swift and fearless.
Name is taken from the daughter of Minos, king of Crete, who saved Theseus.
1  1776 6th rate (20) of 432 tons built at Chatham. Saw much active service. Sold 1814.
5  1816 6th rate (20) of 511 tons built at Pembroke. Guns increased to 26 then 28. Captained at one time by the novelist Frederick Marryat.
6  1859 frigate (26) of 3,214 tons. Renamed *Actaeon* 1905. Became a torpedo school at Sheerness.
7  1898 cruiser of 11,000 tons built at Clydebank. Torpedoed while on passage from Humber to Portsmouth in 1917 by a U-boat.
9  1943 minelayer of 4,000 tons built by Stephen. Mediterranean, Pacific and Home fleets 1944–5. Scrapped Dalmuir 1965.
10  1971 general-purpose frigate of 2,500/2,962 tons built by Yarrow.

## ARIEL

## ARIEL

Heligoland 1914
Belgian Coast 1914
Dogger Bank 1915
Jutland 1916
*Invisibilis quaero* = Unseen I seek.
Name derives from fable: the spirit of the air. Or from Shakespeare's sprite in *The Tempest*.
1  1777 sloop (20) of 455 tons built by Perry & Sons on the Thames. Struck to the French *Amazone* 1779.
2  1781 sloop (16) of 312 tons built at Liverpool. Sold 1802.
3  1800 sloop. Sold 1816.
4  Brig of 236 tons built at Deptford. Wrecked off Sable Island 1828 with all hands in a hurricane.
6  1854 screw steam sloop built at Pembroke. Served in anti-slavery and repression of piracy operations.
7  Screw composite gunboat of 406 tons built Chatham. Served off South and West Africa.
9  1897 torpedo-boat destroyer of 310 tons built by Thornycroft at Chiswick. Wrecked off Malta 1907.
10  1911 destroyer built by Thornycroft at Southampton. Sank *U-12* by ramming. Fought at Heligoland and Dogger Bank. Sunk by mine in the North Sea 1918.
12  1942 shore establishment as a training centre at Warrington.

## ARK ROYAL (also Ark Ralegh, Anne Royal)

Armada 1588
Cadiz 1596
Dardanelles 1915
Norway 1940
Spartivento 1940
Mediterranean 1940−1
*Bismarck* Action 1941
Malta Convoys 1941
*Désir n'a pas repos* = Desire (or zeal) has no rest. This was the motto of Lord Howard of Effingham, the Lord Admiral opposing the Armada.
1   1587 ship built at Deptford for Sir Walter Raleigh: 692 tons and 55 guns. Crew comprised 268 mariners, 32 gunners and 100 soldiers. Sold to Queen Elizabeth for £5,000. Renamed *Anne Royal* 1608.
2   1914 seaplane carrier of 7,400 tons. Saw service in eastern Mediterranean 1915−18. Renamed *Pegasus* 1934. Sold 1946 for scrap.
3   1937 aircraft carrier built by Cammell Laird, 22,000 tons. Torpedoed and foundered in western Mediterranean after attack by *U-81*.
4   1950 aircraft carrier built by Cammell Laird, 43,000/50,786 tons. Broken up by Cairn Ryan in 1980.
5   1981 ASW[24] aircraft carrier, 16,000/19,800 tons built by Swan Hunter of Wallsend.

## ARMADA

1   1810 3rd rate. Sold 1863.
2   1943 destroyer of the 'Battle' class, 3,361 tons built by Hawthorn Leslie. Designed for Pacific war service, but only five of this class were completed in time to take part in WWII in the Far East. Scrapped at Inverkeithing 1965.

## ARMERIA

Atlantic 1942−5
Normandy 1944
English Channel 1944−5
1   1941 corvette of 925 tons built by Harland & Wolff. Sold 1947 for merchant service: *Deppie*, 1948; *Canastel*, 1950; *Rio Blanco*, 1952 and *Lillian*, 1955.

## ARROW

Copenhagen 1801
Cape Tenez 1805
San Sebastian 1813
Crimea 1854−5
Atlantic 1940−3
Norway 1940
North Sea 1942
Libya 1942
Malta Convoys 1942
Sicily 1943

Falkland Islands 1982
*Celeriter certus* = Swiftly sure.
1   1796 sloop which surrendered in 1805.
7   1929 destroyer of 1,350 tons built by Vickers Armstrong of Barrow. Scrapped at Taranto in 1949.
8   1974 Type 21 frigate of 2,750/3,250 tons built by Yarrow.

## ARROWHEAD

Atlantic 1941−5
1   1940 corvette of 925 tons built by Marine Industries. Served with RCN 1941−5. Sold after the war and saw merchant service: *Southern Larkspur*, 1948. Scrapped at Odense in 1959.

## ARTEMIS

The name is taken from Greek mythology. Artemis was the goddess of the moon and the chase, and the twin sister of Apollo.
1   1946 submarine of 1,120/1,620 tons built by Scotts. Scrapped in 1972.

## ARTFUL

1   1947 submarine of 1,120/1,620 tons built by Scotts. Disposal List 1969.

## ASCENSION

Armada 1588
Atlantic 1944
North Sea 1944
1   1588: it was a merchant ship of the City of London which served with the fleet at the Armada campaign.
2   1943 frigate of 1,318 tons built by Walsh Kaiser. Ex-*Hargood* and ex-*PF.74*. Returned to USA in 1946.

24   Anti-submarine Warfare Carrier: her primary task is to act as the command ship of an ASW force.

## ASHANTI

Norway 1940
Atlantic 1940
Malta Convoys 1942
North Africa 1942−4
Arctic 1942−3
English Channel 1942−3
Normandy 1944
Biscay 1944
*Kum apim, apim beba* = Kill a thousand,
a thousand will come.
1   1937 destroyer of the famed 'Tribal'
    class, built by Denny. 1,870 tons.
    Saw great deal of war service. Sold
    1949 for scrapping at Troon.
2   1959 frigate, general-purpose 1st
    rate, 2,370/2,700 tons built by
    Yarrow. Disposal List 1980−1.

## ASPHODEL

Atlantic 1940−5
1   1915 sloop of 1,250 tons built by
    Henderson. Sold to Denmark 1920
    and served as *Fylla*.
2   1940 corvette of 925 tons built by
    Brown, Kincaid. Lost 1944.

## ASSISTANCE

Portland 1653
Gabbard 1653
Lowestoft 1665
Orfordness 1666
China 1858−9
1    1650 4th rate. Sunk as a
     breakwater 1745.
2    1805 ex-*Royal Oak*. Broken up
     1815.
10   1900 repair ship. Sold 1935.
11   1945 repair ship of 14,250 tons
     built by Bethlehem (Fairfield). Ex-
     USN repair ship made available
     under Lend/Lease. Returned
     USN 1946.

## ASTER

Dardanelles 1915−16
Atlantic 1941
North Sea 1944
1   1915 sloop of 1,200 tons built by
    Earle. Mined in Mediterranean
    1917.
2   1941 corvette of 925 tons built by
    Harland & Wolff. Scrapped 1946.

## ASTUTE

1   1945 submarine of 1,120/1,620 tons
    built by Vickers Armstrong of
    Barrow. Scrapped 1970.

## ATHELING

Atheling or Aetheling was the Old
English for 'prince'.
1   1942 escort carrier (ex-USN *Glacier*)
    of 11,420 tons built by Seattle-
    Tacoma. Returned to USN 1946.
    Saw service as a merchant vessel
    — *Roma*, 1950.

## ATHERSTONE

English Channel 1940−2
St Nazaire 1942
Sicily 1943
Mediterranean 1943
North Sea 1942−3
Salerno 1943
South France 1944
Adriatic 1944
Atlantic 1943
Name derives from the hunt in
Warwickshire.
1   1916 paddle minesweeper of 810
    tons built by Ailsa Shipbuilders.
    Sold 1927. Served as *Queen of Kent*
    in WWII.
2   1939 destroyer of 'Hunt' class, 907
    tons, built by Cammell Laird.
    Scrapped Port Glasgow 1957.
3   1986 mine counter-measure
    vessel[25] of 615/725 tons built by
    Vosper.

## ATTACK

Heligoland 1914
Dogger Bank 1915
Jutland 1916
1   1804 vessel.
2   1911 destroyer built at Yarrow.
    Mined off Alexandria 1917.
3   1941−5 Coastal Forces base at
    Portland.

## ATTACKER

Salerno 1943
Atlantic 1943−5
South France 1944
Aegean 1944
1   1941 escort carrier of 11,420 tons
    built by Western Pipe:GEC as USN
    *Barnes*. Returned to USN 1946 and

served as merchant ship *Castel
Forte*, 1948.
2   1983 coastal training boat of 34 tons
    for RNR training.

## AUBRETIA

Atlantic 1941−5
North Africa 1942−3
South France 1944
Mediterranean 1944
1   1916 sloop of 1,250 tons. Built by
    Blyth Shipbuilding Co. Sold 1922
    for breaking up.
2   1940 corvette of 925 tons built by
    Brown:Kincaid. Sold 1947.

## AUCKLAND

China 1856−60
Atlantic 1939
Norway 1940
Greece 1941
Crete 1941
Libya 1941
1   1899 trawler of 155 tons. Saw WWI
    service.
2   1938 sloop of 1,200 tons built by
    Denny. Ex-*Heron*. Lost in June
    1941.

## AUDACITY

Atlantic 1941
1   1941 escort carrier. Torpedoed
    1941.

## AURICULA

Atlantic 1941−2
Diego Suarez 1942
1   1917 sloop of 1,290 tons built by
    Armstrong. Sold 1923 for scrap.
2   1940 corvette of 925 tons built by
    Brown: Kincaid. Mined and sunk
    1942.
3   1979 trials ship of 940/1,118 tons
    built by Ferguson Bros, Glasgow.
    Based at Portland.

## AURIGA

The name refers to the constellation.
1   1945 submarine of 1,120/1,620 tons
    built by Vickers Armstrong at
    Barrow.

25   MCMV of 'Hunt' class.

## AUROCHS

The name comes from the wild ox, now extinct.
1 1945 submarine of 1,120/1,620 tons built by Vickers Armstrong at Barrow. Scrapped 1967 at Troon.

## AURORA

St Lucia 1778
Minorca 1798
Guadeloupe 1810
China 1900
Dogger Bank 1915
Norway 1940
*Bismarck* Action 1941
Malta Convoys 1941
Mediterranean 1941−3
North Africa 1942−3
Sicily 1943
Salerno 1943
Aegean 1943−4
South France 1944
*Post tenebras lux* = After darkness light.
The name derives from the goddess of dawn.
1 1758 prize. Broken up 1762.
2 1766 5th rate. Lost at sea 1769.
4 1793 5th rate prize.
5 1814 5th rate prize. Scrapped 1851.
7 1887 cruiser. Scrapped 1907.
8 1913 cruiser of 3,500 tons built by Devonport Dockyard. Transferred to RCN 1920. Sold 1927.
10 1936 cruiser of 5,270 tons built by Portsmouth: Wallsend. Distinguished WWII career. Sold to Nationalist China 1948 and became successively *Chungking*, then under the Communists *Tchoungking*. She was lost, then salvaged; afterwards served under three new names before becoming a harbour hulk.
11 1962 frigate, improved Type 12,

2,300/2,800 tons built by John Brown, of 'Leander' class. Armed with Ikara missiles.

## AVENGER

Martinique 1794
Arctic 1942
North Africa 1942
Falkland Islands 1982.
1 1779 sloop.
2 1794 sloop taken as prize. Foundered 1803.
4 1845 frigate. Wrecked 1847.
5 1915 armed merchant cruiser of 15,000 tons, ex-*Aotearoa*. Sunk by torpedo from *U-69* in the Atlantic in 1917.
6 1940 escort carrier of 8,200 tons built by Sun Shipbuilding. Ex-*Rio Hudson*. Torpedoed and sunk November 1942.
7 1947 landing ship. Sold to India 1949.
8 1975 frigate, Type 21, 2,750/3,250 tons built by Yarrow.

## AVON

Atlantic 1943−4
Okinawa 1945
1 1805 vessel.
5 1896 destroyer built by Vickers. Broken up 1922.
7 1943 frigate of 1,370 tons built by Hill: Bellis & Morcom. Sold to Portugal 1949 and renamed *Nuño Tristão*.
8 1961 amphibious ship (ramp powered lighter), 100 tons built by White: Saunders Roe, Isle of Wight. Disposal List 1982−3.

## AVON VALE

Atlantic 1941−3
Malta Convoys 1941−2
Libya 1941−2
Sirte 1942
North Africa 1942−3
Adriatic 1944
English Channel 1943−4
Name derives from a hunt in Hampshire.
1 1940 destroyer of the 'Hunt' class of 1,050 tons built at Clydebank. Distinguished WWII career. Scrapped at Sunderland 1958.

## AWE

Atlantic 1944
1 1943 frigate of 1,370 tons built by Fleming & Ferguson. Sold to Portugal 1949 and renamed *Diego Gomes*.

## AYLMER

Normandy 1944
Atlantic 1944−5
Named after Admiral Lord Aylmer, who fought at Barfleur.
1 1943 frigate of 1,300 tons built by Bethlehem: Hingham. Returned to USN 1945.

## AZALEA

Atlantic 1941−3
Normandy 1944
English Channel 1944−5
1 1915 sloop of 1,200 tons built by Barclay Curle. Sold 1923.
2 1940 corvette of 925 tons. Sold 1946. Lost 1955 as merchant ship.

## BACCHANTE

Cattaro 1814
Heligoland 1914
Dardanelles 1915−16
Named after the female followers of Bacchus.
1 1803 6th rate prize. Sold 1809.
2 1811 5th rate. Scrapped 1857.
3 1959 frigate. Scrapped 1869.
4 1876 corvette. Sold 1897.
5 1901 cruiser of 12,000 tons built by John Brown. Sold 1909.
6 1939−45 naval base at Aberdeen.
7 1968 frigate, general-purpose, 2,450/2,860 tons built by Vickers. RNZN in 1982.

## BADGER

Baltic 1855
Heligoland 1914
Jutland 1916
1 1745 vessel.[26]
10 1911 destroyer built by Denny. Sold 1921.
11 1939−46 naval base at Harwich.

26 Nos. 2-9 were all small vessels. No. 2 was a brig commanded by Lieutenant Horatio Nelson 1778-9.

## BADSWORTH

Atlantic 1941−3
Malta Convoys 1942
Arctic 1942
Name is derived from a hunt in
Yorkshire.
1   1941 destroyer of 1,050 tons of the
    'Hunt' class, built by Cammell
    Laird. Transferred to Royal
    Norwegian Navy as *Arendal* 1946.
    Scrapped 1961.

## BAHAMA(S)

Arctic 1944
Atlantic 1944−5
1   1805 prize taken at Trafalgar.
    Scrapped 1814.
2   1943 frigate of 1,318 tons built by
    Walsh Kaiser. Ex-*Hotham*.
    Returned USN 1946.

## BALFOUR

Atlantic 1944
Normandy 1944
English Channel 1944
Named after Captain George Balfour
of the *Conqueror* at the battle of The
Saintes.
1   1912 Admiralty trawler of 285 tons.
    Sunk in collision 1918.
2   1943 frigate of 1,300 tons built by
    Bethlehem: Hingham. Ex-*DE.73*.
    Returned USN 1945.

## BALLINDERRY

Atlantic 1943−5
1   1942 frigate of 1,370 tons built by
    Hawthorn Leslie: Blyth. Scrapped
    1961.

## BALSAM

Atlantic 1943−5
Normandy 1944
English Channel 1944−5
1   1942 corvette of 925 tons built by
    Brown: Clark, ex-*Chelmer*.
    Scrapped Newport 1947.

## BAMBOROUGH CASTLE

Atlantic 1944
Arctic 1944−5
1   1944 corvette/frigate of 1,010 tons

built by Lewis. Scrapped Llanelly
1959.

## BANFF

Atlantic 1941−3
North Africa 1942−3
Sicily 1943
Scottish coastguard station.
1   1941 cutter, ex-USN *Saranac*, of
    1,546 tons, built by GEC. Returned
    to USN to become USCG *Tampa*,
    1946.

## BANN

Sicily 1943
Burma 1945
1   1814 6th rate. Sold 1829.
3   1942 frigate of 1,370 tons built by
    Hill: Bellis & Morcom. Transferred
    to RIN as *Tir* 1945.

## BARBADOS (Barbadoes)

Martinique 1762
St Lucia 1778
1   1757 sloop. Sold six years later.
4   1804 5th rate prize named *Brave*.
    Wrecked 1812.
5   1813 sloop. Renamed *Hind*. Sold
    1829.
7   1943 sloop of 1,318 tons built by
    Walsh Kaiser. Ex-*Halstead*, ex-
    *PF.76*. Returned USN 1946.

## BARFLEUR

Vigo 1702
Velez Malaga 1704
Cape Passero 1718
St Kitts 1782
The Saintes 1782
Glorious First of June 1794
Groix 1795

St Vincent 1797
China 1900
Commemorates the victory of Admiral
Russell in 1692 off Barfleur. The badge
is taken from the crest of Russell, later
Earl of Orford.
1   1697 2nd rate (90) of 1,476 tons.
    Flagship of Shovel at Malaga in
    1704 and Sir George Byng off
    Syracuse 1718.
2   1768 2nd rate (98) of 1,947 tons.
    Commanded at one time by
    Collingwood. Distinguished
    career. Broken up 1819.[27]
3   1892 battleship of 10,500 tons built
    at Chatham. Sold 1910.[28]
4   1943 destroyer of the 'Battle' class,
    of 2,325 tons, built by Swan
    Hunter of Wallsend. Scrapped
    Dalmuir 1966.

## BARHAM

Jutland 1916
Matapan 1941
Crete 1941
Mediterranean 1941
*Tout bien ou rien* = Everything good, or
nothing.
Named after Admiral Charles
Middleton, Lord Barham, and First
Lord of the Admiralty at the time of
Trafalgar.
1   1811 3rd rate. Scrapped 1840.
2   1889 cruiser. Sold 1914.
3   1914 battleship of 27,500 tons built
    by John Brown. Torpedoed and
    sunk November 1941 by *U-331* in
    central Mediterranean.

## BARLE

Atlantic 1943
1   1914 trawler of 283 tons. Hired by
    Admiralty and returned to owners
    1919.
2   1942 frigate (ex-USN) built by
    Canadian Vickers. Returned USN
    1946.

27   Also commanded by Sir Edward Berry: she was struck by lightning in the Mediterranean.

28   Midshipman Basil J.D. Guy won the VC aboard her at Peking 1900.

## BARROSA

Benin 1897
South Africa 1899–1901
Commemorates the battle in the Peninsula 1811.
1 1812 5th rate. Sold 1841.
2 1860 corvette. Broken up 1877.
3 1889 cruiser. Sold 1905.
4 1945 destroyer of the later 'Battle' class of 2,780/3,430 tons built by John Brown: Clydebank. Broken up at Blyth in 1978.

## BASILISK

Martinique 1762
Havana 1762
Baltic 1854–5
Dardanelles 1915–16
Norway 1940
Dunkirk 1940
A mythical beast.
 1 1695 vessel.
 4 1779 sloop/fireship. Sold 1783.
 8 1889 sloop. Sold 1905.
 9 1910 destroyer built by White. Sold for scrapping in Sunderland.
10 1930 destroyer of 1,360 tons built by Clydebank. Sunk near Dunkirk 1940.
11 1943 name given to the base at Port Moresby.

## BATH

Atlantic 1941
1 1940 destroyer of 1,060 tons acquired from USN (ex-*Hopewell*) built in 1918 by Newport News. Transferred to Royal Norwegian Navy 1941 and sunk 1941.

## BATTLEAXE

1 1918 minor war vessel.
2 1945 destroyer of 2,935 tons of 'Weapon' class built by Yarrow. Fleet Radar Picket. Badly damaged in collision. CTL 1962. Scrapped 1964.
3 1977 frigate, Type 22, 3,500/4,200 tons built by Yarrow.

## BATTLER

Atlantic 1942–5
Salerno 1943
1 1942 escort carrier of 11,420 tons built for USN ex-*Altamaha*, and returned to USN 1946.
2 1947 landing-ship.

## BAYNTUN

Atlantic 1943–5
North Sea 1945
Named after Henry William Bayntun, who commanded the *Leviathan* at Trafalgar.
1 1942 frigate of 1,050 tons built at Boston for USN. Returned to USN 1945.

## BAZELY

Atlantic 1943–5
Arctic 1945
Named after Captain Bazely, who commanded the *Bombay* at the bombardment of Algiers 1816.
1 1942 frigate of 1,050 tons of the 'Captain' class built at Boston for the USN. Returned to USN 1945.

## BEAGLE (Golden Beagle)

Basque Roads 1809
San Sebastian 1813
China 1856–60
Crimea 1854–5
Dardanelles 1915–16
Norway 1940

Atlantic 1940–5
North Africa 1942
Arctic 1942–4
English Channel 1943
Normandy 1944
To a finish.
1 1804 sloop. Sold 1814.
3 Surveying brig used for Darwin's voyage in 1831.
7 1909 destroyer built by John Brown. Sold 1921 for scrapping at Sunderland.
8 1930 destroyer of 1,360 tons built at Clydebank. Scrapped at Rosyth 1946.
9 1968 (commissioning date) coastal survey ship 860/1,088 tons built by Brooke Marine, Lowestoft.

## BEAUFORT

Sirte 1942
Libya 1942
Malta Convoys 1942
Mediterranean 1942
Sicily 1943
Salerno 1943
Aegean 1943–4
Anzio 1944
South France 1944
1 1919 surveying vessel named after Sir Francis Beaufort, Hydrographer of the Navy 1829–55. Sold 1938.
2 1941 destroyer of the 'Hunt' class named after the Duke of Beaufort's hunt, 1,050 tons, built by Cammell Laird. Loaned to Royal Norwegian Navy in 1954 and renamed *Haugesund*. Scrapped 1965.

## BEAVER

Louisburg 1758
Heligoland 1914
Atlantic 1942
*Athalante* 1804
 1 1656 vessel.
10 1911 destroyer built by Denny. Sold in 1921 for scrapping by Hayle.
11 1939–45 naval base in the Humber.

12  1982 frigate, Type 22 of 4,100/
    4,900 tons built by Yarrow.

# BEDALE

Named after the hunt in North
Yorkshire.
1   1941 escort destroyer of the 'Hunt'
    class of 1,050 tons built by
    Hawthorn Leslie. Loaned to the
    Polish Navy as *Slazak* (1942–6).
    Later loaned to the RIN 1953 and
    renamed *Godavari*. Scrapped 1959.

# BEDOUIN

Narvik 1940
Norway 1940–1
Atlantic 1940–1
Arctic 1941–2
Malta Convoys 1942
Honour and chivalry.
1   1902 trawler of 188 tons. Mined
    1915 and sunk.
2   1937 destroyer of 'Tribal' class of
    1,870 tons built by Denny.
    Torpedoed and sunk by Italian
    aircraft after being damaged by
    Italian cruiser.

# BEGONIA

Atlantic 1941
North Sea 1941
1   1915 sloop of 1,200 tons built by
    Barclay Curle. Decoy ship 1917.
    Sunk in collision with *U-151* off
    Casablanca, 1917.
1   1940 corvette of 925 tons. Became
    USN *Impulse* 1942. Sold 1946 and
    became a merchant ship: *Begonlock*
    1946; *Fundiciones Molinão* 1949;
    *Astiluzu* 1951, *Rio Mero* 1956.

# BEGUM

Rise and strike.
A Hindu lady of high rank.
1   1942 escort carrier of 11,420 tons,
    ex-USS *Balinas*, built by Seattle-
    Tacoma. Returned to USA 1946.
    Mercantile service: *Raki*, 1948.
    Scrapped in the Far East in 1974.

# BELFAST

Arctic 1943
North Cape 1943
Normandy 1944
Korea 1950–2
*Pro tanto quid retribuamus* = We give as
good as we get.
1   1938 cruiser of 11,550/14,930 tons

built by Harland & Wolff.
Preserved as a department of the
Imperial War Museum in the Pool
of London 1971.

# BELLEROPHON

Glorious First of June 1794
Cornwallis's Retreat 1795
Nile 1798
Trafalgar 1805
Syria 1840
Crimea 1854
Jutland 1916
Name is taken from Greek mythology:
he was the hero who slew the monster
Chimaera.
1   1786 3rd rate. Conveyed Napoleon
    to England after his surrender in
    1815. Scrapped 1836.
3   1865 ironclad ship. Renamed *Indus*
    1904.
4   1907 battleship of 18,600 tons built
    at Portsmouth Dockyard. Sold
    1921 and broken up in Germany.
6   1950 name given to the Reserve
    Fleet at Portsmouth.

# BELLONA

Copenhagen 1801
Basque Roads 1809
Jutland 1916
Normandy 1944
Biscay 1944
Norway 1944–5
Arctic 1944–5
*Courageux* 1761

Battle is our business.
Named after the goddess of war.
1   1747 6th rate prize named *Bellone*.
    Sold the following year.
7   1805 5th rate prize. Renamed
    *Blanche* 1809.
9   1890 cruiser. Sold 1906.
10  1909 cruiser of 3,300 tons built at
    Pembroke Dockyard. Sold 1921.
14  1942 cruiser of 5,770 tons built by
    Fairfield. Loaned to RNZN
    1947–56. Scrapped 1959.

# BELLWORT

Atlantic 1941–5
1   1941 corvette of 925 tons built by
    Brown: Kincaid. Sold to the
    Republic of Ireland 1946 and
    renamed *Cliona*.

# BELMONT

Atlantic 1941
1   1906 hired trawler, used for WWI
    service and returned to owners
    1919.
2   1940 destroyer ex-USN, ex-
    *Satterlee*, built 1918 by Newport
    News. Torpedoed and sunk in the
    Atlantic 1941.

# BELVOIR

Sicily 1943
Salerno 1943
Aegean 1943
South France 1944
Adriatic 1944
Named after the hunt in
Leicestershire.
1   1917 minesweeper of 750 tons built
    by the Ailsa Shipbuilding Co. Sold
    1922.
2   1941 escort destroyer of the 'Hunt'
    class built by Cammell Laird, 1,087
    tons. Scrapped 1957.

# BENBOW

Syria 1840
Jutland 1916
*Usque ad finem* = To the very end.
Named after Vice Admiral John
Benbow.
1   1813 3rd rate. Sold 1894.
3   1913 battleship of 25,000 tons built
    by Beardmore. Sold 1931 for
    scrapping at Rosyth.
4   1941–7 naval base at Trinidad.

## BENTINCK

Atlantic 1943–5
Arctic 1945
Named after Captain John A. Bentinck
of the *Niger* in the Seven Years' War.
1  1943 frigate of 1,300 tons built by
Bethlehem: Hingham. Ex-*DE.52*.
Returned to USN 1946.

## BENTLEY

Normandy 1944
Atlantic 1944
Named after Sir John Bentley,
Anson's flag captain at Finisterre,
1747. He also commanded the
*Warspite* at Quiberon Bay and Lagos in
1759.
1  1943 frigate of 1,300 tons built by
Bethlehem: Hingham. Ex-*DE.74*.
Returned to USN 1945.

## BERGAMOT

Atlantic 1941–5
Arctic 1942–3
Sicily 1943
1  1917 sloop of 1,290 tons built by
Armstrong. Sunk by *U-84* in the
Atlantic in 1917.
2  1941 corvette of 925 tons built by
Harland & Wolff. Sold 1946 to the
merchant navy. She served as
*Syros*, 1947; *Delphini*, 1951; *Delfini*,
1955; *Ekaterini*, 1955.

## BERKELEY

North Sea 1942
English Channel 194
Dieppe 1942
*Dieu avec nous* = God with us.
Name is taken from the two hunts in
Gloucestershire.
1  1940 escort destroyer of the 'Hunt'
class of 907 tons built by Cammell
Laird. Lost at Dieppe 1942.
2  1986 MCMV of 615/725 tons built
by Vosper Thornycroft.

## BERKELEY CASTLE

Atlantic 1944
1  5th rate (48) of uncertain date.
Surrendered 1694.
2  1943 corvette/frigate of 1,010 tons
built by Barclay Curle. Scrapped at
Grays 1955.

## BERMUDA

North Africa 1942
Arctic 1943
Atlantic 1943
1  1795 sloop. Foundered in the
following year.
8  1941 cruiser of 11,000 tons built at
Clydebank. Scrapped at Briton
Ferry 1965.

## BERRY

Atlantic 1943–4
Biscay 1943
Named after one of Nelson's 'Band of
Brothers', Sir Edward Berry, flag
captain in the *Vanguard* at The Nile
and captain of the *Agamemnon* at
Trafalgar.
1  1942 frigate of 1,085 tons, ex-*DE.3*,
built at Boston. Returned to USN
1946.

## BERRY HEAD

1  1944 maintenance and repair ship,
9,000/11,270 tons, built by North
Vancouver Ship Repairers.
Disposal List 1977–8.

## BERWICK

Barfleur 1692
Vigo 1702
Gibraltar 1704
Velez Malaga 1704
Dogger Bank 1781
Atlantic 1939
Spartivento 1940
Norway 1940
Arctic 1941–4
*Victoriae gloria merces* = Glory is the
reward for victory.
1  1679 3rd rate. Scrapped 1742.
4  1775 3rd rate. Wrecked 1805.
Salved by the French and gave
ten years service before being

recaptured at Trafalgar.
9  1902 cruiser of 9,800 tons built by
Beardmore. Sold in 1920 and
scrapped in Germany 1922.
10  1926 cruiser of 9,750 tons built by
Fairfield. Scrapped at Blyth 1948.
11  1958 anti-submarine frigate of
2,380/2,800 tons built by Harland
& Wolff. Disposal List 1982–3.

## BETONY

Atlantic 1943
North Sea 1943
1  1943 corvette of 980 tons built by
Hall. Sold to Thailand 1947.

## BEVERLEY

Atlantic 1940–3
Malta Convoys 1942
Arctic 1942
1  1940 destroyer ex-USN *Branch*, of
1,190 tons, built at Newport News
1918. Torpedoed and sunk 1943.

## BICESTER

North Africa 1942–3
Malta Convoys 1942
Mediterranean 1943–4
South France 1944
Adriatic 1944
Aegean 1944
Named after the hunt in Oxfordshire.
1  1917 minesweeper of 750 tons built
by Ailsa Shipbuilders. Sold 1923.
2  1941 escort destroyer of the 'Hunt'
class of 1,050 tons built by
Hawthorn Leslie. Scrapped at
Grays 1956.
3  1986 minehunter of 615/725 tons
built by Vosper Thornycroft. A
'Hunt' class MCMV.[29]

## BICKERTON

Normandy 1944
Arctic 1944
Atlantic 1944
English Channel 1944
Named after Sir Richard Bickerton,
captain of the *Terrible* at Ushant 1779.
1  1943 frigate ex-*DE.75* built by
Bethlehem: Hingham. 1,300 tons.
Sunk 1944.

---

29   The breed of warship with the generic title Mine Counter Measure Vessel.

## BIDEFORD

Atlantic 1939–45
Dunkirk 1940
North Africa 1942
Biscay 1943
English Channel 1945
Bide your time.
1   1695 6th rate. Wrecked 1699.
2   1712 6th rate. Lost 1736 but salved.
3   1740 6th rate. Scrapped 1754.
4   1756 sloop. Wrecked 1761.
5   1932 sloop of 1,045 tons built at Devonport. Sold 1949 for scrapping at Milford Haven.

## BIGBURY BAY

1   1944 frigate of 1,580 tons built by Hall Russell. Ex-*Loch Carloway*. Sold to Portugal 1959 and renamed *Pacheco Pereira*.

## BIRMINGHAM

Heligoland 1914
Dogger Bank 1915
Jutland 1915
Norway 1940
Korea 1952–3
Forward. The badge crest is taken from that of the city of Birmingham.
1   1913 cruiser of 5,440 tons built by Armstrong. Sold 1931 for scrapping at Pembroke Dock. Rammed and sank *U-15* 1914.
2   1936 cruiser of 9,100 tons. Scrapped at Inverkeithing 1960.
3   1973 Type 42 destroyer of 3,500/4,100 tons built by Cammell Laird.

## BITER

Baltic 1855
North Africa 1942
Atlantic 1943–4
1   1797 vessel.
4   1942 escort carrier, ex-mercantile *Rio Parana*, of 8,200 tons, built by Sun Shipbuilding 1940. Sold to France 1945 and renamed *Dixmude*.

5   1986 coastal training craft of 43 tons.

## BITTERN

Burma 1853
China 1856–60
Ashantee 1873–4
Alexandria 1882
Norway 1940
*Rostro vinco* = I conquer with beak.
A marsh bird.
1   1796 vessel.
4   1897 destroyer built by Vickers. Sunk in collision with ss *Kenilworth* in the Channel 1918.
6   1937 sloop of 1,190 tons built by White. Sunk by bombing 1940.

## BITTERSWEET

Atlantic 1941–5
1   1940 corvette of 925 tons built by Marine Industries. Served with RCN 1941–5. Sold 1947 and scrapped at Charlestown.

## BLACKMORE

Atlantic 1943
Salerno 1943
South France 1944
Adriatic 1944
Named after the hunt, the Blackmore Vale, in Dorsetshire.
1   1941 escort destroyer of 1,050 tons built by Stephen. Lent to the Danish navy and renamed *Esbern Snare*. Scrapped 1966.

## BLACKPOOL

Dieppe 1942
English Channel 1942
Normandy 1944
1   1940 minesweeper. Sold to Norway 1945.
2   1957 frigate of 2,800 tons built by Harland & Wolff. Scrapped in 1978.

## BLACK PRINCE

Jutland 1916
Normandy 1944
South France 1944
Arctic 1944
English Channel 1944
Aegean 1944
Okinawa 1945
With high courage. Named after Edward, Prince of Wales, eldest son of King Edward III.
1   1650 vessel.
3   1861 iron frigate. Renamed *Emerald* 1903.
4   1904 cruiser of 13,550 tons built by Thames Iron Works. Sunk at Jutland 1916.
5   1942 cruiser of 5,770 tons built by Harland & Wolff. Served with RNZN 1948. Sold 1962 and scrapped in Japan.

## BLACK SWAN

Norway 1940
North Sea 1940
Atlantic 1941–3
Korea 1950–1
1   1939 sloop of 1,250 tons built by Yarrow. Scrapped Troon 1956.

## BLACKWOOD

Normandy 1944
Atlantic 1943–4
English Channel 1944
Named after Nelson's favourite frigate captain Henry Blackwood, who commanded *Euryalus* at Trafalgar.
1   1944 frigate of 1,085 tons, ex-*DE.4* of USN, built 1942 by Boston Shipbuilders. Torpedoed and sunk 1944.
2   1955 frigate of 1,536 tons built by Thornycroft: Type 14 anti-submarine. Scrapped in 1976.

## BLAKE

Named after the famous General-at-sea Robert Blake.

1   1808 3rd rate. Broken up 1858.
2   1889 cruiser of 9,000 tons built at Chatham. Destroyer depot ship 1907. Sold 1922.
3   1945 cruiser, originally *Tiger* then named *Blake*, of 9,550/12,080 tons built by Fairfield. Work stopped 1946 till completed to new design 1955. Converted HM Dock Yard Portsmouth to command helicopter cruiser 1965–9. Disposal List 1980–1.

## BLANCHE

Copenhagen 1801
Jutland 1916
*Pique* 1795
*Dum spiro spero* = While I breathe I hope.

1   1779 prize lost at sea the following year.
2   1786 frigate. Wrecked 1799.
3   1800 frigate. Surrendered 1805.
4   1804 frigate taken as prize. Wrecked 1807.
5   1806 frigate renamed *Salsette* 1808.
6   1809 vessel, taken as prize 1805 with the name *Bellone*, renamed *Blanche* in 1809 and broken up 1814.
9   1889 cruiser. Sold 1905.
11  1911 cruiser of 3,350 tons built by Pembroke Dockyard. Sold 1921 for scrapping at Sunderland.
12  1930 destroyer of 1,360 tons built by Hawthorn Leslie. Mined 1939.

## BLANKNEY

Atlantic 1941–3
Malta Convoys 1942
Arctic 1942–3
Sicily 1943
Salerno 1943
Normandy 1944
Mediterranean 1944
Named after the hunt in Lincolnshire.

1   1940 escort destroyer of the 'Hunt' class, of 1,050 tons, built on Clydebank. Distinguished war service in WWII. Scrapped at Blyth 1959.

## BLEAN

North Sea 1942
North Africa 1942
Adriatic 1944
Named after a hunt in Kent.

1   1942 escort destroyer of the 'Hunt' class, of 1,087 tons, built by Hawthorn Leslie. Torpedoed 1942.

## BLEASDALE

English Channel 1942–4
Dieppe 1942
North Sea 1943–5
Normandy 1944
Atlantic 1944

1   1942 destroyer of the 'Hunt' class of 1,087 tons, built by Vickers Armstrong, Tyne. Scrapped Blyth 1956.

## BLENCATHRA

North Sea 1941–5
English Channel 1942–5
Sicily 1943
Salerno 1943
Aegean 1943
Normandy 1944
Mediterranean 1944
Named after the hunt in Cumberland.

1   1940 escort destroyer of the 'Hunt' class of 1,000 tons, built by Cammell Laird. Scrapped at Barrow 1957.

## BLENHEIM

Genoa 1795
St Vincent 1797
China 1841
Baltic 1854–5
Dardanelles 1915–6
*Amat victoria curam* = Victory and prudence are friends.
The name commemorates Marlborough's victory of 1704.

1   1706 2nd rate ex-*Windsor Castle*. Broken up 1763.
2   1761 2nd rate. Foundered 1807.
4   1890 cruiser. Sold 1926 for scrapping.
5   1940 depot ship for destroyers. Originally built by Scotts 1919, purchased 1940. 16,600 tons. Ex-*Achilles*. Scrapped at Barrow 1948.

## BLIGH

Normandy 1944
Atlantic 1944–5
English Channel 1945
Named after Admiral William Bligh (1754–1817).

1   1943 frigate of 1,300 tons built by Bethlehem, Hingham; ex-*DE.76*. Returned to USN 1945.

## BLUEBELL

Atlantic 1940–4
Sicily 1943
Normandy 1944
Mediterranean 1944
Arctic 1945
Ring true.

1   1915 sloop of 1,200 tons built by Scotts. Sold 1930 for scrapping.
5   1940 corvette of 925 tons built by Fleming & Ferguson. Lost 1945 by torpedo attack.

## BOADICEA

Burma 1824–6
Jutland 1916
Atlantic 1941–3
North Africa 1942
Arctic 1942–4
Normandy 1944
*Vincta sed invicta* = Bound yet unconquered.
Named after the Queen of the Iceni who fought the Romans in AD 60.

1   1797 5th rate. Scrapped 1858.
3   1908 cruiser of 3,300 tons built by Pembroke Dock Yard. Attached to Grand Fleet battle squadrons 1914–19. Sold 1926 for scrapping at Alloa, Rosyth.
5   1930 destroyer of 1,360 tons built by Hawthorne Leslie. Torpedoed and sunk by aircraft off Portland 1944.

## BONAVENTURE

Lowestoft 1665
Four Days' Battle 1666
Orfordness 1666
Solebay 1672
Schooneveld 1673
Texel 1673
Barfleur 1692
Malta Convoys 1941–2

1   1489 vessel.
2   1577 Queen's ship. Condemned 1618.
4   1621 5th rate. Surrendered 1652.
5   1660 ex-*President*.
8   1711 4th rate. Renamed *Argyle* 1716.

9 1892 cruiser of 4,360 tons. Sold in 1920 for scrapping.
10 1939 cruiser of 5,450 tons built by Scotts. Torpedoed and sunk 1941 by Italian submarine *Ambra* off Sollum.
11 1942 depot ship for submarines, 10,423 tons, built at Greenock and purchased for the Navy. Returned to merchant trade 1948 as *Clan Davidson*.

## BORAGE

Atlantic 1942−5
English Channel 1943
Biscay 1943
Arctic 1943−4
North Sea 1944
Normandy 1944
1 1941 corvette of 925 tons built by Brown: Kincaid. Sold to the Republic of Ireland in 1946 and renamed *Macha*.

## BOREAS

Louisburg 1758
Havana 1762
English Channel 1940
Atlantic 1941−2
North Africa 1942−3
Name is derived the god of the north wind.
1 1757 6th rate. Sold 1770.
3 1806 sloop. Wrecked 1807.
5 1930 destroyer built by Palmers, 1,360 tons. Transferred to the Greek navy 1944−51 and renamed *Salamis*. Scrapped at Troon 1952.

## BOSCAWEN

Quebec 1759
Baltic 1854
Named after the victor of the battle of Lagos, 1759, Admiral the Hon. Edward Boscawen.
1 1748 vessel.
2 1844 3rd rate. Renamed *Wellesley* 1874.
3 One of three ships forming the training establishment. Sold 1905.
4 From 1932 till 1947 it was the name of the naval base at Portland.

## BOSTON

Atlantic 1942
Malta Convoys 1942
Sicily 1943
Normandy 1944
English Channel 1945
1 1748 6th rate. Broken up 1752.

2 1762 5th rate. Broken up 1811.
3 1940 minesweeper of 656 tons built by Ailsa. Scrapped at Charlestown 1949.

## BOXER

Crimea 1855
Sicily 1943
Salerno 1943
Anzio 1944
*Praemonitus praemunitus* = Forewarned is forearmed.
1 1797 small vessel.
7 1894 destroyer built by Thornycroft. Sunk in collision with ss *Patrick* in the Channel 1918.
8 1942 tank assault ship built by Harland & Wolff, 8,970 tons: she became a radar training ship, a fighter direction ship and was scrapped at Barrow in 1958.
9 1981 Type 22 frigate of 4,100/4,900 tons built by Yarrow.

## BRADFORD

Atlantic 1941−3
North Africa 1942
English Channel 1943
1 1658 6th rate. Renamed *Success* 1660.
3 1940 destroyer ex-USN *McLanahan*, built by Bethlehem: Squantum in 1918 at 1,190 tons. Scrapped at Troon 1946.

## BRAITHWAITE

Normandy 1944
Atlantic 1944
North Sea 1945
Named after the captain of the *Kingston* under Sir Charles Wager.
1 1943 frigate, ex-*DE.77* of 1,300 tons, built by Bethlehem: Hingham. Returned to USN 1945.

## BRAMBLE

Arctic 1941−2
1 1656 Ostend privateer (14) captured then expended as a fireship against the Dutch in the Medway, 1667.
2 1808 schooner (10). Sold 1815.
3 1822 cutter (10) survey vessel. Lent to Colonial service 1853 and used as a diving-bell vessel at Sydney. Sold 1876 as a light-ship.
5 1886 gunboat of 715 tons built by Harland & Wolff. Renamed *Cockatrice* in 1896 and sold ten years later.
6 1898 gunboat of 710 tons built by Potter of Liverpool. Sold in 1920 at Bombay.
8 1938 minesweeper of 875 tons built at Devonport Dock Yard. Sunk in Battle of the Barents Sea 1942.
9 1945 minesweeper of 'Algerine' class built by Lobnitz. Scrapped in 1961 at Gateshead.

## BRAMHAM

Arctic 1942
North Africa 1942
Malta Convoys 1942
Named after the Bramham Moor hunt in Yorkshire.
1 1942 escort destroyer of the 'Hunt' class. built by Stephen, 1,050 tons. Transferred to the Greek navy 1943 and renamed *Themistocles*. Scrapped 1960.

## BRAVE

Armada 1588
Cadiz 1596
South France 1944
1 1588 vessel hired by the city of London.
2 1796 frigate taken as prize. Sold 1825.
4 1805 prize named *Formidable*. Broken up 1816.
5 1806 3rd rate prize. Wrecked the same year.
7 1943 minesweeper. Renamed *Satellite* while she served as the drillship for the Tyne Division RNVR.
8 1983 Type 22 frigate of 4,100/4,800 tons built by Yarrow.

## BRAZEN

Norway 1940
English Channel 1940
*Audax omnia perpeti* = Daring to suffer all things.

1  1781 vessel.
2  1799 prize sloop named *Bonaparte*. Wrecked 1800.
3  1808 sloop. Broken up 1848.
5  1898 destroyer built by Thomson. Sold 1919 for scrapping.
6  1930 destroyer of 1,360 tons built by Palmers. Bombed by German aircraft and foundered in tow off Dover, 1940.
7  1980 Type 22 frigate of 3,500/4,200 tons built by Yarrow.

# BRECON

English Channel 1943
Sicily 1943
Salerno 1943
South France 1944
Mediterranean 1944
Aegean 1944
Atlantic 1945
By luck and good guidance. The badge is derived from the seal of Brecon, Wales.
1  1942 escort destroyer of the 'Hunt' class, built by Thornycroft, 1,175 tons. Scrapped at Faslane 1962.
2  1978 MCMV of the 'Hunt' class, 615/725 tons built by Vosper Thornycroft.

# BRIDGEWATER

Porto Farina 1655
Santa Cruz 1657
North Sea 1942
Atlantic 1942−3
*Stet fortuna nostra* = May our fortune stand.
1  1654 vessel (52). She was renamed *Ann* in 1660.
3  1740 3rd rate. Lost in 1743.
4  1744 6th rate which was destroyed in 1758.
5  1928 sloop of 1,045 tons built by Hawthorn Leslie. Sold in 1947 for scrapping at Gelleswick Bay.

# BRIGHTON

1  1795 vessel.
4  1940 destroyer, ex-USS *Cowell*, built by Fore River in 1918. Acquired for the RN in 1940. Served as Russian *Zharki* from 1944−49. Scrapped in 1949.
5  1959 anti-submarine frigate of 2,800 tons built by Yarrow. Converted to target ship in 1985−6.

# BRILLIANT

Belgian Coast 1914
Zeebrugge 1918
Atlantic 1941−3
English Channel 1940−2
Falkland Islands 1982
*Ea nostra vocamus* = We call these ours.
1  1696 6th rate prize. Sold in 1698.
2  *c*.1730 sloop.
4  1779 6th rate. Scrapped in 1811.
6  1814 5th rate which was renamed *Briton* in 1889.
7  1891 cruiser of 3,600 tons built by Sheerness Dock Yard. Depot ship on the Tyne 1914−15: at Lerwick 1915−18. Sunk as a blockship at Zeebrugge in 1918.
8  1930 destroyer of 1,360 tons built by Swan Hunter at Wallsend. Scrapped at Troon in 1948.
9  1978 Type 22 frigate of 3,500/4,200 tons built by Yarrow.

# BRISSENDEN

Atlantic 1943
Arctic 1943
English Channel 1943−5
Sicily 1943
Normandy 1944
Biscay 1944
Named after the hunt in Kent.
1  1942 escort destroyer of the 'Hunt' class, 1,175 tons built by Thornycroft. Scrapped Dalmuir 1965.

HMS BRILLIANT (No. 9)

# BRISTOL

Santa Cruz 1657
Lowestoft 1665
Four Days' Battle 1666
Orfordness 1666
Solebay 1672
Texel 1673
Finisterre 1747
Falklands 1914
Falkland Islands 1982

1   1653 4th rate. Sunk in 1709.
4   1809 3rd rate, ex-*Agincourt*. Sold in 1814.
5   1861 frigate. Sold in 1883.
6   1910 cruiser of 4,800 tons built by John Brown. Sold in 1921 to Ward at Hayle for scrapping.
7   1943 training establishment at Bristol.
8   1969 Type 82 destroyer of 6,300/7,100 tons built by Swan Hunter.

# BRITANNIA

Barfleur 1692
Ushant 1781
Genoa 1795
St Vincent 1797
Trafalgar 1805
Crimea 1854
The badge is derived from the royal coat of arms.
From the Roman name for Britain.

1   1682 1st rate (100) rebuilt at Chatham 1703 by Phineas Pett. Scrapped 1749.
2   1762 1st rate (100) 2,091 tons. Renamed *St George* 1812. Saw a great deal of active service.
5   1820 1st rate (120) 2,616 tons, built at Plymouth. Scrapped 1869.
6   1869 screw ship, ex-*Prince of Wales*. Sold 1916.
7   1904 battleship of 16,350 tons built by Portsmouth Dock Yard. Torpedoed and sunk by *U-50* off Cape Trafalgar, 1918.
11  RN College Dartmouth.
12  1953 royal yacht. Originally a naval hospital-ship of 4,961 tons built by John Brown.

# BROADSWORD

Falkland Islands 1982

1   1946 destroyer of the 'weapons' class of 2,280/2,935 tons; the first RN ship built around an all-missile weapons system. Built by Yarrow. Fleet Radar Picket ship. Scrapped Inverkeithing in 1968.
2   1976 Type 22 frigate of 3,500/4,200 tons built by Yarrow.

# BROADWATER

Atlantic 1941

1   1940 destroyer of 1,190 tons (ex-USS *Mason*) built by Newport News 1919 and acquired by the RN 1940. Sunk the following year by *U-101* off S. Ireland.

# BROADWAY

Atlantic 1941–3
North Sea 1944

1   1940 destroyer of 1,190 tons, ex-USS *Hunt*, built by Newport News 1920 and acquired by the RN 1940. Scrapped at Charlestown 1947.

# BROCKLESBY

English Channel 1942–3
Dieppe 1942
Sicily 1943
Salerno 1943
Atlantic 1943
Adriatic 1944
*Vincit amor patriae* = Love of country conquers.
Named after a hunt in Lincolnshire.

1   1940 escort destroyer of the 'Hunt' class, 1,000 tons, built by Cammell Laird. Scrapped at Faslane 1968.
2   1983 (commissioning date) minehunter of 615/725 tons built by Vosper Thornycroft. A 'Hunt' class MCMV.

# BROKE

Jutland 1916
Dover 1917
Belgian Coast 1917–18
North Sea 1939
Atlantic 1939–42
Arctic 1942
North Africa 1942
*Saevumque tridentem servamus* = We keep the dread trident.
Named after Rear Admiral Sir Philip Broke of the frigate *Shannon*.

1   1913 flotilla leader of 1,704 tons built by White. Sold to Chile 1920 and renamed *Amirante Uribe*.
2   1920 flotilla leader of 1,480 tons built by Thornycroft. Ex-*Rooke*. Damaged by shore batteries off Algiers and foundered in tow following day, 1942.

# BRUCE

*Tentata attingo* = By attempt I attain.
Named after Robert Bruce, victor of the battle of Bannockburn 1314.

1   1918 flotilla leader of 1,800 tons built by Cammell Laird. Sunk as a target off the Isle of Wight in 1939.
2   1947–9 training establishment at Crail.

# BRUISER (Bruizer)

Sicily 1943
Salerno 1943
Anzio 1944
South France 1944
Atlantic 1944
Aegean 1944

1   1798 vessel.
5   1895 destroyer. Sold 1914.
6   1942 tank assault ship built by Harland & Wolff, Fighter Direct ship 1944. Served with mercantile marine: *Lilla* (1947) and later *Silver Star*.
7   1947 landing ship. Sold 1954.

# BRYONY

Arctic 1942–3
Atlantic 1943
Sicily 1943
*Floreo dum vigilo* = I flourish while I watch.

1   1917 sloop of 1,290 tons built by Armstrong. Sold 1938 to Cashmore for scrap.
2   1941 corvette built by Harland & Wolff. Became a weather reporting station 1946. Royal Norwegian Navy 1947 with the name *Polarfront II*.

## BUCEPHALUS

Java 1811
Normandy 1944
Alexander the Great's horse.
1   1808 5th rate. Broken up 1834.
2   1944 trawler, ex-*Venture*, built 1905
    and requisitioned by the Navy
    1944. 193 tons. Returned to Esso
    1945.

## BUGLOSS

Atlantic 1944
1   1943 corvette built by Crown: Clark
    NE Marine, 980 tons. Transferred
    to RIN 1945, renamed *Assam*.
    Scrapped 1948.

## BULLDOG

St Lucia 1796
Baltic 1854−5
Dardanelles 1915−16
English Channel 1915−16
Atlantic 1941−5
Arctic 1942−4
Hold fast.
1   1792 sloop. Scrapped 1829.
3   1845 sloop. Blown up 1865.
6   1909 destroyer built by John
    Brown. Sold to Ward, Rainham for
    breaking up 1920.
7   1930 destroyer of 1,360 tons built
    by Swan Hunter of Wallsend.
    Scrapped 1946 at Rosyth.
8   1968 (commissioning date) coastal
    survey ship of 860/1,088 tons built
    by Brooke Marine of Lowestoft.

## BULLEN

Atlantic 1944
Named after Charles Bullen, flag
captain to the Earl of Northesk at
Trafalgar.
1   1943 frigate of 1,300 tons ex-
    *DE.78*,built by Bethlehem:
    Hingham. Torpedoed by *U−775*
    NW Scotland 1944.

## BULWARK

1   1807 3rd rate. Broken up 1826.
2   1885 1st rate ex-*Howe*. Renamed
    *Impregnable* following year. Sold in
    1920 as *Bulwark*.
3   1899 battleship of 15,000 tons built
    by Devonport Dock Yard. Blown
    up 1914 by internal explosion in
    the Medway.
4   1948 aircraft carrier, later
    commando carrier and helicopter
    carrier of 23,300/27/705 tons built
    by Harland & Wolff. Scrapped by
    Cairn Ryan 1984.

## BURDOCK

Atlantic 1941−4
Normandy 1944
Arctic 1944
English Channel 1944−5
1   1940 corvette of 925 tons built by
    Crown: NE Marine. Broken up at
    Hayle, 1946.

## BURGES

Atlantic 1943−5
North Sea 1944
English Channel 1945
Named after Captain Richard Rundell
Burges, killed in action at
Camperdown.
1   1943 frigate of 1,085 tons, ex-
    *DE.12*, built by Boston. Returned
    to USN 1946.

## BURGHEAD BAY

1   1945 frigate of 1,580 tons, ex-*Loch
    Harport*, built by Hill: Robey.
    Portuguese *Alvares Cabral*, 1959.

## BURNHAM

Atlantic 1941−3
1   1918 vessel.
2   1940 destroyer, ex USS *Aulick*,
    1,190 tons, built by Bethlehem
    1919. Broken up at Pembroke 1948.

## BURWELL

Atlantic 1942−5
1   1940 destroyer, ex-USS *Laub*, 1,190
    tons, built by Bethlehem:
    Squantum 1918. Sold 1947 and
    scrapped the same year at Milford
    Haven.

## BUTTERCUP

Normandy 1944
1   1915 sloop of 1,250 tons built by
    Barclay Curle. Sold to Hughes and
    Co for scrapping 1920.
2   1941 corvette of 925 tons built by
    Harland & Wolff. Sold to Norway
    1942. Mercantile marine: *Nordkyn*,
    1946; *Thoris*, 1957.

## BUXTON

Atlantic 1941−3
1   1940 destroyer, ex-USS *Edwards*,
    acquired by the RN 1940, built by
    Bethlehem: Squantum 1918, 1,190
    tons. RCN 1943−5. Sold 1946 for
    scrapping.

## BUZZARD

1   1806 prize named *Lutine* but not
    renamed *Buzzard* till 1813.
3   1849 sloop. Broken up 1883.
4   1887 sloop. Renamed *President*
    about 1910.
6   1940−4 RNAS, Jamaica.

## BYARD

Atlantic 1943−4
Named after Captain Sir Thomas
Byard of the *Bedford* at Camperdown.
1   1943 frigate of 1,300 tons, ex-
    *DE.55*, built by Bethlehem:
    Hingham. Returned to USN 1945.

## BYRON

English Channel 1944
Arctic 1944
Atlantic 1944−5
North Sea 1944−5
1   1943 frigate of 1,300 tons, ex-
    *DE.79*, built by Bethlehem:
    Hingham. Returned to USN 1945.

## CACHALOT

Atlantic 1939
Biscay 1940−4
Norway 1941
Malta Convoys 1941
*Nec pluribus impar* = A match for many.
1   1915 Admiralty whaler of 237 tons built by Smith's Dock. Sold in 1933.
2   1937 submarine of 1,520/2,157 tons built by Scotts. Rammed and sunk by Italian TB *Papa* off Cyrenaica in 1941.
3   1957 attack submarine of 1,600/2,030 tons built by Scotts. Scrapped at Blyth in 1980.

## CADIZ

*Ad omnia paratus* = Ready for anything.
There are no battle honours for this name, but a *Cadiz Merchant* has the battle honour Barfleur 1692.
The name commemorates the raids on Cadiz in the sixteenth century.
1   1944 destroyer of the 'Battle' class of 3,361 tons built by Fairfield. Sold to Pakistan in 1956 and renamed *Khaibar*.

## CADMUS

North Sea 1942
North Africa 1942−3
Sicily 1943
Salerno 1943
Anzio 1944
Named after a mythological King of Thebes.
1   1807 vessel.
2   1856 corvette. Scrapped in 1870.
3   1903 sloop of 1,070 tons built by Sheerness Dock Yard. Sold to Hong Kong in 1921.
4   1942 minesweeper. Sold to Belgium 1950.

## CAESAR

Glorious First of June 1794
Gut of Gibraltar 1801
Bay of Biscay 1805
Basque Roads 1809
Baltic 1854−5
Arctic 1944
*Veni, vidi,vici* = I came, I saw, I conquered.
(Words attributed to Julius Caesar).
1   1642 vessel.
3   1853 screw ship. Sold 1870.
4   1896 battleship of 14,900 tons, built by Portsmouth Dock Yard. Sold 1921 for breaking up in Germany.
6   1944 destroyer ex-*Ranger* of 2,600 tons built at Clydebank. Scrapped at Blyth 1967.

## CAICOS

Atlantic 1944
1   1943 frigate, ex-*PF.77*, 1,318 tons, built by Walsh Kaiser. Returned to USN 1945. Mercantile *Santissima Trinidad*, Argentinian, 1947.

## CAIRO

Norway 1940
Atlantic 1940−1
Malta Convoys 1942
1   1918 cruiser of 4,290 tons built by Cammell Laird. Torpedoed and sunk 1942 by Italian submarine *Axum*, north of Bizerta.

## CAISTOR CASTLE

North Sea 1945
1   1944 corvette/frigate of 1,010 tons built by Lewis. Scrapped 1956 at Troon.

## CALCUTTA

Baltic 1855
China 1856−8
Norway 1940
Dunkirk 1940
Greece 1941
Crete 1941
Libya 1941
Malta Convoys 1941
Mediterranean 1941
*Per ardua stabilis* = Steadfast in difficulties.
1   1795 6th rate. Surrendered 1805.
2   1831 2nd rate. Sold 1908.
3   1909 ironclad *Hercules* renamed. Renamed again to *Fisgard III* in 1914.
4   1918 cruiser of 4,290 tons built by

Armstrong: Vickers. Bombed and sunk by German aircraft NW of Alexandria in 1941.

## CALDER

Atlantic 1943−5
Named after Admiral Sir Robert Calder, captain of the fleet to Jervis at St Vincent.
1   1943 frigate of 1,300 tons, ex-*DE.58*, built by Bethlehem: Hingham. Returned to USA in 1945.

## CALDWELL

Atlantic 1940−3
1   1940 acquisition of four-funnelled US destroyer of 1,090 tons built by Bath Iron Works in 1919. Served with RCN 1942−4. Sold 1945 and scrapped by Granton.

## CALEDON

Mediterranean 1940
South France 1944
Aegean 1944
*In utrumque parata* = Ready for anything.
1   1810 vessel.
2   1916 cruiser of 4,180 tons built by Cammell Laird. Scrapped in 1948 at Dover.

## CALEDONIA

Basque Roads 1809
Name comes from the Roman word for Scotland.
1   1808 1st rate. Renamed *Dreadnought* nearly fifty years later.
2   1862 ironclad. Sold 1885.
4   1888 ex-*Kent*. Disposed of 1906.
9   1937 ex-liner *Majestic*, destroyed by fire 1939.
10   1943 shore establishment at Oban.
11   1946 marine engineering school, Rosyth.

## CALENDULA

Atlantic 1940−1
1   1940 corvette of 925 tons built by Harland & Wolff. USS *Ready* in 1942. Sold in 1946 to mercantile marine: *Villa Cisneros* (1948) and *Villa Bens* (1949).

## CALLIOPE

China 1841–2
New Zealand 1846–7
Jutland 1916
1   1808 vessel.
2   1837 6th rate. Scrapped 1883.
3   1884 corvette. She escaped the infamous Apia hurricane. Scrapped 1951.
4   1914 cruiser of 3,750 tons built by Chatham Dock Yard. Sold 1931 to Ward, Inverkeithing for scrapping.
6   1951 ex-*Falmouth* RNVR drillship at Newcastle.

## CALPE

Gut of Gibraltar 1801
Dieppe 1942
English Channel 1942
North Africa 1942
Mediterranean 1943
Sicily 1943
Salerno 1943
Aegean 1944
South France 1944
1   1800 prize named *San Josef*. This sloop was renamed *Calpe*, taking the Roman name for Gibraltar.
2   1941 destroyer of the 'Hunt' class, 1,050 tons, built by Swan Hunter: Wallsend. Lent to Denmark and renamed *Rolf Krake* in 1952.

## CALYPSO

*Cave quod recondo* = Beware of what I hide.
In Greek mythology, a nymph or goddess, daughter of Atlas.
1   1783 sloop, destroyed in a collision at sea 1803.
2   1805 sloop. Scrapped 1821.
5   1845 corvette. Scrapped 1865.
7   1883 corvette. Renamed *Briton* in 1902.
8   1917 cruiser of 4,180 tons built by Hawthorn Leslie. Torpedoed and sunk by Italian submarine *Bagnolini*, south of Crete 1940.

## CAM

Normandy 1944
Atlantic 1944
1   1943 frigate of 1,370 tons built by Brown: Parsons. Scrapped in 1945 on the Tyne.

## CAMBRIAN

Navarino 1827
China 1860

Arctic 1944
*Parvus pars magna* = Of a small people, I am a great part.
Derived from the Roman name for Wales, Cambria.
1   1797 5th rate. Wrecked in 1828.
2   1841 frigate. Sold in 1892.
3   1893 cruiser of 4,360 tons built by Pembroke Dock Yard and renamed *Vivid* in 1921. Scrapped 1923.
4   1916 cruiser of 3,750 tons built by Pembroke Dock Yard. Sold in 1934 to Metal Industries of Rosyth for scrapping.
7   1943 destroyer, ex-*Spitfire*, of 2,600 tons built by Scotts. Scrapped Briton Ferry, 1971.

## CAMBRIDGE

Orfordness 1666
Solebay 1672
Schooneveld 1673
Texel 1673
Barfleur 1692
Vigo 1702
Velez Malaga 1704
Havana 1762
Syria 1840
Belgian Coast 1915
Practice makes perfect.
1   1666 3rd rate. Lost in a gale in 1694.
2   and 3 were also 3rd rates.
4   1815 2nd rate became the gunnery school at Devonport in 1856. Scrapped 1869.
5   1869 the name given to the *Windsor Castle*. Sold before WWI.
7   1956 name given to the gunnery range at Wembury, near Plymouth — the RN's Systems and Weapons Training base.

## CAMELEON (Chameleon)

Egypt 1801
Burma 1945
2   1780 sloop. Sold 1783.
3   1795 sloop. Broken up 1811.
7   1860 sloop. Sold 1882.
8   1910 destroyer built by Fairfield. Sold 1921 for scrapping at Devonport.
9   1944 minesweeper of the 'Algerine' class built by Harland & Wolff. Scrapped 1966.

## CAMELLIA

Atlantic 1940–5
Arctic 1942–5
Sicily 1943
Normandy 1944
North Sea 1944
1   1915 sloop built by Bow

McLachlan, 1,200 tons. Sold 1923 to Unity Ship Breaking Co.
4   1940 corvette of 925 tons built by Harland & Wolff. Sold 1947 to mercantile marine: *Hetty W. Vinke*, 1948.

## CAMERON

1   1940 destroyer ex-USS *Welles*, acquired 1940 but built 1919 by Bethlehem, 1,190 tons. CTL after bombing 1940.

## CAMPANIA

Norway 1944–5
Atlantic 1944
Arctic 1944–5
Of one company. Badge is based on the Cunard Company's badge.
1   1915 seaplane carrier of 18,000 tons, originally built 1893 by Fairfield. Converted 1915–16. Could fly off aircraft. Sunk in collision with *Royal Oak* and *Glorious* in a gale in the Firth of Forth.
3   1943 escort carrier of 12,450 tons built by Harland & Wolff for Shaw Savill & Albion Line. Ferried men and materials to Montebello Island off Australia for atomic explosion experiments. Sold in 1955 for scrapping at Blyth.

## CAMPANULA

Atlantic 1940–4
Arctic 1942
English Channel 1944–5
Normandy 1944
1   1915 sloop of 1,250 tons built by Barclay Curle. Sold 1922.
3   1940 corvette of 925 tons built by Fleming & Ferguson. Broken up Dunston 1947.

## CAMPBELL

Norway 1940
Atlantic 1940—43
North Sea 1941—5
Arctic 1942
Normandy 1944
English Channel 1942—4
Dinna forget.
1   1796 vessel.
2   1918 flotilla leader of 1,530 tons
    built by Cammell Laird. Broken up
    Rosyth 1948.

## CAMPBELTOWN

Atlantic 1941—2
St Nazaire 1942
1   1940 destroyer ex-USS *Buchanan*
    acquired 1940 but built 1919 by
    Bath Iron Works. 1,090 tons.
    Expended as assault ship St
    Nazaire 1942.
2   1987 frigate of the Type 22
    'Broadsword' class: 4,200/4,900
    tons. Built by Cammell Laird.

## CAMPERDOWN

Name derives from the victorious
battle in 1797 and from Admiral
Duncan, who took the name Viscount
Duncan of Camperdown. The badge
derives from the admiral's arms.
1   1797 1st rate prize, *Jupiter*, taken at
    Camperdown. Sold 1817.
3   1825 2nd rate ex-*Trafalgar*.
    Renamed *Pitt* 1882.
4   1885 battleship. Sold 1911 for
    scrapping.
6   1944 destroyer of the 'Battle' class
    of 3,361 tons built by Fairfield and
    scrapped 1970 at Faslane.

## CAMPION

Atlantic 1941—5
1   1941 corvette of 925 tons built by
    Crown: Clark and broken up in
    1947 at Newport.

## CANDYTUFT

Atlantic 1940—1
1   1917 sloop of 1,290 tons built by
    Armstrong. Torpedoed and
    stranded near Bougie, N. Africa,
    1917.
2   1940 corvette of 925 tons. USS
    *Tenacity*, 1942. Mercantile marine
    *Maw Hwa*, 1947.

## CANOPUS

San Domingo 1806
Dardanelles 1916
Name chosen by Nelson for a prize at
The Nile. It is geographical — an
Egyptian city.
1   1798 2nd rate prize, *Franklin*. Sold
    1887.
2   1897 battleship of 12,950 tons built
    by Portsmouth Dock Yard. Sold
    1920.
3   1940 training establishment at
    Alexandria till 1945.

## CAPEL

Normandy 1944
Atlantic 1944
English Channel 1944
Named after Captain the Hon.
Thomas B. Capel, who commanded
the *Phoebe* at Trafalgar.
1   1943 frigate, ex *DE 266*, built by
    Boston, 1,085 tons. Torpedoed and
    sunk by *U-486* off Cherbourg.

## CAPETOWN

Mediterranean 1940
Normandy 1944
*Spes bona* = Good hope.
1   1919 cruiser of 4,250 tons built by
    Cammell Laird. Broken up by
    Preston 1946.

## CAPRICE

Arctic 1944
1   1943 destroyer, ex-*Swallow*, of
    2,020/2,600 tons built by Yarrow
    and scrapped 1979.

## CARADOC

Crimea 1854—5
Atlantic 1940
Britain first.
Named after a knight of the Round
Table.
1   1847 vessel.
2   1916 cruiser of 4,180 tons built by

Scotts and scrapped at Briton
Ferry, 1946.

## CARDIFF

Falkland Islands 1982
*Acris in cardine rerum* = Keen in
emergency.
1   1652 prize, *Fortune*. Scrapped 1656.
2   1917 cruiser of 4,190 tons built by
    Fairfield and scrapped at Troon,
    1946.
3   1974 Type 42 destroyer of 3,500/
    4,100 tons built by Vickers.

## CARDIGAN BAY

Korea 1950—3
1   1944 frigate, ex-*Loch Laxford*, of
    2,420 tons, built by Robb.
    Scrapped Troon, 1946.

## CARISBROOKE CASTLE

Atlantic 1944
1   1943 corvette/frigate of 1,010 tons
    built by Caledon: Clark. Scrapped
    Faslane 1958.

## CARLISLE

Norway 1940
Greece 1941
Crete 1941
Libya 1941—2
Sirte 1942
Malta Convoys 1941—2
Sicily 1943
Aegean 1943
Be just and fear not.
1   1693 4th rate, wrecked three years
    later.
2   1698 4th rate, blown up two years
    later.
3   1918 cruiser of 4,290 tons, ex-
    *Cawnpore*, built by Fairfield. CTL
    1945 and scrapped at Alexandria
    1949.

## CARNARVON BAY

1  1945 frigate of 1,435 tons, ex-*Loch Maddy*, built by Robb and scrapped at Spezia 1959.

## CARNATION

Atlantic 1941−2
1  1807 sloop lost by surrender the following year.
2  1813 sloop. Sold 1836.
5  1915 sloop of 1,200 tons built by Greenoch Grangemouth and sold 1922 for scrapping.
6  1940 corvette of 925 tons built by Grangemouth NE Marine. Transferred to Netherlands navy 1943−5. Mercantile marine *Southern Laurel*, 1949.

## CAROLINE

Banda Neira 1810
Java 1811
Jutland 1916
*Tenax propositi* = Firm of purpose.
Named after Queen Caroline, wife of George IV.
1  1795 5th rate, scrapped in 1815.
5  1882 corvette, renamed *Ganges* about 1908.
6  1914 cruiser of 3,750 tons built by Cammell Laird. Became the drillship for the Ulster Division RNVR in 1924.

## CARRON

Baltic 1855
1  1813 vessel.
2  1944 destroyer, ex-*Strenuous* of 2,020/2,600 tons, built by Scotts and scrapped Inverkeithing 1967.
3  1983 minesweeper of 890 tons built by Richards Ltd of Great Yarmouth.

## CARYSFORT

Syria 1840
Belgian Coast 1916
*Manus haec inimica tyrannis* = This hand is deadly to tyrants.
Named after the first Baron, created 1752.
1  1767 6th rate. Sold 1813.
3  1878 corvette. Sold 1861.
4  1914 cruiser of 3,750 tons built by Portsmouth Dock Yard and sold in 1931 for scrapping by McLellan.
6  1944 destroyer, ex-*Pique* of 2,020/2,600 tons built by White. Disposed of in 1970.

## CASSANDRA

Arctic 1944
*Furiosior undis* = More mad than the waves.
Named after the prophetic daughter of the King of Troy.
1  1805 vessel.
2  1916 cruiser of 4,120 tons built by Vickers. Mined in the Baltic in 1918.
5  1943 destroyer ex-*Tourmaline* of 2,020/2,600 tons built by Yarrow and scrapped Inverkeithing 1967.

## CASTLETON

Atlantic 1940−2
North Sea 1942−4
1  1940 destroyer ex-*Aaron Ward*, acquired 1940 but originally built by Bath Iron Works in 1919, 1,090 tons. Sold for scrap 1947.

## CATO

Atlantic 1943
Normandy 1944
Named after the Roman statesman Marcus Porcius Cato.
1  1782 50-gun ship. Lost at sea the following year.
2  1782 prize, *Caton*. Sold 1815.
3  1943 minesweeper of 890 tons built by Associated Shipbuilding, Seattle. Sunk by human torpedoes off Normandy 1944.

## CATTERICK

Salerno 1943
Aegean 1944
Normandy 1944
Named after the hunt in Yorkshire.
1  1941 destroyer of the 'Hunt' class, 1,087 tons, built by Vickers Armstrong, Barrow. Sold to the Greek navy 1946 as *Hastings*, and was scrapped in Greece in 1963.

## CATTISTOCK

North Sea 1941−5
English Channel 1942−4
Normandy 1944
1  1917 minesweeper, sold for scrapping 1923.
2  1940 destroyer of the 'Hunt' class, 907 tons, built by Yarrow. Wrecked in 1957 on the way to the breakers.
3  1982 (commissioning date) minehunter of 615/725 tons built by Vosper Thornycroft. A 'Hunt' class MCMV.

## CAVALIER

Arctic 1945
1  1944 destroyer, ex-*Pellew*, of 2,020/2,600 tons built by White. Disposal List 1975−6.

## CAVENDISH

*Cavendo tutus* = Safe by taking care.
Named after the famous navigator Thomas Cavendish.
1  1918 cruiser converted to the carrier *Vindictive*. Originally the *Sibyl* of 9,750 tons built by Harland & Wolff. Sold in 1946 and broken up Blyth.
2  1944 destroyer of 2,020/2,600 tons built at Clydebank and scrapped at Blyth 1967.

## CAWSAND BAY

1  1945 frigate, ex-*Loch Rowan* of 1,850 tons, built by White and scrapped in Genoa 1959.

## CAYMAN

Atlantic 1944
1  1943 'Colony' class frigate, ex-*Harland*, ex-*PF 78* built by Walsh Kaiser and returned to the USA 1946.

## CELANDINE

Atlantic 1941−5
English Channel 1944
Normandy 1944
1  1916 sloop of 1,250 tons built by Barclay Curle and scrapped 1923 by Unity Ship Breaking Co.
2  1940 corvette of 925 tons built by Grangemouth: Ailsa. Scrapped Portaferry 1948.

## CENTAUR

Havana 1762
St Kitts 1782
The Saintes 1782
Minorca 1798
Baltic 1855
China 1860
Belgian Coast 1916−17
*Curieux* 1804
*Sevolod* 1808
*Celeriter ferox* = Swiftly fierce.
A mythical creature, half man, half
horse, living in Thessaly.
1  1746 6th rate (24) of 504 tons built
   at Hull and captained by Henry
   Cobby. Sold 1761.
2  1759 3rd rate prize *Centaure* taken
   in Boscawen's action off Lagos
   1759. Anglicized name adopted
   following year. She captured a 64
   off Jamaica 1762, fought at Ushant,
   Martinique and with Graves at the
   Chesapeake; with Hood off St
   Kitts; and at the Saintes.
   Foundered in a hurricane in 1782
   with only Captain Inglefield and
   eleven men surviving.
3  1797 3rd rate (74) of 1,842 tons built
   at Woolwich. Saw action at
   Minorca, off France, in West
   Indies. Helped capture four 40s off
   France 1806. At Copenhagen 1807
   and helped capture *Sevolod* (74) in
   the Baltic. Broken up 1819.
4  1845 paddle-wheel steam frigate.
   Broken up 1864.
5  1916 cruiser of 3,750 tons built by
   Armstrong Whitworth. Kings of
   Denmark and Sweden hoisted
   their flags in her in early 1930s as
   Honorary Admirals of the Fleet.
   Scrapped Troon 1934.
6  1947 aircraft carrier of 27,000 tons
   built by Harland & Wolff. Disposal
   List 1974−5.

## CENTURION

Armada 1588
Cadiz 1596
Dover 1652
Gabbard 1653
Portland 1653
Santa Cruz 1657

Lowestoft 1665
Orfordness 1666
Barfleur 1692
Velez Malaga 1704
Finisterre I 1747
Louisburg 1758
Quebec 1759
Havana 1762
St Lucia 1778
China 1900
Jutland 1916
Normandy 1944
*N. S. de Covadonga* 1743
One in a hundred.
Name derives from the commander of
a hundred men in the Roman army.
1  1588 merchant ship of City of
   London.
2  1650 5th rate. Wrecked 1689.
3  1691 4th rate. Broken up 1728.
4  1732 4th rate. Anson's flagship
   during his circumnavigation.
   Scrapped 1769.
5  1774 4th rate, scrapped 1823.
6  1826 4th rate (50) ex-*Clarence*.
   Scrapped 1828.
7  1844 2nd rate, sold in 1870.
8  1892 battleship, sold 1910.
9  1911 battleship of 25,000 tons
   built by Hawthorn Leslie,
   Devonport. Became wireless-
   controlled target ship. During
   WWII acted as dummy *King
   George V*, and was later expended
   as part of the Mulberry
   breakwater 1944.
10 1970: *Centurion* was
   recommissioned at Gosport: she
   maintains the computer record of
   the Navy, and is the Pay and
   Drafting Centre.

## CERES

St Lucia 1778
Egypt 1801
Atlantic 1939
Normandy 1944
*Tu ne cede malis* = Do not yield to evil.
Named after the goddess of the
harvest.
1  1777 sloop (18) of 361 tons built at
   Woolwich. Captured by French
   1778 off St Lucia when
   commanded by Captain Dacres,
   but recaptured 1782 and renamed
   *Raven*.
2  1781 5th rate (32) of 689 tons built
   at Liverpool. Became victualling
   depot at Sheerness. Broken up
   1830.
5  1917 cruiser of 4,190 tons built by
   John Brown. Sold 1946 for
   breaking up.
6  1946 Supply Officer's training
   establishment at Wetherby, ex-
   *Demetrius*.

## CEYLON

Sabang 1944
Burma 1945
Korea 1950−2
1  1805 East Indiaman named *Bombay*
   and renamed *Ceylon* in 1808. Sold
   1875 for scrapping.
3  1942 cruiser of 8,800 tons built by
   Stephen. Sold Peru 1959 as *Coronel
   Bolognesi*.

## CHALLENGER

San Sebastian 1813
Cameroons 1914
*Depugnare superbos* = To fight the
proud.
Name is taken from Landseer's
picture *The Challenger*.
1  1806 vessel.
3  1826 6th rate. Wrecked 1835.
4  1858 corvette.
5  1902 cruiser. Sold to Ward, Preston
   for breaking up 1920.
6  1931 survey ship of 1,140 tons built
   at Chatham and scrapped at Dover
   in 1954.
7  1981 seabed operations vessel of
   6,500/7,185 tons built by Scotts of
   Greenock.

## CHAMOIS

Normandy 1944
Atlantic 1944
1  1896 destroyer which foundered in
   1904.
2  1942 minesweeper ex-*BAM 12* of
   890 tons built by Associated
   Shipbuilding Co. CTL 1944 but
   entered mercantile marine as
   *Morning Star*, 1948, then
   abandoned and scrapped.

## CHANTICLEER

Sicily 1943
Atlantic 1943
*Vigilantibus non dormientibus* = To
watchers, not to sleep.

1 1808 sloop which became a watch vessel 1833.
2 1861 sloop, broken up 1871.
4 1942 sloop of 1,350 tons built by Denny and renamed *Lusitania* in 1943. CTL 1943. Hulked. Scrapped Lisbon 1946–7.

## CHAPLET

1 1944 destroyer of 2,020/2,600 tons built by Thornycroft and scrapped Blyth 1965.

## CHARGER

1 1801 vessel.
4 1894 destroyer, sold for scrapping 1912.
5 1947 landing-ship.
6 1986 coastal patrol craft of 43 tons.

## CHARITY

Lowestoft 1665
Korea 1950–3
The greatest of these.
1 1242 vessel is recorded.
5 1944 destroyer of 1,710 tons built by Thornycroft and scrapped Blyth 1965.

## CHARLESTOWN

Atlantic 1941–2
North Sea 1943–4
1 1780 5th rate *Boston* taken as prize, and sold three years later.
2 1940 destroyer ex-USS *Abbott* of 1,090 tons acquired 1940 but built 1918 by Newport News. Sold 1947 for scrapping at Sunderland.

## CHARLOCK

Normandy 1944
North Sea 1944
Arctic 1944
Atlantic 1944–5
1 1943 corvette of 980 tons built by Ferguson. Transferred to RIN in 1946 as *Mahratta*.

## CHARWELL (Cherwell)

Normandy 1944
1 1801 sloop prize, *Aurore*, sold in 1813.
3 1815 sloop, sold in 1837.
5 1903 destroyer built by Palmer and sold in 1919 for scrapping by Ward of Rainham.

## CHARYBDIS

Malta Convoys 1942
North Africa 1942
Salerno 1943
Atlantic 1943
English Channel 1943
Biscay 1943
In Greek mythology, a terrible whirlpool, across a strait from the monster Scylla.
1 1809 vessel.
3 1859 corvette. Sold 1884.
4 1893 cruiser. Sold in 1922 for breaking up in Holland, 1923.
5 1940 cruiser of 5,450 tons built by Cammell Laird. Sunk by German E-boats off north coast France 1943.
6 1968 general-purpose frigate of 2,500/2,962 tons built by Harland & Wolff. 'Leander' class, armed with Exocet missiles.

## CHASER

Atlantic 1943
Arctic 1944
Okinawa 1945
1 1781 sloop purchased in the East Indies. Captured 1782 by the French in Bay of Bengal. Recaptured the following year and sold in 1784.
2 1942 escort carrier of 11,420 tons, ex-USS *Breton*, ex-*Mormacgulf*, lent/leased, to RN and returned to USA 1946. Mercantile service as *Aagtekerk*.
3 1947 ex-LST 3029 built by Stephen in 1945. Sold in 1962 for scrapping in Spezia.

## CHATHAM

Quiberon Bay 1759
Dardanelles 1915–16
1 1666 vessel.
5 1691 4th rate. Became a breakwater in 1749. Scrapped 1762.
6 1694 hulk; survived till 1813 before being scrapped.
17 1809 3rd rate prize named *Royal Hollandais* taken while still under construction at Walcheren. Shipped to Woolwich and launched 1812. Sold in 1817.
18 1813 3rd rate. Scrapped in 1876.
19 1911 cruiser of 5,400 tons built by Chatham Dock Yard. RNZN 1920. Scrapped 1926 by Ward at Pembroke Dock.
20 1987 Type 22 frigate of 4,200/4,900 tons built by Cammell Laird.

## CHELMER

Dardanelles 1915
Atlantic 1943–5
English Channel 1944
North Sea 1944
Normandy 1944
1 1904 destroyer. Sold for scrapping 1920.
2 1943 frigate of 1,370 tons built by Brown: Parsons. Scrapped Charlestown 1957.

## CHELSEA

Atlantic 1940–3
1 1940 destroyer acquired 1940 but built in 1919 by Bath Iron Works. 1,090 tons. Transferred to RCN 1942–3, then to Russia, as *Derzki*, 1944–9. Sold and scrapped.

## CHEQUERS

Named after the official country residence of the prime minister.
1 1944 destroyer ex-*Champion* of 2,020/2,600 tons built by Scotts. Scrapped at Newport 1966.

## CHESTERFIELD

Atlantic 1941–3
1 1745 5th rate. Lost at sea 1762.
4 1940 destroyer ex-*Wood* acquired in 1940 but built 1920. 1,190 tons. Sold 1947 for scrapping on the Tyne.

## CHEVIOT

1 1944 destroyer of 1,710 tons built by Stephen. Scrapped Inverkeithing 1962.

## CHEVRON

1 1944 destroyer of 2,020/2,600 tons built by Stephen. Scrapped 1969.

## CHICHESTER

Quiberon Bay 1759
Belleisle 1761
Egypt 1801
*Vincit amor patriae* = Love of country prevails.
1 3rd rate. 1695.
2 3rd rate. 1753.
3 3rd rate. 1785.
4 1809 prize, *Var* (26). Wrecked 1811.
6 1955 frigate for AA Direction of

2,330 tons built by Fairfield.
Broken up by Queenborough 1982.

## CHIDDINGFOLD

Norway 1941
English Channel 1945
Named after the hunts in Surrey.
1  1941 destroyer of the 'Hunt' class
   of 1,050 tons built by Scotts. Sold
   to the RIN 1953 as *Ganga*.
2  1984 (commissioning date)
   minehunter of 615/725 tons built by
   Yarrow. A 'Hunt' class MCMV.

## CHIEFTAIN

1  1914−18 minor war vessel.
3  1945 destroyer of 2,020/2,600 tons
   built by Scotts. Scrapped
   Sunderland 1961.

## CHILDERS

China 1842
1  1778 sloop. Scrapped 1811.
5  1945 destroyer of 2,020/2,600 tons
   built by Denny and scrapped at
   Spezia in 1963.

## CHIVALROUS

1  1945 destroyer of 2,600 tons built
   by Denny. Lent to Pakistan in 1954
   as *Taimur*.

## CHRYSANTHEMUM

*Floret qui vigilet* = He flourishes who
keeps watch.
1  1917 sloop and then the RNVR
   drillship of the London Division.
2  1941 corvette of 925 tons built by
   Harland & Wolff. Served in the
   French navy as *Commandante
   Drogou*, then sold to the mercantile
   marine 1948−59.

## CHURCHILL

Atlantic 1941−4
*Veteris vestigia flammae* = A spark of
the old flame (from Virgil's *Aeneid*).
1  1940 destroyer ex-*Herndon*
   acquired 1940 but built 1919. 1,190
   tons. Lent to Russian navy 1945 as
   *Deiatelnyi*, but lost at sea 1945.
2  1968 nuclear-powered submarine
   of 4,000/4,400/4,900 tons built by
   Vickers at Barrow.

## CICERO

1  1918 sloop of 1,320 tons built by
   Swan Hunter. Sold 1921 to
   Cashmore for scrapping.
3  1945 LSI of 11,650 tons, built in
   1943 by Consolidated Steel
   Corporation as *Empire Arquebus*.
4  1947 naval establishment at
   Braintree, Essex.

## CIRCE

Camperdown 1797
Martinique 1809
Sicily 1943
Salerno 1943
Anzio 1944
*Semper circiter* = Always somewhere
about.
A mythological enchantress.
1  1785 6th rate, wrecked in 1803.
4  Minesweeper of 810 tons built by
   Sheerness Dock Yard and broken
   up 1920.
5  1939 minesweeper of 778 tons,
   requisitioned 1939, became *Medea*,
   served in RAN 1942 and returned
   to owners 1945.
6  1942 minesweeping sloop of 850
   tons built by Harland & Wolff.
   RNVR drillship *Tay* 1955. Scrapped
   1966 Dalmuir.

## CLARE

Atlantic 1940−3
North Africa 1942−3
Sicily 1943
1  1940 destroyer ex-*Upsher* acquired
   in 1940 but built by Newport News
   1920. 1,190 tons. Scrapped after
   WWII.

## CLARKIA

Atlantic 1940−4
English Channel 1944−5
Normandy 1944
1  1940 corvette of 925 tons built by
   Harland & Wolff. Scrapped at
   Hayle 1947.

## CLEMATIS

Atlantic 1940−5
English Channel 1944−5
Normandy 1944
*In arduis floreo* = I flourish in difficult
circumstances.
1  1915 sloop of 1,200 tons built by
   Greenoch Grangemouth. Scrapped
   at Sunderland.
2  1940 corvette of 925 tons built by

Hill Richardson Westgarth Clark
and scrapped Charlestown 1949.

## CLEOPATRA

Dogger Bank 1781
Martinique 1809
Burma 1853
Belgian Coast 1916
Malta Convoys 1942
Sirte 1942
Sicily 1943
*Invicta ut olim* = Unconquered as ever.
Named after the famous Queen of
Egypt, lover of Mark Antony.
1  1779 5th rate (32) of 689 tons built
   at Bristol. Captured by a French 46
   in 1805 and recaptured by the
   *Leander* in 1809. Broken up 1814.
2  1835 6th rate (28) of 918 tons at
   Pembroke. Captured a slaver and
   released 284 slaves 1841. Sold 1862
   for scrapping.
3  1878 light cruiser of 2,380 tons built
   at Glasgow. Sold 1931 as part of
   *Defiance*.
4  1915 cruiser of 3,750 tons built at
   Devonport. Rammed and cut in
   half German destroyer *G 194*. Sold
   1931.
7  1940 cruiser of 5,540 tons built by
   Hawthorn Leslie. Broken up 1958
   at Newport.
8  1964 general-purpose frigate of
   2,450/3,200 tons built at
   Devonport. 'Leander' class, armed
   with Exocet missiles.

## CLEVELAND

Atlantic 1942
English Channel 1942−3
North Sea 1943
Sicily 1943
Salerno 1943
South France 1944
Aegean 1944
Adriatic 1944
Named after the notorious Barbara
Villiers, Duchess of Cleveland
(1641−1709), except fourth ship which
takes its name from the hunt in
Yorkshire.

1 1671 vessel.
4 1940 destroyer of the 'Hunt' class of 907 tons built by Yarrow. Wrecked in 1957 on her way to the shipbreakers.

## CLIO

China 1842
Mesopotamia 1915
Suez Canal 1915
Named after the first of the nine Muses.
1 1807 sloop. Scrapped 1847.
3 1903 sloop of 1,070 tons built at Sheerness. Sold to Bombay 1920.
4 1939−45 naval base at Barrow.

## CLOVER

Atlantic 1941−5
Normandy 1944
North Sea 1944
1 1941 corvette of 925 tons built by Fleming & Ferguson. Mercantile marine 1947 as *Clover Lock*, then to Chinese Communists as *Kai Feng*.

## CLYDE

Norway 1940
Mediterranean 1941
Malta Convoys 1942
Be strong.
1 1796 5th rate. Sold for scrapping in 1814.
5 1934 submarine of 1,850/2,723 tons built by Vickers Armstrong at Barrow. Sold in 1946 for scrapping at Durban.
6 Coastal minesweeper, tender to Clyde Division RNVR.
7 1961−7 ramp powered lighter of the 'Avon'class, 100 tons, built by White and Saunders Roe.

## COCHRANE

Jutland 1916
Named after the renowned Admiral Thomas Cochrane, Earl Dundonald (1775−1860).
1 1905 cruiser of 13,380 tons built by Fairfield. Stranded and wrecked in the Mersey in 1918.
2 1938 naval base at Rosyth.

## COCKADE

Korea 1950−3
1 1944 destroyer of 2,106/2,749 tons built by Yarrow. Scrapped in 1964 at Newport.

## COCKATRICE

Arctic 1943−4
Normandy 1944
A fabulous reptile.
1 1781 vessel.
7 1912 destroyer of about 950 tons built by Hawthorn Leslie and sold in 1921 to Ward at Hayle for scrapping.
8 1942 minesweeper of the 'Algerine' class built by Fleming & Ferguson.

## CODRINGTON

Dunkirk 1940
Norway 1940
*Vultus in hostem* = Face to the foe.
Named after Admiral Sir Edward Codrington, one of Nelson's captains at Trafalgar and commander of the Allied fleet at the battle of Navarino, 1827.
1 1929 flotilla leader of 1,540 tons built by Swan Hunter of Wallsend and sunk by bombing in Dover Harbour, 1940.

## COLLINGWOOD

Jutland 1916
Atlantic 1941−4
*Ferar unus et idem* = I shall carry on regardless.
Named after Vice Admiral Lord Collingwood, second-in-command to Nelson at Trafalgar.
1 1841 2nd rate. Sold 1867.
2 1882 battleship, sold for breaking up 1909.
3 1908 battleship of 19,250 tons built by Devonport Dock Yard. Sold in 1922 for scrapping by Cashmore.
4 1939 training establishment at Fareham, Hants, for new-entry seamen and later Weapon and Electrical Engineering Branch training establishment. In 1979 the Engineering Branch was restructured; *Collingwood* retained the Weapon Engineering Sub Branch.

## COLOMBO

Atlantic 1939−44
Sicily 1943
Aegean 1944
South France 1944
Adriatic 1944
1 1918 cruiser of 4,290 tons built by Fairfield. Broken up at Newport in 1948.

## COLOSSUS

St Vincent 1797
Groix 1795
Trafalgar 1805
Baltic 1855
Jutland 1916
Named after the enormous Colossus at Rhodes, one of the seven wonders of the world. This giant bronze figure of Helios was destroyed by earthquake in 224 B.C.
1 1787 3rd rate, wrecked in 1798.
4 1882 battleship, sold for scrapping 1908.
5 1910 battleship of 20,000 tons built by Scotts and sold in 1928 to the Alloa Ship Breaking Co of Rosyth.
6 1943 aircraft carrier of 13,190 tons built by Vickers Armstrong, Tyne. Transferred to France about 1946 and renamed *Arromanches*.

## COLTSFOOT

Atlantic 1941−5
Malta Convoys 1942
North Africa 1942
1 1941 corvette of 925 tons built by Hall. Sold 1947. Became *Alexandra* 1947, then *Hermopoulis*, 1953. Lost 1954.

## COLUMBINE

China 1841−2
Atlantic 1940−4
South France 1944
Kua Kam 1949 (Single-ship Action)
1 1806 vessel.
2 and 3 were sloops.
4 1912 sloop ex-*Wild Swan*. Sold for scrap 1920.
5 1914 depot ship, ex-*Mercury*, at Rosyth. Sold 1919.
7 1940 corvette of 925 tons built by Hill: Richardson Westgarth & Clark. Sold 1947 and became *Lief Welding* in 1949.

## COMBATANT

Atlantic 1944
1  1804 sloop. Sold in 1816.
2  1942 minesweeper, ex-*BAM 14*, built in USA by Associated Shipbuilding of Seattle. 890 tons. Returned to USA in 1946.

## COMET

Glorious First of June 1794
Mesopotamia 1914−15
*Sylphe* 1808
Follow the light.
1  1695 vessel.
5  Sloop, surrendered to the French 1803.
7  1807 prize 6th rate (20).
11  1910 destroyer built by Fairfield. Sunk 1918 by Austrian submarine in the Mediterranean.
12  1931 destroyer transferred to RCN 1937.
14  1944 destroyer of 2,106/2,749 tons built by Yarrow. Scrapped in 1964 at Newport.

## COMUS

China 1856−60
Jutland 1916
Korea 1950−3
*Frederickscoarn* 1807
Lead on apace.
Mythological god of revelry. Milton represents him as a male Circe.
1  1806 sloop which was wrecked in 1816.
2  1828 sloop ex-*Comet*.
3  1878 corvette, sold for scrapping 1904.
4  1914 cruiser of 3,750 tons built by Swan Hunter. Sold in 1934 for breaking up by Ward, Barrow.
5  1945 destroyer of 2,106/2,749 tons built by Thornycroft and scrapped at Newport in 1958.

## CONCORD

Korea 1950−3
Peace with honour.
1  1646 vessel.
2  1649 prize taken from the Dutch and sold 1659.
3  1783 prize, 5th rate.
7  1916 cruiser of 3,750 tons built by Armstrongs. Sold to Metal Industries of Rosyth in 1935 for breaking up.
10  1945 destroyer of 2,106/2,749 tons, ex-*Corso*, built by Thornycroft. Broken up at Inverkeithing 1962.

## CONDOR

Alexandria 1882
*Sors varia opus idem* = Our lot varies, our task is the same.
1  1876 vessel.
2  1898 sloop which foundered in 1901.
6  1940 RN Air Station at Arbroath. Paid off 1971. Now RM Barracks.

## CONN

English Channel 1944
Arctic 1944
North Sea 1944−5
Atlantic 1944−5
Named after Captain John Conn of the *Dreadnought* at Trafalgar.
1  1943 frigate, ex-*DE.80*, of 1,300 tons built by Bethlehem: Hingham and returned to the USA 1946.

## CONQUEROR

Lagos 1759
The Saintes 1782
Trafalgar 1805
Jutland 1916
North Sea 1942−3
English Channel 1943−5
Biscay 1944
Atlantic 1944−5
Falkland Islands 1982
*Tempus omnia vincit* = Time conquers all things.
1  1745 vessel.
2  1758 3rd rate wrecked only two years later.
4  1798 3rd rate *Conquérant*, prize taken at The Nile. Scrapped 1803.
6  1855 2nd rate, wrecked in 1861.
7  1862 1st rate ex-*Waterloo*, subsequently renamed *Warspite* in 1877.
8  1881 turret ship. Sold for scrapping 1905.
9  1911 battleship of 22,500 tons built by Beardmore. Sold in 1922 to Cox & Danks of Upnor for scrapping.
14  1969 nuclear-powered submarine

of 4,000/4,300/4,800 tons built by Cammell Laird. Sank the Argentinian cruiser *General Belgrano* in the Falklands, 1982.

## CONSORT

Korea 1950−3
Loyal and steadfast.
1  1944 destroyer of 2,106/2,749 tons built by Stephen. Scrapped at Swansea in 1961.

## CONSTANCE

Jutland 1916
Korea 1950−2
1  1797 6th rate prize, lost in 1806.
4  1880 corvette, sold for breaking up 1899.
5  1915 cruiser of 3,750 tons built by Cammell Laird and sold for scrap 1936.
7  1944 destroyer of 2,106/2,749 tons built by Vickers Armstrong, Tyne and sold in 1956 for scrapping at Inverkeithing.

## CONTEST

Basque Roads 1809
Burma 1853
Jutland 1916
1  1797 vessel.
8  1894 destroyer. Sold for breaking up 1911.
9  1913 destroyer of *c*.950 tons built by Hawthorn Leslie. Torpedoed and sunk in 1917 in the Channel by a U-boat.
10  1944 destroyer of 2,106/2,749 tons built by White and scrapped at Grays in 1960.

## CONVOLVULUS

Atlantic 1941−4
North Africa 1942
Sicily 1943
English Channel 1945
1  1917 sloop of 1,290 tons built by Barclay Curle. Sold in 1921 for breaking up at Stanlee the following year.
2  1940 corvette of 925 tons built by Hill: Richardson, Westgarth & Clark. Broken up at Newport in 1947.

## COOK

Named after Captain James Cook, the navigator.

1 1945 frigate, ex-*Pegwell Bay*, ex-*Loch Mochrun*, of 2,230 tons built by Pickersgill. Completed conversion to a survey ship 1950.

## COOKE

Normandy 1944
Atlantic 1944
English Channel 1944–5
Named after Captain John Cooke of the *Bellerophon* at Trafalgar.
1 1943 frigate, ex-*DE.267*, of 1,085 tons, built by Boston. Returned to USA 1946.

## COREOPSIS

Atlantic 1940–3
North Africa 1942
1 1917 sloop of 1,290 tons built by Barclay Curle. Broken up in 1924.
3 1940 corvette of 925 tons built by Inglis: Kincaid. Transferred to the Greek navy as *Kriezis*, 1943–5, and scrapped at Sunderland 1952.

## CORNFLOWER

True blue.
1 1916 sloop. Lost to the Japanese at Hong Kong 1941.

2 1950 minesweeper, ex-*Lysander*. Reverted to *Cornflower* the following year.

## CORNWALL

Falklands 1914
Dardanelles 1915
One and all.
Badge derives from the arms of Cornwall.
1 1692 3rd rate, broken up 1761.
2 1761 3rd rate, destroyed in 1780.
3 1809 3rd rate, renamed *Wellesley* in 1868.
5 1902 cruiser, sold in 1920 to Ward, Briton Ferry for breaking up.
6 1926 cruiser of 9,750 tons built by Beardmore, Devonport. Sunk in the Indian Ocean by Japanese aircraft 1942.
7 1985 frigate of 'Broadsword' class of 4,200/4,900 tons built by Yarrow.

## CORUNNA

Named after Sir John Moore's victory over the French in 1809.
1 1945 destroyer later 'Battle' class of 2,780/3,430 tons built by Swan Hunter, Wallsend. Broken up at Blyth 1975.

## COSBY

English Channel 1944
North Sea 1944
Atlantic 1944–5
Named after Captain Phillips Cosby of the *Robust*.
1 1943 frigate, ex-*Reeves*, ex-*DE.94*, built by Bethlehem: Hingham, and returned to the USA 1946.

HMS CORUNNA (No. 1)

## COSSACK

Baltic 1855
Belgian Coast 1914–16
Narvik 1940
Norway 1940
Atlantic 1940–1
*Bismarck* Action 1941
Malta Convoys 1941
Korea 1950–3
1  1807 vessel.
2  1854 corvette. Sold in 1875.
3  1886 cruiser. Sold in 1905.
4  1907 destroyer of *c*.885 tons built
   by Cammell Laird and sold in 1919
   for breaking up by Ward, Preston.
5  1937 destroyer of 1,870 tons of the
   famous 'Tribal' class built by
   Vickers Armstrong. Took part in
   the *Altmark* incident off Norway,
   1940. Sunk by torpedo from *U-563*
   in the Atlantic 1941.
6  1944 destroyer of 2,106/2,749 tons
   built by Vickers Armstrong, Tyne
   and scrapped at Troon in 1961.

## COTSWOLD

North Sea 1941–5
English Channel 1943
Normandy 1944
Named after the hunts in
Gloucestershire.
1  1917 minesweeper of 750 tons built
   by Bow McLachlan and sold in
   1923 to Alloa of Charlestown for
   breaking up.
2  1940 destroyer of the 'Hunt' class,
   907 tons, built by Yarrow. Became
   a breakwater at Harwich before
   being scrapped a year later in 1957
   at Grays.

## COTTESMORE

North Sea 1941–5
Normandy 1944
English Channel 1942–4
Named after the hunt in Rutland.
1  1917 minesweeper. Sold for scrap
   1922.
2  1940 destroyer of the 'Hunt' class,
   907 tons, built by Yarrow. Sold to
   Egypt. She become the *Ibrahim-el-
   Awal*, 1950, and was still in service
   six years later.
3  1983 (commissioning date)
   minehunter of 615/725 tons built by
   Yarrow. A 'Hunt' class MCMV.

## COTTON

Atlantic 1944
Arctic 1945
Named after Captain Sir Charles

Cotton of the *Majestic* at the Glorious
First of June.
1  1943 frigate, ex-*DE.81*, of 1,300
   tons built by Bethlehem: Hingham.
   Returned to the USA 1946.

## COURAGEOUS (Courageux)

Ushant 1781
Genoa 1795
Bay of Biscay 1805
Falkland Islands 1982
*Fortiter in angustis* = Bravely in
difficulties.
1  1761 3rd rate prize *Courageux*.
   Wrecked in 1796.
2  1800 3rd rate, sold for scrapping
   1832.
3  1916 light battlecruiser later
   converted to aircraft carrier. Built
   by Armstrong: Parsons, 22,500
   tons. Conversion carried out
   1924–30. Torpedoed by *U-29* west
   of Ireland in 1939.
4  1970 nuclear-powered fleet
   submarine of 4,00/4,900 tons built
   by Vickers Armstrong, Barrow.

## COVENTRY

Quiberon Bay 1759
Trincomalee 1782
Spartivento 1940
Atlantic 1940
Norway 1940
Greece 1941
Crete 1941
Libya 1941
Mediterranean 1941
Falkland Islands 1982
*Fortis fert securitatem* = The strong
carries safety.
1  1658 prize, *St Michael*. Surrendered
   1666.
2  1695 4th rate. Surrendered in 1704
   and subsequently retaken in 1709,
   but she was not recommissioned.
3  1757 5th rate. Surrendered 1783.
4  1917 cruiser, ex-*Corsair* of 4,190
   tons built by Swan Hunter,
   Wallsend. Her distinguished
   WWII career compensated for the
   three surrenders of her

predecessors. She was finally
overwhelmed by bombers and
sunk off Tobruk in 1942.
5  1974 Type 42 destroyer of 3,500/
   4,100 tons built by Cammell Laird.
   Sunk by Argentinian forces 1982
   off the Falklands.
6  1985 Type 22 frigate of 4,100/4,800
   tons built by Swan Hunter.

## COWDRAY

Arctic 1942
North Africa 1942
Atlantic 1943
English Channel 1944
North Sea 1944–5
Named after the hunt in Sussex.
1  1941 destroyer of the 'Hunt' class,
   1,050 tons built by Scotts and
   scrapped at Gateshead.

## COWSLIP

Atlantic 1941–5
1  1917 sloop of 1,290 tons built by
   Barclay Curle. Torpedoed and
   sunk in 1918 by *U-105* off Cape
   Spartel.
2  1941 corvette of 925 tons built by
   Harland & Wolff. Sold in 1948 for
   scrapping the following year at
   Troon.

## CRANE

Cadiz 1596
Belgian Coast 1914–17
Biscay 1943
Sicily 1943
Atlantic 1943–4
Normandy 1944
English Channel 1944
Okinawa 1945
Korea 1952–3
1  1590 vessel of 24 guns.
6  1896 destroyer of *c*.400 tons built
   by Palmers and sold in 1919 for
   scrapping by Ward, New Holland.
7  1942 sloop of 1,350 tons built by
   Denny. Scrapped Queenborough
   1965.

## CRANSTOUN

North Sea 1944
Atlantic 1945
English Channel 1944–5
Named after Lord Cranstoun, who
captained the *Formidable* at The
Saintes.
1  1943 frigate, ex-*DE.82* of 1,300 tons
   built by Bethlehem: Hingham and
   returned to the USA in 1945.

## CREOLE

1  1803 prize frigate, but she foundered in the following year.
2  6th rate.
3  6th rate.
5  1945 destroyer of 2,106/2,749 tons built by White. Sold to Pakistan in 1956. She was renamed *Alamgir*.

## CRESCENT

Armada 1588
Gabbard 1653
Scheveningen 1653
Martinique 1762
Cape of Good Hope 1795
*Réunion* 1793
*Virtute cresco* = I grow with valour.
1  1588: a coaster from Dartmouth served in the Armada campaign.
5  1758 prize 5th rate, *Rostan*. Sold in 1777.
6  1779 5th rate, surrendered in 1781.
7  1784 5th rate, wrecked 1808.
10  1892 cruiser of 7,700 tons built by Portsmouth Dock Yard. Sold in 1921 for breaking up in Germany.
12  1931 destroyer. Transferred to RCN 1937.
13  1944 destroyer built at Clydebank and transferred to RCN 1945.

## CRESSY

Baltic 1854−5
Heligoland 1914
The name derives from Edward III's victory over the French at Crécy in 1346.
1  1810 3rd rate which was broken up in 1832.
3  1899 cruiser of 12,000 tons built by Fairfield. Torpedoed and sunk by *U-9* in the North Sea in 1914.

## CRISPIN

Atlantic 1941
Faithful to the last.
The name is taken from the Christian martyr who died in A.D.287.
1  1940 vessel.
2  1945 destroyer, ex-*Craccher*, of 2,106/2,749 tons, built by White. Sold to Pakistan in 1956. She became the *Jahangir* in 1958.

## CROCUS

Atlantic 1940−5
1  1808 sloop. Sold about ten years later.
3  1915 sloop of 1,250 tons built by Lobnitz. Sold to Bombay 1930 for scrapping.
4  1940 corvette of 925 tons built by Inglis: Kincaid. Scrapped at Troon in 1949.

## CROOME

Atlantic 1941−2
Libya 1942
Mediterranean 1942
Aegean 1943
Named after the hunt in Worcestershire.
1  1917 minesweeper of 750 tons built by Clyde Ship Builders. Sold in 1922 for scrapping by Stanlee, Dover.
2  1941 destroyer of the 'Hunt' class, 1,050 tons built by Stephen. Scrapped at Briton Ferry in 1957.

## CROSSBOW

1  1914−18 minor war vessel.
2  1945 destroyer built by Thornycroft and later converted to Fleet Radar Picket at 2,935 tons. Disposal List 1974−5.[30]

## CRUSADER

Belgian Coast 1914−18
Korea 1952−3
*Non nobis domine* = Not unto us, Lord.
1  1909 destroyer of *c*.1,000 tons built by White and sold in 1920 to Ward, Preston for breaking up.
2  1931 destroyer, transferred to RCN 1938.
3  1944 destroyer of 1,710 tons built by Clydebank and transferred to RCN 1945.

## CUBITT

Atlantic 1944−5
North Sea 1944−5
Named after Captain John Cubitt, seventeenth-century seaman.
1  1943 frigate, ex-*DE.83*, built by Bethlehem: Hingham. 1,300 tons. Returned to the USA 1946.

## CUCKMERE

Atlantic 1943
Mediterranean 1943
1  1942 frigate of 1,370 tons, ex-USN, built by 'Canadian' Vickers. Returned to the USA 1946.

## CULVER

North Sea 1941
Atlantic 1941−2
Named after the coastguard station on the Isle of Wight.
1  1941 coastguard cutter, ex-USS *Mendota*, built by Bethlehem in 1928. Torpedoed by *U-105* in the Atlantic.

30  I have chosen Jane's as a source. all sources disagree. Confusion often arises with nomenclature: date of Selling or of listing for Disposal or Deletion, or of actual scrapping can all differ. A ship's name placed on the Disposal List may still be there several years later.

## CUMBERLAND

Sadras 1758
Negapatam 1758
Porto Novo 1759
St Vincent 1780
Baltic 1854−5
Cameroons 1915
Arctic 1942−3
North Africa 1942
Sabang 1944
Burma 1945
*Justitiae tenax* = Tenacious of justice.
1   1695 3rd rate of 1,220 tons built by
    Burlesdon.
2   1710 3rd rate (80) of 1,308 tons
    built at Deptford. Scrapped in
    1732.
3   1739 3rd rate (80) of 1,401 tons
    built at Woolwich. Guns reduced
    to 66. Sank at anchor off Goa in
    1760.
5   1774 3rd rate (74) of 1,674 tons
    built at Deptford. Scrapped in
    1804.
6   Schooner of 29 tons used by
    Flinders in surveying Australia.
7   1807 3rd rate (74) of 1,718 tons
    built at Northfleet. Convict hulk
    in 1830. Renamed *Fortitude* in
    1833 and sold in 1870.
8   1842 3rd rate (70) of 2,214 tons
    built at Chatham. Training ship in
    1869. Burned in the Clyde in 1889.
9   1902 cruiser of 9,800 tons built at
    Glasgow. Sold in 1921.
10  1928 cruiser of 10,000 tons built by
    Vickers. Served throughout
    WWII from the Arctic to Sabang.
    Used experimentally post-war for
    radar, radio and stabilizers.
11  1986 Type 22 frigate of
    'Broadsword' class, 4,200/4,900
    tons built by Yarrow.

## CURACOA

Crimea 1854−5
New Zealand 1864
Norway 1940
Atlantic 1940
North Sea 1940−2
Arctic 1942
*Certamine summo* = In the midst of
battle.
Taken from the name of the island
conquered by Rear Admiral Sir C.
Brisbane (1769−1829).
1   1809 5th rate. Scrapped in 1849.
2   1854 frigate. Sold in 1869.
3   1878 corvette. Sold in 1904.
4   1917 light cruiser of 4,290 tons built
    at Pembroke Dock Yard. Mined in
    1919 and refitted. Sunk in collision
    with RMS *Queen Mary* in North-
    West Approaches in 1942.

## CURLEW

Crimea 1854−5
Norway 1940
*Solvitur amibulandus* = (The question
is) solved by going on.
1   1795 sloop. Lost in 1796.
2   Uncertain date of building: a
    sloop. Sold 1810.
6   1854 sloop. Broken up 1865.
9   1917 light cruiser of 4,190 tons,
    built by Armstrong Vickers. Sunk
    by German aircraft off Ofot Fjord,
    Norway 1940.
11  1943−6 harbour defence depot at
    Inellan.

## CURZON

English Channel 1944
North Sea 1944−5
Probably named after Captain the
Hon. Henry Curzon of the *Pallas*, or
Edward Curzon, captain of the *Asia* at
Navarino.
1   1943 frigate, ex-*DE.84*, of 1,300
    tons built by Bethlehem: Hingham,
    and returned to the USA in 1946.
    Two minesweepers, tenders to the
    Sussex Division RNVR, have borne
    this name. Lord Curzon
    commanded the Division for many
    years.

## CYCLAMEN

Atlantic 1940−5
Diego Suarez 1942
English Channel 1943
1   1796 sloop. Sold, unbelievably, in
    the early 1930s.
2   1940 corvette of 925 tons built by
    Lewis. Sold in 1947. Mercantile
    marine:*Southern Briar*, 1948.

## CYCLOPS

Egypt 1801
Syria 1840
Crimea 1854−5
With eye and hand.
Name taken from Greek mythology:
stories of one-eyed giants.
1   1779 6th rate. Sold in 1814.
2   1839 frigate. Sold in 1863.
3   1871 turret ship. Sold in 1903.
4   1905 repair ship of 11,300 tons built
    by James Laing. Her original name
    was *Indrabarah*. Converted into
    depot ship for submarines. Broken
    up in 1947.

## CYGNET

Armada 1588
Portland 1653
Havana 1762
Guadeloupe 1810
Alexandria 1882
Sicily 1943
Atlantic 1944−5
Arctic 1944−5
*Inter pares insignis* = Notable among
her fellows.
1   1585 pinnace (3) of 30 tons.
    Commanded by John Sherriff in
    Drake's expedition to Cadiz.
2   1643 vessel (20) of 233 tons
    bought at Dunkirk. Served at
    Kentish Knock and Portland. Sold
    in 1654.
5   1657 sloop (6) of 60 tons built at
    Chatham. Sold in the mid-1660s.
6   1688 fireship (8) of 100 tons.
    Captured by two French
    privateers. Captain John Perry
    was court martialled.
7   1759 prize sloop (18), the French
    *Guarland* or *Guirlande* of 386 tons.
    Commanded by the Hon.
    Charles Napier at Havana. Sold in
    South Carolina in 1768.
8   1776 sloop (16) of 301 tons built at
    Portsmouth. Sold in 1802.
10  1804 sloop (18) of 365 tons built by
    Palmers of Yarmouth. Captured
    the French *Impériale* in 1806 and
    assisted in the destruction of two
    frigates in 1809. She was at the
    capture of Guadeloupe. Wrecked
    on French New Guinea coast in
    1815.
15  1898 destroyer of 355 tons built by
    Thornycroft. In WWI served in
    the Local Defence Flotilla, The
    Nore. Sold in 1920.
19  1931 destroyer of 1,375 tons.
    Transferred to RCN and renamed
    *St Laurent*, 1937.
20  1942 sloop, later a frigate, built by
    Cammell Laird of Birkenhead.
    Scrapped in 1956.
21  1976 (commissioning date) OPV
    of the 'Bird' class, 194 tons built
    by R. Dunston, Hessle.

## CYNTHIA

Egypt 1801
A name of the moon goddess.
1   1796 vessel.
3   1898 destroyer of c.340 tons built
    by Thornycroft. Sold in 1920 to
    Ward, Rainham for scrapping.
5   1943 minesweeper, ex-*BAM 15* of
    890 tons built by Associated
    Shipbuilding of Seattle. Returned
    to the USA in 1946.

## DACRES

Atlantic 1943
Normandy 1944
Named after Captain James Richard
Dacres of the *Barfleur* at St Vincent.
1   1943 frigate, ex-*DE.268* of 1,085
    tons built by Boston. Returned to
    the USA in 1946.

## DAEDALUS

Egypt 1801
San Domingo 1806
Named after the Athenian craftsman
who escaped from Crete by
constructing wings for himself and his
son Icarus.
1   1780 5th rate. Scrapped in 1811.
3   1811 5th rate (44) prize, *Conona*, but
    wrecked only two years later.
4   1826 5th rate. Became a drillship in
    Bristol in 1861 and was sold 50
    years later.
5   1915 the hulk and ex-floating
    battery *Thunderbolt* was renamed
    *Daedalus* as she became the depot
    ship for the RNAS. She reverted to
    her former name five years later.
6   1939 RN Air Station at Lee-on-
    Solent. Still operational now,
    though not so 1959−65. Technical
    training for FAA ratings.

## DAHLIA

Atlantic 1941−4
Biscay 1943
Normandy 1944
North Sea 1944
English Channel 1944−5
*Dum ferveo floreo* = While I grow, I
flourish.
1   1915 sloop of 1,200 tons built by
    Barclay Curle. Sold in 1932 to
    Metal Industries for scrapping at
    Charlestown.
2   1940 corvette of 925 tons built by
    Lewis. Sold in 1948 for breaking up
    at Gelleswick Bay.

## DAINTY

Atlantic 1940
Mediterranean 1940−1
Calabria 1940
Libya 1940−1
Malta Convoys 1941
*Dulce quod utile* = It is pleasant if it is
useful.
The badge derives from a fan in a
portrait of Elizabeth I.
1   1588 vessel of 350 tons built for Sir
    John Hawkins. Fought three
    Spanish ships off Ecuador for three
    days till all crew of 75 were killed
    or wounded before surrendering.
3   1932 destroyer of 1,375 tons built
    by Fairfield. With *Ilex* sank two
    Italian submarines off Tobruk
    1942. She was sunk by aircraft in
    1942 off Tobruk.
4   1950 destroyer of 2,800/3,600 tons
    built by White. Disposal List
    1969−70.

## DAKINS

Normandy 1944
English Channel 1944
North Sea 1944
Named after the captain of the *Advice*
and other ships during the Dutch
wars.
1   1943 frigate, ex-*DE.85*, 1,300 tons
    built by Bethlehem, Hingham.
    Constructive Total Loss (CTL)
    1945. Scrapped in Holland in 1947.

## DAMPIER

Named after William Dampier
(1652−1715), pirate, RN captain and
hydrographer.
1   1945 frigate, ex-*Herne Bay*, ex-*Loch
    Eli*, of 2,230 tons built by Smith's
    Dock and completed as a
    surveying ship.

## DANAE

Normandy 1944
*Timeant danacios* = Let them fear those
belonging to Danae.
Named after the daughter of Acrisius,
King of Argos, and mother of Perseus.
1   1759 5th rate prize. Scrapped in
    1771.
3   1798 5th rate prize, *Vaillante*. Taken
    by mutineers into Brest in 1800.
4   1867 corvette. Sold c.1905.
5   1918 light cruiser of 4,850 tons,
    built by Armstrong. In Polish
    service as *Conrad* 1944−6. Sold in
    1948 for scrapping at Barrow.
6   1965 anti-submarine general-
    purpose frigate of 2,450/2,860 tons
    built by Devonport Dock Yard.
    'Leander' class armed with Exocet
    missiles.

## DARING

*Splendide audax* = Finely daring.
1   1804 gun brig of 178 tons built at
    Ipswich by Mr Bailey. Blown up on
    west coast of Africa 1813 to avoid
    capture by French frigates.
2   1844 sloop of 426 tons and 12 guns
    built at Portsmouth. Broken up in
    1864.
3   1874 screw composite sloop of 894
    tons and 4 guns built by Wigram of
    Blackwall. Sold to Mr Cohen for
    breaking up in 1889.
4   1893 twin screw TBD of 260 tons
    built by Thornycroft at Chiswick.
    The name was allocated for a
    destroyer of the 1912 programme,
    but the new system of giving
    names with the initial for the year
    (e.g, 1912 = L) forced a change to
    *Lance*.
5   1932 destroyer of 1,370 tons built
    by Thornycroft. Sunk by *U-23* off
    Duncansby Head in 1940.
6   1950 destroyer of 2,800/3,600 tons
    built by Swan Hunter, Wallsend.
    Disposal List 1974−5.

## DART

Copenhagen 1801
Sicily 1943
Atlantic 1944
*Désirée* 1800
Aim high.
1   1782 vessel.
2   1796 corvette, broken up in 1809.
11  1942 frigate of 1,370 tons built by
    Hawthorn Leslie, and scrapped at
    Newport in 1957.
12  1961−67 'Avon' class of ramp
    powered lighters, 100 tons, built
    by White: Saunders Roe.

## DARTMOUTH

Solebay 1672
Navarino 1827
Dardanelles 1915
1 1655 6th rate (30), wrecked in 1690.
3 1693 4th rate. Surrendered 1695 but was recaptured in 1702 at Vigo. She was restored to the RN as *Vigo*.
4 1698 4th rate, blown up and sunk in action in 1747.
7 1911 cruiser of 5,250 tons built by Vickers. Sold in 1930 for scrapping by Alloa of Rosyth.
9 1939–45 naval base at Dartmouth.
10 1953 name given to the *Britannia* RNC at Dartmouth: RN Officers' training establishment.

## DASHER

Java 1811
Atlantic 1942
North Africa 1942
Arctic 1943
1 1797 sloop, broken up in 1838.
3 1893 destroyer. Sold in 1912.
5 1942 escort carrier of 8,200 tons built by Sun Shipbuilding. Sunk by a petrol explosion south of Cumbraes.
6 1986 coastal patrol craft of 43 tons.

## DAUNTLESS

Baltic 1854
Crimea 1855
Atlantic 1939
*Nil desperandum* = Never despair.
1 1804 sloop. Surrendered 1807.
2 1809 sloop.
3 1847 frigate.
4 1918 cruiser of 4,850 tons built by Palmer. Scrapped at Inverkeithing in 1946.
5 1947 WRNS depot at Burghfield, Reading.

## DEANE

English Channel 1944
North Sea 1944
Arctic 1944
Atlantic 1945
Named after Captain John Deane of the *Lowestoffe* and *Bedford* in the late eighteenth century.
1 1943 frigate, ex-*DE.86*, of 1,300 tons built by Bethlehem: Hingham. Returned to the USA 1946.

## DECOY

Ashantee 1873–4
Alexandria 1882
Mediterranean 1940
Calabria 1940
Greece 1941
Crete 1941
Libya 1941–2
Malta Convoys 1941–2
Atlantic 1942
*Cave quod celo* = Beware what I hide.
1 1810 cutter (10) built at Fishbourne. Captured by the French after grounding at Calais.
2 1856 screw gunboat (2) of 212 tons. Broken up at Haslar in 1869.
3 1871 screw gunboat (4) of 408 tons built at Pembroke. Saw action in the Ashantee war, suppressed a rising, bombarded Alexandria, blockaded the Nile, bemedalled for Egypt and Sudan. Sold in 1885 at Malta.
4 1894 destroyer of 260 tons built at Chiswick. Sunk in collision off the Scillies in 1904.
5 1932 destroyer of 1,375 tons built by Thornycroft. Transferred to RCN in 1943 and renamed *Kootenay*. Scrapped in 1946.
6 1949 destroyer of the 'Daring' class, 2,800/3,600 tons built by Yarrow. Ex-*Dragon*. Sold to Peru in 1969, refitted and renamed *Ferŕe* in 1971.

## DEFENCE

St Vincent 1780
Glorious First of June 1794
Nile 1798
Copenhagen 1801
Trafalgar 1805
Jutland 1916
1 1763 3rd rate. Wrecked in 1811.
7 1861 ironclad. Renamed *Indus* in 1904.
8 1907 cruiser of 14,600 tons built at Pembroke Dock Yard. Sunk at Jutland 1916.
9 1944 cruiser of 8,800 tons built by Scotts. Renamed *Lion* in 1957.

## DEFENDER

Heligoland 1914
Dogger Bank 1915
Jutland 1916
Calabria 1940
Spartivento 1940
Matapan 1941
Malta Convoys 1941
Greece 1941
Crete 1941
Libya 1941
*Defendendo vinco* = By defence I conquer.
1 1797 gunboat (12) of 168 tons built on the Thames by Hill & Co. Sold 1802.
2 1804 gun brig (12) of 179 tons built at Chester by Mr Courtney. Wrecked off Cob Point, Felixstowe in 1809.
4 1911 destroyer of 762 tons built by Denny. Towed *Onslow* to safety at Jutland. Sold in 1921.
6 1932 destroyer of 1,375 tons built by Vickers Armstrong. Sunk by aircraft attack off Sidi Barrani in 1941.
7 1944–5 escort base at Liverpool.
8 1950 destroyer of the 'Daring' class: 2,800/3,600 tons built by Stephens of Govan. Disposal List 1974–5.

## DEFIANCE

Orfordness 1666
Barfleur 1692
Finisterre I & II 1747
Louisburg 1758
Quiberon Bay 1759
Havana 1762
Copenhagen 1801
Trafalgar 1805
*Scientia fiducia plena provocare* = With knowledge and confidence to defy.
1 1590 vessel of 500 tons and 32 guns. Sold 1650.
2 1666 3rd rate of 890 tons and 66 guns built at Deptford. She was destroyed in 1668 by a fire while lying at anchor at Chatham.
3 1676 3rd rate built by Phineas Pett

at Chatham. 64 guns.
Commanded by Captain Kirby,
shot for failing to support
Benbow. Ship reconstructed at
Woolwich 1707 to 949 tons.
Served as hulk at Sheerness and
broken up at Chatham in 1749.

4   1744 5th rate saw much action
until sold in 1776.

5   1769 3rd rate (64) of 1,369 tons:
wrecked in 1780.

9   1861 2nd rate (91 — but none
fitted) of 5,270 tons.
Commissioned as a torpedo
school at Devonport. Sold for
breaking up in 1931, together
with the other ships forming the
school.

10   1931 the new *Defiance* comprised
*Andromeda*, *Inconstant* and *Vulcan*.
Scrapped about 1953.

11   Fleet Maintenance Base,
Devonport.

# DELHI

Atlantic 1940
North Africa 1942
Sicily 1943
Salerno 1943
Anzio 1944
South France 1944
Adriatic 1944
*Dilecta non deleta* = Chosen not
destroyed.

1   1918 cruiser of 4,850 tons built by
Armstrong at Wallsend. Broken up
at Newport in 1948.

# DELIGHT

Armada 1588
Cadiz 1596
Norway 1940
*Duris delectat virtus* = Valour delights
in difficulties.

1   1680 vessel.[31]

2   1709 6th rate (14) of 169 tons built
at Woolwich. Sold 1713.

3   1778 sloop (14) of 306 tons built by
Edward Greaves on the Thames.
Lost at sea 1781.

6   1808 prize sloop (14), *Friedland*
captured by HM ships *Standard*
and *Active*. Sold 1814.

12   1932 destroyer of 1,375 tons built
by Fairfield. Sunk off Portland
after air attack in 1940.

13   1950 destroyer of the 'Daring'
class, ex-*Disdain*, 3,600 tons, built
by Fairfield at Govan. Disposal
List 1974−5.

# DELPHINIUM

Atlantic 1940−5
Libya 1942
Sicily 1943
English Channel 1945
*Delphinum non doces natare* = You don't
teach a dolphin to swim.

1   1915 sloop of 1,250 tons built by
Napier and Miller. Sold 1933 for
scrapping by Rees, Llanelly.

2   1940 corvette of 925 tons built by
Henry Robb, and scrapped at
Pembroke Dock in 1949.

# DENBIGH CASTLE

Arctic 1945

1   1944 corvette/frigate of 1,010 tons,
built by Lewis. Grounded after
damage. CTL 1945.

# DEPTFORD

Barfleur 1692
Atlantic 1939−43
North Africa 1942
Mediterranean 1944
English Channel 1945

1   1652 vessel.

4   1732 4th rate. Broken up in 1756.

9   1935 sloop of 990 tons built by
White at Chatham. Sold in 1948 for
scrapping at Milford Haven.

# DERG

1   1943 frigate of 1,370 tons built by
Henry Robb. Became the RNVR
training ship *Cambria* in North
Wales in 1947.

# DERWENT

Atlantic 1942
Malta Convoys 1942
The earlier names are taken from the
river. The latest ship was named after
the hunt in Yorkshire.

1   1807 vessel.

2   1903 destroyer of *c.*550 tons built
by Hawthorn Leslie. Sunk by a
mine off Le Havre in 1917.

5   1941 destroyer of the 'Hunt' class
of 1,087 tons, built by Vickers
Armstrong, Barrow. Broken up at
Penrhyn in 1947.

# DESPATCH

San Sebastian 1813
Atlantic 1939
Spartivento 1940
Normandy 1944
*Festina non lente* = Make haste.

1   1692 vessel.

2   1745 sloop. Sold in 1773.

3   1764 sloop which capsized and
sank in 1780.

10   1812 sloop. Sold 1837.

15   1919 cruiser of 4,540 tons built by
Fairfield but towed to Chatham
for completion in 1922. Sold for
scrapping in 1947.

# DEVERON

Atlantic 1943−5
Normandy 1944
English Channel 1944
Burma 1945

1   1914−18 trawler.

2   1942 frigate of 1,370 tons built by
Smith's Dock. Transferred to India
in 1945, then to Pakistan in 1948.

# DEVONSHIRE

Ushant 1747
Finisterre I 1747
Louisburg 1758
Quebec 1759
Martinique 1762
Havana 1762
Norway 1940
Arctic 1941
Diego Suarez 1942
*Auxilio divino* = By the help of God.

1   1692 3rd rate. She was blown up in
action in 1707.

2   3 and 5 were all 3rd rates from 1710
to 1869.

6   1904 cruiser of 10,850 tons built by
Chatham Dock Yard. Sold in 1921
for breaking up by Ward at Preston
and Barrow.

7   1927 cruiser of 9,850 tons built at
Devonport by Vickers Armstrong.
Converted to a training ship in
1947 and scrapped at Newport in
1954.

8   1960 guided-missile destroyer of
6,200 tons built by Cammell Laird,
Birkenhead. Sunk as a target ship
in 1984.

---

31   The Armada vessel was a 50-ton merchant ship owned by Sir William Wynter. Her captain, William Coxe, was killed in action.

## DIADEM

Genoa 1795
St Vincent 1797
Egypt 1801
Cape of Good Hope 1806
Arctic 1944−5
Normandy 1944
Biscay 1944
Norway 1945
1  1782 3rd rate (64) of 1,869 tons built at Chatham. Broken up in 1832.
2  1801 sloop. She was renamed *Falcon c.*1805.
3  1856 frigate (32) of 2,483 tons built at Pembroke. Sold and broken up by Castle & Sons in 1875.
4  1896 cruiser of 11,000 tons built by Fairfield. Sold in 1921 to Ward, Morecambe for breaking up.
7  1942 cruiser of 5,770 tons built by Hawthorn Leslie. Transferred to the Pakistan navy in 1956 and renamed *Babur.*

## DIAMOND

Armada 1588
Kentish Knock 1652
Portland 1653
Gabbard 1653
Scheveningen 1653
Lowestoft 1665
Four Days' Battle 1666
Orfordness 1666
Solebay 1672
Schooneveld 1673
Texel 1673
Crimea 1854−5

Spartivento 1940
Mediterranean 1941
Malta Convoys 1941
Greece 1941
*Honor clarissima gemma* = Honour is the brightest jewel.
1  1588: a Dartmouth ship of 60 tons fought under Drake.
2  1652 4th rate, surrendered in 1693. She was built by Peter Petts to 548 tons and 48 guns at Deptford. She earned many of the early battle honours.
3  1708 5th rate of 537 tons built at Blackwall. Sold in 1744.
4  1741 5th rate (44) of 697 tons built at Limehouse. Sold 1756.
5  1774 5th rate (32) of 710 tons built at Hull. Sold in 1784.
6  1794 5th rate. Scrapped in 1812.
7  1816 5th rate (46) of 1,076 tons built at Chatham. Accidentally burnt at Portsmouth 1827.
9  1848 frigate (28) of 1,055 tons built at Sheerness. She was renamed *Joseph Straker* in 1868 and was finally sold for scrap in 1885.
10  1874 corvette (14) of 1,405 tons built at Sheerness. Sold in 1889.
11  1904 cruiser of 3,000 tons built by Laird. Sold in 1921 to Ward, Grays for breaking up.
14  1932 destroyer of 1,375 tons built by Vickers Armstrong, Barrow. Sunk by German aircraft south of Morea in 1941.
15  1952 destroyer of the 'Daring' class, 2,800/3,600 tons, built by John Brown on Clydebank. Broken up 1981.

## DIANA

Armada 1588
Louisburg 1758
Quebec 1759
Burma 1824−6
Norway 1940
*Zefier* 1809
*Certo dirigo ictu* = I aim with sure blow.
Name is derived from Greek mythology. Diana (= Artemis) was

the twin sister of Apollo.
1  1588: a City of London vessel fought at the Armada.
2  1757 5th rate (32) of 668 tons built at Limehouse. Sold at Deptford in 1793.
5  1794 5th rate (38) of 998 tons built on the Thames. Sold in 1815 to the Dutch.
7  1822 5th rate (42) of 1,083 tons built at Chatham but never commissioned into the Navy. Finally scrapped 1874.
9  1895 cruiser. Sold in 1920 to Castle of Plymouth for scrap.
12  1912 destroyer of 1,375 tons built by Palmer. Transferred to RCN in 1940, renamed *Margaree*, and lost in the same year.
13  1952 destroyer, ex-*Druid*, of the 'Daring' class of 2,800/3,600 tons built by Yarrow.

## DIANELLA

Atlantic 1941−5
Arctic 1942−4
North Africa 1942
Sicily 1943
English Channel 1943
Normandy 1944
1  1940 corvette, ex-*Daffodil*, of 925 tons, built by Lewis. Sold 1946 for scrapping at Portaferry.

## DIANTHUS

Atlantic 1941−4
English Channel 1944
Normandy 1944
1  1917 sloop of 1,290 tons. Sold in 1921 to the Mexican State Line and renamed *Guerro*.
2  1940 corvette of 925 tons built by Henry Robb. Sold to mercantile marine and renamed *Thorslep*, 1950.

## DIDO

Egypt 1801
Syria 1840

HMS DIDO (No. 7)

China 1842
Crete 1941
Sirte 1942
Mediterranean 1942−4
Malta Convoys 1942
Sicily 1943
Salerno 1943
Aegean 1943
Anzio 1944
South France 1944
Arctic 1944
*Minerve* 1795
Steadfast.
Named after the the princess who founded Carthage and killed herself on a funeral pyre when her lover Aeneas deserted her.

1  1784 6th rate (28) of 595 tons built by Stewart & Hall of Sandgate. In 1804 she became an army prison ship. Sold in 1817.
3  1831 sloop (18) of 734 tons built at Pembroke. She became a coal hulk in 1854, was scuttled on catching fire, salved and finally sold in 1903.
4  1869 sloop of 1,277 tons built at Portsmouth. Renamed *Actaeon* in 1906.
5  1896 cruiser of 5,600 tons built by London & Glasgow. Sold in 1926 to May & Butcher of Maldon for breaking up.
6  1939 cruiser of 5,450 tons built by Cammell Laird. Broken up in 1958 at Barrow.
7  1959 frigate, improved Type 12, of 2,450/2,860 tons built by Yarrow. Sold to New Zealand 1983.

## DILIGENCE

1  1692 vessel.
2  1709 6th rate. Sold in 1780.
3, 4, 5 and 7 were sloops of 1756, 1762, 1795 and 1801.
11  1915 depot ship for destroyers. Launched 1907 but purchased in 1913 and converted. Built by Henderson as *Tabaristan*, 7,100 tons. Scrapped in 1926.
12  1945 depot ship for destroyers. Returned to USA 1946.
13  1953 small ships commissioning base at Hythe.
14  1981 (commissioning date) repair/maintenance ship of 10,595 tons, ex-*Stena Inspector*, built in Sweden.

## DIOMEDE

Cape of Good Hope 1806
*Fortibus feroces frangentur* = The fierce will be broken by the strong.

Name derives from the King of Argos, one of the Greek heroes.
1  1781 4th rate which was wrecked in 1795.
2  1798 4th rate. Scrapped in 1815.
3  1919 cruiser of 4,850 tons built by Vickers. Served with RNZN 1924−37. Scrapped at Dalmuir 1946.
4  1969 general-purpose frigate of 2,500/2,962 tons built by Yarrow at Scotstoun.

## DITTANY

Atlantic 1943−5
1  1942 corvette of 980 tons built by Collingwood. Ex-USS *Beacon*. Returned to USA 1946.

## DOLPHIN

Armada 1588[32]
Portland 1653

32  A City of London merchant ship, *Dolphin of Leigh*, fought against the Armada in 1588.

Gabbard 1653
Lowestoft 1665
Texel 1673
Dogger Bank 1781
Egypt 1801
*Manent optima mari* = The best things are in the sea.
1    1648 vessel.
3    1652 prize (30). Disposed of in 1657.
4    1655 5th rate prize, entered service as *Wexford*. Renamed 1660 and lost by fire 1665.
7    1689 5th rate. Yet another prize. Scrapped in 1730.
8    1731 6th rate. Renamed *Firebrand* in 1747.
20   1882 sloop. Sold 1925 for scrapping.
21   1924 ex-*Pandora* of 4,580 tons built by Raylton Dixon in 1902. Mined in 1939 off Blyth when on passage for conversion to a blockship.
22   Submarine base at Fort Blockhouse, Gosport.

## DOMETT

Atlantic 1943−5
English Channel 1945
Normandy 1944
Named after Sir William Domett of the *Royal George* at the Glorious First of June.
1    1943 frigate, ex-*DE.269*, of 1,085 tons built by Boston. Returned to the USA in 1946.

## DOMINICA

Martinique 1809
Normandy 1944
Biscay 1944
Atlantic 1944−5
English Channel 1945
1    1806 vessel.
5    1943 frigate, ex-*Harman*, ex-*PF.79*, of 1,318 tons built by Walsh Kaiser and returned to the USA in 1946.

## DORSETSHIRE

Gibraltar 1704
Velez Malaga 1704
Cape Passero 1718
Quiberon Bay 1759
*Bismarck* Action 1941
Atlantic 1941
*Raisonnable* 1758
*Pro patria et comitatu* = For country and county.
1    1694 3rd rate. Scrapped in 1749.
2    1757 3rd rate. Scrapped in 1775.
3    1929 cruiser of 9,975 tons built at Portsmouth by Cammell Laird.

Sunk by Japanese aircraft off Ceylon in 1942.

## DOUGLAS

Atlantic 1940−4
Arctic 1942
Forward.
1    1918 flotilla leader of 1,530 tons built by Cammell Laird. Sold in 1945 for scrapping at Inverkeithing.

## DOVEY

Atlantic 1944
1    1943 frigate, ex-*Lambourn* of 1,460/1,865 tons, built by Fleming & Ferguson. Scrapped in 1954.
2    1983 minesweeper of 890 tons built by Richards Ltd.

## DRAGON

Portland 1653
Gabbard 1653
Scheveningen 1653
Lowestoft 1665
Four Days' Battle 1666
Orfordness 1666
Bugia 1671
Barfleur 1692
Belleisle 1761
Martinique 1762
Havana 1762
Egypt 1801
Baltic 1854−5
Arctic 1944
We yield but to St George.
1    1512 vessel.
2    1544 of 45 guns.
3    1647 of 46 guns. Wrecked in 1712.
4    1689 sloop taken as prize. Foundered in 1690.
5    and 6 were 4th rates of 1715 and 1736.
7    and 9 were 3rd rates of 1760 and 1798.
10   1845 frigate. Scrapped 1864.
13   1894 destroyer. Sold in 1912.
14   1917 cruiser of 4,850 tons built by Scotts. Manned by the Polish navy in 1943. Expended after damage by human torpedoes as part of the Mulberry harbour in 1944.

## DRAKE

Lowestoft 1665
Baltic 1855
China 1856−60
*Sic parvis magna* = Thus from small things to great things.
Named after Sir Francis Drake (1540−96).
1    1652 6th rate built at Deptford. Sold in 1690.
2    1694 6th rate built at Rotherhithe. Lost on passage to Ireland in 1695.
4    5, 6, 7 and 9 were all sloops: 1705 (Woolwich), 1729 (Deptford), 1740 (Wapping; wrecked near Gibraltar), and 1743. The only date recorded for No. 9 is 1778, when she surrendered to the American *Ranger*.
10   1779 brig/sloop, paid off in Jamaica in 1860.
11   1799 prize sloop, *Tigre*, wrecked at Nevis in 1804.
12   1808 brig/sloop built at Ipswich and wrecked off Newfoundland in 1822.
19   1901 armoured cruiser of 14,100 tons built by Pembroke Dock Yard. Torpedoed in 1917 by *U-79* in the North Channel: she capsized and sank.
22   1934 Devonport Barracks and Naval Establishment. Now the parent ship, HM naval base, Devonport.

## DREADNOUGHT

Armada 1588
Cadiz 1596
Lowestoft 1665
Four Days' Battle 1666
Orfordness 1666
Solebay 1672
Schooneveld 1673
Texel 1673
Barfleur 1692
Cape Passero 1718
Cape Francois 1757
Trafalgar 1805
Fear God and dread nought.

HMS DREADNOUGHT (No. 9)

1 1573 vessel (32). Scrapped in 1645.
2 1660 3rd rate (64) ex-*Torrington*. Lost at sea in 1690.
3 and 4 were both 4th rates of 1690 and 1742.
6 1801 2nd rate. Scrapped in 1857.
7 1857 1st rate, ex-*Caledonia*. Scrapped in 1875.
8 1875 battleship. Sold for scrapping in 1908.
9 1906 battleship of 17,900 tons, the first all-big-gun battleship that made all other battleships obselete. Built at Portsmouth Dock Yard. Sold in 1921 for scrapping at Inverkeithing.
11 1960 nuclear-powered submarine of 3,000/3,500 tons built by Vickers Armstrong at Barrow. Disposal List 1982. Still at Rosyth pending disposal, 1986−7.

## DRURY

Atlantic 1943−5
Arctic 1945

Named after Captain Thomas Drury (*d*. 1832).
1 1943 frigate of 1,085 tons, ex-*Cockburn*, ex-*DE.46*, built by Philadelphia. Returned to USA in 1946.

## DRYAD

Abyssinia 1868
*Proserpine* 1796
*Nobis tutissimus ibis* = You will go safely with us.

The name is taken from a nymph of the forest.
1 1709 prize, *Driade*, captured from the French.
2 1795 5th rate (36) of 924 tons built on the Thames. She fought the *Proserpine* off Cape Clear. Became a receiving ship at Portsmouth. Scrapped in 1860.
3 1866 sloop (9) of 1,086 tons built at Devonport. Landed parties in Abyssinia and conducted operations against slavery. Sold in 1885.
4 1893 twin-screw gunboat of 1,070 tons built at Chatham. In 1906 she became a navigation school at Portsmouth.
5 1919 navigation school shore establishment, Portsmouth. Now the School of Maritime Operations, Fareham.

## DUCHESS

Portland 1653
Gabbard 1653
Scheveningen 1653

Barfleur 1692
*Duci non trahi* = To be led but not
dragged.
1   1652 prize, *Duchesse* (24). Sold in
    1654.
2   1679 2nd rate (90) of 1,546 tons
    built at Deptford. Renamed
    *Princess Anne* in 1701, then *Windsor
    Castle*, then *Blenheim*.[33]
4   1932 destroyer of 1,375 tons built
    by Palmer. Sunk in collision in
    1939.
5   1952 destroyer of the 'Daring'
    class, 2,800/3,600 tons, built by
    Thornycroft. RAN 1964.

## DUCKWORTH

Atlantic 1943−4
Normandy 1944
Biscay 1944
Arctic 1944
English Channel 1945
Named after Captain John Thomas
Duckworth (1748−1817).
1   1803 vessel.
2   1943 frigate, ex-*DE.61* of 1,300 tons
    built by Bethlehem: Hingham, and
    returned to USA in 1946.

## DUFF

English Channel 1944
Normandy 1944
Named after Captain George Duff of
the *Mars* at Trafalgar.
1   1943 frigate of 1,300 tons built by
    Bethlehem: Hingham. Ex-*DE.64*
    CTL 1944. Returned to USA 1945.

## DUKE

Barfleur 1692
Quiberon Bay 1759
Ushant 1781
The Saintes 1782
1   1682 2nd rate. Renamed *Prince
George* in 1701.
3   1739 2nd rate, ex-*Vanguard*.
6   1777 2nd rate. Scrapped 1843.
9   1941−46 training establishment at
    Great Malvern.

## DUKE OF YORK

Arctic 1942−3
North Africa 1942
North Cape 1943
*Honi soit qui mal y pense* = Shame to
him who thinks evil of it.
The badge was that of King George VI
when he was Duke of York.
1   1763 cutter of 53½ tons purchased
    for naval service.
6   1940 battleship, ex-*Anson*, of 35,000
    tons built at Clydebank. Scrapped
    at Faslane in 1958.

## DULVERTON

Libya 1942
Sirte 1942
Mediterranean 1942
Malta Convoys 1942
Sicily 1943
Salerno 1943
Aegean 1943
Named after the hunts in Somerset.
1   1941 destroyer of the 'Hunt' class,
    1,050 tons built by Stephen. Sunk
    by a glider bomb off Kos in 1943.
2   1983 (commissioning date)
    minelayer of 615/725 tons built by
    Vosper. A 'Hunt' class MCMV.

## DUMBARTON CASTLE

Atlantic 1944−5
Falkland Islands 1982
1   1707 6th rate which surrendered
    the following year.
2   1943 corvette/frigate of 1,010 tons
    built by Caledon: Hargreaves.
    Scrapped in 1961 at Gateshead.
3   1981 OPV of the 'Castle' class,
    1,427 tons built by Hall Russell of
    Aberdeen.

## DUNBAR

North Sea 1942
Normandy 1944
1   1656 3rd rate (64), renamed *Henry*
    in 1660.
2   1941 minesweeper of 656 tons built
    by White at Blyth. Scrapped at
    Southampton in 1948.

## DUNCAN

Spartivento 1940
Malta Convoys 1941
Mediterranean 1941
Atlantic 1941−5
Diego Suarez 1942
*Secundis dubi isque rectus* = Upright in
prosperity and in peril.
Named after Admiral Adam Duncan,
Viscount Duncan of Camperdown
(1731−1804).
1   1805 frigate, renamed *Dover* only
    two years later.
2   1811 3rd rate, scrapped in 1863.
3   1859 2nd rate, renamed *Pembroke* in
    1889.
4   1901 battleship of 14,000 tons built
    by the Thames Iron Works and
    scrapped in 1920.
5   1932 flotilla leader of 1,400 tons
    built by Hawthorn Leslie at
    Portsmouth. Scrapped at Barrow
    in 1945.
6   1957 frigate, Type 14 of 1,180/1,456
    tons built by Thornycroft and
    scrapped at Cawsand in 1984.

## DUNCANSBY HEAD

1   1944−5 depot and repair ship of
    9,000/11,270 tons built by Barrard,
    Vancouver. In 1962 she became
    half of HMS *Cochrane* (SO Reserve
    Ships, Rosyth), then
    accommodation ship, Belfast.

## DUNDAS

Atlantic 1942−5
Named after Sir Richard Dundas, who
commanded the Baltic fleet in 1855,
and Sir James Dundas, who
commanded the Black Sea fleet.
1   1941 corvette of 925 tons with the
    RCN.
2   1953 anti-submarine frigate, Type
    14 of 1,180/1,456 tons built by
    White. Scrapped at Troon in 1983.

33   According to Weightman, No. 3 was a minor vessel of 260 tons commanded by Captain Stephen Courtney, and with the *Duke* made a memorable privateering voyage round the world in 1707−11 during which she rescued Alexander Selkirk, the original Robinson Crusoe, marooned on Juan Fernandez. See Weightman pp.188−9.

## DUNEDIN

Atlantic 1941
*Nisi dominus frusta* = Vainly without the Lord.
1  1910 drifter of 78 tons. Returned to owners 1919. Still listed during WWII.
2  1918 cruiser of 4,850 tons built by Armstrong: Hawthorn Leslie and completed at Devonport. RNZN 1924–37. Torpedoed and sunk off Pernambuco by *U-124* in 1941.

## DUNKIRK

Lowestoft 1665
Orfordness 1666
Solebay 1672
Schooneveld 1673
Texel 1673
Cape Passero 1718
Quiberon Bay 1759
The badge is derived from the crest of Admiral Sir Bertram Ramsay. The name honours the capture of Dunkirk in 1657, and No. 5 commemorates Dunkirk 1940.
1  1660 6th rate (48) ex-*Worcester*. Scrapped in 1750.[34]
3  1705 6th rate (24), *Dunkirk Prize*. Wrecked in 1708, San Domingo.
4  1752 3rd rate (60) and scrapped forty years later at Plymouth.
5  **1945 destroyer of the later 'Battle' class of 2,780/3,430 tons built by Stephen and scrapped at Faslane in 1965.**

## DURBAN

Normandy 1944
*Natalis honore* = For the honour of our country.
1  1897 trawler of 152 tons which saw wartime service 1914–15.
2  1919 cruiser of 4,850 tons built by Scotts. Expended as part of the Mulberry breakwater in 1944.

## EAGLE

Portland 1653
Gabbard 1653
Lowestoft 1665
Orfordness 1666
Barfleur 1692
Gibraltar 1704
Velez Malaga 1704
Ushant II 1747
Sadras 1782
Providien 1782
Negapatam 1782
Trincomalee 1782
Calabria 1940
Mediterranean 1940
Malta Convoys 1942
*Arduus ad solem* = Soaring to the sun.
1  1592 vessel of 894 tons. Became a careening hulk, was laid up at Chatham and sold in 1683.
2  1650 French vessel of 100 tons named *Aigle*.[35]
3  1660 6th rate (28) ex-*Selby*. 299 tons and 22 guns built at Wapping. Condemned in 1694 and sunk as part of a breakwater at Sheerness.
7  1679 3rd rate (70) of 1,047 tons built at Portsmouth. After a distinguished career she went down with all hands with Sir Clowdisly Shovell's squadron in 1707.
9  1744 4th rate (60) of 1,130 tons, launched at Portsmouth as the *Centurion* but renamed *Eagle* the following year.
10  1774 3rd rate (74) of 1,372 tons built on the Thames. Fought in all of Hughes's battles in the East Indies. In 1794 became a lazaretto, then a prison ship, renamed *Buckingham*, then scrapped in 1812.
16  1804 3rd rate (74) of 1,723 tons. Became Mersey RNVR drillship in 1910.
20  1917 aircraft carrier of 22,600 tons built by Armstrong. Started as a battleship in 1914 for Chile, but purchased 1917 for conversion. Torpedoed by *U-73* in 1942 north of Algiers.
23  1946 aircraft carrier of 54,000 tons, ex-*Audacious*, built by Harland & Wolff, Belfast. Broken up by Cairn Ryan in 1978.

## EASTBOURNE

English Channel 1942–4
Dieppe 1942
North Africa 1942
Normandy 1944
1  1914–18 minor war vessel.
2  1940 minesweeper of 672 tons built by Lobnitz. Scrapped Dunston 1948.
3  1955 frigate of 2,800 tons built by Vickers Armstrong. Disposal List 1978–9.

## EASTON

English Channel 1942
North Africa 1943
Mediterranean 1943
Sicily 1943
Aegean 1944
North Sea 1945
Named after the hunt in Essex.
1  1942 destroyer of the 'Hunt' class, 1,087 tons built by White. Scrapped at Rosyth in 1953.

## ECHO

Quebec 1759
Martinique 1762
Havana 1762
Cape of Good Hope 1795
Atlantic 1939
Norway 1940
*Bismarck* Action 1941
Arctic 1941–3
Malta Convoys 1942
Sicily 1943
Salerno 1943
Aegean 1943
*Marte et arte* = By war and art.
1  1758 6th rate prize. Sold in 1770.
2  3, 4 and 6 were all sloops of 1779, 1782, 1797 and 1824.
9  1934 destroyer of 1,375 tons built by Denny. Transferred to the Greek navy as *Navarinon* from 1944 to 1956. Scrapped Dunston 1956.

---

34  She was the flagship of the Earl of Marlborough (1618–65) on his taking possession of Bombay in 1660.

35  See Manning & Walker, p.176: *Aigle's* honours have been assumed by the *Eagle*.

10 1957 surveying vessel of 120/160 tons built by White at Cowes. Disposal List 1985–6.

## ECLIPSE

New Zealand 1863–6
Norway 1940
Arctic 1941–3
Atlantic 1943
Sicily 1943
Salerno 1943
Aegean 1943
*Nunquam* = Never [eclipsed.]
1 1715 vessel.
7 1867 sloop.
8 1894 cruiser of 5,600 tons built at Portsmouth Dock Yard. Depot ship 1916. Sold 1921 to Cohen.
10 1934 destroyer of 1,375 tons built by Denny. Sunk by a mine east of Kalimnos in 1943.

## EDINBURGH

Finisterre II 1747
Cape Francois 1757
Syria 1840
Baltic 1854–5
Norway 1940–1
*Bismarck* Action 1941
Atlantic 1941
Malta Convoys 1941
Arctic 1941–2
1 1707 5th rate, sunk as a breakwater two years later.
2 1716 3rd rate ex-*Warspight*. Scrapped 1771.
4 1882 battleship. Sold for scrapping 1910.
5 1938 cruiser of 10,000 tons built by Swan Hunter, Wallsend. Torpedoed and scuttled two days later after attacked by *U-456* in the Barents Sea, 1942.
6 1983 Type 42 destroyer of 3,500/4,775 tons built by Cammell Laird at Birkenhead.

## EFFINGHAM

Atlantic 1939–40
Norway 1940
*Foy pour devoir* — Faithful in duty.
Named after Lord Howard of Effingham (1536–1624).
1 1921 cruiser of 9,550 tons built by Harland & Wolff at Portsmouth. Wrecked 1940 and sunk by RN.
2 1943 combined operations base.

## EGGESFORD

Sicily 1943
Salerno 1943
Adriatic 1944
South France 1944
Named after the hunt in Devon.
1 1942 destroyer of the 'Hunt' class, 1,087 tons, built by White. Sold to Federal Republic of Germany in 1958 and renamed *Brommy*.

## EGLANTINE

Norway 1941
Atlantic 1941–4
Arctic 1943–5
1 1914–18 minor war vessel.
2 1917 sloop of 1,290 tons built by Barclay Curle. Sold in 1921.
3 1941 corvette of 925 tons built by Harland & Wolff. Manned by the Norwegian navy. Sold in 1947 for mercantile use.

## EGLINGTON

Atlantic 1940
English Channel 1940–4
North Sea 1941–4
Normandy 1944
Named after a hunt in Ayr.
1 1916 minesweeper of 810 tons, built by Ayrshire. Sold in 1922 to King, Garston.
2 1939 destroyer of the 'Hunt' class, 907 tons, built by Vickers Armstrong, Tyne. Scrapped at Blyth in 1968.

## EGRET

Biscay 1943
Atlantic 1939–42
North Africa 1942–3
*Noli mea levitate decipi* = Don't be deceived by my slightness.
1 1899 fishery trawler of 169 tons, sunk in 1918.
2 1899 fishery trawler of 224 tons, in service the same time as No. 1.
3 1938 sloop of 1,200 tons built by White. Sunk by glider bomb off NW Spain.

## EKINS

Atlantic 1944
English Channel 1944
North Sea 1944–5
Named after Captain Sir Charles Ekins of the *Superb*, who bombarded Algiers 1816.
1 1943 frigate of 1,300 tons, ex-*DE.87*, built by Bethlehem: Hingham. CTL 1945. Scrapped 1947 in Holland.

## ELECTRA

Atlantic 1939–40
Norway 1940
*Bismarck* Action 1941
Arctic 1941
*Fulgens ab undis* = Shining from the waves.
Daughter of Agamemnon; assisted her brother Orestes in killing their father.
1 1806 vessel.
3 1837 sloop. Sold for scrapping in 1862.
4 1896 destroyer built by Thomson. Sold in 1920 to the Barking Ship Breaking Co.
7 1934 destroyer of 1,375 tons built by Hawthorn Leslie. Sunk in the battle of the Java Sea 1942.

## EMERALD

Basque Roads 1809
Atlantic 1939–40
Normandy 1944
*Fide et fiducia* = By faith and trust.
1 1757 prize frigate. Scrapped in 1761.
2 1762 5th rate. Scrapped in 1793.
3 1856 frigate. Scrapped in 1869.
6 1876 corvette. Scrapped in 1906.
7 1903 ex-*Black Prince*. Renamed in 1910 as *Impregnable*.
12 1920 cruiser of 7,550 tons built by Armstrong at Wallsend. Scrapped at Troon in 1948.

## EMPEROR

Atlantic 1943–4
Norway 1944
Aegean 1944
Normandy 1944
South France 1944
Malaya 1945
Burma 1945
1 1857 vessel.

3 1942 escort carrier, ex-USS *Pybus* built by Seattle:Tacoma, 11,420 tons. Returned to USA 1946 and scrapped the same year.

## EMPRESS

Atlantic 1944
Burma 1945
1 1809 vessel.
3 1914−18 seaplane carrier.
4 1942 escort carrier, ex-USS *Carnegie* built by Seattle: Tacoma, 11,420 tons. Returned to USA 1946.

## ENARD BAY

1 1944 frigate, ex-*Loch Bracadale*, of 1,580 tons built by Smith's Dock. Scrapped at Faslane in 1957.

## ENCHANTRESS

Atlantic 1939−45
Mediterranean 1942
North Africa 1942−3
1 1805 vessel.
4 1888 ex-*Helicon*, Admiralty yacht. Sold in 1905.
5 1903 Admiralty yacht of 3,470 tons built by Harland & Wolff, Belfast. Laid up during WWI. Sold 1935.
6 1934 Admiralty Yacht (Escort Vessel) ex-*Bittern*, sloop, of 1,190 tons built on Clydebank. Sold out of the Navy 1946, renamed *Lady Enchantress* and used as a pleasure steamer by the Three Star Shipping Company. Scrapped Dunston 1952.

## ENCOUNTER

Cape of Good Hope 1806
Basque Roads 1809
China 1856−60
Ashantee 1873−4
Atlantic 1939
Norway 1940
Spartivento 1940
Libya 1941
Malta Convoys 1941
Mediterranean 1941
Sunda Strait 1942
*Acta non verba* = Deeds, not words.
1 1805 vessel.
2 1846 sloop. Scrapped in 1866.
3 1873 corvette. Sold in 1888.
4 1902 cruiser of 5,650 tons built by Devonport Dock Yard. Transferred to RAN 1912. Dismantled 1929 and hulked. Scuttled off Sydney 1936.
5 1934 destroyer of 1,375 tons built by Hawthorn Leslie. Sunk in the battle of the Java Sea 1942.

## ENDURANCE

Falkland Islands 1982
By endurance we conquer. Motto of the Shackleton family.
1 1967 ice patrol ship, ex-*Anita Dan*, of 3,600 tons, built by Krögerwerft, Rendsburg. Bought from J. Lauitzen Lines, Copenhagen and converted 1967−8 by Harland & Wolff as ice patrol and Antarctic support ship.

## ENGADINE

Jutland 1916
Atlantic 1943
Falkland Islands 1982
1 1911 seaplane carrier. Built as a vessel of 1,676 tons by Denny. Requisitioned 1914 and returned 1919.
2 1941 aircraft transport, ex-*Clan Buchanan* of 7,473 tons, built by Denny: Kincaid. Returned 1946 and scrapped in Spain in 1962.
3 1966 helicopter support ship of *c*.9,000 tons built by Henry Robb, at Leith.

## ENTERPRISE

Havana 1762
Atlantic 1939−40
Norway 1940
Biscay 1943
Normandy 1944
*Spes aspera levat* = Hope lightens danger.
1 1705 6th rate prize. Wrecked two years later.
2 1709 5th rate. Sold forty years later.
3 1944 ex-*Norwich*, 5th rate. Scrapped 1771.
4 and 5 were 6th rates.
9 1862 armoured vessel. Sold 1884.
14 1919 cruiser of 7,850 tons built on Clydebank. Scrapped at Newport in 1946.
15 1957 inshore surveying vessel of 120/160 tons built by M.W. Blackmore of Bideford. All wood construction. Disposal List 1985−6.

## EREBUS

Belgian Coast 1916−18
Zeebrugge 1918
English Channel 1940−4
North Sea 1941
Atlantic 1943
Mediterranean 1943
Sicily 1943
Normandy 1944
Walcheren 1944
*Inimicis nomen explicat* = The name explains itself to enemies. The dark entrance to Hades.
1 1807 vessel.
2 1845−8: the bomb which was lost in the Franklin expedition.
3 1856 floating battery.
4 1905 ex-*Invincible*, but renamed the following year.
5 1916 Monitor of 7,200 tons built by Harland & Wolff. Scrapped at Inverkeithing 1946.

## ERICA

Atlantic 1940−1
Libya 1942
1 1940 corvette of 925 tons built by Harland & Wolff. Mined in 1943.

## ERIDGE

Libya 1941−2
Malta Convoys 1941−2
Sirte 1942
Mediterranean 1942
Named after a hunt in Sussex.
1 1916 minesweeper of 810 tons built by Clyde Ship Builders. Sold to Ward, Inverkeithing for scrapping, 1922.
2 1940 destroyer of the 'Hunt' class, 1,050 tons, built by Swan Hunter, Wallsend. CTL 1942. Scrapped at Alexandria 1946.

## ERNE

North Africa 1942
Atlantic 1942−5
Sicily 1943
*Surtout* = Above all.
1 1813 6th rate which was wrecked in 1819.
3 1903 destroyer *c*.550 tons built by Palmer. Wrecked in 1915 off Rattray Head.
6 1940 sloop of 1,250 tons built at Furness by Richardson, Westgarth. Renamed *Wessex*, and became a drillship for the Solent Division of the RNVR in 1952. Sold as a hulk in 1965.

## ESCAPADE

Atlantic 1939−45
Norway 1940
Arctic 1941−2
Malta Convoys 1942
*Celeriter* = Swiftly.
1 1934 destroyer of 1,375 tons built

by Scotts. Scrapped at Grangemouth in 1947.

## ESCORT

Belleisle 1761
Atlantic 1939–40
North Sea 1940
*Fideliter* = Faithfully.
1   1757 prize *Escorte*.
5   1934 destroyer of 1,375 tons built by Scotts. Torpedoed in 1940 by the Italian submarine *Marconi* off Cyprus and foundered while in tow.

## ESK

Baltic 1855
China 1856–60
New Zealand 1863–6
Atlantic 1939
Norway 1940
Dunkirk 1940
*Fluctuo sed affluo* = I flow, but I flow onward.
1   1813 sloop. Sold in 1829.
2   1854 corvette. Sold about 1870.
4   1934 destroyer of 1,375 tons built by Swan Hunter, Wallsend. Mined in the North Sea in 1940.

## ESKDALE

Arctic 1942
English Channel 1942–3
Named after the hunt in Cumberland.
1   1942 destroyer of the 'Hunt' class, 1,050 tons built by Cammell Laird. Manned by the Norwegian navy — they retained the English name. Torpedoed in 1943.

## ESKIMO

Norway 1940–1
Narvik 1940
Arctic 1942
Malta Convoys 1942
North Africa 1942–3
Sicily 1943
Normandy 1944
English Channel 1944
Burma 1944–5
*Sikum un gasiktum* = Fire in ice.
1   1937 destroyer of the 'Tribal' class 1,870 tons built by Vickers Armstrong, Tyne. Scrapped at Troon in 1949 after a distinguished WWII record.
2   1960 general-purpose frigate,

2,370/2,700 tons, built by White. Disposal List 1980–1.

## ESPIÈGLE

Egypt 1801
Mesopotamia 1914–16
Sicily 1943
Salerno 1943
Anzio 1944
1   1793 prize French brigantine.
3   1804 sloop. Scrapped in 1811.
6   1880 sloop which was renamed *Argo* in 1900.
7   1900 sloop of 1,070 tons built by Sheerness Dock Yard. Sold to Bombay in 1923 for breaking up.[36]
8   1942 minesweeper of 'Algerine' class built by Harland & Wolff. Sold in 1966 for scrapping at Dalmuir.

## ESSINGTON

Biscay 1943–4
Atlantic 1943–5
Arctic 1944
Normandy 1944
English Channel 1944–5
Named after Captain William Essington, who commanded the *Triumph* at Camperdown.
1   1943 frigate, ex*DE.67*, of 1,300 tons built by Bethlehem: Hingham and returned to the USA in 1945.
2   1950s coastal minesweeper of 360/425 tons.

## ETTRICK

Atlantic 1943–5
1   1903 destroyer *c*.550 tons and built by Palmer. Sold in 1919 to the James Dredging Co for scrapping.
3   1943 frigate of 1,370 tons built by Crown: Parsons. Transferred to RCN 1944–5. Scrapped at Grays 1953.

## EUPHRATES

1   1813 frigate, sold only five years later.
2   1866 troopship. Sold in 1895.
5   1941–6 depot at Basra.

## EUROPA

Egypt 1801
1   1673 prize, burnt two years later.

2   1765 3rd rate. Renamed *Europe* in 1778 and finally broken up in 1814.
4   1897 cruiser of 11,000 tons built by John Brown. Depot ship 1915. Sold in 1920 to Malta.
5   1940–6 patrol service based at Lowestoft.

## EURYALUS

Trafalgar 1805
Baltic 1854–5
Heligoland 1914
Dardanelles 1915
Malta Convoys 1941–2
Mediterranean 1941–3
Sirte 1942
Sicily 1943
Salerno 1943
Okinawa 1945
*Omnia audax* = Bold in all things.
Name is derived from Greek mythology: the friend and companion of Diomedes.
1   1803 3rd rate (36) of 944 tons built by Mr Adams at Buckler's Hard. Convict ship from 1826–59 at Sheerness and Gibraltar.
2   1853 frigate of 2,371 tons and 44 guns built at Chatham. Sold to Castle in 1867 for scrapping.
3   1877 second-class screw cruiser of 4,140 tons. Sold in 1897.
4   1901 cruiser of 12,000 tons built by Vickers at Barrow. Sold in 1920 to Castle for scrapping in Germany.
5   1939 cruiser of 5,450 tons built at Chatham by Hawthorn Leslie. Scrapped at Blyth 1959.
6   1963 Improved Type 12 destroyer of 2,450/2,860 tons built by Scotts. 'Leander' class armed with Ikara missiles.

## EXCALIBUR

Named after King Arthur's sword.
1   1955 fast experimental submarine of 780/1,000 tons built by Vickers Armstrong at Barrow.

36   Manning and Walker note that this was probably the last ship in the Royal Navy to have been built with a figurehead.

## EXCELLENT

St Vincent 1797
Belgian Coast 1914−16
1   1787 3rd rate (74) built by Graham, Harwich. Converted to a 4th rate (58) in 1820. Became gunnery-training ship at Portsmouth 1830. Scrapped in 1835.
2   1834 2nd rate, ex-*Boyne*. Scrapped 1861.
3   1859 1st rate, ex-*Queen Charlotte*. Scrapped in 1892.
4   1891 the gunnery training establishment was set up at Whale Island.
5   1918 trawler, renamed *Malvern* in 1946. Scrapped 1954.
6   General Training School, Portsmouth: Whale Island naval leadership school. Much transference of the component parts of this establishment in 1984−5.

## EXE

Atlantic 1942−5
North Africa 1942
1   1903 destroyer c.550 tons built by Palmer and sold in 1920 to Ward for scrapping at Rainham.
3   1942 frigate of 1,370 tons built by Fleming & Ferguson. Scrapped at Preston in 1956.

## EXETER

Sadras 1782
Providien 1782
Negapatam 1782
Trincomalee 1782
River Plate 1939
Falkland Islands 1982
*Semper fidelis* = Ever faithful.
The badge derives from the city arms of Exeter.
1   1680 3rd rate. Scrapped in 1717.
2   and 3 were both 4th rates of 1697 and 1763.
5   1929 cruiser of 8,390 tons built at Devonport:Parsons. Heavily damaged in the *Graf Spee* action and sunk in action in the battle of the Java Sea 1942.
6   1978 Type 42 destroyer of 3,500/4,100 tons built by Swan Hunter.

## EXMOOR

North Sea 1941
Atlantic 1941−2
Libya 1942
Sicily 1943
Salerno 1943
Aegean 1943−4
Mediterranean 1944
Named after the hunt in Somerset.
1   1940 destroyer of the 'Hunt' class, 1,000 tons built by Vickers Armstrong, Tyne. Sunk by E-boats off Lowestoft in 1941.
2   1941 destroyer of the 'Hunt' class, 907 tons built by Vickers Armstrong, Tyne. Lent to Denmark in 1953.

## EXMOUTH

Baltic 1854−5
Belgian Coast 1914
Dardanelles 1915
Atlantic 1939
*Deo adjuvante* = With God's help.
Named after Admiral Edward Pellew, Viscount Exmouth (1757−1833).
1   1854 2nd rate. Sold in 1905.
2   1901 battleship of 14,000 tons built

by Laird. Sold in 1920, then resold for breaking up in Holland.
4   1934 flotilla leader of 1,375 tons built by Fairfield. Torpedoed in 1940 by *U-22* off Moray Firth.
5   1955 anti-submarine frigate, Type 14 of 1,700 tons built by White. Broken up at Briton Ferry in 1979.

## EXPLORER

1   1939 vessel.
2   1954 submarine of 780/1,000 tons built by Vickers Armstrong, Barrow.
3   1986 coastal patrol vessel of 43 tons.

## EXPRESS

Martinique 1809
Dunkirk 1940
*Celeriter ferio* = I strike quickly.
1   1695 vessel.
7   1897 destroyer of c.400 tons built by Laird and sold in 1921 to Clarkson, Whitby.
8   1934 destroyer of 1,375 tons built by Swan Hunter. Transferred to RCN in 1943 as *Gatineau*. Scrapped in Vancouver in 1956.
9   1986 coastal patrol craft of 43 tons.

## EYEBRIGHT

Atlantic 1941−5
1   1940 corvette built by Canadian Vickers. Served with RCN 1941−45 then sold for mercantile service: *Albert W. Vinke*, 1950.

## FAIRFAX

Dover 1652
Portland 1653
Santa Cruz 1657
Orfordness 1666
Solebay 1672
Texel 1673
Atlantic 1944
Named after Thomas, Lord Fairfax (1611−71).
1   1650 vessel (50) lost by fire three years later.
2   1653 2nd rate, wrecked in 1682.
3   1941 mine-destructor ship, originally *Burlington*, built in 1940, 2,068 tons, then *Soothsayer*, then *Fairfax*, then a maintenance ship in 1944. Finally scrapped in 1945.

## FAIRY

1   1778 vessel.
4   1845 royal yacht. Sold in 1868.
6   1897 destroyer *c*.400 tons built by Fairfield. Foundered in 1918 after damage sustained in ramming *UC75* in the North Sea.
7   1943 minesweeper, ex-*BAM 25*, of 890 tons built by Associated Shipbuilders. Returned to USA 1946.

## FAL

Atlantic 1943−5
1   1942 frigate of 1,370 tons built by Smith's Dock. Renamed *Mayu* in 1945 and transferred to the Burmese navy in 1948.

## FALCON

Gabbard 1653
Schooneveld 1673
Texel 1673
Barfleur 1692
Finisterre I 1747
Baltic 1855
New Zealand 1863
Belgian Coast 1914−17
*Celeriter et audaciter* = Swiftly and boldly.
1   1212 vessel.[37]
9   1666 5th rate which surrendered in 1694.
10  1694 6th rate which surrendered in 1695.
12  1704 5th rate which surrendered in 1709.
13  1744 sloop which surrendered in 1745.
14  and 15 were both sloops of 1745 and 1771 and both were lost in 1759 and 1779.
21  1854 sloop. Sold in 1869.
23  1899 destroyer of *c*.400 tons built by Fairfield. Lost in collision with the trawler *John Fitzgerald* in the North Sea in 1918.
27  1946 RN Air Station at Hal Far in Malta.

## FALMOUTH

Portland 1653
Gabbard 1653
Heligoland 1914

Jutland 1916
Fail not.
The badge derives from the seal of Falmouth.
1   1652 prize, *Rotterdam*. Sold in 1659.
2   1693 4th rate which surrendered in 1704.
3   1708 4th rate. Scrapped in 1747.
4   1752 4th rate which was abandoned at Batavia as unseaworthy in 1765.
8   1910 cruiser of 5,250 tons built by Beardmore. She was torpedoed by *U-63* in the North Sea in 1915.
11  1932 sloop which became the RNVR drillship *Calliope* soon after WWII.
12  1959 frigate of 2,800 tons built by Swan Hunter. Disposal List 1982−3. Still held at Portsmouth for disposal 1986−7.

## FAME

Lowestoft 1665
The Saintes 1782
China 1900
Norway 1940
Atlantic 1942−4
Normandy 1944
*Fama si merita* = Fame comes if deserved.
1   1655 prize which was expended as a fireship in 1665.
2   1709 prize 6th rate which surrendered in the following year.
3   1744 sloop which foundered in 1745.
4   1759 3rd rate which was renamed *Guildford* in 1799.
5   1804 Spanish prize named *Fama*. Sold in 1812.
6   1805 3rd rate. Scrapped 1817.
7   1808 Danish prize (18) which was wrecked in 1808.
10  1896 destroyer of *c*.340 tons built by Thornycroft. Sold to Hong Kong in 1920.
13  1934 destroyer of 1,350 tons built by Vickers Armstrong, Tyne. Sold to Dominica in 1949 and renamed *Generalissimo*.

## FANTÔME

Atlantic 1943
1   1809 French prize.

3   1873 sloop. Sold in 1889.
4   1901 sloop/survey vessel of 1,070 tons built by Sheerness Dock Yard. Transferred to RAN and sold to Sydney, NSW, in 1925.
5   1942 minesweeper of 850 tons built by Harland & Wolff. CTL 1943 and scrapped at Milford Haven in 1947.

## FARNDALE

Atlantic 1941
Malta Convoys 1941
Mediterranean 1941
Libya 1941−2
Arctic 1942
North Africa 1942−3
Sicily 1943
Salerno 1943
South France 1944
Aegean 1944
North Sea 1945
Named after the hunt in Yorkshire.
1   1940 destroyer of the 'Hunt' class, 1,050 tons, built by Swan Hunter at Wallsend. Scrapped at Blyth in 1962.

## FARNHAM CASTLE

Arctic 1945
1   1944 corvette/frigate of 1,010 tons built by Crown: Clark. Scrapped at Gateshead in 1961.

## FAULKNOR

Jutland 1916
Belgian Coast 1917−18
Zeebrugge 1918
Ostend 1918
Atlantic 1939−43
Norway 1940
Spartivento 1940
Malta Convoys 1941
Arctic 1942−3
Sicily 1943
Salerno 1943
Aegean 1943
Mediterranean 1943−4
Anzio 1944
Normandy 1944
*Ducit amor patriae* = Love of fatherland leads.
Named after Captain Robert Faulknor (1763−95).[38]
1   1914 flotilla leader of 1,694 tons built by White. Sold to the Chilean

---

37   Manning and Walker record that the name was borne six times before 1600. See p.191.

38   In the duel between his ship *Blanche* and the French *Pique* Faulknor was killed while trying to lash the enemy's bowsprit to his capstan. See Manning and Walker, p.193.

navy and renamed *Almirante Riveros*.

2   1934 flotilla leader of 1,475 tons built by Yarrow. Sold in 1946 for breaking up at Milford Haven.

## FAWN

Martinique 1809
Guadeloupe 1810
Belgian Coast 1914−18
1   1805 brig/sloop prize named *Faune*.
2   1807 sloop (18) built at Topsham, Devon. Sold 1818.
3   1840 brigantine, ex-slaver *Caroline*. Sold 1847.
4   1856 wood steam sloop, 1,045 tons. Sold 1884.
5   1897 destroyer, 300 tons, built by Palmer. Sank *U-8* in Dover Straits 1915. Sold 1919.
9   1968 survey ship of 'Bulldog' class, 800/1,080 tons, built by Brooke Marine, Lowestoft.

## FEARLESS

Heligoland 1914
Jutland 1916
Norway 1940
Atlantic 1941
Malta Convoys 1941
Mediterranean 1941
Falkland Islands 1982
*Explicit nomen* = The name explains itself.
1   1794 vessel.
4   1886 torpedo cruiser. Sold in 1905 for scrapping.
5   1912 cruiser of 3,350 tons built by Pembroke Dock Yard. Sold in 1921 for breaking up in Germany.
7   1934 destroyer of 1,375 tons built by Cammell Laird. Sunk by torpedo aircraft in the Mediterranean in 1941.
8   1963 assault ship (Amphibious Dock Transport Type) of 11,000/12,150 tons[39] built by Harland & Wolff. Disposal List 1983.

39   16,950 tons with the dock flooded.

## FENCER

Atlantic 1943−4
Norway 1944
North Sea 1944
Arctic 1944
*En garde.*
1   1942 escort carrier ex-USS *Croatan* of 11,420 tons built by Western Pipe: GEC. Returned to USA 1946 and entered merchant service as *Sydney*, 1948.
2   1984 coastal training craft of 34 tons.

## FENNEL

Atlantic 1941−5
1   1940 corvette of 925 tons built by Canadian Vickers. Sold in 1947.

## FERNIE

English Channel 1940−4
North Sea 1940−5
Dieppe 1942
Normandy 1944
Named after the hunt in Leicestershire.
1   1940 destroyer of the 'Hunt' class, 907 tons, built on Clydebank. Broken up in 1956 at Port Glasgow.

## FERRET

Havana 1762
Heligoland 1914
Dogger Bank 1915
Belgian Coast 1917
1   1704 sloop which surrendered in 1706.
2   1711 sloop which surrendered in 1718.
3   1721 sloop. Sold in 1731.
5   1760 sloop which foundered in 1776.
16   1893 destroyer. Sold for scrap in 1910.
17   1911 destroyer of *c*.800 tons built by White. Sold in 1921 for scrapping by Ward at Milford Haven.
18   1940 base at Londonderry.

## FIFE

*Tam ratione quam vi* = As much by reason as by strength.
1   1964 guided-missile armed destroyer, Type 42, of 5,440/6,200 tons built by Fairfield at Govan.

## FIJI

Crete 1941
*Rare raka na Kalon Ka Doke na tui* = Fear God and honour the King
1   1939 cruiser of 8,500 tons built on Clydebank. Sunk by German aircraft during the battle for Crete in 1941.

## FINDHORN

Atlantic 1943−4
Okinawa 1945
1   1942 frigate, ex-USN, built by Canadian Vickers, 1,370 tons. Broken up in 1948.

## FINISTERRE

Commemorates the two great naval victories of 1747 by Anson and Hawke.
1   1944 destroyer of the 'Battle' class of 3,361 tons, built by Fairfield. Scrapped at Dalmuir 1967.

## FINWHALE

1   1915 vessel.
2   1959 submarine of 1,600/2,300 tons

built by Cammell Laird. Disposal List 1979–80, and still for disposal 1983.

# FIREDRAKE

Belleisle 1761
Heligoland 1914
Atlantic 1939–42
Norway 1940
Spartivento 1940
Mediterranean 1940–1
Malta Convoys 1941
*Virtute ardens* = Burning with valour.
1  1648 vessel.
5  1912 destroyer of 765 tons built by Yarrow. Sold in 1921 to J. Smith.
6  1934 destroyer of 1,350 tons built by Vickers Armstrong, Tyne. Torpedoed by *U-211* in the North Atlantic in 1942.

# FISGARD

Curaçoa 1807
*Immortalité* 1798
*Singuli in solidum* = United we stand.
1  1797 French prize, *Résistance*. Sold in 1814.
2  1819 5th rate. Became training ship for engineers. Anchored off Woolwich. Scrapped 1879.
3  1910 training establishment for engine-room artificers at Portsmouth.
4  1946 training establishment for artificers at Torpoint. Paid off in 1983.

# FISHGUARD

Atlantic 1941–3
Sicily 1943
Named after the coastguard station in Pembrokeshire.
1  1941 cutter ex-USCGS *Tahoe*. Built in 1927 by Bethlehem, 1,546 tons. Returned to USA 1946.

# FITZROY

Dunkirk 1940
Arctic 1944
English Channel 1944
Atlantic 1944–5
North Sea 1944–5
Watch there, watch.
Named after Vice Admiral Robert Fitzroy (1805–65) of the *Beagle*.
1  1919 survey vessel, ex-*Pinner*, ex-*Portreath*, of 710 tons built by Lobnitz. Served as a minesweeper in WWII and sunk by a mine off Great Yarmouth in 1942.

2  1943 frigate, ex-*DE.88*, of 1,300 tons built by Bethlehem: Hingham. Returned to USA in 1946.

# FLAMINGO

North Sea 1939–40
Norway 1940
Greece 1941
Crete 1941
Libya 1941
Burma 1944–5
1  1876 vessel.
2  1939 sloop of 1,250 tons built by Yarrow. Sold to Federal Republic of Germany and renamed *Graf Spee*, 1958.

# FLEETWOOD

Norway 1940
Atlantic 1940–4
North Africa 1942–3
Mediterranean 1944
English Channel 1945
Onward.
1  1914–18 vessel.
2  1936 frigate/sloop of 990 tons built at Devonport by Thornycroft. Scrapped at Gateshead in 1959.

# FLEUR-DE-LYS

Atlantic 1940–1
Malta Convoys 1941
1  1940 corvette of 925 tons built by Simons. Torpedoed and sunk in 1941.

# FLINT CASTLE

Atlantic 1944–5
1  1914–18 vessel.
2  1943 corvette/frigate of 1,010 tons built by Henry Robb: Plenty. Scrapped at Faslane in 1958.

# FLY

Belleisle 1761
Sicily 1943
Salerno 1943
Anzio 1944
1  1649 vessel.
4  5, 6, 14, 15, 16, and 17 were all sloops of 1732, 1752, 1776, 1804, 1806, 1813 and 1831 which were sold, wrecked, foundered or became a coal hulk.
23  1942 minesweeper of 850 tons built by Lobnitz. Sold to Imperial Persian navy 1949 and renamed *Palang*.

# FOLEY

Atlantic 1943–4
Named after Captain Thomas Foley (1757–1833) of the *Britannia* at St Vincent, *Goliath* at the Nile and *Elephant* at Copenhagen.
1  1943 frigate, ex-*DE.270*, of 1,085 tons built by Boston. Returned to USA in 1945.

# FOLKESTONE

Atlantic 1940–4
*In portu quies* = Rest in harbour.
1  1704 5th rate. Scrapped 1727.
2  1740 5th rate. Sold in 1749.
6  1930 sloop of 1,045 tons built by Swan Hunter & Hawthorn Leslie. Sold in 1947 for breaking up at Gelliswick Bay.

# FORESIGHT

Armada 1588
Portland 1653
Gabbard 1653
Scheveningen 1653
Porto Farina 1655
Santa Cruz 1657
Orfordness 1666
Schooneveld 1673
Texel 1673
Belgian Coast 1914
Dardanelles 1915–16
Atlantic 1941
Mediterranean 1941
Malta Convoys 1941–2
Arctic 1942
*Aevos sequimur* = We follow our ancestors.
1  1570 vessel (36). Condemned in 1604.
2  1650 4th rate which was wrecked in 1698.
3  1934 cruiser of 2,850 tons built by Fairfield. Broken up in 1920.
5  1934 destroyer of 1,350 tons built by Cammell Laird. Torpedoed by Italian aircraft in 1942, and foundered next day.

# FORESTER

Lowestoft 1665
Solebay 1672
Martinique 1809
Guadeloupe 1810
China 1856–60
Heligoland 1914
Dogger Bank 1915
Atlantic 1939–44
Narvik 1940
Norway 1940
Spartivento 1940

Malta Convoys 1941
Arctic 1942−3
Normandy 1944
English Channel 1944
*Audax potentes caedo* = Boldly I cut
down the mighty.
1　1657 vessel (22). Blown up in
　　1672.
9　1911 destroyer of 760 tons built at
　　Cowes. Sold 1921 to Rees,
　　Llanelly for scrapping.
10　1934 destroyer of 1,350 tons built
　　by White at Cowes. After a
　　distinguished WWII record she
　　was scrapped at Rosyth in 1947.

## FORMIDABLE

The Saintes 1782
Matapan 1941
Crete 1941
Mediterranean 1941
North Africa 1942−3
Sicily 1943
Salerno 1943
Okinawa 1945
Japan 1945
1　1759 French prize (80) taken at
　　Quiberon Bay. Scrapped in 1768 at
　　Plymouth.
2　1777 2nd rate (90) of 1,945 tons.
　　Broken up at Plymouth in 1813.
3　1825 2nd rate (84) of 3,594 tons.
　　Scrapped in 1906.
4　1898 battleship of 15,000 tons built
　　by Portsmouth Dock Yard.
　　Torpedoed by *U-24* off Portland
　　Point in 1915.
6　1939 aircraft carrier of 23,000 tons
　　built by Harland & Wolff. She has
　　a distinguished WWII record. Sold
　　in 1953 for scrapping at
　　Inverkeithing.

## FORTH

1　1812 frigate. Scrapped in 1821.
2　1833 5th rate. Later renamed
　　*Jupiter*.
3　1886 cruiser later converted to a
　　submarine depot ship. 4,050 tons,
　　built by Pembroke Dock Yard. Sold

in 1921 to Slough T.C. for breaking
　　up in Germany.
4　1938 depot ship for submarines of
　　10,000/13,000 tons built at
　　Clydebank. Reconstructed
　　1962−66 as a nuclear-powered
　　submarine support ship. Renamed
　　*Defiance* in 1972. Disposal List
　　1978−9.
5　1961−7 'Avon' class ramp
　　powered lighter of 100 tons built
　　by White/Saunders Roe.

## FORTUNE

Armada 1588
Portland 1653
Gabbard 1653
Orfordness 1666
Jutland 1916
Atlantic 1939
North Sea 1940
Malta Convoys 1941−2
*Faveat* = May [fortune] favour you.
1　1512 vessel.
2　1627 prize.
3　1652 prize which surrendered in
　　the same year.
4　1653 prize which was sold the
　　following year.
13　and 14 were sloops of 1756 and
　　1780.
15　1779 prize 5th rate which became
　　a convict ship.
18　1798 corvette prize.
19　1800 5th rate.
21　1913 destroyer built by Fairfield.
　　Sunk at Jutland in 1916.
22　1934 destroyer of 1,350 tons built
　　at Clydebank. Transferred to
　　RCN as *Saskatchewan*, 1943. Sold
　　in 1948.

## FOWEY

Quebec 1759
Atlantic 1939−45
*Tien ta foy* = Hold thy loyalty.
1, 2, 3, and 4 were all 5th rates of
　　1696, 1705, 1709, and 1744, the
　　first two of which surrendered and
　　the last was wrecked.
5　1749 6th rate was destroyed in
　　action in 1781.
8　1930 sloop of 1,045 tons built at
　　Devonport by White. Sold for
　　mercantile service in 1946, *Fowlock*.
　　Scrapped at Mombasa in 1950.
9　1962 anti-submarine frigate of
　　2,300/2,800 tons, renamed *Ajax*.

## FOX

Gabbard 1653
Orfordness 1666

Barfleur 1692
Genoa 1795
St Vincent 1797
Egypt 1801
Burma 1852−3
1　1650 vessel (20) taken as a prize
　　and later expended as a fireship.
5, 6, and 7. were 6th rates of 1705,
　　1708 and 1740.
8　1746 sloop which was lost in a
　　hurricane in 1751.
9　1773 6th rate, surrendered for a
　　second time in 1778.
28　1829 5th rate. Scrapped in 1880.
30　1893 cruiser of 4,360 tons built by
　　Portsmouth Dock Yard. Sold in
　　1920 for scrapping at Cardiff.
31　1939 naval base at Lerwick.
32　1986 coastal survey vessel of 860/
　　1,088 tons built by Brooke Marine
　　of Lowestoft.

## FOXGLOVE

1　1915 sloop of 1,165 tons built by
　　Barclay Curle. CTL 1940 and finally
　　scrapped at Troon in 1946.

## FOXHOUND

Basque Roads 1809
Dardanelles 1916
Atlantic 1939−41
Narvik 1940
Norway 1940
Malta Convoys 1941
Mediterranean 1941
*Acer in venatu* = Keen in the chase.
1　1806 vessel.
5　1909 destroyer of *c*.950 tons built at
　　Clydebank by John Brown. Sold in
　　1921 for scrapping by Fryer of
　　Sunderland.
6　1934 destroyer of 1,350 tons built at
　　Clydebank. Transferred to RCN as
　　*Qu'Appelle*, 1944. Scrapped in 1948.

## FRANKLIN

Normandy 1944
Named after Sir John Franklin, the
famous explorer.
1　1937 survey vessel of 835 tons built
　　by the Ailsa Shipbuilding
　　Company. Scrapped Dunston
　　1956.

## FREESIA

Atlantic 1941−2
Diego Suarez 1942
1　1914−18 vessel.
2　1940 corvette of 925 tons built by
　　Harland & Wolff. Sold in 1946 for

mercantile service as *Freelock,* but lost at sea 1947.

# FRITILLARY

Atlantic 1941−5
Diego Suarez 1942
1   1941 corvette of 925 tons built by Harland & Wolff. Sold in 1946 for mercantile service as *Andria,* 1947, *V.D. Chitambaram,* 1949. Scrapped in India 1955.

# FROBISHER

Normandy 1944
*Semper triumphans* = Always triumphant.
Named after Sir Martin Frobisher (*c.*1535−94).
1   1920 cruiser of 9,860 tons built at Devonport. Scrapped at Newport in 1949.

# FURIOUS

Crimea 1845−5
China 1856−60
Narvik 1940
Norway 1940−4
Malta Convoys 1942
North Africa 1942−3
*Ministrat arma furor* = Fury supplies arms.
1   1794 vessel.
3   1809 French prize, *Furieuse.* Scrapped in 1816.
5   1896 cruiser which was renamed *Forte* in 1915.
6   1916 cruiser or light battlecruiser, completed as an aircraft carrier of 22,450 tons by Armstrong of Wallsend. Scrapped at Dalmuir and Troon (hull only) in 1948.

# FURY

St Lucia 1796
Egypt 1801
Algiers 1816
Kua Kam 1849
Crimea 1854
China 1856−60
Dardanelles 1915−16
Spartivento 1940
Mediterranean 1941
Malta Convoys 1941−2
Atlantic 1941−3
Arctic 1942−3
Sicily 1943
Salerno 1943
Aegean 1943

Normandy 1944
*Sic ad hostem* = Thus [Fury] to the enemy.
1   1779 sloop. Scrapped 1787.
2   and 8 were sloops of 1790 and 1845.
9   1911 destroyer of *c.*750 tons built by Inglis. Sold in 1921 to Rees of Llanelly for breaking up.
10   1934 destroyer of 1,350 tons built by White. CTL after striking a mine off Normandy in 1944. Scrapped at Briton Ferry 1944.

# GABBARD

*Fortiter, fideliter, feliciter* = Boldly, faithfully, successfully.
Named after the Gabbard, Monck's victory at sea in 1653.
1   1945 destroyer of the 'Battle' class of 3,361 tons built at Swan Hunter. Sold to Pakistan in 1957 and renamed *Badr.*

# GALATEA

Groix 1795
Tamatave 1811
Jutland 1916
Norway 1940
*Bismarck* Action 1941
Mediterranean 1941
*Lynx* 1807
*Nobis mare patria* = The sea is our fatherland.
A sea nymph.

1   1776 6th rate, scrapped seven years later.
5   1859 frigate.
6   1914 cruiser of 3,500 tons built by Beardmore. Sold in 1921 to the Multilocular Ship Breaking Co.[40]
7   1934 cruiser of 5,220 tons built by Scotts. Torpedoed by *U-557* in 1941 north-west of Alexandria.
8   1951 Humber Division of RNVR.
9   1963 frigate of Improved Type 12 of 2,450/2,860 tons built by Swan Hunter & Wigham, Richardson of Wallsend. 'Leander' class armed with Ikara missiles. Paid off 1986−7.

# GALLANT

Atlantic 1939
Dunkirk 1940
Spartivento 1940
Mediterranean 1940−1
Malta Convoys 1941
*Fide et fortitudine* = By faith and courage.
1   1797 vessel.
3   1935 destroyer of 1,335 tons built by Stephen. Mined and became CTL 1942 while in Malta. Bombed 1942. Expended as blockship in Malta.

# GAMBIA

Sabang 1944
Okinawa 1945
1   1940 cruiser of 8,000/11,270 tons built by Swan Hunter, Wallsend. Disposal List 1960−1.

# GANGES

St Lucia 1796
Copenhagen 1801
Syria 1840
Wisdom is strength.
1   1782 3rd rate (74) of 1,655 tons presented to the Admiralty by the East India Company. Ex-*Bengal,*

40   She was the first RN ship to sight the enemy at Jutland.

she was built by Randall & Coot at Blackwall on the Thames. She saw much action in Europe and the West Indies. Became a prison ship in 1811, and was scrapped in 1816 at Plymouth.

2  1821 2nd rate (84) of 2,284 tons built of teak at Bombay, intended as a facsimile of the *Canopus* (ex-*Franklin*) captured by Nelson at The Nile. In 1828 she landed RMs at Rio de Janeiro to protect the Emperor of Brazil. She was the last sailing-ship to be used as a sea-going flagship. In 1866 she moored in Carrick Roads, Falmouth as a training ship for boys. In 1899 she was towed to Harwich and with the *Caroline* formed the Harwich Training Establishment for boys. Renamed *Tenedos* in 1906.

4  Boys' training establishment ashore at Shotley Gate near Ipswich until the 1980s.

# GANNET

*Victoria solatium mihi* = Victory is my solace.

1  1800 vessel.
3  1857 sloop. Sold about 1874.
4  1878 sloop which was renamed *President*.
7  1927 'Petrel' class river gunboat. Presented to Nationalist China 1942 and renamed *Ying Shan*. Taken over by Communists in 1947.
8  1943 RN Air Station at Eglington. Paid off 1959. Reopened 1960 as part of HMS *Sea Eagle*. Finally closed 1963.

# GARDENIA

Atlantic 1940−2
North Africa 1942

1  1917 sloop built by Barclay Curle and scrapped in 1923 by Richardson, Westgarth.
2  1940 corvette of 925 tons built by Simons. Sunk after collision with RN trawler off Oran in 1942.

# GARDINER

Atlantic 1943−5
Named after Captain Arthur Gardiner of the *Monmouth*, killed when he captured the *Foudroyant*.

1  1943 frigate, ex-*DE.274*, of 1,085

tons built by Boston. Returned to the USA in 1946.

# GARLAND

Dover 1652
Kentish Knock 1652
Lowestoft 1665
Bugia 1671
Velez Malaga 1704
Cape Passero 1718
Jutland 1916
Atlantic 1940−3
Arctic 1942
Mediterranean 1944
*Qui meruit ferat* = Let him bear it who has deserved it.

1  1242 vessel.
2  1590 vessel (38), condemned in 1618.
3  1620 (34) which surrendered in 1652.
8  1762 prize, *Guirlande*. Sold in 1783.
9,  11 and 12 were all 6th rates of 1795, 1800 and 1807.
15  1913 destroyer of *c*.1,000 tons built by Cammell Laird. Sold to Denmark in 1921.
16  1935 destroyer of 1,335 tons built by Fairfield. Manned by the Polish navy from 1940−6, retaining the British name. Sold to Holland in 1947 and renamed *Marnix*.

# GARLIES

Atlantic 1943−4
Normandy 1944
Captain Lord Garlies commanded the *Lively* and the *Bellerophon*.

1  1943 frigate ex-*DE.271*, of 1,085 tons built by Boston. Returned to USA 1945.

# GARTH

North Sea 1941−5
Dieppe 1942
English Channel 1942−4
Normandy 1944
Named after a hunt in Wales.

1  1917 minesweeper of 750 tons built by Dunlop Bremner. Sold in 1923 to Alloa of Charlestown for scrapping.
2  1940 destroyer of the 'Hunt' class, 907 tons, built at Clydebank. Broken up at Barrow in 1958.

# GENTIAN

Atlantic 1940−4
Normandy 1944
English Channel 1944−5

1  1915 sloop of 1,250 tons built by Greenock & Grangemouth. Mined in the Gulf of Finland in 1919.
2  1940 corvette of 925 tons built by Harland & Wolff. Sold and scrapped in 1947 at Purfleet.

# GEORGETOWN

Atlantic 1940−3

1  1940 destroyer, ex-USS *Maddox*, of 1,060 tons. Built in 1918 at Fore River. Served with RCN 1942−3. With Russian navy as *Zhostki* 1944−52. Scrapped at Inverkeithing in 1952.

# GERANIUM

Atlantic 1940−5
Malta Convoys 1942
North Africa 1942
Normandy 1944
English Channel 1944

1  1915 sloop of 1,250 tons built by Greenoch & Grangemouth. Presented to RAN 1919. Dismantled 1932 and sunk 35 miles off Sydney as a target.
2  1940 corvette of 925 tons built by Simons. Transferred to the Danish navy in 1945 and renamed *Thetis*.

# GHURKA (Gurkha)

Belgian Coast 1914−16
Norway 1940
North Sea 1940
Atlantic 1941
Mediterranean 1941
Malta Convoys 1941−2

1  1907 destroyer of *c*.870 tons built by Hawthorn Leslie. Mined in 1917 off Dungeness.
2  1937 destroyer of the 'Tribal' class of 1,870 tons built by Fairfield. Sunk by German aircraft off Norway in 1940.
3  1940 destroyer, ex-*Larne* of 1,920 tons built by Cammell Laird. Torpedoed by *U-133* off Sollum in 1942.[41]
4  1960 general-purpose frigate of 2,370/2,700 tons built by Thornycroft. Sold to Indonesia 1983.

---

41  Every man in the Gurkha regiments subscribed a day's pay to provide this replacement destroyer. See Manning and Walker, p.208.

## GIPSY

Belgian Coast 1914–17
Atlantic 1939
Trust your luck.
1   1799 vessel.
4   1897 destroyer of *c*.400 tons built
    by Fairfield. Sold to C.A. Beard of
    Teignmouth for scrapping, but the
    hull was left at Dartmouth as a
    jetty.
5   1935 destroyer of 1,335 tons built
    by Fairfield. Mined in the North
    Sea in 1939.

## GIRDLENESS

1   1945 Landing-craft maintenance
    ship. Converted into guided-
    missile ship 1955–6. Disposal List
    1976–7.

## GLADIOLUS

Atlantic 1940–1
1   1915 sloop of 1,250 tons built by
    Connell. Sold to Portugal in 1920
    and renamed *Republica*.
2   1940 corvette of 925 tons built by
    Smith's Dock. Torpedoed in 1941.

## GLAISDALE

English Channel 1942–4
Named after the hunt in Yorkshire.
1   1942 destroyer of the 'Hunt' class,
    1,087 tons built by Cammell Laird.
    Transferred to the Norwegian
    navy in 1946 and scrapped in
    Denmark in 1961.

## GLAMORGAN

Falkland Islands 1982
1   1964 guided-missile armed
    destroyer of the 'County' class,
    5,440/6,200 tons built by Vickers,
    Newcastle. Paid off 1986–7,
    possibly for sale to Chile.

## GLASGOW

Lagos 1759
Havana 1762
Algiers 1816
Navarino 1827
Falkland Islands 1914
Norway 1940
Biscay 1943
Arctic 1943
Normandy 1944
Falklands 1982
*Memor es tuorum* = Be mindful of your
ancestors.
The badge is derived from the arms of
the city.
1   1707 6th rate (24) of 284 tons, ex-
    *Royal Mary* first commissioned in
    1696. Sold 1717.
2   1745 6th rate. Sold in 1759.
3   1757 6th rate (20) of 451 tons
    launched at Hull. Accidentally set
    on fire and destroyed in Jamaica
    1799.
4   1814 5th rate (40) of 1,260 tons built
    at Blackwall. Broken up at
    Chatham 1829.
5   1861 frigate (28) of 3,037 tons built
    at Portsmouth and sold 1884.
6   1909 cruiser of 4,800 tons built by
    Fairfield. She became a stokers'
    training ship at Portsmouth. Sold
    to Ward in 1926 for breaking up at
    Morecambe.
7   1936 cruiser of 9,100 tons built by
    Scotts. Scrapped at Blyth in 1958.
8   1976 Type 42 destroyer of 3,500/
    4,100 tons built by Swan Hunter.

## GLENARM

Atlantic 1943–4
1   1943 frigate, renamed *Strule* in
    1944. Built by Robb: Smiths, 1,370
    tons. Transferred to the French
    navy 1944 and renamed *Croix de
    Lorraine*.

## GLORIOUS

Norway 1940
*Explicit nomen* = The name explains
itself.
1   1782 French 3rd rate (74) prize
    captured at The Saintes.
    Foundered just a few months later.
2   1916 cruiser built by Harland &
    Wolff. Converted to an aircraft
    carrier 1924–30. 22,500 tons. Sunk
    by gunfire in an engagement with
    *Scharnhorst* and *Gneisenau* off
    Norway, 1940.

## GLORY (La Gloire)

Glorious First of June 1794
Martinique 1809
Guadeloupe 1810
Dardanelles 1915
Korea 1950–3
*Per concordiam gloria* = Glory through
unity.
1   1747 5th rate (44) prize, *Gloire*, of
    748 tons. Reduced to 30 guns in
    1757 and sold in 1763. Once
    captained by Lord Howe.
2   1763 3rd rate (32) of 679 tons.
    Renamed *Apollo* in 1774.
4   1788 2nd rate (98) of 1,931 tons.
    Scrapped in 1825.
5   1795 5th rate (42) of 877 tons was a
    prize, *La Gloire,* which served
    under that name.
7   1806: another *La Gloire* prize
    joined the RN under her own
    name. She was a 5th rate (40) and
    1,153 tons. Scrapped 1812.
8   1814: another prize named *La
    Gloire*: 5th rate (38) of 1,066 tons.
    Sold at Plymouth 1817.
9   1899 battleship of 12,500 tons
    built by Laird. Renamed *Crescent*
    in 1920 and sold two years later to
    Granton S.B. Co.
11  1900 ex-Russian cruiser *Askold*
    was commissioned in 1918 as
    HMS *Glory* in Murmansk for
    service in the White Sea. She was
    laid up at the Gareloch 1919.
12  1943 aircraft carrier of 13,190 tons
    built by Harland & Wolff.
    Scrapped in 1961 at
    Inverkeithing.

## GLOUCESTER

Lowestoft 1665
Four Days' Battle 1666
Orfordness 1666
Solebay 1672
Schooneveld 1673
Texel 1673
Ushant 1747
Jutland 1916
Calabria 1940
Matapan 1941
Crete 1941
Malta Convoys 1941
Mediterranean 1941
*Prorsum* = Onwards.
1    1654 5th rate. Wrecked in 1682.
2    3, 4, 5, and 6 were all 4th rates of
     1695, 1699 (she surrendered),
     1711, 1737 (she sank on Anson's
     circumnavigation), and 1744.
7    1812 3rd rate. Sold 1884.
9    1909 cruiser of 4,800 tons built by
     Beardmore and sold in 1921 to
     Ward for breaking up at Briton
     Ferry.
10   1937 cruiser of 9,400 tons built at
     Devonport by Scotts. Sunk by
     German aircraft in 1941 off Crete.
11   1982 Type 42 destroyer of 3,500/
     4,775 tons built by Vosper
     Thornycroft.

## GLOWWORM

Atlantic 1939
Norway 1940
*Admiral Hipper* 1940
*Ex tenebris lux* = Out of darkness,
light.
1    1916 vessel.
2    1935 destroyer of 1,345 tons built
     by Thornycroft. Sunk in action off
     Norway after ramming the *Hipper*
     in 1940.

## GLOXINIA

Atlantic 1940−4
Malta Convoys 1941
Spartivento 1940
Libya 1941−2
Mediterranean 1943
English Channel 1945
1    1940 corvette of 925 tons built by
     Harland & Wolff. Scrapped
     Purfleet in 1947.

## GOATHLAND

Atlantic 1943
English Channel 1943
North Sea 1944
Normandy 1944
Named after the hunt in Yorkshire.
1    1942 corvette of 1,087 tons. Mined
     at Normandy. CTL 1944. Scrapped
     at Troon in 1945.

## GODETIA

Atlantic 1940−3
Biscay 1943
North Sea 1944
Normandy 1944
English Channel 1945
*Per diem in die floreo* = From day to
day, I flourish.
1    1916 sloop of 1,250 tons built by
     Connell. Handed over to Ward,
     Milford Haven in 1937 as part-
     payment for the *Majestic*.
2    1940 corvette of 925 tons built by
     Smith's Dock. Lost in collision
     with ss *Marsa* north of Ireland.
3    1941 corvette of 925 tons built by
     Crown: Clark. Broken up in 1947 at
     Grays.

## GOODALL

Atlantic 1944
Arctic 1945
Named after Captain Samuel
Granston Goodall of the *Defiance*.
1    1943 frigate, ex-*DE.275*, 1,085 tons
     built by Boston. Torpedoed by *U-
     968* in 1945 in the Kola Inlet.

## GOODSON

Atlantic 1944
Normandy 1944
English Channel 1945
Named after Captain William
Goodson.
1    1943 frigate, ex-*DE.276*, 1,085 tons
     built by Boston. Torpedoed by *U-
     984* off Cherbourg. CTL 1944.
     Returned to USA 1946.

## GORE

Atlantic 1943−4
Normandy 1944
Named after Captain Sir John Gore of
the *Triton*.
1    1943 frigate, ex-*DE.277*, 1,085 tons
     built by Boston. Returned to USA
     1946.

## GORGON

Egypt 1801
Syria 1840
Baltic 1854−5
Belgian Coast 1918
Atlantic 1943
Normandy 1944
A monster in Greek mythology.
1    1785 5th rate. Sold in 1817.
2    1837 frigate. Broken up in 1865.
3    1871 turret ship. Sold in 1902.
4    1914 monitor of 5,700 tons built by
     Armstrong. Sold in 1928 for
     breaking up by Ward at Pembroke
     Dock.
5    1943 minesweeper of 890 tons built
     by the Savannah Machinery Co.
     Ex-*BAM 18*. Returned to USA 1946.

## GORLESTON

Atlantic 1941−3
Named after the coastguard station in
Suffolk.
1    1941 cutter, ex-USCG *Itasca*, 1,546
     tons built by GEC in 1929.
     Returned to USA 1946.

## GOSHAWK

Heligoland 1914
Dogger Bank 1915
Jutland 1916
1    1806 vessel.
4    1911 destroyer of *c.*800 tons built
     by Beardmore. Sold to Rees,
     Llanelly in 1921.
6    1940−7 RN Air Station at Trinidad.

## GOSSAMER

Dunkirk 1940
Atlantic 1940−1
Arctic 1941−2
North Sea 1942
1    1937 minesweeping sloop of the
     'Halcyon' class; 835 tons built by
     William Hamilton. Sunk by
     German aircraft in the Kola Inlet in
     1942.

## GOULD

Atlantic 1943−4
Named after Captain Davidge Gould of the *Audacious* at the Nile.
1  1943 frigate, ex-*DE.272*, 1,085 tons built by Boston. Torpedoed in 1944 by *U-358* north of the Azores.
2  1946 naval barracks in Ceylon.

## GRAFTON

Barfleur 1692
Vigo 1702
Gibraltar 1704
Velez Malaga 1704
Cape Passero 1718
Porto Novo 1759
Dardanelles 1915−16
Atlantic 1939
Dunkirk 1940
*Decus virtutis pretium* = Glory is the reward of valour.
Named after Captain Henry Fitzroy, Duke of Grafton. He commanded the first ship named after him.
1  1697 3rd rate. Surrendered in 1707.
3  1709 3rd rate. Scrapped in 1744.
4  1750 3rd rate. Sold in 1767.
5  1772 3rd rate. Scrapped 1816.
6  1892 cruiser. Sold in 1920.
7  1935 destroyer of 1,335 tons built by Thornycroft. Torpedoed at Dunkirk, 1940.
8  1954 anti-submarine frigate, Type 14, of 1,536 tons built by White. Disposal List 1974−5.

## GRAMPUS

Dardanelles 1915
*Grandis inter alios* = Great amongst others.
1  1731 sloop. Lost 1742.
2  and 4 were sloops of 1743 and 1747.
6  1795 5th rate which was wrecked in 1799.
8  1845 frigate, ex-*Tremendous*. Scrapped in 1897.
9  1913 destroyer of c.950 tons built by the Thames Iron Works. Ex-*Nautilus*. Last of the coal-burning class destroyers. Sold in 1920 for breaking up by Ward of Rainham.
10  1936 submarine of 1,520/2,157 tons built at Chatham. Sunk by Italian torpedo-boats *Clio* and *Circe* off Augusta in 1940.
11  1957 submarine of 1,600/2,030 tons built by Cammell Laird. Broken up in 1980.

## GRAPH

Biscay 1942
Arctic 1942−3
North Sea 1943
Her name is that given to the operation in progress at the time of her capture.
1  1941 submarine (U-boat *U-570*) of 769/871 tons built by Blöhm and Voss and captured in 1941. Given the number *P 715* and entered into Royal Naval service. Wrecked in 1944 off west coast of Islay.

## GRASSHOPPER

China 1860
Dardanelles 1915−16
1  1776 sloop. Renamed *Basilisk* in 1779.
6  1909 destroyer of c.950 tons built by Fairfield. Sold in 1921 to Fryer of Sunderland for breaking up.
8  1943−4 coastal forces base at Weymouth.

## GRAVELINES

Zeal rests not.
This is a translation of the French motto of Lord Howard, Lord High Admiral, *Désir n'a repos*.
The badge derives partly from the crest of Lord Howard.
The name commemorates a phase of the Armada campaign.
1  1944 destroyer of the 'Battle' class of 3,361 tons built by Cammell Laird. Scrapped at Rosyth in 1961.

## GREENWICH

Orfordness 1666
Solebay 1672
Schooneveld 1673
Texel 1673
Barfleur 1692
Marbella 1705
*Tempore utimur* = We use the opportunity.
1  1666 4th rate which was wrecked in 1744 when 80 years old.

2  1747 4th rate which surrendered in 1757.
3  1777 5th rate. Sold 1783.
4  1809 4th rate. Sold in 1836.
5  1915 depot ship for destroyers, 8,100 tons, built by Swan Hunter. Sold for mercantile service in 1947 as *Hembury*, 1947 and as *Navem Hembury*, 1955.

## GRENADE

Atlantic 1939
Norway 1940
Dunkirk 1940
*Semper paratus* = Always ready.
1  1914−18 vessel.
2  1935 destroyer of 1,335 tons built by Stephen. Sunk by air attacks at Dunkirk 1940.

## GRENVILLE

Atlantic 1939
English Channel 1943
Mediterranean 1943−4
Anzio 1944
Normandy 1944
Adriatic 1944
Okinawa 1945
*Deo patriae amicis* = For God, country and friends.
Badge is derived from the crest of Sir Richard Grenville, after whom the ships are named. *Revenge* claimed the motto, but conceded it to *Grenville* in 1922.
1  1763 vessel.
2  1916 flotilla leader of 1,687 tons built by Cammell Laird. Sold in 1931 to Rees, Lannelly.
3  1935 destroyer of 1,485 tons built by Yarrow. Mined in the North Sea in 1940.
4  1942 destroyer of 1,710 tons built by Swan Hunter. Broken up in 1983 by Queenborough.

## GREYHOUND

Armada 1588
Dover 1652
Kentish Knock 1652
Four Days' Battle 1666
Barfleur 1692
Martinique 1762
Egypt 1801
Belgian Coast 1915−18
Atlantic 1939
Norway 1940
Dunkirk 1940
Spartivento 1940
Matapan 1941
Crete 1941
Libya 1941

Malta Convoys 1941
Mediterranean 1941
*Certe ac celerite* = Sure and swift.
1  1545 vessel (45) which was wrecked in 1562.[42]
3  1636 6th rate which was blown up in action in 1656.
4  1657 prize expended as a fireship in 1666.
5, 8, 9, 10, and 12, were all 6th rates of 1672, 1713, 1719, 1741 and 1773, two of which were wrecked and one surrendered.
15  1783 5th rate which was wrecked in 1808.
19  1859 sloop.
20  1900 destroyer of *c*.400 tons built by Hawthorn Leslie. Sold in 1919 to Clarkson, Whitby for scrapping.
22  1935 destroyer of 1,335 tons built by Vickers Armstrong of Barrow. Sunk by aircraft off Morea in 1941.

## GRIFFIN

Armada 1588
Barfleur 1692
Vigo 1702
Velez Malaga 1704
Cape Passero 1718
Norway 1940
Mediterranean 1940–1
Matapan 1941
Greece 1941
Crete 1941
Libya 1941–2
Malta Convoys 1941–2
Atlantic 1942
English Channel 1943
*Unguibus ac rostro* = With claws and beak.
This fabled creature had the body of a lion and the wings of an eagle.
1  1588: merchant ship.[43]
2  1656 vessel.
5  1758 vessel (28) which was wrecked in 1760.
9  1816 sloop.
13  1896 destroyer with the name *Griffon*, *c*.400 tons, built by Laird Bros. Sold in 1920 to Castle of Plymouth.
17  1935 destroyer of 1,335 tons built by Vickers Armstrong of Barrow. Transferred to RCN in 1943 and renamed *Ottawa*. Sold in 1946.

## GRIMSBY

Greece 1941
Crete 1941
Libya 1941
*Praemia post ardua* = Rewards [come] after toil.
1  1914–18 vessel.
2  1933 sloop of 990 tons built at Devonport by White. Sunk by air attacks off Tobruk 1941.

## GRINDALL

Atlantic 1943–5
Named after Captain Richard Grindall of the *Prince* at Trafalgar.
1  1943 frigate ex-*DE.273*, 1,085 tons built by Boston. Returned to USA in 1945.

## GROVE

Atlantic 1942
Libya 1942
Arctic 1942
Named after a hunt in Nottinghamshire.
1  1941 destroyer of the 'Hunt' class, 1,050 tons built by Swan Hunter, Wallsend. Torpedoed by *U-77* off Sollum in 1942.

## GUARDIAN

Norway 1940
Sicily 1943
*Acer et vigilans* = Keen and watchful.[44]
1  1784 5th rate (44) of 896 tons, built by Robert Batson on the Thames. On the way to New South Wales in 1789 she struck an iceberg, and was then sold off at the Cape of Good Hope.
2  1932 netlayer[45] of 2,860 tons built at Chatham and Wallsend. Scrapped at Troon in 1962.
3  1983 date of acquisition and commissioning into RN. Built 1975 by Beverley Ship Yard, ex-*Seaforth Champion*. 802 tons gross. Employed on Falklands patrol duties.

## HADLEIGH CASTLE

Atlantic 1943–4
1  1943 corvette/frigate of 1,010 tons built by Smith's Dock. Scrapped at Sunderland in 1959.

## HALDON

Named after a hunt in Devonshire.
1  1916 minesweeper of 810 tons built by Dunlop Bremner. Sold in 1921 to Stanlee for scrapping.
2  1942 destroyer of the 'Hunt' class, 1,087 tons, built by Fairfield. Loaned to the Free French navy as *La Combattante* and sunk in 1945 by a midget submarine in the North Sea.

## HALLADALE

Burma 1945
1  1944 frigate of 1,370 tons built by Inglis: Parsons. Sold for mercantile service in 1949: *Norden*, 1962 and *Turist Expressen*, 1962.

## HALSTED

Normandy 1944
English Channel 1944
North Sea 1944
Named after Captain Lawrence William Halstead of the *Namur*.
1  1943 frigate, ex-*Reynolds*, ex-*DE.19*, of 1,300 tons built by Bethlehem: Hingham. CTL 1944. Cannibalized for spares. Scrapped in Holland 1947.

## HAMBLEDON

North Sea 1941–4
English Channel 1943
Sicily 1943
Salerno 1943
Aegean 1943
Mediterranean 1944
Normandy 1944
Named after a hunt in Hampshire.
1  1917 minesweeper of 750 tons built by Fleming & Ferguson. Sold in 1922 to Stanlees for scrapping.
2  1939 destroyer of the 'Hunt' class, 907 tons built by Swan Hunter of

---

42  No. 2 *Greyhound* was in the Armada campaign, but was not awarded the honour.

43  Two merchant ships named *Griffin* are recorded as having accompanied the fleet against the Armada.

44  There is also *Vigilante salus* = Safety by watching.

45  Nets and Booms: light net defence systems are termed 'nets': heavyweight systems which are more permanent are termed 'booms'.

Wallsend. Hulked in 1955 and scrapped in 1957.

## HAMPSHIRE

Gabbard 1653
Santa Cruz 1657
Lowestoft 1665
Orfordness 1666
Schooneveld 1673
Texel 1673
Jutland 1916
*Aelfred mec heht gewyrcan* = Alfred had me made.
1   1653 4th rate. Sunk in action in 1697.
2   1698 4th rate. Scrapped in 1739.
3   1741 4th rate. Scrapped in 1766.
4   1903 cruiser of 10,850 tons built by Armstrong. Sunk by mine off the Orkneys in 1916. Kitchener was drowned in the tragedy.
6   1960 guided-missile destroyer of 5,440/6,200 tons built by John Brown at Clydebank. Sold for scrapping 1976.

## HANDY

1   1856 vessel.
4   1895 destroyer. Sold for scrapping to Hong Kong in 1916.
5   1939 destroyer, ex-Brazilian *Jurua*, 1,340 tons built by Vickers Armstrong, Barrow. Renamed *Harvester* in 1940.

## HANNIBAL

Portland 1653
Gabbard 1653
Scheveningen 1653
Baltic 1854
Crimea 1855
Named after the Carthaginian general.
1   1650 vessel.
2   1652 vessel (44).
3   1779 4th rate which surrendered in 1782.
5   1786 3rd rate which surrendered in 1801.
7   1810 3rd rate. Scrapped in 1834.
8   1854 2nd rate. Sold 1904.
9   1896 battleship of 14,900 tons built by Pembroke Dock Yard. Sold in 1920 to Yates and broken up in Italy.
10  1943−6 base at Algiers.

## HARDY

Crimea 1855
China 1860
Jutland 1916
Atlantic 1940
Narvik 1940
Arctic 1943−4
*Amicitia et virtute* = With friendship and valour.
Admiral Sir Masterman Hardy is commemorated in ships of this name laid down this century.
1   1797 vessel.
6   1895 destroyer. Sold in 1911.
7   1912 destroyer of *c*.1,000 tons built by Thornycroft. Sold in 1921 to Ward for scrapping at Briton Ferry.
8   1936 flotilla leader of 1,505 tons built by Cammell Laird. Sunk at Narvik in 1940.
9   1943 destroyer of 1,730 tons built at Clydebank. Torpedoed in 1944.
10  1953 frigate, Type 14, 1,180/1,536 tons built by Yarrow. Disposal List 1979−80.

## HARGOOD

Normandy 1944
Atlantic 1944
Named after Captain William Hargood of the *Belleisle* at Trafalgar.
1   1943 frigate, ex-*DE.583*, built by Bethlehem: Hingham. Returned to USA in 1946.

## HARRIER

Baltic 1855
New Zealand 1863−6
Arctic 1941−3
Normandy 1944
*Tenaciter sequor* = I follow tenaciously.
1,   2, 3, and 4 were all sloops of 1804, 1813, 1831 and 1854.
8   1934 minesweeper of 815 tons built by Thornycroft. Scrapped at Gateshead in 1950.
9   1948 training establishment.

## HART

Armada 1588
Atlantic 1944−5
English Channel 1944
Normandy 1944
Korea 1950−1
1   1546 vessel.
2   A coaster from Dartmouth accompanied the fleet at the Armada.
6   1796 sloop.
12  1895 destroyer. Sold in 1912.

14  1943 frigate of 1,350 tons built by Stephen. Sold to Federal German Republic and renamed *Scheer* in 1958.
15  1972 large patrol craft, 194 tons, built by James & Stone, Brightlingsea. ex-*Stirling*.

## HARTLAND

Atlantic 1941−2
English Channel 1942
North Africa 1942
Named after the coastguard station in Devon.
1   1941 cutter, ex-*Ponchartrain* of the US Coast Guard service. Built by Bethlehem in 1928. Salved after sinking at Oran in 1942 but then scuttled in 1949.

## HARTLAND POINT

1   1944 maintenance ship of 8,580/ 10,200 tons built by Barrard, Vancouver.

## HARVESTER

Dunkirk 1940
Atlantic 1940−3
1   1918 sloop of 1,320 tons built by Barclay Curle. Scrapped in 1922 by C.A. Beard.
2   1939 destroyer, ex-*Handy*. Torpedoed in N. Atlantic in 1943.
3   1939 destroyer, ex-Brazilian and ex-*Handy*, of 1,340 tons. Torpedoed in N Atlantic by *U-432* in 1943.

## HASTINGS

Syria 1840
Burma 1852
Baltic 1855
Atlantic 1940−3
Biscay 1943
*Qui vincit regnat* = Who conquers, rules.
1   1695 5th rate which was wrecked in 1698.
2   3 and 4 were all 5th rates of 1698, 1707, and 1740.
5   1819 3rd rate. Sold in 1886.
6   1930 sloop of 1,045 tons built at Devonport. Scrapped at Troon in 1946.
7   1961 frigate of 2,300/2,800 tons built by Yarrow at Scotstoun. Renamed *Dido*.

## HASTY

Atlantic 1939
Spada 1940
Norway 1940
Calabria 1940
Mediterranean 1940−1
Matapan 1941
Greece 1941
Crete 1941
Libya 1941−2
Sirte 1942
Malta Convoys 1941−2
*Certe ac celeriter* = Sure and swift.
1   1798 vessel.
3   1894 destroyer. Sold in 1912.
4   1936 destroyer of 1,335 tons built
    by Denny. With a very
    distinguished WWII record.
    Torpedoed by the German
    destroyer *S-55* in the
    Mediterranean in 1942.

## HAVANT

Atlantic 1940
Dunkirk 1940
1   1919 minesweeper of 800 tons built
    by Eltringham. Sold in 1922 to
    Siam.
2   1939 destroyer, ex-Brazilian *Javary*,
    1,340 tons built by White. Sunk by
    German aircraft in 1940.

## HAVELOCK

Dardanelles 1915−16
Norway 1940
Atlantic 1940−5
Biscay 1943
English Channel 1944
Normandy 1944
Named after Maj. General Sir Henry
Havelock (1795−1857).
1   1915 monitor of 6,150 tons built by
    Harland & Wolff in Belfast. Sold in
    1927 to Ward, Preston for breaking
    up.
2   1939 destroyer, ex-Brazilian *Jutahy*,
    of 1,340 tons built by White.
    Broken up in 1946 at Inverkeithing.

## HAVOCK

Baltic 1855
China 1860
Atlantic 1939
Narvik 1940
Norway 1940
Spada 1940
Mediterranean 1940−1
Matapan 1941
Greece 1941
Crete 1941
Libya 1941−2

Malta Convoys 1941−2
Sirte 1942
*Fiat justitia ruat coelum* = Let justice be
done though the heavens fall in ruins.
1   1796 Dutch prize, *Harvik*. Wrecked
    in 1800.
5   1893 destroyer. Sold in 1911. (The
    first TBD.)
6   1935 destroyer of 1,340 tons built
    by Denny. Wrecked in 1942 off
    Keliba.

## HAWK

Barfleur 1692
Vigo 1702
The earliest names were after the bird;
No. 16 and later ships probably took
the name of Lord Hawke (1705−81).
1   1593 vessel from Bristol.
2   1655 vessel.
5   6, 7, 9, 12 and 14 were all sloops
    of 1721, 1740, 1758, 1793, 1803
    and 1806.
16  1820 3rd rate. Sold about 1866.
20  1891 cruiser of 7,350 tons built by
    Chatham Dock Yard. Torpedoed
    in the North Sea in 1914 by *U-9*.
22  1945 cruiser of 8,800 tons built by
    Portsmouth Dock Yard.
    Cancelled 1946.
23  1946 Upper Yardsmen's College
    at Exbury.

## HAWKINS

Armada 1588
Normandy 1944
*Nil desperandum* = Never despair.
The badge derives from the crest of Sir
John Hawkins (1532−95).
1   1588: *Bark Hawkyns* was a merchant
    ship with the fleet.
2   1917 cruiser of 9,800 tons built at
    Chatham. Broken up in 1948.

## HAYDON

Sicily 1943
Salerno 1943
Aegean 1943

South France 1944
North Sea 1945
Named after the hunt in
Northumberland.
1   1942 destroyer of the 'Hunt' class,
    1,087 tons built by Vickers
    Armstrong, Tyne. Broken up
    Dunston 1958.

## HAZARD

Armada 1588
Martinique 1809
Guadeloupe 1810
Syria 1840
China 1839−42
New Zealand 1845−7
Belgian Coast 1914
Arctic 1941−2
Sicily 1943
Atlantic 1943−4
*Iacta est alea* = The die is cast.
1   1588 coaster of Feversham
    accompanied the fleet.
2   1711 sloop. Wrecked three years
    later.
3   and 4 were sloops of 1744 and
    1749.
5   1756 prize. Sold in 1759.
10  1937 minesweeper of 835 tons.
    Broken up in 1949 at Grays.

## HEARTSEASE

Armada 1588
Gabbard 1653
Atlantic 1940−1
1   1588: a merchant ship.
2   1652 prize (36). Sold in 1656.
3   1940 corvette, ex-*Pansy*, of 925 tons
    built by Harland & Wolff. USS
    *Courage* in 1942. Sold in 1946 for
    mercantile service till lost at sea in
    1958.

## HEATHER

Atlantic 1940−5
Arctic 1943
Normandy 1944
English Channel 1944−5
1   1916 sloop of 1,250 tons built by
    Greenoch & Grangemouth. Sold in
    1932 for scrapping at Plymouth.
2   1940 corvette of 925 tons built by
    Harland & Wolff. Scrapped at
    Grays in 1947.

## HEBE

St Lucia 1796
Egypt 1801
Dunkirk 1940
Arctic 1941−2

Malta Convoys 1942
Sicily 1943
*En attendant* = In attendance.
1   1798 prize (40) which was renamed *Blonde* in 1804.
3   1804 5th rate. Sold in 1813.
5   1826 5th rate. Broken up in 1873.
7   1936 minesweeper of 835 tons built at Devonport. Mined in 1943 off Bari.
8   1962 (commissioning date) store carrier of 2,740/3,173 tons built by Henry Robb of Leith for the British India Steam Navigation Co. 1973 purchased by P. and O. S.N.Co, but remaining on charter to the MOD (N).

# HECATE

Java 1811
Falkland Islands 1982
1   1797 vessel.
3   1839 sloop.
4   1871 turret ship. Sold in 1902.
6   1965 survey ship of 1,915/2,733 tons built by Yarrow at Scotstoun. First RN ship to be designed with an oceanographic and hydrographic role.

# HECLA

Copenhagen 1801
Algiers 1816
Baltic 1854
Alexandria 1882
*De fumo in flammam* = From smoke to flame.
1   1798 vessel.
3   1839 sloop. Sold in 1863.
4   1878 torpedo depot ship. Sold in 1926.
7   1940 depot ship for destroyers, 10,850 tons, built at Clydebank. Torpedoed by *U-515* west of Gibraltar in 1942.
8   1965 survey ship of 1,915/2,733 tons.

# HEDINGHAM CASTLE

1   1944 corvette/frigate ex-*Gorey Castle* of 1,010 tons built by Crown: Clark. Scrapped Granton 1958.

# HELFORD

1   1943 frigate of 1,370 tons built by Hall Russell at Yarrow. Scrapped at Troon in 1956.
2   1984 minesweeper of 890 tons built by Richards Ltd.

# HELIOTROPE

Dardanelles 1915−16
Atlantic 1940−2
*Surgens ad solem* = Rising to the sun.
1   1915 sloop of 1,200 tons built by Lobnitz. Sold in 1935 to Metal Industries of Charlestown.
2   1940 corvette of 925 tons built by Crown: NE Marine. Became USS *Surprise* in 1942. Sold for mercantile use and believed transferred to Communist China.

# HELMSDALE

Atlantic 1943−4
1   1943 frigate of 1,370 tons built by Inglis: Parsons. Scrapped at Faslane in 1957.
2   1985 minesweeper of 890 tons built by Richards Ltd at Lowestoft.

# HEPATICA

Atlantic 1940−5
1   1940 corvette of 925 tons, Canadian-built. Sold in 1948.

# HERALD

China 1841
I proclaim fame.
1   1919 sloop of the '24' class built by Blyth SB & DD Co, ex-*Merry Hampton*, converted to survey ship 1923. Scuttled at Seletar 1942. Salved by Japanese and renamed *Heiyo*. Mined in Java Sea 1944.
2   1973 ocean-going survey ship of 2,000/2,945 tons.

# HERCULES

Armada 1588
Cadiz 1596
Quiberon Bay 1759
The Saintes 1782
Jutland 1916
The badge derives from Greek mythology and the first labour of Hercules, which was to slay a ferocious lion.
1   1588: a City of London merchant ship accompanied the fleet at the Armada battle.
3   1759 3rd rate of 1,608 tons. Sold in 1784.
4   1798 3rd rate prize of 1,878 tons. Broken up at Portsmouth in 1810.
5   1815 3rd rate (74) of 1,750 tons built at Chatham. Receiving ship at Hong Kong c.1855. Sold to the colony ten years later.
7   1868 central battery ship of 5,234 tons. Floating battery at Gibraltar in 1906. Renamed *Calcutta* in 1909.
8   1910 battleship of 20,000 tons built by Palmer at Jarrow. Sold in 1921 to Slough Trading Co. for breaking up in Germany.
13  1945 aircraft carrier of 14,000 tons built by Vickers Armstrong, Tyne: construction suspended until 1957, when completed by Harland & Wolff. Sold to India in 1957, and renamed *Vikrant*.

# HEREWARD

Atlantic 1940
Calabria 1940
Spartivento 1940
Libya 1940
Malta Convoys 1941
Mediterranean 1940−1
Matapan 1941
Greece 1941
Crete 1941
*Vigila et ora* = Watch and pray.
Named after Hereward the Wake.
1   1936 destroyer of 1,340 tons built by Vickers Armstrong, Tyne. Torpedoed by Italian aircraft off Crete, 1941.

## HERMES

Burma 1852
Atlantic 1940
Falkland Islands 1982
*Altiora peto* = I seek higher things.
Badge of the head of Hermes (or
Mercury), the messenger of the gods.
1   1796 sloop (14) of 201 tons prize,
    *Mercurius*. In the following year
    she foundered at sea with the loss
    of all hands.
2   1798 6th rate of 331 tons. Sold in
    1802.
3   1803 purchase date of sloop (16)
    of 339 tons, built in 1801 and sold
    in 1810.
4   1811 6th rate (20) 512 tons built at
    Portsmouth. Disabled and
    grounded at Mobile, USA; was
    destroyed by her crew, 1814.
6   1835 sloop (6) 830 tons. Sold in
    1864 for breaking up.
7   1866 3rd rate of 1,726 tons was
    built in 1816 as *Minotaur*. Became
    cholera hospital ship in 1866 at
    Gravesend. Scrapped at
    Sheerness 1869.
8   1898 cruiser of 5,600 tons built by
    Fairfield. Torpedoed in 1914 by
    *U-27*.
9   1919 aircraft carrier of 10,850 tons
    built by Armstrong. Sunk by
    Japanese aircraft off Trincomalee
    in 1942.
10  1953 aircraft carrier,[46] ex-*Elephant*,
    23,900/28,700 tons built by
    Vickers Armstrong at Barrow.
    Strike carrier, commando carrier
    and in 1974 Anti-submarine/
    VSTOL carrier. Flagship of
    Falklands Task Force 1982.
    Disposal List 1982–3. Sold to
    India 1986.

## HERMIONE

*Bismarck* Action 1941
Mediterranean 1941
Malta Convoys 1941–2

Diego Suarez 1942
Named after the beautiful daughter of
Menelaus and Helen.
1   1782 5th rate. Taken by mutineers
    to La Guayra in 1797. Recovered in
    1799 and renamed *Retaliation*, and
    then in 1800 *Retribution*.
2   1893 cruiser of 4,360 tons built at
    Devonport Dock Yard. Sold and
    became training ship *Warspite*.
    Broken up by Ward at Grays in
    1940.
3   1939 cruiser of 5,450 tons built by
    Stephen. Torpedoed in 1942 by
    *U-205* off Sollum.
4   1967 anti-submarine general-
    purpose frigate of 2,500/2,962 tons
    built by Stephen of Glasgow.
    'Leander' class armed with Exocet
    missiles.

## HERO

Quiberon Bay 1759
Belleisle 1761
Sadras 1782
Providien 1782
Negapatam 1782
Trincomalee 1782
Bay of Biscay 1805
Basque Roads 1809
Narvik 1940
Norway 1940
Calabria 1940
Spada 1940
Greece 1941
Crete 1941
Mediterranean 1941
Libya 1941–2
Malta Convoys 1941–2
Sirte 1942
*Fortes adjuvat fortuna* = Fortune
favours the brave.
1   1759 3rd rate. Renamed *Rochester*
    about forty years later.
2   1793 3rd rate prize but destroyed
    in the same year.
3   and 5 were both 3rd rates of 1803
    and 1815.
6   1858 screw ship. Sold about 1870.
7   1885 turret ship. Sold in 1907.
10  1936 destroyer of 1,340 tons built
    by Vickers Armstrong, Tyne.
    Transferred to RCN in 1943 and
    renamed *Chaudière*. Sold for
    disposal 1946.

## HEROINE

Egypt 1801
Normandy 1944
1   1783 5th rate. Sold in 1806.
2   1807 ex-*Venus*. Sold in 1828.

4   1881 corvette. Sold early in 1900s.
5   1940 trawler, ex-*Hero*, 217 tons,
    built in 1907, requisitioned in 1940
    and returned in 1944.

## HERON

Algiers 1816
Atlantic 1940
1   1804 sloop, ex-*Jason*. Renamed
    *Volcano* and became a bombship in
    1810. Sold 1816.
2   1812 brig-sloop (18), ex-*Rattlesnake*.
    Built by King at Upnow. Scrapped
    in 1831.
3   1847 brig (16) built at Chatham and
    foundered 1859 off West Africa.
7   1937 sloop of 1,200 tons, built by
    Denny Bros and renamed
    *Auckland*. Sunk 1941 by Italian
    aircraft off Tobruk.
9   RN Air Station at Yeovilton. The
    HQ of Naval Air Command and its
    FO since FAA fighter training
    began here in 1940. Base of RN Air
    Commander helicopter and Sea
    Harrier Force.

## HESPERUS

Norway 1940
Atlantic 1940–5
English Channel 1945
Named after the evening star.
1   1939 destroyer ex-*Hearty*, ex-
    Brazilian *Juruena*, of 1,400 tons
    built by Thornycroft. Scrapped in
    1947.

## HEYTHROP

Atlantic 1941
Libya 1941–2
Malta Convoys 1941–2
Named after a hunt in Oxfordshire.
1   1917 minesweeper of 750 tons built
    by Fleming & Ferguson. Sold in
    1922 to Stanlee for scrapping.
2   1940 destroyer of the 'Hunt' class,

---

46   ASW  Commando  Carrier.

1,050 tons built by Swan Hunter of Wallsend. Torpedoed in 1942 by *U-652* off Sollum.

# HIBISCUS

Atlantic 1940−2
1  1917 sloop of 1,250 tons built by Greenock & Grangemouth. Sold in 1923 by Metal Industries of Charlestown.
2  1940 corvette of 925 tons built by Harland & Wolff. Became USS *Spry* in 1942. Sold for mercantile service about 1947 and scrapped in Hong Kong in 1957.

# HIGHFLYER

Crimea 1854−5
China 1856−60
The utmost for the highest.
1  1801 vessel.
3  1851 frigate which was sold about twenty years later.
4  1898 cruiser of 5,650 tons built by Fairfield. Sold in 1921 to Bombay.
5  1943 base at Trincomalee.

# HIGHLANDER

Norway 1940
Atlantic 1940−5
1  1855 vessel.
4  1939 destroyer, ex-Brazilian *Jaguaribe* of 1,340 tons, built by Thornycroft. Sold in 1947 for scrapping at Rosyth.

# HIND

Quebec 1759
Navarino 1827
Baltic 1855
Heligoland 1914
Normandy 1944
1  1545 vessel (28). Sold ten years later.
6  7 and 8 were all 6th rates of 1709, 1709 (a prize) and 1711, all three of which were wrecked.
9  1744 sloop which foundered in 1747.
10  1749 6th rate. Sold in 1784.
11  1785 6th rate which was scrapped in 1811.
14  1814 sloop, ex-*Barbadoes*.
19  1911 destroyer of *c.*800 tons built by John Brown. Broken up at Preston in 1924.
20  1943 sloop of 1,350 tons built by Denny. Scrapped Dunston 1958.

# HOGUE

Baltic 1854−5
Heligoland 1914
Named after the second phase of the battle of Barfleur, 1692. The badge derives from the arms of Admiral Sir George Rooke.
1  1811 3rd rate of 1,750 tons. Converted to a screw ship of 1,846 tons and 60 guns. Scrapped in 1865.
2  1900 cruiser of 12,000 tons built by Vickers at Barrow. She was sunk, together with cruisers *Aboukir* and *Cressy*, off the Dutch coast in 1914 by the single U−boat *U-9*.
3  1944 destroyer of the 'Battle' class of 3,361 tons built by Cammell Laird and sold in 1962 to Singapore.

# HOLCOMBE

Sicily 1943
Salerno 1943
Mediterranean 1943
Named after a hunt in Lancashire.
1  1942 destroyer of the 'Hunt' class, 1,087 tons built by Stephen. Torpedoed in 1943 by *U-593* off Bougie.

# HOLDERNESS

North Sea 1942−5
Named after a hunt in Yorkshire.
1  1779 vessel.
2  1916 minesweeper of 750 tons built by Henderson. Sold to Ward in 1924 for scrapping.
3  1940 destroyer of the 'Hunt' class, 907 tons built by Swan Hunter of Wallsend. Scrapped at Preston in 1956.

# HOLLYHOCK

Atlantic 1940−1
1  1915 sloop of 1,200 tons built by

Barclay Curle. Sold in 1930 to Ward of Pembroke Dock.
2  1940 corvette of 925 tons built by Crown: NE Marine. Sunk by Japanese aircraft east of Ceylon.

# HOLMES

Normandy 1944
North Sea 1945
Atlantic 1944−5
English Channel 1944−5
Named after Sir Robert Holmes, naval commander of the Dutch wars.
1  1671 vessel (24) bought from Sir Robert Holmes.
2  1943 frigate, ex-*DE.572*, built by Bethlehem: Hingham. Returned to USA in 1945.

# HONESTY

Atlantic 1943
1  1942 corvette, ex-USS *Capria* of 980 tons built at Kingston. Returned to USA 1946.

# HONEYSUCKLE

Dardanelles 1915−16
Atlantic 1940−5
Arctic 1942−5
Sicily 1943
Normandy 1944
English Channel 1944
1  1915 sloop of 1,200 tons built by Lobnitz. Sold to Distinn in 1922 for scrapping.
2  1940 corvette of 925 tons built by Ferguson. Scrapped at Grays 1950.

# HOOD

*Bismarck* Action 1941
*Ventis secundis* = With the following winds.
The badge is derived from the crest, and the motto from the coat of arms of Admiral Viscount Hood (1724−1816).
1  1859 screw ship.

2 1891 battleship of 14,150 tons built
  at Chatham Dock Yard. Expended
  as a blockship in 1914 at the
  southern entrance to Portland
  harbour.
3 1918 battlecruiser of 42,100 tons
  built on Clydebank. Sunk in the
  *Bismarck* action, 1941.

## HORNET

China 1856–60
Dogger Bank 1915
*Noli irritare crabrones* = Don't tease
hornets.
1 3, 4 and 8 were all sloops of 1745,
  1776, 1794 and 1864.
11 1893 destroyer. Sold 1909.
12 1911 destroyer of *c*.800 tons built
  by John Brown. Sold in 1921 to
  Ward, Portishead.
13 1925–34 Coastal Forces base at
  Gosport.
14 1939–57 Coastal Forces base at
  Gosport.

## HOSTE

Atlantic 1944
Named after Admiral Sir William
Hoste (1780–1828).
1 1916 flotilla leader of 1,666 tons
  built by Cammell Laird. Lost in
  collision in the North Sea in 1916.
2 1943 frigate ex-*Mitchell*, ex-*DE.521*,
  built by Boston. Returned to USA
  in 1945.

## HOSTILE

Atlantic 1939–40
Narvik 1940
Norway 1940
Calabria 1940
*Vultus ad hostem* = Face the enemy.
1 1936 destroyer of 1,340 tons built
  by Scotts. Mined in 1940 off Cape
  Bon.

## HOTHAM

Normandy 1944
1 1944 frigate of the 'Captain' class,
  1,400 tons, ex-USS *Buckley* and ex-
  *DE-574*. Returned to USA 1946.
  Scrapped in Holland in 1956.

## HOTSPUR

Atlantic 1940–4
Narvik 1940
Spartivento 1940
Mediterranean 1940–1

Matapan 1941
Greece 1941
Crete 1941
Libya 1941–2
Normandy 1944
*Fortiter in re* = Bravely in action.
1 1810 frigate. Broken up ten years
  later.
2 1828 5th rate which was renamed
  *Monmouth* in 1868.
3 1870 turret ship. Sold in 1904.
4 1936 destroyer of 1,340 tons built
  by Scotts. Sold to Dominica and
  renamed *Trujillo* in 1948.

## HOUND

Gabbard 1653
Scheveningen 1653
Lowestoft 1665
Four Days' Battle 1666
Barfleur 1692
Arctic 1943–4
Normandy 1944
1 1652 prize (36). Condemned in
  1656.
6 7, 8, 9 and 10 were all sloops of
  1732, 1745, 1776, 1790 and 1796.
16 1942 minesweeper of the
  'Algerine' class built by Lobnitz.
  Scrapped at Troon in 1962.

## HOWE

Arctic 1942–3
Sicily 1943
Okinawa 1945
*Utcunque placuerit deo* = God's will be
done.
Named after Admiral of the Fleet
Richard, Earl Howe (1726–99).
1 1791 vessel.
3 1815 1st rate. Scrapped in 1854.
4 1860 screw ship which was
  renamed *Bulwark* in 1885.
5 1885 battleship. sold in 1910.
6 1940 battleship, ex-*Beatty*, of 35,000
  tons built by Fairfield. Scrapped at
  Inverkeithing near Rosyth in 1958.

## HUNTER

Gabbard 1653
Scheveningen 1653
Barfleur 1692
Vigo 1702
Velez Malaga 1704
Louisburg 1758
Quebec 1759
Narvik 1940
Atlantic 1939–44
Salerno 1943
South France 1944
Aegean 1944
Burma 1945
Follow on.
1 1646 vessel.
5 1672 5th rate prize.
10 1796 sloop which was wrecked in
  1797.
15 1895 destroyer. Sold in 1912.
17 1936 destroyer of 1,340 tons built
  by Swan Hunter at Wallsend.
  Sunk at Narvik in 1940.
18 1942 escort carrier, ex-*Trailer*, ex-
  *Mormacpenn*, of 11,420 tons built
  by Ingall's SB Corporation.
  Returned to USA in 1945.
19 1947 Landing Ship. Transferred to
  Ministry of Transport about ten
  years later.
20 *c*.1983 coastal training craft of 34
  tons for RNR training.

## HURRICANE

Atlantic 1940–3
Biscay 1943
1 1918 vessel.
2 1939 destroyer, ex-Brazilian
  *Japarva*. Built by Vickers
  Armstrong of Barrow. Torpedoed
  by *U-415* north of the Azores, 1943.

## HURSLEY

Mediterranean 1942–3
Sicily 1943
Aegean 1943
Named after the hunt in Hampshire.
1 1941 destroyer of the 'Hunt' class,
  1,050 tons built by Swan Hunter.

Transferred to Greece and renamed *Kriti*, 1943. Scrapped in Greece in 1960.

## HURST CASTLE

Atlantic 1944
1 1944 corvette/frigate of 1,010 tons built by Thornycroft. Torpedoed in 1944 north-west of Ireland by *U-482*.

## HURWORTH

Atlantic 1941
Libya 1942
Sirte 1942
Mediterranean 1942
Malta Convoys 1942
Sicily 1943
Aegean 1943
Named after the hunt in Durham.
1 1941 destroyer of the 'Hunt' class, 1,050 tons built by Vickers Armstrong, Tyne. Mined in 1943 east of Kalymnos.
2 1985 (commissioning date) minehunter of 615/725 tons built by Vosper. A 'Hunt' class MCMV.

## HUSSAR

Java 1811
Dardanelles 1915–16
North Africa 1942
Arctic 1941–4
Atlantic 1943
Normandy 1944
*Raison* 1795
Forward. The first word of Tennyson's poem 'Balaclava.'
1 2, 5 and 6 were all sloops of 1757, 1763, 1784 and 1799.
7 1807 5th rate was accidentally destroyed by fire in 1861.
9 1934 minesweeper of 815 tons built by Thornycroft. Sunk in error by friendly aircraft off France.

## HYACINTH

China 1841–2
Spartivento 1940
Greece 1941
Malta Convoys 1941
Libya 1941–2
Mediterranean 1941–3
Sicily 1943
1 1692 prize vessel.
2 1806 sloop. Sold in 1820.
4 1881 corvette. Sold in 1902.
5 1898 cruiser of 5,650 tons built by London & Glasgow. Sold in 1923 to Cohen of Swansea.
7 1940 corvette of 925 tons built by Harland & Wolff. Transferred to Greece and renamed *Apostolis* in 1943. Scrapped at Grays in 1950.

## HYDERABAD

Atlantic 1941–5
North Sea 1942
Arctic 1942–3
Barents Sea 1942
English Channel 1943
Sicily 1943
1 1917 Q ship of 595 tons built by Thornycroft. Specially designed as a Q ship. Sold in 1920.
2 1941 corvette, ex-*Nettle* of 925 tons, built by Hall. Renamed as a compliment to the Nizam, who had been generous to the British war effort. Broken up in 1948.

## HYDRA

Syria 1840
Dogger Bank 1915
Jutland 1916
North Sea 1943
Arctic 1943–4
Normandy 1944
Falkland Islands 1982
Like Hercules, persevere.
The nine-headed serpent that was slain by Hercules.
1 1778 6th rate. Sold in 1783.
2 1797 5th rate. Sold in 1820.
4 1871 turret ship. Sold in 1902.
5 1912 destroyer of *c*.800 tons built by John Brown. Sold in 1921 to Ward of Rainham and broken up in the following year.
7 1942 minesweeper of 850 tons built by Lobnitz. CTL 1944. Scrapped Grays 1947.
8 1965 survey ship built by Yarrow at Blythswood, 1,915/2,733 tons.

## HYDRANGEA

Atlantic 1941–4
English Channel 1945
1 1916 sloop of 1,250 tons built by Connell. Sold 1920 to Hong Kong.
2 1940 corvette of 925 tons built by Ferguson. Sold for mercantile service 1948. Lost in 1957.

## HYPERION

Atlantic 1939
Calabria 1940
Spada 1940
Libya 1940
Mediterranean 1940
*Fulget virtus in arduis* = Virtue shines in difficulties.
One of the Titans. The sun god before Apollo.
1 1807 5th rate. Scrapped in 1833.
2 1936 destroyer of 1,340 tons built by Swan Hunter of Wallsend. Sunk by Italian submarine *Serpente* off Pantellaria in 1940.

## IBIS

Atlantic 1941–2
North Africa 1942
Normandy 1944
1 1914–18 vessel.
3 1939 sloop of 1,250 tons built by Richardson, Westgarth. Sunk by air attack in 1942.

## ICARUS

North Sea 1939
Atlantic 1939–44
Narvik 1940
Norway 1940–1
Dunkirk 1940
*Bismarck* Action 1941
Arctic 1941–3
Malta Convoys 1942
Normandy 1944
English Channel 1945
*Bene est tentare* = It is as well to try.
Named after the son of Daedalus.
1 1814 sloop. Sold in 1861.
2 1858 sloop. Sold in 1875.
5 1936 destroyer of 1,370 tons built by Clydebank. Scrapped at Troon in 1947.

## ILEX

Atlantic 1939
Calabria 1940
Spada 1940
Mediterranean 1940–3
Crete 1941

Matapan 1941
Malta Convoys 1941
Sicily 1943
Salerno 1943
*Frangas non flectes* = You may break
but will not bend.
1  1937 destroyer of 1,370 tons built at
   Clydebank. Broken up in Italy in
   1948 after a distinguished WWII
   record.

# ILLUSTRIOUS

Genoa 1795
Basque Roads 1809
Java 1811
Taranto 1940
Mediterranean 1940−1
Malta Convoys 1941
Diego Suarez 1942
Salerno 1943
Sabang 1944
Palembang 1945
Okinawa 1945
1  1789 3rd rate (74) of 1,616 tons built
   at Buckler's Hard. Suffered great
   damage in Hotham's Action, taken
   in tow but broke loose in a gale,
   ran aground and was wrecked,
   1795.
2  1803 3rd rate (74) of 1,746 tons built
   on the Thames. She became a
   training ship at Portsmouth and
   then attached to *Excellent* before
   being broken up in 1868.
3  1896 battleship of 14,900 tons built
   by Chatham Dock Yard. Sold in
   1920 to Ward of Barrow for
   breaking up.
4  1939 aircraft carrier of 23,000 tons
   built by Vickers Armstrong,
   Barrow. Scrapped at Faslane in
   1956.
5  1978 anti submarine warfare carrier
   of 16,000/19,600 tons built by Swan
   Hunter at Wallsend.
   Commissioned in 1985.

# IMOGEN (Imogene)

Atlantic 1939
North Sea 1940
Quit you like men.
Named after the daughter of
Cymbeline.
1  1801 vessel.
3  1831 6th rate. Accidentally
   destroyed by fire in 1840.
6  1936 destroyer of 1,370 tons built
   by Hawthorn Leslie. Sunk in
   collision with *Glasgow* off
   Duncansby Head in 1940.

# IMPERIAL

Atlantic 1939
Norway 1940
Mediterranean 1941
Crete 1941
*Deum cole Regum serva* = Worship
God, serve the King.
1  1936 destroyer of 1,370 tons built
   by Hawthorn Leslie. Bombed off
   Crete in 1941 and scuttled the next
   day.

# IMPLACABLE

Syria 1840
Dardanelles 1915
Norway 1944
Japan 1945
*Sevolod 1808*
*Saeva parens saeviorum* = Fierce parent
of a fiercer offspring.
1  1805 3rd rate (74) prize, *Duguay-
   Trouin*, captured by Strachan after
   Trafalgar and added to the Navy
   1806. Renamed *Lion* in 1855.
   Reverted to *Implacable* just before
   WWI and eventually sunk in 1949.
2  1899 battleship of 15,000 tons built
   by Devonport Dock Yard. Sold to
   the Slough TC for breaking up in
   Germany.
4  1942 aircraft carrier of 26,000 tons
   built by Fairfield. Broken up in
   1955 at Inverkeithing.

# IMPREGNABLE

Glorious First of June 1794
Algiers 1816
1  1786 2nd rate which was wrecked
   in 1799.
2  1810 2nd rate which was renamed
   *Kent* in 1889.
3  1887 ex-*Bulwark*, ex-*Howe*. Sold in
   1929.
4  1947−8 training establishment at
   Devonport.

# IMPULSIVE

Norway 1940
Dunkirk 1940
Arctic 1941−4
Atlantic 1942−3
Normandy 1944
English Channel 1944
*Cor unum, via una* = One heart, one
way.
1  1937 destroyer of 1,370 tons built
   by White. Sold in 1946 for breaking
   up in Sunderland.

# INCONSTANT

Genoa 1795
Egypt 1801
Jutland 1916
Diego Suarez 1942
Arctic 1942−4
Sicily 1943
Atlantic 1943−4
Normandy 1944
English Channel 1944
In constancy, constant.
1  1778 prize frigate. Renamed
   *Convert* about 1782.
2  and 3 were 5th rates of 1783 and
   1836.
4  1868 frigate which became part of
   the *Defiance*
5  1914 cruiser of 3,500 tons built by
   Beardmore. Sold to Cashmore in
   1922 for breaking up.
6  1941 destroyer of 1,360 tons built
   by Vickers Armstrong of Barrow.
   Transferred to Turkey and
   renamed *Mauvenet* in 1946.

# INDEFATIGABLE

Basque Roads 1809
Jutland 1916
Palembang 1945
Okinawa 1945
Japan 1945
*Virginie* 1796
*Droits de l'Homme* 1797
*Deo adjuvante* = With God's help.
The badge derives from the arms of
Admiral Pellew.
1  1783 3rd rate (64) of 1,384 tons built
   by Adams of Buckler's Hard. In
   1794 she was reduced to a frigate
   (38). Commanded by Captain Sir
   Edward Pellew. Scrapped in 1816.
2  1806 French frigate *Infatigable*
   taken.
3  1848 3rd rate (50) of 2,047 tons.
   Sold in 1914.
4  1891 cruiser of 3,500 tons.
   Renamed *Melpomene* in 1910.

5  1909 battlecruiser of 18,800 tons
   built by Devonport Dock Yard.
   Sunk at Jutland in 1916.
6  1942 aircraft carrier of 26,000 tons
   built on Clydebank. Scrapped in
   1956 by Dalmuir and at Troon (hull
   only).

# INDOMITABLE

Dogger Bank 1915
Jutland 1916
Malta Convoys 1942
Diego Suarez 1942
Sicily 1943
Palembang 1945
Okinawa 1945
1  1907 battlecruiser of 17,200 tons
   built by Fairfield. Sold in 1921 for
   scrapping by Stanlee.
3  1940 aircraft carrier of 23,000 tons
   built by Vickers Armstrong of

Barrow. Scrapped at Faslane in
1955.

# INGLEFIELD

Atlantic 1939−43
North Sea 1940
Norway 1940−2
*Bismarck* Action 1941
Malta Convoys 1942
Arctic 1942−3
Sicily 1943
Salerno 1943
Mediterranean 1944
Anzio 1944
The sun my compass.
Named after Admiral Sir Edward
Inglefield (1820−94).
1  1936 flotilla leader of 1,530 tons
   built by Cammell Laird. Sunk by
   glider bomb at Anzio in 1944.

# INGLIS

Atlantic 1944−5
Normandy 1944
Named after Captain John Inglis of the
*Belliqueux*.
1  1943 frigate, ex-*DE.525*, 1,085 tons
   built by Boston. Returned to USA
   in 1946.

HMS INDOMITABLE (No. 1)

## INMAN

Atlantic 1944–5
Named after Captain Henry Inman of the *Désirée* and *Triumph*.

1   1943 frigate, ex-*DE.526*, 1,085 tons built by Boston. Returned to USA 1946.

## INTREPID

Lagos 1759
Quiberon Bay 1759
Havana 1762
St Kitts 1782
Martinique 1794
Zeebrugge 1918
Atlantic 1939–41
Dunkirk 1941
Norway 1941–2
*Bismarck* Action 1941
Arctic 1941–3
Malta Convoys 1942
Sicily 1943
Salerno 1943
Aegean 1943
Falkland Islands 1982
*Cela va sans dire* = That goes without saying.

1   1747 3rd rate prize. Scrapped in 1765.
2   1770 3rd rate. Scrapped in 1828.
6   1891 cruiser. Sunk as a blockship at Zeebrugge in 1918.
7   1936 destroyer of 1,370 tons built by White. Sunk by German aircraft off Leros in 1943.
8   1964 assault ship of 11,000/12,150 tons[47] built by John Brown. Disposal list 1982–3.

## INVER

Atlantic 1943–5

1   1942 frigate of *c.*1,420 tons built by Canadian Vickers. Returned to USA 1945.

## INVINCIBLE

St Vincent 1780
St Kitts 1782
Glorious First of June 1794

HMS INVINCIBLE (No. 6)

47   16,950 tons with the dock flooded.

Alexandria 1882
Heligoland 1914
Falklands 1914
Jutland 1916
Falkland Islands 1982
1   1747 3rd rate prize. Wrecked in
    1758.
2   1765 3rd rate which was wrecked
    in 1801.
3   1808 3rd rate. Scrapped in 1861.
4   1907 ironclad which was renamed
    *Erebus* about 1905.
5   1907 battlecruiser of 17,250 tons
    built by Armstrong. Sunk at
    Jutland in 1916.
6   1977 ASW carrier of 16,000/19600
    tons built by Vickers at Barrow.
    Sale to Australia prevented by
    Falklands war, 1982. Paid off for 2-
    year refit in 1986.

## IRON DUKE

Jutland 1916
*Virtutis fortuna comes* = Fortune is the
companion of valour.
Named after the Duke of Wellington.
1   1870 ironclad. Sold in 1906.
2   1912 battleship of 25,000 tons built
    by Portsmouth Dock Yard.
    Admiral Jellicoe's flagship at
    Jutland. She became a gunnery
    ship in 1931 and a depot ship in
    1936. Sold in 1946 and broken up
    by Metal Industries of Rosyth.

## ISIS

St Lucia 1778
Sadras 1782
Providien 1782
Trincomalee 1782
Negapatam 1782
Camperdown 1797
Copenhagen 1801
Atlantic 1939−43
Norway 1940
Greece 1941
Crete 1941
Mediterranean 1941−3
Sicily 1943
Normandy 1944
*Quod est manet* = That which is,
remains.
Egyptian goddess; the wife of Osiris.
1   1743 vessel.
2   3 and 4 were 4th rates of 1747 (a
    prize), 1774 and 1819.
5   1896 cruiser of 5,600 tons built by
    London & Glasgow. Sold in 1920
    for scrapping by Granton SB Co.
7   1936 destroyer of 1,370 tons built
    by Yarrow. Mined or torpedoed off
    Normandy in 1944.

## ITCHEN

Atlantic 1943
1   1903 destroyer *c*.550 tons built by
    Laird Bros. Torpedoed in the
    North Sea by *U-99* in 1917.
3   1942 frigate of 1,370 tons built by
    Fleming & Ferguson. Torpedoed in
    1943 by *U-260* in the N. Atlantic.
4   1961−7 'Avon' class RPL of 100
    tons built by White: Saunders Roe.

## ITHURIEL

Atlantic 1942
Malta Convoys 1942
North Africa 1942
*Hasta sequente* = With following spear.
Named after one of the angels.
1   1916 flotilla leader of 1,666 tons
    built by Cammell Laird. Sold in
    1921 for breaking up in Germany.
2   1942 destroyer, ex-Turkish *Gayret*,
    1,360 tons built by Vickers
    Armstrong, Barrow. Severely
    damaged by German bombs in
    1942 off Bone. Scrapped in 1945.

## IVANHOE

Atlantic 1939
Norway 1940
Dunkirk 1940
*Primus inter pares* = First among
equals.
Named after the hero of one of Sir
Walter Scott's novels.
1   1914−18 vessel.
2   1937 destroyer of 1,370 tons built
    by Yarrow. Mined off the Texel in
    1940.

## JACKAL

Heligoland 1914
Dogger Bank 1915
Atlantic 1939−41
Norway 1940
English Channel 1940
Crete 1941
Mediterranean 1941
Libya 1941−2
1   1779 vessel whose crew mutinied
    and took her into Brest.
6   1911 destroyer of *c*.800 tons built
    by Hawthorn Leslie. Sold in 1920
    to J.Smith.
7   1938 destroyer of 1,690 tons built
    on Clydebank. Damaged by air
    attack in the Mediterranean and
    later scuttled, 1942.

## JAGUAR

Dunkirk 1940
Atlantic 1940
Spartivento 1940
Matapan 1941
Crete 1941
Mediterranean 1941
Libya 1941−2
Malta Convoys 1941−2
They shall not pass.
1   1938 destroyer of 1,690 tons built
    by Denny. Torpedoed and sunk by
    *U-652* north of Sollum in 1942.
2   1957 frigate of *c*.2,500 tons built by
    Denny. Sold to Bangladesh in
    1978.

## JAMAICA

Copenhagen 1801
Arctic 1942−4
North Africa 1942
Barents Sea 1942
North Cape 1943
Korea 1950
*Non sibi sed patriae* = Not for oneself
but for one's country.
1   1710 sloop which was wrecked in
    1715.
2   1744 sloop which was lost at
    Jamaica in 1770.
3   1779 sloop.
4   1796 6th rate prize. Sold in 1814.
6   1940 cruiser of 8,000 tons built by
    Vickers Armstrong. Scrapped
    Dalmuir 1960 and Troon (hull only)
    in 1962.

## JANUS

Baltic 1854
China 1856−60
Atlantic 1939
Norway 1940
Calabria 1940
Libya 1940
Mediterranean 1940−4
Matapan 1941
Sfax 1941
Crete 1941
Malta Convoys 1941
Adriatic 1944
1   1778 5th rate which was renamed
    *Dromedary* in 1788.
2   1796 5th rate prize. Sold in 1811.
3   1844 sloop. Sold in 1856.
5   1895 destroyer. Sold in 1912.
8   1938 destroyer of 1,690 tons built
    by Swan Hunter at Wallsend.
    Torpedoed by German aircraft at
    Anzio in 1944.

## JASMINE

Atlantic 1941–2
Diego Suarez 1942
1. 1940 corvette of 925 tons built by Ferguson. Scrapped in 1948.

## JASON

Atlantic 1940
North Sea 1941–2
Arctic 1943
Normandy 1944
Name is taken from Greek mythology. Jason led the Argonauts in the quest of the Golden Fleece.
1. 1673 vessel.
2. 1747 5th rate prize. Sold in 1763.
3. 4, 5 and 6 were all 5th rates of 1763, 1794 (wrecked), 1800 (wrecked) and 1804.
8. 1859 corvette. Scrapped in 1877.
12. 1937 minesweeper of 835 tons built by Ailsa: Thornycroft. Sold in 1946 for mercantile service. Scrapped at Grays in 1950.

## JAVELIN

Norway 1940
Dunkirk 1940
Atlantic 1940
Diego Suarez 1942
Arctic 1942
Mediterranean 1942–3
Normandy 1944
English Channel 1944
*Vi et armis* = By force of arms.
1. 1913 vessel.
2. 1938 destroyer, ex-*Kashmir*, of 1,690 tons built on Clydebank. Scrapped at Troon in 1949.

## JED

Dardanelles 1915–16
Atlantic 1943–4
Burma 1945
1. 1903 destroyer *c*.550 tons built by Thornycroft. Sold to Teignmouth in 1920.
2. 1942 frigate of 1,370 tons built by Hill: Bellis & Morcom. Scrapped at Milford Haven in 1957.

## JERSEY

Santa Cruz 1657
Lowestoft 1665
Orfordness 1666
Lagos 1759
Mediterranean 1941
*Garde* = Guard.
1. 1654 4th rate which surrendered in 1691.
2. 1694 6th rate which was renamed in 1698.
4. 1736 4th rate. Sunk and abandoned at New York during the evacuation 1783.
6. 1938 destroyer of 1,690 tons built by White. Mined off Malta in 1941.
7. 1976 (commissioning date) OPV of 'Island' class, 925/1,260 tons, built by Hall Russell.

## JERVIS

Mediterranean 1940–1
Matapan 1941
Libya 1940–2
Sfax 1941
Crete 1941
Malta Convoys 1941–2
Sirte 1942
Sicily 1943
Salerno 1943
Aegean 1943
Anzio 1944
Adriatic 1944
Normandy 1944
Named after Admiral of the Fleet John Jervis, Earl St Vincent (1735–1823).
1. 1938 flotilla leader of 1,695 tons built by Hawthorn Leslie. Scrapped in 1949.

## JEWEL

Armada 1588
1. 1588: a City of London merchant ship accompanied the fleet at the Armada battle.
2. 1809 prize (40).
3. 1944 minesweeper of the 'Algerine' class built by Harland & Wolff. Bought for the Belgian navy in 1949 and renamed *Adrien de Gerlache*. Hulked in 1959. Scrapped in 1966–7.

## JONQUIL

Dardanelles 1915
Atlantic 1941–5
Malta Convoys 1942
North Africa 1942
1. 1915 sloop of 1,200 tons built by Connell. Sold to Portugal and renamed *Carvalho Araujo* in 1920.
2. 1940 corvette of 925 tons built by Fleming & Ferguson. Sold in 1946 for mercantile services. Lost in 1955.

## JUNO

Louisburg 1758
Atlantic 1939
Calabria 1940
Libya 1940
Matapan 1941
Mediterranean 1940–1
Crete 1941
Malta Convoys 1941
Name is taken from Roman mythology. The goddess Juno was the wife of Jupiter.
1. 1757 5th rate which was burnt and abandoned at Rhode Island in 1778.
2. 3 and 4 were all 5th rates of 1780, 1809 (she later surrendered) and 1810.
5. 1844 6th rate was renamed *Atalanta* in 1878.
7. 1895 cruiser of 5,600 tons built by Vickers. Sold in 1920 to Earle & Co: resold for breaking up in Denmark.
8. 1938 destroyer, ex-*Jamaica*, of 1,690 tons built by Fairfield. Sunk by air attack during the battle for Crete 1941.
9. 1965 anti-submarine general purpose frigate of 2,450/2,860 tons built by Thornycroft. Converted to training ship in 1985.

## JUPITER

Cape of Good Hope 1795
China 1839–42
Belgian Coast 1915–16
Mediterranean 1941
Malaya 1942
Named after the Roman supreme god of heaven and earth.
1. 1778 4th rate which was wrecked in 1808.
2. 1813 4th rate. Scrapped in 1870.
3. *c*.1863 vessel, ex-*Forth*. She became a coal hulk.
4. 1895 battleship of 14,900 tons built by Thomson. Sold to Hughes Bolckow for scrapping in 1920.
6. 1938 destroyer of 1,690 tons built by Yarrow. Torpedoed and sunk

by a Japanese destroyer in the battle of the Java Sea, 1942.

7  1950 Reserve fleet in the Gareloch.
8  1967 frigate of 2,500/2,962 tons built by Yarrow at Scotstoun. 'Leander' class armed with Exocet missiles.

## JUTLAND

Named after Sir John Jellicoe's victory over the German High Seas Fleet.
1  1945 destroyer of 2,315 tons built by Hawthorn Leslie but cancelled. Hull scrapped at Rosyth in 1957.
2  1946 destroyer, ex-*Malplaquet*, 2,400 tons built by Stephen. Scrapped at Blyth in 1965.

## KALE

Atlantic 1943
1  1904 destroyer of *c*.550 tons built by Hawthorn Leslie. Mined and sunk in the North Sea in 1918.
2  1942 frigate of 1,370 tons built by Inglis: Hawthorn Leslie. Scrapped at Newport 1957.

## KANDAHAR

Greece 1941
Crete 1941
Libya 1941
Mediterranean 1941
Malta Convoys 1941
Commemorates the relief of Kandahar in 1880.
1  1939 destroyer of 1,690 tons built by Denny. Mined in 1941 off Tripoli and sunk by RN the following day.

## KASHMIR

North Sea 1939
Crete 1941
Mediterranean 1941
1  1939 destroyer, ex-*Javelin*, of 1,690 tons built by Thornycroft. Sunk by

German aircraft during battle for Crete.

## KEATS

Normandy 1944
Atlantic 1944−5
Named after Captain Sir Richard Keats of the *Superb*.
1  1943 frigate, ex-*DE.278*, built by Boston, 1,085 tons. Returned to USA in 1946.

## KEITH

Atlantic 1939−40
Dunkirk 1940
*Fatis fortior virtus* = Valour is stronger than fate.
Named after Admiral George Keith Elphinstone, Lord Keith (1746−1823).
1  1930 flotilla leader of 1,400 tons built by Vickers Armstrong at Barrow. Sunk by air attacks at Dunkirk in 1940.

## KELLY

Atlantic 1939
Norway 1940
Crete 1941
Mediterranean 1941
Named after Admiral Sir John D. Kelly.
1  1938 flotilla leader of 1,695 tons built by Hawthorn Leslie. Commanded by Lord Mountbatten as Captain (D) 5th DF. Sunk by German air attacks during the battle for Crete in 1941.

## KELVIN

Atlantic 1940
Spartivento 1940
Crete 1941
Mediterranean 1941−3
Sirte 1942
Malta Convoys 1942
Normandy 1944
Aegean 1944
Named after Lord Kelvin, inventor of navigational equipment.
1  1914−18 vessel.
2  1939 destroyer of 1,690 tons built by Fairfield. Scrapped at Troon in 1949.

## KEMPENFELT

Jutland 1916
Atlantic 1939
Anzio 1944

Normandy 1944
Okinawa 1945
*Fideliter* = Faithfully.
Named after Admiral Richard Kempenfelt (1718−82).
1  1915 flotilla leader of 1,604 tons built by Cammell Laird. Sold in 1921 for scrapping by Ward, Morecambe.
2  1931 flotilla leader of 1,390 tons built by White. Transferred to RCN and renamed *Assinboine* in 1939. Wrecked on Prince Edward Island in 1945.
3  1943 destroyer, ex-*Valentine*, of 1,730 tons built on Clydebank. Sold to Yugoslavia in 1956/7 and renamed *Kotor*.

## KEMPTHORNE

Atlantic 1944−5
Named after Captain Sir John Kempthorne (1620−79) of the *Mary Rose*.
1  1943 frigate, ex-*DE.279*, built by Boston. Returned to USA in 1945.

## KENILWORTH CASTLE

Atlantic 1944
North Sea 1945
1  1943 corvette/frigate of 1,010 tons built by Smith's Dock. Scrapped at Llanelly in 1959.

## KENT

Porto Farina 1655
Lowestoft 1665
Orfordness 1666
Barfleur 1692
Vigo 1702
Velez Malaga 1704
Cape Passero 1718
Finisterre II 1747
Egypt 1801
Falklands 1914
Atlantic 1940
Mediterranean 1940
Arctic 1942−3
Normandy 1944
*Invicta* = Unconquered.
1  1652 vessel (40) which was wrecked in 1672.
2  4, 5 and 6 were all 3rd rates of 1679, 1746, 1762 and 1798.
8  1888 ex-*Impregnable* but three years later renamed *Caledonia*.
9  1901 cruiser of 9,800 tons built by Portsmouth Dock Yard. Sold to Hong Kong in 1920.
10 1926 cruiser of 9,850 tons built at Chatham by Hawthorn Leslie. Scrapped at Troon in 1948.

11 1961 guided-missile destroyer of 5,440/6,200 tons built by Harland & Wolff, Belfast. Disposal List 1980–1. Alongside training ship 1980. Accommodation ship 1984–5.

## KENYA

Atlantic 1941
*Bismarck* Action 1941
Malta Convoys 1941–2
Arctic 1941–2
Norway 1941
Sabang 1944
Burma 1944–5
Korea 1950–1
1 1939 cruiser of 8,000 tons built by Stephen. Scrapped at Faslane in 1962.

## KEPPEL

Atlantic 1940–3
Malta Convoys 1942
Arctic 1942–5
Normandy 1944
English Channel 1944
*Ne cede malis* = Yield not to misfortune.
Named after Admiral Augustus Keppel, Viscount Keppel (1725–86).
1 *c.*1779 vessel.
2 1920 flotilla leader of 1,480 tons built by Thornycroft. Sold in 1945 for scrapping at Barrow.
3 1954 anti-submarine frigate, Type 14, 1,536 tons, built by Yarrow. Broken up Sittingbourne, 1979.

## KHEDIVE

Aegean 1943
South France 1944
Burma 1945
Taken from the title of a ruler of Egypt.
1 1943 escort carrier, ex-USS *Cordova*, 11,420 tons built by Seattle-Tacoma. Returned to USA in 1946, to mercantile service.

## KIMBERLEY

Narvik 1940
Norway 1940
Greece 1941
Crete 1941
Malta Convoys 1941
Libya 1941–2

Aegean 1944
Adriatic 1944
1 1914–18 more than one small vessel bore the name.
2 1939 destroyer of 1,690 tons built by Thornycroft. Scrapped at Troon in 1949.

## KING ALFRED

Named after Alfred the Great (*c.*849–901).
1 1901 cruiser of 14,100 tons built by Vickers. Sold to Holland in 1921.
2 1939 officer's training establishment at Hove, Transferred to Exbury in 1945. Paid off in 1946.

## KINGCUP

Atlantic 1941–5
North Sea 1944
English Channel 1944–5
Normandy 1944
1 1940 corvette of 925 tons built by Harland & Wolff. Unclear whether she was sold for mercantile service or for scrapping in Holland.

## KINGFISHER

San Domingo 1806
Dunkirk 1940
Sardinia 1681[48]
Swift and sure.
1 *c.*1664, a hired ship.
2 1675 sloop. Sold in 1727 for scrapping.
4 5, 6, 7 and 11 were all sloops of 1745, 1770 (burnt at Rhode Island), 1782, 1804 and 1879.
13 1935 sloop of 510 tons built by Fairfield. Broken up at Thornaby in 1947.
14 1953 ex-*King Salvor*, submarine rescue vessel.

15 1975 OPV of the 'Bird' class, 194 tons, built by R. Dunston, Hessle.

## KING GEORGE V

Jutland 1916
Atlantic 1941
*Bismarck* Action 1941
Arctic 1942–3
Sicily 1943
Okinawa 1945
1 1762 small vessel.
7 1911 battleship of 23,000 tons built by Portsmouth Dock Yard. Sold to Alloa Shipbreaking Co, Rosyth, 1926.
9 1939 battleship of 35,000 tons built by Vickers Armstrong, Tyne. Scrapped in 1959 at Dalmuir and Troon (hull only).

## KINGSMILL

Normandy 1944
English Channel 1944
Walcheren 1944
Named after Captain Sir Robert Kingsmill (1730–1805).
1 1798 vessel.
2 1943 frigate, ex-*DE.280*, of 1,085 tons built by Boston. Returned to USA 1945.

## KINGSTON

Gibraltar 1704
Velez Malaga 1704
Louisburg 1758
Quiberon Bay 1759
Atlantic 1939
North Sea 1939
Greece 1941
Crete 1941
Libya 1941
Malta Convoys 1941–2
Sirte 1942
1 1697 4th rate. Sold in 1762.
2 1814 3rd rate (60). Sold in 1837.
4 1939 destroyer of 1,690 tons built by White. CTL 1942 after bombing attacks and was scrapped at Malta.

## KIPLING

Atlantic 1940
Norway 1940
Crete 1941
Mediterranean 1941
Malta Convoys 1941–2
Libya 1941–2

48 Single-ship action honour.

Sirte 1942
Named after Rudyard Kipling
(1865–1936).
1   1939 destroyer of 1,690 tons built
    by Yarrow. Bombed and sunk by
    German aircraft in Eastern
    Mediterranean in 1942.

## KITE

Biscay 1943
Atlantic 1943–4
Normandy 1944
Arctic 1944
*Milvus ad astra volat* = On kite's wings
to the stars.
1   1764 small vessel.
2   and 3 were both sloops of 1778
    and 1795.
11  1942 sloop of 1,350 tons built by
    Cammell Laird. Torpedoed and
    sunk by *U-344* in the Greenland
    Sea in 1944.

## KITTIWAKE

North Sea 1941–4
English Channel 1942
*Nunquam dormio* = I never sleep.
1   1936 sloop of 530 tons built by
    Thornycroft. Sold in 1946 for
    mercantile service.

## KNARESBOROUGH CASTLE

Atlantic 1944–5
1   1943 corvette/frigate of 1,010 tons
    built by White at Blyth. Scrapped
    in 1956 at Port Glasgow.

## LABUAN

English Channel 1945
1   1943 frigate, ex-*Gold Coast*, of 1,318
    tons built by Kaiser Walsh.
    Returned to USA in 1946.

## LAERTES

Heligoland 1914
Dogger Bank 1915
Named after the father of Ulysses.
1   1913 destroyer, ex-*Sarpedon*,
    *c*.1,000 tons built by Swan Hunter.
    Sold in 1921 for scrapping.
2   1944 minesweeper of the 'Algerine'
    class built by Redfern. Scrapped at
    Barrow in 1959.

## LAFOREY

Heligoland 1914
Dogger Bank 1915
Dardanelles 1915–16
Malta Convoys 1941–2
Atlantic 1942
Diego Suarez 1942
Sicily 1943
Salerno 1943
Mediterranean 1943–4
Anzio 1944
*Fero facem* = I bear the torch.
Named after Captain Sir Francis
Laforey (1767–1835) of the *Spartiate* at
Trafalgar.
1   1913 destroyer, ex-*Florizel, c*.970
    tons built by Fairfield. Sunk by an
    RN mine in the Channel in 1917.
2   1940 destroyer of 1,935 tons built
    by Yarrow. Torpedoed and sunk
    by *U-223* in 1944 off Sicily.

## LAGAN

Atlantic 1943
1   1942 frigate of 1,370 tons built by
    Smith's Dock. Torpedoed by *U-260*
    in 1943 in the N Atlantic. The same
    U-boat sank HMS *Itchen*. CTL 1943.
    Scrapped at Troon in 1946.

## LAGOS

The name commemorates Admiral
Boscawen's victory in 1759.
1   1944 destroyer of the 'Battle' class
    of 3,361 tons built by Cammell
    Laird. Scrapped in 1967.

## LA MALOUINE

Atlantic 1940–3
Arctic 1942
1   1940 corvette originally intended
    for the French navy but taken over
    by the RN with the French name
    retained. 925 tons built by Smith's
    Dock. Scrapped at Gelleswick Bay
    in 1947.

## LAMERTON

Atlantic 1941–2
Arctic 1942
North Africa 1942–3
Sicily 1943
Salerno 1943
Mediterranean 1943
Aegean 1943
Adriatic 1944
Named after a hunt in Devonshire.
1   1940 destroyer of the 'Hunt' class,
    of 1,050 tons built by Swan Hunter
    of Wallsend. Transferred to the
    RIN and renamed *Gomati*, 1953.

## LANCASTER

Louisburg 1758
Camperdown 1797
Atlantic 1941
Arctic 1942
North Sea 1943–5
1   1694 3rd rate. Scrapped in 1773.
2   1797 3rd rate. Sold in 1832.
4   1902 cruiser of 9,800 tons built by
    Armstrong. Sold in 1920 to Ward
    for breaking up at Preston.
5   1940 destroyer, ex-USS *Philip*, of
    1,090 tons built by Bath Iron Works
    in 1918. Acquired in 1940 and sold
    for scrap at Blyth in 1947.

## LANCASTER CASTLE

Arctic 1945
1   1944 corvette/frigate of 1,010 tons
    built by Fleming & Ferguson.
    Scrapped at Gateshead in 1960.

## LANCE

Heligoland 1914
Belgian Coast 1917
Mediterranean 1941
Malta Convoys 1941–2
1   1914 destroyer, ex-*Daring*, of *c*.994
    tons built by Thornycroft. Sold in
    1921 to Granton for scrapping.
2   1940 destroyer of 1,920 tons built
    by Yarrow. Bombed at Malta. CTL
    1942 and broken up at Grays in
    1944.

## LANDGUARD

Atlantic 1941–3
North Africa 1942
Biscay 1943
Named after the coastguard station in
Suffolk.
1   1940 cutter, ex-*Shushone*, built by
    GEC in 1930, 1,546 tons. Scrapped
    in Colombo 1949–50.

## LANDRAIL

Heligoland 1914
Dogger Bank 1915
Jutland 1916.
1  1806 vessel.
5  1914 destroyer, ex-*Hotspur*, of *c*.980
   tons built by Yarrow. Sold in 1921
   for scrapping by Stanlee.
6  1940 RN Air Station at Strabane.


## LAPWING

Heligoland 1914
Belgian Coast 1914
Dogger Bank 1915
Jutland 1916
Normandy 1944
North Sea 1944
Arctic 1944−5
1  1764 vessel.
2  1785 6th rate. Scrapped 1828.
9  1911 destroyer of *c*.800 tons built
   by Cammell Laird. Sold for
   scrapping in 1921 to Barking Ship
   Breaking Co.
11 1943 sloop of 1,350 tons built by
   Scotts. Torpedoed in 1945 off Kola
   Inlet.


## LARGO BAY

1  1944 frigate of 1,580 tons built by
   Pickersgill: Clark, ex-*Loch Fionn*.
   Scrapped at Inverkeithing *c*.1960.


## LARK

Armada 1588
Velez Malaga 1704
Marbella 1705
Baltic 1855
Heligoland 1914
Dogger Bank 1915
Normandy 1944
English Channel 1944
North Sea 1944
Arctic 1944−5
1  1588: a merchant ship
   accompanied the fleet in the
   Armada campaign.
2  1656 vessel.
3  1698 6th rate was sold in this year.
4  5 and 6 were all 5th rates of 1703,
   1744 and 1762 (burnt to avoid
   capture).
7  and 8 were sloops of 1780 and
   1794.
13 1893 training ship, ex-*Cruiser*.
   Sold in 1912.
14 1913 destroyer, ex-*Haughty* of
   *c*.980 tons. Sold in 1923 for
   scrapping by Hayes at Porthcawl.
15 1943 sloop of 1,350 tons built by
   Scotts. CTL when torpedoed by

*U-968* off Kola Inlet in 1945.
Beached at Murmansk. Stripped
and handed over to the Russians,
who renamed her *Neptun*.
Scrapped 1956.


## LARKSPUR

Atlantic 1941
1  1915 sloop of 1,200 tons built by
   Napier & Miller. Sold in 1920 for
   scrapping by Ward at
   Inverkeithing.
2  1940 corvette of 925 tons built by
   Fleming & Ferguson. USS *Fury* in
   1942. Sold for mercantile service in
   1946 and scrapped in Hong Kong
   in 1953.


## LARNE

Burma 1824−5
China 1841
Aegean 1944
Normandy 1944
South France 1944
1  1814 sloop. Sold in 1828.
2  1832 ex-*Lightning*. Scrapped in
   1866.
3  1910 destroyer of *c*.750 tons built
   by Thornycroft. Sold in 1921 for
   scrapping the following year.
4  1943 minesweeper of 850 tons built
   by Lobnitz. Sold to Italy for
   mercantile service from 1946 till at
   least 1951.


## LAUDERDALE

Atlantic 1942
North Sea 1942
Sicily 1943
Mediterranean 1943
South France 1944
Adriatic 1944
Named after the hunt in Berwickshire.
1  1941 destroyer of the 'Hunt' class
   1,050 tons built by Thornycroft.
   Transferred to Greece in 1946 and
   renamed *Aigaion*. Scrapped in
   1960.


## LAUNCESTON CASTLE

Atlantic 1944
1  1943 corvette/frigate of 1,010 tons
   built by White at Blyth. Scrapped
   at St David's-on-Forth in 1959.


## LAVENDER

Atlantic 1941−5
Normandy 1944

English Channel 1944
1  1915 sloop of 1,200 tons built by
   McMillan. Torpedoed in 1917 by
   *UC-75* in the Channel.
2  1940 corvette/frigate of 925 tons
   built by Hall. Sold for mercantile
   service in 1948.


## LAWFORD

Heligoland 1914
Dogger Bank 1915
Dardanelles 1915−16
Normandy 1944
Named after Captain John Lawford of
the *Polyphemus* at Copenhagen.
1  1913 destroyer, ex-*Ivanhoe*, of
   *c*.1,000 tons built by Fairfield. Sold
   in 1922 for breaking up at
   Porthcawl.
2  1943 frigate, ex-*DE.516*, of 1,085
   tons built by Boston. Sunk by
   German aircraft off Normandy,
   1944.


## LAWSON

Atlantic 1944
Normandy 1944
Named after Sir John Lawson, who
commanded the *Fairfax* in the First
Dutch War.
1  1943 frigate, ex-*DE.518*, of 1,085
   tons, built by Boston. Returned to
   USA in 1946.


## LEAMINGTON

Atlantic 1941−3
Arctic 1942
1  1918 minesweeper, ex-*Aldeburgh*
   built by Ailsa Shipbuilding Co.
   Sold in 1928 to Pembroke Dock for
   scrapping.
2  1940 destroyer ex-*Twiggs* from
   USA, built by New York
   Shipbuilding Co in 1919. 1,090
   tons. RCN 1942−3. Russia
   1944−50 with the name of *Zhguchi*.
   Scrapped at Newport 1951.

# LEANDER

Nile 1798
Algiers 1816
Crimea 1854–5
Kula Gulf 1943
*Qui patitur vincit* = Who suffers,
conquers.
The name is taken from Greek
mythology: Leander was the lover of
Hero. He swam the Hellespont each
night to visit her, but was drowned.
1   1780 4th rate with a remarkable
    history: surrendered in 1798.
    Recaptured by the Russians and
    Turks in 1799 in Corfu and
    restored to the RN by the Empress
    of Russia. Renamed in 1813 and
    sold four years later.
3   and 4 were both 4th rates of 1813
    and 1848.
5   1882 cruiser. Sold for scrapping in
    1920.
6   1931 cruiser of 7,270 tons built at
    Devonport by Vickers Armstrong.
    Scrapped at Blyth in 1950.
7   1961 anti-submarine frigate, 1st
    rate, of 2,450/2,860 tons built by
    Harland & Wolff. 'Leander' class
    armed with Ikara missiles. Paid off
    1986–7.

# LEDA

Egypt 1801
Cape of Good Hope 1806
Java 1811
Atlantic 1939–41
Dunkirk 1940
Arctic 1941–2
1   2, 3 and 4 were all 5th rates of 1783
    (foundered), 1800 (wrecked), 1809
    and 1828.
6   1937 minesweeper of 815 tons built
    by Devonport Dock Yard.
    Torpedoed in 1942.

# LEDBURY

Malta Convoys 1942
Arctic 1942–3
Sicily 1943
Salerno 1943
Adriatic 1944
Aegean 1944
Named after the hunts in
Herefordshire.
1   1941 destroyer of the 'Hunt' class,
    1,050 tons built by Thornycroft.
    Broken up at Rosyth in 1958.
2   1981 (commissioning date)
    minehunter of 615/725 tons built by
    Vosper. A 'Hunt' class MCMV.

# LEEDS

North Sea 1941–5
1   1940 destroyer, ex-USS *Conner* of
    1,020 tons. Built by Cramp in 1917.
    Scrapped at Grays in 1947.

# LEEDS CASTLE

Atlantic 1945
Falkland Islands 1982
1   1943 corvette/frigate of 1,010 tons
    built by Pickersgill: Clark.
    Scrapped at Grays in 1948.
2   1980 OPV of the 'Castle' class,
    1,427 tons built by Hall Russell of
    Aberdeen.

# LEGION

Heligoland 1914
Dogger Bank 1915
Cape Bon 1941
Norway 1941
Atlantic 1941
Mediterranean 1941
Malta Convoys 1941–2
Libya 1941–2
Sirte 1942
1   1914 destroyer, ex-*Viola*, of *c*.1,000
    tons built by Denny. Sold in 1921
    to Ward of New Holland.
2   1939 destroyer of 1,920 tons built
    by Hawthorn Leslie. Bombed by
    aircraft in Malta. CTL 1942.

# LEITH

Atlantic 1939–44
North Africa 1942
English Channel 1945
Persevere
1   1782 vessel.
3   1933 sloop of 900 tons built by
    White at Devonport. Sold in 1946
    for mercantile service. Scrapped in
    1955.

# LENOX (Lennox)

Barfleur 1692
Gibraltar 1704
Velez Malaga 1704
Cape Passero 1718
Heligoland 1914
Normandy 1944
Named after Charles Lennox, Duke of
Richmond and illegitimate son of
Charles II.
1   1678 3rd rate which became a
    breakwater at Sheerness in 1756.
2   1758 3rd rate. Scrapped in 1789.
3   1914 destroyer, ex-*Portia*, of *c*.1,000
    tons built by Beardmore. Sold to
    Barking Shipbreaking Co in 1921.
4   1943 minesweeper of the 'Algerine'
    class built by Lobnitz.

# LEONIDAS

Heligoland 1914
A king of Sparta; commander at
Thermopylae, 480 BC.
1   1807 5th rate. Sold in 1894.
2   1913 destroyer, ex-*Rob Roy*, of
    *c*.1,000 tons built by Palmer. Sold
    in 1921 for scrapping by Ward at
    Hayle.
3   1941–5 naval base at Takoradi.

# LEOPARD

Lowestoft 1665
Four Days' Battle 1666
Orfordness 1666
Solebay 1672
Texel 1673
Marbella 1705
Egypt 1801
Baltic 1854
Crimea 1855
1    1635 vessel (35). Surrendered
     1652.
2    1659 hulk, sunk as a foundation
     forty years later.
4    5, 6 and 7 were all 4th rates of
     1703, 1741, 1782 and 1790.
11   1897 destroyer of *c*.400 tons built
     by Vickers and sold in 1919 to J.
     Jackson for scrapping.
12   1940 destroyer, ex-French, of
     2,126/2,700 tons built in 1924 at St
     Nazaire. Manned by Free French
     crew.
13   1955 frigate of *c*.2,500 tons built
     by Portsmouth Dock Yard.
     Scrapped in 1978.

# LEWES

North Sea 1942
*Fidei tenax* = Hold the faith.
1   1664–7 vessel.

3 1940 destroyer, ex-USS *Conway*, ex-*Craven*, of 1,020 tons built in 1918 at Norfolk. Scuttled off Australia in 1946.

## LIBERTY

Martinique 1809
Heligoland 1914
Dogger Bank 1915
Jutland 1916
1 1649 vessel, ex-*Charles*, but wrecked the following year.
8 1913 destroyer, ex-*Rosalind*, of 1,034 tons built by Thornycroft. Sold in 1926 to King of Garston for scrapping.
12 1944 minesweeper of 850 tons built by Harland & Wolff. Hulked in 1959.

## LIDDESDALE

North Sea 1941−3
Atlantic 1943
Sicily 1943
Salerno 1943
South France 1944
Aegean 1944
Mediterranean 1944
Named after the hunt in Roxburgh.
1 1940 destroyer of the 'Hunt' class, 1,000 tons, built by Vickers Armstrong, Tyne. Sold in 1948 for scrapping at Gateshead.

## LIGHTFOOT

Belgian Coast 1916
Zeebrugge 1918
Atlantic 1943
Normandy 1944
1 1915 flotilla leader of 1,608 tons built by White. Sold in 1921 to Ward of New Holland.
2 1942 minesweeper, ex-USN built by Redfern, 850 tons. Sold to Greece in 1947 and renamed *Navamachos*.

## LIGHTNING

Barfleur 1692
Vigo 1702
Velez Malaga 1704
Louisburg 1758
Baltic 1854−5
Malta Convoys 1941−2
Diego Suarez 1942
1 1691 small vessel.
8 1877: the Navy's first torpedo boat. Sold in 1910.
9 1895 destroyer of 350 tons built by Palmer. Mined in 1915 in the North Sea.
10 1940 destroyer of 1,920 tons built by Hawthorn Leslie. Torpedoed by Italian MAS off Algeria in 1942.

## LIMBOURNE

North Sea 1943
English Channel 1942−3
*Famam extendere factis* = Judge us by our deeds.
Named after a hunt.
1 1942 destroyer of the 'Hunt' class, 1,087 tons built by Stephen. Sunk after damage by torpedo from German TBs off north coast of France in 1943.

## LINARIA

Atlantic 1943
1 1942 corvette, ex-USS *Clash*, 980 tons built by Midland. Returned to USA for mercantile use in 1946.

## LINCOLN

Atlantic 1941−3
North Sea 1942−4
*Loyauté n'a honte* = Loyalty knows no shame.
1 1695 vessel which foundered in 1703.
2 1940 destroyer, ex-USS *Yarnall*, built by Cramp in 1918, 1,090 tons. Given to Russia and renamed *Druzni* for cannibalizing the rest of the flotilla in 1944. Scrapped at Blyth in 1952.
3 1959 AA direction frigate of 2,330 tons built by Fairfield. Disposal List 1980−1.

HMS LION (No. 16)

## LION (Golden Lion)

Armada 1588
Cadiz 1596
Portland 1653
Gabbard 1653
Lowestoft 1665
Orfordness 1666
Schooneveld 1673
Texel 1673
Barfleur 1692
Finisterre 1747
Java 1811
Heligoland 1914
Dogger Bank 1915
Jutland 1916
*Santa Dorotea* 1798
*Guillaume Tell* 1800
*Concordant nomine facta* = The facts
agree with the name.
1   1511 vessel.
2   1536 vessel (50).
3   1549 Scottish prize. Lost.
4   1557 vessel. Scrapped in 1609.
5   1640 3rd rate.
7   1710 4th rate.
10  1777 3rd rate.
14  1847 2nd rate. Sold in 1905.
16  1910 battlecruiser of 26,350 tons
    built by Devonport Dock Yard.
    Beatty's flagship of the Grand
    Fleet's Battlecruiser Force. Sold in
    1924 to Hughes Bolckow of
    Jarrow.
17  1957 cruiser, ex-*Defence*.
    Originally launched in 1944 but
    work on her stopped in 1946.
    Restarted about 1955, with Scott
    responsible to hull stage, then
    Swan Hunter, Wallsend
    completing: 9,550/11,700 tons.
    Broken up at Inverkeithing in
    1975.

## LIVELY

St Vincent 1797
Atlantic 1941
Mediterranean 1941
Malta Convoys 1941−2
Sirte 1942
Libya 1942
*Mutine* 1797

*Tourterelle* 1795
1   1689 prize which surrendered in
    the same year.
2   1756 6th rate.
4   1756 sloop.
8   13 and 14 were all 5th rates of
    1794 (wrecked), 1804 (wrecked)
    and 1813 (became receiving hulk).
20  1901 destroyer of 400 tons built by
    Laird Bros. Sold to Castle of
    Plymouth in 1920.
22  1941 destroyer of 1,920 tons built
    by Cammell Laird. Bombed and
    sunk by German aircraft off
    Sollum in 1942.

## LIVERPOOL

Heligoland 1914
Mediterranean 1940
Calabria 1940
Arctic 1942
Malta Convoys 1942
*Deus nobis haec otia fecit* = God gave us
this ease.
1   1741 5th rate. Sold in 1756.
2   1758 6th rate which was wrecked
    in 1778.
3   and 6 were both frigates of 1813
    and 1860.
7   1909 cruiser of 4,800 tons built by
    Vickers and sold to the Slough
    Trading Co for breaking up in
    Germany in 1921.
8   1937 cruiser of 9,400 tons built by
    Fairfield. Scrapped in 1958.
9   1980 destroyer, Type 42 of 3,500/
    4,100 tons built by Cammell Laird.

## LIZARD

Orfordness 1666
Texel 1673
Quebec 1759
Martinique 1762
Havana 1762
Heligoland 1914
Belgian Coast 1914
Jutland 1916
1   1512 vessel.
4   5 and 7 were all 6th rates of 1694
    (wrecked), 1697 and 1757.

12  1911 destroyer of 810 tons built by
    Cammell Laird. Sold in 1921 to
    Rees of Llanelly.
13  1942−5 landing craft base at
    Shoreham.

## LLANDAFF

1   1955 AA direction frigate of 2,330
    tons built by Hawthorn Leslie.
    Sold to Bangladesh in 1976.

## LOBELIA

Atlantic 1941−4
1   1916 sloop of 1,250 tons built by
    Simons. Presented to
    Newfoundland in 1920 and hulked
    in 1924.
3   1941 corvette of 925 tons built by
    Hall. Manned by the Free French
    until 1947, when she was sold for
    mercantile service.

## *LOCH CLASS FRIGATES:*

All had a displacement of 1,435 tons
standard, 2,260 full load, but some
refitted and emerged 1,575/2,400 tons.

## LOCH ACHANALT

English Channel 1945
1   1945 frigate, ex-*Naver* built by
    Robb: Hall Russell. Sold to New
    Zealand in 1948 and renamed
    *Pukaki*. Sold to Hong Kong for
    scrapping in 1966.

## LOCH ACHRAY

Atlantic 1945
1   1944 frigate built by Smith's Dock.
    Sold to New Zealand in 1948 and
    renamed *Kaniere*. Scrapped in
    Hong Kong in 1967.

## LOCH ALVIE

Arctic 1944−5
English Channel 1945
1   1944 frigate built by Barclay Curle.
    Scrapped in Singapore in 1965.

## LOCH ARD

1   1944 frigate built by Harland &
    Wolff. Sold to South Africa and
    renamed *Transvaal*.

## LOCH ARKAIG

1   1945 frigate built by Caledon: BTH. Scrapped at Gateshead in 1960.

## LOCH BOISDALE

1   1944 frigate built by White at Blyth. Sold to South Africa in 1944 and renamed *Good Hope*.

## LOCH CARRON

1   1944 frigate, ex-*Gerrans Bay*. Later renamed *Surprise*. Scrapped in 1965.

## LOCH CRAGGIE

Atlantic 1945
1   1944 frigate built by Harland & Wolff. Scrapped at Lisbon in 1963.

## LOCH CREE

1   1944 frigate built by Swan Hunter. Sold to South Africa and renamed *Natal*.

## LOCH DUNVEGAN

Arctic 1944
North Sea 1945
1   1944 frigate built by Hill: Fletcher. Scrapped at Briton Ferry in 1960.

## LOCH ECK

Atlantic 1945
North Sea 1945
1   1944 frigate built by Smith's Dock. Sold to New Zealand in 1948 and renamed *Hawea*. Scrapped in Hong Kong in 1966.

## LOCH FADA

Normandy 1944
English Channel 1945
Atlantic 1945
1   1943 frigate built at Clydebank. Disposal List 1974−5.

## LOCH FYNE

Atlantic 1945
English Channel 1945
*Dion na mo marbhshruth* = I will leave safety in my wake.
1   1944 frigate built by Rowan,

Burntisland. Scrapped at Newport 1970.

## LOCH GLENDHU

1   1944 frigate built at Burntisland by Rowan. Scrapped Dunston 1957.

## LOCH GORM

1   1944 frigate built by Harland & Wolff. Sold in 1961.

## LOCH INSH

Atlantic 1944
Arctic 1945
1   1944 frigate built by Robb: Whites ME. Sold to Malaysia in 1964 and renamed *Hang Tuah*.

## LOCH KATRINE

1   1944 frigate built by Robb: Plenty. Sold to New Zealand in 1948 and renamed *Rotoiti*. Scrapped in Hong Kong 1967.

## LOCH KILLIN

Normandy 1944
Atlantic 1944
Biscay 1944
English Channel 1945
1   1943 frigate built by Rowan at Burntisland. Scrapped at Newport in 1960.

## LOCH KILLISPORT

1   1944 frigate built by Harland & Wolff. Sources dispute her fate: some say she was scrapped at Blyth in 1970, while Jane's includes her in the 1974−5 Disposal List.

## LOCH LOMOMD

*Si je puis* = If I can.
1   1944 frigate built by Caledon: Duncan Stewart. Scrapped at Faslane in 1968.

## LOCH MORE

Atlantic 1945
1   1944 frigate built by Caledon: Aitchison Blair. Broken up in 1963 at Inverkeithing.

## LOCH MORLICH

1   1944 frigate built by Swan Hunter. Sold to New Zealand in 1949 and renamed *Tutira*. Sold in 1961.

## LOCH QUOICH

Atlantic 1945
1   1944 frigate built by White at Blyth. Scrapped in 1957.

## LOCH RUTHVEN

English Channel 1945
Atlantic 1945
*Persto et presto* = I persevere and I excel.
1   1944 frigate built by Hill: Beliss & Morcam. Scrapped at Plymouth in 1966.

## LOCH SCAVAIG

Atlantic 1945
1   1944 frigate built by Hill: Beliss & Morcam. Scrapped at Genoa in 1959.

## LOCH SHIN

Norway 1940
Atlantic 1945
Arctic 1945
1   1944 frigate by Swan Hunter. Sold to New Zealand in 1948 and renamed *Taupo*. Sold in 1961.

## LOCH TARBERT

1   1944 frigate built by Ailsa Shipbuilding Co. Scrapped at Genoa in 1959.

## LOCH TRALAIG

1   1945 frigate built by Caledon: BTH. Scrapped in 1963.

## LOCH VEYATIE

1   1945 frigate built by Ailsa Shipbuilding Co. Scrapped Dalmuir 1965.

## LOCHINVAR

Belgian Coast 1916−17
1   1915 destroyer, ex-*Malice*, of 994 tons built by Beardmore. Sold in

1921 to Porthcawl for scrapping.
2  1939 training camp at Port Edgar
   which later became the Central
   Minesweeping School.

## LOCHY

Normandy 1944
1  1943 frigate of 1,370 tons built by
   Hall Russell. Scrapped at Troon in
   1956.

## LOCUST

Baltic 1855
Dunkirk 1940
Dieppe 1942
English Channel 1942−4
Normandy 1944
1  1801 vessel.
3  1896 destroyer of 400 tons built by
   Laird. Sold in 1919 to Castle of
   Plymouth for breaking up.
4  1939 gunboat of 585 tons built by
   Yarrow. In 1951 became the
   drillship of the Severn Division
   RNVR.

## LONDON

Kentish Knock 1652
Gabbard 1653
Scheveningen 1653
Lowestoft 1665
Solebay 1672
Schooneveld 1673
Texel 1673
Barfleur 1692
Chesapeake 1781
Groix 1795
Copenhagen 1801
Crimea 1854
Dardanelles 1915
Atlantic 1941
Arctic 1941−3
*Marengo* 1806
*Domine dirige nos* = God guide us.
1  1636 East Indiaman (40) supplied
   by the City of London.

2  1656 vessel (64) which blew up in
   1665.
3  1664−7 hired ship (50).
4  1666 ship (96) named *Loyal
   London*, burnt by the Dutch in the
   Medway in 1667.
5  1670 2nd rate (96) incorporating
   the remains of *Loyal London*.
   Scrapped in 1747.
8  1766 2nd rate. Scrapped in 1811.
9  1840 3rd rate. Scrapped in 1884.
10  1899 battleship of 15,000 tons
    built at Portsmouth Dock Yard.
    Finally sold to Slough TC for
    breaking up in Germany early
    1920s.
11  1927 cruiser of 9,850 tons built at
    Portsmouth by Fairfield. Broken
    up at Barrow in 1950.
13  1961 guided-missile destroyer of
    5,440/6,200 tons built by Swan
    Hunter at Wallsend. Sold to
    Pakistan in 1982.
14  1984 Type 22 frigate, ex-
    *Bloodhound*, of 4,100/4,800 tons
    built by Yarrow.

## LONDONDERRY

Atlantic 1939−45
North Sea 1940
North Africa 1942−3
Normandy 1944
English Channel 1944−5
*Non recedam* = No retreat.

HMS LONDON (No. 8)

1　1935 sloop of 990 tons built at Devonport by White. Scrapped at Llanelly in 1948.
2　1958 frigate of 2,800 tons built by White. Disposal List 1985−6.

## LOOKOUT

Heligoland 1914
Dogger Bank 1915
Diego Suarez 1942
Malta Convoys 1942
Arctic 1942
North Africa 1942−3
Sicily 1943
Salerno 1943
Mediterranean 1943−5
South France 1944
1　1914 destroyer, ex-*Dragon*, of *c*.980 tons built by Thornycroft. Scrapped in 1922 by Hayes at Porthcawl.
2　1940 destroyer of 1,920 tons built by Scotts. Scrapped at Newport in 1948.

## LOOSESTRIFE

Atlantic 1942−5
Normandy 1944
North Sea 1944
English Channel 1944−5
1　1941 corvette of 925 tons built by Hall Russell. Scrapped in 1962.

## LORING

Atlantic 1945
Named after Captain Sir John Loring of the *Niobe*.
1　1943 frigate, ex-*DE.520*, of 1,085 tons built by Boston. Returned to USA in 1947.

## LOSSIE

Atlantic 1943−4
1　1943 frigate of 1,420 tons built by Canadian Vickers. Returned to USA in 1946.

## LOTUS

Arctic 1942−5
Mediterranean 1942
North Africa 1942−3
Sicily 1943
Atlantic 1944−5
1　1942 corvette of 925 tons built by Hill: Ailsa. Transferred to Free French in 1942 and renamed *Commandante d'Estienne d'Orves*. Scrapped at Troon in 1951.

2　1942 corvette of 925 tons, ex-*Phlox* built by Robb: Ailsa & NE Marine. Sold 1947/48 for mercantile service and renamed *Southern Lotus*.

## LOUIS

Heligoland 1914
Dogger Bank 1915
Dardanelles 1915
Atlantic 1944
Biscay 1944
Arctic 1944
Named after Captain Sir Thomas Louis of the *Minotaur* at Trafalgar.
1　1913 destroyer, ex-*Talisman*, of 1,010 tons. Wrecked at Suvla Bay in 1915.
2　1943 frigate, ex-*DE.517* tons built by Boston, 1,050 tons. Returned to USA in 1946.

## LOWESTOFT

Quebec 1759
Genoa 1795
Heligoland 1914
Dogger Bank 1915
Atlantic 1940−5
North Sea 1940−5
*Minerve* 1795
*Point de jour* = Turn out early.
1　1697 5th rate. Sold in 1744.
2　and 3 were both 6th rates of 1742 and 1756 (lost at Quebec in 1760).
4　1761 5th rate which was wrecked in 1801.
5　1913 cruiser of 5,440 tons built by Chatham Dock Yard. Sold in 1931 to Ward of Milford Haven for scrapping.
6　1934 sloop of 990 tons built by White at Devonport. Sold for mercantile service in 1946. Scrapped in Belgium 1955.
7　1960 anti-submarine frigate of 2,700 tons built by Stephen. Disposal List 1982−3. Trials ship for specialist sonar work. Sunk in 1986.

## LOYAL

Sicily 1943
Salerno 1943
Mediterranean 1943
Anzio 1944
Adriatic 1944
1　1913 destroyer, ex-*Orlando*, of 1,010 tons built by Denny. Sold in 1921 to Hayes at Porthcawl.
2　1941 destroyer of 1,920 tons built by Scotts. Mined in the Adriatic. CTL 1944. Scrapped in 1948 at Milford Haven.

## LOYALTY

Gabbard 1653
Normandy 1944
Arctic 1944
1　1649−54 hired ship (34).
2　1694 hulk which foundered in 1701.
3　1943 minesweeper of 850 tons built by Harland & Wolff, ex-*Rattler*. Sunk by torpedo from *U-480* in the Channel in 1944.

## LUDLOW

Atlantic 1941−2
North Sea 1942−5
1　1698 5th rate which surrendered in 1703.
2　1916 minesweeper. Mined and sunk in 1916.
3　1940 destroyer, ex-USS *Stockton* of 1,020 tons built by Cramp *c*.1919. Scrapped in 1945.

## LULWORTH

Atlantic 1941−3
North Africa 1942
Burma 1945
1　1941 cutter, ex-USCG *Chelan* of 1,546 tons, built in 1928 by Bethlehem. Returned to USA 1946.

## LUPIN

1　1919 sloop of the 'Flower' class. 1,175 tons built by William Simons, Renfrew. Scrapped at Portchester 1947.

## LYNESS

1　1966 fleet supply ship of *c*.16,500 tons built by Swan Hunter of Wallsend.

## LYNX

Crimea 1854−5
1　2 and 3 were all sloops of 1761, 1777 and 1794.
11　1894 destroyer. Sold in 1912.
12　1913 destroyer of 957 tons built by Harland & Wolff at Govan. Mined in 1915 in the Moray Firth.
13　1955 AA frigate of *c*.2,500 tons built by John Brown. Sold to Bangladesh in 1982.

## LYSANDER

Heligoland 1914
Dogger Bank 1915
Belgian Coast 1915–16
Named after the Spartan general.
1 1913 destroyer, ex-*Ulysses*, of 1,010 tons built by Swan Hunter. Sold in 1922 to Cashmore for breaking up.
3 1943 minesweeper, ex-RCN *Hespeler*, of the 'Algerine' class built by Port Arthur. Renamed *Cornflower* in 1950 and reverted to *Lysander* in 1951. Scrapped at Blyth in 1957.

## MACKAY

Atlantic 1939–40
Dunkirk 1940
English Channel 1942–5
Arctic 1942
Normandy 1944
1 1918 flotilla leader, ex-*Claverhouse*, of 1,530 tons built by Cammell Laird. Scrapped at Charlestown in 1947.

## MAENAD

Jutland 1916
1 1915 destroyer of 1,025 tons built by Denny. Sold in 1921 to Cohen for breaking up in Germany.
2 1944 minesweeper of the 'Algerine' class built by Redfern Construction Co. Scrapped in 1957.

## MAGIC

Jutland 1916
1 1915 destroyer, ex-*Marigold*, of 1,025 tons built by White. Sold in 1921 to Cohen for breaking up in Germany.
2 1943 minesweeper, ex-*BAM 20*, of 890 tons built by Savannah Machinery Co. Torpedoed in 1944 by human torpedo off Normandy.

## MAGICIENNE

San Domingo 1806
San Sebastian 1813
Syria 1840
Baltic 1854–5
China 1860
1 and 2 were both 5th rates of 1781 (prize, then lost in 1810) and 1812.
3 1849 frigate. Scrapped in 1866.
4 1888 cruiser. Sold in 1905.

---

5 1944 minesweeper of the 'Algerine' class built by Redfern. Scrapped at Newport in 1956.

## MAGNIFICENT

The Saintes 1782
Dardanelles 1915
1 1766 3rd rate which was wrecked in 1804.
2 1806 3rd rate. Sold in 1843.
3 1894 battleship of 14,900 tons built by Chatham Dock Yard. Sold in 1921 for scrapping by Ward of Inverkeithing.
7 1944 aircraft carrier of 19,550 tons built by Harland & Wolff. Transferred to RCN 1946–57. Scrapped at Faslane 1965.

## MAGPIE

Baltic 1855
Benin 1897
Atlantic 1943–4
Normandy 1944
Arctic 1944
1 The first and all subsequent vessels to bear this name have been minor vessels except No. 9.
9 1943 sloop of 1,350 tons built by Thornycroft. Commanded by HRH Duke of Edinburgh. Scrapped at Blyth in 1959.

## MAHRATTA

Arctic 1943–4
1 1889 vessel.
3 1942 destroyer, ex-*Marksman*, of 1,920 tons, built by Scotts. Torpedoed in the Barents Sea in 1944.

## MAIDSTONE

Santa Cruz 1657
Quiberon Bay 1759
North Africa 1942
*Urbis fortuna navis* = The fortune of the city is the fortune of the ship.
1 1654 vessel (40). Renamed *Mary Rose* in 1660.
2 1693 6th rate. Sold in 1714.
3 and 4 were both 4th rates.
5 1758 6th rate. Scrapped in 1794.
6 and 7 were both 5th rates of 1795 and 1811.
8 1912 depot ship for submarines, 3,600 tons built by Scotts. At Harwich throughout WWI. Sold in 1929.
9 1937 depot ship for submarines, 11,000/13,000 tons built at Clydebank. Reconditioned 1958–62 as Nuclear Powered Submarine Supply Ship. Broken up at Rosyth in 1978.

## MAINE[49]

Korea 1950
1 1903 hospital ship presented by the USA at the time of the South African War. Wrecked in 1914.
2 1920 liner purchased, ex-*Panama*. Sold in 1947.
3 1948 liner, ex-*Empire Clyde*, ex-*Leonardo da Vinci*. Sold in 1954.

## MAJESTIC

Glorious First of June 1794
Nile 1798
Baltic 1854–5
Dardanelles 1915
1 1785 3rd rate which grounded and was wrecked in 1816.
2 1843 3rd rate. Sold in 1867.
3 1895 battleship of 14,900 tons built at Portsmouth Dock Yard. Sunk by *U-21* in 1915 off Cape Hellas.
8 1945 aircraft carrier of 14,000 tons built by Vickers Armstrong of Barrow. Transferred to RAN 1955 and renamed *Melbourne*.

## MALAYA

Jutland 1916
Atlantic 1940–1
Calabria 1940
Mediterranean 1940–1
Malta Convoys 1941–2
English Channel 1944
*Malem fera malis* = I bring evil to the

---

49 This is the hospital-ship name in the Navy. See Manning and Walker p. 283.

evil people.
1   1915 battleship of 31,000 tons built
    by Armstrong. She was a gift of the
    Federated Malay States. Scrapped
    at Faslane in 1948.

## MALCOLM

North Sea 1940
Dunkirk 1940
Atlantic 1940−5
Arctic 1942
Malta Convoys 1942
North Africa 1942
English Channel 1943
*In ardua tendit* = He strives in
difficulties.
The second ship was named after
Captain Sir Pulteney Malcolm
(1768−1838) of the *Donegal*.
1   1919 flotilla leader of 1,530 tons
    built by Cammell Laird. Scrapped
    in 1945 at Barrow.
2   1955 frigate, Type 14, of 1,536 tons
    built by Yarrow. Scrapped in 1978.

## MALLARD

North Sea 1941−3
*Ductus non coactus* = Led but not
driven.
1   1801 vessel.
3   1896 destroyer of 340 tons built by
    Thornycroft. Sold in 1920 to the
    South Alloa Ship Breaking Co.
4   1936 corvette of 510 tons built by
    Stephen. Sold in 1947 for
    scrapping at Gateshead.

## MALLOW

Atlantic 1940−3
North Sea 1942
1   1915 sloop. Transferred to RAN in
    1921.
2   1940 corvette of 925 tons built by
    Harland & Wolff. During WWII
    she became the Yugoslavian *Nada*,
    1944. In 1949 she was sold to Egypt
    and renamed *El Sudan*, 1949.

## MAMELUKE

Named after the former slaves who
seized power in Egypt in 1254.
1   1915 destroyer of 1,025 tons built
    by John Brown. Sold in 1921 to
    Cohen for breaking up in
    Germany.
2   1944 minesweeper of the 'Algerine'
    class built by Redfern. Scrapped at
    Middlesbrough in 1950.

## MANCHESTER

Norway 1940
Spartivento 1940
Arctic 1942
Malta Convoys 1941−2
*Sapere aude* = Dare to be wise.
1   1937 cruiser of 9,400 tons built by
    Hawthorn Leslie. Torpedoed by
    Italian *MAS16* and *MAS22* off
    Tunisia in 1942.
2   1980 Type 42 destroyer of 3,500/
    4,775 tons built by Vickers.

## MANDATE

Jutland 1916
1   1915 destroyer of 1,025 tons built
    by Fairfield. Sold in 1921 to Cohen
    for breaking up in Germany.
2   1944 minesweeper of the 'Algerine'
    class built by Redfern. Scrapped at
    Charlestown in 1957.

## MANNERS

Jutland 1916
Atlantic 1944−5
Named after Captain Lord Robert
Manners (1758−82), killed aboard
*Resolution* at The Saintes.
1   1915 destroyer of 1,025 tons built
    by Fairfields. Scrapped by Barking
    SB Co.
2   1943 frigate, ex-*DE.523* built by
    Boston. CTL in 1945 after being
    torpedoed between Falmouth and
    Liverpool. Returned to USA in
    1945.

## MANSFIELD

Belgian Coast 1916−18
Zeebrugge 1918
Norway 1941
Atlantic 1941−4
1   1914 destroyer of 1,010 tons built
    by Hawthorn Leslie. Named after
    Captain Charles J.M. Mansfield of
    the *Minotaur* at Trafalgar. Scrapped
    by Barking SB Co in 1921.
2   1940 destroyer, ex-USS *Evans*,

1,090 tons built by Bath Iron
Works. Royal Norwegian Navy
1940−2. RCN 1942−3. Sold in
Canada in 1944.

## MANXMAN

Malta Convoys 1941−2
*Stabit quocunque jeceris* = It will stand
however it is thrown.
1   1917 seaplane carrier of 2,048 tons
    built by Vickers in 1904. Returned
    to owners in 1920.
2   1940 minelayer of 4,000 tons built
    by Stephen. Became minesweeper
    support ship 1963.

## MAORI

Belgian Coast 1914−15
Norway 1940
*Bismarck* Action 1941
Cape Bon 1941
Atlantic 1941
Malta Convoys 1941−2
*Aki, aki, kia, kaha* = Push on, be brave.
1   1909 destroyer of 1,090 tons built
    by Denny. Mined off the Belgian
    coast in 1915.
2   1937 destroyer of the 'Tribal' class
    of 1,870 tons built by Fairfield.
    Sunk by aircraft at Malta in 1942.

## MARGUERITE

Atlantic 1941
1   1915 sloop of 1,250 tons built by
    Dunlop Bremner. Given to RAN in
    1919.
3   1940 corvette of 925 tons built by
    Hall Russell. Became a weather
    reporting ship, *Weather Observer*, in
    1947. Scrapped at Ghent in 1961.

## MARIGOLD

Armada 1588
Mediterranean 1941
Atlantic 1941−2
North Africa 1942
1   1577−8: vessel in Drake's
    squadron. Lost in 1578.

2  1588: two merchant vessels of this
   name accompanied the fleet at the
   Armada campaign.
3  1650 prize (30). Sold in 1658.
6  1915 sloop, ex-*Ivy*, 1,200 tons built
   by Bow McLachlan. Sold in 1920.
7  1940 corvette of 925 tons built by
   Hall Russell. Torpedoed by Italian
   aircraft in 1942 off Algiers.

## MARKSMAN

Jutland 1916
1  1915 flotilla leader of 1,608 tons
   built by Hawthorn Leslie. Sold in
   1921 to Slough TC for breaking up
   in Germany.
2  1942 destroyer of 1,920 tons built
   by Scotts. Renamed *Mahratta* in
   1942.

## MARLBOROUGH

Martinique 1762
Havana 1762
St Vincent 1780
The Saintes 1782
Glorious First of June 1794
Jutland 1916
He goes to war.
Named after John Churchill, first
Duke of Marlborough (1650–1722).
1  1706 2nd rate ex-*St Michael*,
   abandoned and destroyed 1762.
2  and 3 were both 3rd rates of 1767
   (wrecked in 1800) and 1807.
4  1855 1st rate. Became *Vernon II* in
   1904. Sold in 1924.[50]
5  1912 battleship of 25,000 tons built
   by Devonport Dock Yard.
   Scrapped in 1932 by Metal
   Industries of Rosyth.
7  1942–7 Torpedo school at
   Eastbourne College.

## MARNE

Jutland 1916
Arctic 1942–4
Malta Convoys 1942
North Africa 1942
Aegean 1944
1  1915 destroyer of 1,025 tons built
   by John Brown on Clydebank. Sold
   in 1921 to Cohen for breaking up in
   Germany.
3  1940 destroyer of 1,920 tons by
   Vickers Armstrong, Tyne. Sold to
   Turkey in 1958.

## MARSHAL SOULT

Belgian Coast 1915–18
Zeebrugge 1918
Named after Nicolas Soult, Marshal-
General of France (1769–1851).
1  1915 monitor of 6,670 tons built by
   Palmer. Became a base ship in
   1940. Broken up at Troon in 1946.

## MARTIN

Dover 1652
Portland 1653
Gabbard 1653
Lowestoft 1665
Camperdown 1797
Arctic 1942
North Africa 1942
Atlantic 1943
1  1651 prize. Sold two years later.
2  1652 6th rate. Sold in 1667.
4  5, 6, 7 and 8 were all sloops of
   1761, 1790 (foundered),
   1805 (foundered), 1807 (wrecked),
   1821 (foundered).
11  1910 destroyer of 760 tons built by
    Thornycroft. Sold in 1920 at
    Malta.
12  1940 destroyer of 1,920 tons built
    by Vickers Armstrong, Tyne.
    Torpedoed by *U-431* off Algiers in
    1942.

## MARVEL

Jutland 1916
1  1915 destroyer of 1,025 tons built
   by Denny. Sold in 1921 for
   scrapping by Ward, Hayle.
2  1944 minesweeper of the 'Algerine'
   class built by Redfern. Scrapped at
   Charlestown in 1958.

## MARY ROSE

Armada 1588
Cadiz 1596
Lowestoft 1665
Four Days' Battle 1666
Orfordness 1666
Solebay 1672
Schooneveld 1673
Texel 1673
Jutland 1916
Scandinavian Convoys 1917
The Seven Algerines 1669
1  1509 vessel (60). Capsized in action
   in 1545.
2  1556 vessel (33). Condemned in
   1618 and made into a wharf.
3  1623 vessel (26) which was
   wrecked in 1650.
4  1649–54 hired vessel (32).
5  1660 vessel (40), ex-*Maidstone*
   which surrendered in 1691. It was
   she who won the battle honour for
   the Seven Algerines.
6  1915 destroyer of 1,025 tons built
   by Swan Hunter of Wallsend.
   Sunk in the North Sea in 1917
   when defending her convoy.
7  1943 minesweeper of the 'Algerine'
   class built by Redfern. Scrapped at
   Blyth in 1957.

## MASHONA

Norway 1940
*Bismarck* Action 1941
1  1937 destroyer of the 'Tribal' class
   of 1,870 tons built by Vickers

---

50  She broke in two, capsized and foundered on her way to the shipbreakers. Manning and Walker, p 287.

Armstrong, Tyne. Sunk by German aircraft off south-west Ireland in 1941.

## MATABELE

Norway 1940
Arctic 1941−2
*Hamba gahle* = Go in peace (a Matabele greeting).
1   1937 destroyer of the 'Tribal' class of 1,870 tons built by Scotts. Torpedoed in 1942 by *U-454* in the Barents Sea.

## MATAPAN

*Veni, vidi, vici* = I came, I saw, I conquered.
The name commemorates Admiral Sir Andrew B. Cunningham's victory in 1941. The words were first attributed to Julius Caesar.
1   1945 destroyer of the later 'Battle' class of 2,780/3,430 tons built on Clydebank by John Brown. Scrapped in 1978.

## MATCHLESS

Belgian Coast 1916−18
Zeebrugge 1918
Arctic 1942−4
Malta Convoys 1942
North Cape 1943
1   1914 destroyer of 1,010 tons built by Swan Hunter. Sold in 1921 to

the Barking Ship Breaking Co.
2   1941 destroyer of 1,920 tons built by Stephen. Sold to Turkey in 1957 and renamed *Kilicali Pasha*.

## MAURITIUS

Atlantic 1941
Sicily 1943
Salerno 1943
Mediterranean 1943−4
Anzio 1944
Normandy 1944
Biscay 1944
Norway 1945
1   1939 cruiser of 8,000 tons built by Swan Hunter of Wallsend. She earned all the battle honours awarded to this name. Scrapped in 1965 at Inverkeithing near Rosyth.

## MAYFLOWER

Armada 1588
Scheveningen 1653
Atlantic 1941−3
Normandy 1944
English Channel 1945
1   1588: a merchant vessel of the City of London accompanied the fleet at the Armada campaign.
2   1649 prize (20) named *Fame* which was blown up, then sold as a wreck in 1658.
3   1651 vessel (20) bought but sold again in 1658.
11   1940 corvette of 925 tons, Canadian-built. Scrapped in 1948.

## MEADOWSWEET

Atlantic 1942−4
1   1942 corvette of 925 tons built by Hill: Richardson Westgarth and Clark. Sold in 1951 for mercantile service as *Gerrut W. Vinke*.

## MEDINA

Crimea 1854−5
1   1772 yacht/sloop, ex-*Old Portsmouth*, fitted out for the Governor of the Isle of Wight.
2   1813 sloop. Sold in 1832.
5   1911 liner of the P and O Line commissioned as a Royal Yacht to take King George V and Queen Mary to India in 1911.
6   1916 destroyer, ex-*Redmill*, 1,025 tons built by White. Sold in 1921 to Ward, Milford Haven for scrapping.
7   1939−45 Fleet Air Arm base on the Isle of Wight.

## MEDWAY

Quebec 1759
Ushant 1781
*In medio tutissimus* = Midway (Medway) you will be safest.
The badge derives from the arms and seal of the Rochester Bridge Commissioners, 1598.
1   1693 3rd rate. Scrapped in 1749.
2   1679 4th rate. Expended as a foundation at Sheerness in 1712.
3   1704 prize 6th rate.
4   1742 4th rate. Hulked seven years later.
5   1744 prize. Sold in 1749.
6   1756 4th rate renamed *Arundel* about 1803.
7   1812 3rd rate. Sold in 1865.
9   1916 destroyer, ex-*Redwing*, of 1,025 tons built by White. Sold in 1921 to Ward of Milford Haven for scrapping.
10   1928 depot ship for submarines, 14,650 tons built by Vickers Armstrong of Barrow. Torpedoed in 1942 off Alexandria by *U-372*.
11   1942 shore base as *Medway II* at Beirut and then Malta. Paid off in 1946.
12   1961−7 'Avon' class ramp powered lighter of 100 tons built by White: Saunders Roe.

## MELAMPUS

Belleisle 1761
Donegal 1798
Guadeloupe 1810
Name is taken from Greek mythology: a celebrated prophet and physician.
1   2 and 3 were all 3rd rates of 1757 (prize), 1785 and 1820.
4   1890 cruiser. Sold in 1910.
5   1914 destroyer of 1,040 tons built by Fairfield. Sold in 1921 to Cohen for breaking up in Germany.
6   1941−5 shore base at Bathurst.

## MELBREAK

Normandy 1944
Atlantic 1944−5
English Channel 1943−4
North Sea 1945
Named after the hunt in Cumberland.
1   1942 destroyer of the 'Hunt' class, 1,087 tons built by Swan Hunter at Wallsend. Scrapped in 1956 at Grays.

## MELITA

Normandy 1944
Atlantic 1945

From the Roman name for Malta.
1   1885 sloop. Sold in 1920 and
    renamed *Ringdove*.
3   1942 minesweeper of the 'Algerine'
    class built by Redfern. Scrapped at
    Llanelly in 1959.

## MELVILLE

China 1841
Atlantic 1942−3
Named after Henry Dundas, first
Viscount Melville (1742−1811).
1   1805 prize 5th rate. Sold in 1808.
2   1817 3rd rate. Sold in 1873.
3   1942 shore base in Darwin.

## MENACE

Jutland 1916
1   1915 destroyer of 1,025 tons built
    by Swan Hunter. Sold in 1921 to
    Ward at Grays.
2   1941 2nd Mobile Naval Base.

## MENDIP

North Sea 1941−5
English Channel 1942−3
Salerno 1943
Mediterranean 1943
Sicily 1943
Normandy 1944
Named after the hunt in Somerset.
1   1940 destroyer of the 'Hunt' class,
    907 tons built by Swan Hunter at
    Wallsend. Sold to Nationalist
    China in 1948, then to Egypt in
    1950.

## MENTOR

Dogger Bank 1915
Belgian Coast 1915
Zeebrugge 1918
1   1781 prize, *Aurora*, which was
    wrecked in 1783.
3   1914 destroyer of 1,055 tons built
    by Hawthorn Leslie. Sold in 1921
    to Ward of Hayle.
4   1939−44 shore base at Stornoway.

## MEON

English Channel 1944
Normandy 1944
Atlantic 1944−5
1   1943 frigate of 1,865 tons built by

Fleming & Ferguson. RCN
1944−5. Scrapped at Blyth in 1966.

## MERCURY

Havana 1762
*Celer et fidelis* = Swift and faithful.
Named after the Roman messenger of
the gods.
1    1592 vessel.
5    6 and 7 were all 6th rates of 1745,
     1756 (wrecked) and 1779.
9    1826 5th rate. Sold in 1906.
11   1878 cruiser which was renamed
     *Columbine* in 1914.
14   1941 Signal School at Leydene in
     Hampshire: more properly, the
     Communications and Navigation
     Faculty of Marine Operations,
     Petersfield.

## MERLIN

Armada 1588
Portland 1653
Gabbard 1653
Scheveningen 1653
Porto Farina 1655
Havana 1762
Baltic 1855
Ashantee 1873−4
*Pervigilis usque volat* = Thoroughly
watchful, he flies continuously.
1    1579 vessel.
5    6, 7, 8, 9, 10 and 11 were all sloops
     of 1699, 1744, 1756 (surrendered
     the following year, almost
     immediately retaken and
     renamed *Zephyr*), 1757, 1780, 1796
     and 1803.
14   1901 was also a sloop, of 1,070
     tons but started as a survey
     vessel, built at Sheerness Dock
     Yard. Designated sloop in 1918.
     Sold to Hong Kong in 1923.
16   1939 RN Air Station at
     Donibristle. Paid off 1959.

## MERMAID

Cadiz 1596
Dover 1652
Gabbard 1653
Porto Farina 1655
Belgian Coast 1914−17
Arctic 1944
1    1596: a merchant ship was at
     Cadiz.[51]
2    and 4 were both 5th rates of 1651
     and 1744 (ex-*Ruby*).
5    and 6 were both 6th rates of 1749
     (wrecked 1760) and 1761 (run
     aground 1778).
7    and 10 were both 5th rates of 1782
     and 1825.
13   1898 destroyer of *c*.400 tons built
     by Hawthorn Leslie. Sold to Ward
     of New Holland for scrapping in
     1919.
15   1943 frigate of 1,350 tons built by
     Denny. Sold to Federal Republic
     of Germany in 1958 and renamed
     *Scharnhorst*.
16   1964 coastal minesweeper, ex-
     *Sullington*, 420 tons converted to
     survey ship. Sold to Malaysia in
     1977.

## MERSEY

Belgian Coast 1914−15
*Königsberg* 1915
1   1814 6th rate. Scrapped in 1852.
2   1858 frigate. Sold in 1875.
3   1885 cruiser. Sold 1905.
4   1914 monitor of 1,260 tons built by
    Vickers. Broken up in 1923.
5   1940−6 depot at Liverpool.[52]

## METEOR

Crimea 1855
Dogger Bank 1915
Arctic 1942−4
Atlantic 1942−3
North Africa 1942
Aegean 1944

---

51   See Manning and Walker, p. 296.

52   Two small tenders to the Mersey Division RNVR have borne the name.

Mediterranean 1945
1   1797 small vessel.
6   1855 floating battery. Scrapped in 1861.
7   1914 destroyer of 1,070 tons built by Thornycroft. Scrapped in 1921 by Ward of Milford Haven.
8   1941 destroyer of 1,920 tons built by Stephen. Sold to Turkey in 1958 and renamed *Piyale Pasha*.

## MEYNELL

English Channel 1941−3
North Sea 1941−5
Arctic 1943
Normandy 1944
Named after the hunt in Derbyshire.
1   1917 minesweeper of 750 tons built by Henderson. Sold in 1922 to Col. Lithgow for scrapping.
2   1940 destroyer of the 'Hunt' class, 907 tons, built by Swan Hunter at Wallsend. Sold to Ecuador in 1954 and renamed *Velasco Ybarra*.

## MICHAEL[53]

Jutland 1916
1   1350 vessel.
2   1915 destroyer of 1,025 tons built by Thornycroft. Sold in 1921 to Cohen for breaking up in Germany.
3   1944 minesweeper of the 'Algerine' class built by Redfern. Scrapped in 1956.

## MIDDLETON

Arctic 1942−3
Malta Convoys 1942
Atlantic 1944
Normandy 1944
English Channel 1944
North Sea 1944−5
Named after the hunt in Yorkshire.
1   1941 destroyer of the 'Hunt' class, 1,050 tons, built by Vickers Armstrong, Tyne. Hulked in 1955, became a pontoon at Harwich in 1956 and scrapped in 1957.
2   1984 (commissioning date) minehunter of 615/725 tons built at Yarrow. A 'Hunt' class MCMV.

## MIGNONETTE

Atlantic 1941−5
Normandy 1944
North Sea 1944

English Channel 1945
1   1916 sloop of 1,250 tons built by Dunlop Bremner. Mined in 1917 SW of Ireland.
3   1940 corvette of 925 tons built by Hall Russell: NE Marine. Sold in 1946 for mercantile service. Lost in 1948.

## MILFORD

Lowestoft 1665
Atlantic 1940−5
*Retibus famam retinens* = Holding fame in our nets.
1   1660 5th rate. Burnt at Leghorn in 1673.
2   1689 5th rate which surrendered in 1694.
3   1697 5th rate. She was the *Scarborough*, taken by the French in 1694, but retaken in 1697 and renamed *Milford*. She was lost in 1720.
4   1744 5th rate, ex-*Active*. Sold five years later.
5   1759 6th rate. Sold in 1785.
6   1809 3rd rate. Scrapped in 1848.
7   1932 sloop of 1,045 tons built by Yarrow at Devonport. Sold in 1949 and scrapped at Hayle.

## MILNE

Dogger Bank 1915
Belgian Coast 1916
Arctic 1942−4
North Africa 1942
Atlantic 1942−3
Named after Admiral Sir David Milne (1763−1845).
1   1914 destroyer of 1,010 tons built by John Brown. Sold in 1921 to Cohen for breaking up in Germany.
2   1941 destroyer of 1,920 tons built by Scotts. Sold to Turkey in 1958.

## MIMOSA

Atlantic 1941−2
1   1915 sloop of 1,200 tons built by Bow McLachlan. Sold in 1922 to South Wales Salvage Co.
2   1941 corvette of 925 tons built by Hill: Richardson Westgarth and Clark. Manned by the Free French. Torpedoed in 1942 by *U-124* in the N. Atlantic.

## MINERVA (Minerve)

Quiberon Bay 1759
St Vincent 1797
Egypt 1801
Suez Canal 1915
Dardanelles 1915
Falkland Islands 1982
*Mutine* 1797
Named after the Roman goddess of wisdom.
1    1759 5th rate. Surrendered in 1778 but retaken three years later and renamed *Recovery*.
2    5, 7 and 9 were all 5th rates of 1780, 1795 (prize), 1805 and 1820.
10   1895 cruiser of 5,600 tons built by Chatham Dock Yard. Sold in 1920 to Auten Ltd.
15   1925 monitor, ex-*M.33*, built in 1915 by Workman Clark. Became a minelayer. Hulked in 1943.
16   1964 anti-submarine general-purpose frigate of 2,450/2,860 tons built by Vickers Armstrong, Newcastle. 'Leander' class armed with Exocet missiles.

## MINOS

Dogger Bank 1915
A king (or kings) of ancient Crete.
1   1840 sloop. Sold in 1852.
2   1914 destroyer of 883 tons built by Yarrow. Sold in 1920 to Ward at Hayle for scrapping.
3   1940−5 shore base at Lowestoft.

## MINOTAUR

The Nile 1798
Egypt 1801
Trafalgar 1805
Jutland 1916
*Hostibus minax* = Threatening to enemies.
Named after the monster, half man, half bull, slain by Theseus.

53   Some sources attribute to her the battle honour Espagnol sur Mer 1350.

1 1793 3rd rate which was wrecked in 1810.
2 1816 3rd rate which was renamed *Hermes* in 1866.
3 1863 armoured ship, renamed *Boscawen II* in 1904.
4 1906 cruiser of 14,600 tons built by Devonport Dock Yard. Sold in 1929 to Ward of Milford Haven for scrapping.
5 1943 cruiser of 8,800 tons built by Harland & Wolff. Transferred to RCN 1944 and renamed *Ontario*. Scrapped in Japan in 1960.

## MINSTREL

1 1807 sloop. Sold in 1817.
3 1911 destroyer of 760 tons built by Thornycroft. Sold in 1921 to Stanlee.
4 1944 minesweeper of 850 tons built by Redfern. Sold to Thailand in 1947 and renamed *Phosampton*.

## MIRANDA

Baltic 1854
Crimea 1854−5
New Zealand 1863−6
Dogger Bank 1915
Belgian Coast 1916−18
1 1851 corvette. Sold in 1869.
2 1879 sloop. Sold in 1892.
3 1914 destroyer of 883 tons built by Yarrow. Sold in 1921 to Barking SB Co.
6 1940−5 shore base at Great Yarmouth.

## MISTRAL

1 1819 vessel.
2 1940 ex-French destroyer of 1,390 tons built in 1925. Returned to France 1945.

## MODESTE

Martinique 1762
Egypt 1801
Java 1811
China 1841−2
Crimea 1854
Korea 1953
1 1759 prize of 3rd rate. Scrapped in 1800.
2 and 3 were both prizes taken in 1793 and 1797.
4 and 5 were both corvettes of 1837 and 1873.

6 1944 sloop of 1,350 tons built by Yarrow at Chatham. Scrapped at St David's-on-Forth in 1961.

## MOHAWK

Belgian Coast 1915−16
Norway 1940
Calabria 1940
Libya 1940
Mediterranean 1940−1
Sfax 1941
Matapan 1941
Malta Convoys 1941
Bold, vigilant, brave.
1 1813 vessel.
2 1841 sloop. Sold in 1852.
4 1856 sloop. Sold to China in 1862.
5 1886 cruiser. Sold in 1905.
6 1907 destroyer of 885 tons built by White. Sold in 1919 to Hughes Bolckow for scrapping.
7 1937 destroyer of 1,870 tons built by Thornycroft. Torpedoed in 1941 by Italian destroyer *Tarigo* off Cape Bon.
8 1962 general-purpose frigate of 2,370/2,700 tons built by Vickers Armstrong of Barrow. Disposal List 1980−1.

## MONCK

Lowestoft 1665
Orfordness 1666
Solebay 1672
Schooneveld 1673
Texel 1673
Barfleur 1692
Velez Malaga 1704
Gibraltar 1704
Named after George Monck, Duke of Albemarle, General-at-sea.
1 1659 3rd rate which was wrecked in 1720.
2 1709 prize 6th rate. Sold in 1712.
3 1942−6 Combined Operations base at Largs.

## MONKSHOOD

Atlantic 1941−4
Biscay 1943
1 1941 corvette of 925 tons built by Fleming & Ferguson. Sold in 1948 for mercantile service.

## MONNOW

Atlantic 1944−5
Arctic 1944−5
North Sea 1945
1 1943 frigate of 1,370 tons built by Hill: Bellis & Morcam. RCN 1944−5. Sold to Denmark in 1945.

## MONTBRETIA

Atlantic 1941−2
1 1917 sloop of 1,250 tons built by Irvine. Sold in 1921 to Clan Line and renamed *Chihuahua*.
2 1941 corvette of 925 tons built by Fleming and Ferguson. Manned by Royal Norwegian Navy. Torpedoed and sunk by *U-624* in the Atlantic in 1942.

## MONTGOMERY

Atlantic 1941−3
1 1940 destroyer, ex-USS *Wickes*, 1,090 tons built by Bath Iron Works in 1918. RCN 1942−3. Broken up in the Tyne in 1945.

## MONTROSE

Atlantic 1939−40
Dunkirk 1940
Arctic 1942−3
North Sea 1942−4
English Channel 1943−4
Normandy 1944
*Mare ditat rosa decorat* = The sea enriches; the rose decorates.
1 1918 flotilla leader of 1,530 tons built by Hawthorn Leslie. Scrapped at Blyth in 1946.[54]

## MONTSERRAT

1 1943 frigate of 1,318 tons built by Walsh Kaiser: ex-*Hornby*, ex-*PF-82*. Returned to USA in 1946.

---

54 Two small tenders to the Tay Division RNVR have borne this name. Manning and Walker, p. 304.

# MOON

Armada 1588
Cadiz 1596
Jutland 1916
1   1552 vessel.
3   1915 destroyer of 900 tons built by
    Yarrow. Sold in 1921 for scrapping
    at Briton Ferry.
4   1943 minesweeper of the 'Algerine'
    class built by Redfern. Ex-RCN
    Mimico. Scrapped at Gateshead in
    1957.

# MOORSOM

Jutland 1916
Belgian Coast 1917−18
Zeebrugge 1918
Normandy 1944
Atlantic 1944
North Sea 1944
Named after Captain Sir Robert
Moorsom of the *Revenge* at Trafalgar.
1   1914 destroyer of 1,010 tons built
    by John Brown. Sold in 1921 for
    breaking up in Germany.
2   1943 frigate, ex-*DE.522*, of 1,085
    tons built by Boston. Returned to
    USA 1945.

# MORECAMBE BAY

Korea 1950−3
1   1944 frigate, ex-*Loch Heilen*, of
    2,420 tons built by Pickersgill:
    Clark. Sold to Portugal in 1961.

# MORPETH CASTLE

Atlantic 1944−5
1   1943 corvette/frigate of 1,010 tons
    built by Pickersgill: Clark.
    Scrapped at Llanelly in 1960.

# MOSQUITO

Navarino 1827
Dardanelles 1915
Dunkirk 1940

1   1777 vessel.
10  1910 destroyer of 975 tons built by
    Fairfield. Sold in 1921 for
    scrapping by Ward at Rainham.
12  1942−5 coastal forces base at
    Alexandria.

# MOUNSEY

Jutland 1916
Normandy 1944
Atlantic 1944
Arctic 1944
Named after Captain William
Mounsey.
1   1915 destroyer of 900 tons built by
    Yarrow. Scrapped in Germany in
    1921.
2   1943 frigate, ex-*DE.524*, built by
    Boston. Returned to USA in 1946.

# MOUNT EDGCUMBE

1   1876 training ship, ex-*Conway*, ex-
    *Winchester*. Deleted 1920.
2   1945 barracks at Devonport.

# MOUNTS BAY

Korea 1950−3
1   1945 frigate of 2,420 tons built by
    Pickersgill: Clark. Ex-*Loch Kilbernie*.
    Sold to Portugal in 1961.

# MOURNE

Atlantic 1943−4
Normandy 1944
English Channel 1944
1   1943 frigate of 1,370 tons built by
    Smith's Dock. Torpedoed in 1944
    in the Channel by *U-767*.

# MOYOLA

Atlantic 1943−4
1   1942 frigate of 1,370 tons built by
    Smith's Dock. Transferred to
    France in 1944.

# MURRAY

Belgian Coast 1916
Named after Vice Admiral Sir George
Murray (1759−1819).
1   1914 destroyer of 1,010 tons built
    by Palmer. Scrapped at Briton
    Ferry in 1921 by Ward.
2   1955 anti-submarine frigate, Type
    14, of 1,536 tons built by Stephen.
    Disposal List 1974−5.

# MUSKETEER

Arctic 1942−4
North Cape 1943
Atlantic 1943
Aegean 1944
The badge displays a demi-marine of
1805.
1   1915 destroyer of 900 tons built by
    Yarrow. Sold in 1921 to Hayes of
    Porthcawl for scrapping.
2   1941 destroyer of 1,920 tons built
    by Fairfield. Scrapped at
    Sunderland in 1955.

# MUTINE

Nile 1798
Algiers 1816
Sicily 1943
Salerno 1943
1   1779 vessel.
7   8 and 9 were all sloops of 1859,
    1889 (renamed *Azov*) and 1900.
10  1942 minesweeper of the
    'Algerine' class built by Harland
    & Wolff. Scrapped in 1967 at
    Barrow.

# MYNGS

Zeebrugge 1918
Norway 1944
Arctic 1944−5
Named after Admiral Sir Christopher
Myngs (1625−66), killed in the Four
Days' Battle.
1   1914 destroyer of 1,010 tons built

by Palmer. Sold in 1921 to Ward for scrapping at Rainham.
2    1943 destroyer of 1,730 tons built by Vickers Armstrong, Tyne. Sold to Egypt in 1955.

## MYOSOTIS

Atlantic 1941−3
English Channel 1945
1    1915 sloop of 1,250 tons built by Bow McLachlan. Sold in 1923.
2    1941 corvette of 925 tons built by Lewis. Sold in 1946 for mercantile service.

## MYRMIDON

Belgian Coast 1914−16
Atlantic 1943
Myrmidons were created from ants, to be subject to Achilles.
1    and 2 were both 6th rates of 1781 and 1813.
5    1900 destroyer of c.400 tons built by Palmer. Sunk in collision in the Channel in 1917.
6    1940 destroyer of 1,920 tons built by Fairfield. Served with the Polish navy in 1942 as *Orkan*. Lost in 1943 by torpedo from *U-610* south of Iceland.
7    1944 minesweeper of the 'Algerine' class built by Redfern Construction. Scrapped about 1958.

## MYSTIC

Jutland 1916
1    1915 destroyer, ex-*Myrtle*, of 1,025 tons built by Denny. Scrapped in Germany in 1921.
2    1944 minesweeper of the 'Algerine' class built by Redfern Construction. Scrapped in 1958.

## NABOB

1    1777 vessel.
2    1943 escort carrier, ex-USS *Edisto*, of 11,420 tons built by Seattle-Tacoma. RCN 1943−44. CTL in 1944. Returned to USA in 1945. Still in mercantile service in 1951.

## NADDER

1    1943 frigate of 1,370 tons built by Smith's Dock. Transferred to RIN in 1944 as *Shamsher*. RCN 1944−5. Pakistan navy in 1948.

## NAIAD

Trafalgar 1805
Crete 1941
Mediterranean 1941
Malta Convoys 1941−2
1    1797 5th rate. Sold in 1866.
2    1890 cruiser. Sold in 1922.
3    1939 cruiser of 5,450 tons built by Hawthorn Leslie. Torpedoed and sunk by *U-565* south of Crete in 1942.
4    1962 anti-submarine general-purpose frigate of 2,450/2,860 tons built by Yarrow. 'Leander' class armed with Ikara missiles. Disposal List 1982−3.

## NAIRANA

Atlantic 1944
Arctic 1944−5
Norway 1945
1    1917 seaplane carrier of 3,547 tons built by Denny. Sold in 1921.
2    1943 escort carrier of 14,050 tons built on Clydebank. Lent to the Dutch navy 1946−8 and renamed *Karel Doorman*. Sold for mercantile service *c*.1948 as *Port Victor*.

## NAMUR

Velez Malaga 1704
Finisterre I 1747
Louisburg 1758
Lagos 1759
Quiberon Bay 1759
Havana 1762
The Saintes 1782
St Vincent 1797
Bay of Biscay 1805
1    1697 2nd rate which was wrecked in 1749.
2    1756 2nd rate. Scrapped in 1833.
3    1945 destroyer of 2,380 tons built by Cammell Laird. She was not completed and was used for target trials until scrapped at Barrow in 1951.

## NAPIER

Crete 1941
Libya 1941
Burma 1944−5
Okinawa 1945
Named after Admiral Sir Charles Napier (1786−1860).
1    1915 destroyer of 1,025 tons built by John Brown. Sold to Slough Trading Co. for breaking up in Germany in 1921.
2    1940 destroyer of 1,695 tons built by Fairfield. RAN until 1945. Scrapped at Briton Ferry in 1956.

## NARBOROUGH

Jutland 1916
English Channel 1944
Normandy 1944
Atlantic 1945
Named after Sir John Narborough (1640−86).
1    1916 destroyer of 1,025 tons built by John Brown. Wrecked in 1918 in the Pentland Skerries.
2    1943 frigate of 1,300 tons, ex-*DE-569*, built by Bethlehem: Hingham. Returned to USA in 1946.

## NARCISSUS

Atlantic 1941−5
Normandy 1944
1    1781 6th rate. Wrecked in 1796.
3    1801 3rd rate. Sold in 1837.
4    1859 frigate. Sold in 1883.
5    1886 cruiser. Sold in 1906.
6    1915 sloop of 1,200 tons built by Napier & Miller. Sold in 1922.
8    1941 corvette of 925 tons built by Lewis. Sold in 1946 for mercantile service as *Este*.

## NARWHAL

Jutland 1916
Atlantic 1939
North Sea 1940
Norway 1940
1    1915 destroyer of 1,025 tons built by Denny. Collision in 1920 resulting in CTL. Broken up in Devonport Dock Yard.
2    1935 submarine of 1,520/2,157 tons built by Vickers Armstrong at Barrow. Lost off Norway in 1940.
3    1957 submarine of 1,600/2,030 tons built by Vickers Armstrong. Expended as a target in 1982.

## NASTURTIUM

Atlantic 1940−5
Normandy 1944
English Channel 1944−5
1  1915 sloop of 1,250 tons built by McMillan. Mined in 1916 near Malta.
2  1940 corvette of 925 tons built by Smith's Dock. Ex-French *La Paimpolaise*. Sold in 1946 for mercantile service — as *Cania* in 1948.

## NELSON

Malta Convoys 1941−2
North Africa 1942−43
Mediterranean 1943
Sicily 1943
Salerno 1943
Normandy 1944

*Palmam qui meruit ferat* = Let him bear the palm who has deserved it.
1  1806 vessel.
3  1814 1st rate which was presented as a very old ship to the government of Victoria, Australia, in 1867.
4  1876 cruiser. Sold in 1910.
7  1925 battleship of 33,950 tons built by Armstrong. Scrapped at Inverkeithing in 1949. During WWII she was mined and torpedoed. She — with sister ship *Rodney* — were the first RN ships to mount 16-inch guns. All nine guns of the main armament were grouped forward.
8  1974 Royal Naval School of Educational and Training Technology, ex-*Victory*.

## NENE

Biscay 1943
Atlantic 1943−4
Arctic 1943−4
North Sea 1945
1  1942 frigate of 1,370 tons built by Smith's Dock. RCN service 1944−5. Broken up at Briton Ferry in 1955.

## NEPAL

Burma 1944−5
Okinawa 1945
1  1941 destroyer, ex-*Norseman*, of 1,690 tons built by Thornycroft. Manned by RAN until 1945. Scrapped at Briton Ferry in 1956.

HMS NELSON (No. 7)

## NEPTUNE

Barfleur 1692
Quebec 1759
Trafalgar 1805
Martinique 1809
Baltic 1854
Jutland 1916
Atlantic 1939
Calabria 1940
Mediterranean 1940
*Bismarck* Action 1941
Malta Convoys 1941
*Regnare est servire* = To rule is to serve.
Named after the god of the sea and
brother of Jupiter.
1   1683 2nd rate (90). Built at
    Deptford Dock Yard. Rebuilt 1710
    at Blackwall and again at
    Woolwich 1730. Renamed *Torbay*
    in 1750 and scrapped in 1784.
2   and 3 were also 2nd rates of 1756
    (90) and 1797 (98).
9   1832 1st rate. Sold in 1875.
10  1874 turret ship. Sold in 1803.
13  1909 battleship of 20,000 tons
    built by Portsmouth Dock Yard
    and sold in 1922.
14  1933 cruiser of 7,270 tons built at
    Portsmouth. Mined and sunk off
    Tripoli in 1941.
15  1945 projected cruiser of *c*.9,000
    tons, cancelled in 1946.
16  Submarine base at Faslane on the
    Clyde. The base includes the
    Faslane complex, including
    *Neptune* on Gare Loch, the RNAD
    at Coulport on Loch Long and
    several outstations. There is a
    dockyard, barracks for 250
    officers and 1,500 men, logistics
    and support area and training
    establishment including the RN
    Polaris School and Sub Attack
    Teacher.

## NÉRÉIDE

1   1797 prize 5th rate. Scrapped in
    1812.
2   1810 prize 5th rate. Scrapped in

1816.
3   1910 destroyer of *c*.760 tons built
    by Hawthorn Leslie. Sold in 1921
    for scrapping by Stanlee.
4   1944 frigate of 1,350 tons built by
    Yarrow at Chatham. Scrapped in
    1958.

## NESS

Atlantic 1943−4
English Channel 1945
1   1905 destroyer of *c*.560 tons built
    by White. Sold in 1919.
2   1942 frigate of 1,370 tons built by
    Robb: Plenty. Broken up at
    Newport in 1956.

## NESTOR

Jutland 1916
Atlantic 1941
*Bismarck* Action 1941
Malta Convoys 1941−2
1   1781 prize 6th rate. Sold two years
    later.
2   1915 destroyer of 1,025 tons built
    by Swan Hunter. Sunk at Jutland.
3   1940 destroyer of 1,690 tons built
    by Fairfield. RAN crew, 1941−2.
    Sunk by Italian aircraft in the
    Mediterranean 1942.

## NEWARK

Velez Malaga 1704
Lagos 1759
Atlantic 1941−2
North Sea 1943−4
1   1695 3rd rate. Scrapped in 1787.
2   1918 minesweeper, ex-*Newlyn*, of
    800 tons built by Inglis. Sold in
    1928 to Alloa, Charlestown for
    scrapping.
3   1940 destroyer, ex-USS *Ringgold*, of
    1,060 tons built by Union Iron
    Works in 1918. Broken up in 1947.

## NEWCASTLE

Porto Farina 1655
Santa Cruz 1657
Lowestoft 1665
Orfordness 1666
Schooneveld 1673
Texel 1673
Marbella 1705
Sadras 1758
Negapatam 1758
Porto Novo 1759
Spartivento 1940
Burma 1944−5
Korea 1952−3
*Fortitudine vinco* = By strength I
conquer.
1   1653 4th rate (54) of 641 tons.
    Foundered (with eleven other
    ships) in a storm while lying at
    Spithead and lost 193 out of 233
    ship's company.
2   1704 4th rate (50) of 676 tons.
    Scrapped at Plymouth in 1746.
3   1750 4th rate (50) of 1,052 tons built
    at Portsmouth. She was wrecked
    in a hurricane near Pondicherry in
    1761.
4   1813 4th rate (50) of 1,556 tons built
    at Blackwall. Broken up in 1850.
5   1861 4th rate (31) screw frigate of
    4,020 tons. Scrapped in 1929.
6   1909 second-class protected cruiser
    of 4,800 tons built by Armstrong
    Whitworth. Sold to Ward for
    scrapping in the 1920s.
7   1936 cruiser of 9,100 tons, ex-
    *Minotaur*, built by Vickers
    Armstrong, Tyne. Scrapped at
    Faslane in 1959.
8   1975 destroyer Type 42 of 3,500/
    4,100 tons built by Swan Hunter.

## NEWFOUNDLAND

Mediterranean 1943
Sicily 1943
1  1941 cruiser of 8,800 tons built by
   Swan Hunter of Wallsend. Sold to
   Peru in 1959 and renamed
   *Almirante Grau*.

## NEWMARKET

Atlantic 1941–2
Arctic 1942
1  1914–18 vessel.
2  1940 destroyer, ex-USS *Robinson*,
   1,060 tons built by Union Iron
   Works in 1918. Scrapped at
   Llanelly in 1945.

## NEWPORT

Velez Malaga 1704
Atlantic 1941
English Channel 1942
Arctic 1942
1  1694 6th rate which surrendered in
   1696.
2  1698 6th rate, ex-*Orford*. Sold in
   1714.
4  1940 destroyer, ex-USS *Sigourney*
   of 1,060 tons built by Fore River on
   1917. Sold in 1947 and scrapped at
   Granton.

## NIGELLA

Atlantic 1941–2
Diego Suarez 1942
1  1915 sloop of 1,250 tons built by
   Hamilton. Sold in 1922 to
   Hallamshire Metal Co.
3  1940 corvette of 925 tons built by
   Philip: Clark. Sold in 1947 for
   mercantile service: *Nigel Lock*. Lost
   1955.

## NIGER

Glorious First of June 1794
St Vincent 1797

Egypt 1801
Crimea 1854–5
China 1856–60
New Zealand 1860–1
Dunkirk 1940
Atlantic 1941
Arctic 1941–2
*Nec timeo nec sperno* = I neither fear nor
despise.
1  1759 5th rate. Renamed *Negro* in
   1813.
2  1813 5th rate. Scrapped in 1830.
3  1846 corvette. Sold in 1869.
6  1936 minesweeper of 815 tons built
   by White. Mined in 1942 off
   Iceland.
7  1945 minesweeper, ex-*Disdain*, of
   the 'Algerine' class built by
   Lobnitz. Scrapped in 1966.

## NIGERIA

Atlantic 1941
Norway 1941
Arctic 1942
Malta Convoys 1942
Sabang 1944
Burma 1944–5
1  1939 cruiser of 8,000 tons built by
   Vickers Armstrong on the Tyne.
   Sold to India in 1957 and renamed
   *Mysore*.

## NILE

Baltic 1854–5
The name commemorates Nelson's
victory in Aboukir Bay 1798.
1  1799 vessel.
3  1839 2nd rate. She became the
   training ship *Conway* in 1875.
4  1888 battleship. Sold in 1912.
6  1939 shore establishment at
   Alexandria.

## NIMROD

Basque Roads 1809
China 1841–2
China 1858–9
Belgian Coast 1917
1  1795 vessel.
2  1799 prize (16). Sold 1811.
4  1828 sloop. Sold in 1907.
6  1915 flotilla leader of 1,608 tons
   built by Denny. Sold in 1925 for
   scrapping at Rosyth.
7  1940–6 anti-submarine school at
   Campbeltown.

## NITH

Normandy 1944
Burma 1945

1  1905 destroyer of *c*.550 tons built
   by White. Sold in 1919 to Ward of
   Preston for scrapping.
3  1943 frigate of 1,370 tons built by
   Henry Robb: Yarrow. Sold to
   Egypt in 1948 and renamed
   *Domiat*. Lost in 1956.

## NIZAM

Malta Convoys 1941
Crete 1941
Libya 1941
Okinawa 1945
Named after the ruler of Hyderabad.
The badge derives from his arms.
1  1916 destroyer of 1,025 tons built
   by Stephen. Sold in 1921 to Ward
   of Rainham.
2  1940 destroyer of 1,690 tons built
   by Clydebank. RAN 1941–5.
   Scrapped at Grays in 1955.

## NOBLE

Jutland 1916
1  1915 destroyer, ex-*Nisus*, of 1,025
   tons built by Stephen. Sold in 1921
   to Slough TC for scrapping.
2  1941 destroyer of 1,690 tons built
   by Denny and sold to Holland in
   1941. She was renamed *Van Galen*.
   Scrapped in Holland in 1957.
3  1946 destroyer, ex-*Nerissa*, ex-
   *Piorun* (she was manned by the
   Polish navy under this name from
   1941–6). Returned to RN 1946.
   Scrapped in 1955–6.

## NONPAREIL

Armada 1588
Cadiz 1596
Unequalled.
1   1580 5th rate (38). Originally built
    as *Philip and Mary* in 1554.
    *Nonpareil* from 1580 to 1603, when
    she became *Nonsuch*. At some
    stage of rebuilding her guns were
    increased to 52.
3   1916 destroyer of 1,025 tons built
    by Stephen. Scrapped by Ward at
    Briton Ferry in 1921.
4   1941 destroyer of 1,690 tons built
    by Denny. Transferred to the
    Dutch navy in 1942 and renamed
    *Tjerk Hiddes*. Subsequently sold to
    the Indonesian navy.

## NONSUCH

Kentish Knock 1652
Portland 1653
Gabbard 1653
Texel 1673
St Lucia 1778
The Saintes 1782
Jutland 1916
Royal palace, favourite of Elizabeth I.
1   1603 5th rate, ex-*Nonpareil*.
    Condemned in 1645.
2   1646 5th rate (34) which was
    wrecked in 1664.
4   6 and 7 were all 4th rates of 1668
    (surrendered 1695), 1696 and
    1741.
8   1774 3rd rate. Scrapped in 1802.
9   1915 destroyer, ex-*Narcissus*, of
    1,025 tons built by Palmer.
    Scrapped in 1921 by Ward of
    Milford Haven.
10  1945: name given to ex-German
    destroyer *Z 38*, surrendered in
    1945. Scrapped in 1949.

## NORFOLK

Velez Malaga 1704
Atlantic 1941
*Bismarck* Action 1941
Arctic 1941−3
North Africa 1942
North Cape 1943
Norway 1945
*Serviens servo* = serving, I preserve.
1   1693 3rd rate which was renamed
    *Princess Amelia* in 1755.
2   1757 3rd rate. Scrapped in 1774.
4   1928 cruiser of 9,925 tons built by
    Fairfield. Scrapped at Newport in
    1950.
5   1967 'County' class cruiser of 5,440/
    6,200 tons built by Swan Hunter &
    Wigham Richardson, Wallsend.
    Sold to Chile in 1982.

6   1987 frigate of *c*.3,000/3,700 tons
    standard, built by Yarrow.

## NORMAN

Burma 1944−5
Okinawa 1945
*Cedere nescio* = I know not how to
yield.
1   1916 destroyer of 1,025 tons built
    by Palmer. Scrapped by Ward at
    Milford Haven in 1921.
4   1940 destroyer of 1,690 tons built
    by Thornycroft. RAN 1941−5.
    Scrapped at Newport in 1958.

## NOTTINGHAM

Gibraltar 1704
Velez Malaga 1704
Marbella 1705
Finisterre I & II 1747
Louisburg 1758
Havana 1762
Martinique 1762
Heligoland 1914
Dogger Bank 1915
Jutland 1916
*Magnanime* 1748
1   1703 4th rate. Seventy years later
    she was expended as a breakwater
    at Sheerness.
2   1704 6th rate prize. Sunk at
    Sheerness in 1706.
4   1913 cruiser of 5,440 tons built by
    Pembroke Dock Yard. Sunk by
    torpedo from *U-62* in the North

Sea in 1916.
5   1980 destroyer, Type 42, of 3,500/
    4,100 tons built by Vosper
    Thornycroft.

## NUBIAN

Belgian Coast 1914−15
Norway 1940
Calabria 1940
Libya 1940
Mediterranean 1940−3
Matapan 1941
Sfax 1941
Greece 1941
Crete 1941
Malta Convoys 1941
Sicily 1943
Salerno 1943
Arctic 1944
Burma 1944−5
A native of Nubia, now part of Sudan.
1   1909 destroyer of *c*.1,090 tons built
    by Thornycroft. Torpedoed off
    Belgian coast in 1916. Cannibalized
    with *Zulu* to make *Zubian*: the
    forward part of *Zulu* and the stern
    part, abaft the 3rd and 4th funnel,
    of *Nubian*, created *Zubian* of 1,050
    tons in 1917. She was sold in 1919.
2   1937 destroyer of 'Tribal' class of
    1,870 tons built by Thornycroft.
    She had a particularly
    distinguished WWII career.
    Scrapped at Briton Ferry in 1949.
3   1960 general-purpose First Rate
    frigate of 2,370/2,700 tons, built at
    Portsmouth Dock Yard. Disposal
    List 1980−1.

## NYASALAND

Atlantic 1943−5
1   1943 frigate, ex-*Hoste*, ex-*PF 83*, of
    1,318 tons built by Walsh Kaiser.
    Returned to USA in 1946.

## OAKHAM CASTLE

Atlantic 1945
1   1944 corvette/frigate of 1,010 tons
    built by Inglis: Harland & Wolff.
    She became a weather-reporting
    ship, *Weather Reporter*, in 1958.

## OAKLEY

Arctic 1942
Sicily 1943
South France 1944
North Sea 1945
Named after the hunt in Bedfordshire.
1   1917 minesweeper of 750 tons built
    by Lobnitz. Sold in 1923 for

scrapping by Alloa at Charlestown.
2  1941 destroyer of the 'Hunt' class of 1,050 tons built by Vickers Armstrong on the Tyne. Became Polish *Kujawiak* in 1941. Mined off Malta in 1942 and foundered in tow.
3  1942 destroyer of the 'Hunt' class of 1,025/1,490 tons built by Vickers Armstrong on the Tyne. Sold to Federal Republic of Germany in 1958.

## OBDURATE

Jutland 1916
Arctic 1942−4
Barents Sea 1942
Atlantic 1943
1  1916 destroyer of 1,025 tons built by Scotts. Sold to Cashmore in 1921 for scrapping.
2  1942 destroyer of 1,540 tons built by Denny. Scrapped at Inverkeithing in 1964.

## OBEDIENT

Jutland 1916
Arctic 1942−4
Barents Sea 1942
Atlantic 1943
Normandy 1944
1  1916 destroyer of 1,025 tons built

by Scotts. Sold in 1921 to Hayes of Porthcawl for scrapping.
2  1942 destroyer of 1,540 tons built by Denny Bros. Scrapped at Blyth in 1962.

## OBERON

Crimea 1855
Ever shall be fortunate.[55]
1  1805 vessel.
2  1847 sloop. Sold in 1880.
4  1916 destroyer of 1,025 tons built by Doxford. Sold in 1921 to Ward of Rainham for scrapping.
6  1926 submarine, ex-*O-1* built at Chatham. Scrapped at Rosyth in 1945.
7  1959 attack submarine of 1,610/2,410 tons built by Chatham Dock Yard. Paid off 1986.

## OCEAN

Ushant 1781
Mesopotamia 1914
Suez Canal 1915
Dardanelles 1915
Korea 1952−3
1  1761 2nd rate (98). Scrapped in 1791.
2  1805 2nd rate (98). Scrapped in 1875.
3  1864 ironclad. Sold in 1882.
4  1898 battleship of 12,950 tons built at Devonport. Mined in 1915 at the Dardanelles.
5  1944 aircraft carrier of 13,190 tons built by Stephen. Scrapped at Faslane in 1962.

## OCELOT

1  1962 attack submarine of 1,610/2,410 tons built at Chatham Dock Yard.

## OCTAVIA

Abyssinia 1868
South France 1944
Named after the sister of the Roman Emperor Augustus.
1  1849 4th rate. Scrapped in 1876.
2  1916 destroyer, ex-*Oryx*, of 1,025 tons built by Doxford. Scrapped at Granton SB Co. in 1921.
4  1942 minesweeper of 850 tons built by Redfern. Scrapped at Gateshead in 1950.

## ODIN

Baltic 1854
Crimea 1855
China 1860
Mesopotamia 1914−17
*Attamen video* = In spite of my blind eye, I see.
Name is taken from Norse mythology: the father of the gods.
1  1807 3rd rate prize. Sold in 1825.
2  1846 frigate. Sold in 1864.
3  1901 sloop of 1,070 tons built by Sheerness Dock Yard. Sold to Bombay in 1920.
4  1928 submarine of 1,475/2,030 tons built at Chatham. Sunk by Italian destroyer *Strale* in Gulf of Taranto in 1940.
5  1960 attack submarine of 1,610/2,410 tons built by Cammell Laird.

## ODZANI

Atlantic 1943−5
Named after a river in Mashonaland, the destroyer *Mashona* having been sunk in 1941.
1  1943 frigate of 1,370 tons built by Smith's Dock. Scrapped at Newport in 1957.

55  *A Midsummer Night's Dream*, Act V Sc 1.

## OFFA

Norway 1940
Arctic 1941–5
North Africa 1942–3
Mediterranean 1943
Atlantic 1943
Sicily 1943
Salerno 1943
Normandy 1944
English Channel 1944
Named after the King of Mercia, said to have built Offa's Dyke.
1  1916 destroyer of 1,025 tons built by Fairfield. Sold in 1921.
3  1941 destroyer of 1,540 tons built by Fairfield. Sold to Pakistan in 1949, renamed *Tariq*. Scrapped in Sunderland in 1959.

## OLYMPUS

Malta Convoys 1941–2
*Fulmen e sereno* = A bolt from the blue. Named after Mount Olympus, the mountain home of the gods.
1  1914–18 vessel.
2  1928 submarine of 1,475/2,030 tons built by Beardmore. Mined in 1942 off Malta.
3  1961 attack submarine of 1,610/ 2,410 tons built by Vickers Armstrong.

## ONSLAUGHT

Jutland 1916
Arctic 1942–5
Atlantic 1943
Normandy 1944
Norway 1945
Fierce in action.
1  1915 destroyer of 1,025 tons built by Fairfield. Commanded by Andrew Cunningham at Jutland. Sold in 1921.
3  1941 destroyer, ex-*Pathfinder*, 1,540/2,030 tons built by Fairfield. Sold to Pakistan in 1951 and

renamed *Ghril*.
4  1960 submarine of 1,610/2,410 tons built at Chatham.

## ONSLOW

Jutland 1916
Norway 1941–5
Arctic 1941–5
Atlantic 1942
Malta Convoys 1942
Barents Sea 1942
North Africa 1942
Normandy 1944
Biscay 1944
Named after Admiral Sir Richard Onslow (1741–1817).
1  1916 destroyer of 1,025 tons built by Fairfield. Sold in 1921 to Barking SB Co for scrapping.
2  1941 destroyer of 1,550 tons built on Clydebank. Sold to Pakistan in 1949 and renamed *Tippu Sultan*.

## ONYX

North Sea 1943
Arctic 1944
Normandy 1944
Falkland Islands 1982
*Manly* 1809
1  1942 minesweeper of the 'Algerine' class built by Harland & Wolff.
2  1966 attack submarine of 1,610/ 2,030/2,410 tons built by Cammell Laird at Birkenhead.

## OPOSSUM

China 1856–60
Korea 1952–3
1  1808 vessel.
4  1895 destroyer of *c*.350 tons built by Hawthorn Leslie. Sold in 1920 to Ward of Preston for scrapping.
5  1944 sloop/frigate of 1,430/1,490 tons built by Denny Bros. In reserve in 1949.
6  1963 submarine of 1,610/2,030/ 2,410 tons built by Cammell Laird at Birkenhead.

## OPPORTUNE

Arctic 1942–5
North Africa 1942
Atlantic 1943
North Cape 1943
Normandy 1944
*Felix opportunitate pugnae* = Happy at the chance of a fight.[56]

1  1916 destroyer of 1,025 tons built by Doxford. Sold in 1923 to J.J. King for scrapping.
2  1942 destroyer of 1,450 tons built by Thornycroft. Scrapped at Milford Haven in 1955.
3  1964 attack submarine of 1,610/ 2,030/2,410 tons built by Scott at Greenock.

## ORACLE

1  1961 attack submarine of 1,610/ 2,030/2,410 tons built by Cammell Laird.

## ORCADIA

1  1916 destroyer of 1,025 tons built by Fairfield. Sold in 1921 for scrapping.
2  1944 minesweeper of the 'Algerine' class built by Port Arthur. Scrapped at Briton Ferry in 1958.

## ORCHIS

Atlantic 1941–4
North Sea 1942
Normandy 1944
English Channel 1944
1  1940 corvette of 925 tons built by Harland & Wolff. Mined and became CTL in 1944.

## ORESTES

Arctic 1944
Normandy 1944
Named after the son of Agamemnon and Clytemnestra.
1  1781 vessel.
4  1824 sloop. Sold in 1903.
5  1860 corvette. Scrapped just six years later.
6  1916 destroyer of 1,250 tons built by Doxford. Sold in 1921 to W & A.T. Burden.
7  1942 minesweeper of the 'Algerine' class built by Lobnitz. Scrapped at Troon in 1963.

## ORIBI

Norway 1941
Malta Convoys 1941
Atlantic 1942–3
North Africa 1942
Arctic 1942–4
Normandy 1944

56  Another source gives: Fortunate in the timeliness of her fight.

1 1941 destroyer, ex-*Observer*, of 1,540 tons built by Fairfield. Transferred to Turkey in 1946 and renamed *Gayret*.

## ORIOLE

Dunkirk 1940
1 1914−18 vessel.
2 1916 destroyer of 1,025 tons built by Palmer. Sold in 1921 to Ward of Grays for scrapping.
3 1939 paddle minesweeper, ex-*Eagle III*, of 441 tons. Accommodation ship in 1944. Returned in 1945.

## ORION

Glorious First of June 1794
Groix 1795
St Vincent 1797
Nile 1798
Trafalgar 1805
Baltic 1854−5
Jutland 1916
Atlantic 1939
Calabria 1940
Mediterranean 1940−4
Matapan 1941
Greece 1941
Crete 1941
Malta Convoys 1941
Sicily 1943
Salerno 1943
Anzio 1944
Aegean 1944
Normandy 1944
South France 1944
*Orbe circumcinto* = Over the world, *or* The world encompassed.
1 1787 3rd rate. Scrapped in 1814.
2 1854 screw ship. Scrapped in 1867.
3 1879 central battery ship. Renamed *Orontes* in 1909.
4 1910 battleship of 22,500 tons built by Portsmouth Dock Yard. Sold in 1922 to Cox & Danks for scrapping at Upnor.
6 1932 cruiser of 7,270 tons built by Vickers Armstong. Sold in 1949 for scrapping at Troon after a specially distinguished WWII record.

7 1950: name of the Reserve Fleet at Devonport.

## ORPHEUS

Guadeloupe 1810
*Vestigia nulla retrorsum* = There is no retreat.
1 2 and 3 were all 5th rates of 1770 (abandoned and burnt at Rhode Island in 1778), 1780 (wrecked) and 1809.
4 1860 sloop which was wrecked in 1863.
5 1916 destroyer of 1,025 tons built by Doxford. Sold in 1921 for scrapping by Fryer of Sunderland.
6 1928 submarine of 1,475/2,030 tons built by Beardmore. Sunk by Italian destroyer *Turbine* in the Mediterranean in 1940.
8 1959 submarine built by Vickers Armstrong, 1,610/2,410 tons. Paid off 1986.

## ORWELL

Arctic 1942−5
Barents Sea 1942
Atlantic 1943
Normandy 1944
Norway 1945
1 1865 vessel.
2 1901 destroyer of *c*.400 tons built by Laird Bros. Sold in 1920 for scrapping by Castle of Plymouth.
3 1942 destroyer of 1,540 tons built by Thornycroft. Scrapped at Newport in 1965.
4 1985 minesweeper of 890 tons built by Richards Ltd of Great Yarmouth.

## OSBORNE

1 1854 royal yacht, ex-*Victoria and Albert*. Scrapped in 1868.
2 1870 royal yacht. Sold in 1908.
4 1941 base at Cowes. Renamed *Vectis* in 1942.

5 1942−5 parent ship for all establishments on the Isle of Wight.

## OSIRIS

Mediterranean 1940
Malta Convoys 1941
Sicily 1943
*Resurgam* = I shall rise again.
God of the dead and of resurrection; husband of Isis.
1 1916 destroyer of 1,025 tons built by Palmer. Ward of Rainham scrapped her in 1921.
4 1928 submarine of 1,475/2,030 tons built by Beardmore. Scrapped at Durban in 1946.
5 1949−54 naval base at Fayid in the Canal Zone.
6 1960 attack submarine of 1,610/2,410 tons built by Vickers Armstrong.

## OSPREY

New Zealand 1845−7
*Ne exeat* = Don't let him go!
1 1797 sloop. Broken up in 1813.
4 1876 sloop. Sold in 1890.
5 1897 destroyer of *c*.400 tons built by Fairfield. Sold in 1919 to J.H. Lee for scrapping.
9 1928 the A/S school at Portland was given the name. The school transferred to Dunoon in 1941 till 1946.
10 1946 RN Air Station Portland.

## OSSORY

Barfleur 1692
Jutland 1916
Named after Rear Admiral the Earl of Ossory (1634−80).
1 1682 2nd rate which was renamed *Prince* in 1705.
2 1915 destroyer of 1,025 tons built by John Brown. Sold in 1921 to Slough TC for scrapping.

3   1944 minesweeper of the 'Algerine'
    class built by Port Arthur.
    Scrapped at Troon in 1959.

## OSWALD

Britain first.
The name is taken from the patron
saint for Oswestry: Oswald, King of
Northumbria.
1   1928 submarine of 1,475/2,030 tons
    built by Vickers Armstrong at
    Barrow. Sunk in 1940 by Italian
    destroyer *Vivaldi* south of Calabria.

## OTTER

Copenhagen 1801
Baltic 1854−5
Hard to catch.
1   1700 sloop which surrendered in
    1702.
2   1710 6th rate. Sold in 1713.
3   5, 6 and 9 were all sloops of 1721,
    1742, 1767 and 1805.
12  1896 destroyer of *c*.400 tons built
    by Vickers. Sold in 1916 to King
    for scrapping.
14  1961 attack submarine of 1,610/
    2,410 tons built by Scotts.

## OTUS

Malta Convoys 1941
*De profundis paratus* = Out of the deep
I am ready.
Named after the son of Poseidon.
1   1928 submarine of 1,475/2,030 tons
    built by Vickers Armstrong of
    Barrow. Scuttled off Durban in
    1946.
2   1962 attack submarine of 1,610/
    2,410 tons built by Scotts.

## OTWAY

Atlantic 1940
*Si deus nobiscum quis contra nos* = If
God is with us, who is against us?
Named after Admiral Sir Robert

Waller Otway (1770−1846).
1   1914−18 vessel.
2   1926 submarine, ex-*OA 2*, of 1,475/
    2,030 tons built by Vickers
    Armstrong at Barrow for RAN.
    Became RN in 1931. Scrapped in
    1945 at Inverkeithing.

## OUDENARDE

Named after Marlborough's victory
over the French in 1708.
1   1945 destroyer of 2,380 tons built
    by Swan Hunter but order
    cancelled. Used for target trials.
    Hull scrapped at Rosyth in 1957.

## OWEN

Named after Vice Admiral William
Fitzwilliam Owen (1774−1857).
1   1945 surveying ship, ex-frigate, ex-
    *Thurso Bay*, ex-*Loch Muick*, of 2,230
    tons built by Hall Russell.

## OXFORD CASTLE

Atlantic 1944−5
1   1943 corvette/frigate of 1,010 tons
    built by Harland & Wolff.
    Scrapped at Briton Ferry in 1960.

## OXLEY

*Fortiter in re* = Bravely in action.
Named after the Australian explorer
John Oxley (1781−1828).
1   1926 submarine, ex-*OA 1*, of 1,350/
    1,870 tons built by Vickers
    Armstrong, Barrow. She joined the
    RN in 1931, but was lost in 1939
    when she was rammed in error by
    the submarine *Triton* off Norway.

## OXLIP

Atlantic 1942−5
Arctic 1942−5
Sicily 1943
Normandy 1944
1   1941 corvette of 925 tons built by
    Inglis: Kincaid. Sold to Ireland and
    renamed *Maev*.

## PADSTOW BAY

*Post bellum, para bellum* = After war,
prepare for war.
1   1945 frigate, ex-*Loch Coulside*, of
    1,600 tons built by Robb: Barclay
    Curle. Scrapped at Spezia in 1959.

## PAKENHAM

Diego Suarez 1942
Mediterranean 1942−3
Named after Admiral the Hon. Sir
Thomas Pakenham (1757−1836).
1   1798 vessel.
2   1941 destroyer, ex-*Onslow*, built by
    Hawthorn Leslie. Sunk after
    damage in action from Italian TBs
    *Cassiopea* and *Cigno* off Sicily in
    1943.

## PALADIN

Diego Suarez 1942
Mediterranean 1943
Sicily 1943
Burma 1944−5
Taken from the name given to the
peers of Charlemagne.
1   1916 destroyer of 1,025 tons built
    by Scotts. Sold for scrapping by
    Ward of Rainham.
2   1941 destroyer of 1,540 tons built
    by Clydebank. Scrapped Dunston
    1962.

## PALLISER

Named after Admiral Sir Hugh
Palliser (1723−96).
1   1956 anti-submarine frigate, Type
    14, of 1,536 tons built by Stephen.
    Broken up at Briton Ferry in 1983.

## PANDORA

Mediterranean 1940−1
Malta Convoys 1941−2
Hope on, hope ever.
Named after the woman who opened
the box containing all the evils to
which humanity is subject, allowing
then all to escape — except hope.
1   1779 sloop which was wrecked in
    1791.
2   1795 prize which foundered in
    1797.
3   1806 sloop which was wrecked in
    1811.
7   1900 cruiser. Sold in 1913.
8   1914 depot ship for submarines,

4,580 tons, built by Raylton Dixon. Renamed *Dolphin* in 1924, mined in 1939 on the way to Blyth for conversion to blockship.
9  1929 submarine, ex-*Python*, of 1,475/2,040 tons built by Vickers Armstrong at Barrow. Sunk by bombs at Malta. Salved, but scrapped in 1955.

## PANTHER

Velez Malaga 1704
Diego Suarez 1942
Atlantic 1942−3
North Africa 1942−3
Sicily 1943
Salerno 1943
Mediterranean 1943
Aegean 1943
1  2 and 3 were all 4th rates of 1703 (sold in 1768 as a hulk), 1746 and 1758.
4  1897 destroyer of *c*.400 tons built by Laird Bros. Sold in 1920 to J. Kelly for scrapping.
5  1941 destroyer of 1,540 tons built by Fairfield. Bombed and sunk by aircraft in the Scarpanto Strait, 1943.

## PAPUA

Atlantic 1944−5
1  1943 frigate, ex-*USS Howett*, ex-*PF-84*, of 1,318 tons built by Walsh Kaiser. Returned to USA 1946, then in mercantile service with Egypt 1950. Scrapped 1956.

## PARAGON

Monte Christi 1652
1  1652 vessel.
2  1913 destroyer of *c*.1,000 tons built by Thornycroft. Sunk in action in the Dover Straits in 1917.
3  1939 naval base at Hartlepool.

## PARRET

Atlantic 1943
Okinawa 1945
1  1943 frigate, ex-USN of 1,370 tons, built by Canadian Vickers. Returned to USA in 1946.

## PARTHIAN

Mediterranean 1940−3
Malta Convoys 1942
Sicily 1943
*Telis utrimque* = With darts on both sides.
Named after the warlike nation from the Caspian area.
1  1808 vessel.
3  1916 destroyer of 1,025 tons built by Scotts. Sold in 1921 for breaking up in Germany.
5  1929 submarine of 1,475/2,040 tons built by Chatham Dock Yard. Lost in 1943, presumed mined in the Adriatic.

## PARTRIDGE

Scandinavian Convoys 1917
Malta Convoys 1942
North Africa 1942
Always game.
1  1809 sloop. Scrapped in 1816.
5  1916 destroyer of 1,025 tons built by Swan Hunter. Sunk in action in the North Sea in 1917.
7  1941 destroyer of 1,540 tons built by Fairfield. Torpedoed and sunk by *U-565* west of Oran in 1943.

## PASLEY

Atlantic 1944
Arctic 1945
Named after Admiral Sir Thomas Pasley (1734−1808).
1  *c*.1801 vessel.
2  1916 destroyer of 1,025 tons built by Swan Hunter. Scrapped in 1921 by Ward of Hayle.
3  1943 frigate, ex-*Lindsay*, ex-*DE.519*, built by Boston. Returned to USA in 1945.

## PATHFINDER

Atlantic 1942−3
Malta Convoys 1942
North Africa 1942−3
Sicily 1943
Salerno 1943
Aegean 1943
Burma 1944−5
1  1904 cruiser of 2,940 tons built by Cammell Laird. Torpedoed in 1914 by *U-21* in the North Sea.
2  1941 destroyer, ex-*Onslaught*, of 1,540 tons built by Hawthorn Leslie. Bombed by Japanese aircraft Ramree Island CTL 1945. Scrapped Milford Haven 1948.

## PATROLLER

Atlantic 1944−5
1  1943 escort carrier, ex-*USS Keeweenaw*, of 11,420 tons built by Seattle-Tacoma. Returned to USA in 1946 for mercantile service.

## PEACOCK

Arctic 1944
Atlantic 1945
1  1651 vessel.
6  1943 sloop of 1,350 tons built by Thornycroft. Scrapped at Rosyth in 1958.
7  1984 Far East patrol craft, 690 tons, one of a class of five built by Hall, Russell: no entry for *Swallow*, but see also *Plover*, *Starling* and *Swift*.

## PEGASUS (Pégase)

St Vincent 1780
Glorious First of June 1794
Egypt 1801
Atlantic 1940−1
*Excelsior* = Higher.
Named after the winged horse lent to Bellerophon.
1  1776 sloop which foundered in 1777.
2  1779 6th rate. Sold in 1816.
3  1782 3rd rate prize. Scrapped in 1815.
4  1849 frigate held the name briefly before being renamed *Greenock* in the same year.
5  1878 sloop. Sold in 1892.
6  1897 cruiser of 2,135 tons built by Palmer. Sunk by the *Königsberg* at Zanzibar in 1914.
7  1917 seaplane carrier of 3,300 tons built by John Brown. Sold in 1931 to Ward at Morecambe.
9  1934 seaplane carrier, ex-*Ark Royal*, 6,900 tons built by Blyth Shipbuilding Co. in 1914. Sold in 1946 for mercantile service in 1947. Scrapped at Grays in 1950.

## PELICAN

Armada 1588
Kentish Knock 1652
Portland 1653
Gabbard 1653
Scheveningen 1653
Quebec 1759
St Lucia 1778
St Lucia 1796
Jutland 1916
Norway 1940
Atlantic 1942−4
North Africa 1942
Normandy 1944
English Channel 1944
*Argus* 1813
What I have I hold.
1  *c*.1577 vessel, renamed *Golden Hind*.[57]
2  1588: hired ship at the Armada.
3  *c*.1647 frigate (12).
4  *c*.1650 4th rate of 500 tons

destroyed by fire 1656.

6   1690 fireship of 300 tons, made into a breakwater at Sheerness 1692.
7   1757 bomb vessel of 234 tons, built in 1754 ex-*St George*. Sold 1763.
8   1776 schooner of 150 tons. Sold 1779.
9   1777 6th rate of 520 tons. Lost in a hurricane 1781.
10  *c*.1781 brig/sloop of 202 tons. Sold at Deptford 1783.
11  1795 brig of 365 tons. Sold in Jamaica 1806.
12  1806 brig/sloop, ex-*Voltigeur*. Sold Deptford 1812.
13  1812 brig/sloop of 385 tons. Sold at Rye 1865.
14  1860 steam sloop of 952 tons built at Pembroke. Sold 1867 to Arthur & Co.
15  1877 screw sloop of 1,124 tons built at Deveoport. Sold in 1901 to Hudson Bay Co.
17  1917 TBD of 1,005 tons built by Beardmore. Sold 1921 to Ward of Preston for scrapping.
18  1938 sloop of 1,250 tons built by Thornycroft. Badly damaged 1940. Scrapped at Preston in 1958.

## PELLEW

Scandinavian Convoys 1917
1   1916 destroyer of 1,025 tons built by Beardmore. Named after Sir Edward Pellew, later Lord Exmouth (1757–1833). Sold to Ward, Briton Ferry in 1921 for scrapping.
2   1954 anti-submarine frigate, Type 14, 1,536 tons built by Swan Hunter. Disposal List 1974–5. Named after Captain Israel Pellew (1758–1832), captain of the *Conqueror* at Trafalgar.

## PELORUS[58]

Martinique 1809
Guadeloupe 1810
New Zealand 1860–1
Normandy 1944
Atlantic 1945
From the ancient name for Cape Faro in Sicily.
1   1808 sloop. Sold in 1941.

2   1856 frigate. Scrapped in 1869.
3   1896 cruiser of 2,135 tons built by Sheerness Dock Yard.
4   1944 minesweeper of 850 tons built by Lobnitz. Sold to South Africa in 1947 and renamed *Pietermaritzburg*.

## PEMBROKE

Lowestoft 1665
Vigo 1702
Marbella 1705
Finisterre 1747
Louisburg 1758
Quebec 1759
Havana 1762
Baltic 1855
1   1655 5th rate (22) built at Woolwich. Sunk in collision with *Fairfax* off Portland in 1667.
2   1689 5th rate built at Deptford which surrendered in 1694. She was wrecked the same year.
3   1694 4th rate (60) built by Snelgrave at Deptford. Captured by the French in 1709. Recaptured 1711 but foundered.
4   1710 4th rate (54) built by Plymouth Dock Yard. Scrapped 1726.
5   1733 4th rate (60) built at Woolwich. Foundered in the Medway in 1745 but raised and salved. Wrecked 1749 at Fort St David.
6   1740 prize sloop. Renamed *Vulture* and sold 1744.
7   1757 4th rate (60) built at Plymouth. Hulk in 1776. Scrapped in 1793 at Halifax, Nova Scotia.
8   1812 3rd rate (74) built at Blackwall by Wigram, Wells & Green. Screw ship conversion in 1855. Flagship C-in-C Nore 1869. Base ship Chatham 1873. Renamed *Forte*

1890 and became receiving hulk. Sold 1905.
9   1890 1st rate screw ship (101) of 5,724 tons built at Portsmouth. Ex-*Duncan*. Renamed *Pembroke* 1890 and *Tenedos III* in 1905. Sold in 1910.
In 1891 the name was assumed by the naval depot at Chatham and the following ships bore the name: *Trent*, 1877: *Nymphe*, 1888: *Achilles*, 1863: *Prince Rupert*, 1915: *Stour*. The dates are of launching.

## PENELOPE

Egypt 1801
Martinique 1809
Baltic 1854
Alexandria 1882
Norway 1940
Malta Convoys 1941–2
Mediterranean 1941–3
Sicily 1943
Sirte 1942
Aegean 1943
Salerno 1943
Anzio 1944
Falkland Islands 1982
*Guillaume Tell* 1800
*Constantia et fide* = With constancy and faith.
The name derives from Greek mythology. Penelope was the wife of Ulysses.
1   1778 5th rate which foundered in 1779.
2   4 and 5 were all 5th rates of 1783, 1798 (she was wrecked in 1815), and 1829.
6   1867 central battery ship. Sold in 1912.[59]
7   1914 cruiser of 3,500 tons built by Vickers. Sold to Stanlee in 1924 for scrapping.

---

57   She circumnavigated the world with Drake, and at Queen Elizabeth's instigation she was preserved 'forever' in an earth-filled dry dock at Deptford. 'Forever' lasted nearly a century.

58   *Pelorus* was one of the many warships which qualified for the medal but not the battle honour for South Africa 1899–1900. The honour was only awarded to those ships which landed a naval brigade.

59   She was the first large ironclad to have twin screws. See Manning and Walker, p. 338.

8 1935 cruiser of 5,270 tons built by Harland & Wolff. Saw great deal of action in WWII and earned the nickname HMS *Pepperpot* because of her shrapnel holes. Torpedoed by *U-410* off Anzio in 1944.

9 1962 frigate, improved Type 12, built by Vickers Armstrong. 2,450/2,860 tons. 'Leander' class armed with Exocet missiles.

## PENN

Atlantic 1942–3
Malta Convoys 1942
North Africa 1942–3
Sicily 1943
Salerno 1943
Aegean 1943
Mediterranean 1943
Burma 1945
Named after Sir William Penn, Admiral and General-at-sea (1621–70).

1 1916 destroyer of 1,025 tons built by John Brown. Sold to W. & A.T. Burden in 1921 for breaking up.

2 1941 destroyer of 1,540 tons built by Vickers Armstrong, Tyne. Scrapped at Troon in 1950.

## PENNYWORT

Atlantic 1942–5
North Sea 1942–3
Normandy 1944

1 1941 corvette of 925 tons built by Inglis: Kincaid. Scrapped at Troon in 1949.

## PENSTEMMON

Atlantic 1941–2
North Africa 1942–3
Sicily 1943

1 1916 sloop of 1,250 tons built by Workman Clark. Sold in 1920 for mercantile service and renamed *Lila*.

2 1941 corvette of 925 tons built by Philip: Clark. Sold in 1946 for mercantile service, still serving in 1951.

## PENYLAN

English Channel 1942
Named after the hunt in Wales.

1 1942 destroyer of the 'Hunt' class, 1,087 tons built by Vickers Armstrong at Barrow. Torpedoed in 1942 by an E-boat in the Channel.

## PENZANCE

Martinique 1762
Atlantic 1940
*Diligenter pensa* = Think carefully.

1 1695 6th rate. Sold in 1713.

2 1747 5th rate. Sold in 1766.

3 1930 sloop 1,045 tons built at Devonport. Torpedoed in 1940 by a German U-boat south of Greenland.

## PEONY

Dardanelles 1915
Atlantic 1940
Spartivento 1940
Malta Convoys 1941
Libya 1941–2

1 1915 sloop of 1,200 tons built by McMillan. Sold in 1919 to T.R. Sales, and resold to become *Ardena*.

2 1940 corvette of 925 tons built by Harland & Wolff. Scrapped in 1952.

## PEREGRINE

1 1650 vessel.

2 1700 6th rate. Became the royal yacht *Carolina* in 1716, and the *Royal Caroline* in 1733. Renamed *Peregrine* in 1749. She foundered in 1762.

3 1742 sloop prize. Sold the following year.

6 1916 destroyer of 1,025 tons built by John Brown. Sold in 1921 to Cashmore for scrapping.

8 1939 RN Air Station at Ford in Sussex. Finally paid off 1958.

9 A boom defence vessel.

## PERIM

Atlantic 1944–5
English Channel 1945

1 1943 frigate of 1,318 tons, ex-USS *Sierra Leone*, ex-*Phillimore* and ex-*PF-89*. Built by Walsh Kaiser. Returned to USA in 1946.

## PERSEUS

*Fortiter* = Bravely.
The name is derived from Greek mythology. He slayed the Medusa and turned Atlas into a mountain. He rescued — and married — Andromeda.

1 1776 6th rate of 432 tons. Broken up at Sheerness in 1805.

2 1805 6th rate (22) of 522 tons built

by Sutton's Yard at Ringmore. Became a receiving ship by the Tower on the Thames. Scrapped at Deptford in 1850.

3 1861 sloop (15) of 955 tons built at Pembroke. Renamed *Defiance II* in 1904.

4 1897 third-class protected cruiser of 2,135 tons built by Earle's Shipping Co at Chatham. Sold in 1914.

5 1929 submarine of 1,475/2,040 tons built by Vickers Armstrong of Barrow. Torpedoed and sunk by Italian submarine *Enrico Toti* off Zante in 1941.

6 1944 aircraft maintenance carrier of 13,350 tons built by Vickers Armstrong on the Tyne. Scrapped at Port Glasgow in 1958.

## PERSIAN

Normandy 1944

1 1809 vessel.

3 1943 minesweeper of 990 tons, ex-USN. Returned to USA for mercantile service in 1946.

## PETARD

Jutland 1916
Mediterranean 1942–3
Sicily 1943
Salerno 1943
Aegean 1943
Named after the old bomb-device.

1 1916 destroyer of 1,025 tons built by Denny. Broken up in 1923.

2 1941 destroyer, ex-*Persistent*, of 1,540 tons built by Vickers Armstrong on the Tyne. Scrapped in 1967.

## PETUNIA

Atlantic 1944–5
Normandy 1944
English Channel 1944–5

1 1916 sloop of 1,250 tons built by Workman Clark. Sold in 1922 to Batson Syndicate.

4 1940 corvette of 925 tons built by Robb: Kincaid. Loaned to Nationalist China in 1946. Lost in 1947.

## PEVENSEY CASTLE

Atlantic 1944
1 1914−18 vessel.
2 1944 corvette/frigate of 1,010 tons built by Harland & Wolff. Became *Weather Monitor* in 1960.

## PHAETON

Barfleur 1692
Glorious First of June 1794
Cornwallis' Retreat 1795
Java 1811
Jutland 1916
*San Josef* 1800
*Meliore casu* = Better luck.
1 1691 vessel.
3 1782 5th rate. Sold in 1827.
4 1848 4th rate. Scrapped in 1875.
5 1883 cruiser. Sold in 1913.
6 1914 cruiser of 3,500 tons built by Vickers. Sold in 1923 for scrapping by King of Troon.
7 1934 cruiser of 6,830 tons built by Swan Hunter and transferred to RAN as *Sydney* in 1938. Sunk in action with armed German raider *Kormoran* in S W Pacific.

## PHEASANT

Atlantic 1943−4
Sicily 1943
Okinawa 1945
1 and 3 were both sloops of 1761 (foundered), and 1798.
6 1916 destroyer of 1,025 tons built by Fairfield. Mined and sunk off the Orkneys in 1917.
7 1942 sloop of 1,350 tons built by Yarrow. Scrapped at Troon in 1961.

## PHOEBE

Trafalgar 1805
Tamatave 1811
Java 1811
Benin 1897
Belgian Coast 1917−18
Zeebrugge 1918
Greece 1941
Crete 1941
Malta Convoys 1942
Aegean 1943
Mediterranean 1944
Sabang 1944
Burma 1944−5
*Néreide* 1797
*Africaine* 1801
*Essex* 1814
The name is derived from Greek mythology.
1 1795 5th rate (36) of 926 tons built on the Thames. She enjoyed a distinguished career and earned the three single-ship action medal awards as well as serving at Trafalgar and helping to capture Java and Mauritius. She became a 'slop' ship at Plymouth in 1830 and was sold to Mr J. Cristall in 1841.
3 1854 4th rate (50) of 2,044 tons. Converted to a screw steamer of 2,896 tons and 30 guns. Scrapped in 1875.
4 1890 third-class cruiser of 2,575 tons built at Devonport. Sold in 1906.
5 1916 destroyer of 1,025 tons built by Fairfield. Sold for scrapping to Cashmore in 1921.
7 1939 cruiser of 5,450 tons built by Fairfield. Scrapped at Blyth in 1956.
8 1964 anti-submarine general purpose frigate of 2,450/3,200 tons built by Stephen. 'Leander' class armed with Exocet missiles.

## PHOENIX

Monte Cristi 1652
Gabbard 1653

Scheveningen 1653
Solebay 1672
Vigo 1702
Velez Malaga 1704
Egypt 1801
Bay of Biscay 1805
Syria 1840
China 1900
Heligoland 1914
Dogger Bank 1915
*Didon* 1805
*Resurgam* = I shall rise again.
Named after the mythical bird which could burn itself on a funeral pyre, then rise again from the ashes.
1 1546 6th rate (20) bought in Scotland.
2 1612 6th rate (20). Sold about fifty years later.
3 4, 5, 9 and 10 were all 5th rates of 1649 (38), 1649−54 (34), 1671 (burnt),[60] 1759 (lost in a hurricane), 1783 (wrecked in 1816).
14 15 and 16 were all sloops of 1832, 1879 and 1895, the last two being wrecked.
17 1911 destroyer of *c.*810 tons built by Vickers. Sunk by an Austrian submarine in the Adriatic in 1918.
18 1929 submarine of 1,475/2,040 tons built by Cammell Laird. Sunk by Italian torpedo boat *Albatross* off Sicily in 1940.
19 1940 RN Air Station at Fayid, handed over to RAF in 1946.
20 1949 RN Defence School, Stamshaw until 1957. Integral part of *Excellent*. Closed 1984.

## PICOTEE

Atlantic 1940−1
1 1940 corvette of 925 tons built by Harland & Wolff. Sunk in 1941 by *U-568* off Iceland.

## PIMPERNEL

Atlantic 1941−5
Biscay 1943
1 1914−18 vessel.
2 1940 corvette of 925 tons built by Harland & Wolff. Scrapped at Portaferry in 1948.

## PINCHER

Baltic 1855
Normandy 1944
Atlantic 1945
Burma 1945
1 1794 vessel.

60 The first RN ship to be lead-sheathed. Manning and Walker p. 342.

6  1910 destroyer of *c*.975 tons built
by Denny. Wrecked in 1918 on the
Seven Stones.
7  1943 minesweeper of the 'Algerine'
class built by Harland & Wolff.
Scrapped in 1962.

## PINK

North Sea 1942
Atlantic 1942−4
English Channel 1944
Normandy 1944
1  1942 corvette of 925 tons built by
Robb: Ailsa and NE Marine. CTL
in 1944. Scrapped at Llanelly in
1947.

## PINTAIL

North Sea 1940−1
1  1914−18 vessel.
2  1934 corvette of 580 tons built in
1939 by Denny. Mined in 1941 in
the Humber.

## PIONEER

China 1856−60
1  1804 schooner of 197 tons built at
Upnor in Kent. Sold at Plymouth
in 1849.
3  1850 steamer ex-*Eider* of 342 tons
purchased for Arctic exploration
but foundered in the Arctic in
1854.
Several small vessels followed: a
screw gun ship, a paddle river
gunboat, a small steamer, a
composite steamer built by
Sunderland, a screw river
gunboat built in sections and
shipped to Lake Nyassa.
10  1899 third-class protected cruiser
of 2,000 tons built at Chatham.
Given to the RAN in 1913 and
sold in 1926.
15  1944 light aircraft carrier, ex-*Mars*,
ex-*Ethalion*, built by Vickers
Armstrong at Barrow. Scrapped
at Inverkeithing in 1954.

## PIQUE

Egypt 1801
Syria 1840
China 1856−60
Normandy 1944
1  1795 5th rate prize. Lost in 1798
after action at sea.
2  and 3 were both 5th rates of 1800
and 1834.
4  1890 cruiser. Sold in 1911.
5  1942 minesweeper ex-USS *Celerity*
of 890 tons. Sold to Turkey in 1947.

## PITCAIRN

1  1943 frigate ex-USS *Pilford*, ex-
*PF.85*, built by Walsh Kaiser.
Returned to USA in 1946.

## PLOVER

Portland 1653
China 1842
China 1856−60
Normandy 1944
*Noli me tangere* = Do not touch me.
1  1652 prize. Sold in 1657.
2  1796 sloop. Sold in 1819.
9  1916 destroyer of 1,025 tons built
by Hawthorn Leslie. Sold in 1921
for scrapping by Ward at Hayle.
10  1937 minelayer of 805 tons built
by Denny. Scrapped at
Inverkeithing in 1969.
11  1984 Far East patrol craft, 690
tons, one of a class of five built by
Hall, Russell: no entry for
*Swallow*, but see also *Peacock*,
*Starling* and *Swift*.

## PLUCKY

Normandy 1944
Burma 1945
1  1856 vessel.
3  1916 destroyer of 1,025 tons built
by Scotts. Sold in 1921 and broken
up in 1924.
4  1943 minesweeper of the 'Algerine'
class built by Harland & Wolff.
Scrapped in 1963.

## PLUTO

*De profundis.*
1  1745 vessel.
3  1782 sloop. Sold in 1817.
5  1944 minesweeper of the 'Algerine'
class built at Port Arthur. Disposed
of about 1973.

## PLYM

Sicily 1943
Atlantic 1943
1  1914−18 vessel.
2  1943 frigate of 1,370 tons built by
Smith's Dock. RNVR drill ship in
1948. Expended in atomic bomb
tests in 1952.

## PLYMOUTH

Porto Farina 1655
Santa Cruz 1657
Lowestoft 1665
Four Days' Battle 1666
Orfordness 1666
Solebay 1672
Texel 1673
Falkland Islands 1982
1  1653 3rd rate. Lost at sea 1705.
3  1708 4th rate. Scrapped in 1764.
4  1709 6th rate prize but she herself
surrendered in the same year.
11  1959 frigate, anti-submarine, of
2,380/2,800 tons built by
Portsmouth Dock Yard.

## POLYANTHUS

Atlantic 1941−3
1  1917 sloop of 1,250 tons built by
Lobnitz. Sold in 1921 to the Clan
Line and renamed *Colima*.
2  1940 corvette of 925 tons built by
Robb: Kincaid. Torpedoed and
sunk in the North Atlantic by a U-
boat, 1943.

## POMONE

Named after Pomona, the goddess of
orchards.
1  1761 sloop which was wrecked in
1776.
2  1778 6th rate which was renamed
*Amphitrite* in 1795.
3  5 and 6 were all 5th rates of 1794
(prize), 1805 (wrecked), and 1810
(prize).
7  1897 cruiser of 2,135 tons. She

became a training ship at Dartmouth and was sold in 1922.

9 1943–6 boom defence depot at Scapa.

## POOLE

Diego Suarez 1942
Sicily 1943
Normandy 1944
1 1696 5th rate which was expended as foundations at Harwich in 1737.
2 1745 5th rate. Scrapped in 1765.
3 1941 minesweeper of 650 tons built by Stephen. Scrapped in 1948.

## POPPY

North Sea 1942–4
Arctic 1942–4
Mediterranean 1942–4
North Africa 1942
Atlantic 1943–5
Sicily 1943
Normandy 1944
English Channel 1944
1 1915 sloop of 1,250 tons built by Swan Hunter. Sold in 1922 to Rees of Llanelly for scrapping.
2 1941 corvette of 925 tons built by Hall. Sold in 1946 for mercantile service. Hulked in 1955.

## PORCUPINE

Quebec 1759
Havana 1762
Baltic 1854–5
North Africa 1942
1 4 and 7 were all sloops of 1746, 1777 and 1807.
9 1894 destroyer of 1,540 tons built by Vickers Armstrong on the Tyne. Torpedoed by *U-602* in the Mediterranean in 1943. CTL, but forepart salved and became landing craft base in 1944. Minesweeping base in 1946. Scrapped in 1947.

## PORLOCK BAY

1 1945 frigate of 1,580 tons, ex-*Loch Seaforth*, ex-*Loch Muick*, built by Hill: Robey. Finnish navy 1962.

## PORPOISE

Baltic 1855
Jutland 1916
Norway 1940
Atlantic 1940–1
Malta Convoys 1942
Mediterranean 1942
Purpose is power.
1 1777 sloop which was renamed *Firebrand* in the following year.
5 1886 cruiser. Sold in 1905.
6 1913 destroyer of *c*.1,000 tons built by Thornycroft. Sold to Brazil in 1920.
7 1932 submarine of 1,520/2,157 tons built by Vickers Armstrong of Barrow. Sunk by Japanese aircraft in the Malacca Straits in 1945.
9 1956 submarine of 1,600/2,030 tons built by Vickers Armstrong. Disposal List 1984–5.

## PORTCHESTER CASTLE

Atlantic 1944
1 1943 corvette/frigate of 1,010 tons built by Swan Hunter. Scrapped in 1958 at Troon.

## POSTILLION

Normandy 1944
Atlantic 1944–5
1 1702 6th rate prize which was wrecked in 1709.
2 *c*.1769 frigate. Sold in the following year.
4 1943 minesweeper, ex-USN built by Redfern, 850 tons. Sold to the Greek navy in 1947.

## POTENTILLA

Atlantic 1942–3
Normandy 1944
North Sea 1944
1 1941 corvette of 925 tons built by

Simons. Royal Norwegian navy 1942–4.
Scrapped at Gateshead in 1946.

## POWERFUL

Camperdown 1797
Syria 1840
South Africa 1899–1901
1 1783 3rd rate. Scrapped in 1812.
2 1826 2nd rate. Scrapped in 1864.
3 1895 cruiser of 14,200 tons. Renamed *Impregnable* in 1919. In 1912 the *Powerful* was part of the training ship formed at Devonport.
4 1945 aircraft carrier of 14,000 tons built by Harland & Wolff. Work was suspended and she was not launched till 1952. Became RCN *Bonaventure*. Scrapped at Taiwan in 1971.

## PREMIER

Atlantic 1944
Norway 1945
Arctic 1945
1 1914–18 vessel.
4 1943 escort carrier ex-USS *Estero* of 11,420 tons built by Seattle:Tacoma. Returned to USA 1946 for mercantile service.

## PRESIDENT

Portland 1653
Gabbard 1653
Scheveningen 1653
Java 1811
San Sebastian 1813
1 1646 (20). Known also as *Little* or *Old President*. Sold in 1655.
2 3 and 4 were all 5th rates of 1649 (42), 1806 and 1815.
5 1829 4th rate became a Reserves drill ship in 1861. Sold in 1903.
6 7 and 8 were all sloops of 1903, 1911 and 1921.[61]

61 All naval officers serving at the Admiralty have been borne on the books of the *President* for more than a century — since May 1878. It is still the HQ of London Division RNR. See Manning and Walker, p. 349.

## PRIMROSE

Armada 1588
Cadiz 1596
Atlantic 1940−5
North Sea 1942
Normandy 1944
English Channel 1944
1  1523 vessel. Two merchant ships
   accompanied the fleet at the
   Armada campaign.
5  1651 sloop. Lost in 1656.
9  1915 sloop of 1,200 tons built by
   Simons. Scrapped by Rees,
   Llanelly in 1923.
13  1940 corvette of 925 tons built by
   Simons. Sold in 1949 for
   mercantile service.

## PRIMULA

Atlantic 1940−4
Libya 1942
Sicily 1943
1  1915 sloop of 1,250 tons built by
   Swan Hunter. Torpedoed in the
   Mediterranean by *U-35* in 1916.
2  1940 corvette of 925 tons built by
   Simons. Sold in 1947 for mercantile
   service. Scrapped in 1953 in Hong
   Kong.

## PRINCE OF WALES

St Lucia 1778
Groix 1795
Dardanelles 1915
*Bismarck* Action 1941
Malta Convoys 1941
1  1765 3rd rate. Scrapped in 1783.
4  1794 2nd rate. Scrapped in 1822.
10  1860 1st rate. She became the
   *Britannia* in 1869 for training
   cadets.
11  1902 battleship of 15,000 tons
   built by Chatham Dock Yard.
   Sold in 1920 to Ward of Milford
   Haven for scrapping.
12  1939 battleship of 35,000 tons
   built by Cammell Laird. Sunk by
   Japanese aircraft in company with
   *Repulse* in 1941 in the South China
   Sea.

## PROMPT

Baltic 1955
Atlantic 1945
1  1702 3rd rate prize which was
   scrapped in the following year.
2  1793 6th rate prize. Scrapped in
   1813.
7  1944 minesweeper of 990 tons ex-
   RCN *Huntsville*. Built by Redfern.
   CTL in 1945. Scrapped at Rainham
   in 1947.

## PROSERPINE

Suez Canal 1915
1  1757 vessel.
2  1777 6th rate which was wrecked
   in 1798.
3  4 and 5 were all 5th rates of 1798,
   1807 (she surrendered) and 1830.
6  1896 cruiser of 2,135 tons built by
   Sheerness Dock Yard. Scrapped in
   1919/20 in Genoa.
7  1939−45 naval base at Lyness.

## PROTECTOR

Sadras 1758
Negapatam 1758
Cape of Good Hope 1806
Norway 1940
Libya 1940−1
Faith For Duty.
The name and badge derive from the
Lord Protector of England, 1547−9,
the Duke of Somerset.
1  1749 5th rate (44) Indian built ship
   which foundered off Pondicherry
   in a cyclone in 1761.
2  1758: a fireship of this name was in
   service.
3  1805 gun-brig (12) built by Warren
   of Brightlingsea. Employed as a
   survey vessel 1817. Sold in 1833 for
   scrapping.
4  1861−2 screw gunboat ordered but
   cancelled 1863.
5  1884 gunboat of 920 tons built by
   Armstrong at Elswick and served
   the Australian government.
   Renamed *Cerebus* in 1921 but
   reverted to *Protector* three years
   later. Sold 1924 to J. Hill of
   Melbourne. Resold 1931 as *Sidney*.
6  1936 netlayer of 2,900 tons built by
   Yarrow. Converted to Antarctic
   patrol ship in 1955 and increased
   displacement to 3,450 tons.
7  1983 date of acquisition and
   commissioning into RN. Built 1975
   by Drypool (Selby). 802 tons gross.
   Employed on Falklands Patrol
   duties. Ex-*Seaforth Saga*.

## PROTEUS

Mediterranean 1941−42
Malta Convoys 1942
*Mutare sperno* = I scorn to change.
1  1777 6th rate (26). Scrapped in
   1783.
2  1780 prize, 3rd rate. Scrapped in
   1815.
3  1825 5th rate. Sold in 1832.
4  1929 submarine of 1,475/2,040 tons
   built by Vickers Armstrong at
   Barrow. Scrapped at Troon in 1946.

## PROVIDENCE

Portland 1653
Gabbard 1653
Lowestoft 1665
Orfordness 1666
Schooneveld 1673
1  1637 6th rate (30) which was
   wrecked in 1668.
8  1780 prize 6th rate (28). Sold in
   1784.
18  1943 minesweeper of the
   'Algerine' class built by Redfern,
   ex-RCN *Forest Hill*. Scrapped at
   Sunderland in 1958.

## PUCKERIDGE

English Channel 1942
North Africa 1942−3
Sicily 1943
Named after the hunt in
Hertfordshire.
1  1941 destroyer of the 'Hunt' class
   of 1,050 tons built by White.
   Torpedoed and sunk by *U-617* off
   Gibraltar in 1943.

## PUMA

1  1954 frigate of 2,500 tons built by
   Scotts. Scrapped in 1976.

## PUNCHER

Atlantic 1944
1  1943 escort carrier, ex-USS *Willapa*
   of 11,420 tons built by Seattle:
   Tacoma. Served with RCN.
   Returned to USA in 1946 for
   mercantile service.
2  1986 coastal patrol craft of 43 tons.

## PUNJABI

Narvik 1940
Atlantic 1940−2
Norway 1941

*Bismarck* Action 1941
Arctic 1941−2
1 1937 destroyer of 'Tribal' class of 1,870 tons built by Scotts. Sunk in collision with *King George V* in N Atlantic.

## PURSUER

Atlantic 1943−5
Norway 1944
Normandy 1944
South France 1944
Aegean 1944
1 1942 escort carrier of 11,420 tons, ex-USS *St George*, ex-*Mormacland*, built by Ingalls Shipbuilding. Returned to USA in 1946.
2 1947 landing-ship.
3 1986 coastal patrol craft of 43 tons.

## PYLADES

China 1841
Baltic 1855
Atlantic 1944
Normandy 1944
1 2 and 3 were all sloops of 1781 (prize), 1794 (wrecked but salved) and 1824.
4 1853 corvette. Sold in 1875.
5 1884 corvette. Sold in 1906.
6 1916 destroyer of 1,025 tons built by Stephen. Sold in 1921 to Ward, Hayle for scrapping.
7 1943 minesweeper of 890 tons. Torpedoed in 1944 off Normandy by a human torpedo.

## PYRAMUS

1 1810 5th rate, Sold in 1879.
2 1897 cruiser of 2,135 tons built by Palmer. Sold in 1920 to Holland.
3 1939−45 naval base at Kirkwall.

## PYRRHUS

Named after King Pyrrhus of Epirus. A 'Pyrrhic' victory is one gained at too great a cost.
1 1945 minesweeper of the 'Algerine' class built by Port Arthur. Scrapped at Newport in 1956.

## PYTCHLEY

English Channel 1942−4
North Sea 1942−5
Arctic 1943
Normandy 1944
Named after the hunt in Northamptonshire.

1 1917 minesweeper of 750 tons built by Napier & Miller. Sold to Stanlee in 1932.
2 1940 destroyer of the 'Hunt' class of 907 tons built by Scotts. Scrapped at Llanelly in 1956.

## QUADRANT

Arctic 1942−3
Okinawa 1945
1 1942 destroyer of 1,705 tons built by Hawthorn Leslie. RAN 1945. Sold in 1963 for scrapping.

## QUAIL

Sicily 1943
Salerno 1943
Mediterranean 1943
1 1805 vessel.
4 1895 destroyer of *c*.400 tons built by Laird. Sold in 1919 to Ward, New Holland.
7 1942 destroyer of 1,705 tons built by Hawthorn Leslie. Mined south of Calabria in 1943 and sank in tow in 1944.

## QUALITY

North Africa 1942−3
Sabang 1944
Okinawa 1945
1 1941 destroyer of 1,705 tons built by Swan Hunter at Wallsend. RAN 1945. Scrapped in Japan in 1958.

## QUANTOCK

North Sea 1941−5
Atlantic 1943
Sicily 1943
Salerno 1943
Adriatic 1944
Named after the hunt in Somersetshire.
1 1940 destroyer of the 'Hunt' class, 907 tons built by Scotts. Sold to Ecuador in 1954.

## QUEEN

Ushant 1781
Glorious First of June 1794
Groix 1795
Crimea 1854−5
Dardanelles 1915
Atlantic 1944
Norway 1945
Arctic 1945
1 1216−72: vessel in the reign of Henry III.

2 1693 1st rate (100), ex-*Royal Charles*. Renamed again in 1715 as *Royal George*.
3 1769 2nd rate. Scrapped in 1821.
8 1839 1st rate. Sold in 1871.
9 1902 battleship of 15,000 tons built by Devonport Dock Yard. Sold in 1920 for breaking up by Ward at Birkenhead and Preston.
12 1943 escort carrier, ex-USS *St Andrews* of 11,420 tons built by Seattle:Tacoma. Returned to USA in 1946.

## QUEENBOROUGH

Sadras 1758
Negapatam 1758
Porto Novo 1759
Arctic 1942−3
Sicily 1943
Salerno 1943
Mediterranean 1943
Okinawa 1945
Seek and slay.
1 1671 vessel.
2 1694 6th rate. Sold in 1719.
4 1747 6th rate. Lost in a cyclone in 1761.
6 1942 destroyer of 1,705 tons built by Swan Hunter at Wallsend. RAN 1945.

## QUEEN CHARLOTTE

Glorious First of June 1794
Groix 1795
Algiers 1816
Named after King George III's consort.
1 1790 1st rate. Blown up in 1800.
4 1810 2nd rate which was renamed *Excellent* in 1859 and then scrapped in the same year.
6 1941−6 AA range at Ainsdale.

## QUEEN ELIZABETH

Dardanelles 1915
Crete 1941
Sabang 1944
Burma 1944−5

*Semper eadem* = Always the same.
Named after Elizabeth Tudor.
1   1913 battleship of 32,700 tons built
    by Fairfield at Portsmouth.
    Scrapped at Dalmuir and Troon
    (hull only) in 1948.

## QUENTIN

Atlantic 1942
Mediterranean 1942
Malta Convoys 1942
North Africa 1942
I will be prompt at the signal.
1   1941 destroyer of 1,705 tons built
    by White. Torpedoed by Italian
    aircraft north of Algiers in 1942.

## QUIBERON

Mediterranean 1942
North Africa 1942−3
Atlantic 1943
Okinawa 1945
Named after Admiral Sir Edward
Hawke's famous victory in 1759.
1   1942 destroyer of 1,705 tons built
    by White. Transferred to the RAN
    in 1942. Scrapped in Japan in 1972.

## QUICKMATCH

English Channel 1942
Atlantic 1942
Sabang 1944
Okinawa 1945
1   1942 destroyer of 1,705 tons built
    by White. Transferred to RAN
    1942. Scrapped in Japan in 1972.

## QUILLIAM

Sicily 1943
Salerno 1943
Mediterranean 1943
Sabang 1944

Okinawa 1945
Named after John Quilliam, First
Lieutenant aboard *Victory* at Trafalgar.
1   1941 destroyer of 1,705 tons built
    by Hawthorn Leslie. Sold to
    Holland in 1945 and renamed
    *Banckert*. Scrapped in 1957.

## QUORN

North Sea 1941−4
English Channel 1942−4
Normandy 1944
Named after the hunt in
Leicestershire.
1   1917 minesweeper of 750 tons built
    by Napier & Miller. Sold in 1922 to
    J. Smith for scrapping.
2   1940 destroyer of the 'Hunt' class,
    907 tons built by White. Struck by
    explosive MTB off Normandy and
    sunk 1944.
3   1986 MCMV of 615/725 tons built
    by Vosper Thornycroft.

## RACEHORSE

Quebec 1759
Tamatave 1811
New Zealand 1845−7
China 1856−60
Belgian Coast 1915−16
Atlantic 1943
Sabang 1944
Burma 1945
1   1757 vessel.
2   4, 5, 6 and 7 were all sloops of
    1775 (surrendered), 1781, 1806
    (lost), 1830 and 1860 (wrecked).
10  1900 destroyer of *c.*400 tons built
    by Hawthorn Leslie. Sold in 1920
    for scrapping at Milford Haven.
11  1942 destroyer of 1,705 tons built
    by John Brown. Scrapped at
    Troon in 1950.

## RACER

1   *c.*1793 vessel.
7   1857 sloop. Scrapped in 1876.
10  1939−45 naval base at Larne.

## RAIDER

Arctic 1942−3
Sicily 1943
Salerno 1943
Mediterranean 1943
Sabang 1944

Burma 1944−5
1   1916 destroyer of 1,065 tons built
    by Swan Hunter. Sold in 1927 to
    Cohen for scrapping.
2   1942 destroyer of 1,705 tons built
    by Cammell Laird. RIN 1949 and
    renamed *Rana*.

## RAINBOW

Armada 1588
Cadiz 1596
Portland 1653
Gabbard 1653
Scheveningen 1653
Lowestoft 1665
Four Days' Battle 1666
Orfordness 1666[62]
Solebay 1672
Schooneveld 1673
Texel 1673
Lagos 1759
1   1586 vessel of 54 guns fought at the
    Armada battle. Sunk at Sheerness
    in 1690.
2   1697 5th rate prize. Sold in the
    following year.
3   1747 5th rate. Sold in 1802.[63]
4   and 5 were both 6th rates of 1809
    (prize) and 1823.
7   1891 cruiser which was transferred
    to the RCN in 1910.
9   1930 submarine of 1,475/2,030 tons
    built at Chatham. Sunk in 1940 by
    the Italian submarine *Enrico Toti* off
    Calabria.

## RAJAH

Atlantic 1944
1   1942 escort carrier, ex-USS *Prince*,
    ex-*McClure*, of 11,420 tons built by
    Seattle: Tacoma. Returned to USA
    in 1946.

---

62   Two ships of this name attended the battle. Manning and Walker p.364.

63   The first ship to be armed entirely with carronades. Manning and Walker, p. 363.

## RALEIGH

*Amore et virtute* = By love and valour.
Named after Sir Walter Raleigh
(1552–1618).
1  1771 sloop which was renamed in
   the following year as *Adventure* —
   she then sailed on Cook's second
   voyage of discovery.
2  1778 5th rate prize. Sold in 1783.
4  1845 4th rate which was wrecked
   in 1857.
5  1873 frigate. Sold in 1905.
6  1916 cruiser of 9,750 tons built by
   Beardmore. Wrecked in 1922 in the
   Belle Isle Strait, Labrador.
7  1939 training establishment at
   Torpoint.

## RAME HEAD

1  1944 maintenance and repair ship
   of 9,000/11,270 tons built by
   Barrard of Vancouver. Disposal
   List 1985–6.

## RAMILLIES

Glorious First of June 1794
Copenhagen 1801
Spartivento 1940
Mediterranean 1940
Atlantic 1941
Diego Suarez 1942
Normandy 1944
South France 1944
*Victoria nostrorum victoria nobis* = The
victory of (our forces) is our victory.
The name commemorates the Duke of
Marlborough's victory in 1706.
1  1706 2nd rate, ex-*Royal Katherine*.
   She was wrecked in 1760.
2  and 3 were both 3rd rates of 1763
   (lost in a hurricane) and 1785.
4  1892 battleship of 14,150 tons. Sold
   in 1913.
5  1916 battleship of 29,150 tons built
   by Beardmore. Scrapped in 1948–9
   by Cairn Ryan, and the hull only at
   Troon.

## RAMSEY

Atlantic 1941–2
1  1940 destroyer ex-USS *Meade*, of
   1,190 tons built by Bethlehem:
   Squantum in 1919. Scrapped in
   1947.

## RANEE

Atlantic 1945
*Ex aqua in auras* = Out of the water
into the air.
1  1914–18 vessel.
2  1943 escort carrier, ex-USS *Niantic*,
   of 11,420 tons built by Seattle:
   Tacoma. Returned to USA in 1946.

## RAPID

Atlantic 1943
Sabang 1944
Burma 1944–5
1  1804 brig (12) of 177 tons built at
   Topsham. Sunk by gun batteries in
   the river Tagus in 1808.
2  1808 sloop (16) of 261 tons. Sold in
   1814.
3  1829 brig/sloop (10) which was
   wrecked off Crete in 1838.
6  1860 sloop of 672 tons built at
   Deptford. Scrapped in 1881.
7  1883 single screw composite
   (corvette) (12) of 1,420 tons built at
   Devonport. Hulked at Gibraltar.
8  1916 destroyer of 1,033 tons built
   by Thornycroft. Sold to Cohen in
   1927 for scrapping.
9  1942 destroyer of 2,700 tons built
   by Cammell Laird. Transferred to
   RIN in 1949. Expended as target
   ship in 1982.

## RATTLESNAKE

Martinique 1794
Cape of Good Hope 1795
China 1841–2
Ashantee 1873–4
Dardanelles 1915–16

North Sea 1942
Arctic 1944
Normandy 1944
1  1777 vessel.
2  and 4 were both sloops of 1773 and
   1791.
5  1822 6th rate. Scrapped in 1859.
6  1861 corvette. Scrapped in 1875.
8  1910 destroyer of *c.*975 tons built
   by Harland & Wolff at Govan. Sold
   in 1921 to Ward of Milford Haven.
9  1943 minesweeper of the 'Algerine'
   class built by Lobnitz. Scrapped at
   Grangemouth in 1959.

## RAVAGER

Atlantic 1943
Ruthless unto victory.
1  1942 escort carrier, ex-*Charger*, of
   11,420 tons built by Sun
   Shipbuilding Corporation.
   Returned to USA in 1946.
2  1947 landing ship.

## RAVEN

Portland 1653
Gabbard 1653
Scheveningen 1653
St Vincent 1797
Crimea 1855
1  1652 5th rate (36) prize.
   Surrendered in 1654.
2  and 4 were both sloops of 1745
   and 1771.
5  1782 prize, ex-*Ceres*. Surrendered
   again in 1783.
6  7 and 8 were all sloops of 1796
   (lost), 1799 (prize) and 1804
   (wrecked in 1805).
15 1939–47 RN Air Station at
   Eastleigh.

## READING

Atlantic 1941–2
1  1940 destroyer, ex-USS *Bailey*, of
   1,190 tons built in 1919 by
   Bethlehem: Squantum. Scrapped
   at Inverkeithing in 1945.

## READY

Normandy 1944
Arctic 1944
1  1797 vessel.
4  1916 destroyer of 1,033 tons built
   by Thornycroft. Sold in 1926 to
   King, Garston for scrapping.
5  1943 minesweeper of 990 tons built
   by Harland & Wolff. Sold to
   Belgium in 1951 and scrapped at
   Bruges ten years later.

## REAPER

Atlantic 1944
1  1914–18 vessel.
3  1943 escort carrier, ex-USS *Winjah*, of 11,420 tons built by Seattle: Tacoma. Returned to USA in 1946.

## RECRUIT

Martinique 1809
Crimea 1855
Belgian Coast 1917
Normandy 1944
Atlantic 1945
Burma 1945
1  1806 vessel.
5  1896 destroyer of *c*.400 tons built by Thompson. Torpedoed in 1915 by *UB-16* off the Galloper Light vessel.
6  1916 destroyer of 1,065 tons built by Doxford. Mined in 1917 in the North Sea.
8  1943 minesweeper of the 'Algerine' class built by Harland & Wolff. Scrapped at Barrow in 1965.

## REDMILL

English Channel 1944
Arctic 1944
North Sea 1944–5
Atlantic 1945
Named after Captain Robert Redmill who commanded the *Polyphemus* at Trafalgar.
1  1943 frigate, ex-USS *DE.89*, of 1,300 tons built by Bethlehem: King. Torpedoed in 1945 by *U-1105* west of Ireland. CTL. Returned to USA in 1946.

## REDOUBT

Atlantic 1943
Burma 1945
1  1793 6th rate. Converted to floating battery. Sold in 1802.
2  1916 destroyer of 1,065 tons built by Doxford. Sold in 1926.
3  1942 destroyer of 1,705 tons built at Clydebank. Transferred to RIN in 1949 and renamed *Ranjit*.
4  1956 LCT.

## REDPOLE

Basque Roads 1809
Atlantic 1943–4
Normandy 1944
Burma 1944–5
1  1808 vessel.
4  1910 destroyer of *c*.760 tons built by White. Sold in 1921 for scrapping by Ward at Milford Haven.
5  1943 frigate of 1,350 tons built by Yarrow. Disarmed and became tender to the Navigation school. Scrapped at St David's-on-Forth in 1960.
6  1967 large patrol craft, 194 tons, built by Brooke Marine, Lowestoft, ex-*Sea Otter*.

## REGENT

Mediterranean 1940–1
Falkland Islands 1982
*Serviendo regno* = I rule by serving.
1  1486 vessel which was destroyed by fire in 1512.
3  1930 submarine of 1,475/2,030 tons built by Vickers Armstrong of Barrow. Lost in 1943 when mined in the Taranto Strait.
4  1967 (commissioning date) fleet replenishing ship[64] of 22,890 tons full load built by Harland & Wolff.

## REGULUS

Egypt 1801
*In primus pro patria* = For the Fatherland first.
In 251 BC Regulus returned to Carthage after sabotaging a peace embassy to Rome. He was cruelly killed.
1  1785 5th rate. Scrapped in 1815.
3  1930 submarine of 1,475/2,030 tons built by Vickers Armstrong at Barrow. Lost in the Adriatic in 1940 from an unknown cause.
4  1943 minesweeper, ex-*Longbranch*, of 950 tons. Lost by mine off Corfu in 1945.

## RELENTLESS

Sabang 1944
1  1916 destroyer of *c*.900 tons built by Yarrow. Sold in 1926 to Cashmore for scrapping.
2  1942 frigate of 2,700 tons built by John Brown at Clydebank. Disposal List 1974–5.

## RELIANT

1  1951 air stores supply ship, ex-*Somersby*, of 13,737 tons built by Laing: Hawthorn Leslie. Helicopter Support ship.

## RENOWN

Gabbard 1653
Scheveningen 1653
Ushant 1781
Egypt 1801
Norway 1940
Atlantic 1940
Spartivento 1940
Mediterranean 1941
*Bismarck* Action 1941
Malta Convoys 1941–2
Arctic 1942
North Africa 1942
Sabang 1944
*Antiquae famae custos* = Guardian of ancient renown.

---

64  Official designation is AEFS = Armament, Explosives, Food, Stores ship.

1 1651 6th rate prize (20). Sold three years later.[65]
2 1747 5th rate prize. Scrapped in 1771.[65]
3 1774 3rd rate. Scrapped in 1794.
4 1796 5th rate prize. Scrapped in 1810.[65]
5 1798 5th rate. Scrapped in 1835.
6 1857 2nd rate. Sold in 1870.
7 1895 battleship. Sold in 1913.
9 1916 battlecruiser of 32,000 tons built by Fairfield: Cammell Laird. Scrapped at Faslane in 1948.[66]
10 1967 nuclear-powered ballistic missile submarine (SSBN) of 7,500/8,400 tons built by Vickers Armstrong at Barrow.

## REPULSE

Cadiz 1596
Martinique 1762
The Saintes 1782
Norway 1940
Atlantic 1940
*Bismarck* Action 1941
*Qui tangit frangitur* = Who touches me is broken.
1 1595 vessel (50).
2 *c.*1760 5th rate which foundered about 1776.
3 1780 3rd rate which was wrecked in 1800.
6 1803 3rd rate. Scrapped in 1820.
8 1868 ironclad. Sold in 1889.
9 1892 battleship. Sold in 1911.
10 1916 battlecruiser of 32,000 tons built on Clydebank. Sunk in the S. China Sea by Japanese aircraft in company with *Prince of Wales*, 1941.
11 1967 nuclear-powered ballistic missile submarine (SSBN) 7,500/8,400 tons built by Vickers Armstrong at Barrow.

## RESOLUTION

Kentish Knock 1652
Gabbard 1653
Scheveningen 1653
Lowestoft 1665
Orfordness 1666
Solebay 1672
Schooneveld 1673
Texel 1673
Barfleur 1692
Quiberon Bay 1759
St Vincent 1780
St Kitts 1782
The Saintes 1782
Basque Roads 1809
Atlantic 1939−40
Norway 1940
*A l'outrance* = To a finish.
1 *c.*1650 vessel (55) ex-*Prince*.
2 1660 vessel (50) ex-*Tredagh*. Lost by fire in 1666.
3 4, 5, 6 and 7 were all 3rd rates of 1667 (lost in the great gale of 1703), 1705 (run ashore and fired), 1708 (wrecked), 1756 (wrecked in the Quiberon battle) and 1770.
8 1771 vessel ex-*Drake*. She sailed on Cook's second and third voyages of discovery.
15 1892 battleship. Sold in 1914 for scrapping.
16 1915 battleship of 29,150 tons built by Palmer. In 1944 she became part of the *Impérieuse*. Scrapped at Faslane in 1948.
17 1958 base at Christmas Island.
18 1966 nuclear-powered ballistic missile submarine of 7,500/8,300 tons built by Vickers Armstrong.

## RESOURCE

Egypt 1801
Falkland Islands 1982
*Passim ut olim* = Everywhere as of yore.
1 1778 6th rate which was renamed *Enterprise* in about 1806.
3 1928 repair ship of 12,300 tons built by Vickers Armstrong of Barrow. Scrapped in 1954 at Inverkeithing.
4 1967 (commissioning date) fleet replenishment ship of 22,890 tons built by Scotts of Greenock. Officially an AEFS ship.

HMS RESOLUTION (No. 18)

65 · Incredibly, all three prizes were named *Renommée*.

66 Manning and Walker point out that the *Victoria* (1887), *Empress of India* (1891) and *Revenge* (1915) all bore the name *Renown* but none of them was launched as such.

## RETALICK

Atlantic 1944
Normandy 1944
English Channel 1944
North Sea 1945
Named after Captain Richard Retalick
of the *Defiance* at Copenhagen.
1   1943 frigate of 1,300 tons, ex-
    *DE.90*, built by Bethlehem:
    Hingham. Returned to USA in
    1945.

## REVENGE

Armada 1588
Azores 1591
Lowestoft 1665
Four Days' Battle 1666
Orfordness 1666
Bugia 1671
Schooneveld 1673
Marbella 1705
Quiberon Bay 1759
Trafalgar 1805
Basque Roads 1809
Syria 1840
Belgian Coast 1914−15
Jutland 1916
Atlantic 1939−41
English Channel 1940
*Orphée* 1758
*Intaminatus fulget honoribus* = Shines
with untarnished honour.
1   1577 vessel (46). Drake's famous
    flagship against the Armada.
    With Sir Richard Grenville as
    captain, she surrendered to
    Spanish ships off the Azores and
    foundered in 1591.
2   1650 4th rate, ex-*Marmaduke*.
3   1660 vessel (52), ex-*Newbury*. She
    was condemned in 1678.
4   1699 3rd rate which was renamed
    *Buckingham* in 1711.
5   1715 3rd rate ex-*Swiftsure*.
    Scrapped in 1787.
6   1805 3rd rate. Scrapped in 1849.
7   1859 1st rate which was renamed
    *Empress* in 1890.
10  1892 battleship of 14,150 tons
    built by Palmer. Scrapped by
    Ward at Briton Ferry in 1919.

11  1915 battleship, ex-*Renown*, of
    29,150 tons built by Vickers. In
    1944 she was part of the
    *Impérieuse*. Scrapped in 1948 at
    Inverkeithing.
12  1968 nuclear-powered ballistic-
    missile submarine (SSBN). 7,500/
    8,300 tons.

## RHODODENDRON

Atlantic 1940−5
English Channel 1942
North Africa 1942
Barents Sea 1942
Arctic 1942−5
Sicily 1943
Normandy 1944
1   1917 sloop of 1,290 tons built by
    Irvine. Torpedoed in the North Sea
    by *U-70* in 1918.
2   1940 corvette of 925 tons built by
    Harland & Wolff. Sold in 1947 for
    mercantile service.

## RHYL

English Channel 1942
Dieppe 1942
Sicily 1943
Salerno 1943
South France 1944
1   1940 minesweeper of 672 tons built
    by Lobnitz. Scrapped at Gateshead
    in 1948.
2   1959 anti-submarine frigate, 1st
    rate, 2,800 tons built by
    Portsmouth Dock Yard. Disposal
    List 1980−1.

## RIBBLE

Dardanelles 1915−16
1   1904 destroyer of 590 tons built by
    Yarrow. Scrapped by Ward at
    Preston in 1920.
4   1943 frigate of 1,370 tons built by
    Simons. Royal Netherlands navy
    1943. Scrapped in 1959.
5   1985 minesweeper of 890 tons built
    by Richards Ltd of Great
    Yarmouth.

## RICHMOND

Quebec 1759
Havana 1762
Atlantic 1941−3
Arctic 1942
1   1660 5th rate ex-*Wakefield*. Sold in
    1698.
3   1745 6th rate prize *Dauphin*. Sold
    four years later.
4   1757 5th rate which surrendered in
    1781.
8   1940 destroyer, ex-USS *Fairfax*, of
    1,090 tons built by Mare Island in
    1917. RCN 1942−3. Russian navy
    1944−9 as *Zhivuchi*. Scrapped in
    1949.

## RIFLEMAN

Normandy 1944
Burma 1945
1   1804 vessel.
3   and 4 were sloops of 1846 and
    1872.
6   1910 destroyer of *c*.750 tons built
    by White. Sold for scrapping in
    1921 by Ward of Briton Ferry.
6   1943 minesweeper of the 'Algerine'
    class built by Harland & Wolff.

## RINALDO

Belgian Coast 1914
North Sea 1942
Anzio 1944
South France 1944
Aegean 1944
Named after one of the twelve peers
of Charlemagne's court.
1   2 and 3 were all sloops of 1808,
    1860 and 1900.
5   1943 minesweeper of the 'Algerine'
    class built by Harland & Wolff.
    Scrapped at Gateshead in 1961.

## RIOU

Normandy 1944
North Sea 1945
Named after Captain Henry Riou of
the *Amazon*, killed at Copenhagen in
1801.
1   1943 frigate, ex-USS *DE.92*, of
    1,300 tons built by Bethlehem:
    Hingham. Returned to USA in
    1946.

## RIPLEY

Atlantic 1941−2
1   1940 destroyer of 1,190 tons, ex-
    USS *Shubrick*, built in 1918 by

Bethlehem: Squantum. Scrapped at Sunderland in 1945.

## ROBERTS

Dardanelles 1915–16
North Africa 1942
Sicily 1943
Salerno 1943
Mediterranean 1943
Normandy 1944
Walcheren 1944
Named after Field Marshal Earl Roberts, and the badge is derived from his arms.
1  1915 monitor of 6,150 tons built by Swan Hunter. Originally named *Stonewall Jackson*, then *Lord Roberts* and finally *Roberts*. Sold in 1936 to Ward of Preston for scrapping.
2  1941 monitor of 7,970 tons built at Clydebank. Scrapped in 1965 at Inverkeithing.

## ROCHESTER

Cape Passero 1718
Quiberon Bay 1759
Martinique 1762
Atlantic 1939–44
North Africa 1942
Normandy 1944
*Urbis fortuna navis* = The city's fortune is the ship's fortune.
1  1693 4th rate. Scrapped in 1748.
2  1702 prize. Sold in 1712.
3  1749 prize 4th rate. Sold in 1770.
4  1800 vessel, ex-*Hero*. Scrapped in 1810.
6  1931 sloop of 1,045 tons built by White at Chatham. Scrapped in 1951.

## ROCKET

Baltic 1855
English Channel 1943
Sabang 1944
Burma 1944–5
Upward and onward.
1  1804 vessel of 62 tons. Sold in 1807.
4  1894 destroyer. Sold in 1912.
5  1916 destroyer of 1,065 tons built by Denny of Dumbarton. Sold for scrapping to Ward of Inverkeithing.
6  1942 destroyer, later fast anti-submarine frigate. 2,700 tons, built by Scotts. She was scrapped by Dalmuir in 1967.

## ROCKINGHAM

Atlantic 1941–3
Biscay 1943
1  1940 destroyer, ex-USS *Swasey* of 1,190 tons built in 1919 by Bethlehem: Squantum. Mined in 1944 off the east coast of Scotland.

## ROCK ROSE

Atlantic 1941–2
1  1941 corvette of 925 tons built by Hill: Richardson Westgarth Clark. Transferred to South Africa and renamed *Protea*.

## ROCK SAND

Named after a Derby winner.
1  1918 sloop of 1,320 tons built by Swan Hunter. Sold in 1922.
2  1944 LSI ex-*Empire Anvil*, of 11,650 tons built by Consolidated Steel Corporation. Disposed of in 1946.

## ROCKWOOD

Sicily 1943
Aegean 1943
Atlantic 1944
English Channel 1944
Named after the hunt in Yorkshire.
1  1942 destroyer of 1,087 tons built by Vickers Armstrong at Barrow. Scrapped at Gateshead in 1946.

## RODNEY

Quebec 1759
Syria 1840
Crimea 1854
Norway 1940
Atlantic 1940–1
*Bismarck* Action 1941
Malta Convoys 1941–2
North Africa 1942–3
Sicily 1943
Salerno 1943
Mediterranean 1943
Normandy 1944
English Channel 1944
Arctic 1944
*Non generant aquilae columbas* = Eagles do not breed doves.
Named after Admiral George Brydges, Lord Rodney (1719–92).
1  1759 vessel.
3  1809 3rd rate which was renamed *Greenwich* in 1827.
4  1833 2nd rate. Scrapped in 1884.
5  1884 battleship. Sold in 1909.
8  1925 battleship of 33,900 tons built by Cammell Laird. Scrapped at Inverkeithing in 1948.

## ROEBUCK[67]

Armada 1588
Cadiz 1596
Portland 1653
Gabbard 1653
Barfleur 1692

67  The Armada *Roebuck* was a hired ship of 300 tons which accompanied Drake's squadron. The Cadiz *Roebuck* was a hired ship of 104 tons in Raleigh's squadron, described as *Roebuck* of London.

Velez Malaga 1704
Cape Passero 1718
Martinique 1794
Egypt 1801
China 1860
Sabang 1944
Burma 1944−5
1   1637 vessel.
3   1652 5th rate (34) prize. Sold in 1657.
4   1666 4th rate. Sold in 1683.
6   1690 fireship, upgraded to a 6th rate five years later. Sank at Ascension in 1701.
7   8 and 9 were all 5th rates of 1704, 1743 and 1774.
13  1901 destroyer of c.400 tons built by Hawthorn Leslie. Scrapped at Portsmouth in 1919.
15  1942 destroyer of 2,700 tons built by Scotts. Scrapped at Dalmuir in 1967.
16  1986 (commissioning date) survey ship of 1,280 tons built by Brooke Marine, Lowestoft.

## ROMNEY

Egypt 1801
Diego Suarez 1942
Sicily 1943
Normandy 1944
*Sibylle* 1794
1   1694 6th rate which was wrecked in 1707.
2   1708 4th rate. She sank in Plymouth's basin in 1721 but was salved and rebuilt at Woolwich. Finally sold in 1757.
3   and 4 were both 4th rates of 1762 (wrecked) and 1815.
5   1940 minesweeper of 672 tons built by Lobnitz. Scrapped at Granton in 1950.

## ROMOLA

1   1916 destroyer of 1,065 tons built by John Brown. Sold in 1930 to King of Troon for scrapping.
2   1944 minesweeper of the 'Algerine' class built by Port Arthur. Scrapped at Plymouth in 1957.

## ROOKE

*Clavem teneo* = I hold the key.
Named after Admiral of the Fleet Sir George Rooke (1650−1709).
1   1806 vessel named *Rook*.
3   1920 flotilla leader which was renamed *Broke* in 1925. She was built by Thornycroft. Foundered off Algiers after being damaged by shore batteries in 1942.

4   1940 boom depot at Rosyth which was renamed *Safeguard* in 1946.
5   1946 naval base at Gibraltar, ex-*Cormorant*.

## RORQUAL

Mediterranean 1940−3
Crete 1941
Malta Convoys 1941−2
Sicily 1943
Aegean 1943
Atlantic 1944
*Nec temere nec timide* = Neither rashly nor timidly.
1   1915 vessel.
2   1936 submarine of 1,520/2,157 tons built by Vickers Armstrong at Barrow. Scrapped at Newport in 1946.
3   1956 submarine of 1,600/2,030 tons built by Vickers Armstrong. Scrapped in 1976.

## ROSARIO

South France 1944
1   1797 prize, *Nuestra Señora del Rosario* used as a fireship.
4   1860 sloop. Sold in 1882.
5   1898 sloop of 980 tons built at Sheerness. Depot ship for submarines in 1910. Sold to Hong Kong for scrapping in 1921.
6   1943 minesweeper of 990 tons built by Harland & Wolff. Sold to Belgium and renamed *De Moor* in 1953.

## ROSEBAY

Atlantic 1943
1   1943 corvette, ex-USS *Spendor* of 980 tons built by Kingston. Returned to USA for mercantile service in 1946.

## ROSEMARY

Atlantic 1940
For remembrance.
1   1915 sloop of 1,175 tons built by Richardson Duck at Blair. Scrapped in 1948 at Milford Haven.

## ROTHER

Atlantic 1942−4
North Atlantic 1942−3
1   1904 destroyer of c.560 tons built by Palmer. Sold in 1919 for scrapping by Ward at Briton Ferry.

3   1941 frigate of 1,370 tons built by Smith's Dock. Scrapped at Troon in 1955.

## ROTHERHAM

Sabang 1944
Burma 1945
Named after Captain Edward Rotheram (1753−1830) of the *Royal Sovereign* at Trafalgar. But his name is misspelt.
1   1942 destroyer of 1,750 tons built at Clydebank. Transferred to RIN in 1949 and renamed *Rajput*.

## ROTHESAY

English Channel 1942
North Africa 1942−3
Sicily 1943
Salerno 1943
Anzio 1944
South France 1944
1   1941 minesweeper of 656 tons built by White. Scrapped at Milford Haven in 1950.
2   1957 anti-submarine frigate of 2,380/2,800 tons built by Yarrow.

## ROVER

Mediterranean 1941
*Pro gloria passim* = Everywhere for glory.
1   1777 prize, *Cumberland* (18). Lost at sea 1781.
2   and 6 were both sloops of 1796 and 1832.
8   1874 cruiser. Sold in 1893.
10  1930 submarine of 1,475/2,030 tons built by Vickers Armstrong at Barrow. Scrapped at Durban in 1946.

## ROWENA

North Sea 1944
*Loyal surtout* = Loyalty above all things.
1   1916 destroyer of 1,065 tons built by John Brown. Sold in 1937 for scrapping at Milford Haven.
2   1944 minesweeper of the 'Algerine' class built by Lobnitz. Scrapped at Gateshead in 1958.

## ROWLEY

Normandy 1944
English Channel 1944−5
Atlantic 1945
Named after Sir Joshua Rowley

(1730−90) of the *Montagu* at Quiberon Bay.

1  1943 frigate of 1,300 tons, ex-*DE.95*, built by Bethlehem: Hingham. Returned to USA in 1945.

## ROXBURGH

Atlantic 1941−3

1  1904 cruiser of 10,850 tons built by London & Glasgow. Sold in 1921 to Slough Trading Co for breaking up in Germany.

2  1940 destroyer, ex-USS *Foote*, of 1,060 tons built by Fore River in 1918. Lent to Russia 1944−9 and renamed *Doblestni*. Scrapped in 1949. This destroyer was spelled *Roxborough*.

## ROYAL ARTHUR

Named after Field Marshal HRH Prince Arthur, Duke of Connaught and Strathearn, son of Queen Victoria (1850−1942).

1  1891 cruiser of 7,350 tons built by Portsmouth Dock Yard. Sold to Cohen in 1921 for breaking up in Germany.

2  1939 training establishment at Skegness.

3  Petty Officers' Leadership school at Corsham, Wiltshire.

## ROYALIST

Jutland 1916
South France 1944
Aegean 1944
Burma 1944
*Weser* 1813
*Surtout loyal* = Loyal above all.

1  1796 vessel.

7  1861 screw sloop (11) of 669 tons. Scrapped in 1875.

8  1883 cruiser, barque-rigged of 1,420 tons. She was renamed *Colleen* in 1913.

9  1915 light cruiser of 3,500 tons built by Beardmore. Scrapped by Cashmore in 1922.

11  1942 cruiser of 5,770 tons built by Scotts. RNZN 1956. Scrapped in Japan in 1968.

## ROYAL OAK

Lowestoft 1665
Orfordness 1666
Velez Malaga 1704
Cape Passero 1718
Chesapeake 1781
The Saintes 1782
Jutland 1916
Old but firm.

1  2, 3 and 4 were all 3rd rates of 1664 (burnt by the Dutch), 1674, 1769 (renamed *Assistance* in 1805) and 1809.

5  1862 ironclad. Sold in 1885.

6  1892 battleship of 14,150 tons. Sold in 1914.

7  1914 battleship of 29,150 tons built by Hawthorn Leslie at Devonport. Sunk by *U-47* in Scapa Flow in 1939.

## ROYAL SOVEREIGN
## (Sovereign and Sovereign of the Seas)

Kentish Knock 1652
Orfordness 1666
Solebay 1672
Schooneveld 1673
Texel 1673
Barfleur 1692
Vigo 1702
Glorious First of June 1794
Trafalgar 1805
Calabria 1940
Atlantic 1940−1
*Ducere classem regem sequi* = To lead the fleet, to follow the King.

1  1509 vessel, ex-*Grace Dieu*. Scrapped in 1595.

2  1637 1st rate — the splendid *Sovereign of the Seas*, destroyed by fire in 1696.

3  1701 3rd rate, based on salvaged parts from *Sovereign of the Seas*.

Scrapped in 1763.

4  1786 1st rate which was renamed *Captain* in 1825.

6  1857 armoured ship. She became a turret ship in 1864. Sold for scrapping in 1884.

7  1891 battleship of 14,150 tons. Sold for scrap in 1913.

8  1915 battleship of 29,150 tons built by Portsmouth Dock Yard. Loaned to Russia in 1944 and renamed *Archangelsk*. Scrapped at Inverkeithing in 1949.

9  1973 nuclear-powered submarine, *Sovereign*, of 4,000/4,900 tons built by Vickers Shipbuilding Group at Barrow.

## RULER

Atlantic 1944
Okinawa 1945
Through vigilance.

1  1943 escort carrier, ex-USS *St Joseph*, of 11,420 tons built by Seattle:Tacoma. Returned to USA in 1946 and scrapped.

## RUPERT

Orfordness 1666
Solebay 1672
Schooneveld 1673
Texel 1673
Barfleur 1692
Cape Passero 1718
Normandy 1944
English Channel 1944
Arctic 1944
Atlantic 1945
North Sea 1945
Named after Prince Rupert.

1  1666 3rd rate. Scrapped over a century later in 1769.

2  1692 6th rate named *Rupert Prize*. Sold in 1700.

3  1741 sloop taken as prize and sold two years later.

4  1872 turret ram. Sold in 1907.

5  1943 frigate of 1,500/1,850 tons built by Bethlehem: Hingham. Ship of all-welded construction. Returned to USA in 1946.

## RUSSELL

St Kitts 1782
The Saintes 1782
Glorious First of June 1794
Groix 1795
Camperdown 1797
Copenhagen 1801
Baltic 1855
Belgian Coast 1914
Dardanelles 1915−16

Named after Admiral of the Fleet Edward Russell, Earl of Orford and Viscount Barfleur.

1  1692 3rd rate. Sunk as a breakwater at Sheerness in 1761.
2  and 3 were both 3rd rates of 1764 and 1822.
4  1901 battleship of 14,000 tons built by Palmer. Mined in 1916 off Malta.
6  1954 frigate, anti-submarine, Type 14, of 1,180/1,456 tons built by Swan Hunter. Disposal List 1977−8.

## RUTHERFORD

Atlantic 1944
English Channel 1944
North Sea 1944−5
Named after Captain William George Rutherford (1764−1812) of the *Swiftsure* at Trafalgar.
1  1943 frigate of 1,300 tons, ex-*DE-93*, built by Bethlehem: Hingham. Returned to USA in 1945.

## RYE

Atlantic 1942
Malta Convoys 1942
Sicily 1943
Normandy 1944
1  1696 5th rate which was sunk as a breakwater at Harwich in 1727.
2  1740 6th rate which was wrecked four years later.
3  1745 3rd rate. Sold in 1763.
4  1940 minesweeper of 656 tons built by Ailsa. Scrapped at Purfleet in 1948.

## SABRE

Dunkirk 1940
Atlantic 1940−3
1  1918 destroyer of 905 tons built by Stephen. Scrapped at Grangemouth in 1945.
2  1971 fast training boat of 102 tons built by Vosper Thornycroft: hull of glued laminated construction. Disposal List 1982−3.

## SAFARI

Sicily 1943
Mediterranean 1943
1  1941 submarine, ex-*P211*, ex-*P61*, 715/990 tons built by Cammell Laird. Sank in 1946 while in tow to the ship-breakers.

## SAGA

1  1945 submarine of 715/990 tons built by Cammell Laird. Sold to Portugal in 1948 and renamed *Nautilo*.

## SAHIB

Mediterranean 1943
1  1945 submarine, ex-*P212*, ex-*P62*, 715/990 tons built by Cammell Laird. Lost in 1943 when sunk by Italian corvette *Gabbiano* off Sicily.

## ST ALBANS

Barfleur 1692
Lagos 1759
St Lucia 1778
St Kitts 1782
The Saintes 1782
Atlantic 1941−3
English Channel 1942
Arctic 1942
North Sea 1943
Probably named after Charles Beauclerk, first Duke of St Albans (1670−1726), son of Charles II and Nell Gwyn.[68]
1  1687 4th rate which was wrecked in 1693.
2  1691 6th rate prize. Sold in 1698.
3  and 4 were both 4th rates of 1706 and 1747.
5  1764 3rd rate. Scrapped in 1814.
6  1940 destroyer, ex-USS *Thomas*, 1,060 tons built by Newport News in 1918. Royal Norwegian navy 1940−4. Lent to Russia 1944−9 and renamed *Dostoini*. Scrapped at Charlestown in 1949.

## ST ANGELO

The ancient fortress at Malta.
1  1933 depot at Malta.

## ST AUSTELL BAY

1  1944 frigate, ex-*Loch Lyddoch*, 1,580 tons built by Harland & Wolff. Scrapped at Rosyth in 1959.

## ST BRIDE'S BAY

Korea 1950−3
1  1945 frigate, ex-*Loch Achilty*, 1,580 tons built by Harland & Wolff. Scrapped at Faslane in 1962.

## ST CHRISTOPHER

1  c.1807 vessel (18) ex-*Mohawk*, French privateer presented to the RN by the island of St Christopher.
2  1940−4 Coastal Forces training base at Fort William.

## ST GEORGE

Lowestoft 1665
Four Days' Battle 1666
Orfordness 1666
Solebay 1672
Schooneveld 1673
Texel 1673
Velez Malaga 1704
Genoa 1795
Copenhagen 1801
Baltic 1854
Benin 1897
*Animo opibusque parati* = Prepared in mind and resources.
1  1622 2nd rate. Sunk at Sheerness in 1697 to reinforce the dock.
2  1687 1st rate, ex-*Charles*. Scrapped in 1774.
4  1785 2nd rate which was wrecked in 1811.
6  1812 1st rate, ex-*Britannia*. Scrapped in 1825.
7  1840 1st rate.
8  1892 cruiser of 7,700 tons built by Earle. Scrapped in 1920 by Castle of Plymouth.
9  1939 training establishment in the Isle of Man. This was transferred to Gosport in 1945 and paid off in 1948.

## ST HELENA

English Channel 1945
1  1943 frigate, ex-*Pasley*, ex-*PF.86*, 1,318 tons built by Walsh Kaiser. Returned to USA in 1946.

---

68  Manning and Walker declare this must be the source of the name. See their p. 387.

## ST JAMES

Named after Albemarle's victory over Tromp in 1666.
1   1945 destroyer of the 'Battle' class of 3,361 tons built by Fairfield. Scrapped in 1961 at Newport.

## ST KITTS

Named after Sir Samuel Hood's brilliant action in Frigate Bay in 1782.
1   1944 destroyer of the 'Battle' class of 3,361 tons built by Swan Hunter. Scrapped at Sunderland in 1962.

## ST MARY'S

Atlantic 1942
North Sea 1943
1   1940 destroyer, ex-USS *Doran*, ex-*Bagley*, 1,600 tons, built by Newport News in 1918. Scrapped at Rosyth in 1945.

## ST VINCENT

Baltic 1854
Jutland 1916
The motto is taken from the old steering order: Keep Her Thus.
1   1692 fireship (8) of 200 tons. Captured by the French.
2   1780 prize (14), the *San Vincente* of Spain. Sold in 1784.
3   1815 1st rate (120) named after Admiral of the Fleet John Jervis, Earl of St Vincent (1734–1823). She became a training-ship in 1862. Sold in 1906.
5   1908 battleship of 19,250 tons built at Portsmouth Dock Yard. Scrapped in 1921 by Stanlee.
7   1927 training establishment at Forton, Gosport. In 1942 it became the Preliminary Air Training Establishment.
8   Shore establishment (WRNS) at Furse House, Queensgate Terrace, London.

## SAINTES

The badge derives from the eagle in the arms of Lord Rodney.
1   1944 destroyer of the 'Battle' class of 3,361 tons built by Hawthorn Leslie. Disposal List 1974–5.

## SALADIN

Dunkirk 1940
Atlantic 1940–4

Arctic 1942–3
English Channel 1944
Named after Saladin, sultan of Egypt and Syria (1137–93).
1   1919 destroyer of 905 tons built by Stephen. Scrapped in 1947 at Llanelly.

## SALAMANDER

Armada 1588
Lagos 1759
Burma 1852
Dunkirk 1940
Arctic 1941–2
Normandy 1944
*Per ignes et undas* = Through fire and water.
1   1544 prize vessel.
2   1588: a City of London merchant vessel accompanied the fleet at the Armada battle.
9   1832 sloop. Sold in 1883.
12  1936 minesweeper of 815 tons built by White. Bombed by Allied aircraft off French coast. CTL 1944. Scrapped in 1947 at Blyth.

## SALISBURY

Sadras 1758
Negapatam 1758
Porto Novo 1759
Atlantic 1941–3
1   1698 4th rate which surrendered in 1703.
2   1698 4th rate was No. 1 above, retaken. She was renamed *Preston* in 1716.
3   4, 5 and 6 were all 4th rates of 1707, 1745 (condemned), 1769 (wrecked) and 1814.
7   1940 destroyer, ex-USS *Claxton* of 1,090 tons built by Mare Island in 1919. RCN 1942–3. Sold in Canada in 1944.
8   1953 frigate of 2,330 tons built by Portsmouth Dock Yard. Disposal List 1980–1.

## SALMON

North Sea 1939–40
*Fluctibus floreo* = I flourish in the waves.
1   1895 destroyer. Sold in 1911.
2   1916 destroyer of 1,065 tons built by Harland & Wolff at Govan. Sold for scrapping in 1937 by Ward of Hayle.
3   1934 submarine of 670/960 tons built by Cammell Laird. Lost south-west of Norway in 1940 when struck by a mine.

## SALTASH

Dunkirk 1940
Normandy 1944
1 2 and 3 were all sloops of *c*.1740 (lost in 1742), 1742 (overset off Beachy Head in 1746) and 1746.
4 1918 minesweeper of 1918 of 710 tons built by Murdoch & Murray. She was sold to Belgium in 1947 for mercantile use.

## SANDWICH

Barfleur 1692
Belleisle 1761
St Vincent 1780
Atlantic 1939–44
North Africa 1942
*Fronte leonis* = With a lion's head. Probably named after Edward Montagu, first Earl of Sandwich (1625–72).
1 1679 2nd rate. Scrapped nearly a century later in 1770.
2 1759 2nd rate. Scrapped in 1810.
9 1928 sloop of 1,045 tons built by Hawthorn Leslie. Sold in 1946 for mercantile use.

## SANGUINE

We strike to kill.
1 1945 submarine of 715/990 tons built by Cammell Laird. Sold to Israel and renamed *Rahav*.

## SARACEN

Cattaro 1814
Belgian Coast 1915
Mediterranean 1942
Sicily 1943
1 1804 sloop. Scrapped in 1812.
4 1909 destroyer of *c*.1,090 tons built by White. Scrapped in 1919 by Ward of Preston.
5 1942 submarine, ex-*P213*, ex-*P63*, of 715/990 tons built by Cammell Laird. Lost in 1943 when sunk by Italian corvette *Minerva* off Bastia.

## SARAWAK

Atlantic 1944
1 1943 frigate, ex-USS *Patton*, ex-*PF.87*, of 1,318 tons built by Walsh Kaiser. Returned to USA in 1946.

## SARDONYX

Atlantic 1940–2
Arctic 1942

Name derives from a precious stone.
1 1919 destroyer of 905 tons built by Stephen. Scrapped at Preston in 1945.

## SATELLITE

Abyssinia 1868
1 1806 vessel.
4 1826 sloop. Scrapped in 1849.
5 1855 corvette. Scrapped in 1877.
6 1881 screw cruiser, third class, of 1,420 tons, built at Sheerness. About 1903 she became a drillship for the Tyne RNVR at North Shields. Scrapped in 1947.
7 1954 minesweeper of 900 tons built by White named *Brave*, in 1943 became RNVR drillship for the Tyne Division. Scrapped in 1958.

## SATYR

Belgian Coast 1917
Norway 1944
1 1916 destroyer of 1,065 tons built by Beardmore. Sold in 1926 to Ward of Milford Haven for scrapping.
2 1942 submarine, ex-*P214*, ex-*P64*, of 715/990 tons built by Scotts. Transferred to France from 1952 till 1961 and renamed *Saphir*. Scrapped at Charlestown in 1962.

## SAUMAREZ

Arctic 1943–4
North Cape 1943
Normandy 1944
Malaya 1945
Burma 1945
Named after Admiral Lord Saumarez, (1757–1836).
1 1916 flotilla leader of 1,687 tons built by Cammell Laird. Sold in 1931 to Ward of Briton Ferry for scrapping.
2 1942 destroyer of 1,730 tons built by Hawthorn Leslie. Damaged by mine in the Corfu Channel in 1946. CTL. Scrapped at Charlestown in 1950.

## SAVAGE

Guadeloupe 1810
Arctic 1943–5
North Cape 1943
Normandy 1944
1 and 2 were both sloops of 1749 and 1781.
6 1910 destroyer of 975 tons built by Thornycroft. Sold in 1921 for scrapping to Ward at Portishead.
7 1942 destroyer of 1,730 tons built by Hawthorn Leslie. Distinguished herself in the sinking of the *Scharnhorst* and of the *Haguro*. Scrapped in 1962 at Newport.

## SCARBOROUGH

Louisburg 1758
Quebec 1759
Atlantic 1939–44
North Africa 1942
North Sea 1943
Normandy 1944
English Channel 1944
*Tutus si fortis* = Safe is brave.
1 1691 vessel.
2 1693 5th rate which surrendered in 1694, was retaken three years later, but was added to the Navy as *Milford*.
3 1695 3rd rate which surrendered in 1710. She was retaken the following year but was added as *Garland*.
4 1711 5th rate. Sold in 1737.
6 and 7 were both 6th rates of 1740 and 1756 (she was lost in a hurricane).
8 1812 3rd rate. Sold in 1836.
9 1930 sloop of 1,045 tons built by Swan Hunter: Hawthorn Leslie. Scrapped in 1949 by Thornaby.
10 1955 anti-submarine frigate, 1st rate, of 2,800 tons built by Vickers Armstrong on the Tyne. Scrapped in 1977.

## SCEPTRE

Trincomalee 1782
Cape of Good Hope 1796
Guadeloupe 1810
Norway 1944
Atlantic 1944
Biscay 1944
Honour with authority.
1  1781 1st rate which was wrecked in 1799.
2  1803 3rd rate. Scrapped in 1821.
3  1917 destroyer of 1,065 tons built by Stephen. Sold to Ward of Briton Ferry in 1926 for scrapping.
5  1943 submarine, ex-*P215*, ex-*P65*, of 715/990 tons built by Scotts. Scrapped at Gateshead in 1949.
6  1976 nuclear-powered submarine of 4,000/4,900 tons built by Vickers Ship Building Company at Barrow.

## SCIMITAR

Dunkirk 1940
Atlantic 1940−4
Arctic 1942
English Channel 1943−4
1  1918 destroyer of 905 tons built by Clydebank. Scrapped at Briton Ferry by Ward in 1947.
2  1970 fast training boat of 102 tons built by Vosper Thornycroft: hull of glued laminated construction. Disposal List 1982−3.

## SCORCHER

*Audi, vide, tace* = Listen, see, be silent.
1  1944 submarine of 715/990 tons built by Cammell Laird. Hull retained for experimental purposes but remainder scrapped at Charlestown in 1962.

## SCORPION

Quebec 1759
Guadeloupe 1810
Dardanelles 1915−16
Arctic 1943−5
North Cape 1943
Normandy 1944
*Athalante* 1804
*Oreste* 1810
1  1746 6th rate which was lost at sea in 1762.
2  and 3 were both sloops of 1771 (lost at sea) and 1785.
7  1863 turret ship. Sold in 1905.
8  1910 destroyer of *c*.975 tons built

by Fairfield. Sold in 1921 to Barking SB for scrapping.
11  1942 destroyer, ex-*Sentinel*, of 1,710 tons built by Cammell Laird. Sold to Holland in 1945 and renamed *Kortenaer*. Scrapped in 1963.
12  1946 destroyer, ex-*Tomahawk*, ex-*Centaur*, of 2,935 tons, fleet radar picket, built by White. Disposal List 1974−5.

## SCOTSMAN

1  1918 destroyer of 1,075 tons built by John Brown. Scrapped in 1937 by Ward at Briton Ferry.
3  1944 submarine of 715/990 tons built by Scotts. Scrapped at Troon in 1964.

## SCOTT

Zeebrugge 1918
Norway 1941
Normandy 1944
The first ship was named after Sir Walter Scott. Others take their name from Captain Robert Falcon Scott, the explorer.
1  1917 flotilla leader of 1,800 tons built by Cammell Laird. Torpedoed and sunk in the North Sea, probably by *UC-17*.
3  1938 surveying vessel of 875 tons built by Caledon: Parsons. Scrapped at Troon in 1965.

HMS SCORPION (No. 8)

## SCOURGE

Dardanelles 1914−15
Arctic 1943−5
Normandy 1944
1  1779 sloop which foundered in
   1795.
4  1796 6th rate (22) prize. Sold in
   1802.
7  1844 sloop. Scrapped in 1864.
9  1910 destroyer of c 975 tons built
   by Hawthorn Leslie. Sold in 1921
   to Ward of Briton Ferry for
   scrapping.
11 1942 destroyer of 1,710 tons built
   by Cammell Laird. Sold to
   Holland in 1946 and renamed
   *Evertsen*. Scrapped in 1963.

## SCOUT

Armada 1588
China 1860
Be prepared.
1  1577 vessel.
4  5, 6, 8 and 11 were all sloops of
   1780 (surrendered), 1800 (prize,
   lost at sea), 1801 (prize,
   foundered), 1804 and 1832.
12 1856 corvette. Scrapped in 1877.
14 1885 cruiser. Sold in 1904.
15 1918 destroyer of c.905 tons built
   at Clydebank, Scrapped at Briton
   Ferry by Ward in 1946.

## SCYLLA

North Africa 1942
Arctic 1942−3
Salerno 1943
Atlantic 1943
Biscay 1943
Normandy 1944
*Weser 1813*
*Clara saevitia* = Of famous savagery.[69]
1  1809 sloop. Scrapped in 1846.
2  1856 corvette. Sold in 1882.
3  1892 cruiser. Sold in 1914.
4  1940 cruiser of 5,450 tons built by

Scotts. Scrapped at Barrow in 1950.
5  1968 general-purpose frigate of
   2,500/2,962 tons built by
   Devonport Dock Yard. 'Leander'
   class armed with Exocet missiles.

## SCYTHIAN

Atlantic 1944
Malaya 1945
One of the nomadic conquerors of 9th
— 3rd century BC, principally from
the region north of the Black Sea.
1  1944 submarine, ex-*P237*, of 715/
   990 tons built by Scotts.Scrapped
   in Charlestown in 1960.

## SEA BEAR

1  1918 destroyer of 1,075 tons built
   by John Brown. Sold in 1930 to
   Ward of Grays for scrapping.
2  1943 minesweeper of the 'Algerine'
   class built by Redfern. Ex-RCN *St
   Thomas*. Scrapped at Blyth in 1959.

## SEA DEVIL

*Me timete* = Fear me.
1  1945 submarine of 715/990 tons
   built by Scotts. Scrapped at
   Newhaven in 1966.

## SEA DOG

Arctic 1942−3
Atlantic 1944
1  1942 submarine, ex-*P216*, ex-*P66*,
   of 715/990 tons built by Cammell
   Laird. Scrapped at Troon c.1948.

## SEA HAWK

1  RNAS Culdrose, Helston,
   Cornwall, including RN Helicopter
   School. Largest naval air station in
   the British Isles.

## SEAHORSE

Quebec 1759
Trincomalee 1782
Sadras 1782
Providien 1782
Negapatam 1782
*Bandere Zaffer 1808*
*Eques sit aequus* = Let the knight be
just.
1  1630 vessel.
2  4, 5, 6 and 7 were all 6th rates of
   1654 (prize), 1694 (wrecked), 1709
   (wrecked), 1712 and 1748.
8  and 9 were both 5th rates of 1794
   and 1830 (renamed *Lavinia* in
   1871).
13 1932 submarine of 670/960 tons
   built by Chatham Dock Yard. Lost
   in 1940 in the Heligoland Bight,
   sunk by German minesweeper.

## SEAL

Atlantic 1939
1  1897 destroyer of c.400 tons built
   by Laird Bros. Sold in 1921 for
   scrapping by Ward, Rainham.
2  1938 submarine of 1,520/2,157 tons
   built by Chatham Dock Yard.
   Disabled in shallow waters and
   captured by the German navy.
   Taken into German service as *UB-
   A*. Scuttled in Germany in 1945.

## SEALION

North Sea 1940
Norway 1940−1
Arctic 1941−2
*Sicut leones* = Be like the lions.
1  1914−18 vessel.
2  1934 submarine of 690/960 tons
   built by Cammell Laird. Expended
   as anti-submarine target in 1945.
3  1959 submarine of 1,600/2,030/
   2,410 tons built by Cammell Laird.
   Paid off 1987.

69  Pliny's description of Scylla.

## SEA NYMPH

Arctic 1942−3
Biscay 1943
Atlantic 1945
1   c.1782 vessel.
2   1942 submarine of 715/990 tons
    built by Cammell Laird. Scrapped
    at Troon in 1948.

## SEARCHER

Atlantic 1943−4
Aegean 1944
South France 1944
Norway 1944−5
1   1918 destroyer of 1,075 tons built
    by John Brown. Scrapped by Ward
    at Barrow in 1938.
3   1942 escort carrier of 11,420 tons
    built by Seattle:Tacoma. Returned
    to USA in 1945 for mercantile
    service.
4   1947 Landing-ship. Disposed of in
    1949.

## SEA ROVER

Atlantic 1943−5
*Subter sed super* = Below but superior.
1   1943 submarine, ex-*P218*, ex-*P68*,
    of 715/990 tons built by Scotts and
    completed by Vickers Armstrong
    at Barrow. Scrapped at Faslane in
    1949.

## SEA SCOUT

Atlantic 1944
Malaya 1945
1   1944 submarine of 715/990 tons
    built by Cammell Laird. Scrapped
    at Briton Ferry in 1966.

## SEA WOLF

Norway 1940−1
Atlantic 1941−2
*Non curo numerum* = I count not the
number [of my enemies].

---

1   1918 destroyer of 1,075 tons built
    by John Brown. Sold in 1931 to
    Cashmore for scrapping.
2   1935 submarine of 690/960 tons
    built by Scotts. Sold to RCN in
    1945.

## SELENE

Malaya 1945
1   1944 submarine of 715/990 tons
    built by Cammell Laird. Scrapped
    at Gateshead in 1961.

## SENESCHAL

A medieval official, a major-domo.
1   1945 submarine of 715/990 tons
    built by Scotts. Scrapped in 1960.

## SENNEN

Atlantic 1941−3
North Africa 1942−3
Named after a coastguard station in
Cornwall.
1   1941 cutter, ex-USCG *Champlain*,
    1,546 tons built by Bethlehem in
    1928. Returned to USA in 1946.

## SENTINEL

1   1804 vessel.
2   1904 cruiser of 2,895 tons built by
    Vickers. Sold in 1923 for scrapping
    to Young of Sunderland.
3   1945 submarine of 715/990 tons
    built by Scotts. Scrapped at
    Gillingham in 1962.
4   1984 ex-*Seaforth Warrior* of 1,710
    tons built by Husumwerft,
    Husum. Acquired by RN in 1984.

## SERAPH

North Africa 1942−3
Mediterranean 1943
Sicily 1943
Aegean 1943
*Prosequor alis* = I follow on wings.
1   1918 destroyer of 1,075 tons built
    by Denny. Sold in 1934 to Ward at
    Pembroke Dock for scrapping.
1   1941 submarine, ex-*P219*, ex-*69*, of
    715/990 tons built by Vickers
    Armstrong, Barrow. Scrapped at
    Briton Ferry in 1965.

## SERAPIS

Normandy 1944
Arctic 1944−5

---

*Bonhomme Richard* 1779
*Cornua cave* = Beware my horns.
1   1779 5th rate. She surrendered to
    the American Captain Paul Jones
    in the *Bonhomme Richard* in the
    same year.
2   1782 5th rate. She became a
    storeship in 1826.
3   1866 troopship. Sold in 1894.
4   1918 destroyer of c.1,075 tons built
    by Denny. Sold in 1934 to Rees of
    Llanelly for scrapping.
4   1943 destroyer of 1,710 tons built
    by Scotts. Sold to Holland in 1945
    and renamed *Piet Hein*. Scrapped
    at Ghent in 1962.

## SERENE

*Parva navis magna quies* = A small ship
of great repose.
1   1918 destroyer of 1,075 tons built
    by Denny. Sold to Ward of
    Inverkeithing in 1936.
3   1943 minesweeper of the 'Algerine'
    class, ex-RCN *Leaside*, built by
    Redfern. Scrapped by Rees of
    Llanelly in 1959.

## SEVERN

Algiers 1816
Belgian Coast 1914
Norway 1940
Atlantic 1940−1
Sicily 1943
Aegean 1943
*Königsberg* 1915
*Fides invicta triumphat* = Faith
unconquered triumphs.
1   1695 4th rate which surrendered
    in 1746 but was recaptured at
    Finisterre II in 1747.
2   3 and 4 were all 4th rates of 1747,
    1786 (wrecked) and 1813.
7   1885 cruiser. Sold in 1905.
8   1914 monitor of 1,260 tons built
    by Vickers. Scrapped by Ward,
    Preston in 1923.
9   1934 submarine of 1,850/2,723
    tons built by Vickers Armstrong
    at Barrow. Scrapped at Bombay in
    1946.
10   1979 nuclear-powered submarine,
    4,000/4,900 tons built by Vickers
    Ship Building Group at Barrow.

## SEYCHELLES

Atlantic 1945
1   1943 frigate of 1,318 tons, ex-USS
    *Pearl*, ex-USS *PF.88*, built by Walsh
    Kaiser. Returned to USA in 1946.

## SEYMOUR

Normandy 1944
North Sea 1944—5
1   1916 flotilla leader of *c*.1,687 tons
    built by Cammell Laird. Sold in
    1929 and broken up in the
    following year by Cashmore.
2   1943 frigate named after Captain
    Lord Hugh Seymour of the
    *Leviathan* at the Glorious First of
    June. Ex-*DE-98*, 1,300 tons built by
    Bethlehem: Hingham. Returned to
    USA in 1946.

## SHAH

Burma 1945
*Huascar* 1877
1   1873 armoured frigate, ex-*Blonde*.
    Sold as a coal hulk in 1919. Named
    in honour of the visit of the Shah of
    Persia in 1873.
2   1943 escort carrier, ex-USS *Jamaica*
    of 11,420 tons built by Seattle:
    Tacoma.[70] Returned to USA in
    1945 for mercantile service.

## SHAKESPEARE

Sicily 1943
Salerno 1943
Aegean 1943
Mediterranean 1943
English Channel 1943
Atlantic 1944
By opposing, end them.
Named after the poet and dramatist
William Shakespeare (1564—1616).
1   1917 flotilla leader of 1,750 tons
    built by Thornycroft. Sold in 1936
    for scrapping by Ward at Jarrow.
2   1941 submarine, ex-*P221*, ex-*P71*,
    of 715/990 tons built by Vickers
    Armstrong at Barrow. Sold in 1946
    to Ward at Briton Ferry for
    scrapping.

## SHALIMAR

Atlantic 1944
Named after a garden near Lahore,
Pakistan.
1   1939 vessel.
2   1943 submarine of 715/990 tons
    built by Chatham. Scrapped at
    Troon in 1950.

## SHARK

Crimea 1854
Jutland 1916
North Sea 1940
*Celer et tenax* = Swift and tenacious.
1   1691 vessel.
2   3 and 4 were all sloops of 1699
    (surrendered in 1703), 1711 and
    1732.
5   28 gun 6th rate bought by Rodney
    in the West Indies. She was
    wrecked in 1780.
8   1779 sloop which was wrecked in
    1818.
9   1894 destroyer. Sold in 1911.
10  1912 destroyer of 935 tons built by
    Swan Hunter at Wallsend. She
    was sunk at Jutland, 1916, her
    CO, Commander Loftus Jones,
    winning the VC. Only six men
    were rescued.
11  1918 destroyer of 1,075 tons built
    by Swan Hunter. scrapped in
    1931 by Ward at Inverkeithing.
12  1934 submarine of 670/960 tons
    built by Chatham Dock Yard.
    Sunk in 1940 off Skudesnes in
    Norway by German
    minesweepers.
13  1943 destroyer of 1,710 tons built
    by Scotts. Transferred to Royal
    Norwegian navy in 1944 and
    renamed *Svenner*. Torpedoed and
    sunk by German surface craft off
    Normandy in 1944.

## SHARPSHOOTER

Belgian Coast 1917
Dunkirk 1940
Arctic 1941—3
Atlantic 1942—4
Sicily 1943
Swift and sure.
1   1802 vessel.
2   1846 sloop. Sold in 1869.
4   1917 destroyer of *c*.1,065 tons built
    by Beardmore. Sold in 1927 for
    scrapping by Ward of Briton Ferry.
5   1936 minesweeper of 835 tons built
    by White at Devonport. Renamed
    *Shackleton* in 1953 and scrapped at
    Troon in 1965.

## SHEARWATER

North Sea 1940—5
1   1808 vessel.
3   1861 sloop. Scrapped in 1877.
4   1900 sloop of 980 tons built at
    Sheerness. Transferred to RCN in
    1915. Sold for scrapping in 1922.
5   1939 sloop of 580 tons built by
    White. Sold to Thornaby in 1947
    for scrapping.

## SHEFFIELD

Norway 1940
Spartivento 1940
Atlantic 1941—3
*Bismarck* Action 1941
Mediterranean 1941
Malta Convoys 1941
Arctic 1941—3
North Africa 1942
Barents Sea 1942
Salerno 1943
Biscay 1943
North Cape 1943
Falkland Islands 1982
*Deo adjuvante proficio* = With God's
help I advance.
1   1936 cruiser of standard 9,400 tons,
    12,400 fully loaded. Built by
    Vickers Armstrong on the Tyne.
    She distinguished herself with a
    brilliant WWII record. Scrapped at
    Inverkeithing in 1967.
2   1971 guided-missile armed
    destroyer, Type 42, 3,500/4,1000
    tons. Built by Vickers. Sunk at the
    Falklands in 1982.
3   1985 Type 22 destroyer of 4,100/
    4,800 tons built by Swan Hunter.

## SHELDRAKE

North Sea 1941—5
Atlantic 1942
*Fidelis et paratus* = Faithful and ready.
1   1806 vessel.
6   1911 destroyer of *c*.760 tons built
    by Denny. Sold for scrapping to
    Ward of Grays in 1921.
7   1937 sloop of 530 tons built by
    Thornycroft. Sold in 1946 for
    mercantile service.

## SHERWOOD

Atlantic 1941—3
North Sea 1943
1   1940 destroyer, ex-USS *Rodgers*, ex-
    *Kalk*, built in 1919 by Bethlehem.
    Disposed of in 1945.

---

70   Weightman clearly says built by Kaiser Company of Vancouver, Washington.

HMS SHEFFIELD (No. 2)

## SHIEL

Atlantic 1944
Burma 1945
1   1943 frigate of 1,370 tons built by
    Canadian Vickers. Returned to
    USA in 1946.

## SHIKARI

Dunkirk 1940
Atlantic 1940−3
Good hunting.
1   1914−18 vessel.
2   1919 destroyer of 905 tons built by
    Doxford at Chatham. Scrapped at
    Newport in 1945.

## SHOREHAM

Sicily 1943
Mediterranean 1943
Burma 1944−5
Make sure.
1   1694 5th rate. Sold exactly fifty
    years later.
2   1709 5th rate prize.
3   1744 6th rate. Sold in 1758.
4   1747 prize which was sunk the
    following year at Oporto.
5   1930 sloop of 1,045 tons built by
    White at Chatham. Sold in 1946 for
    mercantile service and scrapped in
    1950.

## SHREWSBURY CASTLE

1   1943 corvette of 1,010 tons built by
    Swan Hunter. Transferred to
    Norway in 1944 and renamed
    *Tunsberg Castle*. Mined in the Kola
    Inlet.

## SHROPSHIRE

Atlantic 1941
Arctic 1941
Leyte Gulf 1945
Lingayen Gulf 1945
*Floreat ambo* = May both flourish.
1   1928 cruiser of 9,830 tons built by
    Beardmore. Scrapped at Dalmuir
    and Troon (hull only) in 1955.

## SICKLE

Mediterranean 1943
Aegean 1943−4
1   1942 submarine, ex-*P224*, 715/990
    tons built by Cammell Laird.
    Mined in Eastern Mediterranean in
    1944.

## SIDON

Crimea 1854−5
Atlantic 1945
*Nemo fatigabit Sidoniam* = None shall
tire Sidon.
1   1846 frigate. Sold in 1864.
2   1944 submarine of 715/990 tons

built by Cammell Laird. Sunk by
explosion, salved, then expended
as a target off Portland in 1957.

## SIKH

Norway 1940
Atlantic 1940−1
*Bismarck* Action 1941
Cape Bon 1941
Libya 1941
Malta Convoys 1941−2
Sirte 1942
Mediterranean 1942
*Sicut leones* = Be like lions.
1   1918 destroyer of 'Tribal' class of
    *c*.1,075 tons built by Fairfield. Sold
    in 1927 to Granton Shipbuilding
    Co for scrapping.
2   1937 destroyer of 1,870 tons built
    by Stephen. Sunk after damaged
    by shore batteries at Tobruk in
    1942.

## SILVERTON

Named after the hunt in Devonshire.
1   1940 destroyer of the 'Hunt' class,
    1,050 tons, built by White. Lent to
    the Polish navy 1941−6 and
    renamed *Krakowiak*. Scrapped at
    Grays in 1959.

## SIMOON

Crimea 1854−5
Ashantee 1873−4
Sicily 1943
Aegean 1943
Mediterranean 1943
Named after the hot, dry wind
experienced in the Arabian desert.
1   1849 frigate. Sold in 1887.
2   1904 turret ship, ex-*Monarch*, but
    sold a year later.
3   1916 destroyer of 1,065 tons built
    by John Brown. Torpedoed by the
    German *S-50* in the North Sea in
    1917.
4   1918 destroyer of 1,075 tons built
    by John Brown. Sold in 1930 to
    Metal Industries of Charlestown
    for scrapping.
5   1942 submarine, ex-*P225*, 715/990
    tons built by Cammell Laird. Lost
    in 1943, probably sunk by *U-565* off
    the Dodecanese.

## SIR BEDIVERE

Falkland Islands 1982
1   1966 Logistic landing ship of 5,674
    tons full load built by Hawthorn
    Leslie. Manned by the RFA.

## SIRDAR

*Honoris causa* = For honour.
The name means a military leader,
usually Indian.
1   1918 destroyer of 1,075 tons built
    by Fairfield. Sold to Cashmore in
    1934 for scrapping.
2   1943 submarine, ex-*P226*, 715/990
    tons built by Scotts. She became an
    experimental boat about 1958 and
    was scrapped in 1965.

## SIR GALAHAD

North Sea 1942
Normandy 1944
Falkland Islands 1982
1   1941 Admiralty trawler of 'Round
    Table' class, 440 tons built by Hall
    Russell. Disposal List 1944.
    Mercantile service: *Star of Freedom*
    (1946), *Robert Limbrick* (1956). Lost
    1957.
2   1966 Logistic landing ship of 5,674
    tons full load. Hit and abandoned
    at the Falklands: towed to sea and
    sunk.
3   1987[71] Logistic landing ship of
    8,500 tons deadweight built by
    Swan Hunter.

## SIR GERAINT

North Sea 1942
Normandy 1944
Falkland Islands 1982
1   1942 Admiralty trawler of 'Round
    Table' class, 440 tons, built by
    Lewis. Mercantile service: *Star of
    the South* (1946).
2   1967 Logistic landing ship of 5,674
    tons built by Alexander Stephen of
    Glasgow.

## SIRIUS

Trafalgar 1805
Belgian Coast 1914
Zeebrugge 1918
Arctic 1942
Malta Convoys 1942
Mediterranean 1942
North Africa 1942−3
Sicily 1943
Salerno 1943
Aegean 1943−4
Normandy 1944
South France 1944
Heaven's light our guide.
Named after the Dog Star — the
brightest star in the sky.
1   1786 armed store ship ex-*Berwick*
    (10) of 512 tons. She carried the
    first governor to New South Wales
    in 1788. Was wrecked off Norfolk
    Island after colonizing it in 1790.
2   1797 5th rate (36) of 1,047 tons built
    by Dudman on the Thames. After
    an exciting life at sea she was
    finally burnt in 1810 to avoid
    capture.
3   1813 5th rate (38) of 1,268 tons built
    by Tyson & Blake, the last ship to
    be built at Burlesden. Scrapped in
    1882.
4   1868 sloop of 1,268 tons built at
    Portsmouth. Sold in 1885.
5   1890 screw cruiser, second class of
    3,600 tons built by Armstrong on
    the Tyne. Sunk as a blockship at
    Ostend in 1918.
6   1940 cruiser of 5,450 tons built at

Portsmouth by Scotts. Scrapped at
Blyth in 1956.
7   1964 anti-submarine general-
    purpose frigate of 2,450/3,200 tons
    built at Portsmouth. 'Leander'
    class armed with Exocet missiles.

## SIR LANCELOT

Normandy 1944
Falkland Islands 1982
1   1941 Admiralty trawler of 'Round
    Table' class, 440 tons built by
    Lewis. Disposal List 1944.
2   1963 Logistic landing ship of 5,550
    tons built by Fairfield for the Army
    but taken over for the RN in 1970.

## SIR PERCIVALE

Falkland Islands 1982
1   1967 Logistic landing-ship of 5,674
    tons built by Hawthorn Leslie.

## SIR TRISTRAM

Normandy 1944
Falkland Islands 1982
1   1942 Admiralty trawler of 'Round
    Table' class, 440 tons, built by
    Lewis. Sold in 1947.
2   1967 Logistic landing ship of 5,674
    tons built by Hawthorn Leslie.
    Seriously damaged in the
    Falklands. Became accommodation
    ship. Returned to UK 1983 for refit
    by Tyne Shipbuilders. Completed
    1985 with improved helicopter
    deck.

## SKATE

Atlantic 1940−4
Arctic 1943
English Channel 1944
*Per aequora labor* = I glide [skate] over
the surface.
1   1895 destroyer. Sold in 1907.
2   1917 destroyer of 1,065 tons built
    by John Brown. Sold to Cashmore
    in 1947 for scrapping.

## SLEUTH

1   1944 submarine of 715/990 tons
    built by Cammell Laird. Scrapped
    at Charlestown in 1958.

71   Launch date was actually 14 December 1986.

## SLINGER

Okinawa 1945
*Debellare superbos* = To overcome the proud. (A phrase from the *Aeneid*)
1   1942 escort carrier, ex-USS *Chatham*, 11,420 tons built by Seattle: Tacoma. Returned to USA in 1946 for mercantile service.
2   1947 Landing-ship.

## SLUYS

*Per medium illorum ibat* = Through the midst of them he went his way.
The badge derives from the arms of Edward III, who won the victory of Sluys in 1340.
1   1945 destroyer of 3,361 tons of the 'Battle' class built by Cammell Laird. Sold to the Iranian navy in 1967.

## SMITER

Atlantic 1944
*Percutimus crebro* = We strike hard and often.
1   1943 escort carrier ex-USS *Vermilion*, 11,420 tons built by Seattle: Tacoma. Returned to USA in 1946 for mercantile service.
2   1947 Landing Ship. Sold in 1949.
3   1986 coastal patrol craft of 43 tons.

## SNAPPER

Baltic 1855
Norway 1940
Atlantic 1940
*Dentibus paratis* = With teeth ready.
1   1782 vessel.
5   1895 destroyer. Sold in 1911.
8   1934 submarine of 670/960 tons built by Chatham Dock Yard. Lost to unknown cause in Bay of Biscay in 1941.

## SNIPE

1   1801 vessel.
7   1945 sloop of 1,375 tons built by Denny. Scrapped in 1960.

## SNOWDROP

Atlantic 1941–4
1   1915 sloop of 1,200 tons built by McMillan. Sold in 1923 to the Unity Ship Breaking Company.
4   1940 corvette of 925 tons built by Scotts. Scrapped on the Tyne in 1949.

## SOLEBAY

St Kitts 1782
The badge derives from the rose of the Duke of York, C-in-C at Solebay, 1672.
1   1694 5th rate (32). She was lost on Christmas Day 1709 with all hands.
2   1711 bomb vessel. Sold in 1748.
3   1742 6th rate (20) which surrendered in 1744. She was retaken in 1746. Sold in 1763.
4   1763 6th rate (28) which was wrecked in 1782.
5   1785 5th rate (32) built at Deptford. Wrecked in 1809 but her crew was saved.
6   5th rate, ex-*Iris*. Scrapped in 1833.
7   1944 destroyer of 'Battle' class of 3,361 tons built by Hawthorn Leslie. Scrapped at Troon in 1967.

## SOLENT

1   1944 submarine 715/990 tons built by Cammell Laird. Scrapped in 1961 at Troon.

## SOMALI

Norway 1940–1
*Bismarck* Action 1941
Arctic 1941–2
Malta Convoys 1942
1   1937 destroyer of 'Tribal' class of 1,870 tons built by Swan Hunter at Wallsend. Torpedoed while escorting Russian convoy QP 14, in 1942 and foundered some days later when in tow.

## SOMALILAND

Atlantic 1944
Arctic 1944
1   1943 frigate of 1,318 tons, ex-USS *Popham*, ex-*PF.90*, built by Walsh Kaiser. Returned to USA in 1946.

## SOUTHAMPTON

Bellisle 1761
Glorious First of June 1794
St. Vincent 1897
Heligoland 1914
Dogger Bank 1915
Jutland 1916
Norway 1940
Spartivento 1940
Malta Convoys 1941
*Émeraude* 1757
*Pro justitia pro rege* = For justice and the King.
1   1693 4th rate. Scrapped as a hulk in 1771.
2   1757 5th rate. Arguably the first genuine frigate built in England.[72] Wrecked in 1812.
3   1820 3rd rate.
4   1912 cruiser of 5,400 tons built by John Brown. Sold in 1926 to Ward for scrapping at Pembroke Dock.
5   1936 cruiser of 9,100 tons, ex-*Polyphemus*. So seriously damaged by air attacks in 1941 that she was scuttled.
6   1979 Type 42 destroyer of 3,500/

---

72   See Walker and Manning, p.411.

4,100 tons built by Vosper Thornycroft.

## SOUTHDOWN

North Sea 1941–5
Normandy 1944
Named after the hunt in Sussex.
1   1916 minesweeper of 750 tons built by Simons. Sold in 1926 to Granton Ship Breaking Company for scrapping.
2   1940 destroyer of the 'Hunt' class 907 tons built by White. Scrapped at Barrow in 1956.

## SOUTHWOLD

Sirte 1942
Malta Convoys 1942
Libya 1942
Named after the hunt in Lincolnshire.
1   1941 destroyer of the 'Hunt' class 1,050 tons built by White. Mined in 1942 off Malta.

## SOVEREIGN *see* ROYAL SOVEREIGN

## SPANKER

South France 1944
1   1794 floating battery. Sold in 1810.
4   1943 minesweeper of 990 tons built by Harland & Wolff. Sold to Belgium in 1951 and renamed *De Brouwer* in 1953.

## SPARK

Armada 1588
Atlantic 1944
1   1588: a merchant ship of this name accompanied the fleet in the Armada campaign.
4   1943 submarine of 750/990 tons, ex-*P236*, built by Scotts. Sold in 1949 for scrapping at Faslane.

## SPARROW

San Sebastian 1813
Korea 1953
1   1653 prize.
3   1805 brig/sloop helped capture the *Étoile* in 1814 and presented her ensign to Earl St Vincent.
8   1946 sloop of 1,350 tons built by Denny. Scrapped at Rosyth in 1958.

## SPARROWHAWK

China 1860
Jutland 1916
Strike once and enough.
1   1807 vessel.
4   1895 destroyer which was wrecked in 1904.
5   1912 destroyer of *c*.957 tons built by Swan Hunter. Sunk at Jutland in 1916.
6   1918 destroyer of 1,075 tons built by Swan Hunter. Sold in 1931 for scrapping by Ward of Grays.
7   1939 RN Air Station at Hatston.
8   1945–6 RN Air Station at Halesworth.
9   1950 ex-German frontier control boat.

## SPARTAN

Burma 1852–3
China 1856–7
Atlantic 1943
Anzio 1944
Mediterranean 1944
Falkland Islands 1982
Courage with great endurance.
Name derives from the inhabitants of Sparta in ancient Greece.
1   1806 5th rate. Scrapped in 1822.
2   1841 6th rate. Sold in 1862.
3   1868 sloop. Sold in 1884.
4   1891 cruiser of 3,600 tons. Renamed *Defiance II* in 1921.
5   1941 cruiser of 5,770 tons built by Vickers Armstrong of Barrow. She was sunk by a glider bomb off Anzio in 1944.
6   1978 nuclear-powered submarine of 4,000/4,900 tons built by the Vickers Ship Building Group.

## SPARTIATE

Trafalgar 1805
1   1798 prize taken at The Nile. Scrapped in 1857.
2   1898 cruiser of 11,000 tons which was renamed *Fisgard II* in 1915. Training ship at Portsmouth in 1932.
3   1939–46 naval base at Glasgow.

## SPEAKER

Dover 1652
Kentish Knock 1652
Portland 1653
Gabbard 1653
Santa Cruz 1657
Atlantic 1944
Okinawa 1945
*Facta non verba* = Deeds not words.

## SPEARFISH

Norway 1940
North Sea 1940
*Latet hasta sub undis* = Beneath the waves there lies in wait a spear.
1   1936 submarine of 670/960 tons built by Cammell Laird. Sunk off Norway in 1940 by *U-34*.

## SPEARHEAD

Atlantic 1945
Strike hard, strike true.
1   1944 submarine of 670/960 tons built by Cammell Laird. Sold to Portugal in 1948 and renamed *Neptuno*.

## SPEEDWELL

Armada 1588
Barfleur 1692
Dunkirk 1940
Atlantic 1941–3
Arctic 1942–4
North Africa 1942–3
Normandy 1944
*Bene festina* = Speed well.
1   1559 vessel. It was a merchant ship that served in the Armada campaign.
2   1607 ship ex-*Swiftsure*. Lost in 1624.
3   1666 ship ex-*Cheriton*. Lost in 1678.
5   1690 5th rate. She became a fireship, and was reduced later to a 6th rate.
6   1708 6th rate prize.
7   and 9 were both sloops of 1744 and 1762.
26  1935 minesweeper of 815 tons built by Hamilton: Beardmore. Sold in 1946 for mercantile service. Wrecked en route to Dutch ship-breakers in 1950.

## SPEEDY

North Sea 1942
Arctic 1942
Malta Convoys 1942
Sicily 1943
*Gamo* 1801

1   1649 3rd rate which was renamed *Mary* in 1660.
2   1652 prize which was renamed *Sophia* in 1660.
4   1943 escort carrier, ex-USS *Delgado*, of 11,420 tons built by Seattle: Tacoma. Returned to USA in 1946 for mercantile service.

*Virtute et labore* = By valour and labour.
1   1782 brig commanded by Lord Cochrane.
6   1918 destroyer of 1,087 tons built by Thornycroft. Sunk in collision with a merchant ship in the Sea of Marmara in 1922.
7   1938 minesweeper of 815 tons built by White. Scrapped at Aden in 1947.

## SPEY

Atlantic 1942−4
North Africa 1942−3
Burma 1944−5
*Mak sicker* = Make sure.
1   1814 sloop. Sold in 1822.
6   1941 frigate of 1,370 tons built by Smith's Dock on Teeside. Sold to Egypt in 1948 and renamed *Rasheed*.
7   1985−6 minesweeper of 890 tons built by Richards Ltd of Lowestoft.

## SPHINX

Cape of Good Hope 1795
Burma 1852−3
Baltic 1854
Crimea 1854−5
China 1860
1   and 2 were both 6th rates of 1748 and 1775.
3   and 4 were both sloops of 1815 and 1846.
7   1939 minesweeper of 875 tons built by White. Sunk by aircraft in 1940 on the Moray Firth.
8   1941−6 shore base in Egypt.

## SPIREA

Atlantic 1942−5
Malta Convoys 1942
North Africa 1942
North Sea 1943
1   1917 sloop of 1,290 tons built by Simons. Sold in 1922.
2   1940 corvette of 925 tons built by Inglis: Kincaid. Transferred to Greece in 1948 and renamed *Thessalonika*.

## SPIRIT

1   1943 submarine of 715/990 tons built by Cammell Laird. Scrapped in 1950 by Ward of Grays.

## SPITEFUL

Martinique 1794
Crimea 1854−5
1   *c*.1794 vessel.
4   1842 sloop. Sold in 1883.
5   1899 destroyer *c*.400 tons built by Palmer. Sold in 1920 for scrapping by Hayes at Porthcawl.
6   1943 submarine, ex-*P227*, 715/990 tons built by Scotts. Lent to France in 1952 and renamed *Sirene*. Returned in 1958 and scrapped at Faslane in 1963.

## SPLENDID

Mediterranean 1942
Falkland Islands 1982
*Splendide audax* = Splendidly audacious.
1   1597 vessel.
2   1918 destroyer of 1,075 tons built by Swan Hunter. Scrapped in 1931 by Metal Industries of Charlestown.
3   1942 submarine, ex-*P228*, 715/990 tons built by Chatham Dock Yard. Sunk by German destroyer *Hermes* off Corsica 1943.
4   1979 nuclear-powered submarine of 4,000/4,900 tons built by Vickers Armstrong at Barrow.

## SPORTSMAN

Sicily 1943
Aegean 1943−4
Mediterranean 1944
Atlantic 1945
1   1942 submarine, ex-*P229*, of 715/990 tons built by Chatham Dock Yard. Sold to France in 1951 and renamed *Sibylle*, Lost in 1952.

## SPRAGGE

Normandy 1944
English Channel 1944
Named after Admiral Sir Edward Spragge, killed while shifting his flag at the Texel, 1673.
1   1943 frigate of 1,300 tons, ex-*DE.563*, built by Bethlehem: Hingham. Returned to USA in 1946.

## SPRINGER

I strike swiftly.
1   1945 submarine of 715/990 tons built by Cammell Laird. Sold to Israel in 1958 and renamed *Tanin*.

## SPUR

*Acheronto movebo* = I shall overcome death.
1   1944 submarine of 715/990 tons built by Cammell Laird. Sold to Portugal in 1948 and renamed *Narval*.

## SQUIRREL

Louisburg 1758
Quebec 1759
*Assiduitate* = By diligence.
1   1694 vessel.
2   3, 4, 5 and 6 were all 6th rates of 1703 (surrendered), 1704 (foundered), 1707, 1755 and 1785.
11  1944 minesweeper of 990 tons built by Harland & Wolff. Sunk by mine off Puket, Thailand, in 1945.
12  13 and 14 were Fishery Protection vessels.

## STAG

Martinique 1762
1   and 2 were both 5th rates of 1758 and 1794 (wrecked).
6   1812 6th rate. Scrapped in 1821.
7   1830 5th rate. Scrapped in 1866.
10  1899 destroyer of *c*.340 tons built by Thornycroft. Sold in 1921 for scrapping by Ward at Grays.
11  1940−9 naval depot in the Suez Canal area.

## STALKER

Atlantic 1943−4
Salerno 1943
South France 1944
Aegean 1944
Burma 1945
*Hostes captamus* = We catch [stalk] the enemy.
1   1914−18 vessel.
2   1942 escort carrier ex-USS *Hamlin*. 11,420 tons built by Western Pipe: GEC. Returned to USA for mercantile service in 1946.
3   1947 Landing Ship, ex-LST (3) 3515; 2,140/5,000 tons full load. Designated submarine support ship 1958. Disposal List 1982−3.

## STANDARD

1   1782 3rd rate. Scrapped in 1816.
2   1941−5 naval camp at Hexham.

## STANLEY

Atlantic 1941
1. c.1778 vessel.
2. 1940 destroyer ex-USS *McAlla* of 1,060 tons built by Bethlehem in 1919. Torpedoed in 1941 in the Atlantic by *U-574* south-west of Portugal.

## STARFISH

Belgian Coast 1917
*Retibus nostris omnia* = All is [fish] for our nets.
1. 1895 destroyer. Sold in 1911.
2. 1916 destroyer of 1,065 tons built by Hawthorn Leslie and Alloa of Charlestown. Sold in 1928 for scrapping.
3. 1933 submarine of 640/927 tons built by Chatham Dock Yard. Lost in 1940 when attacked by German minesweepers in the Heligoland Bight.

## STARLING

China 1841−2
Baltic 1855
China 1856−60
Biscay 1943−4
Atlantic 1943−5
Arctic 1844
Normandy 1944
1. 1801 vessel.
9. 1942 sloop of 1,350 tons built by Fairfield. She was commanded by the legendary 'U-boat killer' Captain Walker. *Starling* was involved in the sinking of fourteen U-boats. She was scrapped at Queenborough in 1965.
10. 1986 Far East patrol craft, 690 tons, one of a class of five built by Hall, Russell: no entry for *Swallow*, but see also *Peacock*, *Plover* and *Swift*.

## START BAY

1. 1945 frigate, ex-*Loch Arklet*, of 1,580 tons built by Harland & Wolff. Scrapped at Newport in 1958.

## STARWORT

Atlantic 1941−5
North Sea 1942−4
Arctic 1942−4
Mediterranean 1942
North Africa 1942
Sicily 1943
Normandy 1944
English Channel 1944
1. 1941 corvette of 925 tons built by Inglis: Kincaid. Sold in 1947 for mercantile service.

## STATESMAN

1. 1943 submarine of 715/990 tons built by Cammell Laird. Lent to France 1952−9 and renamed *Sultane*. Sold in 1961 for scrapping.

## STATICE

Normandy 1944
Atlantic 1944−5
English Channel 1944−5
1. 1943 corvette, ex-USS *Vim*, of 980 tons built by Collingwood. Returned to USA in 1946.

HMS STARLING (No. 9)

## STAYNER

Normandy 1944
English Channel 1944
North Sea 1944
Named after Admiral Richard Stayner
(d. 1662).
1   1943 frigate, ex-*DE.564*, of 1,300
    tons built by Bethlehem: Hingham.
    Returned to USA in 1945.

## STEADFAST

Normandy 1944
Atlantic 1944
Steadfast and true.
1   1915 vessel.
2   1918 destroyer of 1,075 tons built
    by Palmer. Sold in 1934 to Metal
    Industries for scrapping at
    Charlestown.
3   1943 minesweeper, ex-USS *BAM
    31*, of 890 tons built by Gulf
    Shipbuilding of Chickasaw.
    Returned to USA in 1946.

## STERLET

*Nulli secundus* = Second to none.
1   1937 submarine of 670/960 tons
    built by Chatham Dock Yard.
    Destroyed by German anti-
    submarine trawlers in the
    Skagerrak in 1940.

## STEVENSTONE

English Channel 1943−4
North Sea 1944
Normandy 1944
Named after the hunt in Devonshire.
1   1942 destroyer of the 'Hunt' class,
    1,087 tons built by White.
    Scrapped in 1959.

## STOCKHAM

Normandy 1944
English Channel 1944
Named after John Stockham, First
Lieutenant of *Thunderer* at Trafalgar.
He took command in the absence of
the captain — and earned promotion.
1   1943 frigate, ex-*DE.97*, of 1,300
    tons built by Bethlehem: Hingham.
    Returned to USA in 1946.

## STOIC

Atlantic 1945
1   1943 submarine, ex-*P231*, of 715/
    990 tons built by Cammell Laird.
    Scrapped at Dalmuir in 1950.

## STONECROP

Atlantic 1941−5
English Channel 1945
1   1941 corvette of 925 tons built by
    Smith's Dock. Sold for mercantile
    service as *Silver King* (1949) and
    *Marthe Vinke* (1950).

## STONEHENGE

*Fortis per saeculis* = Strong through the
ages.
1   1919 destroyer of 1,075 tons built
    by Palmer. Wrecked near Smyrna
    in 1920.
2   1943 submarine, ex-*P232*, of 715/
    990 tons built by Cammell Laird.
    Lost to unknown cause in 1944 off
    Nicobar Islands.

## STORK

Gabbard 1653
Martinique 1809
Baltic 1855
Zeebrugge 1918
Norway 1940
North Sea 1940
Atlantic 1940−4
North Africa 1942
Normandy 1944
*Altiora peto* = I seek higher things.
1   1652 Dutch prize.
3   1796 sloop. Sold in 1816.
8   1916 destroyer of 1,065 tons built
    by Hawthorn Leslie. Sold in 1927
    to Cashmore for scrapping.
9   1936 sloop of 1,190 tons built by
    Denny as a surveying ship.
    Scrapped at Troon in 1958.

## STORM

Atlantic 1945
1   1943 submarine, ex-*P233*, of 715/
    990 tons built by Cammell Laird.
    Scrapped at Troon in 1949.

## STORMCLOUD

South France 1944
*Omnibus tempestibus* = In all weathers.
1   1919 destroyer of 1,075 tons built
    by Palmer. Sold to Metal Industries
    in 1934 for scrapping at
    Charlestown.
2   1943 minesweeper of the 'Algerine'
    class built by Lobnitz. Sold in 1959
    for scrapping at Gateshead.

## STRATAGEM

English Channel 1944
*Consilio vincimus* = We conquer by
strategy.
1   1943 submarine, ex-*P234*, of 715/
    990 tons built by Cammell Laird.
    Destroyed by Japanese patrol craft
    off Malacca, 1944.

## STRENUOUS

*Per diem in die* = From day to day.
1   1805 vessel.
4   1918 destroyer of 1,075 tons built
    by Scotts. Sold in 1932 to Alloa for
    scrapping at Charlestown.
5   1942 minesweeper, ex-USS *Vital*,
    of 890 tons built by Gulf
    Shipbuilding Company of
    Chickasaw. Scrapped in Germany
    in 1956.

## STRIKER

Atlantic 1943−4
Arctic 1944
Norway 1944
Okinawa 1945
1   1942 escort carrier, ex-USS *Prince
    William*, of 11,420 tons built by
    Western Pipe:GEC. Returned to
    USA in 1946 and scrapped.
2   1947 Landing-ship.
3   *c*.1983 coastal training craft of 34
    tons for RNR training.

## STROMNESS

Falkland Islands 1982
1   1966 fleet supply ship of 16,500
    tons built by Swan Hunter at
    Wallsend. To US Navy in 1983.

## STRONGBOW

Scandinavian Convoys 1917
Atlantic 1944
1   1916 destroyer of 900 tons built by
    Yarrow. Sunk in action in the
    North Sea in 1917.
2   1943 submarine, ex-*P235*, of 715/
    990 tons built by Scotts. Scrapped,
    surprisingly, in 1946 by Ward at
    Preston.

## STRONGHOLD

Strong holds strong.
1   1919 destroyer of 905 tons built by
    Scotts. Sunk in action with
    Japanese forces south of Java in
    1942.

## STUBBORN

Norway 1941
Biscay 1943
Atlantic 1945
*Fortiter in re* = Bravely in action.
1  1942 submarine, ex-*P238*, of 715/990 tons built by Cammell Laird. Expended as an anti-submarine target in 1946.

## STURDY

Atlantic 1939
Malaya 1945
Strong to endure.
1  1919 destroyer of 1,075 tons built by Scotts. Wrecked in 1940 on Tiree.
2  1943 submarine of 715/990 tons built by Cammell Laird. Scrapped in 1958.

## STURGEON

North Sea 1942
Arctic 1942
North Africa 1942−3
*Cave ampiam* = Beware, I shall catch you.
1  1894 destroyer. Sold in 1910.
2  1917 destroyer of 1,065 tons built by Stephen. Sold in 1926 for breaking up at Plymouth.
3  1932 submarine of 670/920 tons built by Chatham Dock Yard. Lent to the Royal Netherlands navy 1943−5 and renamed *Zeehond*. Scrapped in 1947.

## STYGIAN

Atlantic 1944
1  1943 submarine of 715/990 tons built by Cammell Laird. Scrapped at Faslane in 1949.

## SUBTLE

Martinique 1809
Malaya 1944−5
1  1544 vessel.
2  1944 submarine of 715/990 tons built by Cammell Laird. Scrapped in 1959 at Charlestown.

## SUCCESS

Portland 1653
Gabbard 1653
Porto Farina 1655
Lowestoft 1665
Solebay 1672
Texel 1673
Cape Passero 1718
*Finis coronat opus* = The end crowns the work.
1  and 2 were both 5th rates of 1650 (prize) and 1660 (ex-*Bradford* which became wrecked in 1680).
7  8, 10, 11 and 14 were all 6th rates of 1709 (surrendered), 1712, 1740, 1781 and 1825.
15  1901 destroyer of *c*.400 tons built by Doxford. Wrecked in 1914 off Fife Ness.
16  1918 destroyer of 1,075 tons built by Doxford. Transferred RAN in 1919. Sold in 1937 to Penguins Ltd, Sydney for scrapping.
19  1943 destroyer of 1,760 tons built by White, but she never actually served in the RN. She transferred to the Royal Norwegian Navy in 1943 and was renamed *Stord*. Scrapped in 1959.

## SUFFOLK

Barfleur 1692[73]
Gibraltar 1704
Velez Malaga 1704
Norway 1940
*Bismarck* Action 1941
Arctic 1941−2
Burma 1945
*Nous maintiendrons* = We shall maintain.
1  and 3 were both 3rd rates of 1680 and 1765.
5  1805, ex-*Sultan* a 3rd rate. Scrapped in 1816.
6  1903 cruiser of 9,800 tons built by Portsmouth Dock Yard. Broken up in Germany in 1922.
7  1926 cruiser of 9,750 tons built by Portsmouth DY : Parsons. Scrapped at Newport in 1948.

## SULTAN

Providien 1782
Negapatam 1782
Trincomalee 1782
Alexandria 1882
*Pededemptim* = Step by step.
1  1775 3rd rate which was renamed *Suffolk* in 1805.

2  1807 3rd rate. Scrapped in 1864.
3  1870 ironclad which became part of *Fisgard* in 1906. She was not scrapped until 1946.
5  1940 depot at Singapore until 1946.
6  1956 mechanical training establishment at Gosport. More properly it is the RN School of Marine Engineering, sited on an old WWI airfield.

## SUNFISH

North Sea 1940
Norway 1940−1
1  1896 destroyer of *c*.350 tons built by Hawthorn Leslie. Sold to J. Kelly for scrapping in 1920.
2  1936 submarine of 715/990 tons built by Chatham Dock Yard. Lent to Russia in 1944 and renamed *B 1* but she was sunk in error on passage by British aircraft.

## SUNFLOWER

Atlantic 1941−5
Normandy 1944
North Sea 1944
English Channel 1944−5
1  1915 sloop of 1,200 tons built by Henderson. Sold in 1921 to the Rangoon Port Commissioners.
2  1940 corvette of 925 tons built by Smith's Dock. Scrapped at Hayle in 1947.

## SUPERB

Cape Passero 1718
Sadras 1782
Providien 1782
Negapatam 1782
Trincomalee 1782
Gut of Gibraltar 1801
San Domingo 1806
Algiers 1816

---

73  *Suffolk* clearly appears in lists of ships attending Barfleur, but curiously, she is omitted from the Admiralty list for the battle honour.

Alexandria 1882
Jutland 1916
With sword and courage.
The badge is derived from the crest of Admiral Sir Richard Goodwin Keats (1757−1834).

1   1710 4th rate prize of 1,021 tons taken by the *Kent* in the Channel. She was the French *Superbe*. Rebuilt in 1736−8 to 1,068 tons. Scrapped in 1757.
2   1760 3rd rate (74) of 1,612 tons built by A. Hayes of Deptford. Wrecked in 1783 at Telicherry.
3   1795 prize corvette (22) which became a prison ship at Martinique. She was disposed of in 1798.
4   1798 3rd rate (74) of 1,916 tons built by Dudman on the Thames. Commanded by Captain R.G. Keats and flagship of Vice Admiral Sir J.T. Duckworth at San Domingo. Scrapped in 1826.
5   1842 2nd rate (98) of 2,589 tons built at Pembroke. Became a cholera hospital ship in 1866 at Sheerness. Scrapped in 1869.
6   1878 central battery ship, ironclad, of 9,179 tons built for Turkey as *Hamidieh*. Sold in 1906.
7   1907 battleship of 18,000 tons built by Armstrong at Elswick. Served at Jutland. Sold in 1919 as a gunnery training ship. Scrapped in 1922 by Stanlee.
8   1943 cruiser of 8,800 tons built by Swan Hunter at Wallsend. Scrapped Dalmuir 1960 and Troon, hull only, in 1961.
9   1974 nuclear-powered submarine of 4,000/4,900 tons built by Vickers Ship Building Group at Barrow.

## SUPREME

Atlantic 1944
1   1944 submarine of 715/990 tons built by Cammell Laird. Scrapped at Troon in 1950.

## SURF

Aegean 1943
Atlantic 1944
*Perpetuum mobile* = Always on the move.
1   1914−18 vessel.
2   1942 submarine, ex-*P239*, of 715/990 tons built by Cammell Laird. Scrapped at Faslane in 1949.

## SURPRISE

Dogger Bank 1781
China 1956−60
Belgian Coast 1917
Atlantic 1941−2
North Sea 1942
*Hermione* 1799
*Sola nobilitas virtus* = Valour is the only nobility.

1   1745 6th rate (24) of 508 tons built at Bewley. Sold at Deptford in 1770.
2   1774 6th rate (28) of 594 tons built at Woolwich. She was at Quebec. Sold in 1783.
3   1778 prize, USS *Bunkers Hill* (16 or 18). Sold at Sheerness in 1783.
7   1796 5th rate (28) prize, the French *Unité* captured by HMS *Constant*. Captain Hamilton won a knighthood for his *Hermione* exploit at Puerto Cabello in Venezuela.
9   1812 5th rate built at Milford Haven. Sold in 1837.
10  1856 first-class screw vessel of 680 tons which saw much anti-pirate action off China. Scrapped in 1860.
12  1885 screw despatch vessel of 1,650 tons built at Jarrow. Renamed *Alacrity* in 1913.
13  1916 destroyer of 885 tons built by Yarrow on the Clyde. Mined in the North Sea in 1917.
15  1940 yacht originally built in 1896, fitted out for anti-submarine service. Caught fire and capsized in Lagos in 1942.
16  1945 frigate, ex-*Loch Carron*, ex-*Gerrans Bay*, of 1,580 tons built by Smith's Dock. Scrapped in 1965.

## SUSSEX

Portland 1653
Gabbard 1653
Norway 1940
Burma 1945
*Fortiter in re* = Bravely in action.
1   1652 4th rate. Blown up in the following year.

2   1653 3rd rate which was wrecked in 1694.
3   1802 cruiser ex-*Union* hospital ship. Scrapped in 1816.
4   1928 cruiser of 9,830 tons built by Hawthorn Leslie. Scrapped at Dalmuir in 1955.

## SWALE

North Africa 1942
Atlantic 1942−4
1   1905 destroyer of *c.*560 tons built by Palmer. Sold in 1919 to Ward of Preston.
2   1942 frigate of 1,370 tons built by Smith's Dock. Scrapped at Faslane in 1955.

## SWEETBRIAR

Atlantic 1941−5
Arctic 1942
Normandy 1944
1   1917 sloop of 1,290 tons built by Swan Hunter. Sold in 1927 to Cashmore for scrapping.
2   1941 corvette of 925 tons built by Smith's Dock. Sold for mercantile service and named *Star IX* in 1949.

## SWIFT

Dover 1917
Belgian Coast 1917−18
Zeebrugge 1918
Normandy 1944
Arctic 1944
1   1549 vessel.
2   1689 prize which was sunk as a breakwater in 1695.
6   1704 6th rate. Sold in 1719.
7   8, 9, 10, 11 and 20 were all sloops of 1721, 1741, 1763 (lost at sea), 1777 (surrendered), 1783 (foundered) and 1807.
26  1907 flotilla leader of 2,170 tons built by Cammell Laird. Sold in 1921 to Rees of Llanelly for scrapping.
28  1942 destroyer of 1,710 tons built by White. Mined off Normandy in 1944.
29  1985 Far East patrol craft, 690 tons, one of a class of five built by Hall, Russell : no entry for *Swallow*, but see also *Peacock*, *Plover* and *Starling*.

## SWIFTSURE

Armada 1588
Cadiz 1596
Santa Cruz 1657
Lowestoft 1665
Four Days' Battle 1666
Schooneveld 1673
Texel 1673
Barfleur 1692
Vigo 1702
Gibraltar 1704
Velez Malaga 1704
Lagos 1759
Quiberon Bay 1759
Belleisle 1761
Nile 1798
Egypt 1801
Trafalgar 1805
Suez Canal 1915
Dardanelles 1915–16
Okinawa 1945

1   1573 ship (41) of 400 tons built at Deptford. Served under Captain Edward Fenner at the Armada. Rebuilt in 1592 and again in 1607 when she was renamed *Speedwell*.
2   1621 3rd rate (60) of 898 tons built at Deptford. Commanded by Earl of Essex at Cadiz in 1725. Flagship of Admiral Sir W. Berkeley at Lowestoft and was taken by the Dutch at the Four Days' Battle, when the admiral was killed.
3   1673 3rd rate (70) of 978 tons built at Harwich. She was renamed *Revenge* in 1715.
4   1750 3rd rate (70) of 1,426 tons built at Deptford. Sold in 1773.
5   1787 3rd rate (74) of 1,521 tons built on Thames. She surrendered in 1801, was retaken at Trafalgar and added to the Navy as *Irresistible*.
6   1804 3rd rate (74) built at Buckler's Hard. Used in 1845 as a target then scrapped.
7   1870 ironclad screw battleship of 6,910 tons built by Palmer at Jarrow. She was renamed *Orontes* in 1904.
8   1903 battleship of 11,800 tons built by Armstrong Whitworth. Sold to Stanlee for scrapping in 1920.

9   1943 cruiser of 8,800 tons (full displacement 11,240 tons). Built by Vickers Armstrong on the Tyne. Scrapped at Inverkeithing in 1962.
10  1971 nuclear-powered submarine of 4,000/4,900 tons built by Vickers Armstrong at Barrow.

## SWORDFISH

English Channel 1940
*Ense et animo* = With sword and with courage.
1   1895 destroyer. Sold in 1910.
2   1916 submarine of 932/1,470 tons built by Scotts. She was an experimental steam submarine. Sold to Hayle of Porthcawl in 1923. She was known for a short time as *S 1*.
3   1931 submarine of 670/990 tons built by Chatham. Lost to unknown causes off Ushant in 1940.

## SYBILLE (Sybil and Sibyl)

St Kitts 1782
China 1856–60
Sicily 1943
Aegean 1943–4
*Forte* 1799
1   and 2 were both 6th rates of 1774 and 1779 (renamed *Garland*).
3   and 4 were both 5th rates of 1794 (prize) and 1847.
5   1890 cruiser which was wrecked in 1901.
6   1917 destroyer of *c*.900 tons built by Yarrow. Sold in 1926 to Cashmore for scrapping.
7   1942 submarine, ex-*P217*, ex-*P67*, of 715/990 tons built by Cammell Laird. Scrapped at Troon in 1948.

## SYLVIA

*Echo* 1810
1   1806 vessel.
5   1897 destroyer of *c*.400 tons built by Doxford. Sold in 1919 to Ward of New Holland.
6   1944 minesweeper of the 'Algerine' class built by Lobnitz. Scrapped at Gateshead in 1958.

## SYRTIS

*Feriendo defendo* = In destroying, I preserve.
1   1942 submarine of 715/990 tons built by Cammell Laird. Lost in 1944 when mined off Bodö.

## TABARD

My cloak the sea.
1   1945 submarine of 1,090/1,575 tons built by Scotts. Used as training boat 1969 prior to scrapping.

## TACITURN

Atlantic 1945
Deeds not words.
1   1944 submarine of 1,090/1,575 tons built by Vickers Armstrong at Barrow. Disposal List 1974–5.

## TACTICIAN

Sicily 1943
Mediterranean 1943
Checkmate.
1   1918 destroyer of 1,075 tons built by Beardmore. Sold in 1931 for scrapping by Metal Industries of Charlestown.
2   1942 submarine of 1,090/1,575 tons, ex-*P314*, ex-*P94*, built by Vickers Armstrong at Barrow. Scrapped at Newport in 1963.
3   1983 nuclear-powered submarine of 4,200/5,208 tons built by Vickers Armstrong at Barrow.

## TAFF

Burma 1945
1   1943 frigate of 1,370 tons built by Hill: Bellis & Morcom. Scrapped in 1957 at Newport.

## TAKU

Norway 1940–4
Mediterranean 1941
*Virtute adepta* = Won by valour. Named after the attack on the Taku Forts in 1900.
1   1900 destroyer captured at the attack on the Taku Forts. Originally built in 1898 by Schichau as the 305-ton Chinese *Hai-Nju*. Sold in 1916 to Hong Kong.
2   1939 submarine of 1,090/1,575 tons built by Cammell Laird. Scrapped at Llanelly in 1946.

## TALBOT

Armada 1588
Navarino 1827
Syria 1840
Dardanelles 1915–16
1   1585 vessel.

3  1807 sloop. Sold in 1815.
4  1834 6th rate. Sold in 1896.
5  1895 cruiser of 5,600 tons built by Devonport Dock Yard. Scrapped in 1921.
7  1941 submarine depot at Malta, ex-minelayer *Medusa*. She was sunk by bombing in 1942.
8  1944 naval base at Sardinia.

## TALENT

1  1943 submarine, ex-*P322*, of 1,090/1,575 tons built by Vickers Armstrong at Barrow. Lent to R. Netherlands navy 1944–53. Disposal List 1974–5.
2  Nuclear-powered submarine of 4,100/5,208 tons ordered in 1984 and being built by Vickers Armstrong at Barrow.

## TALISMAN

Mediterranean 1941
Malta Convoys 1941
1  1915 destroyer of 1,098 tons built by Hawthorn Leslie. Sold in 1921 to Ward of Grays for scrapping.
2  1940 submarine of 1,090/1,575 tons built by Cammell Laird. Lost in the Mediterranean in 1942.

## TALLY HO

Biscay 1943
Malaya 1943–4
1  1914–18 vessel.
2  1942 submarine, ex-*P317*, ex-*P97*, of 1,090/1,575 tons built by Vickers Armstrong at Barrow. Scrapped in 1967 by Ward at Briton Ferry.

## TALYBONT

North Sea 1943–4
Normandy 1944
English Channel 1943–4
Named after the hunt in Cambridgeshire.
1  1943 destroyer of the 'Hunt' class, 1,050 tons built by White. Scrapped at Charlestown in 1961.

## TAMAR

Burma 1824–6
Ashantee 1873–4
*Tam marte tam pace* = Alike in war and peace.
1  1758 sloop which was renamed *Pluto* in 1778.
2  1796 5th rate. Scrapped in 1809.

3  1814 6th rate. Sold in 1837.
4  1863 troopship which eventually became a depot ship at Hong Kong. Sunk by the Japanese in 1941.
5  1945 depot ship at Hong Kong.
6  HM Naval Base Hong Kong. HQ of CAPICHHK (Captain in Charge, Hong Kong). Base for five 'Ton' class patrol vessels.

## TANATSIDE

Atlantic 1943
English Channel 1943–5
Normandy 1944
Biscay 1944
Named after the hunt in North Wales.
1  1942 destroyer of the 'Hunt' class, 1,050 tons built by Yarrow. Lent to the Greek navy in 1946 and renamed *Adrias*. Scrapped in 1964.

## TANTALUS

Sabang 1944
Named after the son of Zeus who was punished by being unable to drink, although surrounded by water.
1  1943 submarine, ex-*P318*, ex-*P98*, of 1,090/1,575 tons built by Vickers Armstrong at Barrow. Scrapped at Milford Haven in 1950.

## TANTIVY

Atlantic 1945
1  1943 submarine, ex-*P319*, ex-*P99*, of 1,090/1,571 tons built by Vickers Armstrong at Barrow. Expended as a target in 1951.

## TAPIR

Norway 1945
*Arte percutimus* = We shatter by craft.
1  1944 submarine of 1,090/1,571 tons built by Vickers Armstrong at Barrow. Lent to Royal Netherlands Navy 1948–53 and renamed *Zeehond*. Scrapped at Faslane in 1966.

## TARBATNESS

1  1967 fleet supply ship of 16,500 tons built by Swan Hunter at Wallsend. To USN and renamed *Speca* in 1981.

## TARPON

Norway 1940
Well played.
1  1917 destroyer of *c*.1,065 tons built by John Brown. Sold in 1927 to Cashmore for scrapping.
2  1939 submarine of 1,090/1,575 tons built by Scotts. Lost in 1940 when attacked by German minesweeper *M 6* in the North Sea.

## TARTAR

Velez Malaga 1704
Ushant 1781
Baltic 1855
South Africa 1899–1900
Belgian Coast 1914–16
Norway 1940–1
*Bismarck* Action 1941
Arctic 1942
Malta Convoys 1942
North Africa 1942–3
Sicily 1943
Salerno 1943
Mediterranean 1943
Normandy 1944
English Channel 1944
Biscay 1944
Burma 1945
1  and 2 were both 5th rates of 1702 and 1756 (wrecked).
3  1757 prize 6th rate which was wrecked in 1759.
4  1759 prize.
11  1801 6th rate which was wrecked ten years later.
12  1814 5th rate. Scrapped in 1859.
13  1854 corvette. Scrapped in 1866.
15  1886 cruiser. Sold in 1906 for scrapping.
16  1907 destroyer of *c*.885 tons built by Thornycroft. Sold in 1921 to Ward of Hayle.
17  1937 destroyer of 'Tribal' class of 1,870 tons built by Swan Hunter at Wallsend. Scrapped in 1948 at Newport.
18  1960 general-purpose frigate of 2,370/2,700 tons built by Devonport Dock Yard. Sold to Indonesia in 1983.

## TATTOO

Atlantic 1944
1  1918 destroyer of 1,075 tons built by Beardmore. Presented to RAN in 1919 and sold to Penguins Ltd, Sydney, for scrapping.
2  1943 minesweeper, ex-*BAM 23*, built by the Gulf Shipping Co of Chickasaw. Returned to USA and sold by them to Turkey and renamed *Carsamba* in 1947.

## TAURUS

Belgian Coast 1917
Arctic 1942−3
Sicily 1943
Mediterranean 1943
Malaya 1943−5
Atlantic 1944−5
*Perfingam* = I shall break through.
Named after the constellation, the
second sign of the Zodiac.
1   1917 destroyer of 1,065 tons built
by Thornycroft. Sold in 1930 to
Metal Industries of Charlestown
for scrapping.
2   1942 submarine of 1,090/1,575
tons, ex-*P313*, ex-*P93*, built by
Vickers Armstrong of Barrow. Lent
to Holland in 1948 and renamed
*Dolfjin*. Scrapped at Dunston in
1960.

## TAVY

Atlantic 1943−4
Normandy 1944
English Channel 1944
Arctic 1944
1   1943 frigate of 1,370 tons built by
Hill: Bellis & Morcom. Scrapped at
Newport in 1955.

## TAY

Atlantic 1942−5
1   1814 sloop which was wrecked just
two years later.
3   1942 frigate of 1,370 tons built by
Smith's Dock. Scrapped at Rosyth
in 1956.

## TEAZER

Zeebrugge 1918
Mediterranean 1943
Adriatic 1944
South France 1944
Aegean 1944
1   1794 vessel.
5   1894 destroyer. Sold in 1912.
6   1917 destroyer of 1,065 tons built

by Thornycroft. Sold in 1930 to
Metal Industries of Charlestown
for scrapping.
8   1943 destroyer of 1,710 tons built
by Cammell Laird. Scrapped at
Dalmuir in 1965.

## TEES

Burma 1824−6
Atlantic 1943−5
1   1817 6th rate. In 1872 she sank at
her moorings.
3   1943 frigate of 1,370 tons built by
Hall Russell. Scrapped in 1955 at
Newport.

## TELEMACHUS

Malaya 1944
Korea 1953
*Per me tuties* = Safe through me.
Named after the son of Ulysses and
Penelope.
1   1795 vessel.
2   1917 destroyer of 1,065 tons built
by John Brown. Sold in 1927 to
Hughes Bolckow for scrapping.
3   1943 submarine of 1,090/1,575
tons, *ex-P321*, built by Vickers
Armstrong at Barrow. Scrapped at
Charlestown in 1961.

## TEME

Normandy 1944
1   1943 frigate of 1,370 tons built by
Smith's Dock. RCN 1944−5. CTL
1945 after being torpedoed by *U246*
off Falmouth. Scrapped at Llanelly
in 1946.

## TÉMÉRAIRE

Belleisle 1761
Martinique 1762
Havana 1762
Trafalgar 1805
Alexandria 1882
Jutland 1916

1   1759 3rd rate captured from the
French by Boscawen at Lagos.
2   1798 2nd rate, she featured in
Turner's famous painting 'The
Fighting *Téméraire*', which
portrayed her being brought up to
Rotherhithe in 1838 for breaking
up.
3   1876 ironclad battleship of 8,540
tons built at Chatham. She was
renamed *Indus II* in 1904, later
*Akbar* and sold in 1921.
4   1907 battleship of 18,600 tons built
by Devonport Dock Yard. She
served at Jutland. Sold in 1921 to
Stanlee for scrapping.
5   1971 RNSPT = Royal Naval School
of Physical Training.

## TEMPEST

Zeebrugge 1918
1   1917 destroyer of 1,065 tons built
by Fairfield. Sold in 1937 to Ward
of Briton Ferry for scrapping.
2   1941 submarine of 1,090/1,575 tons
built by Cammell Laird. Sunk in
1942 by the Italian torpedo boat
*Circe* off Taranto.

## TEMPLAR

Sicily 1943
Sabang 1944
1   1942 submarine, ex-*P316*, ex-*P96*,
of 1,090/1,575 tons built by Vickers
Armstrong at Barrow. Scrapped at
Troon in 1959.

## TENACIOUS

Adriatic 1944
Mediterranean 1944
South France 1944
Okinawa 1945
Hold fast.
1   1917 destroyer of 1,065 tons built
by Harland & Wolff. Sold in 1928
to Ward of Briton Ferry for
scrapping.
2   1943 destroyer of 1,710 tons built

by Cammell Laird. Scrapped at Troon in 1965.

## TENBY

Normandy 1944
1  1914−18 vessel.
2  1941 minesweeper of 656 tons built by Hamilton: White. Scrapped at Dunston in 1948.
3  1955 frigate of 1,800 tons built by Cammell Laird. Scrapped in 1974.

## TENEDOS

*Alter aut uterque* = Either or both.
1  1812 5th rate. Scrapped in 1875.
2  1870 corvette. Sold in 1887.
3  1906 training establishment for boy artificers till 1910.
4  1918 destroyer of 905 tons built by Hawthorn Leslie. Sunk by Japanese aircraft at Colombo in 1942.

## TEREDO

*Transfigam* = I shall pierce.
Named after the shipworm (really a mollusc) which lives in ships' timbers.
1  1945 submarine of 1,090/1,575 tons built by Vickers Armstrong of Barrow. Scrapped at Briton Ferry in 1965.

## TERMAGANT

Egypt 1801
Baltic 1854
Jutland 1916
Zeebrugge 1918
Belgian Coast 1918
Arctic 1943
Mediterranean 1943−4
Adriatic 1944
South France 1944
Aegean 1944

Okinawa 1945
1  1780 6th rate. Sold in 1795.
2  1796 sloop. Sold in 1819.
3  1822 6th rate which was renamed two years later *Herald*.
5  1847 frigate. Sold in 1867.
6  1915 destroyer of 1,098 tons built by Hawthorn Leslie. Sold in 1921 to Ward for scrapping at Grays.
7  1943 destroyer of 1,710 tons built by Denny. Sold for scrapping at Dalmuir in 1965.

## TERPSICHORE

Adriatic 1944
South France 1944
Aegean 1944
*Mahonesa* 1796
*Saltando ducam* = I'll lead them a dance.
The name is taken from the Muse of choral song and dancing.
1  1760 prize (20). Sold six years later.
2  1785 5th rate. Scrapped in 1830.
3  1847 corvette. Scrapped in 1866.
4  1890 cruiser. Sold in 1914 for scrapping.
5  1943 frigate of 1,710 tons built by Denny. Scrapped at Troon in 1966.

## TERRAPIN

Norway 1944
1  1943 submarine, ex-*P323*, of 1,090/1,575 tons built by Vickers Armstrong at Barrow. Depth charged in South Pacific and became CTL in 1945. Scrapped at Troon in 1946.

## TERRIBLE

Vigo 1702
Louisburg 1758
Quebec 1759
St Vincent 1780
Genoa 1795

Crimea 1854−5
South Africa 1899−1900
China 1900
1  1694 fireship. She became a 6th rate two years later, reverted to a fireship in 1703 and was re-rated to 5th rate in 1710, in which year she surrendered.
3  1747 3rd rate taken at Finisterre II. Scrapped in 1763.
4  1762 3rd rate which was so unserviceable she was burnt in 1781.
5  1785 3rd rate. Scrapped in 1877.
6  1845 frigate, the first four-funnelled ship in the RN.[74]
7  1895 cruiser of 14,200 tons built by Thomson. Renamed *Fisgard III* c.1920. Sold to Cashmore for scrapping in 1932.
8  1944 aircraft carrier of 14,000 tons built by Devonport: Parsons. Transferred to RAN 1948 and renamed *Sydney*.

## TERROR

Velez Malaga 1704
Copenhagen 1801
Belgian Coast 1916−18
Zeebrugge 1918
Libya 1940−1
Mediterranean 1941
*Vobis non nobis* = [Terror] To you, not us.
1  1696 vessel.
7  1856 floating battery. Depot at Bermuda from 1857 to 1901.
8  1901 depot at Bermuda, ex-*Malabar*, troopship.
9  1916 monitor of 8,000 tons built by Harland & Wolff at Belfast. Sunk by aircraft off Derna in 1941.
10  1946 depot at Singapore.

## TEST

Atlantic 1943
Sicily 1943
Burma 1945
1  1909 destroyer of 570 tons built by Laird Bros. Sold in 1919 to Loveridge & Co for scrapping.
4  1942 frigate of 1,370 tons built by Hall Russell. Served with RIN 1946−7 and renamed *Neza*. Scrapped at Faslane in 1955.

## TETCOTT

Libya 1942
Mediterranean 1942

---

74  See Manning and Walker, p. 438.

Sicily 1943
Salerno 1943
Aegean 1943–4
Anzio 1944
Adriatic 1944
Named after the hunt in Devonshire.
1 1941 destroyer of the 'Hunt' class, 1,050 tons built by White. Scrapped at Milford Haven in 1956.

## TETRARCH

Zeebrugge 1918
Norway 1940
Mediterranean 1940–1
*Celeribus palma* = Reward to the swift.
Named after the Roman governor of a fourth part of a province.
1 1917 destroyer of 1,065 tons built by Harland & Wolff at Govan. Sold in 1934 to Metal Industries of Charlestown.
2 1939 submarine of 1,090/1,575 tons built by Vickers Armstrong of Barrow. Lost to unknown cause in Mediterranean in 1941.

## TEVIOT

Sicily 1943
Burma 1945
1 1903 destroyer of 590 tons built by Yarrow. Sold in 1919 to Ward for scrapping at Morecambe.
3 1942 frigate of 1,370 tons built by Hall Russell. Scrapped in 1955 by Ward at Briton Ferry.

## THAMES

Gut of Gibraltar 1801
*Tametsi* = Notwithstanding.
1 and 2 were both 5th rates of 1758 and 1805.
5 1823 5th rate which was sunk at Bermuda and the wreck blown up in 1863.
7 1885 cruiser. Sold to South Africa in 1920.
9 1932 submarine of 1,850/2,723 tons built by Vickers Armstrong of Barrow. Lost when she was mined off Norway in 1940.
10 and 11 minesweepers attached to London Division RNVR.

## THANE

Atlantic 1944
1 1943 escort carrier, ex-USS *Sunset*, of 11,420 tons built by Seattle: Tacoma. CTL in 1945 when she was returned to USA, but scrapped at Faslane.

## THANET

*In hoc signo* = By this sign you will conquer.
1 1914–18 vessel.
2 1918 destroyer of 905 tons built by Hawthorn Leslie. Sunk by the Japanese off Malaya in 1942.

## THERMOPYLAE

The great battle between the Spartans and the Persians in 480 B.C.
1 1914–18 vessel.
2 1945 submarine of 1,090/1,575 tons built by Chatham Dock Yard. Scrapped at Troon 1970.

## THESEUS

Nile 1798
Acre 1799
Basque Roads 1809
Benin 1897
Dardanelles 1915–16
Korea 1950–1
Action always.
1 1786 3rd rate (74) of 1,680 tons. Nelson's flagship as Rear Admiral at Santa Cruz de Tenerife. Scrapped in 1814.
2 1892 cruiser of 7,350 tons built at the Thames Iron Works. Sold in 1921 for breaking up in Germany.
3 1944 aircraft carrier of 13,190 tons built by Fairfield. Scrapped at Inverkeithing in 1962.

## THETIS

Lagos 1759
Egypt 1801
Guadeloupe 1810
Zeebrugge 1918
*Bouffone* 1761
*Prévoyante* 1795
I bide my time.
Mother of Theseus in Greek mythology.
1 1717 vessel.
2 3, 4, 9 and 10 were all 5th rates of 1747 (hospital ship in 1767), 1773 (wrecked), 1782, 1817 (wrecked) and 1846. She was swopped for two gunboats from the Prussian government in 1855.
11 1871. Sold six years later.
12 1890 cruiser which was expended as a blockship at Zeebrugge.
13 1938 submarine of 1,090/1,575 tons built by Cammell Laird. Sank in Liverpool Bay in 1939 while on trials. Raised and renamed *Thunderbolt*. She was sunk by the Italian corvette *Cicogna* off Sicily in 1943.

## THISBE

Egypt 1801
1 1783 6th rate. Sold in 1815.
2 5th rate of 1824. Sold in 1892.
3 1917 destroyer of 1,065 tons built by Hawthorn Leslie. Sold in 1936 to Ward of Pembroke Dock.
4 1943 minesweeper of the 'Algerine' class. Disposal List 1958.

## THISTLE

Baltic 1855
Norway 1940
*Havik* 1810
*Nemo me impune lacessit* = No one hurts me with impunity.
1 1808 small vessel.[75]
13 1938 submarine of 1,090/1,575 tons built by Vickers Armstrong of Barrow. Lost in 1940 when torpedoed by *U-4* off Skudesnes.

## THORN

Mediterranean 1941–2
1 1779 sloop. Sold in 1816.
2 1900 destroyer of *c*.400 tons built by Thomson. Scrapped in 1919 at Portsmouth.

75 A 14th ship of this name was a drifter lost in WWII. Other than the submarine, all vessels have been of no significance. See Manning and Walker, p 441.

3  1941 submarine of 1,090/1,575 tons
built by Cammell Laird. Lost in
1942 when attacked by Italian
torpedo boat *Pegaso* off Tobruk.

## THORNBOROUGH

Normandy 1944
English Channel 1944
Atlantic 1945
North Sea 1945
Named after Admiral Sir Edward
Thornborough (1754−1834), captain
of the *Robust* in 1798.
1  1943 frigate of 1,300 tons, ex-*DE-565*, built by Bethlehem: Hingham.
Returned to USA in 1947.

## THOROUGH

Malaya 1944−5
*Perfice* = Be thorough.
1  1943 submarine, ex-*P324*, of 1,090/
1,575 tons built by Vickers
Armstrong at Barrow. Scrapped at
Dunston in 1961.

## THRACIAN

Thrust on.
1  1809 sloop. Scrapped in 1829.
2  1920 destroyer of 905 tons built by
Hawthorn Leslie. Beached and
abandoned to the Japanese at
Hong Kong in 1942.[76] Retaken in
1945 at Tokyo, but scrapped in
1946.

## THRASHER

Mediterranean 1941−2
Atlantic 1944
1  1804 vessel.
3  1896 destroyer of *c*.400 tons built
by Laird, Fryer. Scrapped in 1919
at Sunderland.
4  1940 submarine of 1,090/1,575 tons
built by Cammell Laird. Scrapped
at Briton Ferry in 1947.

## THRUSTER

Belgian Coast 1917
Sicily 1943
Salerno 1943
Anzio 1944
South France 1944
Aegean 1944
1  1917 destroyer of 1,065 tons built
by Hawthorn Leslie. Sold in 1935

HMS THUNDERER (No. 5)

to Ward at Grays for scrapping.
2  1942 tank assault vessel. Sold to
Holland in 1945.
3  1947 Landing-ship.

## THULEN (Thule)

Atlantic 1944
Malaya 1944−5
Press on.
1  1796 prize 5th rate. Scrapped in
1811.
2  1942 (*Thule*) submarine, ex-*P325*, of
1,090/1,575 tons built by
Devonport Dock Yard. Scrapped at
Inverkeithing in 1962.

## THUNDERBOLT

Biscay 1940
Malta Convoys 1941−2
Mediterranean 1942
1  1696 5th rate. Broken up in 1731.
2  1842 sloop which was wrecked in
1847.
3  1856 floating battery that was
never completed. In 1873 she was
attached to the floating pier at
Chatham until sold in 1949 nearly a
century after building. She was
renamed *Daedalus* in 1920.
5  1940 submarine, ex-*Thetis*, of 1,090/
1,575 tons built by Cammell Laird.
Lost in 1943.

## THUNDERER

Lake Champlain 1776
Glorious First of June 1794
St Lucia 1796
Trafalgar 1805
Syria 1840
Jutland 1916
*Achille* 1761
*Eripimus Jovi fulmen* = We snatch the
thunder from Jove.
1  1760 3rd rate of 1,600 tons built at
Woolwich. Foundered in the great .
West Indies hurricane of 1780.
3  1738 3rd rate which served at the
Glorious First of June and at
Trafalgar. Scrapped in 1814.
4  1831 2nd rate which was renamed
*Comet* in 1869.
5  1872 twin-screw, armour-plated
battleship. Sold in 1909.
6  1911 battleship to be built on the
Thames. Sold in 1926 to Hughes
Bolckow for scrapping. At one
time the flagship of Prince Louis of
Battenberg and of Sir John Jellicoe.
She ran ashore on her way to the
breakers.
7  1946 RN Engineering College at
Manadon, Portsmouth.

## THYME

North Sea 1941
Atlantic 1941−2
Diego Suarez 1942
1  1941 corvette of 925 tons built by
Smith's Dock. Became a weather-
reporting ship in 1946 — *Weather
Reporter*, *Weather Explorer* (1947),
and was in mercantile service in
1958 as *Epos*.

76  Captured by IJN patrol boat No. *101*.

## TIGER (Tigre)

Armada 1588
Portland 1653
Gabbard 1653
Scheveningen 1653
Lowestoft 1665
Orfordness 1666
Solebay 1672
Marbella 1705
Sadras 1758
Negapatam 1758
Porto Novo 1759
Egypt 1801
Dogger Bank 1915
Jutland 1916
*Quis eripet dentes* = Who will draw my teeth ?
1   1546 vessel. Scrapped in 1605.
2   1585–6 hired ship for Drake's West India voyage.
3   4 and 6 were all 4th rates of 1647 (wrecked), 1678 (prize) and 1747.
7   1762 3rd rate prize. Sold in 1783.
8   1782 3rd rate, ex-British *Ardent*, recaptured at The Saintes and added to the Navy as *Tiger*, but sold the following year.
11  1849 sloop. Ran ashore in 1854 and was destroyed by gunfire.
13  1900 destroyer of *c*.400 tons. Sunk in collision in 1908.
14  1913 battlecruiser of 28,500 tons built by John Brown. Scrapped in 1932 at Inverkeithing.
16  1945 cruiser, ex-*Bellerophon*, of 9,500/12,080 tons built by John Brown. Work stopped 1946 till completed 1955 to new design. Converted to command helicopter cruiser by HM Dock Yard Portsmouth 1968–72. Bought by Spain for scrapping in 1986.

## TIGRIS

Norway 1940
Arctic 1941–2
Mediterranean 1942
1   1813 5th rate, but sold only five years later.
3   1938 submarine of 1,090/1,575 tons built by Chatham Dock Yard. Lost to unknown cause in the Mediterranean in 1943.

## TINTAGEL CASTLE

Atlantic 1944–5
1   1943 corvette/frigate of 1,010 tons built by Ailsa Ship Builders. Scrapped in 1958 at Troon.

## TIPTOE

Malaya 1945
1   1944 submarine of 1,090/1,575 tons built by Vickers Armstrong at Barrow. Scrapped in 1970.

## TIRELESS

*Esto perpetua* = Be perpetual.
1   1943 submarine of 1,090/1,575 tons, ex-*P327*, built at Portsmouth. Scrapped at Newport in 1968.
2   1984 nuclear-powered submarine of 4,200/5,208 tons built by Vickers Shipbuilding Group, Barrow.

## TOBAGO

Atlantic 1944
1   1777 vessel.
3   1918 destroyer of 1,087 tons built by Thornycroft. Mined at Malta in 1920, became CTL and was sold in 1922.
5   1943 frigate, ex *Hong Kong*, ex-*Holmes*, ex-*PF.81*, built by Walsh Kaiser. Returned to USA. Sold to Egypt 1950 and scrapped 1956.

## TOKEN

1   1914–18 vessel.
2   1943 submarine, ex-*P328*,1,090/1,575 tons built at Portsmouth. Scrapped in 1970 by Cairn Ryan.

## TORBAY

Vigo 1702
Velez Malaga 1704
Quiberon Bay 1959
Belleisle 1761
St. Kitts 1782
The Saintes 1782
Mediterranean 1941–3
Arctic 1942–3
Sicily 1943
Aegean 1943
Atlantic 1944
English Channel 1944
*Je maintendrai* = I will maintain.
The name commemorates the landing of William III at Torbay in 1688.
1   1693 3rd rate. Scrapped in 1749.
2   1754 3rd rate. Sold in 1784.
3   1919 destroyer of 1,087 tons built by Thornycroft. Presented to Canada in 1928 and renamed *Champlain*. Scrapped in 1937.
5   1939 submarine of 1,090/1,575 tons built by Chatham Dock Yard. Scrapped at Briton Ferry in 1945.
6   1985 nuclear-powered submarine

of 4,200/5,208 tons built by Vickers Shipbuilding Group, Barrow.

## TORMENTOR

Martinique 1794
1   *c*.1794 vessel.
2   1917 destroyer of 1,065 tons built by Stephen. Wrecked while in tow off South Wales to Troon for scrapping, 1929.
3   1940–6 raiding craft base at Hamble.

## TORQUAY

1   1954 anti-submarine frigate of 2,800 tons built by Harland & Wolff. Disposal List 1982–83.

## TORRINGTON

Normandy 1944
Atlantic 1944
English Channel 1944
North Sea 1944–5
Later ships were named after Admiral George Byng, first Viscount Torrington (1663–1733).
1   1654 3rd rate which was renamed *Dreadnought* in 1660.
2   and 3 were both 5th rates of 1729 and 1742.
4   1943 frigate of 1,300 tons, ex-*DE-568*, built by Bethlehem: Hingham. Returned to the USA in 1946.

## TORTOLA

Arctic 1944
Atlantic 1944–5
1   1943 frigate of 1,318 tons built by Walsh Kaiser, ex-*PF91*, ex-*Peyton*. Returned to USA in 1946.

## TOTEM

1   1914–18 vessel.
2   1943 submarine of 1,090/1,575 tons built by Devonport Dock Yard. Sold to Israel in 1957 and renamed *Dakar*, but lost the following year.

## TOTLAND

Atlantic 1941–4
Named after the coastguard station on the Isle of Wight.
1   1941 coastguard cutter, ex-USCG *Cayuga*, of 1,546 tons built by Bethlehem in 1931. Returned to USA in 1946.

## TOURMALINE

Atlantic 1943
*Ex tenebris lux* = Out of darkness light.
1   1875 corvette. Sold in 1920.
2   1919 destroyer of 1,087 tons built by Thornycroft. Sold in 1931 to Ward for scrapping at Grays.
4   1935 trawler, ex-*Berkshire*, 641 tons, lost to enemy aircraft in 1941.
5   1942 minesweeper of 890 tons, ex-USS *Usage*, built by Gulf Shipbuilding of Chickasaw. Returned to USA in 1947 for mercantile service. Became Turkish *Cardak* in 1947.

## TOWER

1   1668 vessel.
3   1917 destroyer of 1,087 tons built by Swan Hunter. Sold in 1928 to Cashmore for scrapping.
4   1940−6 auxiliary patrol depot in London.

## TOWY

Atlantic 1943−5
English Channel 1945
1   1943 frigate of 1,370 tons built by Smith's Dock. Scrapped at Port Glasgow in 1956.

## TRACKER

Atlantic 1943−4
Arctic 1944
Normandy 1944
*Re Rawita.*
1   1914−18 vessel.
2   1942 escort carrier, ex-USS *Mormacmail*, of 11,420 tons built by Seattle: Tacoma. Returned to USA in 1945.
3   1947 Landing-ship, ex-LST (3) 3522, 2,140/5,000 full load. Accommodation ship 1954 then net and boom carrier 1964. Disposal List 1982−3.

## TRADEWIND

Malaya 1944
*Ventis semper secundis* = With winds ever fair.
1   1919 Admiralty drifter.
2   1942 submarine, ex-*P329*, of 1,090/1,575 tons built by Chatham Dock Yard. Scrapped at Charlestown in 1955.

## TRAFALGAR

Crimea 1854
1   1820 2nd rate which was renamed *Camperdown* in 1825.
2   1841 1st rate which was renamed *Boscawen* in 1873.
3   1887 battleship. Sold in 1911.
4   1944 destroyer of the 'Battle' class of 3,361 tons built by Swan Hunter. Scrapped at Dalmuir in 1970.
5   1981 nuclear-powered submarine of 4,200/5,208 tons built by Vickers Shipbuilding Group at Barrow.

## TRAVELLER

*Fidenter perge viator* = Push forward in faith, traveller.
1   1835 vessel.
2   1941 submarine of 1,090/1,575 tons built by Scotts. Lost to unknown causes in the Mediterranean in 1942.

## TREMADOC BAY

1   1945 frigate, ex-*Loch Arnish*, of 1,580 tons built by Harland & Wolff. Scrapped at Genoa in 1959.

## TRENCHANT

Malaya 1944−5
1   1916 destroyer of 1,085 tons built by White. Sold in 1928 to Plymouth & Devon Ship Breaking Company.
3   1943 submarine of 1,090/1,575 tons built by Chatham Dock Yard. Scrapped at Faslane in 1963.
4   1986 nuclear-powered submarine of 4,200/5,208 tons built by Vickers Ship Building Group at Barrow.

## TRENT

Louisburg 1758
Quebec 1759
Havana 1762

Sicily 1943
Atlantic 1943
Burma 1945
1   1757 6th rate. Although sold only six years later, she won three battle honours.
2   1796 5th rate. Scrapped in 1823.
6   1942 frigate of 1,370 tons built by Hill: Bellis & Morcom. Transferred to RIN in 1946 and renamed *Kukri*: later served with Pakistan navy as *Investigator*, 1948.

## TRESPASSER

Sicily 1943
Aegean 1943
Malaya 1944
Nothing venture, nothing have.
1   1942 submarine of 1,090/1,575 tons built by Vickers Armstrong at Barrow. Scrapped at Gateshead in 1961.

## TRIAD

Dardanelles 1915
Norway 1940
Mediterranean 1940
Forewarned is thrice armed.
1   1915 vessel.
2   1939 submarine of 1,090/1,575 tons built by Vickers Armstrong at Barrow. Lost to unknown cause in the Mediterranean in 1940.

## TRIBUNE

Baltic 1854
Crimea 1854−5
China 1856−60
Arctic 1942
North Africa 1942
Sicily 1943
*Par droit d'armes* = By right of arms. Named after the Roman official elected by the people to defend their rights.
1   1796 5th rate prize which was wrecked in the following year.
2   1803 5th rate which was wrecked in 1839.
3   1853 frigate. Sold in 1866.
4   1891 cruiser. Sold in 1911.
5   1918 destroyer of 1,075 tons built by White. Sold in 1931 for scrapping by Cashmore.
7   1938 submarine of 1,090/1,575 tons built by Scotts. Scrapped at Milford Haven in 1947.

## TRIDENT

Quebec 1759
Cape of Good Hope 1795
Zeebrugge 1918
Ostend 1918
Norway 1940−1
Arctic 1941−2
North Sea 1942
Sicily 1943
Mediterranean 1943
Atlantic 1944
1   1695 4th rate prize which was sunk as a breakwater at Harwich in 1702.
2   and 3 were both 3rd rates of 1747 (prize) and 1768.
5   1845 sloop, said to have been the first iron ship built for the RN.[77] She was scrapped in 1866.
6   1915 destroyer of 1,098 tons built by Hawthorn Leslie. Sold in 1921 to Ward for scrapping at Grays.
8   1938 submarine of 1,090/1,575 tons built by Cammell Laird. Scrapped in 1946 at Newport.

## TRINIDAD

Arctic 1942
Have faith.
1   1805 vessel.
2   1918 destroyer of 1,075 tons built by White. Scrapped by Ward at Inverkeithing in 1932.
3   1939 cruiser of 8,000 tons built by Hawthorn Leslie. Sunk by own forces two weeks after being bombed in the Barents Sea in 1942.

## TRITON

Velez Malaga 1704
St Vincent 1780
The Saintes 1782
Norway 1940
Mediterranean 1940
*Vigilans de profundis* = Watching from the deep.
Named after the son of Poseidon and Amphitrite in Greek mythology.
1   1702 4th rate prize which was sold five years later.
2   1705 6th rate prize. Sold in 1713.
3   *c*.1741 sloop.
4   and 5 were both 6th rates of 1745 (destroyed 1758) and 1773.
6   1796 5th rate. Sold in 1814.
7   1846 sloop. Sold in 1871.
10  1937 submarine of 1,095/1,579 tons built by Vickers Armstrong at Barrow. Sunk in the Adriatic in

1940 by the Italian torpedo boat *Clio*.
11  1942 trawler of 230 tons, built in 1939 and returned to owners in 1945.

## TRIUMPH

Armada 1588
Dover 1652
Portland 1653
Gabbard 1653
Scheveningen 1653
Lowestoft 1665
Four Days' Battle 1666
Orfordness 1666
Solebay 1672
Schooneveld 1673
Texel 1673
Cornwallis' Retreat 1795
Camperdown 1797
Dardanelles 1915
Malta Convoys 1941
Mediterranean 1941
Korea 1950
We shall triumph.
1   1561 great ship (42) of 1,100 tons commanded by Martin Frobisher at the Armada battle. Frobisher was knighted by the Lord Admiral aboard *Ark Royal*.
2   1623 vessel of 42 guns, later increased to 60, 66 and 70. Built by Durell of Deptford, 921 tons. In 1627 she was flagship of Duke of Buckingham, Lord High Admiral, and later of Earl of Northumberland, and in 1652 of Robert Blake, Admiral and General of the Fleet. At Portland she was flagship of Blake and of Deane: at Gabbard of Vice Admiral Sir James Peacock and at the Texel, where the admiral was killed. At Lowestoft Vice Admiral Myngs wore his flag aboard her. After the Four Days' Battle and St James' Day Battle she was laid up in the Medway, where she was sunk in shallow water, but salved. Sold to the Office of Ordnance in 1688.
3   1698 2nd rate (90−96) of 1,482 tons built at Chatham by Robert Lee, onetime flagship of Shovell. Renamed *Prince* in 1714.
5   1764 3rd rate (74) of 1,825 tons had an active career. Onetime flagship of Collingwood. From 1815 till her scrapping in 1859 she was a lazaretto at Milford Haven.
6   1870 ironclad of 6,640 tons which was renamed *Tenedos* in 1904.
7   1903 battleship built for the

Chilean navy but bought and named *Triumph*. 11,985 tons, built by Vickers Armstrong at Barrow. Torpedoed and sunk in the Dardanelles in 1915 by *U-21*.
10  1938 submarine of 1,090/1,575 tons, built by Vickers Armstrong at Barrow. Lost in 1942 in the Aegean to unknown cause.
11  1944 aircraft carrier, 13,350 tons, built by Hawthorn Leslie. Major conversion to Heavy Repair Ship at Portsmouth 1958−64. Disposal List 1980−1, and later scrapped in Spain.
12  Building: Commissioning date 1990. Nuclear-powered submarine of 4,200/5,208 tons, by Vickers of Barrow.

## TROLLOPE

Normandy 1944
English Channel 1944
Named after Admiral Sir Henry Trollope (1756−1839).
1   1943 frigate, ex-*DE.566*, of 1,300 tons built by Bethlehem: Hingham. CTL in 1944. Scrapped at Troon in 1951.

## TROOPER

Sicily 1943
Aegean 1943
Mediterranean 1943
1   1915 vessel.
2   1942 submarine of 1,090/1,575 tons built by Scotts. Lost to unknown cause in the Mediterranean in 1943.

## TROUBRIDGE

Sicily 1943
Salerno 1943
Mediterranean 1943
Aegean 1944
South France 1944
Adriatic 1944

77   Manning and Walker, p. 450.

Okinawa 1945
Named after Rear Admiral Sir Thomas Troubridge (1758–1807).
1 1806 vessel.
2 1942 destroyer of 1,730/2,880 tons built by John Brown at Clydebank. Scrapped at Newport in 1970.

## TROUNCER

Atlantic 1944
1 1943 escort carrier, ex-USS *Perdita* of 11,420 tons built by Seattle: Tacoma. Returned to USA in 1946 and sold for mercantile service at least until 1959.
2 1947 Landing-ship.

## TRUANT

Norway 1940
Mediterranean 1940–1
Atlantic 1944
1 1918 destroyer of 1,075 tons built by White. Sold in 1931 to Rees of Llanelly for scrapping.
2 1939 submarine of 1,090/1,575 tons built by Vickers Armstrong of Barrow. Wrecked in 1946 en route to the breakers.

## TRUCULENT

Belgian Coast 1917
Zeebrugge 1918
Arctic 1943
Atlantic 1944
Is in her name.
1 1917 destroyer of *c*.900 tons built by Yarrow. Sold in 1927 to Cashmore for scrapping.
2 1942 submarine, ex-*P315*, ex-*P95*, of 1,090/1,575 tons built by Vickers Armstrong at Barrow. Sunk in 1950 in collision with a Swedish vessel in the Thames. Salved but then scrapped by Ward at Grays.

## TRUELOVE

Cadiz 1596
Schooneveld 1673
Texel 1673
1 1596 vessel.
2 20-gun vessel of the Commonwealth period.
8 1943 minesweeper of the 'Algerine' class built by Redfern. Scrapped at Blyth in 1957.

## TRUMP

Malaya 1945
1 1944 submarine of 1,090/1,575 tons built by Vickers Armstrong at Barrow. Disposal List 1974–5. Scrapped at Newport.

## TRUMPETER

Atlantic 1943–4
Arctic 1944–5
Norway 1945
1 1914–18 vessel.
2 1942 escort carrier, ex-USS *Lucifer*, ex-USS *Bastian*, of 11,420 tons built by Seattle: Tacoma. Returned to USA in 1946 for mercantile service.
3 1947 Landing-ship, 2,140/5,000 tons full load. Became *Empire Fulmar* when commercially chartered.
4 *c*.1986 coastal patrol craft.

## TRUNCHEON

1 1944 submarine of 1,090/1,575 tons built by Devonport Dock Yard. Sold to Israel and renamed *Dolphin* in 1968.

## TRUSTY

Egypt 1801
Malta Convoys 1941
*Fiducia non terrore* = By trust and not by fear.
1 1782 4th rate. Scrapped in 1815.
2 1855 floating battery which was scrapped nine years later.
3 1918 destroyer of 1,075 tons built by White. Scrapped in 1936 by Ward at Inverkeithing.
4 1941 submarine of 1,090/1,575 tons built by Vickers Armstrong at Barrow. Scrapped at Milford Haven in 1947.

## TUDOR

Malaya 1944–5
*Fide et consilio* = By faith and good counsel.
1 1942 submarine, ex-*P326*, of 1,090/1,575 tons built by Devonport Dock Yard. Scrapped at Faslane in 1963.

## TULIP

Portland 1653
Gabbard 1653
Scheveningen 1653
1 1652 prize of 32 guns. Sold five years later.
4 1916 sloop of 1,250 tons built by Richardson Dock. Torpedoed and sunk in the Atlantic by *U-62*.
6 1940 corvette of 925 tons built by Smith's Dock. Sold in 1950 for mercantile service and still at sea in 1957.

## TUMULT

Atlantic 1943
Sicily 1943
Salerno 1943
Aegean 1943–4
Mediterranean 1943–4
Adriatic 1944
South France 1944
*Tumultu utamur* = Let us use this tumult [to our advantage].
1 1918 destroyer of 930 tons built by Yarrow. Scrapped in 1928 by Alloa of Charlestown.
2 1942 destroyer of 1,710 tons built by John Brown at Clydebank. Scrapped at Dalmuir in 1965.

## TUNA

Biscay 1940–3
Norway 1941
Arctic 1943
1 1915 vessel.
2 1940 submarine of 1,090/1,575 tons built by Scotts. Scrapped at Briton Ferry in 1946.

## TURBULENT

Jutland 1916
Mediterranean 1942
*Absit nomen* = May [turbulence] be absent.
1   1805 vessel.
2   1916 destroyer of 1,098 tons built by Hawthorn Leslie. Sunk at Jutland in 1916.
3   1919 destroyer of 1,075 tons built by Hawthorn Leslie. Sold in 1926 to Ward of Inverkeithing for scrapping.
4   1941 submarine of 1,090/1,575 tons built by Vickers Armstrong at Barrow. Sunk by Italian MAS off Sardinia in 1943.
5   1982 nuclear-powered submarine of 4,200/5,208 tons built by Vickers Shipbuilding Group at Barrow.

## TURPIN

Named after the highwayman Richard Turpin (1706−39).
1   1944 submarine of 1,090/1,575 tons built by Chatham Dock Yard. Sold to Israel in 1964 and renamed *Leviathan*.

## TUSCAN

Adriatic 1944
South France 1944
Aegean 1944
I hold what I take.
The badge derives from the arms of Tuscany.

1   1808 prize captured from Napoleon's Italian fleet.
2   1919 destroyer of 930 tons built by Yarrow. Sold in 1932 to Metal Industries of Charlestown for scrapping.
3   1942 destroyer of 1,710 tons built by Swan Hunter at Wallsend. Scrapped in 1966.

## TWEED

Biscay 1943
Atlantic 1943−4
1   1757 5th rate. Sold in 1776.
3   1823 6th rate. Sold in 1852.
5   1942 frigate of 1,370 tons built by Inglis: Parsons. Torpedoed and sunk south-west of Ireland by *U-305* in 1944.

## TYLER

Normandy 1944
English Channel 1944−5
Atlantic 1945
Named after Admiral Sir Charles Tyler (1760−1835).
1   1943 frigate, ex-*DE.567*, of 1,300 tons built by Bethlehem: Hingham. Returned to USA in 1945.

## TYNE

Baltic 1854
Korea 1953
1   1814 sloop. Sold in 1825.
2   1826 6th rate. Sold in 1962.
3   1878 store ship of 3,560 tons built by Armstrong. Became a destroyer depot ship. Foundered at her moorings in 1920 at Sheerness while on sale list for Stanlee.
4   1940 depot ship for destroyers. 11,000/14,600 tons, built by Scotts.

## TYNEDALE

St Nazaire 1942
English Channel 1942−3
Sicily 1943
Named after the hunt in the dale of the river Tyne.
1   1940 destroyer of the 'Hunt' class of 907 tons built by Stephen. Torpedoed and sunk in the Mediterranean off Bougie by *U-593* in 1943.

## TYRIAN

Atlantic 1943
Sicily 1943

Salerno 1943
Mediterranean 1943
Adriatic 1944
South France 1944
Aegean 1944
Tireless ever.
1   1808 vessel.
4   1918 destroyer of 930 tons built by Yarrow. Sold in 1930 to Metal Industries of Charlestown for scrapping.
5   1942 destroyer of 1,710 tons built by Swan Hunter of Wallsend. Scrapped at Troon in 1965.

## UGANDA

Sicily 1943
Salerno 1943
Mediterranean 1943
Atlantic 1943
Okinawa 1945
1   1942 cruiser of 8,800 tons built by Vickers Armstrong on the Tyne. Transferred to RCN in 1944 and renamed *Quebec*. Scrapped at Osaka in 1961.

## ULSTER

English Channel 1943
Adriatic 1944
Mediterranean 1944
Normandy 1944
Okinawa 1945
1   1917 destroyer of 1,085 tons built by Beardmore. Sold in 1928 to Ward of Pembroke Dock for scrapping.
3   1942 destroyer of 1,710 tons built by Swan Hunter. Scrapped at Inverkeithing in 1980.

## ULTIMATUM

Mediterranean 1942−4
Atlantic 1944
1   1941 submarine, ex-*P34*, of 545/740 tons built by Vickers Armstrong at Barrow. Scrapped in 1949 at Port Glasgow.

## ULTOR

Sicily 1943
Mediterranean 1943–4
Anzio 1944
Atlantic 1944
*Resurgam prudenter* = I shall rise again discreetly.
1   1942 submarine of 545/740 tons, ex-*P53*, built by Vickers Armstrong at Barrow. Scrapped in 1946 by Ward at Briton Ferry.

## ULYSSES

Martinique 1794
Egypt 1801
Arctic 1944
Normandy 1944
The name of Ulysses (or Odysseus) is taken from Greek literature: one of the most famous of Greek heroes, husband of Penelope.
1   1779 5th rate. Sold in 1816.
2   1917 destroyer of 1,085 tons built by Doxford. Sunk in 1918 in collision in the Clyde.
3   1942 destroyer of 1,710 tons built by Cammell Laird. Scrapped at Plymouth in 1970.

## UMBRA

Mediterranean 1942
The name of the shadow cast by the earth or moon in a total eclipse.
1   1941 submarine of 545/740 tons built by Vickers Armstrong at Barrow. Ex-*P35*. Scrapped at Blyth in 1946.

## UMPIRE

*Sans faveur* = Without favour.
1   1917 destroyer of 1,085 tons built by Doxford. Sold to Metal Industries of Charlestown in 1930.
2   1940 submarine, ex-*P31*, of 540/730 tons built by Chatham Dock Yard. Sunk in collision with an RN trawler in the Wash in 1941: rammed in error.

## UNA

Burma 1945
Name is taken from a character ('Truth') in Spenser's *Faerie Queene*.
1   1941 submarine, ex-*P30*, of 540/730

tons built by Chatham Dock Yard. Scrapped at Llanelly in 1949.[78]

## UNBEATEN

Mediterranean 1941–2
Malta Convoys 1941–2
Biscay 1942
1   1940 submarine, ex-*P33*, built by Vickers Armstrong at Barrow. Lost in 1942 when she was bombed in error by British aircraft in the Bay of Biscay.

## UNBENDING

Mediterranean 1942
1   1941 submarine, ex-*P37*, of 545/740 tons built by Vickers Armstrong at Barrow. Scrapped on the Tyne in 1950.

## UNBROKEN

Sicily 1943
*Frango infractus* = I break, but am not broken.
1   1941 submarine, ex-*P42*, built by Vickers Armstrong at Barrow. 545/740 tons. Launched by Mrs Linton, wife of one of WWII's greatest submarine commanders. *Unbroken*

sank some 30,000 tons of enemy shipping and crippled two cruisers. She was handed to Russia in 1944, together with *Ursula*, *Unison* and *Royal Sovereign*. She was returned in 1949 and scrapped on the Tyne the following year.

## UNDAUNTED

Dogger Bank 1915
Belgian Coast 1916
Normandy 1944
Okinawa 1945
1   1794 5th rate prize, *Bienvenue*, taken by Captain Robert Faulknor and given its command by the C-in-C, Sir John Jervis. 'Named after you, sir,' he declared in giving the commission: '*Undaunted*.'
2   1795 prize 5th rate taken in 1793, added in 1795 and wrecked the next year.
3   1807 5th rate. Conveyed Napoleon to Elba in 1814. Scrapped in 1860.
4   1861 frigate, Scrapped in 1882.
5   1886 cruiser. Sold in 1907.
6   1914 cruiser of 3,500 tons built by Fairfield. Sold in 1923 to Cashmore for scrapping.
7   1940 submarine, ex-*P34*, of 540/730 tons built by Vickers Armstrong at Barrow. Lost in 1941 to unknown cause off Gibraltar.
8   1943 destroyer of 1,710 tons built by Cammell Laird. Expended as a target ship in 1978.

## UNDINE

Mediterranean 1944
Normandy 1944
Adriatic 1944
Okinawa 1945
Name derives from the water nymph.
1   1847 vessel.
4   1917 destroyer of 1,085 tons built by Fairfield. Wrecked off Horse Fort in 1928 and the wreck sold to Middlesbrough Salvage Company.
5   1937 submarine of 540/730 tons built by Vickers Armstrong at Barrow. Lost in 1940 to German minesweepers off the Heligoland Bight.
6   1943 destroyer of 1,710 tons built by Thornycroft. Scrapped at Newport in 1965.

78   Weightman refers to 'an unusual craft built in Burma' and a German yacht captured by the RAN in 1941. Weightman, p. 439.

# UNICORN

Armada 1588
Cadiz 1596
Porto Farina 1655
Santa Cruz 1657
Lowestoft 1665
Orfordness 1666
Solebay 1672
Schooneveld 1673
Texel 1673
Basque Roads 1809
Salerno 1943
Okinawa 1945
Korea 1950–3
*Vestale* 1759
*Tribune* 1796
Named after the mythical one-horned beast.

1   1544 vessel (36) taken from the Scots at Leith by Lord Lisle's fleet.[79]
2   1588: coaster of 130 tons served in the Armada campaign.
5   1633 5th rate prize, commissioned as a frigate, converted to a fireship and expended in the Four Days' Battle.
8   1748 6th rate (28) of 481 tons built at Plymouth. Fought the single-ship action with *Vestale*. Broken up at Sheerness in 1771.
9   1776 6th rate (20) of 433 tons built on the Thames. Saw much action before being scrapped at Deptford in 1787.
10   1782 5th rate built at Burlesden but renamed *Thalia* the same year.
11   1794 5th rate (32) of 791 tons built at Chatham. She fought the single-ship action *Tribune*. Scrapped in 1815 at Deptford.
12   1824 5th rate (46) of 1,084 tons built at Chatham. Powder hulk at Woolwich in 1863. Finally became a drillship at Dundee, but her name was wanted for the FAA supply ship in the 1938 programme so she became *Unicorn II*, then *Cressy* in 1941. She was then the oldest serving ship in the Navy apart from *Victory*.
14   1943 aircraft maintenance ship of 14,750 tons built by Harland & Wolff at Belfast. Scrapped in 1959.

# UNION

Quiberon Bay 1759
Ushant 1781

1   1709 2nd rate prize, ex-*Albemarle*. Scrapped in 1749.
2   1757 2nd rate which was renamed *Sussex* about 1801. Scrapped in 1816.
9   1811 3rd rate. Scrapped in 1833.
11   1940 submarine of 540/730 tons, ex-*P35*, built by Vickers Armstrong at Barrow. Lost in 1941 when sunk by Italian patrol craft in the Mediterranean.

# UNIQUE

Mediterranean 1941
Malta Convoys 1941
Biscay 1942
Arctic 1942

1   *c*.1804 prize.
3   1940 submarine, ex-*P36*, of 540/730 tons built by Vickers Armstrong at Barrow. Lost in 1942 to unknown cause off Gibraltar.

# UNISON

Sicily 1943

1   1914–18 vessel.
2   1941 submarine of 540/730 tons, ex-*P43*, built by Vickers Armstrong. Lent to Russia 1944–9 and renamed *B3*. Scrapped at Stockton in 1950.

# UNITED

Sicily 1943
Mediterranean 1943

1   1941 submarine of 540/730 tons, ex-*P44*, built by Vickers Armstrong at Barrow. Scrapped at Troon in 1946.

# UNITY (Unité)

Armada 1588
Orfordness 1666
Pelagosa 1811
Jutland 1916

1   and 2 were both hired ships.

3   1665 prize of 32 guns, *Eendracht*, but surrendered the following year.
8   and 9 were both 5th rate prizes of 1796 and 1793.
10   1913 destroyer of *c*.1,000 tons built by Thornycroft. Sold in 1922 to Rees for scrapping at Llanelly.
14   1938 submarine of 540/730 tons built by Vickers Armstrong at Barrow. Lost in collision in 1940 west of Gibraltar.

# UNIVERSAL

Sicily 1943
Mediterranean 1944
Atlantic 1944

1   1942 submarine, ex-*P57*, of 540/730 tons built by Vickers Armstrong at Barrow. Scrapped at Milford Haven in 1946.

# UNRIVALLED

Sicily 1943
Aegean 1943
Mediterranean 1943

1   1942 submarine, ex-*P45*, of 540/730 tons built by Vickers Armstrong at Barrow. Scrapped at Briton Ferry in 1946.

# UNRUFFLED

Sicily 1943

1   1941 submarine, ex-*P46*, of 545/740 tons built by Vickers Armstrong of Barrow. Scrapped at Troon in 1946.

# UNRULY

Arctic 1942–3
Sicily 1943
Aegean 1943–4
Atlantic 1944

1   1942 submarine of 545/740 tons, ex-*P49*, built by Vickers Armstrong of Barrow. Scrapped at Inverkeithing in 1946.

# UNSEEN

Sicily 1943
Mediterranean 1943
English Channel 1944

1   1942 submarine of 545/730 tons, ex-*P51*, built by Vickers Armstrong at Barrow. Scrapped in 1949 at Hayle.

79   Thirty iron guns and six brass. Weightman, p. 445.

## UNSHAKEN

Sicily 1943
Mediterranean 1943
1  1942 submarine of 545/740 tons, ex-
   *P54*, built by Vickers Armstrong at
   Barrow. Scrapped at Troon in 1946.

## UNSPARING

Sicily 1943
Aegean 1943−4
Atlantic 1944
1  1942 submarine of 545/740 tons, ex-
   *P55*, built by Vickers Armstrong on
   the Tyne. Scrapped at
   Inverkeithing in 1946.

## UNSWERVING

Aegean 1943
Atlantic 1945
1  1943 submarine of 545/740 tons, ex-
   *P63*, built by Vickers Armstrong on
   the Tyne. Scrapped at Newport in
   1949.

## UNTAMED

1  1942 submarine, ex-*P58*, of 545/740
   tons built by Vickers Armstrong on
   the Tyne. Sunk in 1943 while on
   trials. Salved and renamed *Vitality*.

## UNTIRING

Mediterranean 1943−4
Atlantic 1944
1  1943 submarine, ex-*P59*, of 545/740
   tons built by Vickers Armstrong on
   the Tyne. Lent to the Greek navy
   and renamed *Amfitriti* (1945−52).
   Expended as a target in 1957.

## UPHOLDER

Mediterranean 1941−2
Malta Convoys 1941−2
1  1940 submarine, ex-*P37*, of 540/730
   tons built by Vickers Armstrong at
   Barrow. Commanded by Wanklyn,
   who won the VC for his exploits in
   her. Lost in 1942 when attacked by
   the Italian torpedo boat *Pegaso*.
2  1987 Type 2400 patrol submarine of
   2,400 tons dived displacement
   built by Vickers Shipbuilding
   Group at Barrow. *Unseen*, *Ursula*
   and *Unicorn* of this class all ordered
   1986.

## UPRIGHT

Mediterranean 1941
Malta Convoys 1941
1  1940 submarine of 540/730 tons, ex-
   *P38*, built by Vickers Armstrong at
   Barrow. Scrapped at Troon in 1946.

## UPROAR

Sicily 1943
Mediterranean 1943−4
1  1940 submarine, ex-*Ullswater*, ex-
   *P31* (ii), of 545/740 tons built by
   Vickers Armstrong at Barrow.
   Scrapped at Inverkeithing in 1946.

## UPSHOT

One aim.
1  1944 submarine of 545/740 tons
   built by Vickers Armstrong at
   Barrow. Scrapped at Preston in
   1949.

## UPSTART

Atlantic 1944
Mediterranean 1944
1  1942 submarine, ex-*P65*, of 545/740
   tons built by Vickers Armstrong at
   Barrow. Lent to the Greek navy
   (1945−52) and renamed *Xifias*.
   Reverted to *Upstart* on rejoining.
   Sunk as a target in 1957.

## URANIA

Normandy 1944
Okinawa 1945
1  1797 5th rate prize. Sold in 1807.
3  1943 destroyer of 1,710 tons built
   by Vickers Armstrong at Barrow.
   Scrapped at Faslane in 1971.

## URCHIN

Egypt 1801
Anzio 1944
Mediterranean 1944
Adriatic 1944
Normandy 1944
Okinawa 1945
*Armatus ad defendum* = Armed to
defend.
1  1797 vessel.
3  1917 destroyer of 1,085 tons built
   by Palmer. Sold in 1930 to Metal
   Industries for scrapping at
   Charlestown.
4  1940 submarine, ex-*P39* of 540/730
   tons built by Vickers Armstrong at
   Barrow. Served in the Polish navy
   from 1941−6 and renamed *Sokol*.
   Returned to the RN and scrapped
   in 1949.
5  1943 destroyer of 1,710 tons built
   by Vickers Armstrong at Barrow.
   Scrapped at Troon in 1967.

## URGE

Malta Convoys 1941
Mediterranean 1941−2
1  1940 submarine, ex-*P40*, of 540/730
   tons built by Vickers Armstrong at
   Barrow. Sunk in the
   Mediterranean in 1942 by the
   Italian torpedo boat *Pegaso*.

## URSA

Biscay 1944
Normandy 1944
Okinawa 1945

1 1917 destroyer of 1,085 tons built by Palmer. Sold in 1926 to J. Smith for scrapping.
2 1943 destroyer of 1,710 tons built by Thornycroft. Scrapped at Newport in 1967.

## URSULA

North Sea 1939
Norway 1940
Mediterranean 1941
Malta Convoys 1941
Arctic 1942
North Africa 1942
Bear up.
Named after St Ursula, the virgin and martyr.
1 1917 destroyer of 1,085 tons built by Scotts. Sold in 1929 to Cashmore for scrapping.
3 1938 submarine of 540/730 tons built by Vickers Armstrong at Barrow. Lent to Russia (1944–9) and renamed *B 4*. Returned in 1949 and scrapped the following year at Grangemouth.

## URTICA

This nettle — danger.[80]
The name is Latin for nettle.
1 1944 submarine of 545/740 tons built by Vickers Armstrong at Barrow. Scrapped at Milford Haven in 1950.

## USK

Dardanelles 1915–16
Atlantic 1943–4
1 1903 destroyer of 590 tons built by Yarrow. Scrapped in 1920 by Ward of Morecambe.
2 1943 frigate of 1,370 tons built by Smith's Dock. Sold to Egypt in 1950 and renamed *Abikir*. Scuttled in 1956, salved and scrapped in the following year.

## USURPER

Sicily 1943
1 1942 submarine, ex-*P56*, of 545/740 tons built by Vickers Armstrong on the Tyne. Lost in 1943 in Gulf of Genoa to patrol-boat attacks.

## UTHER

Named after King Arthur's father, Uther Pendragon.
1 1943 submarine, ex-*P62*, of 545/740 tons built by Vickers Armstrong on the Tyne. Scrapped at Hayle in 1950.

## UTMOST

Mediterranean 1941
Malta Convoys 1941–2
1 1940 submarine, ex-*P42*,[81] of 540/730 tons built by Vickers Armstrong at Barrow. Lost in 1942 west of Sicily when attacked by Italian torpedo boat *Groppo*.

## VALENTINE

Atlantic 1939
*Valens et volens* = Fit and willing.
1 1418 vessel.
2 1917 destroyer of 1,090 tons built by Cammell Laird. Bombed and stranded at the mouth of the Schelde 1940. Salved and scrapped 1953.
3 1943 destroyer, ex-*Kempenfelt*, of 1,710 tons built by Clydebank. RCN 1944 and renamed *Alongquin*.

## VALIANT

Belleisle 1761
Havana 1762
Ushant 1781
The Saintes 1782
Glorious First of June 1794
Groix 1795
Basque Roads 1809
Jutland 1916
Norway 1940
Mediterranean 1940–3
Malta Convoys 1941
Matapan 1941
Crete 1941
Sicily 1943
Salerno 1943
Sabang 1944
Falkland Islands 1982
Valiant for truth.
1 1759 3rd rate. Scrapped in 1826.
3 1807 3rd rate. Scrapped in 1823.[82]
5 1863 armoured ship of 6,710 tons. She became a hulk in 1897, called *Valiant III*. Oil hulk at Devonport in 1924. Sold in 1956, nearly a century old.
6 1914 battleship of 32,700 tons built by Fairfield. Most distinguished career, earning nine of the battle honours over a period of nearly 30 years. Became *Impérieuse* in 1946. Scrapped by Cairn Ryan in 1948 and the hull only at Troon in 1950.
7 1963 nuclear-powered submarine of 4,000/4,800 tons built by Vickers Armstrong at Barrow.

---

80 'Out of this nettle, danger, we pluck this flower, safety' (I *Henry IV*, ii.3).

81 Note: Several 'U' class submarines with the pennant P were put into service without being named, and six of them were sunk. All were boats of 545/740 tons built by Vickers Armstrong at Barrow.
*P32* built 1940. Lost 1941 when mined off Tripoli.
*P33* built 1941. Lost 1941 when mined off Tripoli.
*P36* built 1941. Lost when bombed in Malta. Salved but scrapped in 1958.
*P38* built 1941. Sunk 1942 by Italian TBs *Circe* and *Usodimare* off Tunisia.
*P39* built 1941. Bombed at Malta in 1942.
*P48* built 1941. Lost in 1942.

82 There is no explanation for this apparent anomaly of perhaps three vessels sharing the same name.

## VALKYRIE

*Retia belli teximus* = We weave the nets of battle.
1   1917 destroyer of *c*.1,300 tons built by Denny. Sold to Ward of Inverkeithing for scrapping in 1936.
3   1941–6 radar school in the Isle of Man.

## VALOROUS

Baltic 1854
Crimea 1854–5
North Sea 1940–5
*Valenter, volenter* = Strongly and willingly.
1   1804 6th rate. Sold in 1817.
3   1816 6th rate. Scrapped in 1829.
4   1851 frigate. Sold in 1891.
5   1917 destroyer of 1,090 tons built by Denny. Scrapped by Thornaby in 1947.

## VAMPIRE

Calabria 1940
Libya 1940–1
Greece 1941
Crete 1941
Aegean 1944
1   1917 destroyer of 1,090 tons built by White. RAN 1932. Sunk by Japanese aircraft east of Ceylon 1942.
2   1943 submarine of 545/740 tons built by Vickers Armstrong of Barrow. Scrapped at Gateshead in 1950.

## VANDAL

Named after the race that ravaged many lands.
1   1942 submarine, ex-*P64*, of 545/740 tons built by Vickers Armstrong at Barrow. Wrecked in the Firth of Clyde in 1943.

## VANESSA

Atlantic 1939–43
*Quandmême j'arrive* = I get there all the same.
1   1918 destroyer of 1,090 tons built by Beardmore. Scrapped at Charlestown in 1949.

## VANGUARD

Armada 1588
Cadiz 1596
Portland 1653
Gabbard 1653
Scheveningen 1653
Lowestoft 1665
Four Days' Battle 1666
Orfordness 1666
Barfleur 1692
Louisburg 1758
Quebec 1759
Martinique 1762
Nile 1798
Syria 1840
Jutland 1916
We lead.
1   1586 galleon (42) of 500 tons built by Matthew Baker at Woolwich. At the Armada campaign she was flagship of Sir William Wynter. She was captained by Sir Robert Mansell at Cadiz. She was rebuilt in 1599 and 1615. Onetime flagship of Sir Richard Hawkins.
2   1631 2nd rate (40–60) of 563–751 tons. She earned all the battle honours of the Dutch Wars.[83] Evidence suggests she was sunk or scuttled in the Medway in 1667.
3   1678 2nd rate (90) of 1,357 tons built at Plymouth. Overset in the great storm of November 1703 in the Medway, salved many years later and then renamed *Duke* in 1728.
4   1748 3rd rate (70) of 1,419 tons built at Cowes, earned four battle honours and was scrapped in 1774.
6   1787 3rd rate (74) of 1,609 tons built at Deptford. She was Nelson's flagship at The Nile. Scrapped in 1821.
7   1835 2nd rate (80) of 2,609 tons built at Pembroke. Renamed *Ajax* in 1867.

8   1868–70 ironclad of 3,774 tons built at Birkenhead. She sank after collision with the *Iron Duke* off the coast of Ireland in 1875.
9   1909 battleship of 19,250 tons built at Barrow. She was blown up by an internal explosion at Scapa in 1917.
13  1944 battleship of 42,500 tons built at Clydebank. Her 15in guns were first mounted in the *Glorious* and *Courageous* of 1917. She was scrapped in 1960 at Faslane.
14  1986 nuclear-powered ballistic-missile submarine of *c*.15,000 tons, dived, building by Vickers at Barrow. In March 1982 the government announced its intention to procure the Trident II weapon system with the D5 missile in a force of four submarines for the mid-1990s. *Vanguard* is the first of these four SSBNs.

## VANITY

North Sea 1939–45
English Channel 1943
*Vanitas vanitatum* = Vanity of vanities.
1   *c*.1649–54 vessel.
2   1918 destroyer of 1,090 tons built by Beardmore. Scrapped at Grangemouth in 1947.

## VANOC

Atlantic 1939–44
Norway 1940
North Africa 1942–3
English Channel 1943–4
Named after one of King Arthur's knights.
1   1917 destroyer of 1,090 tons built at Clydebank. Foundered while en route to Penryn to the breakers in 1946.

## VANQUISHER

Atlantic 1939–45
Dunkirk 1940
English Channel 1943–4
Normandy 1944
*Pugna vinco pugno* = I conquer in battle with my fist.
1   1917 destroyer of 1,090 tons built at Clydebank. Scrapped in 1948 at Charlestown.

83   Sources differ as to Nos. 1 and 2. Manning and Walker consider No. 1 to have survived till scuttled in the Medway in 1667, but Weightman gives convincing evidence of No. 2 having fought in the Dutch Wars. It seems inconceivable that No. 1 should have been battleworthy at the age of eighty, despite three rebuilds. See Manning and Walker, p. 465 and Weightman, pp. 452–3.

## VANSITTART

Atlantic 1939−43
Norway 1940
Malta Convoys 1942
North Africa 1942
*Grata quies si merita* = Rest is pleasant
if deserved.
1   1821−4 hired vessel.
2   1919 destroyer of 1,120 tons built
     by Beardmore. Scrapped at
     Newport in 1946.

## VARANGIAN

This curious name was chosen by
prime minister Winston S. Churchill.
From the Scandinavian bodyguard to
the Greek emperors of Byzantium.
1   1943 submarine, ex-*P61*, of 545/740
     tons built by Vickers Armstrong on
     the Tyne. Scrapped at Gateshead
     in 1949.

## VARNE

1   1943 submarine, ex-*P66*, of 545/740
     tons built by Vickers Armstrong at
     Barrow. Transferred to the
     Norwegian navy in 1943, and
     renamed *Ula*.
2   1944 submarine, ex-*P66*, of 545/740
     tons built by Vickers Armstrong on
     the Tyne. Scrapped at Troon in
     1958.

## VECTIS

*Vectes vectis* = The bars of Vectis [the
sea.]
From the Roman name for the Isle of
Wight.
1   1917 destroyer of 1,090 tons built
     by White at Cowes. Sold in 1936
     for scrapping at Inverkeithing.
2   1942−5 base, ex-*Osborne*, at the Isle
     of Wight.

## VEGA

North Sea 1940−5
*Praeclare fulgens* = Shining brightly.
Named after the star in the
constellation of Lyra.
1   1860 slaver captured by the *Lyra*.
2   1917 destroyer of 1,090 tons built
     by Doxford. Scrapped at Dunston
     in 1948.

## VELOX

Belgian Coast 1918
Zeebrugge 1918
Ostend 1918
Atlantic 1940−3
North Africa 1942−3
Swift to avenge.
1   1902 destroyer of *c.*400 tons built
     by Hawthorn Leslie. Mined off the
     Nab in 1915.
2   1917 destroyer of 1,090 tons built
     by Doxford. Scrapped at
     Charlestown in 1947.

## VENERABLE

Camperdown 1797
Gut of Gibraltar 1801
Belgian Coast 1914−15
Dardanelles 1915
*Quid non venerabilis audet* = What will
not the venerable dare?
1   1784 3rd rate which was wrecked
     in 1804.
2   1808 3rd rate. Scrapped in 1838.
3   1899 battleship of 15,000 tons built
     by Chatham Dock Yard. Broken up
     in Germany in 1920.
4   1943 aircraft carrier of 13,190 tons
     built by Cammell Laird.
     Transferred to Holland in 1948 and
     renamed *Karel Doorman*.

## VENGEANCE

Quiberon Bay 1759
Martinique 1794
St Lucia 1796
Crimea 1854
Dardanelles 1915
I strike, I cover.
1   1758 6th rate (28) of 533 tons. She
     was the French prize taken off the
     Lizard by HMS *Hussar*. Expended
     as a breakwater at Plymouth in
     1766.
2   1744 3rd rate (74) of 1,627 tons built
     on the Thames. Dismasted in the
     Great Storm of October 1780. Saw
     much action in the West Indies.
     Became a prison ship for POWs.
     Scrapped in 1816.
4   1800 frigate (40) of 1,370 tons taken
     as prize from the French. Used as a
     hulk for prisoners in Jamaica.

Believed disposed of in 1814.
5   1824 2nd rate (84) of 2,284 tons
     built at Pembroke. From 1861 she
     was a receiving hulk at Devonport.
     Scrapped in 1897.
6   1899 battleship of 12,950 tons built
     by Vickers. Sold in 1921 for
     scrapping by Stanlee.
7   1944 aircraft carrier of 13,190 tons
     built by Swan Hunter. Transferred
     to RAN 1952−55. Sold to Brazil in
     1956 and renamed *Minas Gerais*
     when refit was completed in 1960.

## VENGEFUL

Atlantic 1945
1   1944 submarine of 545/740 tons
     built by Vickers Armstrong at
     Barrow. Transferred to Greece
     1944−57 and renamed *Delfin*.
     Scrapped at Gateshead in 1958.

## VENOMOUS

Atlantic 1940−3
Dunkirk 1940
Arctic 1942
Malta Convoys 1942
North Africa 1942
Sicily 1943
*Hostibus nocens amicis innocuus* =
Deadly to foes, harmless to friends.
1   1918 destroyer, ex-*Venom*, of 1,120
     tons built by Clydebank. Scrapped
     in 1948.

## VENTURER

Norway 1944−5
I advance.
1   1799 prize, ex-British *Ranger*,
     renamed *Venturer*.
3   1943 submarine of 545/740 tons
     built by Vickers Armstrong at
     Barrow. Transferred to Norway in
     1946 and renamed *Utstein*.
     Two minesweepers of this name,
     tenders to the Severn Division
     RNVR, have been listed since.

# VENUS

Quiberon Bay 1759
St Lucia 1778
Glorious First of June 1794
Arctic 1943−4
Normandy 1944
Malaya 1945
Burma 1945
Named after the Roman goddess of love.
1  1758 5th rate which was renamed *Heroine* in 1809.
4  1807 frigate prize. Sold in 1815.
6  1820 5th rate. Scrapped in 1865.
8  1895 cruiser of 5,600 tons built by Fairfield. Bought by Cohen for breaking up in Germany in 1921.
11 1943 destroyer of 1,710 tons built by Fairfield. Disposal List 1974−5.

# VERBENA

Atlantic 1941
*Virtute bene donata* = Well endowed with virtue.
1  1915 sloop of 1,250 tons built by Blyth. Sold in 1933 to Rees of Llanelly for scrapping.
2  1940 corvette of 925 tons built by Smith's Dock. Scrapped at Blyth in 1951.

# VERDUN

North Sea 1940−5
Arctic 1942
*On ne passe pas.*
Named after the fortress and town heroically defended in 1916.
1  1916: date of acquisition of the paddle minesweeper built in 1888, 804 tons. Sold in 1922.
2  1917 destroyer of 1,090 tons built by Hawthorn Leslie. Scrapped in 1946.

# VERITY

Atlantic 1939−45
North Sea 1940
Dunkirk 1940
North Africa 1942−3
*Prevalebit* = [Truth] shall prevail.
1  1919 destroyer of 1,120 tons built by Clydebank. Scrapped at Newport in 1947.

# VERNON

Named after Admiral Edward Vernon (1684−1757).
1  1781 vessel.
4  1832 4th rate which was renamed *Actaeon* in 1886. Ten years later she became the first torpedo school. Sold in 1922.
5  1886 vessel, ex-*Donegal*, named *Vernon I*. Sold 1925.
6  1904 vessel, ex-*Marlborough*, named *Vernon II*. Sold 1924.
7  Ex-*Warrior*, named *Vernon III* in 1904.
8  1923: the *Vernon* torpedo school establishment was moved on shore in 1923. Now Seamanship and Diving School, Portsmouth.

# VERONICA

Atlantic 1941
*Vera sequor* = I follow the truth.
1  1915 sloop of 1,200 tons built by Dunlop Bremner. Sold to Cashmore in 1935 for scrapping.
2  1940 corvette of 925 tons built by Smith's Dock. USS *Temptress* (1942). Mercantile service post WWII. Lost in 1947 but salved, then scrapped at Blyth in 1951.

# VERSATILE

Atlantic 1939−45
North Sea 1941−5
Normandy 1944

English Channel 1944−5
1  1917 destroyer of 1,090 tons built by Hawthorn Leslie. Scrapped by Granton in 1949.

# VERULAM

Arctic 1944
Normandy 1944
Norway 1944
Malaya 1945
Burma 1945
Named after Verulamium, the Roman city of St Albans.
1  1917 destroyer of 1,300 tons built by Hawthorn Leslie. Mined in 1919 in the Gulf of Finland.
2  1943 destroyer of 1,710 tons built by Fairfield. Disposal List 1974−5.

# VERVAIN

Atlantic 1941−5
Normandy 1944
1  1941 corvette, ex−*Broom*, of 925 tons built by Harland & Wolff. Torpedoed and sunk in 1945.

# VERYAN BAY

1  1944 frigate of 1,580 tons built by Hill: Clark. Ex-*Loch Swannay*. Scrapped at Charlestown in 1959.

# VESPER

Atlantic 1938−45
English Channel 1940−5
North Sea 1941−2
Normandy 1944
*Nescis quod vesper vehat* = You know not what the evening brings forth.
1  1917 destroyer of 1,090 tons built by Stephen. Scrapped at Inverkeithing in 1947.

## VESTAL

Egypt 1801
Belgian Coast 1914
Normandy 1945
Burma 1945
*Bellone* 1759
1   1757 5th rate. Scrapped in 1775.
2   1777 6th rate which foundered in
    the same year.
3   and 4 were both 6th rates of 1779
    and 1833.
5   1865 sloop. Sold in 1884.
6   1900 sloop of 980 tons built by
    Sheerness Dock Yard. Sold in 1921
    to W. Thomas of Anglesey for
    scrapping.
7   1943 minesweeper of the 'Algerine'
    class built by Harland & Wolff.
    Sunk by Japanese aircraft in 1945
    off Puket.

## VETCH

Atlantic 1941−3
North Africa 1942
Sicily 1943
Mediterranean 1943
1   1941 corvette of 925 tons built by
    Smith's Dock. Transferred to
    Greece for mercantile service,
    *Patria* (1948): *Olympic Hunter* (1951)
    and Japanese *Otori Maru No. 18*
    (1956).

## VETERAN

Martinique 1794
Camperdown 1797
Copenhagen 1801
Atlantic 1939−42
Norway 1940
North Sea 1940
*Laudator temporis acti* = Proud of
former deeds.
1   1787 3rd rate. Scrapped in 1816.
3   1919 destroyer of 1,120 tons built
    by Clydebank. Torpedoed and
    sunk in the North Atlantic in 1942
    by *U-404*.

## VICEROY

North Sea 1942−5
Sicily 1943
In the King's name.
1   1917 destroyer of 1,100 tons built
    by Thornycroft. Scrapped by
    Granton in 1948.

## VICTORIOUS (Victorieuse)

St Lucia 1796
Egypt 1801
*Bismarck* Action 1941
Norway 1941−2
Arctic 1941−2
Malta Convoys 1942
North Africa 1942
Biscay 1942
Sabang 1944
Palembang 1945
Okinawa 1945
Japan 1945
*Rivoli* 1812
1   1783 (or 1785) 3rd rate of 1,659 tons
    built at Blackwall. Scrapped at
    Lisbon in 1803.
3   1808 3rd rate (74) of 1,724 tons built
    at Buckler's Hard. She fought the
    single-ship action with *Rivoli*, the
    French 74. In 1835 she was fitted as
    a receiving ship. Scrapped in 1868.
4   1895 battleship of 14,900 tons built
    by Chatham Dock Yard. Renamed
    *Indus II* in 1920, and finally sold in
    1923 to Stanlee for scrapping at
    Dover.
5   1939 aircraft carrier of 23,000 tons
    built by Vickers Armstrong.
    Distinguished WWII record.
    Rebuilt at Portsmouth Dock Yard
    1950−8 with increased
    displacement of 35,500 tons.
    Scrapped at Faslane in 1969.

## VICTORY

Armada 1588
Dover 1652
Portland 1653
Gabbard 1653
Scheveningen 1653
Four Days' Battle 1666
Orfordness 1666
Solebay 1672
Schooneveld 1673
Texel 1673
Barfleur 1692
Ushant 1781
St Vincent 1797
Trafalgar 1805
1   1588: the Armada battle honour

was awarded to *Victory*. She was
probably scrapped in 1608.
2   1620 vessel. Scrapped in 1690.
6   1691 1st rate, ex-*Royal James*.
    Renamed *Royal George* in 1714, but
    reverted to *Victory* the following
    year. Scrapped in 1721.
7   1737 1st rate which was wrecked in
    1744.
9   1765 1st rate of 2,162 tons (104). In
    1798 she was unseaworthy and
    became a prison hulk at Chatham.
    She was refitted, and in 1803 went
    to sea again as Nelson's flagship.
    From 1812 to 1922 she was moored
    in Portsmouth Harbour as a
    training ship. She then became
    preserved as a national
    monument. She was bomb-
    damaged in WWII, but is still
    preserved in Portsmouth. She is
    flagship of C-in-C Naval Home
    Command.

## VIDAL

Named after Vice Admiral A.T.E.
Vidal (1792−1863).
1   1951 survey ship of 2,230 tons built
    by Chatham Dock Yard. Scrapped
    in 1976.

## VIDETTE

Atlantic 1940−4
Spartivento 1940
Malta Convoys 1942
Normandy 1944
English Channel 1944
*Vigilate* = Watch!
1   1800 prize.
2   1918 destroyer of 1,090 tons built
    by Stephen. Scrapped at
    Grangemouth in 1947.

## VIGILANT

Arctic 1943−4
Normandy 1944
Malaya 1945
Burma 1945
1   1745 4th rate prize. Sold in 1759.

HMS VICTORY (No. 9)

2 1774 3rd rate. Scrapped in 1816.
3 1777 vessel, condemned and burnt in 1780.
15 1901 destroyer of *c*.400 tons built by Thomson. Sold in 1920 to South Alloa SB Co.
19 1942 destroyer of 1,710 tons built by Swan Hunter at Wallsend. Scrapped at Faslane in 1965.

# VIGO

The name recalls Admiral Sir George Rooke's exploits in Vigo Bay in 1702.
1 1703 4th rate prize taken after Vigo. She was the ex-RN *Dartmouth* taken in 1695. She was

wrecked in 1703.
2 1810 2nd rate. Sold in 1865.
3 1865 3rd rate, ex-*Agincourt*. Sold in 1884.
4 1945 destroyer of the 'Battle' class of 3,361 tons built by Fairfield. Scrapped at Faslane in 1964.

# VIGOROUS

Aegean 1944
*Vigor vincit* = Strength conquers.
1 1914–18 vessel.
2 1943 submarine of 545/740 tons built by Vickers Armstrong at Barrow. Sold for scrapping in 1949.

# VIKING

Belgian Coast 1914–15
1 1909 destroyer of *c*.1,090 tons built by Palmer. Sold in 1919.
4 1943 submarine of 545/740 tons built by Vickers Armstrong at Barrow. Transferred to Norway in 1946 and renamed *Utvaer*.

# VIMIERA

Guadeloupe 1810
North Sea 1941–2
*Sicut olim* = [Victory] as formerly.
Named after Sir Arthur Wellesley's victory (also called Vimeiro) over Junot in 1808.
1 1808 prize, *Pylades*. Sold in 1814.
2 1917 destroyer of 1,090 tons built by Swan Hunter at Wallsend. Mined in the Thames estuary in 1942.

# VIMY

Atlantic 1949–45
Dunkirk 1940
Normandy 1944
English Channel 1944–5
North Sea 1944–5
*Audaces fortuna juvat* = Fortune favours the brave.
Named after the Canadian Army victory in 1917.
1 1928 destroyer, ex-*Vancouver*, of 1,300 tons originally built in 1917, taken over by the RCN. Built by Beardmore. Scrapped in 1948 at Rosyth.

## VINDEX

Atlantic 1944
Arctic 1944−5
*Die noctuque mari coeloque* = By day
and by night — by sea and by sky.
1  1915 seaplane carrier of 1,950 tons
   built by Armstrong. Sold in 1920 to
   the Isle of Man for scrapping.
2  1943 escort carrier of 13,455 tons
   built by Swan Hunter. Sold in 1947
   for mercantile use as *Port Vindex*.

## VINDICTIVE

Zeebrugge 1918
Ostend 1918
Norway 1940
*Vindicavi* = I have made good.
1  1779 vessel.
2  1796 6th rate prize. Broken up in
   1816.
3  1813 3rd rate which was wrecked
   in 1871.
4  1897 cruiser of 5,750 tons built by
   Chatham Dock Yard. Sunk as a
   blockship at Ostend in 1918.
5  1918 cruiser/carrier of 9,750 tons.
   She was originally named
   *Cavendish*, but after launching was
   renamed to honour her
   predecessor's exploits. She was
   built by Harland & Wolff as a
   cruiser, but completed as a carrier.
   In 1925 she was rebuilt as a cruiser.
   Training ship in 1937. Repair ship
   in 1940. Sold in 1946 for scrapping
   at Blyth.

## VINEYARD

Armada 1588
Cadiz 1596
1  1588: a merchant ship of this name
   served with the fleet in the
   Armada campaign.
2  1944 submarine of 545/740 tons
   built by Vickers Armstrong at
   Barrow. Lent to France 1944−7 and
   renamed *Doris*. Scrapped at
   Charlestown in 1950.

## VIOLET

Armada 1588
Cadiz 1596
Gabbard 1653
Atlantic 1941−4
North Africa 1942
North Sea 1943−4
1  1588: 1596: a hired ship served at
   both the Armada and Cadiz.
2  1652 prize 5th rate (44). Scrapped
   in 1672.
8  1897 destroyer of *c*.400 tons built

by Doxford. Sold to Montrose in
1920 for scrapping.
12  1940 corvette of 925 tons built by
   Simons. Sold in 1947 for
   mercantile service as *La Aguera*
   (1947) and *La Guera* (1949).

## VIRAGO

Arctic 1943−4
North Cape 1943
Normandy 1944
Malaya 1945
Burma 1945
1  1803 vessel.
2  1842 sloop. Scrapped in 1876.
3  1895 destroyer of *c*.400 tons built
   by Laird. Sold to Hong Kong in
   1919.
4  1943 destroyer of 1,710 tons built
   by Swan Hunter at Wallsend.
   Scrapped at Faslane in 1965.

## VIRTUE

Aegean 1944
1  1943 submarine of 575/740 tons
   built by Vickers Armstrong at
   Barrow. Scrapped Cochin 1946.

## VIRULENT

1  1944 submarine of 545/740 tons
   built by Vickers Armstrong on the
   Tyne. Transferred to Greece and
   renamed *Argonaftis* (1946−58).
   Scrapped Pasajes in 1961.

## VISCOUNT

Atlantic 1939−4
Biscay 1943
*Nobile qui nobilis* = Handsome is as
handsome does.
1  1917 destroyer of 1,120 tons built
   by Thornycroft. Scrapped on the
   Tyne in 1947.

## VISIGOTH

Atlantic 1944
We hide and seek.
Named after the ancient Germanic
tribe.
1  1943 submarine of 545/740 tons
   built by Vickers Armstrong at
   Barrow. Scrapped at Hayle in 1950.

## VITALITY

1  1914−18 vessel.
2  1943 submarine, ex-*Untamed*, ex-
   *P58*, of 574/740 tons built by
   Vickers Armstrong at Barrow. Lost
   on trials in 1943. Salved and
   renamed *Vitality*, Scrapped at
   Troon in 1946.

## VIVACIOUS

Atlantic 1939−40
Dunkirk 1940
North Sea 1942−5
Arctic 1943
English Channel 1943−4
Normandy 1944
1  1917 destroyer of 1,090 tons built
   by Yarrow. Scrapped at
   Charlestown in 1948.

## VIVID

Aegean 1944
1  1848 vessel. This ship and No. 2
   were used as admiral's yachts at
   Plymouth.
5  1921 cruiser, ex-*Harlech*, ex-
   *Cambrian*, 4,360 tons built at
   Pembroke. Scrapped at
   Sunderland in 1923.
6  1922 monitor, ex-*Marshal Ney*,
   6,670 tons, renamed *Drake* in 1934
   and scrapped at Milford Haven in
   1957.
7  1943 submarine of 545/740 tons
   built by Vickers Armstrong on the
   Tyne. Scrapped at Faslane in 1950.

## VIVIEN

North Sea 1940−5
Trust me all in all.
1  1918 destroyer of 1,090 tons built
   by Yarrow. Scrapped at Rosyth
   and Charlestown in 1948.

## VOLAGE

Lissa 1811
Aden 1839
Baltic 1855
Arctic 1944
1  1798 6th rate prize. Scrapped in 1804.
2  and 3 were also 6th rates of 1807 and 1825.
4  1869 corvette. Sold in 1904.
5  1943 destroyer of 1,710 tons built by White. Scrapped in 1976.

## VOLATILE

1  1944 submarine of 545/740 tons built by Vickers Armstrong on the Tyne. Transferred to Greece and renamed *Triaina* (1946–58). Returned in 1958 and scrapped.

## VOLUNTEER

Atlantic 1939–45
English Channel 1940–5
Arctic 1942
Biscay 1943
Normandy 1944
North Sea 1945
1  1804 vessel.
2  1806 5th rate prize. Scrapped in 1816.
4  1919 destroyer of 1,120 tons built by Denny Bros. Scrapped by Granton in 1948.

## VORACIOUS

Atlantic 1944
*Adversarios devorabo* = I will devour my enemies.
1  1943 submarine of 545/740 tons built by Vickers Armstrong on the Tyne. Scrapped Cochin 1946.

## VORTIGERN

Atlantic 1939–40
North Sea 1941–2
*Virtus a majoribus* = Our valour is from our ancestors.
1  1918 destroyer of 1,090 tons built by White. Torpedoed and sunk by a German E-boat off Cromer in 1942.

## VOTARY

*Causam susceptam defendo* = I defend the cause I have undertaken.
1  1944 submarine of 545/740 tons built by Vickers Armstrong on the Tyne. Transferred to Norway in 1946 and renamed *Uthaug*.

## VOX

Aegean 1944
1  1943 submarine, ex-*P67*, of 545/740 tons transferred to French Navy and renamed *Curie* (1943–6). Returned and renamed *Vox*, then scrapped in 1949 at Milford Haven.
2  1943 submarine of 545/740 tons built by Vickers Armstrong at Barrow. Scrapped Cochin 1946.

## VULPINE

*Astu vincere* = By craft to conquer.
1  1943 submarine of 545/740 tons built by Vickers Armstrong on the Tyne. Lent to Denmark 1947–58 and renamed *Storen*. Scrapped in 1959 at Faslane.

## VULTURE

Barfleur 1692
Vigo 1702
Velez Malaga 1704
Baltic 1854–5
1  1648 vessel.
2  1656 prize.
5  6, 7 and 8 were all sloops of 1744, 1763, 1776 and 1803.
9  1843 frigate. Sold in 1863.
11 1898 destroyer of *c*.400 tons built by Thomson. Sold in 1919 to Hong Kong.
13 1940 RN Air Station at St Merryn. Recommissioned as HMS *Curlew* Dec. 1952. Paid off Jan. 1956.

## WAGER

Okinawa 1945
*Sponsione provoco* = I challenge with a wager.
1  1739 vessel (24) lost during Anson's voyage in 1741.
2  1744 6th rate. Sold in 1763.
3  1943 destroyer of 1,710 tons built at Clydebank. Named after Admiral Sir Charles Wager (?1666–1743). Sold to Yugoslavia in 1956 and renamed *Pula*.

## WAKEFUL

Atlantic 1939–40
Dunkirk 1940
North Sea 1944
*Si dormiam capiar* = Catch a weasel asleep!.
1  1917 destroyer of 1,300 tons built by John Brown. Torpedoed and sunk by E-boats off Dunkirk in 1940.
2  1943 destroyer, ex-*Zebra*, of 1,710 tons built by Fairfield. Scrapped at Inverkeithing in 1971.[84]
3  1974 submarine support vessel, ex-*Dan*, ex-*Heracles*, *c*.900 tons originally built as a tug by Cochranes of Selby for a Swedish company. Purchased in 1974 for naval service. Now employed as a submarine target ship in the Clyde.

## WALDEGRAVE

Normandy 1944
English Channel 1944
Named after Admiral William Waldegrave, 1st Baron Radstock (1753–1825).
1  1943 frigate, ex-*DE.570*, of 1,300 tons built by Bethlehem: Hingham. Returned to USA in 1945.

84  Colledge quotes 1959.

## WALKER

Atlantic 1939–43
Norway 1940
Normandy 1944
English Channel 1944
Arctic 1944–5
Named after Rear Admiral James
Walker (1764–1831).
1  1917 destroyer of 1,100 tons built
   by Denny Bros. Scrapped at Troon
   in 1946.

## WALLACE

North Sea 1941–5
Sicily 1943
*Pro patria* = For my country.
Named after Sir William Wallace
(*c.*1272–1305), the great Scots patriot.
1  1918 flotilla leader of 1,480 tons
   built by Thornycroft. Scrapped in
   1945.

## WALLFLOWER

Atlantic 1941–5
North Sea 1942
Arctic 1943–4
Normandy 1944
*Passim floreo* = I flourish everywhere.
1  1915 sloop of 1,250 tons built by
   Irvine. Sold in 1931 for scrapping
   at Inverkeithing.
2  1940 corvette of 925 tons built by
   Smith's Dock. Sold in 1946 for
   mercantile service: *Asbjorn Larsen*
   (1949).

## WALNEY

Atlantic 1941–2
North Africa 1942
Named after the Lancashire
coastguard station.
1  1941 US coastguard cutter, ex-
   *Sebago*, of 1,546 tons built by GEC
   in 1930. Sunk at Oran in 1942.

## WALPOLE

Atlantic 1939–43
English Channel 1942–4
North Sea 1942–4
Normandy 1944
Named after Sir Robert Walpole, first
Earl of Orford, and usually termed
first British prime minister.
1  1918 destroyer of 1,100 tons built
   by Doxford. Scrapped at Grays in
   1945.

## WALRUS

*Cave dentes* = Beware my tusks.
1  1917 destroyer of *c.*1,300 tons built
   by Fairfield. Wrecked in Filey Bay
   but salved and scrapped at
   Dunston in 1938.
2  1959 submarine of 1,600/2,030/
   2,410 tons built by Scotts. Paid off
   1987.

## WANDERER

Guadeloupe 1810
China 1842
Atlantic 1939–44
Norway 1940
Sicily 1943
Normandy 1944
Arctic 1944
English Channel 1944
*Vagantes nunquam erramus* =
Wandering, we never stray.
1  1806 vessel (20). Sold in 1817.
5  1883 sloop. Sold in 1907.
7  1919 destroyer of 1,120 tons built
   by Fairfield. She participated in the
   destruction of five U-boats during
   the Atlantic battle. She was
   scrapped in 1946 at Blyth.

## WARRIOR

The Saintes 1782
Copenhagen 1801
Jutland 1916
*Arma virumque* = Arms and the man.[85]
1  1781 3rd rate (74) of 1,621 tons built
   at Portsmouth. Scrapped in 1857.
2  1860 ironclad frigate of 6,121 tons
   and forty 68pdr guns, built at
   Blackwall. Renamed *Vernon III* in
   1904. Bought by HMS *Warrior*
   Preservation Trust, 1979.
   Transferred from Hartlepool to
   Portsmouth, 1987.
3  1905 cruiser of 13,550 tons built at
   Pembroke Dock Yard. Severely
   damaged at Jutland, and had to be
   abandoned and sunk.

7  1944 aircraft carrier, ex-*Brave* of
   13,350 tons built by Harland &
   Wolff. RCN 1946–8. Modernized
   1952–3. Sold to Argentina in 1958
   and renamed *Independencia*.
8  HQ of C-in-C Fleet, Northwood.
   Also Allied C-in-C Channel and C-
   in-C Eastern Atlantic Area, FO
   Submarines and
   COMSUBEASTLANT.

## WARSPITE

Cadiz 1596
Orfordness 1666
Solebay 1672
Schooneveld 1673
Texel 1673
Barfleur 1692
Velez Malaga 1704
Marbella 1705
Lagos 1759
Quiberon Bay 1759
Jutland 1916
Atlantic 1939
Norway 1940
Narvik 1940
Libya 1940–2
Calabria 1940
Mediterranean 1940–3
Matapan 1941
Crete 1941
Malta Convoys 1941
Sicily 1943
Salerno 1943
Normandy 1944
Walcheren 1944

---

85  Opening words of Virgil's *Aeneid*.

HMS WARRIOR (No. 2)

English Channel 1944
Biscay 1944
*Belli dura despicio* = I despise the
hardships of war.

The two ship's badges call for
comment. The Elizabethan form of the
ship's name was spelled Warspight,
the 'spight' expressing defiance or
contempt. The first, and perhaps
more official, badge shows a ship's
gun which most clearly illustrates the
defiance or contempt alluded to.
However, there is a second meaning
to the word spight: in Elizabethan
days it was a colloquial term for the
green woodpecker. Captain Roskill

tried desperately hard to establish a
credible link between the two origins,
but he is unconvincing.[86] The squat
Elizabethan gun badge is the
Admiralty version, but with typical
British sailor obstinacy the
woodpecker badge was retained in
*Warspite* No.7 — on the guns'
tampions and the boats' bows, while
even the dance band was called The
Woodpeckers. It would be
contentious to omit the woodpecker
badge here.
1　1596 vessel (36) of 650 tons.
2　1666 3rd rate (64) of 898 tons.
　　Modernized in 1702 to 70 guns and
　　952 tons. Renamed *Edinburgh* in
　　1715.

3　1758 3rd rate (74) of 1,890 tons. Her
　　first captain was the Hon. Henry
　　Blackwood, Nelson's 'favourite
　　frigate captain'.[87] Lent to Marine
　　Society in 1872 to train youngsters:
　　an eighteenth-century form of the
　　RNVR. Burnt in 1876. Replaced
　　promptly by:
5　1876 vessel of 2,845 tons, ex-
　　*Conqueror*. Burnt in 1918.
6　1884 cruiser. Sold in 1905.
7　1913 battleship of 30,600 tons built
　　by Devonport Dock Yard. One of
　　the world's most renowned
　　warships, whose WWII battle
　　honours testify to her exploits.
　　Flagship of Admiral Sir Andrew
　　Cunningham during the thickest
　　fighting of the Mediterranean war;
　　she led the surrendered Italian
　　fleet into the anchorage 'under the
　　guns of the fortress of Malta'. She
　　found a distinguished writer —
　　Captain S. W. Roskill — as her
　　biographer: *HMS Warspite*.
8　1965 nuclear-powered submarine
　　of 4,000/4,300/4,800 tons built by
　　Vickers Armstrong at Barrow.

## WARWICK

Zeebrugge 1918
Ostend 1918
Atlantic 1939–44
Biscay 1943
*Ea nostra vocamus* = We claim the
deeds of our ancestors.
1　1643 vessel (22), also known as *Old
　　Warwick*. Scrapped in 1660.
2　3 and 4 were all 4th rates of 1696,
　　1733 (surrendered in 1756,
　　recaptured five years later but
　　never re-added), and 1767.
5　1917 destroyer of 1,100 tons built
　　by Hawthorn Leslie. Torpedoed in
　　1944 by *U-413* off N. Cornwall.

## WASP

1　3 and 5 were all sloops of 1749
　　(burnt), 1801 (prize) and 1850.
8　1940 −4 Coastal Forces base at
　　Dover.

## WATCHMAN

China 1860
Atlantic 1940–4
Normandy 1944
Arctic 1944

86　See *HMS Warspite* by Captain S.W. Roskill, (Collins, 1957), Chapter One.

87　*Op. cit.* p. 70.

HMS WARSPITE (No. 7)

**English Channel 1944−5**
1   1917 destroyer of 1,100 tons built at
    Clydebank. Scrapped at
    Inverkeithing in 1945.

# WATERWITCH

**Anzio 1944**
1   1832 vessel.
2   1864 armoured vessel. Sold in
    1890.
5   1943 minesweeper of 'Algerine'
    class built by Lobnitz.
6   1959 survey vessel of 160 tons built

by White, former minesweeper of
the 'Ham' class, ex-*Powerham*,
seconded to Port Auxiliary service
in 1968. Disposal List 1985−6

## WAVENEY

**Atlantic 1942−3**
**Biscay 1943**
**Normandy 1944**
**Burma 1945**
1   1903 destroyer of *c*.560 tons built
    by Hawthorn Leslie. Sold in 1920
    to Ward of Grays for scrapping.
4   1942 frigate of 1,370 tons built by
    Smith's Dock. Scrapped at Troon
    in 1957.
5   1983 minesweeper of 890 tons built
    by Richards Ltd.

## WEAR

**Dardanelles 1915−16**
**Atlantic 1943−4**
**Biscay 1943**
1   1905 destroyer of *c*.560 tons built
    by Palmer. Sold in 1919 to Ward of
    Grays for scrapping.

4   1942 frigate of 1,370 tons built by
    Smith's Dock. Scrapped in 1957 at
    Sunderland.

## WELFARE

**South France 1944**
1   1348 vessel.
3   1943 minesweeper of the 'Algerine'
    class built by Redfern. Scrapped at
    Grays in 1957.

## WELLESLEY

**China 1840−2**
1   1815 3rd rate built in Bombay and
    renamed *Cornwall* in 1868.
2   1868 vessel, ex-*Cornwall*. Scrapped
    in 1875.
3   1875 3rd rate, ex-*Boscawen*. Burnt in
    1910.
4   1940−5 training establishment at
    Liverpool.

## WELLINGTON

Atlantic 1939−45
*Suprema ut olim* = Supreme as ever.
Named after the Duke of Wellington.
1 1810 prize sloop (16) of 312 tons taken by the *Scorpion* from the French off Guadeloupe, but scrapped two years later.
2 1816 3rd rate (74) of 1,757 tons, ex-*Hero* built at Deptford. Became coastguard ship. In 1862 renamed *Akbar*. Sold in 1908 to Ward for scrapping.
6 1934 sloop of 990 tons built by White at Devonport. Became HQ and Hall of the Honourable Master Mariners' Company in 1947.

## WELLS

Atlantic 1941−2
Arctic 1942
North Sea 1943−4
1 1764 vessel.
2 1940 destroyer, ex-USS *Tillman*, of 1,090 tons built by Charleston in 1919. Scrapped at Troon in 1945.

## WELSHMAN

Malta Convoys 1942
1 1940 minelayer of 2,650 tons built by Hawthorn Leslie. Torpedoed and sunk off Crete in 1943 by *U-617*.

## WENSLEYDALE

Atlantic 1943−4
English Channel 1943−4
North Sea 1943−4
Normandy 1944
Named after the hunt in Yorkshire.
1 1942 destroyer of the 'Hunt' class, 1,087 tons built by Yarrow. Scrapped at Blyth in 1946.

## WESSEX

Atlantic 1939−40
Okinawa 1945
*Proles militum* = Offspring of soldiers.
Named after the kingdom of the West Saxons.
1 1918 destroyer of 1,100 tons built by Hawthorn Leslie. Bombed and sunk off Calais in 1940.
2 1943 destroyer, ex-*Zenith*, of 1,710

tons built by Fairfield. Sold to South Africa in 1950 and renamed *Jan Van Riebeeck*.
3 1951 drill ship of the Solent Division RNVR, ex-sloop *Erne*, built in 1940, 1,250 tons. Sold as a hulk in 1965.

## WESTCOTT

Norway 1940
Atlantic 1940−3
Malta Convoys 1942
North Africa 1942−3
Arctic 1943−5
English Channel 1943
Normandy 1944
*Quo duxit sequimur* = Where he led, we follow.
Named after Captain George Blagdon Westcott (c.1745−98). He was killed while commanding the *Majestic* at The Nile.
1 1918 destroyer of 1,120 tons built by Denny Bros. Scrapped at Troon in 1946.

## WESTMINSTER

North Sea 1942−5
English Channel 1943
*Pro populo et gloria* = For the people and for glory.
1 1918 destroyer of 1,100 tons built by Scotts. Scrapped at Rosyth in 1948.

## WESTON

North Sea 1940
Atlantic 1940−4
English Channel 1945
The name was originally *Weston-super-mare* at the request of A.V. Alexander, First Lord of the Admiralty , but she was launched as *Weston*.[88]
1 1932 sloop of 1,060 tons built by Yarrow at Devonport. Sold in 1947 for scrapping at Gelleswick Bay.

## WEYMOUTH

Sadras 1758
Negapatam 1758
Porto Novo 1759
Valour buildeth the bridge.
1 1652 prize taken from the Royalists. Sold in 1662.
2 3 and 4 all were 4th rates of 1693,

1736 (wrecked) and 1752.
5 1795 6th rate which was wrecked in 1800.
6 1804 5th rate. Sold in 1866.
7 1910 cruiser of 5,250 tons built by Armstrong. Sold in 1928 to Hughes Bolckow for scrapping.
8 1961 general-purpose anti-submarine frigate of the 'Leander' class, 2,450/2,860 tons full load built by Harland & Wolff.

## WHADDON

North Sea 1941−3
Sicily 1943
Salerno 1943
Mediterranean 1943
South France 1944
Aegean 1944
Adriatic 1944
Named after the hunt in Buckinghamshire.
1 1940 destroyer of the 'Hunt' class, 907 tons built by Stephen. Scrapped at Faslane in 1959.

## WHEATLAND

Arctic 1942
North Africa 1942−3
Mediterranean 1943
Sicily 1943
Salerno 1943
Adriatic 1944
Named after the hunt in Shropshire.
1 1941 destroyer of the 'Hunt' class, 1,050 tons built by Yarrow. Hulked in 1955 and became a pontoon at Harwich. Scrapped in 1959.

## WHELP

Portland 1653
Gabbard 1653
Okinawa 1945

88 Manning and Walker, p.484.

1   1627: there were ten *Lion's Whelp* vessels, the last of which was sold in 1655.[89]
11  1943 destroyer of 1,710 tons built by Hawthorn Leslie. Transferred to South Africa in 1953 and renamed *Simon Van Der Stel*.

## WHIMBREL

Sicily 1943
Atlantic 1943−4
Normandy 1944
English Channel 1944
Arctic 1944
Okinawa 1945
1   1942 sloop of 1,300 tons built by Yarrow. Sold to Egypt in 1949 and renamed *El Malek Farouq*. In 1954 she was *Tarik*.
2   1970 experimental trials vessel of 300 tons, ex-*NSC* (E), basically LCT (3) class, employed by Underwater Weapon Establishment, Portland.

## WHIRLWIND

Zeebrugge 1918
Ostend 1918
Atlantic 1939−40
Norway 1940
Okinawa 1945
*Tot itinera tot venti* = Every voyage has its gales.
1   1917 destroyer of 1,100 tons built by Swan Hunter at Wallsend. Torpedoed in 1940 by *U-34* south-west of Ireland.
2   1943 anti-submarine frigate of 1,710 tons built by Hawthorn Leslie. Scrapped in 1974.

## WHITAKER

Atlantic 1944
Normandy 1944
English Channel 1944
Named after Admiral Sir Edward Whitaker (1660−1735).
1   1943 frigate of 1,300 tons built by Bethlehem: Hingham. Ex-*DE.571*. Torpedoed in 1944 by *U-483* off Malin Head. CTL. Returned to USA in 1947.

## WHITBY

Atlantic 1944−5
1   1780 vessel.
3   1954 frigate of 2,800 tons built by Cammell Laird. Scrapped in 1979 at Queenborough.

## WHITE BEAR

Armada 1588
Burma 1944−5
1   1563 vessel. Served at the Armada. Sold in 1629.
2   1908 vessel of *c*.1,800 tons, ex-*Iolanda*, built by Ramage and Ferguson. Submarine tender in 1940. Survey vessel in 1944. Sold in 1947 for scrapping.

## WHITEHALL

Atlantic 1939−43
Dunkirk 1940
Arctic 1943−5
Normandy 1944
English Channel 1944
*Nisi domini frustra* = Without My Lords [of the Admiralty], in vain.
1   1919 destroyer of 1,120 tons built by Swan Hunter, Wallsend. Scrapped at Barrow in 1945.

## WHITESAND BAY

Korea 1950−3
1   1944 frigate of 1,580 tons, ex-*Loch Lubnaig*, built by Harland & Wolff. Scrapped at Charlestown in 1956.

## WHITLEY

*Facta non verba* = Deeds, not words. The name should have been *Whitby*, but a typist's error caused her to be launched as *Whitley*.[90]
1   1918 destroyer of 1,100 tons built by Doxford. Beached after being bombed near Ostend in 1940.

## WHITSHED

Atlantic 1940
Dunkirk 1940
North Sea 1941−5
English Channel 1942−4
Normandy 1944
Named after Admiral of the Fleet Sir

James Hawkins Whitshed (1762−1849).
1   1919 destroyer of 1,120 tons built by Swan Hunter at Wallsend. Sold in 1947 for scrapping at Gateshead.

## WIDEMOUTH BAY

1   1944 frigate of 1,580 tons, ex-*Loch Frisa*, built by Harland & Wolff. Scrapped at Blyth in 1957.

## WIDGEON

Benin 1897
North Sea 1941−5
*Alis et animo* = With wings and courage.
1   1806 vessel.
5   1938 coastal corvette of 530 tons built by Yarrow. Scrapped by Redhaugh in 1947.

## WIGTOWN BAY

1   1945 frigate of 1,580 tons, ex-*Loch Garasdale*, built by Harland & Wolff. Scrapped at Faslane in 1959.

## WILD GOOSE

Atlantic 1943−4
Biscay 1943
Normandy 1944
Arctic 1944
English Channel 1945
Alert to evil.
1   1942 sloop of 1,300 tons built by Yarrow. One of the Navy's most famous anti-submarine vessels of WWII: she was involved in the sinking of eleven U-boats. Scrapped in 1956.

## WILD SWAN

Dunkirk 1940
Atlantic 1940−2
*Rara avis navis rarior* = A rare bird, a rarer ship.
1   1876 sloop which was renamed *Columbine* in 1912.
2   1919 destroyer of 1,120 tons built by Swan Hunter at Wallsend. Sunk by aircraft in the Bay of Biscay in 1942.
3   A patrol boat.

89  Manning and Walker, p. 485.

90  Manning and Walker, p. 486.

## WILLOWHERB

Atlantic 1943—5
1   1943 corvette of 980 tons built by
    Midland Shipbuilders. Ex-USS
    *Vitality*. Returned to USA in 1946,
    and scrapped in 1961 at Hamburg.

## WILTON

Arctic 1942
Malta Convoys 1942
North Africa 1942—3
Sicily 1943
Aegean 1943
Mediterranean 1944
Adriatic 1944
North Sea 1945
Named after the hunt in Wiltshire.
1   1941 destroyer of the 'Hunt' class,
    1,050 tons built by Yarrow.
    Scrapped at Faslane in 1959.
2   1972 minehunter of 450 tons built
    by Vosper Thornycroft. The first
    all-GRP vessel — glass-reinforced
    plastic.

## WINCHELSEA

Martinique 1794
Egypt 1801
Atlantic 1939—44
Dunkirk 1940
North Sea 1942
*Filia classium matris* = Daughter of the
Mother of Fleets.
1   2 and 3 were all 5th rates of 1694
    (surrendered), 1706 (lost in a
    hurricane) and 1707.
4   1740 6th rate, possibly a rebuild of
    No. 3. Scrapped in 1761.[91]
6   1764 5th rate. Sold in 1814.
7   1917 destroyer of 1,120 tons built
    by Denny Bros. Scrapped at Troon
    in 1960.

## WINCHESTER

Burma 1852—3
China 1856—60
North Sea 1940—4
English Channel 1943
Atlantic 1944
Valour makes the man.
1   2, 3 and 4 were all 4th rates of 1693
    (wrecked), 1698 (scrapped as a
    hulk), 1744 and 1822 (renamed
    *Conway*).
5   1861 6th rate, ex-*Conway*. Scrapped
    ten years later.

7   1918 destroyer of 1,100 tons built
    by White. Scrapped in the Forth
    1946.

## WINDFLOWER

Atlantic 1941
1   1918 sloop of 1,290 tons built by
    Workman Clark. Sold in 1927 to
    Cashmore for scrapping.
2   1940 corvette of 925 tons built by
    Davie Shipbuilding. RCN 1940.
    Lost in collision off Newfoundland
    in 1941.

## WINDSOR

Finisterre 1747
Ushant 1747
Atlantic 1939—40
Dunkirk 1940
Arctic 1942
English Channel 1942—3
North Sea 1942—5
Normandy 1944
*Stet fortuna domus* = May the fortune
of the house stand.
1   1695 4th rate. Scrapped in 1777.
3   1918 destroyer of 1,100 tons built
    by Scotts. Scrapped at
    Charlestown in 1947.

## WISHART

Atlantic 1939—44
Spartivento 1940
Mediterranean 1942
Malta Convoys 1942
North Africa 1942—3
Sicily 1943
*Clementia victis* = Mercy to the
vanquished.
Named after Admiral Sir James
Wishart (*d.* 1723).
1   1919 destroyer of 1,140 tons built
    by Thornycroft. Scrapped at
    Inverkeithing in 1945.

## WITCH

Atlantic 1939—43
Norway 1940
North Sea 1944
I'll do and I'll do.[92]
1   1919 destroyer of 1,140 tons built
    by Thornycroft. Scrapped by
    Granton in 1946.

## WITHERINGTON

Atlantic 1939—44
Norway 1940
English Channel 1940
1   1919 destroyer of 1,120 tons built
    by White. Lost on passage to the
    shipbreakers in 1945.

## WIVERN (Wyvern)

Atlantic 1939—43
North Africa 1942—3
North Sea 1944—5
A heraldic monster.
1   1863 turret ship. Sold in 1922.
2   1919 destroyer of 1,120 tons built
    by White. Scrapped at
    Charlestown in 1948.

## WIZARD

Endless endeavour.
1   1805 vessel.
4   1895 destroyer of *c*.350 tons built
    by Hanna. Sold in 1920 to Ward of
    Rainham for scrapping.
5   1943 destroyer of 1,710 tons built
    by Vickers Armstrong at Barrow.
    Scrapped at Inverkeithing in 1967.

## WOLFHOUND

Dunkirk 1940
North Sea 1943—5
In at the death.
1   1918 destroyer of 1,100 tons built
    by Fairfield. Scrapped by Granton
    in 1948.

## WOLSEY

Dunkirk 1940
Atlantic 1940—2
North Sea 1941—5
English Channel 1943

---

91   Manning and Walker identify differing Admiralty information about this vessel. See p. 488.

92   *Macbeth*, Act 1 Sc 2.

To the last penny — 'tis the King's.[93]
Named after Cardinal Thomas Wolsey
(c.1471–1530).
1   1918 destroyer of 1,120 tons built
    by Thornycroft. Scrapped at
    Sunderland in 1947.

## WOLVERINE (Wolverene)

Martinique 1809
Dardanelles 1915–16
Atlantic 1943–5
Norway 1940
Malta Convoys 1942
*Avidus laboris gloriae avidus* = Greedy
of work, greedy of glory.
1   1798 vessel.
5   1863 corvette which was handed
    over to New South Wales in 1881.
6   1910 destroyer of c.975 tons built
    by Cammell Laird. Lost in collision
    with *Rosemary* in 1917 off NW
    Ireland.
7   1919 destroyer of 1,120 tons built
    by White. Scrapped at Troon in
    1946.

## WOODCOCK

China 1856–60
Atlantic 1943–5
English Channel 1944
Okinawa 1945
1   1806 vessel.
4   1942 sloop of 1,300 tons built by
    Fairfield. Scrapped at Rosyth in
    1955.

## WOODPECKER

Biscay 1943
Atlantic 1943–4
*Inveniet qui exquirit* = He who seeks
carefully shall find.
1   1942 sloop of 1,300 tons built by
    Denny Bros. Torpedoed by *U-764*
    in the N. Atlantic in 1944.

## WOODRUFF

Atlantic 1941–5
1   1941 corvette of 925 tons built by
    Simons. Sold in 1946. Scrapped at
    Odense in 1959.

## WOOLSTON

Atlantic 1941
North Sea 1941–5
Arctic 1942

Sicily 1943
*Quo majores ducunt* = Where our
forefathers lead [we follow.]
Named after Messrs Thornycroft's
Woolston yard at Southampton.
1   1918 destroyer of 1,120 tons built
    by Thornycroft. Scrapped at
    Grangemouth in 1948.

## WOOLWICH

Barfleur 1692
Martinique 1762 and 1794
St Lucia 1796
Egypt 1801
*Sua tela tonanti* = Our bolts are those
of the Thunderer.
1   1673 sloop built at Woolwich but
    wrecked only two years later.
2   1674 sloop built at Woolwich. Sold
    in 1747.
3   1748 5th rate. Sold in 1762.
4   1785 5th rate which was wrecked
    in 1813.
6   1912 depot ship for destroyers,
    3,380 tons built by London &
    Glasgow. Sold in 1926 for
    scrapping at Ward, Hayle.
7   1934 depot ship for destroyers,
    8,750 tons built by Fairfield.
    Scrapped in 1962 at Dalmuir.

## WORCESTER

Dover 1652
Portland 1653
Gabbard 1653
Scheveningen 1653
Porto Farina 1655
Santa Cruz 1657
Porto Bello 1739
Sadras 1782
Providien 1782
Negatapatam 1782
Trincomalee 1782
Dunkirk 1940
Atlantic 1940
North Sea 1940–3
English Channel 1942–3
Arctic 1942–3
*In bello in pace fidelis* = Faithful in peace
and war.
1   and 2 were both 4th rates of 1651
    (renamed *Dunkirk*) and 1698.
3   1705 6th rate prize. Surrendered in
    1708.
4   1735 4th rate. Scrapped 1765.
5   1769 3rd rate. Scrapped in 1816.
6   1843 4th rate. Sold in 1885.
7   1876 3rd rate, ex-*Frederick William*,
    the famous cadet training ship
    even used throughout WWII, and
    sold in 1948.

8   1919 destroyer of 1,120 tons built
    by White. Renamed *Yeoman* in
    1945. Scrapped at Grays in 1946.

## WRANGLER

Baltic 1854
Crimea 1855
The first and last word.
1   1797 small vessel.
7   1943 destroyer of 1,710 tons built
    by Vickers Armstrong at Barrow.
    Sold to South Africa in 1957 and
    renamed *Vrystaat*.

## WREN

Atlantic 1939–45
Norway 1940
Biscay 1943–4
Normandy 1944
Arctic 1944
*Ex parvulis magna* = Great things
develop from small.
1   1653 vessel.
3   1919 destroyer of 1,120 tons built
    by Yarrow. Sunk off Aldeburgh by
    bombing in 1940.
4   1942 sloop of 1,250 tons built by
    Denny. Scrapped at Rosyth in
    1956.

## WRESTLER

Mediterranean 1940–2
Atlantic 1940–3
Malta Convoys 1942
North Africa 1942
Sicily 1943
Arctic 1943–4
Normandy 1944
English Channel 1944
*Nitendo vincimus* = By doing our
utmost we win.
1   1918 destroyer of 1,100 tons built
    by Swan Hunter at Wallsend. CTL
    1944 after damaged by a mine.
    Scrapped at Newport in 1944.

## WRYNECK

Libya 1941
Mediterranean 1941
Greece 1941
Lay on.
1   1918 destroyer of 1,100 tons built
    by Palmer. Sunk in the Greek
    campaign south of Morea by
    bombing in 1941.

93   *Henry VIII*, Act 3 Sc 2.

## WYE

North Sea 1944
1  1814 6th rate. Scrapped in 1862.
4  1943 frigate of 1,370 tons built by Robb: Lobnitz. Scrapped at Troon.

## YARMOUTH

Lowestoft 1665
Orfordness 1666
Solebay 1672
Schooneveld 1673
Texel 1673
Gibraltar 1704
Velez Malaga 1704
Finisterre 1747
Ushant 1747
Sadras 1758
Negatapatam 1758
Porto Novo 1759
The Saintes 1782
Jutland 1916
Falkland Islands 1982
*Rex et jura nostra* = Our King and laws.
1  1653 4th rate built at Yarmouth.
2  1694 3rd rate which was made a hulk in 1740.
3  1745 3rd rate. Scrapped in 1811.
4  1807 prize 3rd rate ex-*Waldemar*. Scrapped in 1816.
6  1911 cruiser of 5,250 tons built by London & Glasgow. Sold to Alloa, Rosyth for scrapping in 1929.
7  1959 frigate of 2,800 tons built by John Brown at Clydebank.

## YORK

Lowestoft 1665
Orfordness 1666
Solebay 1672
Schooneveld 1673
Texel 1673
Barfleur 1692
Louisburg 1758
Martinique 1809
Atlantic 1939
Norway 1940
Mediterranean 1940−1
Malta Convoys 1941
*Bon espoir* = Good hope. Motto of Edmund Langley, first Duke of York

(1341−1402), the fifth son of Edward III.
1  1660 3rd rate, ex-*Marston Moor*, which was wrecked in 1703.
2  1706 4th rate which was sunk as a breakwater at Sheerness in 1751.
4  1753 4th rate. Scrapped in 1772.
6  1777 sloop which surrendered two years later.
8  1796 3rd rate which foundered in 1804.
9  1807 3rd rate. Scrapped in 1854.
11  1928 cruiser of 8,250 tons built by Palmers. CTL and abandoned in Suda Bay, Crete in 1941 after attack by Italian explosive MTB. Subsequently bombed. The wreck was sold in 1947.
12  1982 Type 42 destroyer of 3,500/ 4,775 tons built by Swan Hunter.

## ZAMBESI

Norway 1944
Arctic 1945
1  1943 destroyer of 1,710 tons built by Cammell Laird. Scrapped at Briton Ferry in 1959.

## ZANZIBAR

Atlantic 1944
English Channel 1945
1  1943 frigate ex-USS *Prowse*, ex-*PF92*, of 1,318 tons built by Walsh Kaiser. Returned to USA in 1946.

## ZEALOUS

Nile 1798
Norway 1945

Arctic 1945
The badge derives from the arms of Captain S. Hood of the *Zealous* at The Nile.
1  1785 3rd rate which led the fleet at The Nile. Scrapped in 1816.
2  1864 ironclad. Sold in 1886.
3  1944 destroyer of 1,710 tons built by Cammell Laird. Sold to Israel in 1955 and renamed *Elath*.

## ZEBRA

The Saintes 1782
Martinique 1794
Copenhagen 1801
Syria 1840
Arctic 1945
1  1777 sloop which was wrecked in the following year.
2  1780 sloop. Sold in 1812.
4  1860 sloop. Sold in 1873.
5  1895 destroyer of c 350 tons. Scrapped in 1914.
6  1944 destroyer, ex-*Wakeful*, of 1,710 tons built by Denny. Scrapped in 1959.

## ZENITH

This above all.
1  1918 vessel.
2  1944 destroyer, ex-*Wessex*, of 1,710 tons built by Denny. Sold to Egypt in 1955 and renamed *El Fateh*.

## ZEPHYR

Quebec 1759
Martinique 1762
Copenhagen 1801
Baltic 1854
Arctic 1945
Named after the west wind,
Zephyrus.
1  1756 sloop which surrendered in
   1778.
2  1779 sloop which was renamed
   *Navy Transport* in 1782.
8  1895 destroyer of *c*.350 tons built
   by Donald Hanna. Sold in 1920 to
   Ward of Rainham for scrapping.
9  1943 destroyer of 1,710 tons built
   by Vickers Armstrong at Barrow.
   Scrapped Dunston 1958.

## ZEST

Arctic 1945
Norway 1945
1  1943 destroyer of 1,710 tons built
   by Thornycroft. Scrapped at
   Dalmuir in 1970.

## ZETLAND

Atlantic 1942−5
Malta Convoys 1942
North Africa 1942−3
Mediterranean 1943−4
Aegean 1944
Adriatic 1944
South France 1944
Named after the hunt, itself named
after the Marquess of Zetland.
1  1917 minesweeper of 750 tons built
   by Murdoch & Murray. Sold in
   1923 for scrapping at West
   Hartlepool.
2  1942 destroyer of the 'Hunt' class,
   1,050 tons built by Yarrow.
   Transferred to the Norwegian
   navy in 1954 and renamed *Tromsö*.
   Scrapped in 1965.

## ZINNIA

Atlantic 1941
1  1915 sloop of 1,200 tons built by
   Swan Hunter. Sold to Belgium in
   1920.
2  1940 corvette of 925 tons built by
   Smith's Dock. Torpedoed in the N.
   Atlantic in 1941.

## ZODIAC

Arctic 1945
Faythe hath no fear.
1  1944 destroyer of 1,710 tons built
   by Thornycroft. Sold to Israel in
   1955 and renamed *Yaffa*.

## ZULU

Belgian Coast 1915−16
Norway 1940
Atlantic 1941
*Bismarck* Action 1941
Malta Convoys 1941−2
Libya 1942
Sirte 1942
Mediterranean 1942
1  1909 destroyer of *c*.1,090 tons built
   by Hawthorn Leslie. Severely
   disabled by a mine in 1916. The
   bow section of *Zulu* was joined to
   the stern section of *Nubian* and a
   new ship of 1,050 tons, the *Zubian*,
   emerged in 1917. This ship was
   sold to Fryer of Sunderland in
   1919.
2  1937 destroyer of 'Tribal' class of
   1,870 tons built by Stephen.
   Bombed and sunk off Tobruk in
   1942.
3  1960 frigate of 2,370/2,700 tons
   built by Stephen. Sold to Indonesia
   in 1983.

# SECTION 3
# NAVAL BATTLES

# NAVAL BATTLES

For God's sake, if you should be so lucky as to get sight of the enemy, get as close to him as possible. Don't let them shuffle with you by engaging at a distance but get within musket shot if you can: that will be the only way to gain great honour and to make the victory decisive.

Lord Hawke to Geary, *26 August 1780.*

No captain can do wrong if he places his ship alongside that of an enemy.

Vice Admiral Nelson, *9 October 1805.*

The whole fortunes of our race and Empire, the whole treasure accumulated during so many centuries of sacrifice and achievement would perish and be swept utterly away if our naval supremacy were to be impaired.

Winston S. Churchill, *9 February 1912.*

## INTRODUCTION

This dictionary describes the battles in which the Royal Navy has participated since the year 1588. What is included and what is excluded is largely a matter of definition and of selection. In general, the guiding principle for inclusion has been a battle fought at sea between a fleet or squadron of the Royal Navy and an enemy. If this is strictly observed, it eliminates landing assaults such as combined operations, single or very-few-ship actions, evacuations and air-sea engagements. Patently, this is not good enough.

I confess to inconsistency here. No such compilation could excuse omitting the clash of Force Z and Japanese aircraft in the South China Sea, when the battleship HMS *Prince of Wales* and the battlecruiser HMS *Repulse* were sunk in December 1941, simply because no enemy ships were engaged. The engagement was a benchmark in naval history: two capital ships apparently adequately armed, with plenty of sea room, with well-trained crews and good visibility, succumbed to the assault. The operation a year earlier by the Fleet Air Arm at Taranto and the almost simultaneous attack on Pearl Harbour were against capital ships secured in port, and in one case officially at peace. The Force Z clash and the Taranto attack both merit inclusion here.

For equally strong reasons, no true battle list can exclude a paragraph or two on the evacuations from Dunkirk (1940) and Crete (1941), although the principal enemy forces were German aircraft.

It is purely a matter of selection which determines the inclusion of the Battle of Savo Island (1942) in which the 'British' element was Australian, and similarly The Sunda Strait (1942) which sacrificed HMAS *Perth* and the USS *Houston*: and the lesser-known battle at Kolombangara (1943) in which the light cruiser *Leander* figured — earning her captain, historian Stephen W. Roskill, the DSC.

On a grander scale, the World War I operations in the Dardanelles are excluded, while only brief references are made to World War II amphibious operations involving landings of invasion forces in the course of which some naval and some air-sea clashes occurred.

Convoy battles deserve full classification in their own right, especially those in the Atlantic battle. Churchill wrote of this battle: 'A war of groping and drowning, of ambuscade and stratagem, of science and seamanship.' On another occasion he wrote: 'The only thing that really frightened me during the war was the U-boat peril.' But it is evident that this is not the place for full classification: hundreds of convoys were operated during World War II, with scores of them resulting in significant engagements. Space limitations apply, so a few convoy battles from the Russian, Malta and Atlantic fronts have been selected to bring home the anguish, violence and horror of these clashes.

Curiously, all these exclusions and limitations mean the total exclusion of British submarine activity: this will not do, so Commander Martin Nasmith's exciting and extraordinary foray into the Sea of Marmara in HM Submarine *E 11* during World War I and Lieut.-Commander Wanklyn's gallant exploits in *Upholder* in the Mediterranean during World War II earn a mention to redress the balance.

Such limitations also exclude single-ship actions, yet these were the dominant feature of the Naval War of 1812 against America: so one has been included — the most celebrated, *Chesapeake* v *Shannon*. This was not selected chauvinistically because it was the first British victory after a series of five incredible American single-ship successes. It has just about all the qualities needed in fighting at sea in the days of sail.

# CHRONOLOGY
# of Sea Battles of the Royal Navy since 1588

**War** (bold type)
Battle[1] (Roman type) *British/Allied Commander* (italic type)

## War with Spain
1588 Spanish Armada *Lord Howard of Effingham*
1591 Azores *Sir Richard Grenville*
1596 Cadiz *Lord Howard of Effingham*

## First Dutch War 1652–4
1652 Dover *General-at-sea Robert Blake*
1652 Montecristi *Captain Richard Badiley*
1652 Kentish Knock *General-at-sea Robert Blake*
1653 Portland (The Three Days' Battle) *General-at-sea Robert Blake*
1653 The Gabbard (North Foreland) *Generals-at-sea George Monck/Richard Deane*
1653 Scheveningen (First Texel) *General-at-sea George Monck*
1655 Porto Farina *General-at-sea Robert Blake*
1657 Santa Cruz *General-at-sea Robert Blake*

## Second Dutch War 1665–7
1665 Lowestoft *James, Duke of York*
1666 Four Days' Battle *Duke of Albemarle*
    Orfordness (St James's Day or North Foreland) *Prince Rupert/Duke of Albemarle*
    Holmes's Bonfire *Sir Robert Holmes*
1667 Nevis *Captain Berry*
    Medway (De Ruyter in the Thames)

## Mediterranean Piracy
1671 Bugia *Vice Admiral Sir Edward Spragge*

## Third Dutch War 1672–4
1672 Solebay (Southwold Bay) *James, Duke of York*
1673 Schooneveld I *Prince Rupert*
    Schooneveld II *Prince Rupert*
    The Texel *Prince Rupert*

1 Alternative titles are given in parentheses.

**War of the English Succession 1689–97**[2]

1689 Bantry Bay *Admiral Arthur Herbert (later Earl of Torrington)*
1690 Beachy Head *Admiral Arthur Herbert (later Earl of Torrington)*
1692 Barfleur *Admiral Sir Edward Russell*
    La Hogue *Admiral Sir Edward Russell*
1693 Lagos I (Disaster of the Smyrna Convoy) *Vice Admiral Sir George Rooke*

**War of the Spanish Succession 1702–13**

1702 Santa Marta *Vice Admiral John Benbow*
    Vigo Bay *Admiral Sir George Rooke*
1704 Gibraltar *Admiral Sir George Rooke*
    Malaga *Admiral Sir George Rooke*
1705 Marbella (Action off Cabrita or Cabareta Point) *Admiral Sir John Leake*
1708 Cartagena (Wager's Action) *Commodore Charles Wager*

**War for Sicily 1718–20**

1718 Cape Passero *Admiral Sir George Byng (later Viscount Torrington)*

**War of 1739–48**[3]

1739 Puerto Bello *Vice Admiral Edward Vernon*
1744 Toulon *Admiral Thomas Mathews*
1746 Fort St David (Negapatam) *Commodore Edward Peyton*
1747 Finisterre I *Rear Admiral George Anson*
1747 Finisterre II *Rear Admiral Sir Edward Hawke*
1748 Havana I *Rear Admiral Charles Knowles*

**Seven Years' War 1756–63**

1756 Minorca I *Vice Admiral John Byng*
1757 Cap François *Captain Arthur Forrest*
1758 Ile d'Aix *Admiral Sir Edward Hawke*
    Cuddalore I (Sadras) *Vice Admiral George Pocock*
    Louisburg *Admiral the Hon. Edward Boscawen*
    Negapatam I *Vice Admiral George Pocock*
1759 Lagos II *Admiral the Hon. Edward Boscawen*
    Pondicherry *Vice Admiral George Pocock*
    Quebec *Vice Admiral Sir George Saunders*
    Quiberon Bay *Admiral Sir Edward Hawke*
1761 Belleisle I *Commodore the Hon. Augustus Keppel*
1762 Martinique I *Rear Admiral George B. Rodney*
    Havana II *Admiral Sir George Pocock*

**American War of Independence 1775–83**

1776 Lake Champlain
1778 Ushant I *Admiral Augustus Keppel*
    St Lucia I *Rear Admiral Samuel Barrington*
1779 Grenada *Vice Admiral John Byron*

---

2   Also War of the League of Augsburg. The War of the Grand Alliance, The Nine Years' War, King William's War.

3   Also War of the Austrian Succession. The War of Jenkins's Ear (1739–41) merged into this war. Jenkins alleged his ear was cut off by the Spanish in 1731, but public indignation was aroused in 1738 when he related his story to the House of Commons.

Flamborough Head *Captain Richard Pearson*
1780 Cape St Vincent I (The Moonlight Battle) *Admiral Sir George Rodney*
    Monte Christi I *Captain William Cornwallis*
    Monte Christi II *Captain William Cornwallis*
    Dominica I *Admiral Sir George Rodney*
1781 Chesapeake I (Action off Cape Henry) *Rear Admiral Marriott Arbuthnot*
    Porto Praya *Vice Admiral Sir Edward Hughes*
    Martinique II *Admiral Sir George Rodney*
    Dogger Bank I *Captain Hyde Parker*
    Chesapeake II *Rear Admiral Thomas Graves*
    Ushant II *Rear Admiral Kempenfelt*
1782 St Kitts *Rear Admiral Sir Samuel Hood*
    Sadras *Vice Admiral Sir Edward Hughes*
    Dominica II *Admiral Sir George Rodney*
    The Saintes[4] *Admiral Sir George Rodney*
    Providien *Vice Admiral Sir Edward Hughes*
    Negapatam II *Vice Admiral Sir Edward Hughes*
    Trincomalee *Vice Admiral Sir Edward Hughes*
1783 Cuddalore II *Vice Admiral Sir Edward Hughes*

**French Revolutionary War 1793−1802**
1794 Martinique III *Vice Admiral Sir John Jervis*
    Glorious First of June *Admiral Earl Howe*
1795 Gulf of Genoa (Hotham's First Action) *Vice Admiral William Hotham*
    Belleisle II (Cornwallis's Retreat) *Vice Admiral William Cornwallis*
    Île de Groix (Bridport's Action) *Admiral Lord Bridport*
    Hyères (Hotham's Second Action) *Vice Admiral William Hotham*
    Cape of Good Hope I *Vice Admiral Sir George Elphinstone*
1796 St Lucia II *Rear Admiral Sir Hugh C. Christian*
1797 Cape St Vincent II *Admiral John Jervis*
    Camperdown *Admiral Duncan*
1798 The Nile (Aboukir Bay) *Rear Admiral Horatio Nelson*
    Minorca II *Commodore John Duckworth*
    Donegal (Warren's Action) *Rear Admiral Warren*
1799 Acre *Captain Sir Sidney Smith*
1801 Copenhagen *Admiral Sir Hyde Parker*
    Algeciras and the Straits (Gut of Gibraltar) *Rear Admiral Sir James Saumarez*

**Napoleonic War 1803−15**
1805 Cape Tenez *Commander Richard B. Vincent*
    Calder's Action (Cape Finisterre) *Vice Admiral Sir Robert Calder*
    Trafalgar *Vice Admiral Lord Nelson*
    Cape Ortegal (Strachan's Action; Bay of Biscay) *Captain Sir Richard Strachan*
    Cape of Good Hope II *Commodore Sir Home Riggs Popham*
1806 San Domingo *Vice Admiral Sir John Duckworth*
1807 Curaçoa *Captain Brisbane*
1809 Cayenne *Captain James L. Yeo*
    Martinique IV *Rear Admiral the Hon. Sir Alexander Cochrane*
    Basque and Aix Roads *Admiral Lord Gambier*
1810 Cape Town *Commodore Sir Home Riggs Popham*

---

4  Variously called Les Saintes, The Saints, but preferably The Saintes.

Guadeloupe *Vice Admiral the Hon. Sir Alexander Cochrane*
Amboina *Captain Edward Tucker*
Banda Neira *Captain Christopher Cole*
Ternate *Captains Tucker and Forbes*
1811 Lissa *Captain William Hoste*
Tamatave *Captain Charles Schomberg*
Java *Rear Admiral the Hon. R. Stopford*
Pelagosa *Captain Murray Maxwell*
1813 *Chesapeake* v *Shannon: Captain Peter Broke*
1814 Glückstadt *Captain Arthur Farquhar*
Cattaro *Captain William Hoste*
1816 Algiers *Admiral Lord Exmouth*

### Greek War of Independence 1821–9
1827 Navarino *Vice Admiral Sir Edward Codrington*

### 19th Century
1839 Aden *Captain Henry Smith*
1840 Syria *Admiral the Hon. Sir Robert Stopford*
1849 Kua Kum *Commander John C. D. Hay*
1858 Lucknow *General Sir Colin Campbell*
Amorha *Captain E. S. Sotheby*
1868 Abyssinia *Lieut.-Gen Sir Charles Napier*
1882 Alexandria *Admiral Sir Frederick B. Seymour*
1897 Benin *Rear Admiral Sir Harry Rawson*
1900 Taku Forts *Commander Christopher G.F.M. Cradock*

### World War I 1914–18
1914 Heligoland Bight *Rear Admiral Sir David Beatty*
Cameroons *Captain Cyril T.M. Fuller*
Coronel *Rear Admiral Sir Christopher Cradock*
Falklands *Vice Admiral Sir Doveton Sturdee*
1915 Dogger Bank II *Vice Admiral Sir David Beatty*
Suez Canal *Admiral Peirse*
Nasmith's Patrol *Lieut.-Commander Martin Nasmith*
1916 Jutland (Skagerrak) *Admiral Sir John Jellicoe*
1917 Dover Straits *Commander Edward Evans*
1918 Zeebrugge/Ostend *Admiral Sir Roger Keyes*

### World War II 1939-45
1939 The Atlantic Battle till 1945
River Plate (*Graf Spee* Action) *Commodore Henry Harwood*
1940 Narvik I *Captain Warburton Lee*
Narvik II *Vice Admiral Whitworth*
Dunkirk (Operation Dynamo) *Vice Admiral Sir Bertram Ramsay*
Oran (Mers el Kebir) *Vice Admiral Sir James Somerville*
Dakar *Vice Admiral John Cunningham*
Spada (Cape Spada) *Captain John Collins*
Malta Convoys till 1943 *Admiral Sir Andrew Cunningham*
Calabria (Punta Stilo) *Admiral Sir Andrew Cunningham*
Cape Spartivento *Vice Admiral Sir James Somerville*
Taranto *Admiral Sir Andrew Cunningham*

1941 Cape Bon *Commander G.H. Stokes*
    (Cape) Matapan *Admiral Sir Andrew Cunningham*
    Greece *Admiral Sir Andrew Cunningham*
    Sfax *Captain P.J. Mack*
    Greece *Admiral Sir Andrew Cunningham*
    Crete *Admiral Sir Andrew Cunningham*
    *Bismarck* Action (Denmark Strait) *Admiral Sir John Tovey*
    Sirte I *Rear Admiral Sir Philip Vian*
    Force Z (South China Sea) *Rear Admiral Sir Tom Phillips*
    *Upholder* Patrol *Lieut.-Commander D. Wanklyn*
1942 Russian Convoys — PQ 17 *Admiral Sir John Tovey*
    Channel Dash *Vice Admiral Sir Bertram Ramsay*
    Java Sea *Rear Admiral Karel Doorman*
    Sunda Strait *Captain Hector Waller RAN*
    Sirte II *Rear Admiral Sir Philip Vian*
    St Nazaire *Commander R.E.D. Ryder*
1942 Diego Suarez *Rear Admiral E.N. Syfret*
    Coral Sea *Rear Admiral F.J. Fletcher USN*
    Savo Island *Rear Admiral V.A.C. Crutchley RAN*
    Dieppe *Captain J. Hughes-Hallett*
    Barents Sea *Captain R. St V. Sherbrooke*
    North Africa Landings (Operation Torch) *Vice Admiral E.N. Syfret*
1943 Sicily *Admiral Sir Andrew Cunningham*
    Kolombangara *Rear Admiral Ainsworth USN*
    Salerno *Admiral Sir Andrew Cunningham*
    North Cape (*Scharnhorst* Action) *Admiral Sir Bruce Fraser*
1944 Anzio *Rear Admiral Lowry USN*
    Normandy Landings *Admiral Sir Bertram Ramsay*
    Sabang *Admiral Sir James Somerville*
    Leyte Gulf *Rear Admiral Berkey USN*
    Walcheren *Captain A.F. Pugsley*
1945 Lingayen Gulf *Vice Admiral Oldendorf USN*
    Palembang *Vice Admiral Sir H.B. Rawlings*
    *Haguro* Sinking *Captain Manley Power*
    Okinawa *Vice Admiral Sir H. B. Rawlings*
    Sakishima Group *Vice Admiral Sir H.B. Rawlings*

**Korean War 1950–3**
1950 Inchon Landings *Rear Admiral W.G. Andrewes*

**Suez War 1956**
**1956 Suez Canal** *General Sir Charles Keightley*

**Falkland Islands 1982**
1982 Falkland Islands *Rear Admiral John 'Sandy' Woodward*

# THE BATTLES

**ABOUKIR BAY** — *see* NILE, THE

## ABYSSINIA

*13 April 1868*

Magdala was captured by a naval brigade commanded by Lieut.-General Sir Charles Napier. Ships engaged in the operation were *Argus*, *Daphne*, *Dryad\**, *Nymphe*, *Octavia\**, *Satellite\**, *Spiteful*, *Star* and *Vigilant*.

Asterisks denote that these ships landed naval brigades.

## ACRE

*17 March—20 May 1799*

After Napoleon conquered Egypt in 1799 he marched on Turkish forces at St Jean d'Acre. Captain William Sidney Smith arrived before him and fortified the town, landed naval brigades from his own ship, *Tigre* (80), and the *Alliance* and *Theseus*. Smith captured Napoleon's siege train and withstood the siege from March to May.

## ADEN

*19 January 1839*

Ships involved in the capture of Aden were: *Cruizer* and *Volage*, plus the Indian ships *Coote* and *Mahé*. Troops from the Bombay Artillery, 1st Bombay European Regiment and 24th Bombay Native Infantry participated.

## AIX, ILE D'

*4 April 1758*

### Seven Years' War 1756—63

Several naval battles highlighted the Seven Years' War, that war of complex alliances, intrigues and mistrust: Britain and Prussia ranged themselves against the might of Russia, France, Poland, Sweden, Austria and Spain. The war spread to Africa, India (The Black Hole of Calcutta, Clive's victory at Plassey), Canada (capture of Quebec), America (conquest of Pittsburgh) and the major naval success at Quiberon Bay near Lorient.

The confused action of the Ile d'Aix took place in 1758. Admiral Sir Edward Hawke prevented a French squadron from quitting Rochefort to escort a valuable convoy to America. Hawke had seven ships of the line and three frigates when he came upon the convoy on 4 April lying off the Ile d'Aix. Forty merchantmen were escorted by five 74s and 64s and possibly seven frigates. Battle was joined, but the conditions never allowed it to get too damaging. In the confusion many French ships were driven into shoal water and grounded, but most lightened ship and got clear. The convoy never re-formed.

**AIX ROADS** — *see* BASQUE AND AIX ROADS

## ALEXANDRIA

*11 July 1882*

The bombardment of Alexandria, in which Lord Charles Beresford in *Condor* distinguished himself, was effected under the command of Admiral Sir Frederick Beauchamp Seymour in HMS *Alexandra*.

## ALGECIRAS AND THE STRAITS (Gut of Gibraltar)

*6 and 12/13 July 1801*

### French Revolutionary War 1793—1802

Rear Admiral Sir James Saumarez fought two separate actions within a week off Gibraltar against a squadron of French and Spanish ships of the line. The first action had an unhappy outcome for Saumarez. He wore his flag in the *Caesar* (80) with five 74s in company. On the morning of 6 July he encountered an inferior Spanish squadron commanded by Admiral Linois comprising three of the line and a frigate lying at anchor in Algeciras Bay. Linois was forced to run his ships ashore to avoid destruction and gain the sanctuary of shore guns. One of

Saumarez's 74s, the *Hannibal*, also ran aground and was pounded by the batteries into surrender. The British squadron retired to Gibraltar to lick its wounds — and secured its revenge six days later.

Patched and repaired, the British ships sailed and met a combined Franco-Spanish force at dusk on 12 July. It comprised eight of the line and three frigates. At midnight the two Spanish first rates — both of 112 guns, the *Real Carlos* and *San Hermenegildo* — caught fire and collided. They both foundered with heavy loss of life. Soon after the French 74, *St Antoine*, was taken. Several of the British ships were damaged, especially the 3rd rate *Venerable*, but all reached Gibraltar safely.

The battle is also known as the Gut of Gibraltar. When the news reached England Saumarez became a national hero.

## ALGIERS

*27 August 1816*

The bombardment of Algiers arose from the anti-slavery patrols by British ships in the Mediterranean. Lord Exmouth in *Queen Charlotte*, with a Dutch squadron under the command of Vice Admiral Baron von Theodorus van Capellan in *Melampus* supported by troops, sappers and miners, offered treaties to the Deys of Tunis, Tripoli and Algiers if they agreed to prohibit the taking of Christian slaves. The Dey of Algiers refused. The port was well defended, but Exmouth mounted a brilliant attack and reduced the port and town to near-rubble. 1,200 Christian slaves were released. The Dey surrendered his studded scimitar as a token of his complete capitulation.

## AMBOINA

*17 February 1810*

The town of Amboina in the Moluccas (Indonesia) was captured by a detachment of the Madras European Regiment supported by the *Cornwallis*, *Dover* and *Samarang*.

## AMORHA

*5 March 1858*

A naval brigade from HMS *Pearl* with detachments of Bengal Yeomanry, Military Police and Gurkhas comprehensively defeated 14,000 Indian rebels during the Indian Mutiny.

## ANZIO

*22 January 1944*

Operation 'Shingle' was the landing of substantial forces for an assault on Rome, covered by large concentrations of ships. On the first day 36,034 troops and 3,069 vehicles were landed. During the battle for Anzio ships of the RN came under heavy air attack, and the following ships were sunk: *Inglefield*, *Janus*, *Penelope* and *Spartan*.

## ARCTIC CONVOYS — *see* RUSSIAN CONVOYS

## (SPANISH) ARMADA

*July/August 1588*

The Spanish Armada comprised about 130 ships including 33 galleons and 4 galleasses. It was commanded by the Duke of Medina Sidonia. He sighted the Lizard on 19 July. He intended sailing the Armada up the Channel to link up with Parma's invasion force already assembled at Calais.

The English fleet, the main part of which was assembled at Plymouth, was commanded by Lord Howard of Effingham, with Francis Drake as his vice admiral.

For nine days there followed a running battle as the Armada sailed slowly up Channel in a huge crescent formation with the English ships engaging when possible.

On 21 July the Spaniards lost the *Nuestra Senhōra del Rosario* and the *San Salvador*. Two days later Frobisher's squadron got the better of a sharp engagement off Portland Bill. Another fierce scrap took place off Dunnose Head, Isle of Wight, on the 25th. But Sidonia found a good anchorage at Calais on 27 July.

The English fleet was now joined by a squadron from the Downs under Lord Henry Seymour and Sir William Wynter.

In order to prevent the embarkation of the invasion forces, the Spanish ships were attacked by fireships on the night of 28/29, with remarkable results. Panic set in among the Spaniards: cables were cut and the ships fell into complete confusion as they attempted to avoid the fireships.

The decisive battle — off Gravelines — was fought the next day. Three or four Spanish galleons were lost, and many others seriously damaged. The wind and current were driving the Spanish ships towards the lee shore of the Flemish shoals, but a sudden change of wind enabled the fleet to claw off the dangerous shallows.

Sidonia could not fight his way back down Channel, so he determined upon a return to Spain north-about Scotland and Ireland, a voyage of tragic consequences. Howard pursued the Spanish ships as far north as the Firth of Forth. Of the original 130 ships, some 70 finally reached home.

## ATLANTIC, THE

*1939—45*

### World War II 1939—45

This was the longest-lasting battle of WWII. It is impossible in a matter of a few paragraphs to epitomize such a vast and complex battle, the fortunes of which swayed first one way and then the other. A huge bibliography on the subject exists, which covers the drama and horror of the long-drawn-out battle in all its facets, from both the British and the German viewpoints. The barest outline is given of three con-

**British, Allied & Neutral Merchant Ship Losses 1939—45 Atlantic Theatre.**
Extracted from the Official History, *War at Sea*, S.W. Roskill, Vols 1—3, HMSO. All Causes: U-boats, aircraft, mines, surface ships & unknown causes.

| Year | Tons | % of world-wide losses | British merchant ship losses by all causes | Crews lost |
|------|------|------------------------|---------------------------------------------|------------|
| 1939 | 754,686 | 99.9 | 95 | 495 |
| 1940 | 3,654,511 | 91.6 | 511 | 5,622 |
| 1941 | 3,295,909 | 76.1 | 568 | 7,838 |
| 1942 | 6,150,340 | 79.0 | 590 | 9,736 |
| 1943 | 453,752 | 37.2 | 266 | 4,606 |
| 1944 | 339,052 | 63.9 | 102 | 1,512 |
| 1945 | 366,852 | 83.9 | 45 | 323 |

**GERMAN U-BOAT LOSSES 1939—45.**
Extracted from *U-Boote,*
by Dr Jürgen Rohwer.

**1. On Operations:**

| | On way to or from base | North Sea Baltic Arctic | North & South Atlantic | Med. | Indian Ocean | Total |
|--|------------------------|--------------------------|------------------------|------|--------------|-------|
| 1939—45 | 186 | 58 | 324 | 50 | 12 | 630 |

**2. By Other Causes:**

| | |
|--|--|
| In Home Waters/at base by air attack/mines | 81 |
| In Home Waters/at base by accident | 42 |
| In evacuating forward bases/scuttling at end of war | 215 |

**3. Remainder:**

| | |
|--|--|
| Irreparable damage/obsolescence | 38 |
| Captured by enemy/damaged in neutral harbours | 11 |
| Surrendered at end of war | 153 |

TOTAL 1,170

voy battles in order to indicate the bitterness of the Atlantic battle. Perhaps the stark figures in the tables above will also help give a glimpse of the horror of this long campaign. 'The Battle of the Atlantic', Churchill wrote, 'was the dominating factor all through the war. Never for one moment could we ever forget that everything elsewhere depended upon its outcome.'

## CONVOY HX 79
### October 1940

This convoy battle was one of the first fought by a Wolf Pack: it included U-boats commanded by the 'aces' Günther Prien, Heinrich Bleichrodt, Engelbert Endrass and Joachim Schepke. The homebound convoy HX 79 was escorted by ten RN vessels led by the old destroyer HMS *Whitehall.* Several of these German commanders — and Otto Kretschmer, the most successful of all the war — had finished attacking a slow convoy, SC 7 (Kretschmer himself

had sunk six ships totalling about 80,000 tons), and now they could hardly believe their luck when they came upon the hapless HX 79.

The convoy comprised 49 ships, ten escorts and the Dutch submarine *O—14*, but the latter contributed nothing to the defence of the convoy. In five hours on the night of 19—20 October 1940 these U-boat aces ran alongside the columns of ships firing to port and starboard, sinking 60,000 tons of shipping.

The significance of the mauling of these two convoys was the prime minister's and the government's immediate and positive reaction: destroyers were transferred from anti-invasion duties to supplement convoy escorts; radar for escorts became top priority; a new high-powered and independent command, C-in-C Western Approaches, was brought into being with a large operational HQ at Liverpool; a radical change in anti-submarine training and the setting up in Tobermory Bay of a rigorous course for escorts and their officers in convoy duties and A/S tactics. All of these contributed towards the subsequent victory in the Atlantic battle.

## CONVOY HG 76
### December 1941

German Focke-Wulf Kondor long-range aircraft homing U-boats on to Gibraltar convoys in 1941 decided the Admiralty to suspend sailings, especially after the loss of five merchant ships and the destroyer *Cossack* in HG 75. Two points in particular influenced this decision: firstly, Coastal Command was unable to give cover along the whole route of the convoys; secondly, agents in nearby Algeciras with powerful binoculars could give accurate intelligence of all Gibraltar shipping movements.

Convoy HG 76 comprising 31 ships was a resumption of these suspended convoys. It sailed from Gibraltar on 14 December. Lieutenant-Commander F.J. (Johnny) Walker, the Navy's leading A/S tactician, in his sloop, *Stork*, commanded the 3rd Escort Group. Sixteen escorts gave strong cover: 2 destroyers, 4 sloops, 9 corvettes, the escort carrier *Audacity* and the CAM ship *Darwin*.

Dönitz deployed seven U-boats of his *Seeräuber* Group, and homed them on to the convoy by Kondors of 1KG 40 from Bordeaux. One of the U-boat commanders was the ace Endrass in *U-567*.

It was dusk on the second night when the first, most southerly U-boat contacted the convoy, soon joined by a second. The following morning *U-131* was spotted and attacked by Martlets from *Audacity*, then attacked and sunk by destroyers. *U-434* was sunk the following day, soon after the destroyer *Stanley* had been torpedoed and blown up with a huge sheet of flame. Walker raced to counter-attack, forced *U-434* to the surface, rammed and depth-charged her to destruction.

The U-boats scored their greatest success when they torpedoed and sank *Audacity*, a great loss to the defenders' firepower. Soon Walker's sloop was in collision with the *Deptford*, but both survived. Unknowingly *Deptford* had already destroyed Endrass's *U-567* in an earlier attack.

Despite the loss of *Audacity* and *Stanley*, the scales balanced strongly in favour of Walker and his escorts: four out of seven U-boats were sunk, against the loss of only one ship of the convoy.

## CONVOY ONS 5
### April/May 1943

The battle element of this convoy passage was fought over a period of six consecutive days between the B7 Escort Group led by Captain Peter Gretton, assisted by the US Navy's 3rd Support Group, and a wolf pack of about forty U-boats. Twelve merchant ships were sunk for the loss of seven U-boats, five to enemy action and two by collision. But most significantly, it was a decisive victory over wolf-pack tactics

and the end of the pack's ascendancy over escorts.

The convoy was a slow one of 6 knots, westbound, comprising 42 ships, with Gretton commanding the destroyer *Duncan*, a frigate and 4 corvettes. Seas were rough, weather bad and visibility poor — which grounded Iceland-based aircraft. Dönitz had organized a formidable concentration of forty U-boats which he named the *Fink* Group, comprising U-boats of the *Amsel* Group off Newfoundland, and of the *Star* and *Specht* Groups, to the north and east respectively.

Five attacks were fought off before a sixth sank a freighter at dawn on 29 April. Shortage of fuel compelled Gretton to hand over command to Lieutenant-Commander Sherbrooke in the frigate *Tay*. Other escorts were also detached, but reinforcements came with the US 3rd Escort Group.

By 5 May the U-boats gained an advantage and sank five ships in two hours, but the escorts' counter-measures damaged at least four U-boats. RCAF Catalinas helped keep U-boats submerged, as did continuing storms, but these same storms scattered the convoy. Two more ships were picked off in the main body of the convoy, and another two stragglers. Two more ships were lost that night, when the storm worked more to the radar advantage of the escorts than the part-blinded U-boats.

Five U-boats were sunk during 24 attacks on the convoy. *Oribi* and *Sunflower* rammed one each: *Snowflake* destroyed one with depth-charges. *Loosestrife* forced another to the surface with depth charges, and she then blew up. And *Vidette* sank one with her hedgehog. Several more were damaged, and another two collided and foundered.

May was the turning-point in the Atlantic battle, with U-boats being sunk at the rate of one a day.

## AZORES
### 31 August 1591

This action was fought between an English squadron of seven sail commanded by Lord Thomas Howard and a far superior Spanish squadron under Don Alonso de Bazan. *Defiance*, *Revenge* (flag of Sir Richard Grenville), *Nonpareil*, *Bonaventure*, *Lion*, *Foresight* and *Crane* had waited weeks off Flores to intercept a Spanish treasure fleet. But they were surprised on 31 August at anchor. Howard hurriedly stood out to sea with his ships and engaged in a running fight till darkness cloaked his escape — all except the *Revenge*: she remained to fight the Spaniards. She was hopelessly outnumbered. She fought for 15 hours. She sank two of the enemy. By daylight she was totally dismasted, all upperworks shot away, 40 crew killed and six feet of water in her hold. The severely wounded Grenville struck. Two days later he died — and the *Revenge* foundered in a storm.

## BANDA NEIRA

*9 August 1810*

This island of the Moluccas was captured by troops of the Madras European Regiment supported by *Caroline*, *Piedmontaise* and *Barracouta*.

## BANTRY BAY

*1 May 1689*

### War of the English Succession 1689—97

An unhappy engagement for the British commander, Admiral Arthur Herbert (later Earl of Torrington), who found his force outnumbered, badly positioned to leeward of the enemy in narrow waters with little sea-room. His force had been assembled hurriedly in Portsmouth, and it comprised the 70-gun *Elizabeth* (flag), sixteen more of the line (mainly smaller 50s and 60s) and three bomb vessels. The enemy was the Frenchman the Comte de Châtaurenault, who commanded a powerful fleet of twenty-four of the line and ten fireships. He had been dispatched by Louis XIV in April 1689 to Bantry Bay in Ireland with supplies and reinforcements further to support the exiled James II. This was the fleet discovered by Herbert on the morning of 1 May.

Châteaurenault weighed rapidly and with a favourable wind bore down on Herbert's ships, but despite holding all the trump cards he failed to win. Unco-operative subordinates and the absence of his fireships (which continued to unload stores) led the Frenchman to break off the engagement prematurely. Herbert, not believing his good fortune, turned about and got clear away.

## BARENTS SEA

*31 December 1942*

### World War II 1939—45

Captain R. St V. Sherbrooke earned a Victoria Cross for his gallantry in command of his destroyer flotilla in defence of Convoy JW 51B from Loch Ewe to Russia. Sherbrooke's own destroyer was the *Onslow* (1,540 tons, four 4.7"). Toward the end of 1942 the Admiralty adopted the plan of dispatching smaller groups of ships as convoys to Russia. Thus JW 51A was the first half of a convoy which reached Kola Inlet on Christmas Day: it was quickly followed by the other half, JW 51B. The awful severity of the Arctic weather, it was agreed, would help reduce the danger of air and U-boat attacks.

Sherbrooke led his six destroyers and five smaller warships from the anchorage with fourteen merchant ships. A severe gale part-scattered the convoy on the very day that Rear Admiral R.L. Burnett with the cruisers *Sheffield* (9,100 tons, 12—6") and *Jamaica* (8,000 tons, 12—6") left Kola to meet Sherbrooke halfway and give support.

Unluckily for them, *U-354* sighted the convoy on 30 December. Vice Admiral Kummetz, with his flag in the heavy cruiser *Admiral Hipper* (12,500 tons, eight 8") led the *Lützow* (12,750 tons, eight 8") and six destroyers to intercept. This force split. Burnett's cruisers had not established contact, and a day of utter confusion developed in atrocious weather conditions.

*Hipper* located the convoy, severely damaged the *Onslow*, blinding Sherbrooke in one eye, and overwhelmed the minesweeper *Bramble*. Snow squalls prevented the *Lützow* from annihilating the convoy and warships. *Hipper* attacked again, crippling the destroyer *Achates* (1,350 tons, 4—4.7") which continued to fight for another two hours before sinking.

Then fortune turned. Burnett came on the scene and promptly sank a destroyer and scored three hits on the *Hipper*. Kummetz turned about and headed back to Alten Fjord. *Lützow* fired from long range, but the action was over. The convoy reached Kola unharmed. The Germans suffered the price of hesitancy and the igominy of failure to press home their attack, for the convoy had been at their mercy.

## BARFLEUR

*19—22 May 1692*

### War of the English Succession 1689—97

Two years earlier the French admiral the Comte de Tourville had wrested superiority in the Channel from the English by his victory off Beachy Head. Now Barfleur and its dramatic sequel at La Hogue a few days later regained not only the Channel superiority for the English but settled decisively the Anglo-French naval struggle during the War of English Succession.

Exiled James II was preparing to regain his throne from a base in Cherbourg by invading England. Tourville awaited reinforcements, but as these failed to materialize he weighed from Brest with forty-four of the line (a few authorities have thirty-eight), entering the Channel on 17 May, but without the Toulon fleet back-up.

Unknown to him, Admiral Sir Edward Russell (later Lord Orford) had mustered a huge Anglo-Dutch fleet of just under one hundred ships of the line at Portsmouth. The two battle fleets sighted each other off Cap Barfleur on the Cotentin Peninsula. Russell wore his flag in the *Britannia* (100) and Tourville in his flagship, the *Soleil Royal* (104).[5] The two battle lines engaged, and fierce fighting ensued. Early in the afternoon a dense fog settled over the battle area. Tourville skilfully extricated his fleet and slowly drew away to the west. Both fleets anchored at nightfall, neither having lost a ship.

---

5  Depends which source you select for number of guns. Most sources vary between 102 and 106. I have chosen David Hannay's 104.

# THE DUTCH                    THE ENGLISH                    THE FRENCH

| White Squadron | Guns | Red Squadron | Guns | Blue Squadron | Guns | | Guns |
|---|---|---|---|---|---|---|---|
| The Zealand | 90 | The Royal William | 100 | The Victory | 100 | Bourbon | 64 |
| Konig Wilhelm | 92 | London | 100 | Albemarle | 90 | Monarque | 90 |
| Brandenburg | 92 | Britannia | 100 | Windsor Castle | 90 | Aimable | 68 |
| West Friesland | 84 | St. Andrew | 100 | Neptune | 90 | Saint Louis | 60 |
| Printz | 92 | Royal Sovereign | 100 | Vanguard | 90 | Diamant | 60 |
| Printzess | 92 | St. Michael | 90 | Duchess | 90 | Gaillard | 68 |
| Bexhirmer | 84 | Sandwich | 90 | Ossory | 90 | Terrible | 76 |
| Casteel Medenblick | 86 | Royal Catherine | 90 | Duke | 90 | Merveilleux | 94 |
| Captain General | 84 | Cambridge | 70 | Resolution | 70 | Tonnant | 76 |
| North Holland | 68 | Plymouth | 60 | Monk | 60 | Saint-Michel | 60 |
| Erste Edele | 74 | Breda | 80 | Expedition | 70 | Sans-Pareil | 62 |
| Munickendam | 72 | Kent | 70 | Royal Oak | 74 | Foudroyant | 82 |
| Gelderland, A | 72 | Swiftsure | 70 | Northumberland | 70 | Brilliant | 68 |
| Stadt Meeyden | 72 | Hampton Court | 70 | Lion | 60 | Fort | 60 |
| Etswout | 72 | Grafton | 70 | Berwick | 70 | Henri | 64 |
| Printz Casimir | 70 | Restoration | 70 | Defiance | 70 | Ambitieux | 96 |
| Frisia | 70 | Eagle | 70 | Montague | 60 | Couronne | 76 |
| Riddershap | 72 | Rupert | 60 | Warspight | 70 | Maure | 52 |
| De 7 Provintzen | 76 | Elizabeth | 70 | Monmouth | 70 | Sérieux | 68 |
| Zurick Zee | 60 | Burford | 70 | Edgar | 70 | Courageux | 58 |
| Gelderland, R | 64 | Captain | 70 | Stirling Castle | 70 | Perle | 56 |
| Vere | 62 | Devonshire | 80 | Dreadnought | 60 | Glorieux | 64 |
| Zealand, A | 64 | York | 60 | Suffolk | 70 | Conquérant | 84 |
| Haerlem | 64 | Lenox | 70 | Cornwall | 80 | Soleil Royal | 104 |
| Leyden | 64 | Ruby | 50 | Essex | 70 | Saint-Philippe | 84 |
| Amsterdam | 64 | Oxford | 50 | Hope | 70 | Admirable | 90 |
| Velew | 64 | St. Albans | 50 | Chathan | 50 | Content | 64 |
| Maegd van Dort | 64 | Greenwich | 50 | Advice | 50 | Souverain | 84 |
| Tergoes | 54 | Chester | 50 | Adventure | 50 | Illustre | 70 |
| Medenblick | 50 | Centurion | 50 | Crown | 50 | Modéré | 52 |
| Gaesterland | 50 | Bonaventure | 50 | Woolwich | 54 | Excellent | 60 |
| Ripperda | 50 | | | Deptford | 50 | Prince | 60 |
| Schattershoff | 50 | | | | | Magnifique | 76 |
| Stadden Land | 52 | | | | | Laurier | 64 |
| Hoorn | 50 | | | | | Brave | 58 |
| Delft | 54 | | | | | Entend | 60 |
| | | | | | | Triomphant | 76 |
| | | | | | | Orgueilleux | 94 |

The following morning Tourville continued sailing westward to the Channel Islands and Russell began a general chase. After the fleets had anchored again for the night the chase continued the following day (21st). Tourville shifted his flag to the *Ambitieux* (96).

The *Soleil Royal* went aground near Cherbourg, where she was trapped by Vice Admiral Sir Ralph Delavall on the 22nd with the Red Squadron. *Soleil Royal*, *Triomphant* (76) and *Admirable* (90) were all destroyed by fire.

Some 22 ships were chased by Admiral Sir John Ashby (Blue Squadron) through the race of Alderney into St Malo while others escaped towards the Bay of La Hogue, where the battle was fought to a bitter end. See LA HOGUE for the continuation.

The combined assembled fleets for the battle of Barfleur aggregated nearly 140 ships, with possibly the world's greatest clash at sea in prospect: three fleets waiting on a wind for fame or fortune — or crushing defeat. The rival fleets are shown in the table above.[6]

## BASQUE AND AIX ROADS (Oléron Roads)
### 11–16 April 1809

### Napoleonic War 1803–15

Rear Admiral Willaumez sailed with ten of the line from Brest southward to join a smaller French squadron already in the anchorage at Basque and Aix Roads but he was followed by Admiral Gambier's Channel Fleet and blockaded in the Roads.

The Admiralty determined to neutralize this threat in the Bay of Biscay and dispatched Lord Cochrane

6  See David Hannay's *A Short History of the Royal Navy*, Vol II 1689–1815.

with a force of fireships to join Gambier off Roche-fort.

The fireships and explosion vessels, each loaded with several hundred barrels of gunpowder, were launched on the night of 11–12 April. In the confusion of cutting cables and avoiding the dreaded fireships all but two of the French ships ran aground. However, the engagement lacked the success expected. Gambier declined to assist Cochrane till later the following day, when the *Varsovie* (80), *Aquilon* (74) and *Tonnerre* (80) were taken or burnt. Sporadic actions over the next few days were inconclusive. A great opportunity for a crushing victory was lost.

Cochrane opposed a parliamentary vote of thanks to Gambier, citing his excessive caution in battle. But he protested too much, continued to make a nuisance of himself, lost support and ruined his own career.

## BAY OF BISCAY — *see* CAPE ORTEGAL

## BEACHY HEAD
*30 June 1690*

### War of English Succession 1689–97

This battle won for the French temporary ascen-dancy in the Channel and disgrace to the English commander, Arthur Herbert, later Earl of Torring-ton. Herbert's Channel Fleet had been weakened by dispatching a squadron to the Mediterranean and other ships to support William III's vainglorious expedition to Ireland. Support came from an unlike-ly source — the Dutch, for they were allies of the English, and their van squadron under Admiral Cornelis Evertsen 'The Youngest' helped build Tor-rington's combined fleet to fifty-six ships.

The Comte de Tourville was sighted off the Lizard on 21 June with an awesome fleet of 77 ships bent-on blockading the Thames. On 25 June this fleet was off the Isle of Wight. Torrington, exercising his fleet, declined action and retired up-Channel, keeping his fleet 'in being'.

Four days later he received direct orders to engage the enemy. On 30 June, with his flag in *Royal Sovereign* (100), he committed his fleet off Beachy Head. The Allied fleet was ill organized: the Dutch van and English rear made half-hearted attacks independently, and both were mauled. Torrington in the centre kept at a long range to windward. In the evening the Allied fleet retired to the eastward, scuttling their own badly damaged ships — a 72, 70, 64, 60 and a 50 gun ship. De Tourville lost no ships.

When news reached London of the defeat there was panic. But incredibly de Tourville abandoned the pursuit, pleading sickness and lack of stores: he

BEACHY HEAD 1690

turned and headed back down the Channel. He burnt Teignmouth as if in a fit of pique.

When Torrington anchored off the Nore he was relieved of his command, and although acquitted at a later court martial, he was never employed again.

The French refer to the battle of Bévésiers, supposedly a corruption of Pevensey.

## BELLEISLE I

*7 June 1761*

### Seven Years' War 1756–63

The island was captured by troops of the Royal Artillery, Light Dragoons, 2 Marine battalions and numerous foot soldiers supported by ships, frigates, bombs and fireships under the command of Commodore the Hon. Augustus Keppel in HMS *Valiant*. This date is a Memorable Day observed by the Royal Marines.

## BELLEISLE II (Cornwallis's Retreat)

*17 June 1795*

### French Revolutionary War 1793–1802

Cornwallis displayed great skill in extricating his squadron from a superior enemy, without loss.

Vice Admiral William Cornwallis, with his flag in the *Royal Sovereign* (100), had four 74s and two frigates in company north of Belleisle in the Bay of Biscay when he was surprised by a powerful French squadron of twelve of the line, two 50s and nine frigates under Admiral Villaret-Joyeuse.

Cornwallis fled south under full sail, *Bellerophon* (74) and *Brunswick* (74) jettisoning gear to help speed their flight. Joyeuse's ships caught up, and a sporadic action ensued on 17 June in the course of which *Royal Sovereign* rescued the damaged *Mars* (74).

Captain Robert Stopford in the frigate *Phaeton* tricked Joyeuse by signalling to a non-existent British fleet. The French gave up the chase, and Cornwallis escaped, having suffered no ship losses.

## BENIN

*18 February 1897*

Benin in Nigeria was captured by a naval brigade and supporting ships commanded by Rear Admiral Sir Harry Rawson. His ships comprised *Alecto*, *Barrosa*, *Forte*, *Magpie*, *Philomel*, *Phoebe*, *St George*, *Theseus* and *Widgeon*. An Ashantee Medal Clasp 'Benin 1897' was issued.

## 'BISMARCK' ACTION

*23–27 May 1941*

### World War II 1939–45

The pursuit and sinking of the German 45,000-ton battleship *Bismarck* is a textbook model of command of the sea.

Accompanied by the heavy cruiser *Prinz Eugen* (12,750 tons, 8–8″), she broke out from her Gdynia base to attack North Atlantic convoys, under the command of Vice Admiral Lütjens. Both ships were intercepted by the patrolling cruisers *Suffolk* (9,800 tons, 8–8″) and *Norfolk* (9,925 tons, 8–8″) in the Denmark Strait, near the Greenland ice-edge.

Admiral Sir John Tovey, C-in-C Home Fleet, dispatched the battlecruiser *Hood* (42,100 tons, 8–15″) and newly commissioned battleship *Prince of Wales* (35,000 tons, 10–14″) under Vice Admiral Holland, then 220 miles to the SE to intercept the German squadron. Shortly before 6 a.m. on 24 May battle was joined at 25,000 yards. After ten minutes a 15 inch shell from *Bismarck* penetrated one of *Hood's* magazines and she blew up. Only three men out of more than 1,400 survived. *Prince of Wales* was damaged, but she scored two hits on *Bismarck*, one of which created a serious oil leak: small though it was, it became a significant influence in the options open to Lütjens later in the battle. When action was broken off the German admiral abandoned the Atlantic foray and headed for a French port.

Meanwhile Tovey deployed his forces: he sailed in *King George V* (35,000 tons, 10–14″) from Scapa with *Repulse* (32,000 tons, 6–15″, 20–4.5″), the carrier *Victorious* (23,000 tons, 35 aircraft), five cruisers and six destroyers, headed north: from convoy escort duty *Rodney* (33,900 tons, 9–16″) and *Ramillies* (29,150 tons, 8–15″), altered course to intercept. Command of the seas was being exercised.

Lütjens detached *Prinz Eugen* and she reached Brest independently, while *Bismarck* managed to give the slip to the shadowing British cruisers. After intensive searching a Catalina flying-boat of Coastal Command sighted *Bismarck* only 700 miles from Brest. Tovey detached the *Sheffield* to make contact and shadow while *Ark Royal* flew off a strike force of Swordfish aircraft which mistook the cruiser for the *Bismarck* and launched an abortive attack.

Late that evening another strike was launched and a torpedo from one of the fifteen attacking aircraft scored a crucial hit right aft which damaged *Bismarck's* propellers and jammed the rudder. This damage was to prove decisive. It gave Captain Vian commanding the 4th Destroyer Flotilla in the *Cossack* (1,870 tons, 8–4.7″) time to locate the battleship and launch torpedo attacks.

In the early hours of the following day — 27 May — Tovey in the *King George V* with *Rodney* closed with the *Bismarck* and awaited daylight rather than undertake a night action.

For two hours the British heavy ships pounded the German guns to silence. The cruiser *Dorsetshire* (9,975 tons, 8–8″) dispatched her with torpedoes and *Bismarck* sank at 10.36 a.m. 400 miles from Brest with her ensign still flying. Only 110 men from a crew of 2,400 were rescued by the *Dorsetshire* and *Maori* (1,870 tons, 8–4.7″).

Two incidents soured the victory. At Churchill's instigation Admiral Pound ordered *King George V* to remain on the scene even though running out of fuel: 'She must do so even if it means subsequently towing her home.' Had this been done, *Rodney* and the *KGV*, towed at 6–8 knots, would have been sacrificed to the Luftwaffe and Doenitz's U-boats. Pound had the good grace to apologize to Tovey for having allowed the signal to be sent.

The second incident originated in the same way. Churchill persuaded Pound to require Tovey to charge Admiral Wake-Walker of the *Norfolk* and Captain Leach of the *PoW* at court-martial for failing to engage the *Bismarck* during her run south. Tovey took unkindly to this injustice and threatened to haul down his flag so that he might stand as prisoner's friend to both these distinguished officers. That ended the matter.

During the *Bismarck* pursuit the German ship had been hunted by a total of seven battleships or battlecruisers, two aircraft carriers, twelve cruisers and numerous destroyers. She had been in combat at one time or another with the *Hood* and *Rodney*, the modern battleships *KGV* and *PoW*, with the heavy cruisers *Suffolk, Norfolk, Devonshire*; the two carriers *Victorious* and *Ark Royal* and with Vian's five destroyers.

## BRIDPORT'S ACTION — *see* GROIX, ÎLE DE

## BUGIA
*8 May 1671*

### War Against Mediterranean Piracy
Vice Admiral Sir Edward Spragge's squadron of six ships attacked and set afire seven warships and three Algerine corsairs in Bugia Bay (now Port de Bougie) in a daring daylight attack. His squadron also bombarded the town and castle, killing, it was estimated, upward of 360 people. 'Old Treky', as Spragge was known, was wounded in the action.

## CABARETA POINT — *see* MARBELLA

## CABRITA ISLAND — *see* MARBELLA

## CADIZ
*21 June 1596*

Until 1600 it was called Cales.
Lord Howard of Effingham commanded an English squadron which sacked Cadiz after capturing most of the shipping in the harbour. It was valued at the time at 12 million ducats (about £5m.)

## CALABRIA (Punto Stilo)
*9 July 1940*

### World War II 1939—45
The first capital-ship action in the Mediterranean off Calabria established British ascendancy over the Italians at the beginning of the war with Italy. The Royal Navy never relinquished the hold.

Admiral Sir Andrew B. Cunningham with the battleships *Warspite* (30,600 tons, 8—15″), *Malaya* (31,000 tons, 8—15″) and *Royal Sovereign* (29,150 tons, 8—15″), the carrier *Eagle* (36,800 tons, 100 aircraft) with escorting cruisers and destroyers gave cover to

two convoys from Malta to Alexandria.

Admiral Campioni's flagship, the battleship *Giulio Cesare* (23,622 tons, 10—12.6″), fought off an air strike from *Eagle*, but when the cruiser *Bolzano* (10,000 tons, 8—8″) and the flagship herself were struck from shells from *Warspite* Campioni broke off the action.

## CALDER'S ACTION (Cape Finisterre)
*22 July 1805*

### Napoleonic War 1803—15
Vice Admiral Calder's lack of resolution lost an opportunity to gain a significant victory: thus found the court-martial after his action of 22 July.

The action was the result of elaborate and skilful dispositions by Lord Barham at the Admiralty, intended to trap Admiral Villeneuve and prevent the concentration of Franco-Spanish fleets on Villeneuve's return to Europe from the West Indies.

Calder lay off Ferrol with ten of the line, soon reinforced by another five: he cruised 100 miles off Finisterre. Three days after taking up station, he made contact with Villeneuve and an indecisive action followed in the course of which Calder cut out and took two Spanish ships of the line — *Raphael* (80) and *Firme* (71) — and temporarily barred Villeneuve approaching Ferrol. But he evidently failed to demonstrate the offensive spirit the Admiralty deemed necessary. In sending him home for a court-martial, Nelson provided not the usual frigate, but the handsome three-decker *Prince of Wales*, as an unspoken appreciation of Calder's action. Calder was subsequently severely reprimanded at the court-martial.

## CAMEROONS
*September 1914*

### World War I 1914—18
Naval operations against Duala in the French Cameroons began this month. Duala was captured on the 27th. Ships which participated were: *Astraea, Challenger, Cumberland, Dwarf*, the Niger Flotilla comprising: *Alligator, Balbus, Crocodile, Ivy, Molesley, Porpoise, Remus, Vampire, Vigilant* and *Walrus*.

## CAMPERDOWN
*11 October 1797*

### French Revolutionary War 1793—1802
A main plank of the Admiralty's strategy of war was the maintaining of a continuous blockade of enemy ports. This confinement denied the enemy sea time while it ensured tremendous sea experience for the British fleet and its seamen.

Just such a blockade in the summer of 1797 by Admiral Adam Duncan herded the Dutch fleet in the Texel as if in a cattle pen. Even when his fleet retired for necessary refit and stores, Duncan left frigates on patrol: it was a late eighteenth century parallel of the twentieth-century blockading of *Tirpitz* and *Bismarck*.

Sure enough, the Dutch ships moved soon after

CAMPERDOWN 1797

Duncan sailed for the Yarmouth Roads in his flagship *Venerable* (74). The Dutch fleet of sixteen of the line and nine frigates under Vice Admiral Jan de Winter was shadowed by Captain Trollope in the *Russell* (74) with accompanying small squadron.

Duncan joined Trollope on the morning of 11 October and battle was joined soon after noon the same day, about three miles NW of Camperdown (Kamperdujin) on the Dutch coast.

The fleets were fairly evenly matched: eighteen of the line and seven frigates under de Winter: sixteen British of the line and eight frigates under Duncan. Duncan had the advantage of somewhat heavier guns and the weather gage. He closed at once in two squadrons, his own comprising eight of the line in line abreast attacking the Dutch van and Vice Admiral R. Onslow attacking the rear with ten ships.

A ferocious battle ensued over the next three and a half hours. Onslow's success was almost complete: Rear Admiral Reyntjes in the Dutch *Jupiter* (74), *Haarlem* (68), *Alkmaar* (56), *Delft* (56) and *Monnikendam* (44) all struck.

Duncan sought out de Winter's *Vrijheid* (74), lying fifth in the line. After hours of fighting, de Winter surrendered at 3.15 p.m., by which time he was the only unwounded man on deck. By then, too, four more of his ships had struck: *Hercules* (64), *Gelijkheid* (68), *Admiral Tjerk Hiddes de Vries* (68) and *Wassenaer* (64).

So heavy had been the casualties on both sides and so severe the damage to ships that with the approach of darkness Duncan headed off for base, but so damaged were some of the prizes that two

234

sank under tow to England and the others never saw sea service again.

## CAPE BON
*13 December 1941*
### World War II 1939—45
Four Allied destroyers: *Sikh* (1,870 tons, 8—4.7"), *Maori* (1,870 tons 8—4.7"), *Legion* (1,920 tons, 6—4.7") and the Dutch *Isaac Sweers* under the command of Commander G.H. Stokes sank the Italian cruisers *Alberto di Giussano* (5,069 tons, 8—6") and *Alberico da Barbiano* (5,069 tons, 8—6") in a brilliant night action in the early hours of 13 December 1941.

## CAPE FINISTERRE — *see* CALDER'S ACTION

## CAPE HENRY, ACTION OFF — *see* CHESAPEAKE I

## (CAPE) MATAPAN
*28—29 March 1941*
### World War II 1939—45
A night action fought off Cape Matapan by the British Mediterranean Fleet commanded by Admiral Sir Andrew B. Cunningham and units of the Italian Fleet under the overall command of Admiral Iachino.

Intelligence of an intended sortie by Italian naval forces against British convoys to Greece prompted Cunningham to dispatch four cruisers and four destroyers under Vice Admiral Pridham-Wippell to rendezvous with five more destroyers south of Crete.

Meanwhile Cunningham sailed from Alexandria

## BRITISH

*Isis*, 50, Capt. W. Mitchell
*Lancaster*, 64, Capt. J. Wells
*Belliqueux*, 64, Capt. J.Inglis
*Bedford*, 74, Capt. Sir T. Byard
*Ardent*, 64, Capt. R. Burgess
*Venerable*, 74, Adm. Duncan
*Triumph*, 74, Capt. W.H. Essington
*Veteran*, 64, Capt. G. Gregory
*Monarch*, 74, Vice-Adm. R. Onslow
*Powerful*, 74, Capt. W. O'Bryen Drury
*Director*, 64, Capt. W. Bligh
*Russell*, 74, Capt. H. Trollope
*Monmouth*, 64, Capt. J. Walker
*Montagu*, 74, Capt. J. Knight
*Adamant*, 50, Capt. W. Hotham
*Agincourt*, 64, Capt. J. Williamson

## DUTCH

*\*Gelijkheid*, 68, Capt. Ruyse
*Beschermer*, 56, Capt. Hinxtt
*\*Hercules*, 64, Capt. Rysoort
*\*De Vries*, 68, Capt. J.B. Zegers
*\*Vrijheid*, 74, Adm. de Winter
*States General*, 74, Adm. Storij
*\*Wassenaer*, 64, Capt. Holland
*Cerberus*, 68, Capt. Jacobson
*\*Jupiter*, 74, Adm. Reyntjes
*\*Haarlem*, 68, Capt. Wiggerts
*\*Alkmaar*, 56, Capt. Kraft
*\*Delft*, 56, Capt. Verdoorn
*\*Monnikendam*, 44, Capt. Lancaster
+*\*Embuscade*, 32, Capt. Huys
*Batavier*, 56, Capt. Souters
*Brutus*, 74, Adm. Bloys
*Leyden*, 68, Capt. Musquetier
*Mars*, 44, Capt. Kolff

## Frigates

*Beaulieu*
*Rose*
*King George*
*Active*
*Diligent*
*Speculator*
*Circe*
*Martin*

## Frigates

*Waaksaamheid*
*Minerva*
*Galatea*
*Atalanta*
*Heldin*
*Daphne*
*Ajax*

*Signifies captured ships.
+There is some doubt whether this ship participated in the battle.

CAPE MATAPAN 1941

with his flag in the *Warspite* (30,600 tons, 8–15"), *Barham* (31,100 tons, 8–15") and *Valiant* (32,700 tons, 8–15"), the carrier *Formidable* (23,000 tons, 36 aircraft) and nine escorting destroyers to give distant cover to Pridham-Wippell.

Air reconnaissance located an enemy force but it was not till after noon on 28 March that Cunningham knew this to be the battleship *Vittorio Veneto* (35,000 tons, 9–15"), nine cruisers and fourteen destroyers. Iachino realized he had lost the element of surprise, and being without air cover, he headed for base.

*Formidable* flew off a strike of torpedo aircraft to try to slow down the battleship, but it was the second strike at 3.15 which scored a hit on her port quarter and reduced her speed to 19 knots. A third strike failed to hit the enemy flagship, but the heavy cruiser *Pola* (10,000 tons, 8–8") was struck by a torpedo which brought her to a stop. Iachino detached the 8" heavy cruisers *Fiume* and *Zara* and a division of destroyers to stand by the stricken ship while he continued his westerly flight.

The British cruisers in the van of the British fleet reported at 9 p.m. a darkened ship as they sped past. It was the *Pola*.

Cunningham prepared to open fire when two more cruisers suddenly appeared, crossing the flagship's bows. Cunningham turned to starboard and the British battleships opened fire with their 15" broadsides at a point-blank range of 3,500 yards. Searchlights exposed the *Fiume* and *Zara* with guns trained fore and aft, totally unprepared for action. Both ships were reduced to blazing hulks and sank. An Italian destroyer, the *Vittorio Alfieri*, attempted a brave torpedo attack but was overwhelmed by gunfire from *Barham*. Another destroyer, the *Giosue Carducci*, was also sunk. Both were ships of 1,709 tons and 4–4.7" guns.

Later the crippled *Pola* was located and sunk, many of her crew being rescued.

Cunningham, characteristically, was disappointed that the damaged battleship had escaped destruction; but Matapan was a well-earned victory at a time when victories for Britain were hard to come by.

## CAPE OF GOOD HOPE I

*16 September 1795*

Vice Admiral Sir George Elphinstone (later Lord Keith) captured the Cape of Good Hope, commanding his squadron from HMS *Monarch*. The naval brigade which took part in the operations ashore came under the shore commander General Alfred Clark.

## CAPE OF GOOD HOPE II

*8–18 January 1806*

### Napoleonic War 1803–15

An expedition to capture Cape Town from the Dutch was assembled under the command of Commodore Sir Home Riggs Popham in the *Diadem* (64) with

*Raisonnable* (64), *Belliqueux* (64), *Diomède* (64) *Leda* (38), *Narcissus* (32), *Espoir* (18), *Encounter* (14) and later the brig *Protector*. This squadron covered the landing of an assault force of about 5,000 men under Major-General Sir George M. Keith. Most of the ships engaged shore batteries. The Dutch burnt their ship *Bato* (68) in Simon's Bay to avoid capture. The British naval losses were nil, and casualties were minimal.

## CAPE ORTEGAL (Strachan's Action; Bay of Biscay)

*4 November 1805*

### Napoleonic War 1803–15

Captain Sir Richard Strachan would have known the aphorism about what comes after the Lord Mayor's Show: the same could be applied to his action after Trafalgar. Fourteen days after the great battle Strachan in *Caesar* (80) led three 74s and four frigates straight into an encounter off Cape Ortegal, the north-west shoulder of Spain, with four French of the line, escapees from Trafalgar. The French declined action and a long chase ensued. Eventually Rear Admiral Dumanoir Le Pelley was compelled to fight, and after a fierce encounter all his ships struck: *Formidable* (80), *Duguay-Trouin* (74), *Mont Blanc* (74) and *Scipion* (74).

The *Duguay-Trouin* was eventually put into RN service as a boy's training ship, the *Implacable*, at Devonport from 1855 until as recently as 1949.

## CAPE PASSERO

*11 August 1718*

### War for Sicily 1718–20

Admiral Sir George Byng, later Viscount Torrington, won a significant sea victory over the Spanish even though the two countries were not at war.

The battle followed the Spanish invasion of Sicily and the foundation of the Quadruple Alliance in 1718. A large English fleet was dispatched to the Mediterranean with Byng wearing his flag in the *Barfleur* (90): altogether nineteen ships of the line.

The force arrived at Messina on 9 August 1718 and contact was made on the following day — over four months before a declaration of war — with a Spanish squadron off Cape Passero on the southern tip of Sicily. Vice Admiral Castañete's force comprised twelve of the line and several smaller ships. He wore his flag in the *Real San Felipe* (74).

Battle was joined on 11 August, and Byng's fleet overwhelmed the opposition in convincing style. No less than twenty-two Spanish ships were taken, burned or sunk, and the admiral himself died of wounds he received.

## CAPE ST VINCENT (The Moonlight Battle)

*16 January 1780*

### American War of Independence 1775–83

This was the renowned 'Moonlight Battle' that Rodney won while confined to his cabin with gout.

Admiral Sir George Rodney left Plymouth on 29 December 1799 with a powerful fleet of twenty-two of the line and nine frigates: this force escorted a convoy of reinforcements for besieged Gibraltar and the trade for the West Indies — where Rodney was to take command of the Leeward Islands station.

An enemy force, known as the Caracca fleet, commanded by Commodore Don Juan de Yardi, comprised the *Guipuscoana* (64), six frigates and a merchant convoy of sixteen ships bound for Cadiz with wheat and naval stores. On 8 January Rodney's fleet intercepted this force and captured it intact.

Rodney continued heading southward and eight days later when 12 miles south of Cape Finisterre he encountered a Spanish fleet commanded by Admiral Don Juan de Langara: it comprised eleven of the line and two frigates. Rodney immediately gave chase before a strong westerly wind and his van engaged the Spanish rear at about 4 p.m. An hour later the Spanish *San Domingo* (70) blew up with what must have been as shattering a blow as the loss of the *Hood* in 1941. Only one man survived from the 600 crew.

The battle continued though darkness fell, the blustery weather allowing a fine moon. Rodney exercised his two-to-one superiority, and by dawn six Spanish of the line had been taken: *Fenix* (80, and Langara's flagship), *San Julian* (70), *San Eugenio* (70), *Monarca* (70), *Princessa* (70) and *Diligente* (70).

The weather worsened, two of the prizes had to be abandoned, and only good seamanship extricated the British fleet from the dangerous lee shore.

## CAPE ST VINCENT II

*14 February 1797*

### French Revolutionary War 1793 – 1802

Jervis's naval victory at St Vincent was a classic. The enemy fleet was twice the size of his own. The number of guns marshalled by the Spanish ships of the line totalled 2,308, including the incredible 136 of the massive *Santissima Trinidad*. Jervis could muster 1,232.

But he could also muster a 'band of brothers' of incomparable courage and tactical skills: Commodore Nelson in his *Captain* (74) twice excelled himself in the battle, ensuring victory; Troubridge in *Culloden* (74); Parker in the *Prince George* (98); James Saumarez in *Orion* (74); Collingwood in the *Excellent* (74).

A large but undermanned Spanish fleet under Admiral de Cordova left Cartagena for Cadiz. He commanded twenty-seven of the line — including his great flagship and six 112s — plus twelve frigates.

Jervis weighed from Lisbon's Tagus on 18 January in the *Victory* (100), plus fourteen of the line and four frigates and sailed to cruise off Cape St Vincent and intercept Cordova. On 13 February he was joined by Nelson from Gibraltar.

When the fog lifted off Cape St Vincent the following morning the Spanish fleet was seen to be straggling in two divisions. Jervis's fleet attacked at the gap between divisions, and *Culloden* led to attack the weather division. Confusion spread among the Spanish ships, but led by the *Santissima Trinidad* they threatened to escape astern of the English column.

Nelson, in his *Captain*, third ship from the English rear, saw the threat, pulled out of line across *Excellent's* bows and at great risk of being blown to smithereens, crossed the line of advance of Cordova's giant flagship and 112s. Perhaps more importantly, Nelson's tactic was totally contrary to the *Fighting Instructions*. No signal had yet been broken out that ships might act independently, however obvious the need. Nelson had the courage to do so. The *Captain* had her wheel and foremast shot away, but Nelson managed to place her alongside the *San Nicolas* (84) which herself had fouled the 112 *San Josef*. Both were heavily engaged with HMS *Prince George*.

Nelson boarded and captured the *San Nicolas*, then, using her as his 'patent bridge for capturing enemies', boarded and captured the *San Josef* too.

This brilliant tactic increased the enemy confusion, and Jervis took advantage of it. After an hour of battle the *Salvador del Mundo* (112) and *San Ysidro* (74) struck. At one time the *Santissima Trinidad* was threatened with capture but managed to extricate herself. Cordova made good his escape to Cadiz and Jervis was happy enough with his four great prizes and returned home in triumph.

## LIST OF SHIPS ENGAGED AT THE BATTLE OF ST VINCENT[7]

### BRITISH

| Ship | Guns | Commander |
|---|---|---|
| *Victory* | 100 | Admiral Sir John Jervis |
| | | Captain R. Calder |
| *Captain* | 74 | Commodore H. Nelson |
| | | Captain R.W. Miller |
| *Blenheim* | 90 | T.L. Frederick |
| *Culloden* | 74 | T. Troubridge |
| *Excellent* | 74 | C. Collingwood |
| *Irresistible* | 74 | G. Martin |
| *Prince George* | 98 | Rear-Admiral Parker |
| | | Captain V.T. Irwin |
| *Orion* | 74 | Sir J. Saumarez |
| *Goliath* | 74 | Sir C.H. Knowles |
| *Namur* | 90 | J.H. Whitshed |
| *Barfleur* | 98 | Vice-Admiral Waldegrave |
| | | Captain J.R. Dacres |
| *Colossus* | 74 | G. Murray |
| *Diadem* | 64 | G.H. Towry |
| *Egmont* | 74 | J. Sutton |
| *Britannia* | 100 | Vice-Admiral Thompson |
| | | Captain T. Foley |

7  The best source is Oliver Warner's *Camperdown and St Vincent*, Batsford, 1963, though there are several compelling rival accounts.

| | | |
|---|---|---|
| Lively | 32 | Lord Garlies |
| La Minerve | 38 | G. Cockburn |
| Niger | 32 | E.J. Foote |
| Southampton | 32 | J. McNamara |
| La Bonne Citoyenne | 18 | C. Lindsay |
| Raven brig | 18 | W. Prowse |
| Fox cutter | 12 | Lt.Gibson |

## SPANISH

| | | |
|---|---|---|
| Atlante | 74 | G. Vallego |
| Bahama | 74 | Admiral D.de Nava |
| Pelayo | 74 | C. Valdes |
| San Pablo | 74 | B.de Cisneros |
| Neptuno | 84 | J.L. Goicoechea |
| Concepcion | 112 | Admiral Morales de los Rios |
| San Domingo | 74 | M. de Torres |
| Conquistadore | 74 | J. Butler |
| San Juan Nepomuceno | 74 | A. Boneo |
| San Genaro | 74 | A. Villavicencio |
| Mexicano | 112 | Admiral P. de Cardenas |
| Terrible | 74 | F. Uriarte |
| Oriente | 74 | J. Suarez |
| Soberano | 74 | J.V. Yanez |
| Santissima Trinidad | 136 | Admiral J. de Cordova |
| *San Nicolas | 84 | T. Geraldino |
| *San Ysidro | 74 | D.T. Argumosa |
| *Salvador del Mundo | 112 | D.A. Yepes |
| *San Josef | 112 | Admiral F.J. Winthuysen |
| San Ildefonso | 74 | R. Maestre |
| Conde de Regla | 112 | Admiral P. de Cardenas |
| San Firmin | 74 | J.de Torres |
| Principe de Asturias | 112 | Admiral J.J. Moreno |
| San Antonio | 74 | S. Medina |
| San Francisco de Paulo | 74 | J. de Guimbarda |
| Firme | 74 | B. Ayala |
| Glorioso | 74 | J. Aguizze |

### Frigates

| | | | | |
|---|---|---|---|---|
| Brigida | 34 | | Asuncion | 28 |
| Perla | 34 | | San Justa | 18 |
| Mercedes | 34 | | San Balbino | 20 |
| Vigilante brig | 12 | | San Paulo | 20 |
| Matilda | 34 | | Atocha | 34 |
| Diana | 34 | | Ceres | 34 |

*Signifies captured ship

## CAPE SPADA — see SPADA

## CAPE SPARTIVENTO
*27 November 1940*
### World War II 1939−45
Admiral Sir James Somerville commanding Force H was entrusted with the passage of a convoy of three important merchant ships carrying tanks and other mechanical transport to the Middle East. With his flag in *Renown* (32,000 tons, 6−15"), he had in company *Ark Royal* (22,000 tons, 36 aircraft), two cruisers and nine destroyers. Four corvettes gave close escort to the merchantmen.

Off Cape Spartivento an Italian squadron commanded by Admiral Campioni was encountered. It consisted of the two battleships *Vittorio Veneto* (35,000 tons, 9−15") and *Guilio Cesare* (23,622 tons, 10−12.6"), seven heavy cruisers and sixteen destroyers.

An hour's engagement in which the *Berwick* (9,750 tons, 8−8") and the Italian destroyer *Lanciere* (1,620 tons, 4−4.7") were damaged and two air strikes failed, proved inconclusive to both sides. Campioni broke away, and because Somerville failed to pursue, a Board of Enquiry arrived in Gibraltar even before Somerville had returned to port to question the correctness of putting the safety of the convoy as the first consideration. Cunningham objected at this iniquitous action by the Admiralty. The Board's decision was totally in favour of Somerville's action.

## CAPE TENEZ
*4 February 1805*
### Napoleonic War 1803−15
*Arrow* (18) and *Acheron* (8) were giving protection to a convoy of 32 sail in a position about 30 miles NW off Cape Tenez in Algeria when they were attacked by the superior French ships *Hortense* and *Incorruptible*. Three of the merchant ships were taken as well as the two warships, *Arrow* sinking immediately after capture and *Acheron* fired by the French.

## CAPE TOWN
*10 January 1810*
### Napoleonic War 1803−15
The town capitulated to land forces under the command of Major-General Sir David Baird and seaborne forces commanded by Commodore Sir Home Riggs Popham in HMS *Diadem*. A naval brigade landed. The following ships took part: *Belliqueux, Diadem, Diomède, Encounter, Espoir, Leda, Protector* and *Raisonnable*.

## CAP FRANÇOIS
*21 October 1757*
### Seven Years' War 1756−63
Captain Arthur Forrest commanded a small squad-

ron comprising *Augusta* (60), *Edinburgh* (64) and *Dreadnought* (60) which fought gallantly against a more powerful French squadron off the north coast of San Domingo near the French naval base of Cap François. Forrest awaited a convoy, but met instead Admiral de Kersaint's squadron of *Intrépide* (74), *Sceptre* (74), *Opiniâtre* (64), a 50 and three frigates. A fierce 2½-hour engagement followed and both sides suffered severe damage. De Kersaint retired to his base and Forrest to Port Royal where it took weeks to restore the ships to fighting fitness. By which time the French convoy had made good its departure.

## CARTAGENA (Wager's Action)
*28 May 1708*

### War of the Spanish Succession 1702—13

Commodore Charles Wager with the *Expedition* (70), *Kingston* (60), *Portland* (50) and a fireship encountered a Spanish treasure squadron off Cartagena. The enemy force comprised two 64s, two 5th rates and eight smaller vessels.

After sunset on 28 May Wager brought the enemy flagship to action, and after 90 minutes the *San Josef* blew up, taking with her 600 men and a fortune in treasure. Another ship was captured, but she was treasureless, while yet another was run aground and lost.

The captains of the *Kingston* and *Portland* failed to give Wager the support he expected: they were both court-martialled and dismissed their ships.

## CATTARO
*5 January 1814*

### Napoleonic War 1803—15

*Bacchante* and *Saracen* captured the town and port of Cattaro (Kotor) in Yugoslavia.

## CAYENNE
*14 January 1809*

### Napoleonic War 1803—15

Captain James Lucas Yeo in HMS *Confiance* supported by Portuguese troops captured Cayenne in French New Guinea.

## CHANNEL DASH
*12 February 1942*

### World War II 1939—45

An audacious and meticulously planned 'escape' of the German battlecruisers *Scharnhorst* and *Gneisenau* (both 31,800 tons, 9—11″) and the heavy cruiser *Prinz Eugen* (12,750 tons, 8—8″) occurred in the Channel, as humiliating as Tromp's broom at the masthead.

Vice Admiral Ciliax commanded the operation, taking the German squadron from the Atlantic port of Brest up-Channel through the narrow waters of the Straits of Dover to Wilhelmshaven and Kiel. The force was escorted by six destroyers, MTBs, minesweepers and aircraft of Luftflotte 3.

British opposition took the form of coastal batter-

CARTAGENA 1708

ies near Dover, attacks by MTBs, destroyer torpedo attacks from a flotilla of six from Harwich and attacks by torpedo-carrying Swordfish in the course of which Lieutenant-Commander Esmonde won a posthumous VC.

All these endeavours failed to stop the warships. In addition *Scharnhorst* was struck by three mines and *Gneisenau* by one. The Channel Dash was a masterly German success.

## CHESAPEAKE I (Action off Cape Henry)
### 16 March 1781

### American War of Independence 1775—83

This first, and unsatisfactory, encounter at sea in the American War of Independence took place about 40 miles NE of Cape Henry in Chesapeake Bay. It was fought between a French squadron commanded by Commodore des Touche, who on balance won a tactical victory, and a British squadron commanded by Rear Admiral Marriott Arbuthnot, who was left with temporary command of the bay.

The French flagship *Duc de Bourgogne* (80) with seven more of the line and two frigates met Arbuthnot's eight of the line and four frigates in thick haze off Cape Henry. And thus began the first of two naval encounters in the bay in 1781 between French and British squadrons, both arising from British attempts to prevent French aid reaching America.

After an hour's exchange of gunfire the French line broke and the French ships stood out to sea to clear the battle area. Arbuthnot's leading ships were severely disabled, having borne the brunt of the battle. As each squadron lost the other in the haze, the encounter petered out. Neither commander could be overly pleased with his performance, but at least Arbuthnot stood in command of the bay. Nevertheless, because of his failure to achieve a conclusive victory, the battle was to have significant consequences.

## CHESAPEAKE II
### 2 September 1781

### American War of Independence 1775—83

This second Chesapeake battle was more crucial than the first. If ever an admiral helped to lose a land battle, then Rear Admiral Thomas Graves was such a man. The pity of it was that the land commander was Cornwallis, his surrender was at Yorktown, and with it American independence from the British was assured.

By the time the battle was fought there had been a concentration of enemy land forces investing the British troops at Yorktown.

At sea the French Admiral Comte de Grasse had brought his Caribbean fleet of twenty-four of the line to Chesapeake Bay. In response Admiral Rodney despatched his second-in-command, Rear Admiral Samuel Hood, with fourteen of the line to reinforce Graves, who eventually assumed command of a force comprising nineteen of the line in the *London* (98), with Hood commanding the rear and Rear Admiral Drake the van.

De Grasse's fleet was located at anchor just inside the bay. Graves was well aware of the gravity of the battle in prospect. He may well have had in mind Byng's end after his tactical blunder at Minorca in 1756. Yet, despite having the advantage of weather, of formation and of surprise, he made a faulty approach, so that after two and half hours of indecisive action Hood's division had not yet become engaged. The action had called for a Jervis or Collingwood; the Nelson touch. It got instead indecision and lack of resolution, and it brought about a spasmodic battling over several days, in the course of which the badly damaged *Terrible* (74) had to be sunk.

De Grasse himself seemed reluctant to engage too closely, but his primary task was to reinforce the besieged American armies. On 11 September he re-entered the bay. Graves held a Council of War on the 13th: in view of the poor state of the British ships, the lack of bread and water, it was resolved to return to New York to refit. Graves retired north and left de Grasse in command of Chesapeake Bay. The way was clear for Cornwallis's defeat and surrender in the following month — and the loss of the American colonies.

## 'CHESAPEAKE' v 'SHANNON'
### 1 June 1813

In the Naval War of 1812 the few ships of the new United States Navy took on the might of the Royal Navy in a long series of mainly single-ship actions which included the following:

> British frigate *Guerrière* (46 small guns) captured by the superior American ship *Constitution* (54), August 1812.
> British brig *Frolic* captured by the American sloop *Wasp*, October 1812.
> British frigate *Macedonia* taken by the American ship *United States*, mounting large carronades, after a two-hour action, October 1812.
> British frigate *Java* taken by the American ship *Constitution* after an engagement of three-quarters of an hour manoeuvring and two hours' battle at close range, December 1812.
> British sloop *Peacock* captured by the American ship *Hornet:* she finally sank with a heavy loss of life.

The battle between the *Chesapeake* and the *Shannon* was in a class of its own. The American frigate was one of six original frigates authorized in 1794 as the basis of the United States Navy. Though often classified as a 50-gun ship, she was in fact fitted out with 36. She carried 376 men, and she was commanded by Captain James Lawrence.

The British ship was a 38-gun frigate manned by 330 men, and commanded by Captain Peter Vere

CHESAPEAKE v. SHANNON 1813

Broke. Broke sought out the *Chesapeake* (which was lying off Boston) and sent Lawrence a challenging letter: 'Sir, As the *Chesapeake* appears now ready for sea, I request that you will do me the favor to meet the *Shannon* with her ship to ship to try the fortune of our respective ships . . . ' So began his courteous letter.

Lawrence sailed that day, and fate ensured him fame and honour in the most celebrated single-ship action in the annals of the Royal Navy.

After an eleven-minute battle of the fiercest intensity imaginable[8] Broke's men boarded the battered US frigate, and after another four minutes the *Chesapeake* struck. Lawrence was mortally wounded. Broke took the captured frigate to Halifax, and later she was brought to Britain.

## CHINA SEA — *see* FORCE Z

## COPENHAGEN
*2 April 1801*

### French Revolutionary War 1793–1802

This celebrated British naval victory is attributed to Nelson's meticulous planning and tenacious execu-

tion, but it is also well known as the occasion of his blind eye gesture. The battle came about through the British efforts to obstruct a coalition of northern powers.

Admiral Sir Hyde Parker commanded a Baltic Fleet comprising eighteen of the line and thirty-five smaller vessels. Vice Admiral Nelson was second-in-command. Their orders were to attack the Danish fleet in the strongly defended harbour of Copenhagen. Hyde Parker allocated twelve of the line, five frigates, two sloops, five bomb vessels and two fireships to Nelson, who was to lead the attack.

On 1 April 1801 Nelson negotiated the Outer Channel and positioned his squadron just two miles from the formidable Danish line of eighteen warships, hulks and floating batteries. Moored near the Trekroner fortress by the harbour entrance lay four battleships and supporting vessels.

Nelson's plan was to lead ten of his ships plus all the frigates in the narrow King's Deep Channel and anchor the *Edgar* (74) opposite the Danish fifth in line while each succeeding ship passed her on the disengaged side to take up position.

The operation began on the morning of 2 April, but before *Edgar* was in position the plan had already gone awry, in part at least; *Bellona* (74) and *Russell*

---

8    In the eleven minutes of battle between Cape Ann and Cape Cod more men were killed or wounded per minute (10 per minute) than in all of Nelson's and Villeneuve's great ships combined at the battle of Trafalgar. See Peter Padfield's *Broke And The Shannon*, p.244.

(74) were stranded on the Middle Ground Shoal and *Agamemnon* (74) was unable to occupy her position.

With the remaining ships in position a fierce bombardment of the Danish defences began. When the Danish Admiral Fischer's flagship *Dannebrog* was set ablaze he shifted his flag to the *Holstein.*

Soon Hyde Parker signalled 'Discontinue the engagement' and Nelson employed his blind-eye act, though Captain Riou of the *Amazon* (38) obeyed and was withdrawing his frigate when he was killed.

Danish resistance began to falter; the burning flagship blew up; two more ships cut their cables and foundered. Sporadic fire came from various ships as English boats sought prizes, but a cease fire was agreed and Nelson began a difficult extrication of his ships, two more of which ran aground.

Casualties on both sides were very heavy because the Danish resistance was more defiant than expected. A commander other than Nelson could well have withdrawn early, with no discredit.

## CORAL SEA
*4−8 May 1942*

### World War II 1939−45

A battle south of the Solomon Islands waged by Task Force 17 under the command of Rear Admiral F.J. Fletcher USN, which defeated a force of Japanese ships and thus removed the threat of invasion from North Australia. It was the first major action in which only aircraft carriers were engaged and in which the heavy surface escorts never sighted each other. The two Australian cruisers engaged were *Australia* and *Hobart.*

## CORNWALLIS'S RETREAT — *see* BELLEISLE II

## CORONEL
*1 November 1914*

### World War I 1914−18

The battle of Coronel was a decisive defeat for the Royal Navy redeemed only by the retaliatory victory of the Falklands one month later.

The German Vice Admiral Graf von Spee wore his flag in the armoured cruiser *Scharnhorst* (11,420 tons, 8−8"): he had under his command the *Gneisenau,* the flagship's sister-ship, and the light cruiser *Nürnberg* (3,350 tons, 10−4.1"), the three of them forming the East Asiatic Squadron. At the outbreak of war von Spee was obliged by British and Japanese naval superiority to operate in South American waters. En route there he was reinforced at the Easter Islands by the light cruisers *Dresden* and *Leipzig* (both 3,544 tons, 12−4.1").

Rear Admiral Sir Christopher Cradock commanded the South American squadron comprising the old armoured cruisers *Good Hope* (flagship, 14,100 tons, 2−9.2" and 16−6") and *Monmouth* (9,800 tons, 14−6"), the light cruiser *Glasgow* (4,800 tons, 2−6" & 10−4"), and an armed merchant cruiser, the *Otranto* (12,128 tons, 8−4.7"). The Admiralty was aware of von Spee's movements and reinforced Cradock with the old and slow pre-dreadnought *Canopus* (12,950 tons, 4−12" and 12−6"). Comfortingly, she had 12" guns.

Cradock sailed — without the *Canopus* — from the Falklands to locate von Spee, and von Spee left Valparaiso and headed south. The opposing squadrons met at nearly 5 p.m. on 1 November, fifty miles off Coronel, each flagship believing the other to be a single ship unaccompanied. Von Spee had every advantage: power, speed, modernity, setting sun silhouetting the British ships.

The accuracy of the German gunnery was awe-inspiring: the British futile. By 8 p.m. the *Good Hope* had blown up, and an hour later the *Monmouth* went down. No one survived. The *Glasgow* and *Otranto* managed to escape under cover of darkness. The German ships suffered neither casualties nor damage.

## CRETE
*May 1941*

### World War II 1939−45

The Royal Navy fought vicious battles against the German Luftwaffe during the evacuation of troops from Greece, the defence of the island of Crete and the subsequent evacuation of British and Commonwealth troops from the island. The battles were spread over many days and resulted in heavy losses and casualties to the Mediterranean Fleet, commanded by Admiral Sir Andrew Cunningham from the naval base at Alexandria.

The admirals most closely associated with these actions were Vice Admiral Pridham-Wippell, Rear Admiral King, Rear Admiral Rawlings and Rear Admiral Glennie. The destroyer flotillas most heavily engaged were the 5th (Mountbatten), 10th (Walker) and 14th (Mack). The cost of the defence of the island of Crete[9] and evacuations from both Greece and Crete in terms of ships and personnel is as follows:

**Warships Sunk:**
**Cruisers:**
*Calcutta* (4,200 tons) *Gloucester* (9,600 tons) — 725 men lost with her. *Fiji* (8,000 tons)

**Destroyers:**
*Kashmir* (1,690 tons) *Hereward* (1,340 tons)
*Kelly* (1,695 tons) *Greyhound* (1,335 tons)
*Juno* (1,690 tons) *Diamond* (1,370 tons)
*Imperial* (1,370 tons) *Wryneck* (1,100 tons)

---

9 The German capture of the island was a triumph. Never before nor since has an island been conquered from the air. It was a decisive success for the Luftwaffe, a damaging defeat for the Mediterranean Fleet: an important signpost to the dominance of air power at sea.

**Ships damaged included:**

*Warspite, Valiant, Barham, Formidable, Orion, Ajax, Perth, Dido, Naiad, Coventry, Carlisle* and nine other destroyers.

**Killed and Missing:** 2,261 — with many hundreds more wounded.

## CUDDALORE I (Sadras)

*29 April 1758*

### Seven Years' War 1756−63

This was hardly a battle, more like a scrappy indecisive encounter, with some damage to both sides.

The French had a base at Pondicherry on the Coromandel coast of SE India, and the British had one at nearby Cuddalore, south of Madras fronting on to the Bay of Bengal. The French Admiral Comte D'Aché in his flagship *Zodiaque* (74) and Vice Admiral Pocock with the *Yarmouth* (64) commanded the respective light squadrons.

In this encounter, both admirals surprised each other and neither could gain an advantage. If anything D'Aché came off best, having forced two British frigates ashore, but it was he who called off the fight and retired north to Pondicherry.

## CUDDALORE II

*20 June 1783*

### American War of Independence 1775−83

It was Vice Admiral Hughes's misfortune in war to fight no less than five naval battles, all of them against the French, but worst of all, all against that brilliant tactician Admiral Suffren. (See SADRAS, PROVIDIEN, NEGAPATAM and TRINCOMALEE). Cuddalore was the last of the five.

Sir Edward Hughes wore his flag in the *Superb* (74) and he had eighteen of the line with him as he sought Pierre André de Suffren with his fifteen of the line outside Cuddalore, which was presently occupied by the French. Nearly three days were spent in manoeuvring for advantage in the unfavourable conditions. Then on 20 June battle was joined. It ended three hours later with no losses on either side. Hughes retired north to Madras, having yet again failed to gain an advantage over the Frenchman. A little later Suffren was able to raise the blockade of Cuddalore.

## CURAÇOA

*1 January 1807*

### Napoleonic War 1803−15

The island was captured by the ships *Anson, Arethusa, Fisgard, Latona* and *Morne Fortunée*.

## DAKAR

*23−25 September 1940*

### World War II 1939−45

An attempt to land troops to take possession of the French African colonies and to take charge of French warships at the fall of France led to the action at Dakar.

Vice Admiral John H.D. Cunningham commanded a force comprising the battleships *Barham* (31,100 tons, 8−15″), *Resolution* (29,150 tons 8−15″), the carrier *Ark Royal* (22,000 tons, 36 aircraft), the heavy cruiser *Devonshire* (9,850 tons, 8−8″), *Cumberland* (9,750 tons, 8−8″), and *Australia* (9,870 tons, 8−8″) and six destroyers.

At Dakar the French had an unseaworthy battleship, *Richelieu* (35,000 tons, 8−15″), the cruisers *Georges Leygues* (7,600 tons, 9−6″) and *Montcalm* (7,600 tons, 9−6″), two destroyers and three submarines.

Over a period of two days the submarines *Persée* and *Ajax* and the destroyer *L'Audacieux* (2,569 tons, 5−5.5′) were sunk and many other ships damaged. The *Resolution* received a torpedo hit, the *Barham* and *Cumberland* were both damaged. Cunningham abandoned the unhappy operation and withdrew.

## DENMARK STRAIT — *see* 'BISMARCK' ACTION

## DE RUYTER IN THE THAMES — *see* MEDWAY

## DIEGO SUAREZ

*5−7 May 1942*

### World War II 1939−45

Madagascar was occupied by Vichy French forces, and the decision was taken to capture the island by a direct attack on Diego Suarez. It capitulated on 7 May after 60 hours of attack. Rear Admiral E.N. Syfret commanded the operation aboard HMS *Ramillies* while Major-General R.G. Sturges commanded the troops and RMs. *Devonshire* and destroyers covered the landings. Aircraft from *Illustrious* and *Indomitable* attacked the harbour and airfield.

The destroyer *Anthony* landed 50 marines at the Naval Base and they were embarrassed by the large number of prisoners. Ten minutes' bombardment of the coastal defences by *Ramillies* soon secured surrender. The only British loss of ships was the corvette *Auricula* sunk by a mine.

## DIEPPE

*19 August 1942*

### World War II 1939−45

The assault by seaborne forces on Dieppe was a rehearsal for the Second Front. It was commanded by Captain J. Hughes-Hallett aboard HMS *Calpe* and Major-General J.H. Roberts (Canadian Division). Operation Jubilee was mounted specially to give battle experience to Canadian troops and to test techniques and weaponry. 237 naval vessels were employed. 4,961 Canadians plus 1,057 Commandos and some US Rangers were used. 67 squadrons of aircraft were also employed in the battle. Fighting was fierce and casualties were very heavy. The *Berkeley* was sunk. 33 landing-craft were lost. 3,363 Canadians and 607 Commandos became casualties. 106 British aircraft were lost. The Germans lost 48 aircraft and suffered only 600 casualties from all services.

19 August is the Memorable Date for 40 Commando Royal Marines. Many important lessons were learnt and probably thousands of lives saved in future operations such as Normandy two years later by the sacrifices at Dieppe.

## DISASTER OF THE SMYRNA CONVOY —
*see* LAGOS I

## DOGGER BANK I
*5 August 1781*

### American War of Independence 1775—83

A bitterly fought action off the Dogger Bank about 60 miles east of Northumberland between Captain (later Admiral Sir) Hyde Parker and the traditional enemy — the Dutch — in the form of Rear Admiral Zontman, each admiral escorting a convoy of merchantmen.

They were evenly matched antagonists: *Fortitude* (74) and six of the line against *Admirael de Ruijter* (68) and six of the line.

Each convoy managed to disperse clear of the battle area, the British to England and the Dutch to the Texel.

The battle saw neither side gain an advantage, and though losses were small each exhausted squadron was relieved to break off the action. The Dutch *Hollandie* (64) suffered so severely that she failed to make port.

## DOGGER BANK II
*24 January 1915*

### World War I 1914—18

Although this was a British naval victory, a tactical error saved the German squadron from suffering a considerable mauling.

Rear Admiral Franz von Hipper sailed from Wilhelmshaven with the objective of attacking British patrols in the area of the Dogger Bank. He took a formidable force of battlecruisers: the First Scouting Group, *Seydlitz* (flag: 25,000 tons, 10—11″), *Moltke* (23,000 tons, 10—11″), *Derfflinger* (28,000 tons, 8—12″), together with the armoured cruiser *Blücher* (15,500 tons, 12—8.2″) accompanied by four light cruisers and two destroyer flotillas.

Acting Vice Admiral Sir David Beatty's battlecruiser force was despatched from Rosyth, augmented by the Harwich force commanded by Commodore R.Y.Tyrwhitt. It was Beatty's purpose to position his force between Hipper and his base. Beatty had the battlecruisers *Lion* (26,350 tons, 8—13.5″), *Tiger* (27,000 tons, 8—13.5″), *Princess Royal* (same class as *Lion* ), *New Zealand* (18,800 tons, 8—12′) and *Indomitable* (17,250 tons, 8—12″), escorted by the 1st Light Cruiser Squadron and torpedo boats.

Hipper's force was sighted early on 24 January and a high-speed action ensued in the course of which the *Seydlitz* was struck by a 13.5″ shell from *Lion*, silencing her X and Y turrets and killing 160 men. The *Blücher* was also hit and began to lose way. The German force seemed to be in grave danger.

Then three shells struck *Lion* and she rapidly fell astern. Rear Admiral Arthur Moore in *New Zealand* assumed command of the pursuit, but concentrated the fire of his whole squadron on the crippled *Blücher* instead of pursuing the remainder of Hipper's force. *Blücher* capsized and sank after three hours of indescribable punishment: only 189 of her crew were rescued. By then the opportunity of destroying the rest of the squadron had gone.

*Lion* was towed back to harbour. The total British casualties were 15 killed and 80 wounded. Hipper lost 954 killed and hundreds more wounded. Germany learned a lesson from the battle, the need to prevent flash from bursting shells reaching magazines: their capital ships were rendered safe. Not so the British, and it cost the Navy five major capital ships at Jutland 16 months later.

## DOMINICA I
*17 April 1780*

### American War of Independence 1775—83

Misinterpretation of a crucial signal denied Admiral Rodney a victory over the French Admiral de Guichen.

Rodney's appointment as C-in-C of the Leeward Islands station coincided with the arrival of strong French reinforcements in the West Indies. On 13 April de Guichen left Fort Royal with no less than 23 of the line, five frigates and merchantmen crammed with 3,000 troops to attack Barbados.

Three days later this force was intercepted by Rodney in the *Sandwich* (90) plus twenty of the line. There was plenty of sea-room, two great naval tacticians, and the prospect of battle. After much fleet manoeuvring, Rodney — whose intention was to attack the enemy's rear and centre — signalled 'Every ship to bear down and steer for her opposite in the enemy's line', followed five minutes later with 'Engage'. The signals were completely misunderstood. Captain Carkett in the *Stirling Castle* leading the van division took it to mean his numerical opposite in the order, and maintained full sail to reach that position, followed by the rest of his division.

Rodney intended the signal to mean the opposite in the line at the time of the 'Engage'. The result was a scrappy, disjointed attack, lacking concentration.

De Guichen bore up and took advantage by running down wind and making good his escape. No losses were suffered on either side, but Rodney's flagship was severely damaged. Later he bitterly criticized his captains for their actions.

DONEGAL 1798

## DOMINICA II
*9 April 1782*

### American War of Independence 1775–83

All seemed set for a battle royal, yet in the end it fizzled out like a spent flare with the opposing fleets losing no ships at all. The French Admiral de Grasse with thirty-five of the line lay at Fort Royal,[10] Martinique, preparing to combine with the Spaniards for an attack on Jamaica.

Admiral Rodney's look-out frigate kept him informed of the French movements while his thirty-six of the line lay at Castries in St Lucia. As soon as de Grasse weighed anchor Rodney too made his move, and the two fleets were in contact by dusk on 9 April.

The bulk of the French fleet became becalmed in the lee of Dominica, as did Rodney with his centre and rear. Indeed, all twelve of the rear and four of the centre never got into the battle at all. However, both vans, the French under Vandreuil in *Triomphant* and Rear Admiral Sir Samuel Hood in *Barfleur* (90), engaged in a long-range exchange, with the French failing to employ their advantage in numbers.

De Grasse managed to protect the convoy in his charge, and even to work his ships to windward to attack Hood, but was unable to get to close grips. In the afternoon Rodney contrived to find the wind and

came up to support Hood. Both sides were content to break off the action, with neither side having lost a ship.

## DONEGAL (Warren's Action)
*12 October 1798*

### French Revolutionary War 1793–1802

A splendid action in which Commodore Sir John Warren defeated a French invasion force trying to take advantage of unrest in Ireland during the Revolutionary War.

The invasion force comprised the French ship of the line *Hoche*, commanded by Commodore Bonpart, leading eight frigates packed with 3,000 troops. Warren displayed greater power: three of the line and eight frigates.

The two squadrons met in foul weather — the gale-force winds had already removed *Hoche's* main topmast — at 11 a.m. on 11 October. Warren ordered 'General chase' and overhauled the French ships the following morning when both forces were in a straggling order.

By 11 a.m. the *Hoche* had struck, and by early afternoon three frigates had also struck and prize crews were aboard them. Three more were captured a few days later, and only two managed to return to France.

10   Now Fort-de-France.

245

## DOVER I

*19 May 1652*

### First Dutch War 1652—4

The battle was fought between a British fleet commanded by General-at-sea Robert Blake and a Dutch fleet commanded by Marten Tromp.[11] It was a battle brought about by 'the honour of the flag': the English demanded that all foreign ships in English waters should lower topsails and dip flags to English ships. It was a provocative demand, especially to the Dutch who were loath to conform. Relationships between the two seafaring nations were, to use a modern phrase, trigger-happy.

A full month before official hostilities between the two nations, the Dutch fleet in the Channel encountered Blake's fleet. On coming within hail the Dutch started lowering topsails but were slow in dipping Tromp's flag. Blake — perhaps precipitately — opened fire. A general action followed. Two Dutch ships struck (one recovered later after being abandoned by the prize crew), and England won the day.

## DOVER II

*20—21 April 1917*

### World War I 1914—18

A brilliant night action between six British and twelve German destroyers took place in the Channel. Admiral Reginald H. Bacon made his usual dispositions unaware of an impending German attack.

Commanders Evans and Peck, of the flotilla leaders *Broke* (1,704 tons, 6—4") and *Swift* (2,170 tons, 4—4") respectively, distinguished themselves in the ensuing violent, high-speed action in which the German Commodore lost two of his ships, the *G 42* and *G 85*.

*Broke* suffered serious damage and forty casualties in an action which typified the dashing destroyer work of the Navy, and which earned the commander renown as Evans of the *Broke*.

## DUNKIRK (Operation Dynamo)

*28 May—4 June 1940*

### World War II 1939—45

The evacuation of troops of the British Expeditionary Force at the Fall of France from Dunkirk and other French coastal locations across the Channel while under heavy air attacks from the Luftwaffe was effected at heavy cost to the Navy.

In a period of eight days 338,266 men were lifted in 848 craft of all types, some naval, most non-military. Almost all equipment and arms were left in France, but the rescued troops formed the basis of new armies which went back to France during Operation Overlord in Normandy 1944, four years later almost to the day.

Naval vessels played a large and vital role in the evacuation. More than fifty destroyers were engaged in the operation and nine of them were sunk and nineteen damaged. Destroyers lifted a total of 102,843 men.

**Destroyers sunk during the Operation were:**

*Valentine* (1,090 tons). Lost 15 May. Later salved.
*Whitley* (1,120 tons). Lost 19 May.
*Wessex* (1,100 tons). Lost 24 May.
*Wakeful* (1,100 tons). Lost 29 May.
*Grafton* (1,335 tons). Lost 29 May.
*Grenade* (1,335 tons). Lost 29 May.
*Basilisk* (1,360 tons). Lost 1 June.
*Keith* (1,400 tons). Lost 1 June.
*Havant* (1,335 tons). Lost 1 June.

## FALKLANDS

*8 December 1914*

### World War I 1914—18

Only days after the defeat at Coronel, Winston Churchill (First Lord) and Admiral Fisher (First Sea Lord), despatched with all haste from Plymouth the two powerful battlecruisers *Invincible* and *Inflexible* (both 17,250 tons, 8—12") to the South Atlantic. Vice Admiral Sir Doveton Sturdee was given command.

Sturdee rendezvoused with Rear Admiral Stoddard, who had assembled all available warships at Montevideo and the force proceeded south to the Falklands, arriving at Port Stanley on 7 December.

Meanwhile the victorious Admiral Graf von Spee made a crucial decision: to attack and destroy the base installations at the Falklands which he believed to be undefended, before breaking out into the Atlantic, through the British blockade and back to Germany.

He detached *Gneisenau* (11,420 tons, 8—8") and *Nürnberg* (3,350 tons, 10—4.1") to reconnoitre Port Stanley ahead of the squadron, and the gunnery officer of *Gneisenau* saw with horror the distinctive tripod masts of two battlecruisers in the outer anchorage. Von Spee turned and sped south-east as fast as he could.

Sturdee had also been unprepared for the sighting. Several of his ships were coaling, but within two hours all ships had steam up and set off on a long pursuit. Both von Spee and the British knew that the battlecruisers' superior fire power (a total of 16—12" guns) and speed (they had been designed for just such an eventuality) would be decisive, and that probably only darkness would save the German squadron.

But by 1 p.m. on that same day of 8 December the

---

11 In the Netherlands Tromp is always known, and always signed himself, without the 'van' or 'van der', though technically his father was van der Tromp. Curiously, De Ruyter (known as such to history) also always signed and called himself Ruyter, without the *particule*.

flagging *Leipzig* (3,544 tons, 12−4.1″) was coming under British fire. Von Spee ordered his light cruisers to disperse, while his heavier ships, *Scharnhorst* and *Gneisenau* (both with 8−8″ guns) engaged the powerful British battlecruisers. The outcome was inevitable. The German flagship sank with all hands at 4.15 p.m. and the *Gneisenau* followed at 6 p.m.

The pursuit of the light cruisers was equally devastating. The *Glasgow* (4,800 tons, 2−6″ and 10−4″) and *Cornwall* (9,800 tons, 14−6″) sank the *Leipzig*. The *Kent* (9,800 tons, 14−6″) sank the *Nürnberg* after a tremendous chase. Only the *Dresden* (3,544 tons, 12−4.1″), escaped, but three months later she was found in the port of Mas a Fuera by the *Kent* and *Glasgow* and she scuttled herself. Thus the whole of von Spee's squadron had been eliminated in one of the most startling episodes of revenge at sea.

## FALKLAND ISLANDS
*2 April−14 June 1982*
### Falkland Islands War 1982
Britain's first missile war started when 2,500 Argentinians invaded the Falkland Islands, claiming sovereignty over what they called 'the Malvinas'. The islands were defended by a token force of 84 Royal Marines. Within a few days twenty ships had left Portsmouth, including the carriers *Invincible* and *Hermes,* under the overall command of Rear Admiral J.F. Woodward, to undertake the biggest British naval/military operation since the end of WW II, the recapture of the islands. Royal Marines and Paras fought a sharp, skilful and speedy land action and recovered the islands. The P & O cruise liner *Canberra* (48,000 gross registered tonnage) and the *Queen Elizabeth II* (65,863 grt) were requisitioned for trooping/accommodation duties.

The Navy was subjected to bomb and missile attacks and suffered serious losses, including the sinking of the *Sheffield, Ardent, Antelope, Coventry, Atlantic Conveyor, Sir Tristram* and *Sir Galahad*. The *Plymouth* and *Glamorgan* were both damaged. SSN *Conqueror* torpedoed and sank the Argentinian cruiser *General Belgrano,* and the submarine *Santa Fe* was abandoned and wrecked. At midnight on 14 June Brigadier General Menendez surrendered all Argentinian forces on the islands.

## FINISTERRE — *see* CALDER'S ACTION (Cape Finisterre)

## FINISTERRE I
*3 May 1747*
### War of 1739−48
Rear Admiral Anson scored a resounding victory off the NW coast of Spain in the Bay of Biscay in May 1747. Anson wore his flag in the *Royal George* (90). He had with him twelve of the line, cruising in search of French convoys.

On 3 May a large concentration of ships was encountered. It comprised two convoys, one bound for India and the other for Canada, all under the protection of Admiral de la Jonquierre with a totally inadequate escort which he bravely formed into line of battle.

In a hopelessly one-sided battle Anson captured four ships of the line and two frigates, before turning his attention to the fleeing convoy which he chased, capturing seven of them. Another twenty-odd made good their escape in darkness. But Anson and his crews added considerably to their share of prize money as well as winning a victory at sea.

## FINISTERRE II (battle honour USHANT)
*14 October 1747*
### War of 1739−48
Rear Admiral Sir Edward Hawke endured eight weeks of exhaustive patrolling between Ushant and Finisterre hoping to intercept a French convoy known to be assembling, and which rewarded his patience on 14 October. He was delighted to see that he heavily outnumbered the French squadron escorting the convoy by about two to one.

The French Admiral L'Etendierre commanded eight of the line and the Indiaman *Content* (64) which he despatched with the dispersing convoy. Although fewer in number, the French ships were more powerfully armed. (The opposing squadrons are set out in the table below.)

The French admiral fought his line courageously in a nine-hour running battle, enabling the whole of the convoy to escape. But the price he paid for the convoy's safety was high. Only his flagship, the *Tonnant* (80) and the *Intrépide* (74), both badly damaged, escaped the ferocious British attacks, and limped into Brest. The other six were all taken by the British.

## BRITISH[12]

| | | |
|---|---|---|
| *Kent* | (64) | Captain Thomas Fox |
| *Eagle* | (60) | Captain George B. Rodney |
| *Defiance* | (60) | Captain John Bentley |
| *Portland* | (50) | Captain Charles Steevens |
| *Nottingham* | (60) | Captain Philip Saumarez |
| *Edinburgh* | (64) | Captain Thomas Cotes |
| *Devonshire* | (66) | Admiral Edward Hawke |
| | | Captain John Moore |
| *Yarmouth* | (64) | Captain Charles Saunders |
| *Windsor* | (60) | Captain Thomas Hanway |
| *Gloucester* | (50) | Captain Philip Durell |

12   Apart from Saumarez (killed 14 October), Hanway and Scott, all the British captains attained flag rank, an indication of the quality of fighting captains available in the service at this time.

| | | |
|---|---|---|
| *Tilbury* | (60) | Captain Robert Harland |
| *Lyon* | (60) | Captain Arthur Scott |
| *Monmouth* | (64) | Captain Henry Harrison |
| *Princess Louisa* | (60) | Captain Charles Watson |

## FRENCH

| | |
|---|---|
| *Intrépide* | (74) |
| *Terrible* | (74) |
| *Trident* | (64) |
| *Tonnant* | (80) |
| *Monarque* | (74) |
| *Severn* | (50) |
| *Fougueux* | (64) |
| *Neptune* | (70) |

The French frigate *Castor* accompanied the convoy. The British frigate *Hector* (40), Captain Stanhope, carried despatches.

## FLAMBOROUGH HEAD

*23 September 1779*

### American War of Independence 1775–83

One of the bitterest encounters at sea of not only the American War of Independence but of the whole eighteenth century.

FLAMBOROUGH HEAD 1779

John Paul Jones — born in Scotland, but enlisted into the American navy — was given command of the 900-ton *Bonhomme Richard* in 1779, together with the new frigate *Alliance* (commanded by a half-mad Frenchman, Pierre Landais), the frigate *Pallas* and two smaller vessels, all flying the American ensign.

This squadron sailed round the British Isles, raiding and skirmishing till 23 September found them encountering a Baltic convoy of forty-four sail escorted by the newly built frigate *Serapis* (50),[13] Captain Richard Pearson, and the sloop *Countess of Scarborough* (22).

Pearson gave cover to the convoy which escaped northward. The American frigate *Pallas* took the British sloop, but the *Alliance* seems to have taken little or no part in the engagement.

The duel — off Flamborough Head — between the two major ships was historic. The *Serapis* raked the *Bonhomme Richard*, then grappled her for boarding, but was unable actually to put a party aboard because of the fierce opposition. The two ships fought muzzle to muzzle for two hours. The American had all her guns knocked out except two, and she was on the brink of defeat when the *Serapis* burst into flame, Jones managed to get a boarding party aboard and Pearson struck. He had lost 128 men killed and wounded, while the American casualties numbered 150.

The *Bonhomme Richard* sank two days later, Jones transferred to the *Serapis* and put in at the Texel to a hero's welcome. Pearson was also received as a hero: he was court-martialled, acquitted and knighted.

13   Rated a 44, but she actually carried 50 guns.

Jones, of course, went on to greatness in the American navy.

## FORCE Z (South China Sea; Gulf of Siam)
*10 December 1941*
### World War II 1939–45
Force Z comprised the battleship *Prince of Wales* (35,000 tons: Captain J.C.Leach) the battlecruiser *Repulse* (32,000 tons: Captain W. Tennant) and four destroyers, *Express, Electra, Vampire* and *Tenedos.* The C-in-C, Acting Admiral Sir Tom Phillips, wore his flag in the battleship. In a period of just under two and a half hours — from 11 a.m. till 1.20 p.m. on 10 December — these two splendid capital ships were sunk in the South China Sea by Japanese bombers and torpedo-bombers of the 22nd Air Flotilla based in Indo-China. In this terrible disaster 327 men were lost in the battleship, in addition to the C-in-C and his flag captain, with another 513 of the *Repulse's* ship's company. This one strike denied the Navy their operations east of Singapore for three years: naval superiority in the area had been seized by Japanese aircraft.

This loss was the culmination of a series of unfortunate circumstances over the previous months: differences between the prime minister, Winston Churchill, and the Admiralty; the grounding in Kingston, Jamaica, of the carrier *Formidable* prevented her presence with Force Z; the underestimating of Japanese aircraft performance and of the pilots' skills and of air power generally; a false report of Japanese troops landing at Kuantan; Phillips's determination to maintain radio silence; and pure chance which allowed some Japanese aircraft to make a sighting of the British ships.

But the sinkings had far-reaching repercussions which resulted in the development of new weapons, techniques and tactics, and ultimately in the control of the sea and air by the USN in the great battles of the Pacific three years later.

## FORT ST DAVID (Negapatam)
*25 June 1746*
### War of 1739–48
Commodore Edward Peyton's feeble efforts off the Coromandel coast of southern India seem hardly worthy of inclusion when compared with many of the everyday convoy battles of World War II.

The Frenchman La Bourdonnais, in his *Achille* (70) and accompanied by seven armed merchantmen, encountered Peyton in his *Medway* (60) with three 50s and two smaller vessels. There was little wind to give any advantage, but Peyton failed to use his greater power, and Bourdonnais extricated his force.

The East India Company duly censured Peyton for his conduct and failure to annihilate the French force.

## FOUR DAYS' BATTLE
*1–4 June 1666*
### Second Dutch War 1665–7
A prolonged and fierce battle, one of the classics of naval history, fought in the southern North Sea betwen an English fleet of fifty-six ships under the command of the Duke of Albemarle and a massive Dutch fleet of eighty-five ships commanded by Admiral De Ruyter. Prince Rupert commanded the White squadron which had been detached to the west, down-Channel to intercept a supposed French fleet which did not in fact materialize.

Despite his inferiority in numbers, Albemarle attacked soon after noon on 1 June in thick weather off the North Foreland, with light winds in his favour. A running battle ensued. Cornelis Tromp's squadron was chased close to the French coast.

De Ruyter joined action later in the afternoon, and soon Albemarle's flagship was badly mauled. Admiral Sir William Berkeley was killed and his *Swiftsure* (64) surrendered. Rear Admiral Sir John Harman's flagship *Henry* (64) had a narrow escape from Evertsen's division of ships.

At the end of the first day Albemarle stood off to the west to repair damage. The second day found him with only about forty ships seaworthy against De Ruyter's eighty-odd. Nevertheless, battle was again joined, the fleets engaging on opposite tacks, but the English were unable to take advantage of confusion in the Dutch line. By the end of the second day Albemarle was in full retreat.

The retreat continued throughout the third day when three disabled ships were burnt to avoid capture. Then disaster struck when Admiral Sir George Ayscue's flag, the *Royal Prince* (90), ran aground on the Galloper Sand, was captured and burnt.

That night Prince Rupert joined Albemarle, which allowed the English to muster about sixty ships against seventy-eight Dutch sail on the fourth day of battle.

Another day of bitter fighting ensued: Rupert's *Royal James* (82) and Albemarle's *Royal Charles* (80) were both badly damaged, and Admiral Sir Christopher Myngs was killed aboard the *Victory.*

Both fleets became exhausted. As the day wore on Albemarle gained the weather advantage, and safety. The battle was over; De Ruyter retired that evening. The losses were horrific. The English lost seventeen ships (including two flagships) and about 8,000 men. The Dutch had about 2,000 casualties and lost six ships.

The English powers of recovery were remarkable: in seven weeks they fought another major battle at Orfordness.

## GABBARD (North Foreland)
*2–3 June 1653*
### First Dutch War 1652–4
The name is taken from the Gabbard Sands off

FOUR DAYS' BATTLE 1666

Orfordness, Suffolk. The English fleet comprised 100 ships and 5 fireships under the joint command of Generals-at-sea George Monck and Richard Deane. The opposing Dutch fleet of 98 ships and 6 fireships was commanded by Marten Tromp, with De Ruyter and De With as his vice admirals.

The fleets sighted each other at dawn on 2 June but light winds delayed action being joined till 11 o'clock. The first broadside killed Richard Deane. This first day of battle found the Dutch hard pressed and they suffered losses of 3 or 4 ships.

Blake arrived on the scene with 18 sail on the following day and the Dutch were routed. All told they lost about twenty ships — eleven were taken (including a vice admiral), six sunk and three blown up. There were no English losses, although 126 men were killed and 236 wounded. 1,360 Dutch prisoners were taken.

## GENOA — *see* GULF OF GENOA

## GIBRALTAR
*24 July 1704*

### War of Spanish Succession 1702—13
An English naval force commanded by Admiral Sir George Rooke with his flag in the *Royal Katherine* was accompanied by the Prince of Hesse-Darmstadt. Gibraltar was bombarded and its defences severely impaired, but stout defence caused numerous casualties among the storming English and Dutch marines. The Allied losses were 60 killed and 217 wounded. The governor surrendered the town on the 25th. The RMs observe the 24th as a Memorable Date, and the name Gibraltar is the only one worn on their badge. Gibraltar has stood many sieges and reliefs since 1704.

## GIBRALTAR (GUT OF) — *see* ALGECIRAS

## GLORIOUS FIRST OF JUNE, THE
*1 June 1794*

### French Revolutionary War 1793—1802
This battle in the North Atlantic between Admiral Lord Howe and the French Admiral Villaret-Joyeuse was the first major encounter at sea between the warring countries. The outcome is not easy to assess: on the face of it Howe triumphed — as is implied in the name given to the battle, which had no geographic location other than a chart reference — by taking six valuable prizes and sinking a seventh ship of the line. But Joyeuse's objective was to give cover to a large convoy of grain ships from America to starving France. Despite Howe's naval victory, every merchantman reached France safely.

The battle was the culmination of weeks of patient patrolling in the Western Approaches by Howe's fleet of thirty-four of the line. Reward came on 28 May in heavy seas when Howe's flagship, *Queen Charlotte* (100) sighted Joyeuse's fleet of twenty-six of the line. Joyeuse had the weather gage and for three days fended off Howe's attempts to reach the grain convoy away to the south. Skirmishing occurred during these days with casualties, damage and losses to both sides, but the Frenchman was unexpectedly reinforced by another four of the line under Rear Admiral Neilly.

1 June dawned clear; the opposing fleets were about four miles apart. Howe, having gained the windward position, bore down on the French line, intending to break through at all points and attacking from leeward. The *Queen Charlotte, Marlborough, Defence, Royal George* and *Queen* did just that, but other admirals and captains either misunderstood the intentions or baulked the issue and failed to break through. The result was a mêlée.

Six French of the line struck, two of them 80s, and *Le Vengeur du Peuple* (74) foundered after a monumental duel with the *Brunswick*. Joyeuse's flagship, *Montagne* (120), was heavily damaged and suffered 300 men killed.

Weeks of patrolling and days of battling took their toll: Howe, at sixty-eight, was exhausted. Had he had the stamina of a younger man he might well have captured the convoy too. It is the view of many that he should have done so anyway.

The King visited the fleet at Spithead at the end of June, and the occasion is captured by Sir William Dillon, then a midshipman.[14]

To the noble and gallant Lord Howe, His Majesty presented a diamond-hilted sword of the value of 3,000 guineas; also a gold chain to be worn round the neck . . . The two next senior Admirals, Graves and Hood were created Irish peers: the four Rear Admirals, baronets. All the Flag Officers received gold chains similar to that given to Lord Howe, and the Captains received medals — at least a certain number of them.[15] Pensions were settled on all that were wounded. All the Senior Lieutenants of the ships of the line that were in action received the rank of Commander. The Master of the *Queen Charlotte*, Mr Bowen, was made a Lieutenant.[16]

## GLÜCKSTADT
*5 January 1814*

### Napoleonic War 1803—15

Glückstadt in Holstein was captured by a British squadron comprising *Blazer, Désirée, Hearty, Piercer, Redbreast, Shamrock* and several gunboats.

## 'GRAF SPEE' ACTION — *see* RIVER PLATE

## GREECE
*April 1941*

### World War II 1939—45

Greece was attacked on 6 April 1941 by German troops and aircraft, and that night the port of Piraeus was put out of action when the ammunition ship *Clan Fraser* was struck by a bomb; the resulting explosion also sank another ten ships.

A fortnight later the decision was taken to mount Operation Demon, the evacuation of Greece by British troops. The operation started on 24/25 April. Only minor ports and beaches could be used, and the round trip to Egypt was about 1,000 miles. Germany enjoyed almost complete air supremacy. During seven nights of evacuation 50,732 troops were saved for the loss of four transports and two destroyers.

## GRENADA
*6 July 1779*

### American War of Independence 1775—83

The French Admiral D'Estaing was riding high: he had taken the island of St Vincent in the West Indies. Three weeks later, at the beginning of July, he sailed with twenty-five of the line and an expeditionary force and took the island of Grenada. The French influence in the Caribbean was about to soar, and it would remain in the ascendancy for nearly three years.

The recently appointed C-in-C Leeward Islands was Vice Admiral Byron. When he learnt of the Grenada capture he sailed from St Lucia with his whole fleet, its main strength being twenty-one of the line. He caught the French fleet in some confusion trying desperately to form line of battle in St George's Bay, Grenada, on 6 July.

By 11 a.m. both fleets were in line ahead sailing roughly parallel NNW, though the *Lion, Fame, Grafton* and *Cornwall* lay well astern, badly damaged. Both vans became heavily engaged, but later in the afternoon the fire became desultory, the French turned south and broke off the action.

---

14  *Dillon's Narrative*, Navy Records Society, 1953. Vol 1, p.150.

15  Strangest omission was that of Captain Cuthbert Collingwood. But he was awarded one later. This medal is of historical interest on a number of points. It was the first of all naval medals. Over fifty years later — in 1848 — when the Naval General Service medal was issued, it dated back to 1 June 1794, and the ribbon selected was the same white and blue.

16  Bowen became a Commissioner and a Rear Admiral, a rare achievement for a warrant officer in those days.

D'Estaing patently failed to exploit an advantageous situation, for he should have taken the four damaged ships, yet in spite of this failure the French still enjoyed a naval superiority in the Caribbean.

## GROIX, ÎLE DE (Bridport's Action)
*23 June 1795*

### French Revolutionary War 1793–1802

A battle between Admiral Bridport's Channel Fleet and a squadron under Admiral Villaret-Joyeuse off Quiberon Bay.

Bridport had been giving distant cover to the landing of a force of French royalist exiles in Brittany. On 22 June he sighted nine French ships of the line which immediately turned and headed for Lorient when they sighted the British ships. Bridport gave chase and overhauled the French squadron, engaging the ships early the next morning off the Île de Groix.

In a spirited action three of the rear Frenchmen struck: *Alexandre* (74), *Tigre* (74) and *Formidable* (74). Bridport was content with this and made off with his prizes. Joyeuse considered himself lucky to have escaped further destruction or loss, and made for Lorient.

## GUADELOUPE
*5 February 1810*

### Napoleonic War 1803–15

The island was captured by forces under the command of Lieutenant-General Sir George Beckwith and naval support commanded by Vice Admiral the Hon Sir Alexander Cochrane in HMS *Pompée*.

## GULF OF GENOA (Hotham's First Action)
*13–14 March 1795*

### French Revolutionary War 1793–1802

This was an unsatisfactory action between a French squadron under Rear Admiral Martin with fifteen ships of the line and Vice Admiral William Hotham with fourteen of the line from his Mediterranean Fleet.

Martin was escorting an assault force from Toulon to recapture Corsica when he encountered Hotham's squadron cruising in the Gulf of Genoa. Two days of manoeuvring like shadow boxing followed, with Hotham showing little inclination to close.

On 13 November the French 84 *Ça Ira* rammed her next ahead, the *Victoire*, losing her fore and main topmasts. The British frigate *Inconstant* quickly closed and engaged her, swiftly followed by Captain Nelson in *Agamemnon* (60), who meted out great punishment to the bigger adversary.

The following day's action was indecisive. Martin stood away to the west under full sail — and Hotham let him go, satisfied, it seems, with capturing the *Ça Ira* and the *Centaur* (74) which had her in tow.

## GULF OF SIAM — *see* FORCE Z

## GUT OF GIBRALTAR — *see* ALGECIRAS

## 'HAGURO' SINKING
*15–16 May 1945*

### World War II 1939–45

A battle between the 26th Destroyer Flotilla commanded by Captain Manley L. Power and His Imperial Japanese Majesty's heavy cruiser *Haguro* (13,380 tons, 10–8") commanded by Captain Kajuh Sugiura during a night action in the Straits of Malacca 55 miles WSW of Penang.

The 26th DF comprised the leader *Saumarez* (1,730 tons, 4–4.7") *Venus*, *Virago*, *Verulam* and *Vigilant* (all 1,710 tons, 4–4.7").

The *Haguro* was a fine, powerful, battle-hardened veteran of the Pacific war: she was powerfully armed and well armoured, her 1940 refit leaving her bristling with secondary and tertiary guns. She could not, however, match the high (36-knot) speed of the British destroyers. At the time of the battle she wore the flag of Rear Admiral Hashimoto.

She had in company the destroyer *Kamikaze* (1,400 tons, 3–4.7"), Lieutenant-Commander K. Kasuga.

Power's flotilla established radar contact with *Haguro* after a pursuit of several hours. Action was joined when Power activated his plan for a synchronized torpedo attack by the whole flotilla. Within minutes the heavy cruiser had been torpedoed several times. The *Kamikaze* failed to live up to its name and sped off in the confusion and escaped.

*Haguro* lost way and began to settle. *Venus* administered two torpedoes as a *coup de grâce*. No survivors were picked up — a measure of the fearsome antagonism between Allied and Japanese warships: later the *Kamikaze* returned and collected about 400 survivors.

*Saumarez* was struck by 8" and 5" shells and suffered serious damage forward, and to a boiler. But the British casualties were minimal. The 26DF were the victors of the last major torpedo action of World War II.

## HAVANA I
*1 October 1748*

### War of 1739–48

The last battle of this war between Britain and Spain was fought between a squadron of six of the line commanded by Rear Admiral Charles Knowles and a similar squadron (two 74s and four 64s) under Vice Admiral Reggio. Knowles was C-in-C of the Jamaica station. He had intelligence of a Spanish treasure fleet, and weighed from Fort Royal in his flagship, the *Cornwall* (80), with the rest of his squadron to cruise off the Tortuga Banks.

When Knowles sighted Reggio's squadron he had what wind advantage there was. Battle was joined at 2.30 p.m. except for *Warwick* and *Canterbury*, which were still a couple of hours astern.

After some fierce fighting the Spanish *Conquistador* (64) struck. By 8 p.m. Reggio was withdrawing towards Havana, but his flagship *Africa* (74) was so badly damaged that she anchored in a cove to make repairs. Two days later she was discovered there by the British ships, and her crew burnt their ship to avoid capture.

Knowles was subsequently court-martialled and reprimanded for his failure to get his squadron into action earlier and for his poor tactics.

## HAVANA II

*13 August 1762*

### Seven Years' War 1756–63

After two months of investment and attack Havana was captured by Admiral Sir George Pocock in *Namur*, supported by Admiral Keppel and his brother the Earl of Albemarle.

## HELIGOLAND BIGHT

*28 August 1914*

### World War I 1914–18

The battle was fought between British and German light forces within three weeks of the outbreak of war.

The Admiralty planned a raid on German patrols in the Heligoland Bight. The British force comprised the Harwich Force — the light cruisers *Arethusa* (3,500 tons, 2–6″ and 6–4″) and *Fearless* (3,300 tons, 10–4″) leading twenty-one destroyers in two flotillas commanded by Commodore R.T. Tyrwhitt. He was covered by the 1st Battle Cruiser Squadron (Vice Admiral David Beatty) and the 1st Light Cruiser Squadron (Commodore W.E. Goodenough).

The battle started when Tyrwhitt entered the Bight at dawn and sighted two patrolling destroyers, one of which was promptly sunk. German light cruisers appeared on the scene and Tyrwhitt found himself embroiled in several high-speed actions, opposed by no less than six light cruisers: *Stettin* (3,350 tons, 10–4.1″), *Frauenlob* (2,715 tons, 10–4.1″), *Mainz* (4,350 tons, 12–4.1″), *Köln* (4,350 tons, 12–4.1″), *Stralsund* (4,450 tons, 12–4.1″) and *Ariadne* (2,660 tons, 10–4.1″). Rear Admiral Maas's flag was in the *Köln*.

Beatty responded to a call for assistance, and his force's appearance was timely and decisive. The light cruisers *Köln*, *Ariadne* and *Mainz* were sunk. The remainder scattered into the mist and escaped. British casualties amounted to 35 killed and 40 wounded. The Germans lost over 1,200 men killed and taken prisoner.

## HOLMES'S BONFIRE

*8–9 August 1666*

### Second Dutch War 1665–7

Sir Robert Holmes (1622–92) commanded a few 'lesser' frigates, fireships and a considerable number of ketches in a mini-fleet endeavouring to burn a huge fleet of Dutch merchantmen sheltering in the river Vlie. The action followed a fortnight after the victory of Orfordness.

A huge assemblage of ships still laden with imports from the east 'that would feed Dutch industry and keep the Dutch export trade going for a year to come, lay at Terschelling'.

Holmes attacked them with his mini-fleet of ships and boats manned by carefully picked, skilled commandos, and succeeded in setting ablaze two Dutch warships and no less than 165 merchant ships in an unprecedented conflagration. The incident was given the name Holmes's Bonfire.

Troops and marines then went ashore and pillaged and fired the houses, public buildings and richly stocked warehouses of the town of Terschelling.

## HOTHAM'S ACTIONS — *see* GULF OF GENOA and HYÈRES

## HYÈRES (Hotham's Second Action)

*13 July 1795*

### French Revolutionary War 1793–1802

Battle fought between the British and French Mediterranean Fleets under the commands of Vice Admiral William Hotham and Vice Admiral Martin respectively, the old antagonists of the Gulf of Genoa battle four months previously.

Hotham had the advantage of twenty-three of the line against Martin's seventeen. The opposing fleets met near Hyères Island off Provence. Hotham again displayed a reluctance to act decisively. Martin, wisely perhaps, attempted to avoid entanglement. Hotham signalled 'General chase', but some of his ships never got within range of the enemy ships. The British van — including Nelson's *Agamemnon* (60) — managed to engage the French ships, and one of them, the *Alcide* (74), struck. The wind changed, and fearful of being blown ashore, Hotham ordered disengage — and another opportunity was lost.

## JAVA

*18 September 1811*

### Napoleonic War 1803–15

The reduction of Java was accomplished by troops under the command of Lieutenant-General Sir Samuel Auchmuty and naval forces commanded by Rear Admiral the Hon. Robert Stopford with his flag in the *Scipion*.

## JAVA SEA

*27 February 1942*

### World War II 1939–45

A battle fought against a Japanese amphibious invasion of the island of Java by an Allied squadron commanded by the Dutchman Rear Admiral Karel Doorman. The Japanese squadron was commanded

| ALLIED | | | JAPANESE |
| --- | --- | --- | --- |
| Commander | Doorman (Neth.) | | Takagi |
| Heavy Cruiser | *Houston* | USN | *Nachi* |
| | *Exeter* | RN | *Haguro* |
| Light Cruiser | *Perth* | RAN | *Jintsu* |
| | *De Ruyter* | Neth. | *Naka* |
| | *Java* | Neth. | |
| Destroyers | 9 (3−RN, 2−Neth. and 4−USN) | | 14 |

by Admiral Takagi and the rival forces are shown above.

The Allied force was a makeshift one, without a common signalling system, and it operated under air dominated by the Japanese.

Doorman led his fleet in *De Ruyter* from Sourabaya to meet the approaching Takagi force. A long-range gunnery duel developed, with mass torpedo attacks from destroyers. *Exeter* (8,390 tons, 6−8″) suffered damage and fell out of line. The RN destroyer *Electra* (1,375 tons, 4−4.7″) and Dutch *Kortenaer* (1,310 tons, 4−4.7″) were sunk, obliging Doorman to break off the action and try to work round the covering force to get at the troop convoy.

The four US destroyers, having expended all their torpedoes, were detached back to Sourabaya. The RN destroyer *Jupiter* (1,690 tons, 6−4.7″) struck a mine and foundered.

After dark another clash of the cruisers occurred: *De Ruyter* and *Java* both sank with enormous loss of life. The Battle of the Java Sea was at a virtual end.

Captain Waller RAN in *Perth* (6,830 tons, 8−6″) took command of the remaining ships and withdrew. The following day the *Perth, Houston,* (9,050 tons, 9−8″), the destroyers *Encounter* (1,375 tons, 4−4.7″) and *Pope* (1,190 tons, 4−4″) all tried to escape the Java Sea, but were intercepted, fought with great gallantry and were sunk with heavy loss of life. See SUNDA STRAIT. The Japanese victory was comprehensive and complete. Java was lost.

# JUTLAND (Skagerrak)
*31 May 1916*

## World War I 1914−18

The greatest battle at sea of World War I, fought between the main fleets of the Royal Navy and the Imperial German Navy. Both opposing fleets were divided into two distinct advance forces consisting on the one hand of battlecruisers, cruisers and destroyers under the command of Vice Admiral David Beatty and Vice Admiral Franz von Hipper, and on the other hand the main fleets of battleships, cruisers and destroyers commanded by Admiral Sir John Jellicoe and Vice Admiral Reinhard Scheer.

The German plan was to lure the British Grand Fleet to sea from its bases over carefully positioned U-boats which could then launch torpedo attacks. But this ill-conceived plan suffered many defects and misfired in many respects. Yet Jutland (or Skagerrak,

as the Germans call it), was a contest between mighty Britain and the newcomer — a battle where curiously, the most modern weapons, submarines and aircraft, were not employed. This clash of the capital ships was to be the first major battle of its kind, and the last. Jutland was unique — and will ever remain so.

It was also a chapter of might-have-beens: one thing is certain. The German High Seas Fleet should never have escaped the annihilation that faced it in the murky wastes of the North Sea in 1916.

Hipper put to sea with his Scouting Force, followed by Scheer's Main Battle Fleet about 60 miles astern.

Intelligence of these moves became known to the Admiralty, and the Grand Fleet (always ready at short notice for sea) sailed. Beatty's force left harbour ahead of Jellicoe, who like Scheer followed his main force about 60 miles astern.

On that day most of the world's capital ships were at sea, seeking battle, none of them knowing the strength of the opposition, or their exact whereabouts.

Action started almost by accident. HMS *Galatea* (3,520 tons, 2−6″) and 6−4″) on the port wing of the advanced cruiser screen turned to investigate a Swedish merchant ship almost at the same time as a German warship on the port wing of their advance screen did the same. In a few minutes 'Enemy in sight' was being flashed to the battle fleets.

Beatty's Battlecruiser Force (less the battleships) and Hipper's Battlecruiser Scouting Force were soon engaged, the latter trying to lure Beatty to the south towards Scheer's battleships. In this phase of the engagement six British and five German battlecruisers were exchanging shots.

Within a short time the *Indefatigable* (18,750 tons, 8−12″) had been pounded to destruction by the accurate shelling of *Von der Tann* (21,000 tons, 8−11″). The *Queen Mary* (27,000 tons, 8−13.5″), battered by the *Seydlitz* (25,000 tons, 10−11″) and the *Derfflinger* (28,000 tons, 8−12″), blew up with frightening suddenness. Beatty then found himself confronted with Scheer's battle force.

He turned his battlecruisers away to the northward, hoping to draw Scheer towards Jellicoe's main Battle Fleet. Hipper and Scheer, neither aware that Jellicoe was at sea, complied: they expected to destroy Beatty's battlecruisers.

JUTLAND 1916

# THE BRITISH GRAND FLEET

## The Battle Fleet

### BATTLESHIPS

SECOND BATTLE SQUADRON[A]

| | |
|---|---|
| *King George V* | Captain F.L. Field[B] |
| | (Flagship of Vice-Admiral Sir Martyn Jerram) |
| *Ajax* | Captain G.H. Baird |
| *Centruion* | Captain M. Culme-Seymour |
| *Erin* | Captain The Hon. V.A. Stanley |
| *Orion* | Captain O. Backhouse |
| | (Flagship of Rear-Admiral A.C.Leveson) |
| *Monarch* | Captain G.H. Borrett |
| *Conqueror* | Captain H.H.D. Tothill |
| *Thunderer* | Captain J.A. Fergusson |

FOURTH BATTLE SQUADRON[A]

| | |
|---|---|
| *Iron Duke* | Captain F.C. Dreyer |
| | (Fleet flagship of Admiral Sir John Jellicoe) |
| *Royal Oak* | Captain C. Maclachan |
| *Superb* | Captain E. Hyde-Parker |
| | (Flagship of Rear-Admiral A.L. Duff) |
| *Canada* | Captain W.C.M. Nicholson |
| *Benbow* | Captain H.W. Parker |
| | (Flagship of Vice-Admiral Sir Doveton Sturdee) |
| *Bellerophon* | Captain E.F. Bruen |
| *Téméraire* | Captain E.V. Underhill |
| *Vanguard* | Captain J.D. Dick |

A   Of the 24 battleships 9 were armed with 10−12″ guns, one with 14, 11 with 10−13.5″, one with 10−14″ and two with 8−15″ guns.

B   First Sea Lord 1930−2

FIRST BATTLE SQUADRON[A]

| | |
|---|---|
| *Marlborough* | Captain G.P. Ross |
| | (Flagship of Vice-Admiral Sir Cecil Burney) |
| *Revenge* | Captain E.B. Kiddle |
| *Hercules* | Captain L. Clinton-Baker |
| *Agincourt* | Captain H.M. Doughty |
| *Colossus* | Captain A.D.P.R. Pound[C] |
| | (Flagship of Rear-Admiral E.F.A. Gaunt) |
| *Collingwood* | Captain J.C. Ley |
| *Neptune* | Captain V.H.G. Bernard |
| *St Vincent* | Captain W.W. Fisher[D] |

## BATTLECRUISERS[E]

THIRD BATTLECRUISER SQUADRON

| | |
|---|---|
| *Invincible* | Captain A.L. Cay |
| | (Flagship of Rear-Admiral The Hon. H.L.A. Hood) |
| *Inflexible* | Captain E.H.F. Heaton-Ellis |
| *Indomitable* | Captain F.W. Kennedy |

## ARMOURED CRUISERS[F]

FIRST CRUISER SQUADRON

| | |
|---|---|
| *Defence* | Captain S.V. Ellis |
| | (Flagship of Rear-Admiral Sir Robert Arbuthnot) |
| *Warrior* | Captain V.B. Molteno |
| *Duke of Edinburgh* | Captain H. Blackett |
| *Black Prince* | Captain T.P. Bonham |

SECOND CRUISER SQUADRON

| | |
|---|---|
| *Minotaur* | Captain A.C.S.H. D'Aeth |
| | (Flagship of Rear-Admiral H.L. Heath) |
| *Hampshire* | Captain H.J. Savill |
| *Cochrane* | Captain E. La T. Leatham |
| *Shannon* | Captain J.S. Dumaresq |

## LIGHT CRUISERS[G]

FOURTH LIGHT CRUISER SQUADRON

| | |
|---|---|
| *Calliope* | Commodore C.E. Le Mesurier |
| *Constance* | Captain C.S. Townsend |
| *Caroline* | Captain H.R. Crooke |
| *Royalist* | Captain The Hon. H. Meade |
| *Comus* | Captain A.G.Hotham |

ATTACHED

| | |
|---|---|
| *Active* | Captain P. Withers |
| *Bellona* | Captain A.B.S. Dutton |
| *Blanche* | Captain J.M. Casement |
| *Boadicea* | Captain L.C.S. Woollcombe |
| *Canterbury* | Captain P.M.R. Royds |
| *Chester* | Captain R.N. Lawson |

C   First Sea Lord during much of World War II.

D   C-in-C Mediterranean during the early 1930s.

E   Armed with 8−12″ and 16−4″.

F   Armed with a wide variety of 9.2″, 7.5″ and 6″ guns.

G   Chiefly for repeating visual signals between units of the battle fleet.

## DESTROYERS[H]

FOURTH FLOTILLA
*Tipperary* (Captain C.J. Wintour), *Acasta, Achates, Ambuscade, Ardent, Broke, Christopher, Contest, Fortune, Garland, Hardy, Midge, Ophelia, Owl, Porpoise, Shark, Sparrowhawk, Spitfire, Unity*

ELEVENTH FLOTILLA
*Castor* (light cruiser: Commodore J.R.P. Hawskley) *Kempenfelt, Magic, Mandate, Manners, Marne, Martial, Michael, Milbrook, Minion, Mons, Moon, Morning Star, Mounsey, Mystic, Ossory*

TWELFTH FLOTILLA
*Faulknor* (Captain A.J.B. Stirling), *Maenad, Marksman, Marvel, Mary Rose, Menace, Mindful, Mischief, Munster, Narwhal, Nessus, Noble, Nonsuch, Obedient, Onslaught, Opal*

## MISCELLANEOUS

*Abdiel* (Minelayer)
*Oak* (Destroyer-tender to fleet flagship)

# The Battlecruiser Fleet

## BATTLECRUISERS

| | |
|---|---|
| *Lion* | Captain A.E.M. Chatfield[I] |
| | (Flagship of Vice-Admiral Sir David Beatty) |

FIRST BATTLECRUISER SQUADRON
| | |
|---|---|
| *Princess Royal* | Captain W.H. Cowan |
| | (Flagship of Rear-Admiral O.de B. Brock) |
| *Queen Mary* | Captain C.I. Prowse |
| *Tiger* | Captain H.B. Pelly |

SECOND BATTLECRUISER SQUADRON
| | |
|---|---|
| *New Zealand* | Captain J.F.E. Green |
| | (Flagship of Rear-Admiral W.C. Pakenham) |
| *Indefatigable* | Captain C.F. Sowerby |

## FAST BATTLESHIPS

FIFTH BATTLE SQUADRON[J]
| | |
|---|---|
| *Barham* | Captain A.W. Craig |
| | (Flagship of Rear-Admiral H. Evan-Thomas) |
| *Valiant* | Captain M. Woollcombe |
| *Warspite* | Captain E.M. Phillpotts |
| *Malaya* | Captain The Hon. A.D.E.H. Boyle |

## LIGHT CRUISERS

FIRST LIGHT CRUISER SQUADRON[K]
| | |
|---|---|
| *Galatea* | Commodore E.S. Alexander-Sinclair |
| *Phaeton* | Captain J.E. Cameron |
| *Inconstant* | Captain B.S. Thesiger |
| *Cordelia* | Captain T.P.H. Beamish |

H   Almost all armed with 2−3 4″ guns and 2−21″ torpedo tubes.

I   First Sea Lord as Lord Chatfield 1932−5.

J   Armed with 8−15″ and 14−6″ guns.

K   Armed with 2−6″ and 6−4″ guns.

SECOND LIGHT CRUISER SQUADRON[L]
| | |
|---|---|
| *Southampton* | Commodore W.E. Goodenough |
| *Birmingham* | Captain A.A.M. Duff |
| *Nottingham* | Captain C.B. Miller |
| *Dublin* | Captain A.C. Scott |

THIRD LIGHT CRUISER SQUADRON[M]
| | |
|---|---|
| *Falmouth* | Captain J.D. Edwards |
| | (Flagship of Rear-Admiral T.D.W. Napier) |
| *Yarmouth* | Captain T.D. Pratt |
| *Birkenhead* | Captain E. Reeves |
| *Gloucester* | Captain W.F. Blunt |

**SEAPLANE-CARRIER**

*Engadine*

**DESTROYERS**

FIRST FLOTILLA
*Fearless* (light cruiser: Captain C.D. Roper), *Acheron, Ariel, Attack, Badger, Defender, Goshawk, Hydra, Lapwing, Lizard*

NINTH AND TENTH FLOTILLAS (combined)
*Lydiard* (Commander M.L. Goldsmith), *Landrail, Laurel, Liberty, Moorsom, Morris, Termagant, Turbulent*

THIRTEENTH FLOTILLA
*Champion* (light cruiser: Captain J.U. Farie), *Moresby, Narborough, Nerissa, Nestor, Nicator, Nomad, Obdurate, Onslow, Pelican, Petard*


# THE GERMAN HIGH SEAS FLEET

## The Battle Fleet

**BATTLESHIPS**

THIRD BATTLE SQUADRON[N]
| | |
|---|---|
| *König* | Captain Brüninghaus |
| | (Flagship of Rear-Admiral Paul Behncke) |
| *Grosser Kurfürst* | Captain E. Goette |
| *Kronprinz Wilhelm* | Captain C. Feldt |
| *Markgraf* | Captain Seiferling |
| *Kaiser* | Captain F. von Kayserlink |
| | (Flagship of Rear-Admiral Nordmann) |
| *Kaiserin* | Captain Sievers |
| *Prinz Regent Luitpold* | Captain K. Heuser |

FIRST BATTLE SQUADRON[N]
| | |
|---|---|
| *Friedrich der Grosse* | Captain T. Fuchs |
| | (Fleet flagship of Vice-Admiral Reinhard Scheer) |
| *Ostfriesland* | Captain von Natzmer |
| | (Flagship of Vice-Admiral E. Schmidt) |
| *Thüringen* | Captain H. Küsel |
| *Helgoland* | Captain von Kameke |
| *Oldenburg* | Captain Höpfner |

---

L  Armed with 8−6″ guns except *Birmingham* and *Nottingham* with 9 each.

M  Armed with a variety of 4″, 5.5″ and 6″ guns.

N  Four armed with 12−11″ guns, four with 12−12″, others with 10−12″. All a secondary armament of 14−5.9″ guns.

| | |
|---|---|
| *Posen* | Captain Lange |
| | (Flagship of Rear-Admiral Engelhardt) |
| *Rheinland* | Captain Rohardt |
| *Nassau* | Captain H. Klappenbach |
| *Westfalen* | Captain Redlich |

SECOND BATTLE SQUADRON[O]
| | |
|---|---|
| *Deutschland* | Captain H. Meurer |
| | (Flagship of Rear-Admiral Mauve) |
| *Hessen* | Captain R. Bartels |
| *Pommern* | Captain Bölken |
| *Hannover* | Captain W. Heine |
| | (Flagship of Rear-Admiral F. von Dalwigk zu Lichtenfels) |
| *Schlesien* | Captain F. Behnche |
| *Schleswig-Holstein* | Captain Barrentrapp |

## LIGHT CRUISERS

FOURTH SCOUTING GROUP
| | |
|---|---|
| *Stettin* | Captain F. Regensburg |
| | (Broad pendant of Commodore von Reuter) |
| *München* | Commander O. Böcker |
| *Hamburg* | Commander von Gaudecker |
| *Frauenlob* | Captain G. Hoffman |
| *Stuttgart* | Captain Hagedorn |

## TORPEDOBOATS[P]

| | |
|---|---|
| *Rostock* (light cruiser) | Captain O. Feldmann |
| | (Broad pendant of Commodore Michelson) |

FIRST FLOTILLA (half)
4 boats under Commander Albrecht (in G39)

THIRD FLOTILLA
7 boats under Captain Hollman (in S53)

FIFTH FLOTILLA
11 boats under Captain Heinecke (in G11)

SEVENTH FLOTILLA
9 boats under Captain von Koch (in S24)

# The Battlecruiser Force

## BATTLECRUISERS

FIRST SCOUTING GROUP[Q]
| | |
|---|---|
| *Lützow* | Captain Harder |
| | (Flagship of Vice-Admiral Franz Hipper)[R] |
| *Derfflinger* | Captain Hartog |
| *Seydlitz* | Captain M. von Egidy |
| *Moltke* | Captain von Karpf |
| *Von der Tann* | Captain Hans Zenkert |

O   Pre-dreadnoughts with 4−11" and 14−6.7" guns.

P   Vary from 800−1,800 tons, with 3−12pdrs to 3−4" guns and 3−Torpedo tubes.

Q   *Lützow* and *Derfflinger* armed with 8−12": *Seydlitz* and *Moltke* with 10−11" and *Von der Tann* 8−11".

R   Hipper's senior staff officer was Commander Erich Raeder, later Grand Admiral in Hitler's Navy.

## LIGHT CRUISERS

**SECOND SCOUTING GROUP**

| | |
|---|---|
| *Frankfurt* | Captain T. von Trotha |
| | (Flagship of Rear-Admiral Bödicker) |
| *Wiesbaden* | Captain Reiss |
| *Pillau* | Captain Mommsen |
| *Elbing* | Captain Madlung |

## TORPEDOBOATS

| | |
|---|---|
| *Regensburg* | |
| (light cruiser) | Captain Heuberer |
| | (Broad pendant of Commodore Heinrich) |

SECOND FLOTILLA
10 boats under Captain Schuur (in *B98*)

SIXTH FLOTILLA
9 boats under Captain Schultz (in *G41*)

NINTH FLOTILLA
11 boats under Captain Goehle (in *V28*)

At 6 p.m. about 80 miles west of the Jutland peninsula the two main fleets clashed. Soon the cruiser *Wiesbaden* sank. Minutes later the armoured cruiser *Defence* (14,600 tons, 4—9.2" and 10—7.5") exploded and sank. *Derfflinger,* assisted this time by *Lützow* (28,000 tons, 8—12"), again demonstrated her accurate gunnery by inflicting terrible damage on the *Invincible* (17,250 tons, 8—12"), which soon blew up. However, the *Lützow* was so seriously pummelled in this phase that she sank the following day.

Jellicoe deployed his fleet into line of battle on the port wing column, a masterly move which put his fleet across Hipper's line of retreat and crossed the German's T. The scene was all set for a resounding British victory. But it was not to be.

The battle continued in a confused fashion throughout the night. During this night phase Hipper avoided being trapped by Jellicoe and extricated his forces, only encountering light British forces. The old pre-dreadnought *Pommern* (13,200 tons, 14—6.7") suffered much damage in the night and finally sank at 4.10 a.m.

The light cruiser *Frauenlob* (2,715 tons, 10—4.7") took a lot of punishment and sank. The German destroyer *Elbing* was rammed and sunk by a German battleship and the light cruiser *Rostock* (4,900 tons, 12—4.1") sank after a fierce duel with British destroyers. HMS *Black Prince* (13,550 tons, 6—9.2" and 10—6") had to be abandoned when the fires gained control, and she sank.

When daylight came on 1 June the German fleet had reached the safety of its own minefield in the Heligoland Bight. Jellicoe and the British found themselves gazing at an empty sea.

The losses sustained were as follows:

| **BRITISH** | **GERMAN** |
|---|---|
| 3 Battlecruisers | 1 Pre-dreadnought |
| 3 Armoured cruisers | 1 Battlecruiser |
| 8 Destroyers | 4 Light cruisers |
| | 5 Destroyers |
| 6,090 men killed | 2,550 men killed |

The place of Jutland in the war is debated to this day, more than seventy years later. Tactically and in material terms the rewards went to Scheer and Hipper. Strategically, the British retained command of the sea and the German High Seas Fleet never again came out to dispute control. As one journalist put it: 'The German fleet has assaulted its gaoler, but is still in prison.'

## KENTISH KNOCK

*28 September 1652*

### First Dutch War 1652—4

The battle was named after the sandbank of that name in the southern North Sea. The English fleet comprised 68 ships commanded by General-at-sea Robert Blake. He defeated a Dutch fleet of 59 ships commanded by Admiral Witte de With. The Dutch ships were sighted at about noon 18 miles east of North Foreland. Action was joined at 5 p.m. when Blake and his vice admiral William Penn engaged the van and centre divisions of de With's ships, followed by the rear. The battle ended with darkness. The English losses were minimal. The Dutch lost two ships and suffered considerable damage and casualties.

## KOLOMBANGARA

*13 July 1943*

### World War II 1939−45

This battle was one of the numerous clashes between predominantly US naval forces and Japanese ships brought about by the Japanese need to replenish their forces in the Guadalcanal area in what was nicknamed the Tokyo Express. On the night of 12−13 July there was a brief but bloody encounter between one such Japanese force and TF 36.1 under the command of Rear Admiral Ainsworth USN. It comprised the US cruisers *Honolulu* and *St Louis*, *Leander* (Captain Roskill) and Desron 21 and 12, totalling 9 destroyers. All three Allied cruisers were torpedoed and one destroyer sunk.

## KOREA

*1950−1*

### Korean War 1950−3

The Inchon landings and subsequently the Inchon evacuation were two main features of the naval war in Korean waters. In 1950 70,000 men of the US 10th Corps were landed from 550 landing-craft. British naval support was given by the *Jamaica* and *Kenya* to the Gun Fire Support Group. During the operation *Jamaica* fired 1,290 rounds of 6" and 393 of 4"; *Kenya* fired 1,242 rounds of 6" and 205 rounds of 4". *Jamaica* also became the first United Nations ship to shoot down an enemy aircraft.

In the evacuation from Inchon in the following year these British ships participated: *Kenya*, *Ceylon* and the Australian destroyers *Warramunga* and *Bataan*.

## KUA KUM

*20 October 1849*

During anti-slavery operations in the Far East no fewer than 58 Chinese junks were destroyed in the Kua Kum, Indo-China, by *Columbine*, *Fury*, *Phlegethon* (of the Bengal Marine) and a boarding party from *Hastings*.

## LAGOS I (Disaster of the Smyrna Convoy)

*17−18 June 1693*

### War of English Succession 1689−97

This was a battle in defence of an important convoy between an attacking French squadron and a defending Anglo-Dutch squadron.

In June 1693 an attempt was made to pass an extremely large and enormously valuable convoy of 400 merchantmen down-Channel to the Mediterranean. The merchant ships were English, German, Dutch, Danish and Swedish.

The escort was provided as far as Ushant by the main Anglo-Dutch fleets, which returned to their bases on completing this phase of the operation.

Vice Admiral Sir George Rooke and Rear Admiral van der Goes took over responsibility after Ushant. All went reasonably well until about noon on 17

June, when south of Cape St Vincent Rooke found himself confronted by a vast fleet of about 80 French warships.

Unknown to Rooke, the French were well aware of the passage of the convoy, and instructions had been issued to Admiral Tourville in Brest and Admiral D'Estrées at Toulon to rendezvous at Lagos Bay just to the east of Cape St Vincent and there to lay in wait.

Rooke did all in his power to avoid action, and two Dutch ships gallantly sacrificed themselves and were taken: *Zeeland* (64) and *Wapen van Medemblik* (64). In vain: the French ships got among the convoy and in all sank or captured ninety-two of the vessels. Rooke managed to collect another fifty-four into a small convoy and provided them with an escort. Others scattered to Gibraltar, to Cadiz, Malaga and Madeira.

The total financial loss to the Allies has been variously computed between £1 million and £6 million, a huge sum then. Whatever the sum, in all senses the battle was a disaster of great proportions.

## LAGOS II

*18−19 August 1759*

### Seven Years' War 1756−63

An important naval battle fought off Lagos in southern Portugal between a British squadron under Admiral Edward Boscawen and a French squadron under Commodore De la Clue.

Boscawen had been blockading De la Clue in Toulon for some time. While the latter was refitting his ships in Gibraltar he slipped away to join the French main fleet at Brest with ten of the line, two 50s and three frigates.

As soon as Boscawen received intelligence of this move he sailed westward from Gibraltar with fifteen of the line and several frigates. He wore his flag in *Namur* (90).

Early on 18 August seven French ships were sighted off the Portuguese coast, the remainder of the French force having made for Cadiz without orders. Action began in the afternoon. The French *Centaure* (74) was taken and the *Namur* much disabled aloft. Boscawen transferred his flag to the *Newark* (80). The boat in which he transferred was hit by a round shot, and the admiral plugged the hole with his wig. The chase continued through the night until four of the Frenchmen found sanctuary in Lagos Bay while the other two escaped in the darkness. So hurried was the flight of the French flagship, the *Océan* (80), that she ran aground in the bay under full sail, her three masts going by the board. She struck her colours, her crew fled ashore and she was set ablaze.

The other three Frenchmen in the bay anchored under the Portuguese shore batteries. Boscawen adopted the principle of 'hot chase' and pursued the enemy into the bay. The next morning he captured the *Téméraire* (74) and *Modeste* (64) while the 74 *Redoutable* was wrecked and burnt by her crew.

De la Clue was carried ashore during the battle, mortally wounded. Boscawen enjoyed the fruits of a splendid and incredibly well-conducted victory.

## LAKE CHAMPLAIN
*11 and 13 October 1776*

### American War of Independence 1775−83

The first battle on Lake Champlain occurred on 11 October when a British and an American lake flotilla clashed. The second battle took place two days later, and the result was a defeat for the Americans. The British ships comprising the flotilla were: *Carleton, Inflexible, Loyal Convert, Maria, Thunderer.* Troops of the Royal Artillery also served.

## LA HOGUE
*23−24 May 1692*

### War of the English Succession 1689−97

See BARFLEUR. The battle of La Hogue was the continuation of the battle of Barfleur between an Anglo-Dutch fleet and a French fleet.

On 23 May Sir Clowdisley Shovel, Rear Admiral commanding the Red Squadron, was ordered to destroy the French ships left at anchor off La Hogue. But Shovel had been severely cut by a large splinter wound in the thigh, so his place was taken by Vice Admiral Sir George Rooke, commanding the Blue Squadron.

Fifteen French ships of the line had been caught by the flood tide and lay at anchor in the bays of La Hogue and Cherbourg. Three of them had already been dispatched — the flagship *Soleil Royal, Admirable* and *Triomphant* — as we have read: the remaining twelve sailed deeper into the bay, among the scores of transports assembling for an attempted invasion of England by James II.

British and Dutch fireships and boats as well as the ships of the line pursued the French ships and transports, wreaking dreadful destruction by fire and shot. Every one of the twelve ships of the line was destroyed. So close inshore was the battle being fought that crowds watched from ashore, including, it is said, James II himself. The Allied boats and fireships operated in such shallow waters that French cavalry were dispatched to attack them. We have the remarkable record of French troopers being pulled off their horses by seamen with boathooks.

The Allies gained a stunning victory. It was complete. It proved decisive in the direction and outcome of the war.

LA HOGUE 1692

## LEYTE GULF
*20—27 October 1944*

This great naval battle was fought between the US 3rd and 7th Fleets and a Japanese battlefleet, and resulted in a convincing American victory. RAN ships which served with the US forces were: *Arunta, Ariadne, Australia, Gascoyne, Warramunga* and *Shropshire*. On the 21st five kamikaze bombers caused damage to the *Australia* and she withdrew from the battle, escorted by the *Warramunga*.

## LINGAYEN GULF
*5—9 January 1945*

### World War II 1939—45

This battle covered operations in the Philippines. The following RAN ships participated: *Arunta, Australia, Warramunga, Gascoyne, Shropshire* and *Warrego*.

## LISSA
*13 March 1811*

### Napoleonic War 1803—15

A most creditable victory for a small British squadron of four frigates over a stronger force of three French frigates (each with 44 guns), three Venetian frigates and four or five smaller vessels.

Captain William Hoste with the *Amphion, Active* and *Cerberus* (all 5th rates[17]) and the 6th rate *Volage*, were using Lissa Island off the Dalmatian coast as a base.

Commodore Dubourdieu was dispatched from Ancona with his mixed squadron plus 500 troops to occupy Lissa.

The squadrons sighted each other north of the island at dawn on 13 March. Dubourdieu, having the weather gage, bore down on the British ships in two divisions. Hoste was one of Nelson's protégés: he rallied his squadron with the signal 'Remember Nelson' and a spirited battle followed. After three hours the French flagship had been driven ashore and blown up, killing the commodore. Three other frigates were taken, and the remainder of the force fled.

## LOUISBURG
*8 June—26 July 1758*

### War of American Independence 1775—83

Louisburg and the whole of Cape Breton Island were captured by Admiral and the Hon. Edward Boscawen in *Namur* and troops under the command of Major-General Jeffrey Amherst.

## LOWESTOFT
*3 June 1665*

### Second Dutch War 1665—67

One of the great classic battles of sail, fought on an enormous scale between an English fleet of 109 ships commanded by James, Duke of York and 103 ships of a Dutch fleet commanded by Admiral Opdam (or Obdam) Jacob van Wassenaer, off the Suffolk coast about 40 miles south-east of Lowestoft.

The Dutch fleet was marauding near the Dogger Bank at the end of May, capturing a convoy of twenty English merchant ships, when James, Duke of York, received intelligence of the enemy activity. James in his flagship the *Royal Charles* (80) led the English fleet in weighing anchor from the Gunfleet and proceeding to Southwold Bay. James had with him, commanding two of the enormous squadrons, the Earl of Sandwich (Montagu) and Prince Rupert, two of the famous Generals-at-sea.

Two days of manoeuvring these vast fleets preceded the battle, which was joined at 4 a.m. on 3 June, each fleet passing the other on opposite tacks, each ship engaging as enemy ships came into range. Soon the battle had degenerated into a mêlée on a grand scale.

In the centre the two flagships, *Royal Charles* and *Eendracht* (76), fought a bitter battle, the latter just failing in an attempt to board James's ship. At one stage a chain shot killed many officers and men alongside James, who was spattered with their blood. A chronicler (probably James's flag captain Sir William Penn), wrote: 'At 12 came A shot from Opdam yt killed ye Earl of Falmouth [Charles Berkeley] Lord Musgrave [Muskerry] and Mr Boyle [younger son of the Earl of Burlington].'

*Eendracht* then received a shot in her powder room and exploded with devastating force. Only five of her complement of many hundreds of men were rescued. With the death of Wassenaer, Vice Admiral Jan Evertsen took command. Another demoralizing blow to the Dutch was the death of Vice Admiral Kortenaer aboard the *Groot Hollandia*.

The English gradually gained the upper hand and the Dutch began to give way. Ships fouled each other, and no less than seven Dutch ships were lost by fire in this way.

With great skill Jan Evertsen and Cornelis Tromp marshalled the Dutch fleet into a controlled withdrawal towards the Texel and Maas estuary, which was reached by the late evening. They had lost thirty-two ships, only nine of which were taken as prizes; their casualties amounted to about 4,000 killed and 2,000 taken prisoner.

The English losses were amazingly light by comparison. The *Charity*, captured early in the battle, was the only ship lost. In terms of seamen lost, 283 were killed and 440 wounded.

---

17   5th rates carried between 32 and 44 guns with a weight of broadside between 636 and 350lb. A 6th rate carried between 20 and 28 guns with a broadside between 250 and 180lb.

LOWESTOFT 1665

## LUCKNOW
*16 March 1858*

### Indian Mutiny 1857–8

A naval brigade from HMS *Shannon* accompanied forces under the command of General Sir Colin Campbell at the capture of Lucknow.

## MALAGA
*13 August 1704*

### War of the Spanish Succession 1702–13

A grand but undistinguished battle between an Anglo-Dutch fleet of fifty-three ships of the line and a Franco-Spanish fleet of fifty of the line.

Admiral Sir George Rooke commanded the Anglo-Dutch fleet, with Admiral Clowdisley Shovel leading the van and the Dutch Admiral Callenburgh the rear squadron.

The Allies had captured Gibraltar only the previous month. The French Admiral Comte de Toulouse sailed from Toulon with the purpose of gaining a naval victory and recapturing Gibraltar.

Battle was joined off Malaga on 13 August and it developed into a long day's artillery duel with no ships being taken, burnt or sunk, though damage was severe and casualties enormous.

The following day Toulouse made no attempt to renew the battle and Rooke was content to return to Gibraltar for repairs.

Despite its being a drawn contest, the battle left Britain and the Netherlands with the ascendancy, for the Allied superiority at sea was not seriously challenged again for the rest of the war, which ran for another nine years. The retention of Gibraltar as a base helped dominate and command the western basin of the Mediterranean.

## MALTA CONVOYS
*1940–3*

### World War II 1939–45

On 10 June 1940 Italy opened hostilities with Britain in the Mediterranean, where Admiral Sir Andrew B. Cunningham was C-in-C. The Italian navy enjoyed considerable strength on paper: 6 battleships, 7 heavy cruisers, 14 light cruisers, 59 destroyers and 108 submarines.

This fleet lacked the fighting spirit of the Royal Navy, whose aggression and resolution found no match in Mussolini's navy. The impressive Italian fleet of submarines achieved so little in comparison with German U-boat commanders that Germany augmented the Italian submarines with German U-boats. It is a matter of fact that two of the greatest achievements in terms of submarine warfare in the Mediterranean, the sinking of *Ark Royal* and of *Barham*, were both German achievements.

The greatest danger to the Royal Navy in the Mediterranean came from bombers and dive bombers of the Luftwaffe, and the damage and losses sustained by the Navy were considerable. Convoys from Gibraltar and Alexandria to beleagured Malta took on the role of a fleet operation: capital ships to defend the convoy from marauding Italian capital ships; aircraft carriers to provide fighter protection against the high-level bombers of the Italian air force and the dive bombers of Germany; cruisers and AA cruisers to give AA protection to the capital ships and merchantmen; destroyers for escort and AA duties. To illustrate the ferocity of some of these battles, three such convoy operations are described here.

## MALTA: OPERATION EXCESS
### 10–11 January 1941

A battle fought between Force H from Gibraltar under the command of Admiral Sir John Somerville, units of the Mediterranean Fleet under the command of Admiral Sir Andrew Cunningham and the German Fliegerkorps X based in Sicily.

The action arose over the passage of four merchantmen in a convoy: one ship destined for Malta and the other three for the Piraeus. Force H covered the passage as far as the Straits of Sicily; there the cruisers *Southampton* (9,100 tons, 12–6″) *Gloucester* (9,400 tons, 12–6″) and *Bonaventure* (5,450 tons, 10–5.25″) and five destroyers took over responsibility. Long-range cover was given by the battleships *Valiant* (32,700 tons, 8–15″) and *Warspite* (30,600 tons, 8–15″), the carrier *Illustrious* (23,000 tons, 36 aircraf) and accompanying cruisers and destroyers.

Aircraft from Fliegerkorps X struck on 10 January. *Illustrious* was hit six times and her armoured flight deck failed to prevent serious damage. An eye witness reported seeing a bomb 'bounce like a ball' along the flight deck. The carrier limped into the questionable safety of Malta for repairs. *Warspite* was also hit. The following day *Southampton* and *Gloucester* were heavily bombed and *Southampton* had to be abandoned.

The four merchantmen reached their destinations.

## MALTA: OPERATION HARPOON
### 12–16 June 1942

A joint convoy operation attempting to fight through to Malta a convoy from Gibraltar simultaneously with one from Alexandria.

After heavy fighting with Axis light surface units, U-boats and aircraft, the Alexandria convoy was aborted with the loss of two of the freighters. Although heavy units of the Italian fleet were at sea, they were not committed to the battle.

The Gibraltar element of the operation suffered even more heavily. Four out of six freighters were sunk during the attacks together with the light cruiser *Hermione* (5,450 tons, 10–5.25″). Furthermore, five destroyers and a cruiser were damaged. The Italians lost the cruiser *Trento* (10,000 tons,

8–8″) while the flagship, the battleship *Littorio* (35,000 tons, 9–15″), suffered damages from bomb hits and a torpedo.

## MALTA: OPERATION PEDESTAL
### 10–15 August 1942

A bitter battle developed over several days when the Royal Navy attempted to fight through a convoy of fourteen freighters from Gibraltar to Malta, just two months after the fierce experience of the Harpoon convoy. Central to the whole saga was the British-manned US oil tanker *Ohio*, laden with fuel oil desperately needed by the defending aircraft at Malta.

Vice Admiral Sir Neville Syfret commanded the British force which consisted of:

**Carriers:**
*Indomitable* (Rear Admiral D. W. Boyd): 50 aircraft
*Eagle:* 16 aircraft
*Victorious* (Rear Admiral Sir A.L. St A. Lister): 34 aircraft
*Furious* 42 Spitfires for Malta: 4 aircraft

**Battleships:**
*Nelson* (Vice Admiral Sir Neville Syfret; 33,950 tons)
*Rodney* (33,900 tons: both ships 9–16″ and 12–6″)

**Cruisers:** *Nigeria* (Rear Admiral H.M. Burroughs: (8,000 tons, 12–6″)
*Kenya* (8,000 tons, 12–6″)
*Manchester* (9,400 tons, 12–6″)
*Cairo* (4,290 tons, 8–4″)
*Phoebe* (5,450 tons, 10–5.25″)
*Sirius* (5,450 tons, 10–5.25″)
*Charybdis* (5,450 tons, 10–5.25″)

**Destroyers:** 28

**Submarines:** 9

The bulk of the Italian fleet remained in harbour due to lack of oil supplies but heavy and sustained air attacks were launched by Italian and German aircraft from Sardinian and Sicilian bases in the course of which the *Indomitable* was damaged and the *Victorious* was struck by two bombs which bounced along the armoured flight deck. The convoy and escorts were also subjected to submarine and E-boat attacks. The carrier *Eagle* was sunk by *U-73* (Herbert Rosenbaum). The Italian submarine *Axum* fired a salvo of four torpedoes which struck the *Nigeria*, *Cairo* and the tanker *Ohio*. The *Cairo* had to be sunk by torpedo and gunfire from HM ships. In a daring night attack Italian E-boats torpedoed the *Manchester*: she had to be scuttled later. A stray aircraft torpedo struck the *Foresight* and she was subsequently sunk by the *Tar.* by the *Tartar*.

Nine of the fourteen merchant ships were sunk and most of the remaining five were damaged. Despite the *Ohio*'s extensive damage she made an epic arrival at Valetta, barely afloat, lashed to rescue vessels either side of her to give buoyancy and steerage way.

Operation Pedestal had been a desperately fierce encounter, but the Royal Navy — at great sacrifice — had raised the siege of Malta.

## MARBELLA (Action off Cabrita or Cabareta Point)
*10 March 1705*

### War of the Spanish Succession 1702—13

This action resulted from a French attempt to land troops for the recapture of Gibraltar. It was fought between a squadron of French of the line under the command of Admiral de Pointis, and a similar squadron under the command of Admiral Sir John Leake.

The French squadron arrived in Gibraltar Bay, but a rising gale drove his force to leeward towards Marbella. The British squadron lay off Cabrita Point; Leake had with him five of the line. At daybreak on 10 March Leake surprised de Pointis. Leake had every advantage, and he pressed home his attack with speed and vigour. In a swift and skilful action the British took the *Ardent* (66), *Marquis* (66) and *Arrogant* (60). Two more of the line, the flagship *Magnanime* (74) and *Lys* (66), were driven ashore and burnt by their crews to avoid capture.

Leake had not only scored a remarkable victory but had saved Gibraltar from attack and had enhanced his own already high reputation.

## MARTINIQUE I
*16 February 1762*

### Seven Years' War 1756—63

The island was captured by naval forces under the command of Rear Admiral George Brydges Rodney with his flag in *Marlborough,* and military forces under the command of Major-General the Hon. Robert Monckton.

## MARTINIQUE II
*29 April 1781*

### American War of Independence 1775—83

The battle was fought when Rear Admiral Samuel Hood with eleven ships of the line met a greatly superior French squadron under Admiral Comte de Grasse comprising twenty of the line escorting a convoy of 150 sail.

Admiral Sir George Rodney was in command of the naval forces in the Caribbean, with Hood as his second-in-command. Rodney ordered Hood to take his squadron to join Rear Admiral Drake's squadron at Fort Royal, Martinique, then to cruise to windward of the island in the hopes of intercepting de Grasse.

On 28 April Hood sighted the much superior French fleet and spent the night and the next morning skilfully manoeuvring his ships to gain whatever advantage he could. But when battle was joined it was mainly at long range, with the advantage of fire power with the French.

Hood's ships *Russell, Centaur* and *Intrepid* (all 3rd rates) suffered severe damage but managed to reach port safely. De Grasse safeguarded his convoy, which reached its destination unscathed, and perhaps for this reason alone he can be regarded as the victor of the battle of Martinique.

## MARTINIQUE III
*5—22 March 1794*

### French Revolutionary War 1793—1802

Vice Admiral Sir John Jervis commanded a squadron which captured the French *Bienvenue* in Fort Royal Harbour. She was abandoned temporarily but retaken on 20 March.

## MARTINIQUE IV
*24 February 1809*

### Napoleonic War 1803—15

Rear Admiral the Hon. Sir Alexander Cochrane commanded the naval forces in his flagship *Neptune,* which helped capture the island. The military forces were commanded by Lieutenant-General George Beckwith.

## MATAPAN — *see* CAPE MATAPAN

## MEDWAY (De Ruyter in the Thames)
*June 1667*

### Second Dutch War 1665—7

A Dutch fleet of warships under the command of Admiral De Ruyter audaciously sailed up the Thames and into the Medway, burned or captured many English ships, blockaded London and created panic in the streets of the city.

No British forces opposed the marauders, primarily because of a bankrupt Treasury: this had resulted in the English ships not being fitted out in the spring of 1667, and the ships were left in 'ordinary' — in other words, they were in reserve with all their stores taken ashore. Furthermore, incredible though it may seem, hundreds of English seamen whose pay was months in arrears had deserted to serve in the Dutch navy.

De Ruyter commanded twenty-four of the line, twenty smaller vessels and fifteen fireships; they entered the Thames estuary. A chain boom at Sheerness was broken, Sheerness captured, guardships battered into submission and shore batteries silenced. Armed parties landed and destroyed more batteries at Upnor.

Nearby sixteen English of the line were captured or burnt. Humiliatingly, the *Royal Charles* (80), Albemarle's flagship in recent battles against the Dutch, was taken and towed to Holland with the royal standard still flying at the main as a tremendous prize of war. Although the ship was

MEDWAY 1667

broken up in 1673 the magnificent carving from the stern is still preserved in the Rijksmuseum.

De Ruyter continued to blockade the Thames and London for a month, during which time there were bouts of panic. Samuel Pepys recorded in his *Diary* that he sent his wife and father out of London with as much gold as they could carry to bury in his father's garden in Huntingdonshire.

## MERS EL KEBIR — *see* ORAN

## MINORCA I

*20 May 1756*

### Seven Years' War 1757—63

It was this indecisive clash which resulted in the celebrated loss of Minorca and its valuable harbour at Port Mahon and in the court-martialling and shooting of Vice Admiral John Byng.

Admiral the Marquis de la Galissonière captured the island of Minorca in April 1756 with a squadron of twelve of the line and 15,000 French troops. They invested the naval base at Port Mahon, whose garrison held out bravely.

A hard-pressed Admiralty raised a weak and inefficient force of thirteen ships of the line under the command of Vice Admiral the Hon. John Byng to relieve the garrison.[18]

On 20 May Byng encountered La Galissonière's squadron about 30 miles east of Port Mahon and an indecisive action followed, largely due to Byng's tactical error in angle of approach. The French drew off and Byng made no positive effort to engage them again. Neither did he make an effort to land his troops to relieve the garrison or even to bombard the transports supplying the island.

Byng held a Council of War aboard his flagship which resolved to draw back to Gibraltar to await reinforcements from Britain. He therefore retired from Minorca, and as a result the garrison had no option but to surrender — with the loss of Minorca.

The Admiralty did not await Byng's despatch but sent Vice Admiral Sir Edward Hawke to relieve him and recapture the island. But the situation was irretrievable.

Byng returned to England to face public outcry and a court martial which found him guilty of neglect of duty and sentenced him to execution. He

18   The numbers of ships are often misquoted. Byng set out from Gibraltar with thirteen of the line plus three frigates. The latter were dispatched to contact the garrison ashore. When battle commenced, such was Byng's elementary, child-like knowledge of sea warfare, he had one ship too many in his line to fight ship-to-ship with the French line; thus he ordered *Deptford* out of the line; thus twelve British ships took part in the battle. See Hannay's *A Short History of the Royal Navy 1689—1815*, Vol II 1909, p.152.

was shot on 14 March 1757 at Portsmouth, a fate which aroused great public condemnation.[19]

## MINORCA II
*15 November 1798*
### French Revolutionary War 1793—1802
Commodore John Duckworth with his flag in *Leviathan* commanded the naval forces which helped capture the island. Seamen and marines were landed from ships. *Argo, Aurora, Centaur, Constitution, Cormorant, Leviathan* and *Petrel* participated. The military forces were commanded by General the Hon. Charles Stuart.

## MONTE CHRISTI I
*20 March 1780*
## MONTE CHRISTI II
*20 June 1780*
### American War of Independence 1775—83
Two actions, and both were contested by Captain William Cornwallis and French commanders in the West Indies off the northern coast of the island of San Domingo.

In the first encounter Cornwallis was cruising with three small ships of the line when he met a French convoy escorted by four of the line and three frigates on its way to nearby Cap François. In the running fight which continued throughout the night the British *Janus* was badly damaged. Reinforcements arrived too late to prevent the French escaping.

The second encounter was similarly lightweight. Cornwallis in the *Lion* (64) with four ships of the line in support fought an inconclusive action with Commodore de Ternay, who had a force of seven of the line escorting a valuable convoy. The Frenchman failed to press home an attack in which he had most advantage, and the engagement was noted mainly for the good work Cornwallis put in in rescuing the damaged *Ruby* (64).

## MONTECRISTI
*28 August 1652*
### First Dutch War 1652—3
Captain Richard Badiley commanded a small squadron of ships comprising *Paragon, Phoenix, Constant Warwick* and *Elizabeth* escorting a convoy of four sail south of Leghorn near Montecristi, when he was attacked by a small Dutch squadron commanded by Captain Johan van Galen. Tactical skirmishing took place on the 27th but battle was joined on the 28th. The convoy was successfully protected, and it made good its escape. In the engagement Badiley got the upper hand and one Dutch ship — curiously also named *Phoenix* — struck.

## MOONLIGHT BATTLE — *see* CAPE ST VINCENT

## NARVIK I
*10 April 1940*
### World War II 1939—45
Narvik is a seaport of northern Norway, and it was the scene of two naval battles among its fjords during World War II.

At the time of the German invasion of Norway a force of ten German destroyers was dispatched to capture the town and port. Commodore Bronte commanded the operation.

In the first action on 10 April the British 2nd Destroyer Flotilla under Captain (D) B.A.W. Warburton-Lee in the 1,505-ton *Hardy* (5—4.7″) with *Havock, Hunter, Hostile* and *Hotspur* (all 1,350 tons, 4—4.7″) entered the fjord leading to Narvik at dawn and engaged and sank two German destroyers, the *Wilhelm Heidkamp* (2,411 tons, 5—5″) and *Anton Schmidt* (2,411 tons, 5—5″), killing the commodore. Several supply ships were also sunk, and damage was inflicted to other destroyers.

On the return journey down Ofot Fjord five more modern destroyers were encountered, and in a high-speed action the *Hunter and Hardy* were so badly damaged that they were beached. Warburton-Lee was fatally wounded when a shell struck the bridge and wheelhouse of *Hardy*. He was awarded a posthumous VC. The rest of the flotilla made good its escape.

## NARVIK II
*13 April 1940*
### World War II 1939—45
The second battle was fought three days later when the veteran battleship *Warspite* (30,600 tons, 8—15″), wearing the flag of Vice Admiral Whitworth, entered the approaches to Narvik with an escort of destroyers.

The eight remaining German destroyers known to be in hiding in the various inlets in the fjords of Narvik were sought out with the aid of reconnaissance aircraft from the *Warspite* and brought to action. All were either sunk or otherwise destroyed at no loss to the Royal Navy. Furthermore, a U-boat which had taken shelter at the head of a fjord was also sunk: she was the *U-64*.

While both battles of Narvik were conspicuous successes for the Royal Navy, they failed to prevent the Germans from capturing the seaport and town of Narvik, and eventually the whole of Norway.

---

19   Voltaire commented contemptuously: *'Dans ce pays-ci il est bon de tuer de temps en temps un amiral pour encourager les autres.'*

## SHIPS ENGAGED IN NARVIK I AND II

| Ship | Displacement | Main guns | T/T | Comments |
|---|---|---|---|---|
| BRITISH | | | | |
| *Hardy* | 1,505 | 5−4.7″ | 8−21″ | Sunk |
| *Havock* | 1,340 | 4−4.7″ | 8−21″ | |
| *Hostile* | 1,340 | 4−4.7″ | 8−21″ | |
| *Hotspur* | 1,340 | 4−4.7″ | 8−21″ | Damaged |
| *Hunter* | 1,340 | 4−4.7″ | 8−21″ | Sunk |
| *Warspite* | 30,600 | 8−15″ | | |
| *Bedouin* | 1,870 | 8−4.7″ | 8−21″ | |
| *Cossack* | 1,870 | 8−4.7″ | 8−21″ | |
| *Eskimo* | 1,870 | 8−4.7″ | 8−21″ | |
| *Punjabi* | 1,870 | 8−4.7″ | 8−21″ | |
| *Forester* | 1,375 | 4−4.7″ | 8−21″ | |
| *Foxhound* | 1,375 | 4−4.7″ | 8−21″ | |
| *Hero* | 1,340 | 4−4.7″ | 8−21″ | |
| *Icarus* | 1,530 | 4−4.7″ | 10−21″ | |
| *Kimberley* | 1,690 | 6−4.7″ | 10−21″ | |
| GERMAN | | | | |
| *Wilhelm Heidkamp* | 2,411 | 5−5″ | 8−21″ | |
| *Hermann Kunne* | 2,411 | 5−5″ | 8−21″ | |
| *Hans Ludemann* | 2,411 | 5−5″ | 8−21″ | |
| *Deither von Roeder* | 2,411 | 5−5″ | 8−21″ | All sunk or otherwise destroyed |
| *Anton Schmidt* | 2,411 | 5−5″ | 8−21″ | |
| *Bernd von Arnim* | 2,230 | 5−5″ | 8−21″ | |
| *Erich Giese* | 2,230 | 5−5″ | 8−21″ | |
| *Erich Koellner* | 2,230 | 5−5″ | 8−21″ | |
| *Georg Thiele* | 2,230 | 5−5″ | 8−21″ | |
| *Wolfgang Zenker* | 2,230 | 5−5″ | 8−21″ | |

## NASMITH'S PATROL

*May−June 1915*

### World War I 1914−18

Admiral Sir Martin Dunbar-Nasmith VC, KCB was less resplendent when he was a young Lieutenant-Commander, nor did he affect a hyphenated surname. There was a dash and élan about him during the patrol by *E 11*,[20] the submarine he commanded in the Sea of Marmara in the Dardanelles campaign, that resulted in the award of the VC — the third submarine commander to earn the award in that theatre.

He entered the Dardanelles on 19 May, went to 80 ft. off Achi Baba and passed under two minefields — and then a third — in order to attack a Turkish battleship, but when he surfaced the target had moved out of range. However there was no shortage of destroyers, two of which spotted his periscope and attempted to ram. The glassy flat water of the inland sea was a grave hazard for a submarine, so Nasmith captured a dhow and lashed it to the part-submerged conning tower to disguise his progress through the Sea.

The next day he put a boarding party on to a sailing ship, torpedoed a Turkish gunboat and took a bullet right through *E 11's* periscope.

On the 24th Nasmith intercepted a vessel which he ordered to be abandoned: it was loaded with arms, gun spares and 6″ shells. A demolition charge sent it to the bottom: 'the vessel exploded with a loud report . . .'

After chasing another loaded vessel into the port of Rodosto Nasmith torpedoed her as she secured alongside. Yet another extraordinary event on this same day was the prize he captured which ran itself ashore: his prize crew were driven off by rifle fire from a cavalry unit ashore!

On the 25th Nasmith was off Constantinople, relishing the prospect of masses of shipping in the Bosporus. One torpedo was fired, but it developed a gyro failure and circled round the harbour, narrowly missing *E 11* itself. Another torpedo exploded against the transport *Stamboul* while she was alongside the harbour wall. Constantinople panicked. Shops shut. Troops aboard transports were disembarked and all sailings cancelled. The city came to a standstill.

After a day ashore on an island, resting and washing, *E 11* tackled a battleship, but was driven off by a destroyer. She then brushed with a Turkish Q-ship — but escaped.

On 28 May a large transport was sunk by demolition charges on the same day that a spent torpedo, complete with live firing pistol, was recovered and safely taken aboard after Nasmith himself had swum to the torpedo to make it safe — taking care not to touch the 'whiskers' of the firing pistol.

20   Displacement tonnage 725/810: 4 TT.

On his return passage to base Nasmith sank another transport, then passed through some more minefields: a mine mooring-cable fouled one of the forward hydroplanes but Nasmith managed to get clear. During his 20-day patrol Nasmith had sunk one gunboat, two transports, two ammunition ships, two supply ships ( a third had been driven ashore), had paralysed lines of communication and blockaded the Turkish army.

Nasmith won accelerated promotion to commander and an award of the VC.

# NAVARINO
*20 October 1827*

### Greek War of Independence 1821−9

This was a battle fought between a combined British, French and Russian fleet commanded by Vice Admiral Sir Edward Codrington and a Turco-Egyptian fleet under Ibrahim Pasha, who was trying to restore Turkish rule over Greece. The Allied fleet comprised:[21]

| Ships of the line | | Frigates | Others | Commander |
|---|---|---|---|---|
| British | 4 | 3 | 4 | Codrington |
| French | 4 | 1 | 2 | De Rigney |
| Russian | 4 | 4 | | Heyden |
| Total | 12 | 8 | 6 | |

The Turco-Egyptian fleet comprised seven of the line, fifteen frigates, twenty-six corvettes and seventeen others. It lay at anchor in Navarino Bay on the south-west coast of the Peloponnese in a roughly horseshoe formation.

Codrington had Admiralty instructions to use force only as a last resort because of the political sensitivity of the situation. But the impression one gets is that the provocation on both sides was more than a saint could bear. Codrington, it is clear, wanted action. He ordered his fleet to anchor right inside the bay, almost within the horseshoe of ships, and started parleying.

There was much to-ing and fro-ing of boats. One such was fired upon by Turkish musketeers who believed it to be a boarding party; a British ship replied with a shot, which echoed round the bay. Soon other shots followed, action broke out everywhere and a battle ensued which lasted about four hours.

The Pasha's fleet was decisively punished, losing one ship of the line, twelve frigates and twenty-two corvettes: casualties amounted to about 4,000 men. No Allied ships were sunk, though many suffered extensive damage.

Codrington was recalled to London and was lucky to be cleared of charges of disobeying orders.

The battle was the last major battle of sail of the line: the next major clash at sea would be the battle of Jutland, eighty-nine years later, but aeons ahead in terms of technological and scientific advances.

# NEGAPATAM (25 June 1746 — *see* FORT ST DAVID)

# NEGAPATAM I
*3 August 1758*

### Seven Years' War 1756−63

Three months after the indecisive encounter off Cuddalore in SE India, another inconclusive action occurred between a British squadron commanded by Vice Admiral George Pocock and a French squadron commanded by Admiral Comte D'Aché off nearby Negapatam. It could well have been named Pocock's Pursuit.

Pocock, in his flagship *Yarmouth* (64) and with another six of the line, chased the Comte's nine of the line for several days before the Frenchmen were finally brought to action at noon on 3 August.

A shot from *Yarmouth* carried away *Zodiaque's* (74) wheel, which caused the French flagship to collide with the *Duc d'Orléans*. Both survived the experience. D'Aché managed to disentangle, and later to disengage his ships. Under cover of darkness he thereupon retired to the north.

No ships had been sunk, but casualties on both sides were heavy.

# NEGAPATAM II
*6 July 1782*

### American War of Independence 1775−83

This was the third encounter between Admiral Sir Edward Hughes's British squadron and Admiral Suffren's French squadron off south-east India in 1782. See SADRAS and PROVIDIEN.

The battle arose from Suffren's preparations to capture the British base at Negapatam. Hughes received intelligence of these plans and sailed from Trincomalee on Ceylon's east coast to frustrate the French assault.

When the two squadrons — each comprising eleven of the line — clashed a battle royal was in prospect, but although it was fiercely fought, and the casualties were heavy, no ship was taken or sunk.

At one time Captain de Cillart of the French *Sévère* (64) struck to the British *Sultan* (74), but his men refused to surrender, won the day and rejoined their squadron.

In the evening both squadrons lay inshore and

---

21 Sources differ surprisingly in figures of ships comprising both the Allied and the Turco-Egyptian fleets. These are taken from Kemp's *Oxford Companion*.

anchored as if for a well-earned breathing space. Suffren then retired north to Cuddalore, thwarted in his attempted assault.

## NEVIS
*20 May 1667*

### Second Dutch War 1665–7

This battle was an English defeat in the West Indies when a Franco-Dutch squadron of seventeen of the line commanded by Admiral de la Barre and Admiral Crijnssen encountered Captain Berry's squadron of twelve ships off Nevis Point in the Leeward Islands.

The Franco-Dutch force was carrying more than 1,000 soldiers to capture the island of Nevis itself. In the ensuing battle Captain Berry in the *Coronation* (56) fought bravely but lost three of his ships, while the enemy suffered no loss. Nevertheless, the invasion attempt was thwarted, the enemy force retired to Martinique and Nevis remained in English hands.

## NILE, THE (Aboukir Bay)
*1 August 1798*

### French Revolutionary War 1793–1802

This classic battle at sea was fought between the well-ordered fleet commanded by Rear Admiral Sir Horatio Nelson on the one hand and the French Admiral d'Aigalliers Brueys with his much less well-ordered squadron.[22] Nelson won a splendid victory due primarily to his audacious and brilliant handling of a squadron disciplined and exercised in the skills of war at sea.

Nelson had scoured the Mediterranean for weeks for the French Toulon fleet and its convoy of transports for the invasion of Egypt, which carried with it none other than Napoleon Bonaparte.

The French expeditionary force eluded Nelson's squadron and landed at Aboukir Bay 15 miles east of Alexandria, while the fleet anchored in the bay, close inshore. Nelson's force arrived off Alexandria on 1 August and sighted the French fleet at anchor.

| | BRITISH | | | FRENCH | |
|---|---|---|---|---|---|
| **Ship** | **Guns** | **Admiral & Captain** | **Ship** | **Guns** | **Admiral & Captain** |
| *Goliath* | 74 | T. Foley | *Guerrier* | 74* | Trullet |
| *Zealous* | 74 | S. Hood | *Conquérant* | 74* | D'Albarade |
| *Orion* | 74 | J. Saumarez | *Spartiate* | 74* | Eimeriau |
| *Audacious* | 74 | D. Gould | *Aquilon* | 74* | Thevenard |
| *Theseus* | 74 | R.W. Miller | *Peuple Souverain* | 74* | Raccord |
| *Vanguard* | 74 | H. Nelson E. Berry | *Franklin* | 80* | B. du Chayla Gillet |
| *Minotaur* | 74 | T. Louis | *L'Orient* | 120+ | Brueys Casabianca |
| *Bellerophon* | 74 | H.D.E. Darby | *Tonnant* | 80* | Duguay-Trouin Thouard |
| *Defence* | 74 | J. Peyton | *L'Heureux* | 74* | Etienne |
| *Majestic* | 74 | G.B. Westcott | *Timoléon* | 74+ | L. Trullet |
| *Alexander* | 74 | Alex J. Ball | *Guillaume Tell* | 80 | Villeneuve Saunier |
| *Swiftsure* | 74 | B. Hallowell | *Mercure* | 74* | Cambon |
| *Leander* | 50 | T.B. Thompson | *Généreux* | 74 | Lejoille |
| *Culloden* | 74 | T. Troubridge | *Sérieuse* | 36+ | |
| | | | *Artémise* | 36+ | Rear Admiral |
| | | | *Diane* | 48* | Decrès |
| | | | *Justice* | 44* | |
| Total Guns | 1,012 | 8,068 men | | 1,190 | 11,230± men |
| Casualties | 218 k. | 678 w. | 1,451 k. | 1,479 w. | |

\* Signifies captured
\+ Signifies burnt or destroyed
± Nominal strength: actual was about 7,850

22  Brueys had no confidence in his revolutionary captains: he thought them ignorant and boors. His ships were badly undermanned, some lacking a third or quarter of their complement. Discipline was poor. Brueys knew his squadron was unequal to a British squadron of the same strength.

Nelson was in command of what many consider to have been the finest squadron of its size ever assembled in the age of sail. These magnificent 74s were commanded by skilled professionals, a 'band of brothers' who knew Nelson's mind, his unswerving adherence 'to use your utmost endeavours to take, burn, sink or destroy'.

Admiral Brueys sighted Nelson's ships but was not unduly troubled. True, while he was at anchor he must be at a tactical disadvantage — and further handicapped with watering and stores parties ashore. But he had carefully selected the anchorages for his ships, anchorages which even the most critical eye might deem impregnable: they were protected on two sides by shoals and breakers, flanked by frigates and a land battery on Aboukir Island. In guns, he had a heavier weight in metal than Nelson. Furthermore, even the time of day was advantageous to him, for sunset was not many hours away.

Nelson thought otherwise. He determined to attack then, not to delay till tomorrow. He also detected an opening, small, but an opening none the less, allowing of penetration on the enemy's blind side — between the ships at anchor and the shoals.

Captain Foley's *Goliath* led the squadron with the NNW breeze at his back, passed along the centre and van of the French line, *crossed the van and attacked from the leeward side.* Within two hours the first five French ships had been carronaded and shot into submission, and had struck.

In the centre there was a terrible struggle. Brueys's giant 120-gun *L'Orient* blasted Captain Darby's *Bellerophon* with a thunderous broadside which dismasted and almost wrecked his ship, killing 200 men in just a moment of time. The *Majestic* too suffered cruelly and Captain Westcott was killed.

Brueys was struck and killed by a shot from *Swiftsure*, and later the flagship *L'Orient* was seen to be ablaze. She blew up at 10 p.m. and this seemed to signal a significant moment in the battle. Although the *Franklin* and *Tonnant* continued to fight gallantly, the French were beaten. With the collapse of their centre the British ships passed down the line to engage the enemy rear, but by then the British were exhausted. Even so, three more 74s were taken or burnt.

All told the French lost eleven of the line and two frigates. The intrepid Rear Admiral Villeneuve in *Guillaume Tell* (80) and the *Généreux* (74)[23] and two frigates managed to escape destruction.

Nelson's brilliant victory established British naval supremacy in the Mediterranean and effectively stranded Napoleon's expeditionary force in Egypt. Gone were his dreams of conquering India. Napoleon's political standing also suffered a severe check. For the first time he was shown to be vulnerable, not the invincible conqueror whom all of Europe believed him to be.

## NORMANDY LANDINGS
*6 June 1944*
### World War II 1939—45

Commander of the naval forces participating in Operation Neptune was Admiral Sir Bertram Ramsay. Ships taking part were:[24]

| | |
|---|---|
| Warships | 1,212 |
| Landing Ships and Craft | 4,026 |
| Ancilliaries | 731 |
| Merchant vessels | 864 |
| *Total* | 6,833 |

78% were British; 17% were USA; 5% were French, Norwegian, Dutch, Polish and Greek.

Over 10,000 marines took part. Marines manned no less than two-thirds of the landing craft. The day is observed as a Memorable Date by 48 Commando RM.

From D-Day to the capture of Le Havre in September:
750 bombardments had been carried out by cruisers and larger ships. The expenditure of ammunition by destroyers and larger ships was:

| | |
|---|---|
| 16" and 15" rounds | 3,371 |
| 7.5" to 5.25" | 31,250 |
| 4.7" to 4" | 24,000 |
| *Total* | 58,621 |

In addition: 609 mines were swept, and 28 surface actions took place. During this same three-month period the following were landed in Normandy:

352,570 men
1,410,600 tons of stores
152,000 vehicles

## NORTH AFRICA LANDINGS (Operation Torch)
*November 1942*
### World War II 1939—45

The struggle to seize North Africa in November 1942 (known by the codename Operation Torch) was waged between formidable Allied forces and the Vichy French forces, supported by units of the French fleet operating from their colonial empire. The Operation was not simply a military battle: it was an enterprise hedged about with diplomatic and political intrigue — even to the extent of trying to

---

23  Within eighteen months even these two ships met their end in the Mediterranean.

24  *The Royal Navy Day By Day*, ed. R.E.A. Shrubb and A.B. Sainsbury (1979)

satisfy Russia by providing a species of second front — something for which they had been clamouring to relieve their beleagured armies on the Eastern Front. Some critics claimed that the whole Operation was an unnecessary enterprise: that these colonial nonentities would have fallen like ripe fruit had the energies and forces used to displace them been properly employed elsewhere.

The armed forces employed in the assaults are listed in the table below.

About 65,000 men, not counting follow-up forces, were landed on beaches. All told, in addition to the more than 300 warships tabled below about 370 merchant ships were employed. Air support initially came from carriers, but by D + 3 160 fighters were ashore at Casablanca, another 160 at Oran and 90 at Algiers.

Opposition from French forces was not strong or prolonged, although the sinking of the two ex-USCG cutters *Walney* and *Hartland* in Oran harbour was a fierce engagement. Within a few days all French forces under the command of Admiral Darlan had surrendered.

Only Tunisia, defended by German forces, resisted stoutly, and it was to be six months before the North African campaign was brought to an end on 12 May 1943.

| Class of Ship | Western Naval Task Force (Morocco) Rear Adml Hewitt USN | Central Naval Task Force (Oran) Commodore Troubridge | Eastern Naval Task Force (Algiers) Vice Adml Burrough | Force H & Fuelling Force Vice Adml Syfret |
|---|---|---|---|---|
| HQ Ship | | *Largs* | *Bulolo* | |
| Aircraft Carriers | *Ranger* | *Argus* | | *Victorious* *Formidable* *Furious* |
| Escort Carriers | *Santee, Chenango Sangamon, Suwannee* | *Biter Dasher* | *Avenger* | |
| Battleships & Battlecruisers | *Massachusetts Texas, New York* | | | *Duke of York Renown Rodney* |
| Cruisers | *Augusta, Wichita, Tuscaloosa, Philadelphia, Savanah, Brooklyn, Cleveland* | *Aurora, Jamaica* | *Sheffield, Scylla, Charybdis* | *Bermuda, Argonaut, Sirius* |
| Destroyers | 38 | 13 | 13 | 17 |
| Submarines | 4 | 2 | 3 | |
| Corvettes | | 6 | 4 | 1 |
| Sloops | | 2 | 3 | |
| Minesweepers | 11 | 8 | 7 | |
| Landing Ships Tanks | | 3 | | |
| Landing Ships Infantry | | 15 | 11 | |
| Combat Loaders | 23 | | 4 | |

In addition, there were 109 other vessels such as trawlers, tankers etc.

## NORTH CAPE ('Scharnhorst' Action)

*26 December 1943*

### World War II 1939—45

This engagement was in the time-honoured naval style, with British forces defending an important convoy from attacks by a marauding force of German ships. The antagonists comprised a squadron of the Home Fleet under the command of Admiral Sir Bruce Fraser with a detached cruiser force under Rear Admiral Burnett, and a battle group of the German navy commanded by Rear Admiral Erich Bey.

On 20 December 1943 Convoy JW 55B comprising nineteen ships sailed from Loch Ewe for Russia via the North Cape. Two days later Convoy RA 55A of twenty-two ships left Kola Inlet in North Russia homeward-bound. Both convoys had heavy close destroyer escorts.

A covering force of the 10th Cruiser Squadron consisted of *Belfast* (11,500 tons, 12—6"), *Norfolk*

NORTH CAPE 1943

(9,925 tons, 8—8") and *Sheffield* (9,400 tons, 12—6"). Distant cover was given by the Home Fleet squadron, comprising the battleship and flagship *Duke of York* (35,000 tons, 10—14"), the cruiser *Jamaica* (8,000 tons, 12—6") and four destroyers.

The battlecruiser *Scharnhorst* (31,800 tons, 9—11") was known to be in Alten Fjord at the northern extremity of Norway. Rear Admiral Bey (Flag Officer Destroyers) was deputizing for Vice Admiral Kummetz (FOC Battle Group). On Boxing Day at 4 a.m. *Scharnhorst* and five destroyers left harbour and headed for the convoys in bitter weather and atrocious sea conditions. Convoy JW55B was being trailed by *U-601*. Burnett's cruiser squadron was 150 miles east of the enemy and Fraser's battle group was about 220 miles to the south-west of the convoy: *Scharnhorst* was about 100 miles south-east of the convoy.

That morning Burnett picked up *Scharnhorst* by radar, closed at full speed and opened fire at 13,500 yards. The first salvoes struck home and among other damage destroyed the battlecruiser's forward radar installation. Bey was taken completely by

surprise, turned away and escaped in the appalling weather conditions and Arctic darkness. So bad were the weather conditions that Bey detached his destroyers to base and operated alone. This needs no comment other than to record that not only did the British destroyers remain at sea, but they participated fully in the battle that followed.

Burnett guessed that Bey would work round and head for the convoy, and he acted accordingly. Sure enough, when *Scharnhorst* spotted the convoy it was Burnett's cruisers which emerged from the gloom and engaged him for twenty minutes, inflicting more damage. Bey broke off the action and headed south-east — unwittingly, directly towards Fraser's battle group.

*Duke of York's* radar picked up *Scharnhorst* four hours later at the extreme range of 44,000 yards. She and *Jamaica* closed the range to 12,000 yards before *Belfast* illuminated the target with a starshell and opened fire.

For the second time that day Bey was totally surprised. His guns were seen to be trained fore and aft. There began a systematic battering of this fine ship by a display of accurate gunfire rarely matched in battle: of the 52 broadsides fired by *Duke of York* 31 scored straddles, with enough hits to put turrets A and B out of action and rupture steam pipes to reduce her speed. Altogether she was struck by about thirty 14" shells plus 6" and 8" shells; she was also hit by eleven torpedoes out of 55 fired at her. As an eye-witness recorded, she 'must have been a hell on earth.'

A feature of the early evening battle was the destroyer attack launched by the *Savage, Saumarez, Scorpion* and *Stord,* which closed as near as 3,000 yards under heavy secondary armament fire to launch their torpedoes.

A little later the other destroyer division comprising *Musketeer, Opportune, Virago* and *Matchless* attacked from even shorter ranges. The target was now a dull red glow in a black pall of smoke. At 7.45 p.m. she blew up and sank. Only 36 men from a crew of 1,986 were rescued from the icy Arctic sea.

## BRITISH

| | | | | |
|---|---|---|---|---|
| *Duke of York* | Battleship | 35,000 | 10−14" | Admiral Sir B. Fraser |
| | | | 16−5.25" | Captain Hon G.H. Russell |
| *Jamaica* | Cruiser | 8,000 | 12−6" | Captain Hughes-Hallett |
| *Belfast* | Cruiser | 11,500[1] | 12−6" | Captain E.R. Parham |
| *Sheffield* | Cruiser | 9,400 | 12−6" | Captain C.T. Addis |
| *Norfolk* | Cruiser | 9,925 | 8−8" | Captain D.K. Bain |
| *Matchless* | Destroyer | 1,920 | 6−4.7"[2] | |
| *Musketeer* | Destroyer | 1,920 | 6−4.7" | Commander R.L. Fisher |
| *Opportune* | Destroyer | 1,540 | 4−4.7" | |
| *Saumarez* | Destroyer | 1,710 | 4−4.7" | |
| *Savage* | Destroyer | 1,710 | 4−4.7" | Commander M. G. Meyrick |
| *Scorpion* | Destroyer | 1,710 | 4−4.7" | |
| *Stord*[3] | Destroyer | 1,710 | 4−4.7" | |
| *Virago* | Destroyer | 1,710 | 4−4.7" | |

## GERMAN

| | | | | |
|---|---|---|---|---|
| *Scharnhorst* | Battlecruiser | 31,800 | 9−11" | Rear Admiral Bey |
| | | | 12−6" | Captain F. Hintze |
| *Z 29*[4] | Destroyer | 2,603 | 5−5.9" | |
| *Z 30* | Destroyer | 2,603 | 5−5.9" | |
| *Z 33* | Destroyer | 2,603 | 5−5.9" | |
| *Z 34* | Destroyer | 2,603 | 5−5.9" | |
| *Z 38* | Destroyer | 2,603 | 5−5.9" | |

1   After breaking her back on a magnetic mine in November 1939 her tonnage was increased from 10,000.

2   All destroyers, German and British, also carried 8−21" TTs.

3   *Stord* was Royal Norwegian Navy.

4   As the narrative shows, these destroyers took no part in the actual battle.

**NORTH FORELAND** — *see* ORFORDNESS

## OKINAWA
*24 March — 21 June 1945*
### World War II 1939—45
The last great naval/military battle in the Pacific before the planned assault on Japan itself in WW II (made unnecessary by the explosion of the first two atomic bombs — 'Little Boy' on Hiroshima and 'Fat Boy' on Nagasaki in August 1945). The British Pacific Fleet — operating as TF 57 — under Vice Admiral Rawlings comprised the four carriers *Indomitable*, *Victorious*, *Illustrious* (later relieved by *Formidable*) and *Indefatigable* with 218 aircraft, the battleships *King George V* and *Howe* with five cruisers and several destroyers. This fleet reinforced Vice Admiral Mitscher's Task Force 58, the USN carrier force which comprised the main element in Admiral Spruance's 5th Fleet. The landing fleet (TF 51) comprised 430 transports and large landing-ships, 10 battleships, 13 cruisers, 18 escort carriers with 540 aircraft. Landings were made on 1 April. Five days later the Japanese began a six-week-long series of kamikaze attacks involving 2,000 planes. 26 ships were sunk (none of them larger than a destroyer) and 164 damaged, including three carriers and three battleships. TF 57 began its attacks on the Sakishima Group on 26 March. On 1 April the *Indefatigable* and *Ulster* were damaged, and five days later *Formidable* and *Victorious* were struck. Organized resistance on the islands ceased on 21 June. The Total US casualties in capturing them amounted to 48,000 killed and wounded.

## OLÉRON ROADS — *see* BASQUE AND AIX ROADS

## OPERATION DYNAMO — *see* DUNKIRK

## OPERATION OVERLORD — *see* NORMANDY LANDINGS

## OPERATION TORCH — *see* NORTH AFRICA LANDINGS

## ORAN (Mers el Kebir)
*3 July 1940*
### World War II 1939—45
A melancholy action between heavy units of the Royal Navy and the bulk of the French fleet at the naval base of Mers el Kebir near Oran in Algeria. With the fall of France in 1940 it became imperative that the French navy should not be surrendered to Germany.

The French Admiral Gensoul commanded the battleships *Dunkerque* (26,500 tons, 8—13") and *Strasbourg* (as her sister ship), the old battleships *Bretagne* and *Provence* (22,100 tons, 10—13.4"), eleven destroyers and five submarines. Admiral Sir John Somerville commanding Force H offered Gensoul three options on 2 July:

1  Join the British forces.

2  Sail to a British port or the West Indies under escort.
3  Scuttle his ships within six hours.

Otherwise Somerville would be compelled to use force — and he had with him *Hood* (42,100 tons, 8—15"), *Valiant* (32,700 tons, 8—15"), *Resolution* (29,150 tons, 8—15") and *Ark Royal* (22,000 tons, 72 aircraft).

Gensoul finally rejected the ultimatum and at 6 p.m. on 3 July Somerville's ships opened fire. A 15" shell from *Hood* blew up the *Bretagne*, killing about 950 Frenchmen. *Dunkerque* and *Provence* and a 2,884-ton destroyer, *Mogador*, were severely damaged and beached. The *Strasbourg* and four destroyers managed to escape to either Toulon or Algiers.

This tragic rift in Anglo-French naval relationships has left scars that even time finds difficult to heal.

## ORFORDNESS (St James's Day or North Foreland)
*25—26 July 1666*
### Second Dutch War 1665—7
This was a battle fought between an English fleet of 89 ships and 17 fireships jointly commanded by Prince Rupert and the Duke of Albemarle, and a Dutch fleet of 85 ships, 20 fireships and 10 smaller vessels, all under the command of Admiral De Ruyter, the Dutch Nelson. The result was a brilliant victory for the English, particularly important because it came so soon after the defeat in the Four Days' Battle.

The long-drawn-out battle began at about 10 a.m. on St James's Day, 26 July, in the North Sea about 40 miles south-east of Orfordness in Suffolk. After two hours battling Admiral Cornelis Tromp's rear squadron sailed out of line, broke through the English line and became locked in combat with the English Blue squadron — the rear squadron under Admiral Sir Jeremy Smythe in the *Resolution* (74). Smythe gained the upper hand, and this battle-within-a-battle became a pursuit of De Ruyter, progressing westward in a confused mêlée, while the main battle between the opposing vans and centres headed nearly due east. The Dutch van was in full flight by 3 p.m. and an hour later the centre gave way too, three flag officers including Jan Evertsen being killed. But by then the English were too exhausted to take advantage.

Although retreating, De Ruyter handled the situation in a disciplined and masterly fashion, even after his own flagship had been severely damaged.

Sporadic skirmishing occurred throughout the night and action flared up briskly in the early daylight hours, but the Dutch continued their retreat to the shoals of their coastline. The battle and pursuit were over.

The Dutch losses were considerable: 20 ships were lost, with 4,000 men killed or drowned and 3,000 wounded. The only English ship lost was Smythe's *Resolution*, and the casualties in men were considerably lighter than the enemy's.

## PALEMBANG
*24 and 29 January 1945*
### World War II 1939—45
This attack on Japanese oil installations in Sumatra was carried out by a British fleet designated Force 63, commanded by Admiral Philip Vian. It was opposed by four fighter squadrons of the 9th Air Division of the Japanese 7th Area Army and by heavy AA batteries. The fleet comprised virtually the whole of the British Pacific Fleet except the battleship *Howe*.

> 1st Aircraft Carrier Squadron: *Indomitable* (flag), *Illustrious*, *Victorious* and *Indefatigable*: battleship *King George V*.
> 4th Cruiser Squadron: *Argonaut*, *Black Prince*, *Euryalus*, *Ceylon*.
> 25th Destroyer Flotilla: *Grenville* (D), *Undine*, *Ursa*, *Undaunted*.
> 27th Destroyer Flotilla: *Kempenfelt* (D), *Wakeful*, *Whirlwind*, *Wager*, *Wessex*, *Whelp*.

This force carried 239 aircraft and was supported by an oiling group, Force 69 (*Urchin*, *Echodale*, *Wave King*, *Empire Salvage* and — later — *Arndale*).

Meridian One was the codename for the strike at the Royal Dutch Oil refinery at Pladjoe (24 January), the largest and most important refinery in the Far East, and Meridian Two (29 January) for the second largest at the Standard Oil refinery at Soengi Gerong. These strikes were the two largest undertaken by the FAA in WWII.

Enormous damage was inflicted, the effects of which lasted for months. 68 Japanese aircraft were also destroyed. British losses amounted to: 16 aircraft lost in battle, 11 ditched, 14 destroyed in deck crashes: a total of 41 aircraft from 378 sorties. Personnel lost only amounted to 30 aircrew.

## PASSERO — *see* CAPE PASSERO

## PELAGOSA
*29 November 1811*
### Napoleonic War 1803—15
This was a spirited action between two small squadrons of British and French ships in the Adriatic near Lissa, where Captain Murray Maxwell commanded the *Alceste* (38), the *Active* (48: Captain James Alexander Gordon), *Unité* (36: Captain Edwin H. Chamberlayne) and *Acorn* (20: Captain George Miller Bligh). The French squadron was commanded by Commodore Montfort in the *Pauline* (40), accompanied by the *Pomone* (40) and *Persanne* (26). HMS *Acorn* had been detached to remain in Lissa harbour

to defend the area. Action at sea began at 11 a.m. and continued till late afternoon. *Unité* chased the *Persanne*, which failed to keep up with her consorts, and stood away to the north-east. *Persanne* was overtaken, and when badly damaged she struck.

*Active* and *Alceste* engaged the other two ships fiercely. After *Pomone* had lost two of her masts (the third was to come down later) she struck: she had 50 killed and wounded out of a crew of 332. But the two British ships were themselves too badly damaged to pursue *Pauline* and she made good her escape. *Active* lost 7 killed and had 13 wounded from 218 men aboard, and *Alceste* suffered 8 killed and 27 wounded.

## PONDICHERRY
*10 September 1759*
### Seven Years' War 1756—63
The third and final clash between a squadron of seven of the line commanded by Vice Admiral Pocock and a French squadron of eleven of the line under the Comte D'Aché in the Indian Ocean off the Coromandel coast. (See CUDDALORE and NEGAPATAM).

A running battle ensued with both squadrons formed into line ahead on a parallel course.

The accuracy and speed of the British gunnery outweighed the enemy's superiority in numbers, and the climax came when D'Aché's flagship *Zodiaque* (74) was severely damaged and hauled out of line with her captain killed and the admiral wounded.

The English ships suffered considerable damage to rigging and sails. The battle ended with the Frenchmen managing to get into the safety of Pondicherry, at a cost of about 1,500 casualties.

Soon after this defeat D'Aché's squadron was recalled to France and she abandoned the Indian station.

## PORTLAND (The Three Days' Battle)
*18—20 February 1653*
### First Dutch War 1652—4
The battle was fought between a fleet of 80 English ships under the command of General-at-sea Robert Blake, supported by Monck, Deane and William Penn, and a Dutch fleet of equal size escorting a fleet of about 150 merchantmen, all under the command of Tromp. The English ships assembled at Portsmouth as the Dutch fleet approached the Channel.

Action was joined on the 18th off Portland and it soon developed into a long running battle. Tromp was supported by De Ruyter and Evertsen, but they were all hampered by having to protect the convoy. Tromp displayed great skill and seamanship in keeping his losses to a minimum and reaching the safety of Gravelines. All told he lost 8 warships and 30 merchantmen. Blake lost only one ship. His was a decisive victory, and it represented a turning-point in the war with the Netherlands.

**PORTO BELLO** — *see* PUERTO BELLO

## PORTO FARINA
*4 April 1655*

General-at-sea Robert Blake wore his flag in the *George* when he commanded a force of fifteen warships which destroyed the forts at Porto Farina in Tunisia and sank 9 Algerian warships.

## PORTO PRAYA
*16 April 1781*

### American War of Independence 1775–83

This action took place in the Porto Praya roads on the south coast of St Jago in the Cape Verde Islands, between a small British squadron commanded by Commodore Johnstone and an even smaller squadron under the great French admiral (then Commodore) Pierre André de Suffren.

Johnstone's force comprised five of the line, several smaller warships and some troop transports en route to take the Dutch colony at the Cape of Good Hope.

Suffren left Brest for India with five of the line. Just two of these ships surprised Johnstone's — and these two, both of them 74s and one of them Suffren's flagship, the *Héros*, and the other the *Annibal* — launched a furious attack, taking Johnstone completely unawares. After seriously damaging the British ships Suffren wisely retired.

While Johnstone remained to make good the damage sustained, Suffren hurried to the Cape and seized it from the Dutch before Johnstone could get a look in!

## 'PRINCE OF WALES' AND 'REPULSE' — *see* FORCE Z

## PROVIDIEN
*12 April 1782*

### American War of Independence 1775–83

This was the second clash in the Hughes/Suffren series of battles for supremacy in the Indian Ocean 1782–3. Admiral Sir Edward Hughes commanded eleven of the line and was reinforcing Trincomalee in Ceylon, which he had captured earlier in the year.

Admiral Pierre Suffren — destined to go down as one of France's greatest admirals — commanded an equal number of ships. It was his good fortune to encounter Hughes's squadron on a lee shore with little sea room off Providien to the north of Trincomalee.

A bitter struggle developed between the French *Héros* (flag: 74), *L'Orient* (74), and *Brillant* (64), and the British *Superb* (flag: 74) and *Monmouth* (64). The latter was carronaded almost to a wreck but refused to strike.

Fighting continued until exhaustion set in. Both sides anchored for the night but neither resumed

action the following morning. They licked their wounds in sight of each other for a week, then Suffren sailed north and Hughes south for Trincomalee.

## PUERTO BELLO
*22 November 1739*

### War with Spain and France 1739–48

Vice Admiral Edward Vernon with his flag hoisted in the *Burford* commanded six ships which captured Puerto Bello, Panama.

## PUNTA STILO — *see* CALABRIA

## QUEBEC
*13 September 1759*

### Seven Years' War 1756–63

The Seven Years' War started with French settlers in Canada fortifying a number of posts against the advance of English settlers. As the war developed it was clear that the French city of Quebec 'was the key to the conquest of upper Canada'. The attempt to capture the city from the French resulted in a brilliant exploit by Major-General James Wolfe and Vice Admiral Charles Saunders in the *Neptune*. The British fleet under Saunders carried an army up the St Lawrence, brilliantly navigated by Master (later Captain) James Cook. The fleet dominated the river and landed 17,000 men below the Plains of Abraham. Seamen landed guns and hauled them up the Heights of Abraham. A splendid victory was achieved.

## QUIBERON BAY
*20 November 1759*

### Seven Years' War 1756–63

One of the most celebrated naval battles in the Royal Navy's history was fought between a British force — the Western Squadron — under Admiral Sir Edward Hawke commanding twenty-three of the line with his flag in the *Royal George* (100), and Admiral the Comte de Conflans with twenty-one French of the line including his flagship the *Soleil Royal* (80), and three frigates. Hawke's force was augmented by a squadron of ten small ships commanded by Commodore Duff.

The French were planning an invasion of Ireland. Conflans evaded the British blockade of Brest and took his squadron to strengthen the invasion forces. In a rising westerly gale he sought sanctuary in Quiberon Bay, where the squadron hove to west of Belle Isle.

Admiral Hawke learnt of Conflans's escape from Brest and set off in pursuit. He located the Frenchman's ships in the treacherous, rock-strewn shoal waters of the bay. The master of Hawke's flagship dared to warn the admiral of the dangerous shallows, but the latter replied: 'You have done your duty in pointing out to me the danger. Now lay me

## HAWKE'S FLEET

| Ship | Guns | Commander | Ship | Guns | Commander |
|---|---|---|---|---|---|
| The Royal George | 100 | Sir E. Hawke Capt. Campbell | Hero | 74 | Hon G. Edgecumbe |
| Union | 90 | Sir C. Hardy Capt. J. Evans | Swiftsure | 70 | Sir T. Stanhope* |
| Duke | 90 | T. Graves | Dorsetshire | 70 | P. Denis |
| Namur | 90 | M. Buckle | Burford | 70 | J. Gambier |
| Mars | 74 | Commodore James Young | Chichester | 70 | E.S. Willet |
| Warspight | 74 | Sir John Bentley* | Temple | 70 | Hon. W. Shirley |
| | | | Revenge | 64 | J. Storr |
| Hercules | 74 | E. Fortescue | Essex+ | 64 | L. O'Brien |
| Torbay | 74 | Hon. A. Keppel | Kingston | 60 | T. Shirley |
| Magnanime | 74 | Lord Howe | Intrepide | 60 | J. Maplesden |
| Resolution+ | 74 | H. Speke | Montagu | 60 | J. Rowley |
| | | | Dunkirk | 60 | R. Digby |
| | | | Defiance | 60 | P. Baird |

## DUFF'S SHIPS AND THE FRIGATES

| Ship | Guns | Commander | Ship | Guns | Commander |
|---|---|---|---|---|---|
| Rochester | 50 | Capt. R. Duff | Venus | 36 | T. Harrison |
| Portland | 50 | M. Arbuthnot | Vengeance | 28 | G. Nightingale |
| Falkland | 50 | Fr. S. Drake | Coventry | 28 | F. Burslem |
| Chatham | 50 | J. Lockhart | Maidstone | 28 | D. Diggs |
| Minerva | 32 | A. Hood | Sapphire | 32 | J. Strachan |

## CONFLANS'S FLEET

| Ship | Guns | Commander | Ship | Guns | Commander |
|---|---|---|---|---|---|
| Soleil Royal | 80 | Conflans Capt. de Chézac | Juste | 70 | Saint Allouarn |
| Tonnant | 80 | de Beauffremont | Dauphin Royal | 70 | Vicomte d'Urtubie |
| | | | Inflexible | 70 | Chevr. de Caumont |
| | | | Dragon | 70 | Levassor de Latouche |
| Formidable | 80 | Duverger | Eveillé | 70 | Chevr. de Laprévalais |
| Orient | 80 | de Budez | Sphinx | 70 | Chevr. de Coutance-Laselle |
| Intrépide | 74 | Chasteloger | | | |
| Magnifique | 74 | Bigot de Morogues | Solitaire | 70 | Vicomte de Langle |
| Glorieux | 74 | Villars de Labrosse | Brilliant | 70 | Boischateau |
| Thésée | 74 | de Kersaint | Bizarre | 70 | Chevr. de Rohan |
| Héros | 74 | Vicomte de Sanzay | | | |
| Robuste | 74 | Marquis de Vienne | Frigates:— *Vestale, Aigrette* | | |
| Northumberland | 74 | Chevr. de Belingant | Corvettes:— *Calypso, Prince Noir* | | |
| Superbe | 74 | | | | |

* Bentley and Stanhope were both knighted for their parts in the battle of Lagos, and had taken part in the battle of Cape Finisterre II.

+ *Resolution* and *Essex* were Hawke's only losses — both were wrecked by storm rather than the enemy.

alongside the enemy's flagship.'

Conflans believed Hawke would not hazard his ships and attempt to force a battle in such confined waters and dreadful weather. He was wrong.

In bitter fighting the British van mauled the French rear, and during the afternoon and evening the French *Formidable* (80) struck, the battered *Superbe* (74) capsized, the badly damaged *Héros* (74) struck and when the *Thésée* (74) was practically wrecked by the *Torbay* she foundered with the loss of about 700 men.

When darkness fell the British anchored, but some of the French beat out of the bay and escaped south. Others broke their backs on the bar in attempting to shelter in the Vilaine estuary, or became trapped after lightening ship by jettisoning their cannons.

The *Soleil Royal*, flagship, got under way early the following day, but grounded on the Rouelle Shoal and was burnt by her crew to prevent capture. Later the *Juste* (70) foundered in the Loire estuary.

The French lost a total of seven ships of the line and over 2,500 men killed or killed or drowned. Of those ships which survived many were unfit for further sea service. The British lost two ships —

279

*Resolution* (74) and *Essex* (64) — both of which ran aground early in the battle and were wrecked in the continuing storm.

Hawke's was a brilliant victory achieved by skilled seamanship, daring and resolution under most adverse conditions, and off an enemy shore. In achieving this victory he also dispelled the threat of invasion.

## RIVER PLATE ('Graf Spee' Action)

*13 December 1939*

### World War II 1939—45

The first naval battle of World War II took place in the estuary of the river Plate on the east coast of South America. It was fought between a small cruiser force commanded by Commodore H. Harwood and the German pocket-battleship *Admiral Graf Spee* (12,100 tons, 6—11" and 8—5.9"), commanded by Captain H. Langsdorff.

Harwood's cruiser force was one of many searching for the *Graf Spee*, which was on a marauding expedition against Allied merchant shipping. Harwood thought that the busy shipping lanes of the Plate (Montevideo — Buenos Aires — La Plata) would attract Langsdorff, and he proved right when

RIVER PLATE 1939

on 13 December he sighted the *Graf Spee*.

Harwood wore his broad pennant in *Ajax* (6,985 tons, 8—6") and had in company HMS *Exeter* (8,390 tons, 6—8") and HMNZS *Achilles* (7,030 tons, 8—6").

Langsdorff closed the British squadron at full speed. Harwood divided his force, *Exeter* to one side and the two light cruisers to the other, compelling Langsdorff to split his main armament between two forces — or concentrate on one, to the advantage of the other.

Within half an hour *Exeter* was in dire trouble. The heavy 11" shells had silenced all but one of her main guns. *Ajax* and *Achilles* too suffered hits, but they had also struck the *Graf Spee* with their 6" shells. *Ajax* came in for special attention, and when she was badly mauled Harwood called off the action and retired behind smoke.

Curiously, *Graf Spee* did not pursue, and win an outright victory, or even head away to the broad expanse of the South Atlantic. Instead she set course for Montevideo, a neutral port.

British ships began to head for the River Plate while *Graf Spee* remained secured alongside, trapped into believing that a strong force already lay in wait in the estuary.

On 17 December Langsdorff took *Graf Spee* out of harbour to the three-mile limit and scuttled her in the estuary. A few days later he committed suicide.

# RUSSIAN CONVOYS — PQ 17

*2–13 July 1942*

## World War II 1939–45

From the winter of 1941–2 the Royal Navy began escorting convoys to Russia, north-about Bear Island to Murmansk and Archangel. Although the convoys and some escorts were Allied, the predominant content of the convoys and escorts were British. These convoys endured not only appalling weather conditions but the threat of German U-boats, surface units and aircraft. One such convoy was PQ 17.

It comprised thirty-five merchantmen, three rescue ships, two tankers and thirteen close escort vessels. a close support force of four cruisers and three destroyers accompanied the convoy. Long-range cover was provided by units of the Home Fleet under Admiral Sir John Tovey with two battleships, one carrier, two cruisers and fourteen destroyers. Several Allied submarines formed defensive patrol lines off the northern Norway coast in addition to all these other deployments.

The Germans had considerable forces at their disposal in these far northern waters. U-boats *U-334* and *U-456* were supported by six boats of the 'Eiseufel' Group (*U-251*, *U-335*, *U-657*, *U-88*, *U-457* and *U-376*). In Norwegian fjords lay the Trondheim Group of warships comprising the battleship *Tirpitz* (Admiral Schneiwind), heavy cruiser *Hipper*, destroyers *Hans Lody*, *Theodor Riedl*, *Karl Gustar*, *Friedrich Ihn*; T Boats *T 7* and *T 15*. Ships which had left Trondheim for Altenfjord were the pocket battleship *Admiral Scheer* (Vice Admiral Kummetz), heavy cruiser *Lützow*, destroyers *Friedrich Eckholt* and *Erich Steinbrinck*. The Narvik Group destroyers left Narvik for Trondheim: *Z 24*, *Z 27*, *Z 28*, *Z 29*, *Z 30* and *Richard Beitzen*. An indication of the difficulty of piloting through these waters is given by the fact that the destroyers *Lody*, *Riedel* and *Karl Gustar* all ran aground and returned to base, while the *Lützow* also ran aground and took no further part in the operations.

The Admiralty believed that the German North Sea Combat Group — the combination of all these groups or squadrons — had put to sea in the direction of North Cape. With mounting anxiety for the safety of the convoy and its escorting forces, the Admiralty ordered the long-range group to retire to the west and the convoy to disperse, and later to scatter. The Home Fleet units turned about at Bear Island. At that time only three ships had been lost, all to aircraft.

In the meantime the German North Sea Combat Group also turned back to base, judging the condi-

## ABSTRACT OF STATISTICS RELATING TO RUSSIAN CONVOYS 1941–5

Number of convoys escorted to Russia = 40   Total ships = 720
Number of convoys escorted from Russia = 35   Total ships = 680
Allied Merchant Ship Losses

| Category | British | USA | Panama | USSR | Dutch | Norway | Total | Gross Tons |
|---|---|---|---|---|---|---|---|---|
| Eastbound | 21 | 29 | 5 | 2 | 1 | – | 58 | 353,366 |
| Westbound | 6 | 15 | 2 | 5 | – | 1 | 29 | 178,317 |
| Independents | 3 | 1 | – | 2 | – | – | 6 | 42,004 |
| In USSR ports | 3 | 2 | – | – | – | – | 5 | 27,278 |
| Other ways | 2 | – | – | – | – | – | 2 | 4,872 |
| **Totals** | **35** | **47** | **7** | **9** | **1** | **1** | **100** | **605,837** |

*Goods delivered by Great Britain:*

3,830 tanks + 1,388 from Canada
4,932 anti-tank guns
1,800 radar sets
2,000 telephone sets
4 submarines

7,411 aircraft (including 3,129 USA)
4,005 rifles and machine guns
4,338 radio sets
9 MTBs
14 minesweepers

£120 millions-worth of raw materials, foodstuffs, industrial plant, medical and hospital supplies and equipment.

### Royal Navy Ships Lost Escorting Russian Convoys 1941–5

| | |
|---|---|
| Cruisers: | *Trinidad, Edinburgh* |
| Destroyers: | *Matabele, Punjabi, Somali, Achates, Hardy, Mahratta* |
| Sloops: | *Kite, Lapwing* |
| Frigate: | *Goodall* |
| Corvettes: | *Denbigh Castle, Bluebell* |
| Minesweepers: | *Gossamer, Niger, Leda, Bramble* |
| Armed Whaler: | *Shera* |
| Submarine: | *P551* |

### German Warship Losses:

Battleship *Tirpitz*; Battlecruiser *Scharnhorst*; 3 destroyers and 32 U-boats

tions and forces employed unlikely to prove rewarding.

In the event the now unprotected and scattering convoy suffered terrible losses and casualties. All told twenty-three of the merchant ships — two-thirds of those in the convoy — were sunk by either torpedo or bomb, plus one of the rescue ships, altogether totalling 144,000 tons: in addition, of course, all the cargoes were lost. Five German aircraft were shot down.

This disastrous episode will long be debated in naval circles. What is not any longer disputed is the fact that the sailing of PQ 17 was an unsound operation of war, but political considerations made it paramount.

> **Summary of the Losses:**
> Of the 35 merchant ships, 2 turned back, 8 were sunk by aircraft, 9 sunk by U-boats, 7 damaged by aircraft then sunk by U-boats. Stores lost: 430 tanks, 210 aircraft, 3,350 vehicles, 99,316 tons cargo. 153 merchant seamen were lost, 1,300 were rescued.

# SABANG

*25 July 1944*

## World War II 1939—45

This operation was an air strike and naval bombardment of Japanese-occupied installations at Sabang, Sumatra. Surface ships of the Eastern Fleet engaged Japanese shore batteries. Operation Crimson was under the command of Admiral Sir James Somerville in the *Queen Elizabeth*. It was an impressive fleet which assembled for the operation, officially designated Force 62.

# SADRAS (20th April 1758) — *see* CUDDALORE I

# SADRAS

*17 February 1782*

## American War of Independence 1775—83

The first of a series of five engagements [25] fought between Vice Admiral Sir Edward Hughes and Commodore the Comte Pierre André de Suffren during 1782—3.

They first met off Madras, when Suffren failed to surprise Hughes. Suffren had with him a small convoy of transports and he was not anxious to join battle. Hughes weighed anchor and set off in pursuit.

On the night of 15/16 July Hughes captured six of the transports. The following day the two squadrons engaged. Suffren had eleven of the line and Hughes nine. Suffren had the wind advantage and concentrated his attack on the last five in Hughes's line.

The *Exeter* (64) suffered seriously and was almost taken, and Hughes's own flagship *Superb* was also badly damaged. The wind suddenly changed and allowed the British van to come up and rescue the flagship. The battle petered out and Suffren was content to get clear of the British. His captains showed little resolution during the fight and failed to turn advantage to victory.

# THE SAINTES (The Saints)

*12 April 1782*

## American War of Independence 1775—83

This great battle was fought between a British fleet under Admiral Sir George Rodney, commanding thirty-six of the line, and a French fleet under the command of Vice Admiral the Comte de Grasse comprising thirty-two ships of the line. The battle settled once and for all the naval dominance of the West Indies. It also added a chapter to the tactics of naval warfare in *Fighting Instructions* by introducing the tactic of breaking the line of battle, sailing through the gap in the line, carronading the enemy as the ship passed through the gap in the line, and even forcing the enemy to engage on both sides of his ship. The traditional and stereotyped line of battle, with both sides' line passing along the other and engaging ships as they came within range of shot, had till now been sacrosanct.

A curtain-raiser to the battle was an encounter four days before the Saintes battle when de Grasse missed a fine opportunity at Dominica (see DOMINICA) to destroy Admiral Hood's van division of Rodney's fleet. Now he found himself lacking the superiority he enjoyed in the earlier encounter. A long, three-day pursuit of Rodney followed.

On 12 April at about 7 a.m. the French fleet with de Grasse in *Ville de Paris* (104), hampered by a large convoy in its charge, was brought to action near a small group of islands in the channel between Guadaloupe and Dominica. The islands are The Saints, or Les Saintes. The opposing lines of battle passed each other slowly on opposite courses, exchanging broadsides.

At 9.15 a.m. the wind veered suddenly four points, the French line grew ragged in the lee of Dominica and developed gaps in the line. Rodney in *Formidable* (90), then the *Duke* (90) and the *Bedford* (74) snatched the opportunity to sail through the breaks in the French line. At the rear of the fleet, second-in-command Admiral Sir Thomas Hood followed suit with all twelve of his division following the *Bedford*. The British thus gained the weather gage and the French tried desperately to reform their line on their leeward-most ships. But they lost the 74s *Glorieux*, *César* and *Hector*, all of which struck. By late afternoon *Ardent* had also been taken and the French flagship was surrounded completely.

Just before 6.30 p.m. the flagship struck: she had no less than 400 men killed aboard her. Hood in

---

25  See PROVIDIEN, NEGAPATAM, TRINCOMALEE and CUDDALORE.

## BRITISH FLEET

| Ship | Guns | Ship | Guns |
|------|------|------|------|
| *Formidable* | 90 | *Marlborough* | 74 |
| *Agamemnon* | 64 | *Monarch* | 74 |
| *Ajax* | 74 | *Montagu* | 74 |
| *Alcide* | 74 | *Namur* | 90 |
| *Alfred* | 74 | *Nonsuch* | 64 |
| *America* | 64 | *Prince George* | 90 |
| *Anson* | 64 | *Prince William* | 64 |
| *Arrogant* | 74 | *Princessa* | 70 |
| *Barfleur* | 90 | *Prothee* | 64 |
| *Bedford* | 74 | *Repulse* | 64 |
| *Belliqueux* | 64 | *Resolution* | 74 |
| *Canada* | 74 | *Royal Oak* | 74 |
| *Centaur* | 74 | *Russell* | 74 |
| *Conqueror* | 74 | *St Albans* | 64 |
| *Duke* | 90 | *Torbay* | 74 |
| *Fame* | 74 | *Valiant* | 74 |
| *Hercules* | 74 | *Warrior* | 74 |
| *Magnificent* | 74 | *Yarmouth* | 64 |

## FRENCH FLEET

| Ship | Guns | Ship | Guns |
|------|------|------|------|
| *Ville de Paris* (Flagship)* | 104 | *Hector** | 74 |
| *Ardent** | 64 | *Hercule** | 74 |
| *Auguste* | 80 | *Languedoc* | 80 |
| *Bourgogne* | 74 | *Magnanime* | 74 |
| *Brave* | 74 | *Magnifique* | 74 |
| *César** | 74 | *Marseillais* | 74 |
| *Citoyen* | 74 | *Neptune* | 74 |
| *Conquérant* | 74 | *Northumberland* | 74 |
| *Couronne* | 80 | *Palmier* | 74 |
| *Dauphin Royal* | 70 | *Pluton* | 74 |
| *Destin* | 74 | *Réfléchi* | 74 |
| *Diadème* | 74 | *Sceptre* | 74 |
| *Duc de Bourgogne* | 80 | *Scipion* | 74 |
| *Eveillé* | 64 | *Souverain* | 74 |
| *Glorieux** | 74 | *Triomphant* | 80 |

*Signifies captured

*Barfleur* (90) accepted the surrender.

De Vandrevil took command of the remainder of the French fleet and establishing some semblance of order led the fleet away. Rodney pursued, but a little half-heartedly, and then gave up the chase, allowing Hood the criticism that many more ships could have been taken if the pursuit had been more vigorous. Indeed, most of Rodney's officers considered that he had 'botched his battle'.[26]

Nevertheless, it was a substantial victory for Rodney: the French losses amounted to five ships and over 2,000 men killed and wounded and many more taken prisoner. The British lost no ships, and their casualties amounted to just over 1,000 men.

**ST JAMES'S DAY** — *see* ORFORDNESS

## ST KITTS
*25–26 January 1782*

### American War of Independence 1775–83

A remarkable battle between a British fleet commanded by Rear Admiral Sir Samuel Hood, commanding twenty-two ships of the line, and the French Comte de Grasse with twenty-four of the line and a large number of transports which had landed 8,000 troops and captured St Kitts in the West Indies. The troops had been landed at the Basseterre anchorage: when de Grasse quit the anchorage to do battle with Hood

26  Captain Cornwallis wrote of the missed opportunity: 'I could think of nothing for a week after 12th April but what could be the motive of his forbearance, having such an opportunity thrown in his way, not to take advantage of it.' *The Life and Letters of Admiral Cornwallis*, G. Cornwallis-West (1927), p.126.

the latter determined to avoid battle and to seize the anchorage itself.

This he did. In a masterly move he took his fleet into the anchorage, and despite the rear being harassed by de Grasse and shore batteries engaging his ships, he had them anchor in succession so that attacking ships would receive full broadsides from the British ships. Hood beat off two or more such attacks and de Grasse lost heart and withdrew, but as the British troops ashore had surrendered Hood found an opportunity to slip away unnoticed and reached safety.

## ST LUCIA I
*15 December 1778*

### American War of Independence 1775−83
St Lucia is one of the smaller islands of the Windward group. In November 1778 Rear Admiral Samuel Barrington, commander of the much weakened naval forces in the area, was reinforced by ships from North America, but almost simultaneously the French naval strength in the area was also increased to about twelve of the line under Admiral D'Estaing.

On 14 December Barrington's small squadron gave support to a British expeditionary force landing troops to capture St Lucia when intelligence was received of the approach of the French squadron. But Barrington's force was protected by a good anchorage — the bay of Grand Cul de Sac — and his guns covered the entrance.

D'Estaing in the *Languedoc* (90), leading a transport fleet of 7,000 troops to retake the island was repulsed at Carenage by shore batteries, and then twice more at Barrington's anchorage. He withdrew and landed the troops farther north at an undefended location, but it was an abortive operation. Within a month the French governor ashore had surrendered and the British occupation was complete.

## ST LUCIA II
*24 May 1796*

### French Revolutionary War 1793−1802
The island was captured by naval forces under the command of Rear Admiral Sir Hugh Cloberry Christian with his flag in the *Thunderer*, and military forces under the command of Lieutenant-General Sir Ralph Abercromby.

## ST NAZAIRE
*28 March 1942*

### World War II 1939−45
An attack upon St Nazaire was carried out by light forces under the command of Commander R.E.D. Ryder (MGB 314). Commandos were under the military control of Lieutenant-Colonel A.C. Newman. The purpose of the attack was to destroy the gates to the Normandie dock, the only one on the Atlantic seaboard capable of accommodating the

*Tirpitz.* HMS *Campbeltown*, an old destroyer commanded by Lieutenant-Commander S.H. Beattie, was modified to ram the dock caisson. Ryder's MGB, an MTB and 16 MLs were used to land the commandos, but the German defences were alerted. The explosives did considerable damage and the raid was very successful, but only four MLs returned home safely. Five VCs were awarded for valour, in this, Operation Chariot.

## ST VINCENT — *see* CAPE ST VINCENT

## SAKISHIMA GROUP
*26 March 1945*

### World War II 1939−45
Operation Iceberg was conducted by naval forces under the command of Vice Admiral Sir Bernard Rawlings. Aircraft of Task Force 57 attacked airfields on Myako and Ishigaki Islands of the Sakishima Group. 1,000 tons of bombs were dropped, 1,000 rockets fired and no less than 5,335 sorties flown by aircraft from *Illustrious, Indomitable, Indefatigable* and *Victorious. Howe* and *KGV* were accompanied by five cruisers, eleven destroyers, with another three with the Fleet Train. 57 enemy aircraft were destroyed in combat, with about the same number destroyed on the ground.

## SALERNO
*9 September−6 October 1943*

### World War II 1939−45
An amphibious assault was launched against the Germans in Italy in the area of Salerno as a first step to capturing Naples. For four days after landing on the 9th, 41 Commando were heavily engaged against crack German divisions. *Warspite* and *Valiant* helped restore the Allied situation ashore by heavy bombardment. 'The margin of success in the landings was carried by the naval guns' reported the naval commander, and the Germans attributed their failure to achieve a breakthrough to the beaches to the devastating effects of the battleships' gunfire. *Warspite* was crippled by a radio-controlled bomb which exploded in a boiler room and passed through the ship's bottom. She was towed to Gibraltar, where large cofferdams were built on her bottom to effect repairs.

## SAN DOMINGO
*6 February 1806*

### Napoleonic War 1803−15
This was a spirited action between a squadron of six of the line and two frigates commanded by Admiral Sir John Duckworth, and Rear Admiral Leissègues, commanding a French squadron comprising the *Impérial* (120), *Alexandre* (80), *Jupiter* (74) and *Diomède* (74), plus two frigates.

Leissègues had escaped the Brest blockade and fled to the West Indies. He was followed from Cadiz

SAN DOMINGO 1806

by Duckworth, who eventually caught up with him in Occa Bay at the eastern end of San Domingo.

After only one and a half hours of furious action Duckworth had routed the French squadron, which had been caught provisioning. The huge *Impérial* and *Diomède* were driven ashore and burnt to avoid capture. The remaining three of the line were captured. Only the two frigates escaped.

## SANTA CRUZ
*20 April 1657*

### War With Spain 1655–60
General-at-sea Robert Blake with his flag in the *George* destroyed sixteen Spanish ships in a fierce battle off Santa Cruz, Teneriffe. On the way home — just off Plymouth — he died.

## SANTA MARTA
*20–24 August 1702*

### War of the Spanish Succession 1702–13
This battle displayed the amazing courage of the English Vice Admiral John Benbow, commanding seven ships of the line, and the cowardice of some of his captains. The adversary was the Frenchman Du Casse, commanding four of the line and a frigate.

The two squadrons met on 20 August and a running fight ensued over the next four days, with Benbow leading his flagship *Breda* (70) supported by the two 48s *Ruby* and *Falmouth*. The rest of his

squadron comprised the *Defiance, Greenwich, Pendennis* and *Windsor*.

Their captains ignored Benbow's signals and took no part in the action. Benbow broke off the action after he was severely wounded by a chain shot that smashed his right leg. The squadron returned to Jamaica, and a few days later Benbow died of his wounds.

The captains of the four ships were court-martialled. Those of the *Defiance* and *Greenwich* were sentenced to death by shooting and the others cashiered.

## SAUMAREZ'S ACTION — *see* ALGECIRAS

## SAVO ISLAND
*9 August 1942*

### World War II 1939–45
This was a disastrous battle for the Allied heavy cruiser squadron giving cover to Guadalcanal landings, when the Japanese Admiral Mikawa's heavy cruiser squadron surprised them at Savo Island.

The Allied squadron was surprised at 2 a.m. Illuminated by starshell, their guns shown to be trained fore and aft, they were blasted to destruction like the Italian cruisers at Cape Matapan. In half an hour the US cruisers *Astoria, Quincy, Vincennes* and HMAS *Canberra* — all 8″ gun ships — were sunk or so crippled that they foundered later. The Allied casualties amounted to 1,023 killed and 709 wounded. The Japanese casualties were negligible. Only the flagship *Chokai* received any damage.

| Allied | | | | | Japanese | | | | |
|---|---|---|---|---|---|---|---|---|---|
| USS | *Astoria* | 9,950 | 9−8″ | | IJN | *Chokai* | 11,350 | 10−8″ | |
| | *Quincy* | 9,375 | 9−8″ | | | *Aoba* | 8,300 | 6−7.9″ | |
| | *Vincennes* | 9,400 | 9−8″ | | | *Kako* | 8,100 | 6−7.9″ | |
| | *Chicago* | 9,300 | 9−8″ | | | *Kinugasa* | 8,300 | 6−7.9″ | |
| HMAS | *Canberra* | 9,850 | 8−8″ | | | *Furutaka* | 8,100 | 6−7.9″ | |
| HMAS | *Australia* | 9,570 | 8−8″ | | | | | | |
| HMAS | *Hobart* | 7,150 | 6−6″ | | | | | | |

Destroyers − 6

Light Cruisers − 2
Destroyers − 1

Rounds fired:  107−8″
              385−5″

Rounds fired:  1,020−8″
               176−5.5″

Torpedoes fired:  8

Torpedoes fired:  61

## 'SCHARNHORST' ACTION — *see* NORTH CAPE

## SCHEVENINGEN I (First Texel)

*31 July 1653*

### First Dutch War 1652−4

This was the last naval battle of this war. An English fleet commanded by General-at-sea George Monck (Blake was ill) fought a bitter battle with a Dutch fleet commanded by Marten Tromp. Both fleets were at sea around the Texel, and both numbered about 100 ships. Admiral De With, with about 27 ships and ten fireships, was blockaded by Monck. The two main fleets sighted each other at about noon on the 29th July. Tromp cleverly lured Monck from his blockading area, and Monck's fleet chased Tromp's, and his leading ships engaged the last in Tromp's line. Only about 30 ships altogether got engaged. De With managed to slip out of harbour with his force and in a rising gale sped to join Tromp. The combined fleets enjoyed a great superiority over the English.

At about 7 a.m. on the 31st the fleets came to close action off the tiny harbour of Scheveningen. For six hours the battle raged. Tromp was killed by a musket ball shot to the heart. Jan Evertsen assumed command. After hours of desperately hard fighting, the English secured ascendancy, and by 8 p.m. the Dutch were in full flight and the battle was over. The English lost 250 killed including a vice admiral, a rear admiral and five captains. Another 700 men were wounded, and two ships were lost. The Dutch lost at least 14 ships,[27] eight captains and 1,300 prisoners. It was a disastrous outcome for the Dutch: the only crumb of comfort was that they had raised the siege of the Hague.

## SCHOONEVELD I

*28 May 1673*

### Third Dutch War 1672−4

The Schooneveld is (or was) a long basin guarding the entrance to the Scheldt estuary. Two battles were fought here: the first between an Anglo-French fleet commanded by Prince Rupert, with Admiral Sir Edward Spragge as second-in-command, and a Dutch fleet commanded by the redoubtable Admiral De Ruyter. The composition of these two fleets was as set out below.

After days of reconnoitring and manoeuvring Prince Rupert determined to attack De Ruyter's fleet on 28 May, but the Dutchman emerged from the

| | Anglo-French | Netherlands |
|---|---|---|
| Ships of the line | 54 British | 52 |
| | 27 French | |
| Frigates | 11 | 12 |
| Fireships | 35 | 25 |
| Flags | Prince Rupert (van) | Tromp (van) |
| | d'Estrées (centre) | De Ruyter (centre) |
| | Spragge (rear) | Banckerts (rear) |

---

27   According to *Salt In Their Blood* by Francis Vere, Cassell (1955), Monck claimed 20 to 30 Dutch ships were taken or destroyed.

shoals with a favourable wind to meet the Allied combined fleet approaching in line abreast. For nine hours a fierce battle ensued, in the course of which De Ruyter broke the French line but had to fall back to aid the hard-pressed Banckerts. Tromp (junior) also got into difficulties with the English van — he was obliged to transfer his flag three times during the day.

The fleets disengaged in the evening and anchored within sight of each other. It was largely an inconclusive battle. The French lost two ships during the day while the Dutch *Deventer* (70) was so badly damaged that she foundered during the night. But strategically, few would argue with the Dutch, who claimed it a victory.

## SCHOONEVELD II

*4 June 1673*

### Third Dutch War 1672−4

Following SCHOONEVELD I the opposing fleets continued repairing their ships for several days, the Dutch having the advantage of home waters.

On 4 June, with an advantageous wind, De Ruyter weighed and suddenly attacked the Anglo-French fleet in almost the same place as the first battle some days earlier. The Allies scuttled about to weigh and engage but they were driven before the Dutch, almost to the English coast. Only Tromp and Spragge entered into serious fighting, but even their action was not closely joined and after six hours De Ruyter recalled his fleet and gave up the chase.

Both battles had demonstrated De Ruyter's brilliance at handling a fleet at sea and in battle: he had frustrated an invasion of the Netherlands, suffered minimal damage and casualties, and, into the bargain, had opened up Dutch ports to precious overseas convoys.

## SFAX

*15−16 April 1941*

### World War II 1939−45

Captain P.J. Mack commanded the 14th DF in the Mediterranean, comprising the *Jervis, Janus, Nubian* and *Mohawk*. The flotilla intercepted an Italian convoy off the Tunisian coast heading for Tripoli at about 2 a.m. on the 16th. It comprised five merchant ships with an escort of one large and two smaller destroyers. Fire was opened at about 2.20 a.m., and within minutes there was a general mêlée and high-speed destroyer night action in which all enemy ships were hit, damaged, sinking or aflame. Then *Mohawk* took two torpedo hits. The second, under her bridge, sank her in seven fathoms, leaving her forepart out of the sea. After an hour's action *Jervis's* log read: 'One destroyer sunk. Two destroyers, four merchantmen burning fiercely. The fifth merchantman (ammunition ship) sunk. *Mohawk* sunk . . .' In fact all the convoy and its escorts were annihilated. Mack returned to Malta in triumph.

## SICILY

*10 July−17 August 1943*

### World War II 1939−45

Operation Husky was the name given to the invasion of Sicily, the first major step from North Africa to the Italian mainland. During the operation 115,000 British troops and 66,000 American troops were landed. Ships involved were:

|  | British | US | Others |
|---|---|---|---|
| Warships | 199 | 68 | 12 |
| Landing and coastal craft | 1,260 | 811 | 3 |
| Merchant and troop ships | 155 | 66 | 16 |

Losses were not heavy. In the first three weeks they were:

> 3 German and 8 Italian U-boats sunk. British losses: 4 merchant ships and 2 LSTs sunk by U-boats, another 2 merchant ships and 2 cruisers damaged. 13 ships sunk by air attack and many more damaged.

## SIRTE I

*17 December 1941*

### World War II 1939−45

This was a brief engagement in which Rear Admiral Philip Vian with a squadron of five cruisers and twenty destroyers giving cover to a convoy to Malta, skirmished with units of the Italian battle fleet under Admiral Iachino. The action took place in the Gulf of Sirte (or Syrte).

The Italian force comprised the four battleships *Littorio* (35,000 tons, 9−15″), *Caio Duilio* (23,000 tons, 10−12″), *Andrea Doria* (23,000 tons, 10−12″) and *Guilio Cesare* (23,000 tons, 10−12″), five cruisers and twenty destroyer escorts covering a convoy to Tripoli.

The Italian force had such enormous superiority in firepower that the British convoy seemed doomed. But Vian attacked persistently with destroyer torpedo strikes and cruiser gunfire through smokescreens. The action — in a rising gale — was a brilliant example of the defence of a convoy in the face of overwhelming enemy superiority. Iachino preferred not to press home his advantage of superior firepower and was impressed by Vian's aggression. The battle never got to very close grips and ended inconclusively.

## SIRTE II

*22 March 1942*

### World War II 1939−45

Three months after SIRTE I Rear Admiral Philip Vian recorded another remarkable success in defending a convoy to Malta with light forces against a superior Italian battleship force.

Vian was commanding the squadron of four light cruisers and ten destroyers, augmented by a cruiser and a destroyer from Malta, giving escort to four important freighters in a convoy from Alexandria to Malta. They were joined later by a 'Hunt' class destroyer of an A/S sweeping patrol.

Admiral Iachino intercepted Vian; he wore his flag in the 35,000 ton *Littorio* (9−15″ and 12−6″), three cruisers and ten destroyers. Vian immediately ordered the convoy with a small escort away from the battle area and made an effective smoke-screen through which he launched a series of determined torpedo attacks. The SSE wind greatly assisted the screen, and the Italians showed a marked reluctance to face the torpedo attacks through the smoke.

Iachino tried to outflank the smoke and Vian several times, but after three hours of skirmishing he called it a day.

The destroyers *Havock, Kingston* and *Lively* (1,340, 1,690 and 1,920 tons respectively) all took 15″ shell-hits, yet survived.

Two of the four freighters were sunk in an air attack later and the other two reached Malta, though both were sunk at their moorings.

## SKAGERRAK — *see* JUTLAND

SOLEBAY 1672

## SOLEBAY (Southwold Bay)
*28 May 1672*

### Third Dutch War 1672−4

This battle was fought between a combined Anglo-French fleet and a huge Dutch fleet in the North Sea. The result was both a tactical and a strategic victory for the redoubtable Dutch Admiral De Ruyter, who frustrated a planned invasion of the Netherlands.

Solebay, off the coast of Suffolk, was then a large curved bay, ideal as a fleet anchorage. At the end of May 1672 James, Duke of York, with his flag in the *Princess Royal* (120) commanded a vast fleet of English and French warships — over seventy ships of the line and more than this number of fireships, transports and smaller vessels. The Earl of Sandwich commanding the rear wore his flag in the *Royal James* (100), and Admiral D'Estrées aboard the *St Philippe* (78) commanded the van. This huge assembly of ships lay at anchor provisioning in Solebay.

The Dutch fleet under De Ruyter in his flagship *Zeven Provincien* (82) discovered the combined fleet and, running before the stiff north-east wind, bore down on the anchorage with his fleet and with fireships.

The English centre division cut cables and stood to the north — with difficulty in face of the wind. D'Estrées managed to get away and fled south-east. De Ruyter detached Banckerts with about twenty

ships to contain him, evening the odds in the rest of his fleet. These two divisions fought a battle of their own and took no part in the main action.

The main Dutch fleet — De Ruyter in the centre, Van Ghent in the rear — included heroes of the Medway (see MEDWAY): Van Brakel who took the *Royal Charles,* Jan Van Rijn who broke the chain boom, 'Devil' Evertsen and his cousin, Cornelis the Younger.

Sandwich and Van Ghent engaged first. Brakel in his *Groot Hollandia* (60) also found himself obliged to engage Sandwich's *Royal James* (100) in a fierce duel. Van Ghent was killed, then as if in retribution Jan Van Rijn's fireships set the *Royal James* ablaze and she had to be abandoned. Sandwich and his son-in-law Sir Phillip Carteret got away in a boat which became so overloaded with survivors that it overturned, everyone aboard being drowned. Sandwich's body was recovered later.

The Duke of York also experienced much action, compelling him to shift his flag three times during the day.

By the evening the Allied fleet was content to disengage and allow the Dutch divisions to withdraw to the Maas. The English losses were four ships and 2,500 men. the Dutch lost two ships, *Jozua* (60) and *Stavoren* (48), and another which blew up in the night. De Ruyter had disabled the English fleet for about a month, had wrested command in the Channel and thwarted an invasion of the Netherlands. Small reason the Dutch regard him as their Nelson.

## SOUTHWOLD BAY — *see* SOLEBAY

## SPADA
*19 July 1940*
### World War II 1939−45
This was an engagement between the cruiser HMAS *Sydney* (Captain J.A. Collins) with the 1,340-ton 4−4.7″ destroyers *Hasty, Havock, Hero* and *Hyperion,* and the *Ilex* (1,370 tons), against the two Italian cruisers *Bartolomeo Colleoni* and *Giovanni delle Bande Nere* (both 5,069 tons, 8−6″).

In a spirited action off Cape Spada on the north coast of Crete the 6,830-ton *Sydney* (8−6″) sank the *Bartolomeo Colleoni.* The other cruiser was damaged but managed to escape destruction, and reached Benghazi in safety.

## SPARTIVENTO — *see* CAPE SPARTIVENTO

## STRACHAN'S ACTION — *see* CAPE ORTEGAL

## SUEZ CANAL
*2−4 February 1915*
### World War I 1914−18
A Turkish attack was launched on the Suez Canal in 1915. It was strongly repulsed with the assistance of naval units and a battle honour was subsequently awarded. A clasp 'Suez Canal' for the British War Medal was approved but never in fact issued.

## SUEZ
*6 November 1956*
Several days after war broke out between Egypt and Israel, Britain and France launched an assault on Egypt in an effort to safeguard the Suez Canal. On 1 November the *Newfoundland* and *Diane* sank the Egyptian frigate *Domiat* (ex-*Nith*). At the assault on the 6th, more than 100 sea craft were involved, including six carriers — *Eagle, Albion, Bulwark, Ocean, Theseus* and *Lafayette. Ocean* and *Theseus* carried RM Commandos and helicopters. RN aircraft flew about 2,000 sorties — and another 400 by helicopters. No.3 Commando Brigade was landed by LST/LCTs, with 45 Commando by air — all in 91 minutes. The naval bombardment or 'softening up' was restricted to nothing larger than 6″ guns in order to minimize damage to civilian properties: wanton damage was carefully avoided. Suez was the first major helicopter-borne assault from ships. It was politically disastrous, and the British and French forces were compelled to withdraw after a short while.

## SUNDA STRAIT
*28 February−1 March 1942*
### World War II 1939—45
The surviving Allied warships of the battle of the Java Sea (see JAVA SEA) all perished in a series of actions within a day or two of the Java Sea battle.

The heavy cruiser USS *Houston* (9,050 tons, 9−8″, but with one turret out of action) and HMAS *Perth* (6,830 tons, 8−6″) sailed from Batavia and endeavoured to clear the zone via the Sunda Strait to the west of Java, but the area was swarming with Japanese warships and the two cruisers were overwhelmed by a Japanese squadron of Admiral Kurita's heavy cruisers, both ships being sunk with heavy losses of men.

The damaged heavy cruiser *Exeter* (8,390 tons, 6−8″), destroyer *Encounter* (1,375 tons, 4−4.7″) and the old USS *Pope* (1,190 tons, 4−4″) left Sourabaya to try to escape but were all overwhelmed by dive bombers and sunk with heavy loss of life. The defeat of the fragmented Allied forces in the Java Sea area was complete. The island of Java fell to the Japanese.

## SYRIA
*4 November 1840*
### War Between Egypt and Turkey 1840
Acre was captured by Admiral the Hon. Sir Robert Stopford and Commodore Charles Napier in *Princess Charlotte.* Their naval forces were supported by Austrian and Turkish ships and troops of the Royal Artillery and Royal Sappers and Miners.

## TAKU FORTS
*17 June 1900*

### Boxer Rising 1900

These forts were bombarded and captured during the rebellion in China. Ships engaged were: *Algerine*, *Lion* (French), *Alacrity*, *Iltis* (German), *Bobr* (Russian), *Giliak* (Russian) and *Koreytz* (Russian). *Fame* and *Whiting* captured four Chinese torpedo boats in the Pei-Ho below Tongku, China.

## TAMATAVE
*20 May 1811*

### Napoleonic War 1803—15

This was a dashing frigate action between three 40-gun French frigates commanded by Commodore Roquebert, and three 36-gun frigates and a sloop commanded by Captain Charles Schomberg.

Schomberg's squadron comprised the *Astraea*, *Phoebe*, *Galatea* and the sloop *Racehorse*. Roquebert's ships were the *Renommée*, *Clorinde* and *Néréide*.

They clashed off Foul Point, north of Tamatave in Madagascar. The *Galatea* suffered serious damage, but when Roquebert was killed the *Renommée* struck. The *Néréide* escaped into Tamatave, then surrendered a few days later. The *Clorinde* got clear away and managed to reach Brest safely.

## TARANTO
*11 November 1940*

### World War II 1939—45

The Fleet Air Arm executed an attack on the Italian battle fleet in an action which helped in one night to redress the balance of naval power in the Mediterranean. The action was fought between aircraft of the Royal Navy carriers *Illustrious* (23,000 tons, 36 aircraft) and *Eagle* (36,800 tons, 100 aircraft) of the Mediterranean Fleet under Admiral Sir Andrew B. Cunningham and the Italian battle fleet at anchor in Taranto harbour.

Air reconnaissance over Taranto showed five of the six Italian battleships in commission lying at anchor in Taranto. Cunningham determined upon an immediate strike. The *Eagle* herself was not available for the attack, so the *Illustrious* was the lone carrier employed, her aircraft augmented by some from *Eagle*.

Twenty-one aircraft flew off from a position 180 miles south-east of Taranto starting at 8.40 p.m., the first wave arriving on target two hours later. Complete surprise was achieved.

Aircraft from FAA Squadrons 813 and 824 (from *Eagle*) and 815 and 819 (from *Illustrious*) armed with torpedoes and bombs carried out Operation Judgement with great determination.

Three battleships were sunk at their moorings, though all were subsequently salvaged: the new *Littorio* (35,000 tons) and the older *Conte di Cavour* (28,700 tons) and *Caio Duilio* (28,700 tons). Two aircraft were lost.

It was at such small cost that this successful operation re-established British command of the Mediterranean.

## TERNATE
*29 August 1810*

### Napoleonic War 1803—15

Ternate lies in the Moluccas. It was captured in 1810 by HMS *Dover* and detachments of the Madras European Regiment and Madras Coastal Artillery.

## TEXEL, THE
*11 August 1673*

### Third Dutch War 1672—4

The Texel was the scene of the last battle of the Third Dutch War with the same adversaries: Prince Rupert, Admiral De Ruyter, the Frenchman D'Estrées, Banckerts, Sir Edward Spragge, Tromp — they had all fought each other a couple of times earlier that summer. Once again the brilliant De Ruyter thwarted an Anglo-French invasion of the Netherlands.

The Allied fleet was commanded by Prince Rupert. It numbered 92[28] warships plus thirty fireships. De Ruyter marshalled a fleet of about 75 sail of the line and frigates, plus about thirty fire-ships.

On the Allied side, Prince Rupert commanded the centre, D'Estrées the van and Spragge the rear division. On the Dutch side, De Ruyter commanded the centre, Banckerts the van and Tromp the rear.

Action was joined on 11 August when De Ruyter, having the weather gage, attacked the superior Allied force. The whole of D'Estrées's van division was separated from the main fleet by Banckerts's van and thrown into confusion, so that it gave no support to the English.

Thus the brunt of De Ruyter's attack fell upon the English centre and rear divisions: both suffered hours of fierce battle and dreadful damage.

Spragge and Tromp had a desperate duel. Each shifted his flag three times during the day. Sadly, Spragge was drowned when the boat in which he was transferring took a shot and sank.

Eventually the two exhausted fleets drew apart, the English abandoning the attempt to land troops, and licking serious wounds. No ships had been lost, but the damage suffered was enormous and the loss in men about 2,000.

De Ruyter's fleet also suffered serious damage, but no ships were lost and his casualties were about half the English.

Prince Rupert was quick to give as the reason for defeat the lack of French participation but the real

---

28  The numbers are difficult to establish with certainty.

reason was the brilliance of De Ruyter's tactics and his skilful handling of huge fleets in action.

## TOULON

*11 February 1744*

### War of 1739—48

This battle was fought between the British Mediterranean fleet of twenty-eight ships of the line commanded by Admiral Thomas Mathews and a combined Franco-Spanish fleet of the same number commanded by the French Admiral La Bruyère de Court and the Spanish Admiral Don Jośe de Navarro commanding the Spanish contingent.[29]

Mathews, leading the centre division in the *Namur* (90), was supported by Rear Admiral Sir William Rowley commanding the van, while Vice Admiral Richard Lestock led the rear division.

After a pursuit of three days, battle was finally joined on 11 February, but so poor was Mathews's approach to the enemy line that while the British had wind advantage — it was only a breeze — and while Mathews's and Rowley's divisions became heavily engaged, Lestock's division was miles astern. His division never in fact took part in the actual battle.

The conflict dragged on throughout the day, and apart from an individual ship action of some consequence the general action ended in confusion and inconclusively. One such individual success was that of Captain Edward Hawke (of future fame) who set a fine example in his *Berwick* in capturing the Spanish *Poder* (60).

The failure at Toulon stirred the country to deep anger. Mathews resigned and came home, and Lestock returned under arrest. A parliamentary enquiry led to a flurry of court-martials. Four lieutenants of the *Dorsetshire* were acquitted. Their captain — Burrish — was cashiered. Captain Williams of the *Royal Oak* was found guilty, as was Captain Ambrose of the *Rupert*. Captain Dilk of the *Chichester* was cashiered and Captain Norris of the *Essex* fled to Spain, never to be heard of again. Five other captains received a variety of sentences. Lestock, the real culprit, the reluctant admiral, the man who chose to misread signals and to avoid action if possible, was tried and acquitted. In due course Mathews stood trial and was cashiered: the result of stupidity more than anything else, for he was a brave enough, if dull, man.

What the courts martial did establish, to the detriment of the Navy for years to come, was that the *Fighting Instructions* were inviolable, omnipotent.

## TRAFALGAR

*21 October 1805*

### Napoleonic War 1803—15

The Trafalgar Campaign started more than seven months before the famous sea battle which was fought on 21 October (Trafalgar Day) off Cape Trafalgar on the south-west coast of Spain. Apart from Admiral Codrington's battle at Navarino Bay in 1827, it was the last major fleet encounter of the days of sail.

The victory of the British fleet at Trafalgar, and the defeat of the combined French and Spanish fleet, effectively put an end to the hopes of Napoleon's invasion of Britain by his Grand Army. It gave to England naval dominance of the Channel, the Atlantic ports and the Mediterranean for the remaining ten years of the Napoleonic War. Thus Trafalgar had far-reaching consequences, both in the short term and in the long term.

The actual battle came about as the result of a complex French plan to keep the Channel clear to allow passage of Napoleon's invasion by his Grand Army. To ensure this it was necessary to secure the Straits of Dover and the Western Approaches to the Channel by defeating Admiral William Cornwallis's watching fleet.

To accomplish this the Comte de Villeneuve broke Nelson's blockade at Toulon, then intended to release squadrons from blockaded Cadiz and Cartegena, though in the event he only picked up a few Spanish ships in Cadiz. Thus he made haste to the West Indies to collect more warships before hastening back to European waters. Off Cape Finisterre he was engaged by Sir Robert Calder (see CALDER'S ACTION), then made port to Cadiz, where Collingwood blockaded him.

Nelson had followed Villeneuve to the West Indies and back, and by the end of September 1805 was with his fleet off Spain. He had a battle plan which enthused his captains. He made no secret of the plan, and when Villeneuve eventually left Cadiz to head south, Nelson's fleet was ready for the encounter.

Nelson's fleet consisted of twenty-seven of the line and Villeneuve had thirty-three, with his flag in the *Bucentaure* (80). Commanding the Spanish (rear) division was Admiral Gravina, while the French van was commanded by Admiral Dumanoir. As soon as the enemy fleet was sighted Nelson implemented his plan of attacking the Franco-Spanish line in two columns with the intention of breaking the enemy line in two places.

'The whole impression of the British fleet,' Nelson had written, 'must be to overpower from two or three ships ahead of their C-in-C (supposed to be in the centre) to the rear of the fleet.'

The *Victory* (100) and the rest of his division would hold the enemy centre and the flagship in battle while Collingwood would engage the enemy's rear, giving Nelson the advantage of powerful strength at the enemy's centre and rear. The enemy van would thus be prevented from aiding the centre. True, the leading ships of the British column would be

---

29  Some sources quote with apparent authority 15 French and 12 Spanish of the line.

subjected to the full force of the enemy broadsides during the hazardous approach and for that reason the toughest ships would lead each column: Nelson in *Victory* with *Téméraire* and *Neptune* while Collingwood would lead the other column in *Royal Sovereign*. Collingwood had fifteen ships in his rear or lee division. Nelson had twelve in his van or weather column.

Three minutes before midday Collingwood came under fire and remained so for ten minutes without support. But soon the enemy line was pierced and once Nelson could bring his column's broadsides to bear the effect was devastating.

In the next four hours the battle continued furiously: at one time no less than twenty of the enemy ships had struck or been taken in prize. The massive four-decker *Santissima Trinidad* (136) was taken and Gravina mortally wounded aboard the *Asturias*. Villeneuve himself was captured when his flagship *Bucentaure* struck.

But early in the action, at about 1.15 p.m., the *Redoutable* grappled with the *Victory* and a marksman in her rigging shot Nelson while he was pacing the quarterdeck with his flag captain Hardy. He was taken below, where he lived for a few hours.

The *Téméraire* (98), commanded by Captain Sir Eliab Harvey, came to *Victory's* assistance and captured the *Redoutable* (74), then went on to capture the *Fougueux* (74). The *Neptuno* (74) and *San Augustino* (74) both struck, and later in the afternoon the burning French *Achille* blew up and sank.

By 4.30 Nelson knew that he had won a great victory, and he died. The Franco-Spanish fleet lost eighteen ships, seventeen of which were in British hands. Only four finally reached Gibraltar, the remainder being run ashore, sunk or recaptured: they suffered 2,600 dead and wounded and 7,000 prisoners on prizes. No British ships were lost, but half of them were severely damaged and 1,700 men were killed or wounded. Five of the damaged ships failed to survive the night storm which deprived Britain of several of its prizes.

The battle's outcome gave Britain undisputed mastery at sea.

---

# TRAFALGAR: Ships engaged

---

### BRITISH WEATHER DIVISION

| | | |
|---|---|---|
| *Victory* | 100 | Vice Admiral Nelson |
| *Téméraire* | 98 | |
| *Neptune* | 98 | |
| *Conquerer* | 74 | |
| *Leviathan* | 74 | |
| *Britannia* | 100 | |
| *Agamemnon* | 64 | |
| *Ajax* | 74 | |

| | | |
|---|---|---|
| *Orion* | 74 | |
| *Minotaur* | 74 | |
| *Spartiate* | 74 | |
| *Africa* | 64 | |

### BRITISH LEE DIVISION

| | | |
|---|---|---|
| *Royal Sovereign* | 100 | Vice Admiral Collingwood |
| *Belleisle* | 74 | |
| *Mars* | 74 | |
| *Tonnant* | 80 | |
| *Bellerophon* | 74 | |
| *Colossus* | 74 | |
| *Achilles* | 74 | |
| *Polyphemus* | 64 | |
| *Revenge* | 74 | |
| *Swiftsure* | 74 | |
| *Defiance* | 74 | |
| *Thunderer* | 74 | |
| *Defence* | 74 | |
| *Dreadnought* | 98 | |
| *Prince* | 98 | |

### FRANCE

| | | |
|---|---|---|
| *Bucentaure* | 80 | Admiral Villeneuve |
| *Redoutable* | 74 | |
| *Indomptable* | 80 | |
| *Neptune* | 80 | |
| *Fougueux* | 74 | |
| *Pluton* | 74 | |
| *Intrépide* | 74 | |
| *Algésiras* | 74 | Rear-Admiral Magon |
| *Berwick* | 74 | |
| *Aigle* | 74 | |
| *Swiftsure* | 74 | |
| *Argonaute* | 74 | |
| *Achille* | 74 | |
| *Scipion* | 74 | |
| *Formidable* | 80 | Rear-Admiral Dumanoir |
| *Mont Blanc* | 74 | |
| *Duguay Trouin* | 74 | |
| *Héros* | 74 | |

### SPAIN

| | | |
|---|---|---|
| *Principe de Asturias* | 112 | Admiral Gravina |
| *Montannes* | 74 | |
| *Argonauta* | 80 | |
| *Bahama* | 74 | |
| *San Juan de Nepumuceno* | 74 | |
| *San Ildefonso* | 74 | |
| *San Justo* | 74 | |
| *Santissima Trinidad* | 136 | Rear-Admiral de Cisneros |
| *San Leandro* | 64 | |
| *Santa Ana* | 112 | Vice-Admiral de Alavo |
| *Monarca* | 74 | |
| *Neptuno* | 74 | |

\* Signifies Badly damaged
○ Signifies Prize

## TRINCOMALEE (12 April 1782) — *see* PROVIDIEN

## TRINCOMALEE
*3 September 1782*

### American War of Independence 1775−83

This was the fourth action between Vice Admiral Sir Edward Hughes and Admiral Pierre Suffren in their series of battles in the East Indies. It took place off Ceylon's eastern anchorage of Trincomalee.

When Hughes arrived off Trincomalee with twelve of the line on 2 September it was to find that Suffren had already captured the base. Suffren — ever ready for action — weighed anchor and set sail with fourteen of the line and battle was joined 25 miles south-east of Trincomalee.

During a three-hour battle during which Suffren lacked support from some of his captains, his flagship *Héros* (74) lost her mainmast and the *Illustre* (74) and *Ajax* (64) were both severely damaged. Later *L'Orient* (74) grounded on a reef and was totally wrecked.

Despite Hughes's success in the action, it was Suffren who retired to Trincomalee and Hughes who had to retire north to Madras.

## 'UPHOLDER'S' PATROL
*May 1941*

### World War II 1939−45

Lieutenant-Commander David Wanklyn VC, DSO commanded HM submarine *Upholder* and has been referred to by fellow submarine commander Alastair Mars as 'the immortal Wanklyn'. He was an outstanding submariner of great skill and daring. By May 1941 he had completed six patrols in the Mediterranean, working out of Gibraltar and Valetta in Malta. In one of these patrols he sank the 5,000-ton *Antonietta Lauro* off Lampedusa, the 2,500-ton German m.v. *Arta* which he boarded and set ablaze, the 2,500-ton *Arcturus* and the 8,000-ton *Leverkusen*.

It was his May 1941 patrol which earned him the highest award for gallantry on patrol in the southern approaches to the Straits of Messina. A defect in a torpedo necessitated changing it — a dreadful job in the confines of a submarine's torpedo compartment forward. On 20 May Wanklyn sighted a 4,000-ton tanker, two supply ships and an escort. He fired four torpedoes, but the bow cap of the fourth tube failed to open. The tanker was hit. In the counter-attack his Asdic and hydrophones were put out of action by the depth charges.

Three days later Wanklyn torpedoed the Vichy French tanker *Alberta*.

Only two torpedoes remained: one was the defect and the other was in the tube with a faulty bow cap. But both were prepared for action. At about 8.30 p.m. on 24 May Wanklyn sighted large vessels while *Upholder* was on the surface charging batteries. There were three ships — all of them liners of about 20,000 tons apiece. They were troopships engaged in a high speed night-time dash to Libya. They were protected by four or five high-speed escorts.

Wanklyn's attack had to be rapid. The enemy ships altered course, giving a more favourable angle of attack; a moderate sea was running; he had no listening gear, and only two torpedoes. He penetrated the escorts' screen and got away both torpedoes. Two explosions were heard. The 17,800-ton *Conte Rosso* was torpedoed and sank. When she went down she was so close to *Upholder* that some of her wires probably scraped the submarine's hull.

*Upholder* endured a heavy and damaging counterattack by thirty-seven depth charges, but the submarine survived and Wanklyn extricated her and made good the escape to Malta. It was for this exploit that Wanklyn won the VC. It was almost exactly a year later when the submarine was lost with all hands.

*Upholder* completed twenty-four patrols, sinking two destroyers and two submarines (*Ammiraglio St Bon* and *Tricheo*). Merchant ships totalling about 82,000 tons were also sunk or seriously damaged, and a cruiser was damaged.

On her loss the Admiralty uniquely issued a statement:

> It is seldom proper for Their Lordships to draw distinction between different services rendered in the course of naval duty, but they take the opportunity of singling out those of HMS *Upholder*, under the command of Lieutenant-Commander Wanklyn, for special mention . . . . Such was the standard of skill and daring, that the ship and her officers and men became an inspiration, not only to their own flotilla, but to the fleet of which it was a part, and Malta, where for so long HMS *Upholder* was based. The ship and her company are gone, but the example and inspiration remain.

## USHANT I
*27 July 1778*

### American War of Independence 1775−83

This encounter had all the ingredients of a battle royal, but it proved inconclusive and left the bitter taste of a prolonged dispute between two English admirals, both of whom were court-martialled.

It was the first clash of fleets from Britain and France in this war and it took place about 70 miles west of Ushant.

Admiral Augustus Keppel in his flagship *Victory* (100) commanded the Channel Fleet comprising twenty-six of the line. He sailed from Portsmouth to seek out Admiral the Comte D'Orvilliers, who commanded the French fleet of thirty-two ships of the line from his flagship *Bretagne* (110).

Four days of manouevring preceded the encounter. On the afternoon of 27 July the two fleets passed each other on opposite tacks, exchanging broadsides and inflicting damage on each other. When Keppel later renewed the action his rear division under the command of Vice Admiral Hugh Palliser in *Formidable* (90) fell badly astern, and seemed to ignore signals to rejoin. By the time Palliser did rejoin, D'Orvilliers had retired in the gathering dusk and the battle was at an end. Neither side had lost a ship, but the casualties of killed and wounded were 700 British and 500 French.

Recriminations between Palliser and Keppel followed, and would not be dispelled until both were court-martialled. Both were acquitted of the charges brought against them, but the recriminations continued. Palliser came off worse than Keppel.

VIGO BAY 1702

## USHANT II

*12 December 1781*

### American War of Independence 1775—83

This battle took place about 150 miles west of Ushant. Rear Admiral Kempenfelt with twelve of the line from the Channel Fleet intercepted a large and valuable French convoy from Brest to the West Indies, escorted by nineteen of the line commanded by Admiral de Guichen. Undeterred, Kempenfelt ordered his squadron to chase the enemy. He noticed that Guichen was positioned far from the convoy, and took advantage of this by skilfully interposing his squadron between the convoy and the escorting force. He cut out no less than fifteen of the French merchant ships, and got clean away without loss.

## VELEZ MALAGA — *see* MALAGA

## VIGO BAY

*12 October 1702*

### War of Spanish Succession 1702—13

Admiral Sir George Rooke undertook an attack upon a Spanish treasure fleet with its escorting French naval squadron of thirteen ships of the line commanded by Admiral Châteaurenault. The treasure ships and escorting squadron lay protectively behind a

harbour boom with fortified batteries guarding the port approaches.

Rooke's assault force of twenty-five Anglo-Dutch ships led by Vice Admiral Hopsonn in *Torbay* (80) and Admiral Van der Goes in *Zeven Provincien* (90) landed troops to secure the batteries. *Torbay* broke through the boom and the squadron forced the harbour.

In a fierce and furious battle the French squadron was savaged. Châteaurenault ordered his ships to be burnt rather than be seized, but even so, the French losses were enormous: ten of the line were captured or destroyed, and about eleven treasure ships taken as rich prizes.[30] The allied losses were nil, and casualties described as light.

## WAGER'S ACTION — *see* CARTAGENA

## WALCHEREN 1944

*1 November 1944*

### World War II 1939–45

Operation Infatuate was launched in an effort to capture Walcheren Island (heavily fortified by the Germans) in order to open up the Scheldt and the port of Antwerp (necessary for logistics) thus giving support to the Allied armies advancing into Flanders. 180 landing craft carried army and RM commandos ashore, supported by the monitors *Erebus* and *Roberts*, by *Warspite* and *Kingsmill*. After two days' heavy fighting the RMs won Churchill's

'The extreme gallantry of the Royal Marines stands forth.' The RMs observe the anniversary as a Memorable Date.

## WARREN'S ACTION — *see* DONEGAL

## ZEEBRUGGE/OSTEND

*23 April – 10 May 1918*

### World War I 1914–18

Both Zeebrugge and Ostend were important ports for German U-boats. Admiral Sir Roger Keyes planned raids to block these ports. At Zeebrugge there was heavy fighting and great gallantry — so much so that eight VCs were awarded, some of them by ballot. Three minelayers — *Intrepid*, *Iphigenia* and *Thetis* — were filled with concrete, then sunk in the canal to block it. The old cruiser *Vindictive* went alongside the Long Mole, held in position by the Mersey ferries *Iris II* and *Daffodil*,[31] and landed the marines packed between decks. The obsolete submarine *C3* was sacrificed to blow up the other end of the mole to prevent German reinforcements arriving. The RMs suffered particularly severely. Never since has there been a Marine battalion numbered 4.

At Ostend matters went less successfully. The blockships were sunk prematurely.

*Vindictive* sailed again despite her damage, as another blockship for Ostend, where a second assault took place on 10 May. Her bows are still preserved there as a war memorial.

---

30  It is only fair to report that figures vary in nearly every account.

31  Renamed *Royal Iris II* and *Royal Daffodil* at the command of King George V.

## GENERAL
Allen, J.*Battles of the British Navy*, 2 vols (1852)
Hannay, D. *A Short History of the Royal Navy 1217–1815*, 2 vols (1909)
Kemp, P. (Ed) *Oxford Companion to Ships And The Sea (1979)*
Marcus, G.J. *A Naval History of England*, 2 vols (1961–71)
Pemsel, H. *Atlas of Naval Warfare* (1977)
Vere, Francis *Salt In Their Blood* (1955)
Warner, O. *The British Navy — A Concise History* (1975)

## RESTORATION
Ollard, R. *Man of War: Holmes and the Restoration Navy* (1969)
Rogers, P.G. *The Dutch in the Medway* (1970)

## WILLIAM III, ANNE & EARLY HANOVERIAN
Richmond, H.W. *The Navy in the War of 1739–48*, 3 vols (1900)

## SEVEN YEARS' WAR
Marcus, G.J. *Quiberon Bay* (1960)

## AMERICAN WAR OF INDEPENDENCE
Gardner, A. *A History of the American Revolution*, Boston (1913)
James, W.M. *The British Navy in Adversity* (1926)
Mackesy, P. *The War For America*
Richmond, H.W. *The Navy in India 1762–1783 (1931)*

## REVOLUTIONARY & NAPOLEONIC WARS
Corbett, J.S. *The Trafalgar Campaign* (1910)
Lloyd, C.C. *St Vincent and Camperdown* (1963)
Lloyd, C.C. *The Nile Campaign* (1973)
Marcus, G.J. *The Age of Nelson* (1971)
Mackesy, P. *The War in the Mediterranean 1803–1810* (1957)
Warner, O. *The Glorious First Of June* (1961)

## AMERICAN WAR OF 1812–15
Forester, C.S. *The Age of Fighting Sail* (1956)
Padfield, P. *Broke and the Shannon* (1968)
Roosevelt, T. *The Naval War of 1812*, New York (1894)

## 19TH CENTURY
Bartlett, C.J. *Great Britain and Sea Power 1815–1853*
Holt, E. *New Zealand — The Strangest War* (1962)
Woodhouse, C.M. *The Battle of Navarino* (1965)

## WORLD WAR I
Bennett, G. *Coronel and the Falklands* (1962)
Bennett, G. *Cowan's War — The Baltic 1918–20* (1964)
Bennett, G. *The Battle of Jutland* (1964)
Bennett, G. *Naval Battles of World War I* (1968)
Corbett, J.S. and Newbolt, H. *Naval Operations* (1920)
Hough, R. *The Pursuit of Admiral Von Spee* (1969)
Irving, J. *The Smokescreen of Jutland* (1966)
James, R.R. *Gallipoli* (1968)
Jellicoe J. *The Grand Fleet* (1919)
Macintyre, D. *Jutland* (1957)
Pitt, B. *Revenge at Sea* (1960)

## WORLD WAR II
Bennett, G. *Naval Battles of World War II (1975)*
Bennett, G. *Battle of the River Plate*
Berthold, W. *The Sinking of the Bismarck* (1958)
Costello, J. and Hughes T. *The Battle of the Atlantic* (1977)
Hough, R. *The Hunting of Force Z* (1967)
Irving, D. *The Destruction of PQ 17* (1968)
Macintyre, D. *The Naval War Against Hitler* (1971)
Macintyre, D. *The Battle of the Atlantic* (1961)
Macintyre, D. *The Battle for the Mediterranean* (1964)
Macintyre, D. *Operation Menace [Dakar and Admiral North]* (1976)
Middlebrook, M. *Battleship* (1978)
Middlebrook, M. *Convoy* (1976)
Pack, S.W.C. *The Battle of Matapan* (1961)
Pope, D. *73 North* (1958)
Pope, D. *The Battle of the River Plate* (1956)
Roskill, S.W. *The War At Sea* (official history) 3 vols (1954–61)
Roskill, S.W. *HMS Warspite* (1957)
Schofield, B.B. *Arctic Convoys* (1977)
Schofield, B.B. *The Loss of the Bismarck*
Schofield, B.B. *The Attack on Taranto* (1973)
Smith, P. *Operation Pedestal* (1970)
Thomas, D.A. *Battle of the Java Sea* (1968)
Thomas, D.A. *Crete 1941: The Battle at Sea* (1972)
Von der Poorten, E.P. *The German Navy in World War II* (1970)
Watts, A.J. *Loss of the Scharnhorst*
Winton, J.*The Forgotten Fleet* (BPF) (1969)
Winton, J. *Freedom's Battle: The War At Sea* (1967)

# SECTION 4
# BATTLE HONOURS

# BATTLE HONOURS

**There never was any appeal made to them for honour, courage or loyalty that did not more than realise my expectations.**

Admiral Lord St Vincent.

**The commanders and companies … behaved with the greatest intrepidity, and gave the strongest proofs of a great British spirit … When I consider the season of the year, the hard gales on the day of action, a flying enemy … and the coast they were on, I can boldly affirm that all that could possibly be done, has been done.**

Lord Hawke's Quiberon Bay despatch to the Admiralty.

**Be pleased to inform Their Lordships that the Italian Fleet now lies at anchor under the guns of the fortress of Malta.**

Admiral Sir Andrew Cunningham to the Admiralty, 1943.

**There seems to be something wrong with our bloody ships today.**

Admiral Beatty at Jutland, 1916.

## INTRODUCTION

The Battle Honours of the Royal Navy date from the Armada, which, as the AFO puts it 'is in all respects worthy of inclusion', even though this predates the generally accepted date of birth of the Royal Navy by some seventy-two years.

A number of points need spotlighting in order to clarify what at first glance appear to be anomalies and difficulties. The document which helps to set out the criteria and lists the awards is AFO 2565/54, Issue 98/54 dated 1 October 1954, and it is entitled *Battle Honours for HM Ships and FAA Squadrons*. Subsequent Orders have added to these lists.

In promulgating this Fleet Order, the Lords Commissioner of the Admiralty approved these Battle Honours for the Navy for the first time in history, and in so doing rationalized what had been for centuries a slipshod arrangement. Commanding officers of HM ships often displayed honours on their own authority, and many inaccuracies were perpetuated. These anomalies have now been remedied.

The Admiralty clearly defined the conditions under which Battle Honours would be awarded: 'successful war service' is a phrase used in the AFO to differentiate from simple presence at an action or operation. 'A Battle Honour will be awarded', the order instructed, 'for those actions which resulted in the defeat of the enemy, or when the action was inconclusive but well fought, and in exceptional cases, where outstanding efforts were made against overwhelming odds.' It was not the intention to award the Honours for a British defeat or when the action was inconclusive and badly fought. But 'successful service' clearly approved 'operations which resulted in the more or less complete frustration of the enemy's intention at the time, although no warship may have been sunk'.

There were six types of service approved by the Lords for rating as a Battle Honour:

1  Fleet or Squadron actions
2  Single Ship or Boat Service actions
3  Major Bombardments
4  Combined Operations
5  Campaign Awards
6  Area Awards

**Fleet and Squadron Actions**   Prior to World War I ships 'participating in an action' needed little definition, but since the introduction of air-sea battles (when opposing fleets or squadrons may not have been in visual contact at all) 'present' is ruled as 'at sea under the direct orders of the Senior Officer controlling the operation...' Thus, ships may have won an award without actually having opened fire on the enemy.

**Single-ship Actions and Bombardments**   These are self-explanatory. Single-ship Actions cite the name of the enemy ship captured or sunk plus the year. For example, in the action between *Bellona* and *Courageux* the *Bellona* is awarded the Honour of *Courageux* 1761. In the case of Bombardments, honours are only awarded where the enemy retaliation was substantial, such as at Algiers 1816.

**Combined Operations**   Manifestly, a large number of seamen, marines, troops have to be landed in order to earn an award: simply transporting troops to the landing area and engaging the enemy as a minor element of the whole operation does not merit an award. The anomaly can exist of a ship not receiving an Honour, while troops landed from her earn after a successful operation the Battle Honour for their regiment. Havana 1762 and St Nazaire 1942 are examples of this class of award. A curious omission from the official list is Corsica 1794. Hood's seamen gave notable service ashore under Captain Horatio Nelson; evidence of the fighting ashore is the loss of sight in Nelson's right eye at the siege of Calvi.

**Campaign Awards**   The First Burma War 1824–6 was the first to be recognized by a Campaign Award[1] — and carried through to the Falkland Islands 1982.[2] It is worth repeating that a Campaign has not earnt an entry in Section 3 — the list of battles — although there are exceptions, such as Malta Convoys, where three

300

individual convoys are included as representative of the campaign as a whole. Thus, there is not necessarily a complete cross-reference between this Battle Honours Section and the Battles Section. Further, it is worth commenting again on curious omissions and inclusions, not only of battles but of individual ships (e.g., *Atlantic Conveyor* in the Falkland Islands 1982.) It was considered that many of the actions in which a ship took part were in themselves of minor importance, though they contributed to the main strategic effort.

This section gives comprehensive details of all ships and FAA Squadrons awarded Battle Honours under the following headings:

    A   Fleet Actions and Campaigns
    B   Single-ship Actions
    C   Fleet Air Arm Squadrons
    D   Naval Honours Won by Army Regiments
    E   Royal Marines

The listing of ships' names under the heading of Battle Honours is not a usual procedure. It is more usual to regard the lists of individual ships' names with their awards as the definitive work. In trying to cross-refer and reconcile the entries of ships and their honours in this Section with those in Section 2 some anomalies have been revealed, and even the Admiralty admits to some inconsistencies. In some cases there are queries against ships' names in this Section; in others, the lists are admittedly incomplete, and in the case of FAA Squadrons' awards, one or two would seem suspect (e.g., 899 Squadron probably ought not to have 'Aegean 1943', and 801 Squadron surely deserves a 'North Africa' honour.) However, these anomalies have been allowed to stand until formally corrected.

---

1  Also, incidentally, the first time the Navy employed a steamship — the *Diana* — on operational service, on the Irrawaddy.

2  *Hansard* 25 October 1983.

# HONOURS AWARDED

# A

## FLEET ACTIONS AND CAMPAIGNS

**ARMADA 1588**
21–29 July
*Achates*
*Advice*
*Aid*
*Antelope*
*Ark (Royal)*
*Brigandime*
*Bull*
*Charles*
*Cygnet*
*Disdain*
*Dreadnought*
*Elizabeth Bonaventure*
*Elizabeth Jonas*
*Fancy*
*Foresight*
*Galley Bonavolia*
*George*
*(Golden) Lion*
*Hope*
*Mary Rose*
*Merlin*
*Moon*
*Nonpareil*
*Rainbow*
*Revenge*
*Scout*
*Spy*
*Sun*
*Swallow*
*Swiftsure*
*Tiger*
*Tramontana*
*Triumph*
*Vanguard*
*Victory*
*(White) Bear*

*White Lion*
158 merchant ships have also
been awarded the honour.

**AZORES 1591**
31 August–1 September
*Revenge*

**CADIZ 1596**
21 June
*Ark Royal*
*Charles*
*Crane*
*Dreadnought*
*Lion*
*Lion's Whelp*
*Mary Rose*
*Mere Honour*
*Moon*
*Nonpareil*
*Quittance*
*Rainbow*
*Repulse*
*Swiftsure*
*Tramontana*
*Truelove*
*Vanguard*
*Warspite*
*Witness*
63 merchant ships now have
the honour.

**DOVER 1652**
19 May
*Adventure*
*Andrew*
*Assurance*
*Centurion*

Fairfax
Garland
Greyhound
Happy Entrance
James
Martin
Mermaid
Portsmouth
Reuben(?)
Ruby
Sapphire
Seven Brothers
Speaker
Triumph
Victory
Worcester(?)

## MONTECRISTI 1652
28 August
Constant Warwick
Elizabeth
Paragon
Phoenix

## KENTISH KNOCK 1652
28 September
Andrew
Diamond
Garland
Greyhound
Guinea
James
London
Nightingale
Nonsuch
Pelican
Resolution
Ruby
Sovereign
Speaker
(List incomplete)

## PORTLAND 1653
18–20 February
Advantage
Adventure
Advice
Amity
Angel
Ann and Joyce
Ann Piercy
Assistance

Assurance
Brazil(?)
Centurion(?)
Charles
Chase
Convert
Convertine
Cullen(?)
Cygnet
Diamond
Discovery
Dolphin
Dragon
Duchess
Eagle
Elizabeth and Ann
Exchange
Expedition
Fairfax
Falmouth
Foresight
Fortune
Gift
Gilliflower
Guinea
Hannibal
Happy Entrance
Katherine
Kentish
Laurel
Lion
Lisbon Merchant(?)
Martin
Mary
Merlin
Nicodemus
Nightingale
Nonsuch
Oak
Old Warwick
Paradox
Paul
Pearl
Pelican
Plover
President
Princess Maria
Prosperous
Providence
Rainbow
Raven
Reformation

Richard and Martha
Roebuck
Ruby
Ruth
Sampson
Sapphire
Satisfaction
Speaker
Speaker's Prize
Success
Sussex
Tenth Whelp(?)
Thomas and Lucy
Thomas and William
Tiger
Triumph
Tulip
Vanguard
Victory
Waterhound
Wiliam and John
Worcester

**GABBARD 1653**
2–3 June
Adventure
Advice
Andrew
Arms of Holland
Amity
Ann and Joyce
Anne Piercy
Assistance
Assurance
Bear
Benjamin
Blossom
Brazil
Centurion
Convert
Convertine
Crescent
Crown
Culpepper
Diamond
Dolphin
Dragon
Dragoneare
Duchess
Eagle
Eastland Merchant
Employment

Essex
Exchange
Expedition
Fair Sisters
Falcon
Falmouth
Foresight
Fortune
Fox
George
Gift
Gilli Flower
Globe
Golden Fleece
Guinea
Hamburg Merchant
Hampshire
Hannibal
Happy Entrance
Heart's Ease
Hopeful Luke
Hound
Hunter
Industry
James
John and Abigail
Jonathan
Kentish
King Ferdinando
Laurel
Lion
Lisbon Merchant
London
Loyalty
Malaga Merchant
Marmaduke
Martin
Mary
Merlin
Mermaid
Middleborough
Nicodemus
Nonsuch
Oak
Paul
Pearl
Pelican
Peter
Phoenix
Portsmouth
President
Princess Maria

Prosperous
Providence
Prudent Mary
Rainbow
Raven
Reformation
Renown
Resolution
Richard and Martha
Roebuck
Ruby
Samaritan
Samuel Talbot
Sapphire
Sarah
Society
Sophia
Speaker
Stork
Success
Sussex
Swan
Tenth Whelp
Thomas and Lucy
Thomas and William
Tiger
Triumph
Tulip
Vanguard
Victory
Violet
Waterhound
Welcome
William
William and John
Worcester

## SCHEVENINGEN 1653
31 July
Advantage
Andrew
Assurance
Crescent
Diamond
Dragon
Duchess
Exeter Merchant
Expedition
Foresight
Gift
Golden Cock
Hannibal

Hound
Hunter
James
John and Katherine
Laurel
London
Malaga Merchant
Mary Prize
Mayflower
Merlin
Norwich
Oak
Phoenix
Portland
Portsmouth
President
Prosperous
Rainbow
Raven
Recovery
Renown
Resolution
Seven Brothers
Sophia
Tiger
Triumph
Tulip
Vanguard
Victory
William
Worcester

## PORTO FARINA 1655
4 April
Amity
Andrew
Bridgwater
Foresight
George
Kent
Merlin
Mermaid
Newcastle
Pearl
Success
Unicorn
Worcester

## SANTA CRUZ 1657
20 April
Bridgwater
Bristol

Centurion
Colchester
Convert
Fairfax
Foresight
George
Hampshire
Jersey
Langport
Lyme
Maidstone
Nantwich
Newbury
Newcastle
Plymouth
Ruby
Speaker
Swiftsure
Unicorn
Winsby
Worcester

## LOWESTOFT 1665

3 June
Adventure
Amity
Anne
Antelope
Assistance
Assurance
Bear
Bendish
Blackamore Merchant
Bonaventure
Breda
Briar
Bristol
Castle Frigate
Centurion
Charity
Clove Tree
Coast Frigate
Colchester
Constant Katherine
Convertine
Diamond
Dolphin
Dover
Dragon
Drake
Dreadnought
Dunkirk

Eagle
Fame
Forester
Fountain
Garland
George
Gloucester
Golden Lion
Guernsey
Guinea
Hambro' Merchant
Hampshire
Happy Return
Henrietta
Henry
Horseman
Hound
Jersey
John and Abigail
John and Katherine
John and Thomas
Katherine
Kent
King
King Ferdinando
Leopard
Lion
London
Loyal George
Loyal Merchant
Maderas
Marmaduke
Martin
Mary
Maryland Merchant
Mary Rose
Milford
Monck
Mountague
Newcastle
Nightingale (?)
Old James
Oxford
Pembroke
Plymouth
Portland
Portsmouth
Providence
Princess
Prudent Mary
Rainbow
Reserve

Resolution
Return
Revenge
Royal Charles
Royal Exchange
Royal James
Royal Katherine
Royal Prince
St Andrew
St George
Sapphire
Satisfaction
Society
Success
Swallow
Swiftsure
Tiger
Triumph
Unicorn
Vanguard
Yarmouth
York
Young Lion

## FOUR DAYS' BATTLE 1666
1−4 June
Amity
Antelope
Assurance
Black Bull
Black Spread Eagle
Bonaventure
Breda
Bristol
Clove Tree
Convertine
Diamond
Dragon
Dreadnought
Essex
Expedition
Gloucester
Greyhound
Happy Entrance
Henrietta
Henry
Hound
House de Swyte
Leopard

Lilly
Little Katherine
Little Unicorn
Loyal George
Mary Rose
Plymouth
Portland
Portsmouth
Princess
Rainbow
Reserve
Revenge
Richard
Royal Charles
Royal James
Royal Katherine
Royal Prince
St George
St Paul
Sevenoaks
Spread Eagle
Swallow
Swiftsure
Triumph
Vanguard
Victorious
Young Prince

## ORFORDNESS 1666
25 July
Abigail
Adventure
Advice
Aleppine
Amity
Anne
Antelope
Assistance
Assurance
Baltimore[3]
Blessing
Bonaventure
Breda
Briar
Bristol
Cambridge
Castle[3]
Centurion
Charles

3  This denotes that vessels were hired for war service.

Charles Merchant[3]
Coronation[3]
Crown
Defiance
Delph
Diamond
Dover
Dragon
Dreadnought
Dunkirk
Eagle
East India London[3]
East India Merchant[3]
Elizabeth
Expedition
Fairfax
Fanfan
Foresight
Fortune
Fox
George[3]
Gloucester
Golden Phoenix
Great Gift
Greenwich
Guilder de Ruyter
Guinea
Hampshire
Happy Return
Helverson
Henrietta
Henry
House of Sweeds
Jersey
John and Thomas[3]
Katherine[3]
Kent
Land of Promise
Leopard
Lion
Lizard
London Merchant[3]
Loyal London
Loyal Merchant[3]
Marmaduke
Mary
Mary Rose
Mathias
Monck
Mountague
Newcastle
Old James

Paul
Plymouth
Portland
Portsmouth
Princess
Providence
Rainbow
Resolution
Revenge
Richard
Richard and Martha
Royal Charles
Royal James
Royal Katherine
Royal Oak
(Royal) Sovereign
Ruby
Rupert
St Andrew
St George
St Jacob
Samuel
Sancta Maria
Slothany
Swallow
Tiger
Triumph
Turkey
Turkey Merchant[3]
Unicorn
Unity
Vanguard
Victory
Virgin
Warspite
Welcome
Yarmouth
York
Zealand

**BUGIA 1671**
8 May
Advice
Dragon
Garland
Little Victory
Mary
Portsmouth
Revenge

## SOLEBAY 1672
28 May

*Adventure*
*Advice*
*Alice and Francis*
*Ann and Judith*
*Anne*
*Antelope*
*Bantam*
*Bonaventure*
*Bristol*
*Cambridge*
*Charles*
*Crown*
*Dartmouth*
*Diamond*
*Dover*
*Dreadnought*
*Dunkirk*
*Edgar*
*Fairfax*
*Forester*
*Fountain*
*French Ruby*
*Gloucester*
*Greenwich*
*Henry*
*Katherine*
*Leopard*
*London*
*Mary*
*Mary Anne*
*Monck*
*Monmouth*
*Montague*
*Old James*
*Phoenix*
*Plymouth*
*Prince*
*Princess*
*Rachel*
*Rainbow*
*Resolution*
*Robert*
*Royal James*
*Royal Katherine*
*Ruby*
*Rupert*
*St Andrew*

*St Michael*
*Sovereign*
*Success*
*Sweepstakes*
*Thomas and Edward*
*Tiger*
*Triumph*
*Unicorn*
*Victory*
*Warspite*
*Yarmouth*
*York*

## SCHOONEVELD 1673
28 May and 4 June

*Advice*
*Anne*
*Assurance*
*Bonaventure*
*Cambridge*[4]
*Charles*
*Constant Warwick*
*Crown*
*Diamond*
*Dreadnought*
*Dunkirk*
*Edgar*
*Falcon*
*Foresight*
*French Ruby*
*Gloucester*
*Greenwich*
*Hampshire*
*Happy Return*
*Henrietta*
*Henry*
*Lion*
*London*
*Mary*
*Mary Rose*
*Monck*
*Newcastle*
*Old Hames*
*Prince*
*Princess*
*Providence*[4]
*Rachel*[4]
*Rainbow*
*Resolution*[4]

---

4   1st Action only.

Revenge
Royal Charles
Royal Katherine
Ruby
Rupert
St Andrew
St George
St Michael
Samuel and Anne[4]
Sovereign
Stavoreen
Sweepstakes
Swiftsure[5]
Triumph
Truelove
Unicorn
Victory
Warspite
Welcome[5]
York

**TEXEL 1673**
11 August
Advice
Anne
Assurance
Blessing
Bonaventure
Bristol
Cambridge
Charles
Crown
Diamond
Dolphin
Dreadnought
Dunkirk
Edgar
Fairfax
Falcon
Foresight
French Ruby
Friendship
Gloucester
Guernsey
Hampshire
Happy Return
Hard Bargain
Henrietta
Henry

Katherine
Leopard
Lion
Lizard
London
Mary
Mary Anne
Monck
Monmouth
Newcastle
Nonsuch(?)
Old James
Pearl
Plymouth
Portland
Portsmouth
Prince
Princess
Prudent Mary
Rainbow
Resolution
Roe
Rose
Royal Charles
Royal Katherine
Ruby
Rupert
St Andrew
St George
St Michael
Society
Sovereign
Stavoreen
Success
Supply
Swallow
Sweepstakes
Swiftsure
Triumph
Truelove
Unicorn
Victory
Warspite
Yarmouth
York

**BARFLEUR 1692**
19–24 May
Adventure

5  2nd Action only.

Advise
Aetna
Albemarle
Berwick
Blaze
Bonaventure
Britannia
Burford
Cadiz Merchant
Cambridge
Captain
Centurion
Charles Galley
Chester
Crown
Defiance
Deptford
Dreadnought
Duchess
Duke
Eagle
Edgar
Elizabeth
Essex
Expedition
Extravagant
Falcon
Flame
Fox
Grafton
Greyhound
Griffin
Half Moon
Hampton Court
Hawk
Hopewell
Hound
Hunter
Kent
Lemfox
Lightning
Lion
London
Mary Galley
Monck
Monmouth
Montague
Neptune
Northumberland
Ossory
Owner's Love
Oxford

Phaeton
Portsmouth
Resolution
Restoration
Roebuck
Royal Katherine
Royal William
Ruby
Rupert
St Albans
St Andrews
St Michael
Sandwich
Sovereign
Speedwell
Spy
Stirling Castle
Strombolo
Swiftsure
Thomas and Elizabeth
Tiger Prize
Vanguard
Vesuvius
Victory
Vulcan
Vulture
Warspite
Windsor Castle
Wolf
Woolwich

**VIGO 1702**
12 October
Association
Barfleur
Bedford
Berwick
Cambridge
Essex
Grafton
Griffin
Hawk
Hunter
Kent
Lightning
Mary
Monmouth
Northumberland
Oxford
Pembroke
Phoenix
Ranelagh

Royal Sovereign[6]
Somerset
Swiftsure
Terrible
Torbay
Vulture

## GIBRALTAR 1704
24 July
Bedford
Berwick
Dorsetshire
Eagle
Essex
Grafton
Kingston
Lenox
Monck
Monmouth
Montague
Nassau
Nottingham
Ranelagh
Royal Catherine
Suffolk
Yarmouth

## VELEZ MALAGA 1704
13 August
Assurance
Barfleur
Bedford
Berwick
Boyne
Burford
Cambridge
Centurion
Charles Galley
Dorsetshire
Eagle
Essex
Firebrand
Firme
Garland
Grafton
Griffin
Hare
Hunter
Jefferies

Kent
Kingston
Lark
Lenox
Lightning
Monck
Monmouth
Montague
Namur
Nassau
Newark
Newport
Norfolk
Nottingham
Orford
Panther
Phoenix
Prince George
Princess Anne
Ranelagh
Roebuck
Royal Katherine
Royal Oak
St George
Shrewsbury
Somerset
Suffolk
Swallow
Swiftsure
Tartar
Terror
Tilbury
Torbay
Triton
Vulcan
Vulture
Warspite
William and Mary
Yarmouth

## MARBELLA 1705
10 March
Antelope
Bedford
Canterbury
Expedition
Greenwich (?)
Hampton Court
Lark

---

6  Not engaged.

*Leopard*
*Newcastle*
*Nottingham*
*Pembroke*
*Revenge*
*Swallow*
*Tiger*
*Warspite*
(List incomplete)

**PASSERO 1718**
31 July
*Argyll*
*Barfleur*
*Breda*
*Burford*
*Canterbury*
*Captain*
*Dorsetshire*
*Dreadnought*
*Dunkirk*
*Essex*
*Garland*
*Grafton*
*Griffin*
*Kent*
*Lenox*
*Loo*
*Montague*
*Orford*
*Ripon*
*Roebuck*
*Royal Oak*
*Rupert*
*Shrewsbury*
*Superb*

**PUERTO (or PORTO) BELLO 1739**
22 November
*Burford*
*Hampton Court*
*Norwich*
*Princess Louisa*
*Strafford*
*Worcester*

**FINISTERRE 1747**
3 May
*Ambuscade*
*Bristol*
*Centurion*

*Defiance*
*Devonshire*
*Falcon*
*Falkland*
*Monmouth*
*Namur*
*Nottingham*
*Prince Frederick*
*Prince George*
*Princess Louisa*
*Vulcan*
*Windsor*
*Yarmouth*

**USHANT 1747**
14 October
*Defiance*
*Devonshire*
*Eagle*
*Edinburgh*
*Gloucester*
*Kent*
*Lion*
*Monmouth*
*Nottingham*
*Portland*
*Princess Louisa*
*Tilbury*
*Weazle*
*Windsor*
*Yarmouth*

**CAP FRANCOIS 1757**
21 October
*Augusta*
*Dreadnought*
*Edinburgh*

**SADRAS 1758**
29 April
*Cumberland*
*Elizabeth*
*Newcastle*
*Protector*
*Queenborough*
*Salisbury*
*Tiger*
*Weymouth*
*Yarmouth*

## LOUISBURG 1758
8 June – 26 July
*Active*
*Beaver*
*Bedford*
*Boreas*
*Burford*
*Captain*
*Centurion*
*Defiance*
*Devonshire*
*Diana*
*Dublin*
*Gramont*
*Halifax*
*Hawke*
*Hunter*
*Juno*
*Kennington*
*Kingston*
*Lancaster*
*Lightning*
*Namur*
*Nightingale*
*Northumberland*
*Nottingham*
*Orford*
*Pembroke*
*Port Mahon*
*Prince Frederick*
*Prince of Orange*
*Princess Amelia*
*Royal William*
*Scarborough*
*Shannon*
*Somerset*
*Squirrel*
*Sutherland*
*Terrible*
*Trent*
*Vanguard*
*York*

## NEGAPATAM 1758
3 August
*Cumberland*
*Elizabeth*
*Newcastle*
*Protector*

*Queenborough*
*Salisbury*
*Tiger*
*Weymouth*
*Yarmouth*

## LAGOS 1759[7]
17 – 18 August
*Active*
*Ambuscade*
*America*
*Conqueror*
*Culloden*
*Edgar*
*Etna*
*Favourite*
*Gibraltar*
*Glasgow*
*Gramont*
*Guernsey*
*Intrepid*
*Jersey*
*Lyme*
*Namur*
*Newark*
*Portland*
*Prince*
*Rainbow*
*St Albans*
*Salamander*
*Shannon*
*Sheerness*
*Swiftsure*
*Tartar's Prize*
*Thetis*
*Warspite*

## PORTO NOVO 1759
10 September
*Cumberland*
*Elizabeth*
*Grafton*
*Newcastle*
*Queenborough*
*Salisbury*
*Sunderland*
*Tiger*
*Weymouth*
*Yarmouth*

---

7  This was the first of the naval honours in what became known as 'The Wonderful Year' or 'The Year of Victories'.

**QUEBEC 1759**
July – 13 September
*Alcide*
*Baltimore*
*Bedford*
*Boscawen*
*Captain*
*Centurion*
*Cormorant*
*Crown*
*Devonshire*
*Diana*
*Dublin*
*Echo*
*Euros*
*Fowey*
*Halifax*
*Hind*
*Hunter*
*Lizard*
*Lowestoffe*
*Medway*
*Neptune*
*Nightingale*
*Northumberland*
*Orford*
*Pelican*
*Pembroke*
*Porcupine*
*Prince Frederick*
*Prince of Orange*
*Princess Amelia*
*Racehorse*
*Richmond*
*Rodney*
*Royal William*
*Scarborough*
*Scorpion*
*Seahorse*
*Shrewsbury*
*Somerset*
*Squirrel*
*Stirling Castle*
*Strombolo*
*Sutherland*
*Terrible*
*Trent*
*Trident*
*Vanguard*

*Vesuvius*
*Zephyr*

**QUIBERON BAY 1759**
20 November
*Burford*
*Chatham*
*Chichester*
*Coventry*
*Defiance*
*Dorsetshire*
*Duke*
*Dunkirk*
*Essex*
*Falkland*
*Hercules*
*Hero*
*Intrepid*
*Kingston*
*Magnanime*
*Maidstone*
*Mars*
*Minerva*
*Montague*
*Namur*
*Portland*
*Resolution*
*Revenge*
*Rochester*
*Royal George*
*Sapphire*
*Swiftsure*
*Temple*
*Torbay*
*Union*
*Vengeance*
*Venus*
*Warspite*

**BELLEISLE 1761**[8]
7 June
*Achille*
*Actaeon*
*Adventure*
*Aetna*
*Aldborough*
*Blast*
*Buckingham*
*Burford*

8   This is the preferred spelling rather than Belle Île.

318

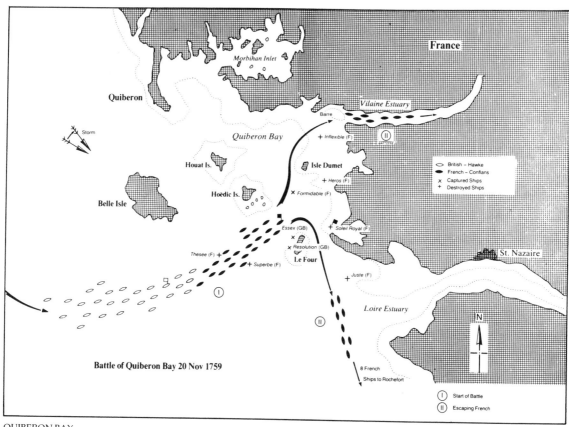

QUIBERON BAY

| | |
|---|---|
| Chichester | **MARTINIQUE 1762** |
| Dragon | 7 January – 16 February |
| Druid | Alcide |
| Escort | Amazon |
| Essex | Antigua |
| Firedrake | Barbados |
| Flamborough | Basilisk |
| Fly | Crescent |
| Furnace | Crown |
| Hampton Court | Culloden |
| Hero | Devonshire |
| Infernal | Dover |
| Launceston | Dragon |
| Lynn | Dublin |
| Melampe | Echo |
| Monmouth | Falkland |
| Prince of Orange | Foudroyant |
| Sandwich | Granado |
| Southampton | Greyhound |
| Swiftsure | Levant |
| Téméraire | Lizard |
| Torbay | Marlborough |
| Valiant | Modeste |
| Vesuvius | Nightingale |
| | Norwich |

Nottingham
Raisonnable
Repulse
Rochester
Rose
Stag
Stirling Castle
Sutherland
Temple
Téméraire
Thunder
Vanguard
Virgin
Woolwich
Zephyr

## HAVANA 1762
6 June – 13 August
Alarm
Alcide
Basilisk
Belleisle
Bonetta
Cambridge
Centaur
Cerberus
Cygnet
Defiance
Devonshire
Dover
Dragon
Echo
Edgar
Enterprise
Ferret
Glasgow
Granado
Hampton Court
Intrepid
Lizard
Lurcher
Marlborough
Mercury
Namur
Pembroke
Porcupine
Richmond
Stirling Castle
Sutherland
Temple
Thunderer

Trent
Valiant
Viper

## LAKE CHAMPLAIN 1776
11 and 13 October
Carleton
Inflexible
Loyal Convert
Maria
Thunderer

## ST LUCIA 1778
15 December
Ariadne
Aurora
Barbados
Boyne
Carcass
Centurion
Ceres
Isis
Pelican
Preston
Prince of Wales
St Albans
Snake
Venus
Weazel

## ST VINCENT 1780
16 January
Ajax
Alcide
Alfred
Apollo
Bedford
Bienfaisant
Culloden
Cumberland
Edgar
Hyena
Invincible
Marlborough
Monarch
Montagu
Pegasus
Prince George
Resolution
Sandwich
Terrible
Triton

## CHESAPEAKE 1781

16 March

*Adamant*
*America*
*Bedford*
*Europe*
*Guadeloupe*
*Irish*
*London*
*Pearl*
*Prudente*
*Robust*
*Royal Oak*

## DOGGER BANK 1781

5 August

*Artois*
*Belle Poule*
*Berwick*
*Bienfaisant*
*Buffalo*
*Cleopatra*
*Dolphin*
*Fortitude*
*Latona*
*Preston*
*Princess Amelia*
*Surprise*

## USHANT 1781

12 December

*Agamemnon*
*Alexander*
*Arethusa*
*Britannia*
*Courageux*
*Duke*
*Edgar*
*Medway*
*Monsieur*
*Ocean*
*Prudente*
*Queen*
*Renown*
*Tartar*
*Tisiphene*
*Valiant*
*Victory*

## ST KITTS 1782

25–26 January

*Ajax*

*Alcide*
*Alfred*
*America*
*Barfleur*
*Bedford*
*Belliqueux*
*Canada*
*Centaur*
*Champion*
*Eurydisis*
*Expedition*
*Gros Inlet*
*Intrepid*
*Invincible*
*Monarch*
*Montagu*
*Nymphe*
*Prince George*
*Prince William*
*Princessa*
*Prudent*
*Resolution*
*Russell*
*St Albans*
*Shrewsbury*
*Sibyl*
*Solebay*

## SADRAS 1782

17 February

*Burford*
*Combustion*
*Eagle*
*Exeter*
*Hero*
*Isis*
*Minorca*
*Monarch*
*Seahorse*
*Superb*
*Worcester*

## THE SAINTES 1782

12 April

*Agamemnon*
*Ajax*
*Alarm*
*Alcide*
*Alecto*
*Alert*
*Alfred*
*America*

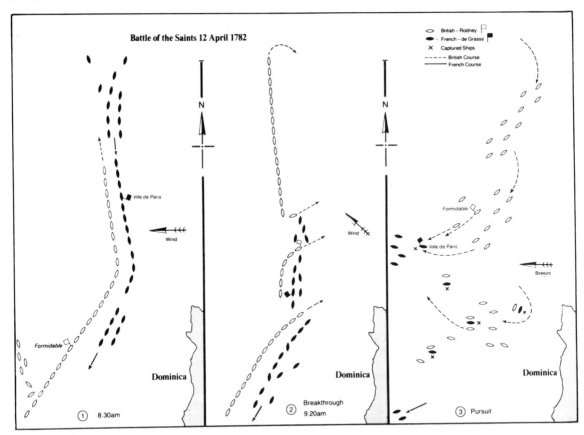

**Battle of the Saints 12 April 1782**

British – Rodney
French – de Grasse
Captured Ships
British Course
French Course

N

Ville de Paris

Wind

Formidable

Dominica

① 8.30am

N

Wind

Breakthrough
② 9.20am

Dominica

Formidable

Ville de Paris

Breeze

③ Pursuit

Dominica

THE SAINTES

Andromache
Anson
Arrogant
Barfleur
Bedford
Belliqueux
Canada
Centaur
Champion
Conqueror
Duke
Endymion
Eurydice
Fame
Flora
Formidable
Hercules
Magnificent
Marlborough
Monarch
Montagu
Namur
Nonsuch
Prince George

Prince William
Prothée
Repulse
Resolution
Royal Oak
Russell
St Albans
Torbay
Triton
Warrior
Yarmouth
Zebra

**PROVIDIEN 1782**

12 April
Burford
Combustion
Eagle
Exeter
Hero
Isis
Magnanime
Monarch
Monmouth
Seahorse

Sultan
Superb
Worcester

## NEGAPATAM 1782

6 July
*Burford*
*Eagle*
*Exeter*
*Hero*
*Isis*
*Magnanime*
*Monarch*
*Monmouth*
*Seahorse*
*Sultan*

Superb
Worcester

## TRINCOMALEE 1782

3 September
*Active*
*Burford*
*Combustion*
*Coventry*
*Eagle*
*Exeter*
*Hero*
*Isis*
*Magnanime*
*Medea*
*Monarch*
*Monmouth*
*San Carlos*

STRUGGLE FOR INDIA (CUDDALORE II)

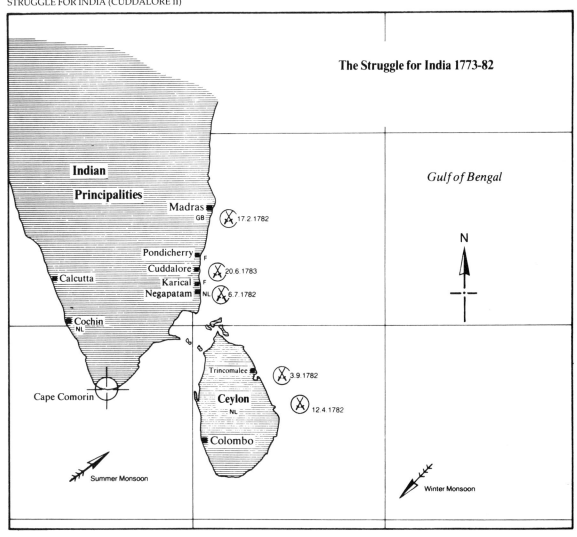

*Sceptre*
*Seahorse*
*Sultan*
*Superb*
*Worcester*

## MARTINIQUE 1794
5–22 March
*Asia*
*Assurance*
*Avenger*
*Beaulieu*
*Blonde*
*Boyne*
*Dromedary*
*Experiment*
*Irresistible*
*Nautilus*
*Quebec*
*Rattlesnake*
*Roebuck*
*Rose*
*Santa Marguerita*
*Sea Flower*
*Spiteful*
*Tormentor*
*Ulysses*
*Vengeance*
*Venom*
*Vesuvius*
*Veteran*
*Winchelsea*
*Woolwich*
*Zebra*

## GLORIOUS FIRST OF JUNE 1794
1 June (and 28–29 May)
*Alfred*
*Aquilon*
*Audacious*
*Barfleur*
*Bellerophon*
*Brunswick*
*Caesar*
*Charon*
*Comet*
*Culloden*
*Defence*
*Gibraltar*
*Glory*
*Impregnable*

*Incendiary*
*Invincible*
*Latona*
*Leviathan*
*Majestic*
*Marlborough*
*Montagu*
*Niger*
*Orion*
*Pegasus*
*Queen*
*Queen Charlotte*
*Ramillies*
*Ranger*
*Rattler*
*Royal George*
*Royal Sovereign*
*Russell*
*Southampton*
*Thunderer*
*Tremendous*
*Valiant*
*Venus*

## GENOA 1795
13–14 March
*Agamemnon*
*Bedford*
*Blenheim*
*Boreas*
*Britannia*
*Captain*
*Centurion*
*Courageux*
*Diadem*
*Egmont*
*Fortitude*
*Fox*
*Illustrious*
*Inconstant*
*Lowestoffe*
*Meleager*
*Moselle*
*Poulette*
*Princess Royal*
*Romulus*
*St George*
*Tarleton*
*Terrible*
*Windsor Castle*

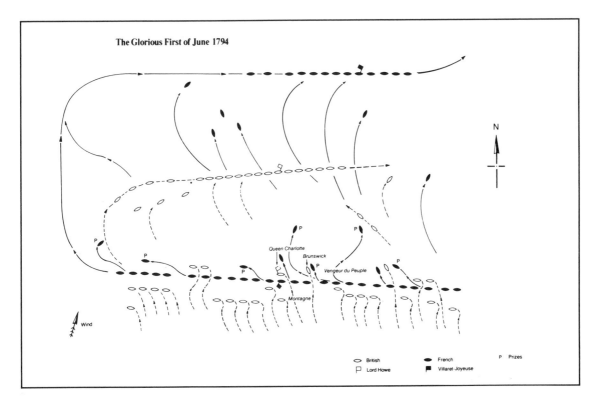

The Glorious First of June 1794

British ⬭    French ⬬    P   Prizes

⊡ Lord Howe    ⚑ Villaret-Joyeuse

GLORIOUS FIRST OF JUNE

## CORNWALLIS'S RETREAT
## 1795
17 June
*Bellerophon*
*Brunswick*
*Mars*
*Pallas*
*Phaeton*
*Royal Sovereign*
*Triumph*

## GROIX ISLAND 1795
23 June
*Aquilon*
*Argus*
*Astraea*
*Babet*
*Barfleur*
*Charon*
*Colossus*
*Dolly*
*Galatea*
*Incendiary*
*Irresistible*
*London*
*Megara*

*Nymphe*
*Orion*
*Prince of Wales*
*Prince George*
*Révolutionnaire*
*Royal George*
*Russia*
*Sanspareil*
*Thalia*
*Valiant*

## CAPE OF GOOD HOPE 1795
14 July – 16 September
*America*
*Crescent*
*Echo*
*Hope*
*Jupiter*
*Monarch*
*Moselle*
*Rattlesnake*
*Ruby*
*Sceptre*
*Sphinx*
*Stately*
*Tremendous*
*Trident*

**ST LUCIA 1796**
27 April – 24 May
*Alfred*
*Arethusa*
*Astraea*
*Beaulieu*
*Bulldog*
*Fury*
*Ganges*
*Hebe*
*Medias*
*Pelican*
*Thunderer*
*Vengeance*
*Victorieuse*
*Woolwich*

**ST VINCENT 1797**
14 February
*Barfleur*
*Blenheim*
*Bonne Citoyenne*
*Britannia*
*Captain*
*Collision*
*Colossus*
*Culloden*
*Diadem*
*Egmont*
*Fox*
*Goliath*
*Irresistible*
*Lively*
*Minerve*
*Namur*
*Niger*
*Orion*
*Prince George*
*Raven*
*Victory*

**CAMPERDOWN 1797**
11 October
*Active*
*Adamant*
*Agincourt*
*Ardent*
*Beaulieu*
*Belliqueux*
*Circe*
*Diligent*
*Director*

*Isis*
*King George*
*Lancaster*
*Martin*
*Monmouth*
*Montagu*
*Powerful*
*Rose*
*Russell*
*Speculator*
*Triumph*
*Venerable*
*Veteran*

**NILE 1798**
1 August
*Alexander*
*Audacious*
*Bellerophon*
*Culloden*
*Defence*
*Goliath*
*Leander*
*Majestic*
*Minotaur*
*Mutine*
*Orion*
*Swiftsure*
*Theseus*
*Vanguard*
*Zealous*

**DONEGAL 1798**
12 October
*Amelia*
*Anson*
*Canada*
*Ethalion*
*Foudroyant*
*Magnanime*
*Melampus*
*Robust*

**MINORCA 1798**
7 – 15 November
*Argo*
*Aurora*
*Centaur*
*Constitution*
*Cormorant*
*Leviathan*
*Petrel*

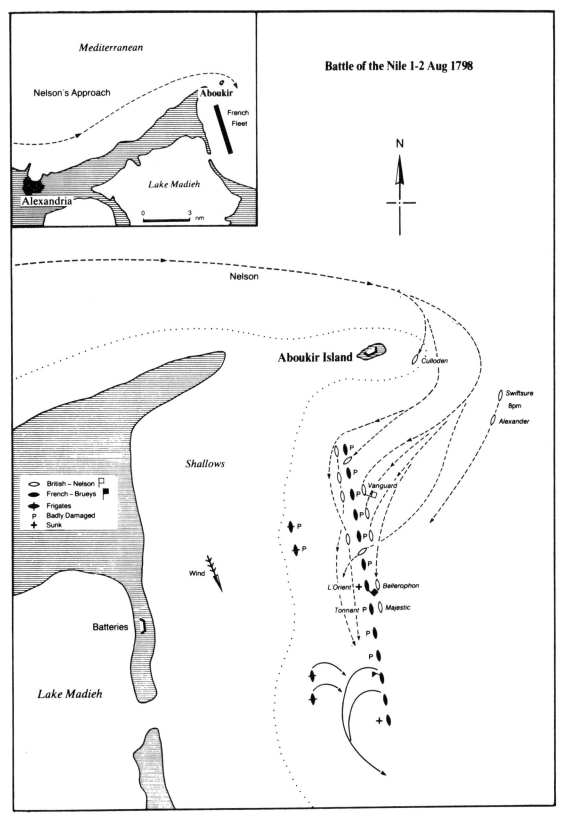

## Battle of the Nile 1-2 Aug 1798

Mediterranean

Nelson's Approach

Aboukir

French Fleet

Lake Madieh

Alexandria

0   3 nm

N

Nelson

Aboukir Island

Culloden

Swiftsure

8pm

Alexander

Shallows

British – Nelson
French – Brueys
Frigates
P   Badly Damaged
+   Sunk

P

P

P

Vanguard

P

P

P

P

P

P

L'Orient   +   Bellerophon

Tonnant   P   Majestic

P

P

Wind

Batteries

Lake Madieh

+

THE NILE

## ACRE 1799

17 March – 20 May

*Alliance*
*Theseus*
*Tigre*

## COPENHAGEN 1801

2 April

*Agamemnon*
*Alcmene*
*Amazon*
*Ardent*
*Arrow*
*Bellona*
*Blanche*
*Cruizer*
*Dart*
*Defence*[9]
*Defiance*
*Désirée*
*Discovery*
*Edgar*
*Elephant*
*Explosion*
*Ganges*
*Glatton*
*Happy*
*Hecla*
*Isis*
*Jamaica*
*London*[9]
*Monarch*
*Otter*
*Polyphemus*
*Raisonnable*[9]
*Ramillies*[9]
*Russell*
*St George*[9]
*Saturn*[9]
*Sulphur*
*Terror*
*Veteran*[9]
*Volcano*
*Warrior*
*Zebra*
*Zephyr*

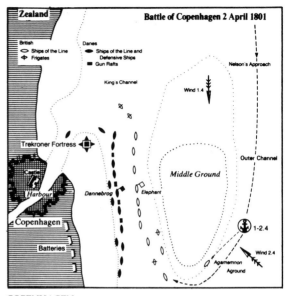

COPENHAGEN

## (GUT OF) GIBRALTAR 1801

12 – 13 July

*Audacious*
*Caesar*
*Calpe*
*Louisa*
*Spencer*
*Superb*
*Thames*
*Venerable*

## EGYPT 1801

8 March – 2 September

*Active*
*Agincourt*
*Ajax*
*Alexander*
*Alligator*
*Asp*
*Astraea*
*Athenian*
*Bebelmandel*
*Ballahou*
*Blonde*
*Bonne Citoyenne*
*Braakel*
*Cameleon*
*Ceres*

---

9  Not engaged: support ships.

Charon
Chichester
Cruelle
Cyclops
Cynthia
Dangereuse
Delft
Déterminée
Diadem
Diane
Dictator
Dido
Dolphin
Dover
Dragon
Druid
El Carmen
Entreprenante
Espiègle
Europa
Eurus
Expedition
Experiment
Flora
Florentina
Foudroyant
Fox
Fulminante
Fury
Gibraltar
Good Design
Gorgon
Gozo
Greyhound
Haarlem
Hebe
Hector
Heroine
Inconstant
Inflexible
Iphigenia
Janissary
Kangaroo
Kent
Leda
Leopard
Madras
Minerve
Minorca
Minotaur
Modeste
Mondovi

Monmouth
Négresse
Niger
Northumberland
Pallas
Pearl
Pegasus
Penelope
Peterel
Phoenix
Pigmy
Pique
Port Mahon
Regulus
Renommée
Renown
Resource
Roebuck
Romney
Romulus
Rosa
Salamine
Santa Dorothea
Santa Teresa
Scampavia
Sensible
Sheerness
Sir Sidney Smith
Spider
Stately
Sultana
Swiftsure
Tartarus
Termagant
Thetis
Thisbe
Tigre
Tourterelle
Transfer
Trusty
Ulysses
Urchin
Vestal
Victor
Victorieuse
Vincejo
Wilhelmina
Winchelsea
Woolwich

**CAPE TENEZ 1805**
4 February
*Acheron*
*Arrow*

**TRAFALGAR 1805**
21 October
*Achilles*
*Africa*
*Agamemnon*
*Ajax*
*Belleisle*
*Bellerophon*
*Britannia*
*Colossus*
*Conqueror*
*Defence*
*Defiance*
*Dreadnought*
*Euryalus*
*Entreprenante*
*Leviathan*
*Mars*
*Minotaur*
*Naiad*
*Neptune*
*Orion*
*Phoebe*
*Pickle*
*Polyphemus*
*Prince*
*Revenge*
*Royal Sovereign*
*Sirius*
*Spartiate*
*Swiftsure*
*Téméraire*
*Thunderer*
*Tonnant*
*Victory*

**BAY OF BISCAY 1805**
4 November
*Aeolus*
*Caesar*
*Courageux*
*Hero*
*Namur*
*Phoenix*
*Révolutionnaire*
*Santa Margarita*

**CAPE OF GOOD HOPE 1806**
8 – 18 January
*Belliqueux*
*Diadem*
*Diomède*
*Encounter*
*Espoir*
*Leda*
*Protector*
*Raisonnable*

**SAN DOMINGO 1806**
6 February
*Acasta*
*Agamemnon*
*Atlas*
*Canopus*
*Donegal*
*Epervier*
*Kingfisher*
*Magicienne*
*Northumberland*
*Spencer*
*Superb*

**CURAÇOA 1807**
1 January
*Anson*
*Arethusa*
*Fisgard*
*Latona*
*Morne Fortunée*

**CAYENNE 1809**
14 January
*Confiance*

**MARTINIQUE 1809**
30 January – 24 February
*Acasta*
*Aeolus*
*Amaranthe*
*Bacchus*
*Belleisle*
*Bellette*
*Captain*
*Cherub*
*Circe*
*Cleopatra*
*Cuttle*
*Demarara*
*Dominica*

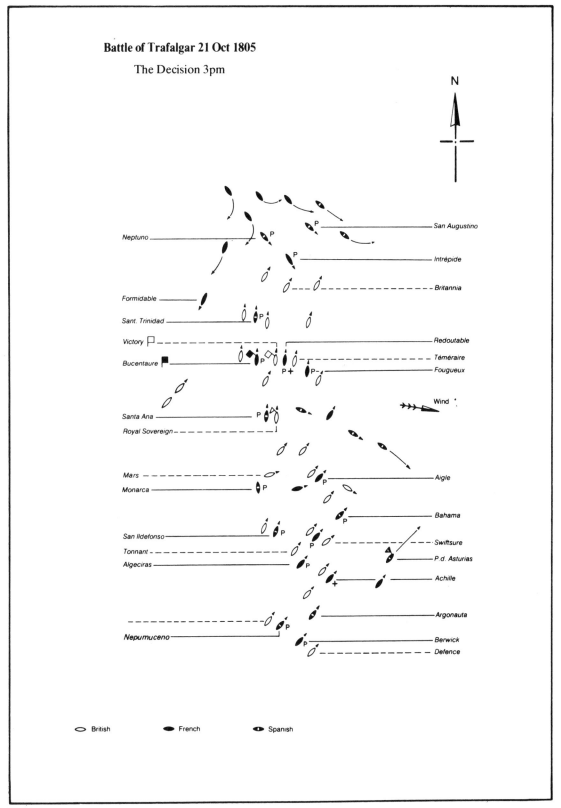

Battle of Trafalgar 21 Oct 1805

The Decision 3pm

N

Neptuno

San Augustino

P

Intrèpide

P

Britannia

Formidable

Sant. Trinidad

P

Victory

Redoutable

Bucentaure

P

Témèraire

Fougueux

P

P

Wind

Santa Ana

P

Royal Sovereign

Mars

Aigle

Monarca

P

Bahama

P

San Ildefonso

P

Swiftsure

Tonnant

P

P.d. Asturias

Algeciras

P

Achille

Argonauta

P

Berwick

Nepumuceno

P

Defence

British     French     Spanish

Eclair
Ethalion
Eurydice
Express
Fawn
Forester
Frolic
Gloire
Gorée
Haughty
Hazard
Intrepid
Liberty
Mosambique
Pelorus
Penelope
Pompée
Port d'Espagne
Pultusk
Recruit
Ringdove
St Pierre
Snap
Star
Stork
Subtle
Supérieure
Surinam
Swinger
Wolverine
York

### BASQUE ROADS 1809
11 April                    ·
Aetna
Aigle
Beagle
Bellona
Caesar
Caledonian
Conflict
Contest
Donegal
Doteral
Emerald
Encounter
Fervent
Foxhound
Gibraltar
Growler
Hero
Illustrious

Impérieuse
Indefatigable
Insolent
King George
Lyra
Martial
Mediator
Nimrod
Pallas
Redpole
Resolution
Revenge
Theseus
Thunder
Unicorn
Valiant
Whiting

### GUADELOUPE 1810
28 January – 5 February
Abercrombie
Achates
Alcmene
Alfred
Amaranthe
Asp
Attentive
Aurora
Bacchus
Ballattou
Belleisle
Blonde
Castor
Cherub
Cygnet
Elizabeth
Fawn
Forester
Freija
Frolic
Gloire
Grenada
Guadeloupe
Hazard
Laura
Loire
Melampus
Morne Fortunée
Netley
Observateur
Orpheus
Pelorus

Perlen
Plumper
Pompée
Pultusk
Ringdove
Rosamund
Savage
Sceptre
Scorpion
Snap
Star
Statira
Surinam
Thetis
Vimiera
Wanderer

**AMBOINA 1810**
17 February
Cornwallis
Dover
Samarang

**BANDA NEIRA 1810**
9 August
Barracouta
Caroline
Piedmontaise

**TERNATE 1810**
29 August
Dover

**LISSA 1811**
13 March
Active
Amphion
Cerberus
Volage

**TAMATAVE 1811**
20 May
Astraea
Galatea
Phoebe
Racehorse

**JAVA 1811**
July−18 September
Akbar
Barracouta
Bucephalus

Cornela
Caroline
Dasher
Doris
Harpy
Hecate
Hesper
Hussar
Illustrious
Leda
Lion
Minden
Modeste
Nisus
Phaeton
Phoebe
President
Procris
Psyche
Samarang
Scipion
Sir Francis Drake

**PELAGOSA 1811**
29 November
Active
Alceste
Unité

**SAN SEBASTIAN 1813**
August−8 September
Ajax
Andromache
Arrow
Beagle
Challenger
Constant
Despatch
Freija
Holly
Juniper
Lyra
Magicienne
President
Révolutionnaire
Sparrow
Surveillant

**GLÜCKSTADT 1814**
5 January
Blazer
Désirée

*Hearty*
*Piercer*
*Redbreast*
*Shamrock*
Some gunboats

## CATTARO 1814
5 January
*Bacchante*
*Saracen*

## ALGIERS 1816
27 August
*Albion*
*Belzebub*
*Britomart*
*Cordelia*
*Fury*
*Glasgow*
*Granicus*
*Hebrus*
*Prometheus*
*Queen Charlotte*
*Severn*
Some rocket boats
(List incomplete)

## BURMA 1824–6
5 March 1824–25 February
   1826
*Alligator*
*Aracne*
*Boadicea*
*Champion*
*Diane*
*Tamer*
*Tees*
(List incomplete)

## NAVARINO 1827
20 October
*Albion*
*Asia*
*Brisk*
*Cambrian*
*Dartmouth*
*Genoa*
*Glasgow*
*Mosquito*
*Philomel*
*Rose*
*Talbot*

## ADEN 1839
19 January
*Coote*
*Cruizer*
*Mahé*
*Volage*

## SYRIA 1840
10 September–9 December
*Asia*
*Bellerophon*
*Benbow*
*Cambridge*
*Carysfoot*
*Castor*
*Cyclops*
*Daphne*
*Dido*
*Edinburgh*
*Ganges*
*Gorgon*
*Hastings*
*Hazard*
*Hydra*
*Implacable*
*Magicienne*
*Phoenix*
*Pique*
*Powerful*
*Princess Charlotte*
*Revenge*
*Rodney*
*Stromboli*
*Talbot*
*Thunderer*
*Vanguard*
*Vesuvius*
*Wasp*
*Zebra*
There was a dispute about
*Hecate*: it was ruled she was
not entitled to the Battle
Honour although awarded the
medal.

## CHINA 1841–2
7 January 1841–21 July 1842
1841
*Alligator*
*Blenheim*
*Conway*
*Cruizer*

Druid
Herald
Larne
Melville
Nimrod
Pylades
Samarang
Sulphur
Wellesley

1841–2
Algerine
Blonde
Calliope
Columbine
Hyacinth
Jupiter
Modeste
Rattlesnake
Starling

1842
Apollo
Belleisle
Childers
Clio
Cornwallis
Dido
Endymion
Harlequin
Hazard
North Star
Plover
Sapphire
Vixen
Wanderer
Young Hebe

## NEW ZEALAND 1845–7

Calliope
Castor
Driver
Elphinstone
Hazard
Inflexible
North Star
Racehorse

## BURMA 1852–3

10 January 1852–30 June 1853
Hastings
Hermes

Rattler
Salamander
Serpent

1852–3
Cleopatra
Contest
Fox
Spartan
Sphinx
Winchester

1853
Bittern
Styx

## BALTIC 1854–5

28 March–20 September 1854
17 April–10 December 1855
1854
Alban
Algiers
Boscawen
Cumberland
Dauntless
Gladiator
Hannibal
Hecla
Janus
Leopard
Miranda
Monarch
Neptune
Odin
Penelope
Pigmy
Prince Regent
Princess Royal
Resistance
Rhadamanthus
Rosamund
Royal William
St George
St Jean d'Acre
St Vincent
Sphinx
Stromboli
Termagant
Tribune
Tyne
Valorous

Wrangler
Zephyr

1854—5
Ajax
Amphion
Archer
Arrogant
Basilisk
Belleisle
Blenheim
Bulldog
Caesar
Conflict
Cressy
Cruizer
Cuckoo
Desperate
Dragon
Driver
Duke of Wellington
Edinburgh
Euryalus
Gorgon
Hogue
Impérieuse
James Watt
Lightning
Locust
Majestic
Magicienne
Nile
Otter
Porcupine
Royal George
Snap
Volcano
Vulture

1855
Aeolus
Badger
Beacon
Biter
Blazer
Calcutta
Carron
Centaur
Colossus
Cornwallis
Cossack
Dapper

Drake
Esk
Exmouth
Falcon
Firefly
Geyser
Gleaner
Grappler
Growler
Harrier
Hastings
Havock
Hawke
Hind
Jackdaw
Lark
Magpie
Manly
Mastiff
Merlin
Orion
Pelter
Pembroke
Pickle
Pincher
Porpoise
Princess Alice
Prompt
Pylades
Redbreast
Redwing
Retribution
Rocket
Ruby
Russell
Sinbad
Skylark
Snapper
Starling
Stork
Surly
Swinger
Tartar
Thistle
Volage
Weazel

**CRIMEA 1854—5**
17 September 1854—
    9 September 1855
(Sea of Azov till 22 November)
1854

Apollo
Arethusa
Bellerophon
Brenda
Britannia
Circassia
Fury
Minna
Modeste
Pigmy
Retribution
Sampson
Sans Pareil
Shark
Trafalgar
Varna
Vengeance

*1854—5*
Agamemnon
Albion
Algiers
Ardent
Arrow
Banshee
Beagle
Caradoc
Curlew
Cyclops
Danube
Dauntless
Diamond
Firebrand
Furious
Gladiator
Harpy
Highflyer
Industry
Inflexible
Leander
London
Lynx
Medaera
Medina
Miranda
Niger
Queen
Rodney
Royal Albert
Simoon
Sphinx
Spitfire

Stromboli
Swallow
Terrible
Tribune
Valorous
Viper
Vulcan
Wasp

*1855*
Boxer
Camel
Clinker
Cracker
Curaçoa
Fancy
Firm
Flamer
Glatton
Grinder
Hannibal
Hardy
Jasper
Leopard
Magnet
Meteor
Moslem
Oberon
Odin
Oneida
Princess Royal
Raven
St Jean d'Acre
Snake
Sulina
Weser
Wrangler

**CHINA 1856—60**
1 October 1856—26 June 1858
1 August—24 October 1860
*1856—60*
Acorn
Actaeon
Adventure
Algerine
Amethyst
Assistance
Auckland
Banterer
Barracouta
Beagle

Belleisle
Bittern
Bustard
Calcutta
Camilla
Clown
Comus
Cormorant
Coromandel
Cruiser
Drake
Elk
Encounter
Esk
Firm
Forester
Furious
Fury
Haughty
Hesper
Highflyer
Hong Kong
Hornet
Inflexible
Insolent
Janus
Kestrel
Lee
Leven
Nanking
Niger
Nimrod
Pioneer
Pique
Plover
Racehorse
Sampson
Sans Pareil
Sir Charles Forbes
Slaney
Spartan
Starling
Staunch
Surprise
Sybille
Tribune
Volcano
Watchful
Winchester
Woodcock

*1860*
Bouncer
Cambrian
Centaur
Chesapeake
Cockchafer
Flamer
Grasshopper
Hardy
Havock
Impérieuse
Magicienne
Odin
Pearl
Retribution
Reynard
Ringdove
Roebuck
Scout
Simoon
Snake
Snap
Sparrowhawk
Sphinx
Urgent
Vulcan
Watchman
Weazel

**LUCKNOW 1857−8**
Indian Mutiny 1857−8
Shannon

**AMORHA 1858**
Indian Mutiny 5 March
Pearl

**NEW ZEALAND 1860−6**
*1860−1*
Cordelia
Iris
Niger
Pelorus

*1863−6*
Curaçoa
Eclipse
Esk
Falcon
Harrier
Himalaya
Miranda

*1865*
*Brisk*

## ABYSSINIA 1868
13 April
*Dryad*
*Octavia*
*Satellite*
The following ships also took part in the campaign but they are not eligible for the Battle Honour because they did not land a brigade: *Argus, Daphne, Nymphe, Spiteful, Star, Vigilant.*

## ASHANTEE 1873–4
9 June 1873–4 February 1874
*1873*
*Rattlesnake*
*Seagull*

*1873–4*
*Active*
*Amethyst*
*Argus*
*Barracouta*
*Beacon*
*Bittern*
*Coquette*
*Decoy*
*Dromedary*
*Druid*
*Encounter*
*Himalaya*
*Merlin*
*Simoon*
*Tamer*

*1874*
*Victor Emmanuel*

## ALEXANDRIA 1882
11 July
*Alexandra*
*Beacon*
*Bittern*
*Condor*
*Cygnet*
*Decoy*
*Hecla*
*Helicon*
*Inflexible*

*Invincible*
*Monarch*
*Penelope*
*Sultan*
*Superb*
*Téméraire*

## BENIN 1897
8–28 February
*Alecto*
*Barossa*
*Forte*
*Magpie*
*Philomel*
*Phoebe*
*St George*
*Theseus*
*Widgeon*

## SOUTH AFRICA 1899–1900
*Barossa*
*Doris*
*Forte*
*Monarch*
*Philomel*
*Powerful*
*Tartar*
*Terrible*
Because they did not land a Naval Brigade the following ships qualified for a medal but not the Battle Honour:
*Barracouta, Beagle, Blanche, Dwarf, Fearless, Gibraltar, Magicienne, Magpie, Naiad, Niobe, Partridge, Pearl, Pelorus, Penelope, Racoon, Rambler, Rattler, Redbreast, Sapphire, Sybille, Thetis, Thrush, Widgeon.*

## CHINA 1900
Boxer Rising. 10 June–31 December
*Alacrity*
*Algerine*
*Aurora*
*Barfleur*
*Centurion*
*Endymion*
*Fame*
*Orlando*

*Phoenix*
*Terrible*
*Whiting*
Because the following ships
did not land a Naval Brigade
they are ineligible for the
Battle Honour, although they
were awarded the medal:
*Arethusa, Bonaventure,*
*Canning, Clive, Dalhousie,*
*Daphne, Dido, Esk, Goliath,*
*Hart, Hermione, Humber, Isis,*
*Linnet, Marathon, Peacock,*
*Pigmy, Pique, Plover, Protector,*
*Redpole, Rosario, Snipe,*
*Undaunted, Wallaroo,*
*Waterwitch, Woodcock,*
*Woodlark.*

## HELIGOLAND 1914
28 August
*Aboukir*
*Acheron*
*Amethyst*
*Archer*
*Arethusa*
*Ariel*
*Attack*
*Bacchante*
*Badger*
*Beaver*
*Birmingham*
*Cressy*
*Defender*
*Druid*
*Euryalus*
*Falmouth*
*Fearless*
*Ferret*
*Firedrake*
*Forester*
*Goshawk*
*Hind*
*Hogue*
*Invincible*
*Jackal*
*Laertes*
*Laforey*
*Lance*
*Landrail*
*Lapwing*
*Lark*

*Laurel*
*Lawford*
*Legion*
*Lennox*
*Leonides*
*Liberty*
*Linnet*
*Lion*
*Liverpool*
*Lizard*
*Llewellyn*
*Lookout*
*Louis*
*Lowestoft*
*Lucifer*
*Lurcher*
*Lydiard*
*Lysander*
*New Zealand*
*Nottingham*
*Phoenix*
*Princess Royal*
*Queen Mary*
*Sandfly*
*Southampton*
Submarines: *D2, D8, E4, E5,*
*E6, E7, E8, E9*

## FALKLANDS 1914
8 December
*Bristol*
*Carnarvon*
*Cornwall*
*Glasgow*
*Inflexible*
*Invincible*
*Kent*
*Macedonia*

## CAMEROONS 1914
*Astraea*
*Challenger*
*Cumberland*
*Dwarf*

## MESOPOTAMIA 1914–17
*Bahrein*
*Bee*
*Blackfly*
*Butterfly*
*Caddisfly*
*Clio*

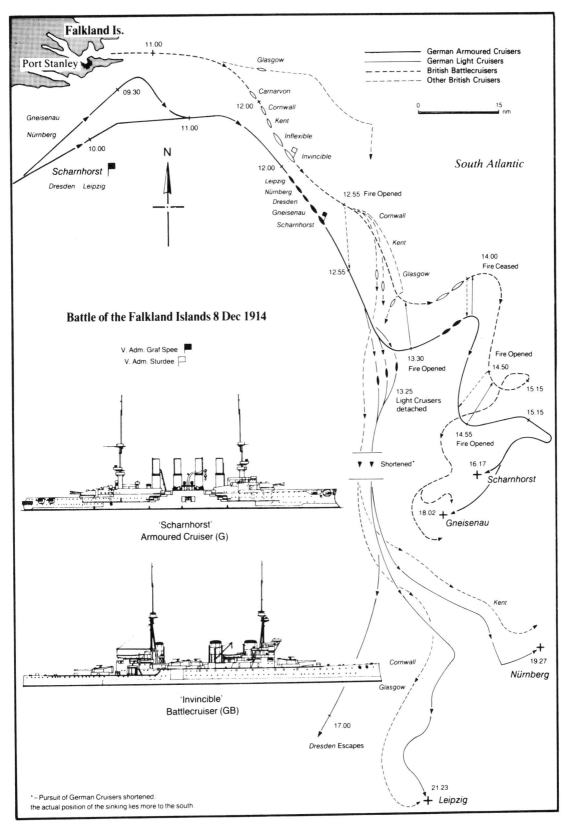

**Falkland Is.**

Port Stanley

11.00

Glasgow

09.30

Carnarvon

12.00    Cornwall

Gneisenau
Nürnberg                    Kent
                    11.00
                    Inflexible
10.00

*Scharnhorst* ⚑                    Invincible    *South Atlantic*

*Dresden Leipzig*    12.00

Leipzig
Nürnberg
Dresden                    12.55  Fire Opened
N                    Gneisenau
                    Scharnhorst    Cornwall

Kent

12.55    Glasgow    14.00
                    Fire Ceased

**Battle of the Falkland Islands 8 Dec 1914**

Fire Opened
14.50

V. Adm. Graf Spee ◼    13.30
V. Adm. Sturdee ▯    Fire Opened    15.15

13.25    15.15
Light Cruisers
detached    14.55
                    Fire Opened

Shortened*    16.17
                    ✚ *Scharnhorst*

18.02 ✚
    *Gneisenau*

*'Scharnhorst'*
Armoured Cruiser (G)

Kent

✚
19.27
*Nürnberg*

Cornwall

Glasgow

*'Invincible'*
Battlecruiser (GB)

17.00
*Dresden Escapes*

21.23
✚ *Leipzig*

\* = Pursuit of German Cruisers shortened:
the actual position of the sinking lies more to the south.

German Armoured Cruisers
German Light Cruisers
British Battlecruisers
Other British Cruisers

0                    15
                    nm

FALKLANDS

341

Comet
Cranefly
Dragonfly
Espiègle
Firefly
Flycatcher
Gadfly
Gnat
Grayfly
Greenfly
Hoverfly
Julnar
Lawrence
Lewis Pelly
Mantis
Massoudieh
Mayfly
Miner
Moth
Muzaffri
Ocean
Odin
Sawfly
Scarab

Sedgefly
Shaitan
Shushan
Snakefly
Stonefly
Sumana
Tarantula
Waterfly

## DOGGER BANK 1915

24 January
Acheron
Arethusa
Ariel
Attack
Aurora
Birmingham
Defender
Druid
Ferret
Forester
Goshawk
Hornet
Hydra
Indomitable
Laertes

DOGGER BANK II

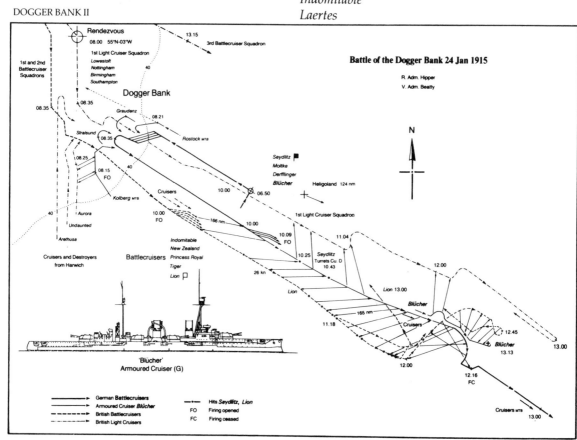

Laforey
Landrail
Lapwing
Lark
Laurel
Lawford
Legion
Liberty
Lion
Lookout
Louis
Lowestoft
Lucifer
Lydiard
Lysander
Mastiff
Mentor
Meteor
Milne
Minos
Miranda
Morris
New Zealand
Nottingham
Phoenix
Princess Royal
Sandfly
Southampton
Tiger
Tigress
Undaunted

## SUEZ CANAL 1915
2–4 February
Clio
Dufferin
Hardinge
Himalaya
Minerva
Ocean
Proserpine
Swiftsure
T.B. 043

## DARDANELLES 1915–16
19 February 1915–8 January
   1916
Abercrombie
Adamant
Agamemnon
Albion
Amethyst

Anemone
Ark Royal
Arno
Aster
Bacchante
Basilisk
Beagle
Ben-My-Chree
Blenheim
Bulldog
Canning
Canopus
Chatham
Chelmer
Colne
Cornwall
Cornwallis
Dartmouth
Doris
Dublin
Earl of Peterborough
Edgar
Endymion
Euryalus
Exmouth
Foresight
Foxhound
Fury
Gazelle
Glory
Goliath
Grafton
Grampus
Grasshopper
Harpy
Havelock
Hector
Heliotrope
Hibernia
Honeysuckle
Humber
Hussar
Implacable
Inflexible
Irresistible
Jed
Jonquil
Kennet
Laforey
Lawford
London
Lord Nelson

Louis
Lydiard
Magnificent
Majestic
Manica
Mars
Minerva
Mosquito
Ocean
Osiris II
Peony
Prince of Wales
Prince Edward
Prince George
Queen
Queen Elizabeth
Queen Victoria
Racoon
Raglan
Rattlesnake
Renard
Ribble
River Clyde
Roberts
Russell
Sapphire
Scorpion
Scourge
Sir Thomas Picton
Staunch
Swiftsure
Talbot
Theseus
Triad
Triumph
Usk
Venerable
Vengeance
Wear
Welland
Wolverine
Monitors: *M15, M16, M17,*
*M18, M19, M21, M29, M31,*
*M32, M33.*
Submarines: *AE2, B6, B11, E2,*
*E7, E11, E12, E14, E15, E20.*
TBs: *O64.*

## JUTLAND 1916
31 May
Abdiel
Acasta

Achates
Acheron
Active
Agincourt
Ajax
Ambuscade
Ardent
Ariel
Attack
Badger
Barham
Bellerophon
Bellona
Benbow
Birkenhead
Birmingham
Black Prince
Blanche
Boadicea
Broke
Calliope
Canada
Canterbury
Caroline
Castor
Centurion
Champion
Chester
Christopher
Cochrane
Collingwood
Colossus
Comus
Conqueror
Constance
Contest
Cordelia
Defence
Defender
Dublin
Duke of Edinburgh
Engadine
Erin
Falmouth
Faulknor
Fearless
Fortune
Galatea
Garland
Gloucester
Goshawk
Hampshire

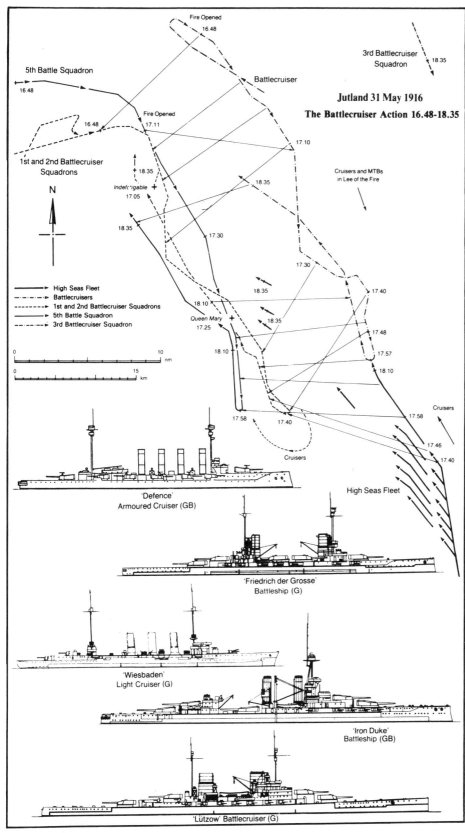

5th Battle Squadron
16.48

Fire Opened
16.48

Battlecruiser

3rd Battlecruiser
Squadron
18.35

Jutland 31 May 1916
The Battlecruiser Action 16.48-18.35

Fire Opened
16.48

17.11

17.10

1st and 2nd Battlecruiser
Squadrons

16.48

Cruisers and MTBs
in Lee of the Fire

N

18.35

Indefatigable
17.05

18.35

18.35

17.30

17.30

18.35

17.40

High Seas Fleet
Battlecruisers
1st and 2nd Battlecruiser Squadrons
5th Battle Squadron
3rd Battlecruiser Squadron

18.10

Queen Mary
17.25

18.35

17.48

17.57

18.10

0        10
                nm
0        15
                km

18.10

17.58

17.40

17.58

Cruisers

17.46

Cruisers

17.40

'Defence'
Armoured Cruiser (GB)

High Seas Fleet

'Friedrich der Grosse'
Battleship (G)

'Wiesbaden'
Light Cruiser (G)

'Iron Duke'
Battleship (GB)

'Lützow' Battlecruiser (G)

JUTLAND

Hardy
Hercules
Hydra
Inconstant
Indefatigable
Indomitable
Inflexible
Invincible
Iron Duke
Kempenfelt
King George V
Landrail
Lapwing
Laurel
Liberty
Lion
Lizard
Lydiard
Maenad
Magic
Malaya
Mandate
Manners
Marksman
Marlborough
Marne
Martial
Marvel
Mary Rose
Menace
Michael
Midge
Milbrook
Mindful
Minion
Minotaur
Mischief
Monarch
Mons
Moon
Moorsom
Moresby
Morning Star
Morris
Mounsey
Munster
Mystic
Narborough
Narwhal
Neptune
Nerissa
Nessus

Nestor
New Zealand
Nicator
Noble
Nomad
Nonsuch
Nottingham
Oak
Obdurate
Obedient
Onslaught
Onslow
Opal
Ophelia
Orion
Ossory
Owl
Pelican
Petard
Phaeton
Porpoise
Princess Royal
Queen Mary
Revenge
Royalist
St Vincent
Shannon
Shark
Southampton
Sparrowhawk
Spitfire
Superb
Téméraire
Termagant
Thunderer
Tiger
Tipperary
Turbulent
Unity
Valiant
Vanguard
Warren
Warspite
Yarmouth

**DOVER 1917**
21 April
Broke
Swift

**ZEEBRUGGE 1918**
23 April
*Zeebrugge*
*Attentive*
*Daffodil*
*Erebus*
*Intrepid*
*Iphigenia*
*Iris II*
*Lingfield*
*Manly*
*Mansfield*
*Melpomeme*
*Moorsom*
*Morris*
*Myngs*
*North Star*
*Phoebe*
*Scott*
*Stork*
*Teazer*
*Termagant*
*Terror*
*Thetis*
*Trident*
*Truculent*
*Ulleswater*
*Velox*
*Vindictive*
*Warwick*
*Whirlwind*
Submarines: C1, C3.
CMBs: *5, 7, 15A, 16A, 17A, 21B, 22B, 23B, 24A, 25BD, 26B, 27A, 28A, 29A, 30B, 32A, 34A, 35A.*
MLs: *79, 110, 121, 128, 223,239, 241, 252, 258, 262, 272, 280, 282, 308, 314, 345, 397, 416, 420, 422, 424, 513, 525, 526, 533, 549, 552, 555, 557, 558, 560, 561, 562.*

*Ostend*
*Afridi*
*Brilliant*
*Faulknor*
*General Crauford*
*Lightfoot*
*Lord Clive*
*Marshal Soult*
*Mastiff*

*Matchless*
*Mentor*
*Prince Eugene*
*Sirius*
*Swift*
*Tempest*
*Tetrarch*
*Zubian*
Monitors: *M21, M24, M26.*
CMBs: *2, 4, 10, 11, 19A, 20A.*
MLs: *11, 16, 17, 22, 23, 30, 60, 105, 254, 274, 276, 279, 283, 429, 512, 532, 551, 556.*

**OSTEND 1918**
10 May
*Faulknor*
*Prince Eugene*
*Trident*
*Velox*
*Vindictive*
*Warwick*
*Whirlwind*
CMBs: *22B, 23B, 24A, 25BD, 26B, 30B.*
MLs: *254, 276.*

**SCANDINAVIAN
CONVOYS 1917**
17 October and 12 December
*Mary Rose*
*Partridge*
*Pellew*
*Strongbow*

**BELGIAN COAST 1914−18**
*Afridi*
*Albyn*
*Amazon*
*Ariel*
*Attentive*
*Botha*
*Brighton Queen*
*Brilliant*
*Broke*
*Bustard*
*Cambridge*
*Carysfoot*
*Centaur*
*Cleopatra*
*Columbia*
*Cossack*

Crane
Crusader
Curran
Devonia
Duchess of Montrose
Erebus
Excellent
Exmouth
Falcon
Faulknor
Fawn
Ferret
Flirt
Foresight
General Craufurd
General Wolfe
Ghurka
Gipsy
Glen Avon
Gorgon
Gransha
Greyhound
Hazard
Humber
Iris
Irresistible
Jupiter II
Kangaroo
Kempton
Lady Ismay
Lance
Lapwing
Laurel
Leven
Lightfoot
Lizard
Lochinvar
Lord Clive
Lucifer
Lysander
Manly
Mansfield
Maori
Marmion II
Marshal Ney
Marshal Soult
Mastiff
Matchless
Medea
Melpomene
Menelaus
Mentor

Mermaid
Mersey
Milne
Miranda
Mohawk
Moorsom
Morris
Murray
Myrmidon
Nimrod
Nubian
Nugent
P11
Peary
Phoebe
Prince Eugene
Prince Rupert
Queen Victoria
Racehorse
Radiant
Ravenswood
Recruit
Redoubtable
Retriever
Revenge
Rinaldo
Riviera
Russell
Sapphire
Saracen
Sargetta
Satyr
Sharpshooter
Sirius
Sir John Moore
Skilful
Springbok
Starfish
Superman
Swift
Syren
Tartar
Taurus
Termagant
Terror
Thruster
Truculent
Undaunted
Ure
Venerable
Velox
Vestal

*Viking*
*Westward Ho*
*Zulu*
Monitors: *M23, M24, M25,*
*M26, M27*
TBs: *4, 24.*
MLs: *103, 105, 110, 239, 252,*
*272, 276, 279, 280, 282, 283,*
*532.*
CMBs: *1, 2, 3, 4, 5, 7, 8, 9, 10,*
*12, 13, 14A, 15A, 16A, 19A,*
*20A, 21B, 22B, 23B, 24A, 25BD,*
*64BD, 66BD, 68B, 70A, 71A,*
*73BD, 74BD, 76A, 86BD,*
*89BD.*

## RIVER PLATE 1939
13 December
*Achilles*
*Ajax*
*Exeter*
FAA Squadron:700

## NARVIK 1940
10 and 13 April
*Bedouin*
*Cossack*
*Eskimo*
*Forester*
*Foxhound*
*Furious*
*Hardy*
*Havock*
*Hero*
*Hostile*
*Hotspur*
*Hunter*
*Icarus*
*Kimberley*
*Punjabi*
*Warspite*

## NORWAY 1940−5
*Acanthus*
*Acasta*
*Acheron*
*Afridi*
*Algonquin*
*Amazon*
*Angle*
*Arab*
*Ardent*

*Arethusa*
*Ark Royal*
*Arrow*
*Ashanti*
*Aston Villa*
*Auckland*
*Aurora*
*Basilisk*
*Beagle*
*Bedouin*
*Bellona*
*Berwick*
*Birmingham*
*Bittern*
*Black Swan*
*Bradman*
*Brazen*
*Cachalot*
*Cairo*
*Calcutta*
*Campania*
*Campbell*
*Cape Chelyuskin*
*Cape Passero*
*Cape Siretoko*
*Carlisle*
*Chiddingford*
*Clyde*
*Codrington*
*Cossack*
*Coventry*
*Curaçoa*
*Curlew*
*Delight*
*Devonshire*
*Diadem*
*Diana*
*Echo*
*Eclipse*
*Edinburgh*
*Effingham*
*Eglantine*
*Electra*
*Ellesmere*
*Emperor*
*Encounter*
*Enterprise*
*Escapade*
*Esk*
*Eskimo*
*Fame*
*Faulknor*

Fearless
Fencer
Firedrake
Flamingo
Fleetwood
Forester
Foxhound
Furious
Galatea
Gaul
Ghurka
Glasgow
Glorious
Glowworm
Grenade
Greyhound
Griffin
Guardian
Hammond
Hasty
Havelock
Havock
Hero
Hesperus
Highlander
Hostile
Icarus
Imperial
Implacable
Impulsive
Inglefield
Intrepid
Iroquois
Isis
Ivanhoe
Jackal
Janus
Jardine
Javelin
Juniper
Kelly
Kent
Kenya
Kimberley
Kipling
Larwood
Legion
Loch Shin
Manchester
Mansfield
Maori
Margaret

Mashona
Matabele
Mauritius
Melbourne
Mohawk
Myngs
Nairana
Narwhal
Nigeria
Norfolk
Northern Gem
Nubian
Offa
Onslaught
Onslow
Oribi
Orwell
Pelican
Penelope
Porpoise
Premier
Prince Charles
Prince Leopold
Prins Albert
Prinses Beatrix
Protector
Punjabi
Pursuer
Queen
Queen Emma
Ranen
Renown
Repulse
Resolution
Rhine
Rodney
Rutlandshire
St Goran
St Magnus
St Sunniva
Satyr
Sceptre
Scott
Sealion
Searcher
Seawolf
Severn
Sheffield
Sikh
Snapper
Somali
Southampton

Spearfish
Stork
Striker
Stubborn
Suffolk
Sunfish
Sussex
Taku
Tapir
Tarpon
Tartar
Terrapin
Tetrarch
Thirlmere
Thistle
Tigris
Triad
Trident
Triton
Truant
Trumpeter
Tuna
Ursula
Valiant
Vandyck
Vanoc
Vansittart
Venturer
Verulam
Veteran
Victorious
Vindictive
Walker
Wanderer
Warspite
Warwickshire
Westcott
Whirlwind
Wisteria
Witch
Witherington
Wren
Wolverine
X 24
York
Zambesi
Zealous
Zest
Zulu

MTBs: *711, 722.*
FAA Squadrons: 700, 701, 800, 801, 802, 803, 804, 806, 810, 816, 817, 818, 820, 821, 823, 825, 827, 828, 829, 830, 831, 841, 842, 846, 852, 853, 856, 880, 881, 882, 887, 894, 896, 898[10], 1770, 1771, 1832, 1834, 1836, 1840, 1841, 1842.

## DUNKIRK 1940
26 May – 4 June
Albury
Amulree
Anthony
Argyllshire
Arley
Basilisk
Bideford
Brock
Blackburn Rovers
Boy Roy
Brighton Belle
Brighton Queen
Calcutta
Calvi
Cape Argona
Cayton Wyke
Chico
Codrington
Comfort
Conidaw
Crested Eagle
Devonia
Duchess of Fife
Dundalk
Eileen Emma
Emperor of India
Esk
Express
Fidget
Fisher Boy
Fitzroy
Fyldea
Forecast
Gallant
Gervais Rentoul

10   898 Sqdn appears in the AFO but not the Admiralty Definitive List.

Girl Gladys
Girl Pamela
Glen Avon
Glen Gower
Golden Eagle
Golden Gift
Golden Sunbeam
Gossamer
Gracie Fields
Grafton
Grenade
Greyhound
Grive
Grimsby Town
Guillemot
Gulzar
Halcyon
Harvester
Havant
Hebe
Icarus
Impulsive
Intrepid
Inverforth
Ivanhoe
Jacketa
Jaguar
Javelin
John Cattling
Keith
Kellett
King Orry
Kingfisher
Kingston Alalite
Kingston Andalusite
Kingston Olivine
Lady Philomena
Leda
Llanthony
Locust
Lord Cavan
Lord Howard
Lord Howe
Lord Inchcape
Lydd
Mackay
Malcolm
Marmion
Medway Queen
Midas
Mona's Isle
Montrose

Mosquito
Nautilus
Netsukis
Niger
Olvina
Oriole
Our Bairns
Pangbourne
Paxton
Plinlimmon
Polly Johnson
Princess Elizabeth
Queen of Thanet
Ross
Royal Eagle
Sabre
Saladin
Salamander
Saltash
Sandown
Saon
Sargasso
Scimitar
Sharpshooter
Shikari
Shipmates
Silver Dawn
Skipjack
Snaefell
Speedwell
Spurs
Stella Dorado
Sutton
The Boys
Thomas Bartlett
Thuringia
Torbay II
Ut Prosim
Vanquisher
Venomous
Verity
Vimy
Vivacious
Wakeful
Waverley
Westella
Westward Ho
Whitehall
Whitshed
Wild Swan
Winchelsea
Windsor

*Wolfhound*
*Wolsey*
*Wolves*
*Worcester*
*Worthing*
*Yorkshire Lass*
*Young Mun*
FAA Squadrons: 801, 806, 825, 826.
Numerous other 'Red Ensign' ships such as personnel ships, hospital carriers and so on, took part in the operation but have not been awarded Battle Honours.

## CALABRIA 1940
9 July
*Dainty*
*Decoy*
*Defender*
*Eagle*
*Gloucester*
*Hasty*
*Hereward*
*Hero*
*Hostile*
*Hyperion*
*Ilex*
*Janus*
*Juno*
*Liverpool*
*Malaya*
*Mohawk*
*Neptune*
*Nubian*
*Orion*
*Royal Sovereign*
*Stuart*
*Sydney*
*Vampire*
*Voyager*
*Warspite*
FAA Squadrons: 813, 824.

## SPADA 1940
19 July
*Hasty*
*Havock*
*Hero*
*Hyperion*
*Ilex*

*Sydney*

## TARANTO 1940
11 November
*Illustrious*
FAA Squadrons: 813, 815, 819, 824.

## SPARTIVENTO 1940
27 November
*Ark Royal*
*Berwick*
*Coventry*
*Defender*
*Despatch*
*Diamond*
*Duncan*
*Encounter*
*Faulknor*
*Firedrake*
*Forester*
*Fury*
*Gallant*
*Gloxinia*
*Greyhound*
*Hereward*
*Hotspur*
*Hyacinth*
*Jaguar*
*Kelvin*
*Manchester*
*Newcastle*
*Peony*
*Ramillies*
*Renown*
*Salvia*
*Sheffield*
*Southampton*
*Vidette*
*Wishart*
FAA Squadrons: 700, 800, 808, 810, 818, 820.

## MATAPAN 1941
28–29 March
*Ajax*
*Barham*
*Defender*
*Formidable*
*Gloucester*
*Greyhound*
*Griffin*

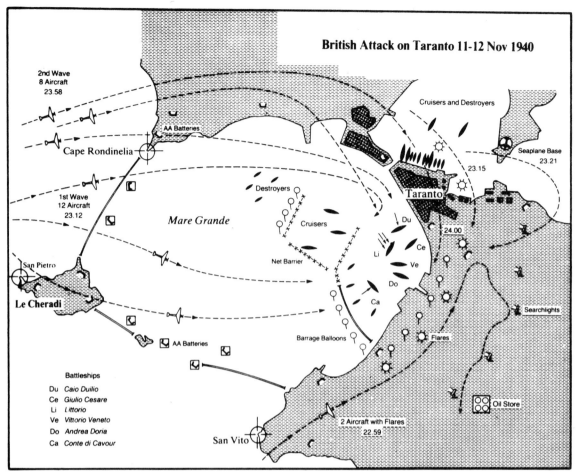

British Attack on Taranto 11-12 Nov 1940

2nd Wave
8 Aircraft
23.58

AA Batteries

Cape Rondinelia

1st Wave
12 Aircraft
23.12

*Mare Grande*

Cruisers and Destroyers

Seaplane Base
23.21

23.15

Taranto

Destroyers

Cruisers

Du

24.00

Ce

Li

Net Barrier

Ve

San Pietro

Do

Le Cheradi

Searchlights

Ca

Barrage Balloons

Flares

AA Batteries

Battleships

Du  *Caio Duilio*
Ce  *Giulio Cesare*
Li  *Littorio*
Ve  *Vittorio Veneto*
Do  *Andrea Doria*
Ca  *Conte di Cavour*

Oil Store

2 Aircraft with Flares
22.59

San Vito

TARANTO

*Hasty*
*Havock*
*Hereward*
*Hotspur*
*Ilex*
*Jaguar*
*Janus*
*Jervis*
*Juno*
*Mohawk*
*Nubian*
*Orion*
*Perth*
*Stuart*
*Valiant*
*Vendetta*
*Warspite*
FAA Squadrons: 700, 803, 806,
815, 826, 829.

**SFAX 1941**
15 − 16 April
*Janus*
*Jervis*
*Nubian*
*Mohawk*

**GREECE 1941**
24 − 29 April
*Ajax*
*Auckland*
*Calcutta*
*Carlisle*
*Coventry*
*Decoy*
*Defender*
*Diamond*
*Flamingo*
*Glenearn*
*Glengyle*
*Griffin*
*Grimsby*

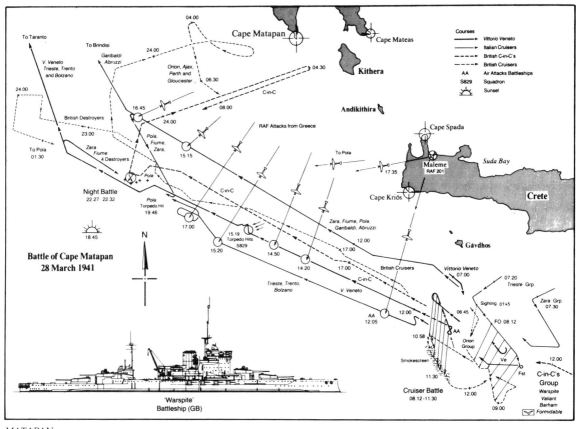

MATAPAN

## CRETE 1941

| MATAPAN | CRETE 1941 |
| --- | --- |
| | 20 May–1 June |
| Hasty | Abdiel |
| Havock | Ajax |
| Hereward | Auckland |
| Hero | Barham |
| Hotspur | Calcutta |
| Hyacinth | Carlisle |
| Isis | Coventry |
| Kandahar | Decoy |
| Kimberley | Defender |
| Kingston | Dido |
| Muroto | Fiji |
| Nubian | Flamingo |
| Orion | Formidable |
| Perth | Glengyle |
| Phoebe | Glenroy |
| Salvia | Gloucester |
| Stuart | Griffin |
| Ulster Prince | Grimsby |
| Vampire | Hasty |
| Vendetta | Havock |
| Voyager | Hereward |
| Waterhen | Hero |
| Wryneck | |

Hotspur
Ilex
Imperial
Isis
Jackal
Jaguar
Janus
Jervis
Juno
Kandahar
Kashmir
Kelly
Kelvin
Kimberley
Kingston
Kipling
Kos 21
Kos 22
Kos 23
Lanner
Naiad
Napier
Nizam
Nubian
Orion
Perth
Phoebe
Queen Elizabeth
Rorqual
Salvia
Stuart
Syvern
Valiant
Vampire
Vendetta
Voyager
Warspite
Waterhen
Widnes
MLs: *1011, 1030, 1032*.
MTBs: *67, 213, 216, 217, 314*.
FAA Squadron: 805

## 'BISMARCK' 1941
23–27 May
Achates
Active
Antelope
Anthony
Ark Royal
Aurora
Cossack

Dorsetshire
Echo
Edinburgh
Electra
Galatea
Hermione
Hood
Icarus
Inglefield
Intrepid
Kenya
King George V
Maori
Mashona
Neptune
Nestor
Norfolk
Prince of Wales
Punjabi
Renown
Repulse
Rodney
Sheffield
Sikh
Somali
Suffolk
Tartar
Victorious
Zulu
FAA Squadrons: 800, 808, 810, 818, 820, 825.

## CAPE BON 1941
13 December
Legion
Maori
Sikh

## LIBYA 1940–2
September 1940–June 1942

*1940*
Hereward
Hyperion
Janus
Juno
Mohawk
Nubian
FAA Squadron: 819.

*1940–41*
Chakla

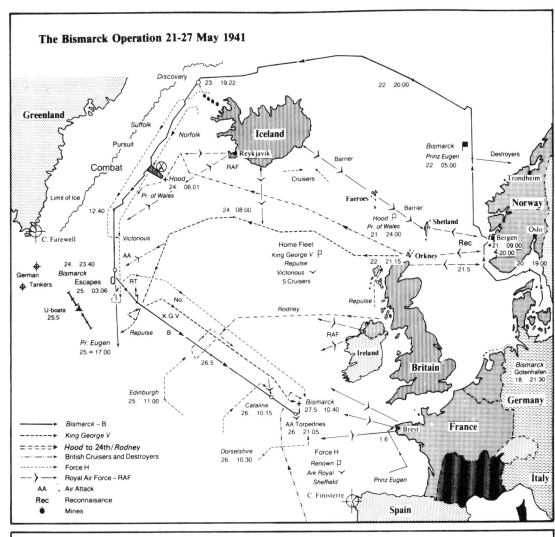

## The Bismarck Operation 21-27 May 1941

**Greenland**

*Discovery* 23. 19.22

*Suffolk*

*Norfolk*

**Iceland**

Reykjavik

RAF

Pursuit

**Combat**

Limit of Ice

12.40

C. Farewell

⊕ *Hood* 24. 06.01

Pr. of Wales

*Victorious*

AA

RT

24. 23.40
*Bismarck*
**Escapes**
25. 03.06

German
Tankers

U-boats
25.5

No.

K.G.V.

B

*Pr. Eugen*
25. ≈ 17.00

*Repulse*

26.5

*Edinburgh*
25. 11.00

*Catalina*
26. 10.15

22. 20.00

*Bismarck*
*Prinz Eugen*
22  05.00

Destroyers

Trondheim

**Norway**

Bergen
21. 09.00
20. 19.00

Oslo

Barrier

Cruisers

**Faeroes**

*Hood*
Pr. of Wales
21. 24.00

Barrier

**Shetland**

**Rec**

Orkney

22  21.15

21.5

Home Fleet
*King George V*
*Repulse*
*Victorious*
5 Cruisers

*Repulse*

*Rodney*

RAF

**Ireland**

**Britain**

*Bismarck*
27.5  10.40

AA Torpedoes
26. 21.05

Brest

**France**

1.6

*Prinz Eugen*

24. 08.00

*Bismarck*
Gotenhafen
18. 21.30

**Germany**

**Italy**

*Dorsetshire*
26. 10.30

**Force H**
*Renown*
*Ark Royal*
*Sheffield*

C. Finisterre

**Spain**

---

| | |
|---|---|
| ──────► | *Bismarck* – B |
| – – – ► | *King George V* |
| ▭▭▭▭► | *Hood* to 24th/*Rodney* |
| · – · – ► | British Cruisers and Destroyers |
| · · · · · | Force H |
| ──►  | Royal Air Force – RAF |
| AA | Air Attack |
| Rec | Reconnaisance |
| ⬤ | Mines |

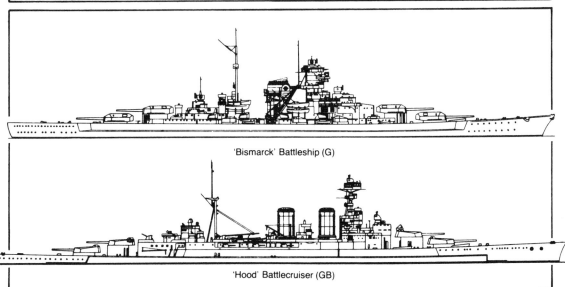

'Bismarck' Battleship (G)

'Hood' Battlecruiser (GB)

'BISMARCK' OPERATION

357

Dainty
Fiona
Ladybird
Protector
Stuart
Terror
Vampire
Vendetta
Voyager
Waterhen
FAA Squadrons: 803, 806, 813,
815, 824.

1940−2
Aphis
Jervis

1941
Abdiel
Arthur Cavenagh
Auckland
Aurora II
Bagshot
Calcutta
Calm
Chakdina
Chantala
Coventry
Cricket
Defender
Encounter
Fareham
Flamingo
Glenearn
Glengyle
Glenroy
Gnat
Greyhound
Grimsby
Hailstorm
Huntley
Kai
Kandahar
Kingston
Kos 21
Latona
May
Milford Countess
Muroto
Napier
Nebb
Nizam

Ouse
Parramatta
Rosaura
Salvia
Sikh
Sindonia
Skudd III
Skudd IV
Soira
Southern Floe
Stoke
Svana
Thorbryn
Thorgrim
Wryneck
Yama
Yarra
MLs: 1012, 1023.
MTBs: 68, 215.

1941−2
Aberdare
Avon Vale
Burgonet
Carlisle
Cocker (ex Kos 19)
Decoy
Eridge
Falk
Farndale
Gloxinia
Griffin
Hasty
Havock
Hero
Heythorp
Hotspur
Hyacinth
Jackal
Jaguar
Kimberley
Kipling
Klo
Legion
Moy
Peony
Protea
Skudd V
Soika
Sotra
Southern Isle
Southern Maid

*Southern Sea*
*Toneline*
*Wolborough*
MLs: *1048, 1051.*
FAA Squadrons: 805, 826.

*1942*
*Airedale*
*Aldenham*
*Antwerp*
*Arrow*
*Beaufort*
*Beves*
*Boksburg*
*Croome*
*Delphinium*
*Dulverton*
*Erica*
*Exmoor*
*Farnham*
*Firmament*
*Gribb*
*Grove*
*Hurworth*
*Imhoff*
*Kingston Coral*
*Kingston Crystal*
*Langlaate*
*Lively*
*Malines*
*Parktown*
*Primula*
*Seksern*
*Snapdragon*
*Southwold*
*Treern*
*Victoria I*
*Vulcan*
*Zulu*
MLs: *266, 267, 348, 355, 1004,*
*1005, 1039, 1046, 1069.*
MTBs: *61, 259, 260, 261, 262,*
*263, 266, 267, 309, 311, 312.*
FAA Squadron: 821.

## SUNDA STRAIT 1942
28 February
*Perth*

## SIRTE 1942
22 March
*Avon Vale*

*Beaufort*
*Breconshire*
*Carlisle*
*Cleopatra*
*Dido*
*Dulverton*
*Eridge*
*Euryalus*
*Hero*
*Hurworth*
*Jervis*
*Kelvin*
*Kingston*
*Legion*
*Lively*
*Penelope*
*Sikh*
*Southwold*
(The Admiralty appears to
have overlooked the active
presence of HMS *Havock* in
this battle.)

## ST NAZAIRE 1942
28 March
*Atherstone*
*Campbeltown*
*Tynedale*
MLs: *156, 160, 177, 192, 262,*
*267, 268, 270, 298, 306, 307,*
*443, 446, 447, 457.*
MGB: *314.*
MTB: *74.*

## DIEGO SUAREZ 1942
5−7 May
*Active*
*Anthony*
*Auricula*
*Bachaquero*
*Cromarty*
*Cromer*
*Cyclamen*
*Devonshire*
*Duncan*
*Freesia*
*Fritillary*
*Genista*
*Hermione*
*Illustrious*
*Inconstant*
*Indomitable*

Jasmine
Javelin
Karanja
Keren
Laforey
Lightning
Lookout
Nigella
Pakenham
Paladin
Panther
Poole
Ramillies
Romney
Royal Ulsterman
Thyne
Winchester Castle
FAA Squadrons: 800, 810, 827, 829, 831, 880, 881, 882.

## CORAL SEA 1942
7 May
*Australia*
*Hobart*

## SAVO ISLAND 1942
9 August
*Australia*
*Canberra*
*Hobart*

## DIEPPE 1942
19 August
*Albrighton*
*Alresford*
*Bangor*
*Berkeley*
*Blackpool*
*Bleakdale*
*Blyth*
*Bridlington*
*Bridport*
*Brocklesby*
*Calpe*
*Clacton*
*Duke of Wellington*
*Eastbourne*
*Felixstowe*
*Fernie*
*Garth*
*Glengyle*
*Ilfracombe*

*Invicta*
*Locust*
*Polruan*
*Prince Charles*
*Prince Leopold*
*Prins Albert*
*Prinses Astrid*
*Prinses Beatrix*
*Queen Emma*
*Rhyl*
*Sidmouth*
*Stornoway*
*Tenby*
MLs: *114, 120, 123, 171, 187, 189, 190, 191, 193, 194, 208, 214, 230, 246, 291, 292, 309, 343, 344, 346.*
MGBs: *50, 51, 312, 315, 316, 317, 320, 321, 323, 326.*
SGBs: *5, 6, 8, 9.*

## BARENTS SEA 1942
31 December
*Achates*
*Hyderabad*
*Jamaica*
*Northern Gem*
*Obdurate*
*Obedient*
*Onslow*
*Orwell*
*Rhododendron*
*Sheffield*

## GUADALCANAL 1942−3
August 1942−February 1943
*Achilles*
*Arunta*
*Australia*
*Canberra*
*Hobart*
*Kiwi*
*Moa*
*Tui*

## NORTH AFRICA 1942−3
8 November 1942−20 February 1943

*1942*
*Abbeydale*
*Aberdeen*

Achates
Algerine
Alynbank
Argonaut
Argus
Avenger
Beagle
Bermuda
Bideford
Biter
Blean
Boadicea
Bradford
Bramham
Broke
Brown Ranger
Bulldog
Bulolo
Burke
Charybdis
Clyne Castle
Coltsfoot
Coreopsis
Cowdray
Cumberland
Dasher
Delhi
Deptford
Derwentdale
Dianella
Duke of York
Eastbourne
Empyrean
Emmerdale
Erne
Exe
Fluellen
Gardenia
Geranium
Glengyle
Hartland
Horatio
Hoy
Ibis
Ilfracombe
Imperialist
Ithuriel
Jamaica
Jonquil
Karenja
Keren
Kingston Chrysolite

Landguard
Largs
Laurel
Leith
Leyland
Lord Hotham
Lulworth
Malcolm
Marigold
Martin
Meteor
Milne
Misoe
Nasprite
Norfolk
Onslow
Opportune
Oribi
Othello
P45
P48
P54
P221
P222
P228
Palomares
Partridge
Pelican
Philante
Poppy
Porcupine
Quentin
Renown
Returno
Rhododendron
Roberts
Rochester
Ronaldsay
Ronsay
Rysa
St Nectar
Sandwich
Scarborough
Scottish
Scylla
Sheffield
Spirea
Starwort
Stork
Swale
Tribune
Tynwald

Ulster Monarch
Ursula
Vansittart
Victoria
Walney
Wrestler
FAA Squadrons: 804, 809, 817,
832, 833, 880, 882, 883, 884,
891.

1942–3
Acute
Alarm
Albacore
Amazon
Antelope
Arctic Ranger
Ashanti
Aubretia
Aurora
Avon Vale
Bachequero
Banff
Bicester
Boreas
Brilliant
Brixham
Bude
Cadmus
Calpe
Cava
Clacton
Clare
Convolvulus
Coriolanus
Dewdale
Dingledale
Easton
Eday
Egret
Elbury
Enchantress
Eskimo
Farndale
Felixstowe
Filey Bay
Fleetwood
Formidable
Foula
Furious
Goth
Hengist

Hunda
Hussar
Inchcolm
Jaunty
Jura
Kerrera
Kintyre
Lammerton
Linnet
Loch Oskaig
Londonderry
Lookout
Lord Nuffield
Lotus
Lunenburg
Maidstone
Mull
Negro
Nelson
Offa
P51
P217
P219 (Seraph)
Panther
Pathfinder
Penn
Penstemon
Polruan
Pozarica
Prescott
Prinses Beatrix
Puckeridge
Quality
Queen Emma
Quiberon
Restive
Rhyl
Rodney
Rother
Rothesay
Royal Scotsman
Royal Ulsterman
Ruskholm
St Day
St Mellons
Samphire
Sennen
Shiant
Sirius
Speedwell
Spey
Stornoway

Stroma
Strongsay
Sturgeon
Tartar
Tasajera
Vanoc
Velox
Venomous
Verity
Vetch
Vienna
Violet
Westcott
Westray
Wheatland
Wilton
Wishart
Wivern
Woodstock
FAA Squadrons: 700, 800, 807,
820, 822, 885, 888, 893.
MLs: 238, 273, 280, 283, 295,
307, 336, 338, 433, 444, 458,
463, 469, 471, 480, 483.
HDMLs: 1127, 1128, 1139.

## SICILY 1943
10 July−17 August
Abdiel
Abercrombie
Acute
Albacore
Aldenham
Alynbank
Antwerp
Aphis
Arrow
Atherstone
Aurora
Banff
Bann
Beaufort
Belvoir
Bergamot
Blankney
Blencathra
Bluebell
Bonito
Boston
Boxer
Brecon
Brissendon

Brittany
Brixham
Brocklesby
Bruiser
Bryony
Bulolo
Burra
Cadmus
Calpe
Camellia
Carlisle
Cava
Cedardale
Cessnock
Chanticleer
Circe
Clacton
Clare
Cleopatra
Cleveland
Cockchafer
Colombo
Convolvulus
Coriolanus
Crane
Cromarty
Cygnet
Dart
Delhi
Delphinium
Derwentdale
Dianella
Dido
Dulverton
Easton
Echo
Eclipse
Eday
Eggesford
Emmerdale
Erebus
Erne
Eskimo
Espiègle
Euryalus
Exmoor
Farndale
Faulknor
Felixstowe
Fishguard
Fly
Formidable

Foxtrot
Fury
Gavotte
Gawler
Geraldton
Glengyle
Grayling
Guardian
Hambledon
Haydon
Hazard
Hebe
Hilary
Holcombe
Honeysuckle
Howe
Hursley
Hurworth
Hyacinth
Hyderabad
Hythe
Ilex
Inchmarnock
Inconstant
Indomitable
Inglefield
Intrepid
Ipswich
Isis
Islay
Jervis
Juliet
Jumna
Keren
Kerrera
King George V
King Sol
Laforey
Lammerton
Largs
Lauderdale
Ledbury
Liddlesdale
Lismore
Lookout
Lotus
Loyal
Man-o-War
Maryborough
Mauritius
Mendip
Mullet

Mutine
Nelson
Newfoundland
Nubian
Oakley
Offa
Orion
Osiris
Oxlip
Paladin
Panther
Parthian
Pathfinder
Pearleaf
Penelope
Penn
Penstemon
Petard
Pheasant
Pirouette
Plym
Polruan
Poole
Poppy
Primula
Prince Charles
Prince Leopold
Prins Albert
Prinses Astrid
Prinses Beatrix
Prinses Josephine Charlotte
Protea
Puckeridge
Quail
Quantock
Queenborough
Queen Emma
Quilliam
Raider
Reighton Wyke
Rhododendron
Rhyl
Roberts
Rockwood
Rodney
Romeo
Romney
Rorqual
Rothesay
Royal Scotsman
Royal Ulsterman
Rye

Safari
Saracen
Scarab
Seaham
Seraph
Severn
Shakespeare
Sharpshooter
Shiant
Shoreham
Sibyl
Simoon
Sirius
Southern Isle
Southern Sea
Sportsman
Starwort
Stella Carina
Stornaway
Stroma
Sutlej
Tactician
Tango
Tartar
Taurus
Templar
Test
Tetcott
Teviot
Thruster
Torbay
Trent
Trespasser
Tribune
Trident
Trooper
Troubridge
Tumult
Tynedale
Tyrian
Uganda
Ulster Monarch
Ulster Queen
Ultor
Unbroken
Unison
United
Universal
Unrivalled
Unruffled
Unruly
Unseen

Unshaken
Unsparing
Uproar
Usurper
Valiant
Venomous
Vetch
Viceroy
Visenda
Wallace
Wanderer
Warspite
Whadden
Wheatland
Whimbrel
Whitehaven
Whiting
Wilton
Wishart
Wolborough
Woolongong
Woolston
Wrestler
MLs: 125, 126, 565, 1158, 1252.
MGBs: 641, 657, 659, 660
MTBs: 57, 62, 63, 75, 77, 81, 82, 84, 85, 260, 265, 288, 289, 290, 295, 313, 316, 633, 640, 665, 670.
FAA Squadrons: 807, 817, 820, 880, 885, 888, 893, 899.

**KULA GULF 1943**
13 July
Leander

**SALERNO 1943**
9 September—6 October
Abercrombie
Acute
Albacore
Alynbank
Antwerp
Atherstone
Attacker
Aurora
Battler
Beaufort
Belvoir
Blackmore
Blankney
Blencathra

Boxer
Brecon
Brittany
Brixham
Brocklesby
Bruiser
Bude
Cadmus
Calpe
Catterick
Charybdis
Circe
Clacton
Cleveland
Coverly
Delhi
Derwentdale
Dido
Dulverton
Echo
Eclipse
Eggesford
Ensay
Espiègle
Euryalus
Exmoor
Farndale
Faulknor
Felixstowe
Fly
Formidable
Fury
Gavotte
Glengyle
Hambledon
Haydon
Hengist
Hilary
Holcombe
Hunter
Ilex
Illustrious
Inglefield
Intrepid
Jervis
Laforey
Lamerton
Ledbury
Liddesdale
Lookout
Loyal
Mauritius

Mendip
Minuet
Mousa
Mutine
Nelson
Nubian
Offa
Orion
Palomares
Panther
Pathfinder
Penelope
Penn
Petard
Pirouette
Polruan
Prince Charles
Prince Leopold
Prins Albert
Prinses Astrid
Prinses Beatrix
Prinses Josephine Charlotte
Quail
Quantock
Queenborough
Quilliam
Raider
Reighton Wyke
Rhyl
Roberts
Rodney
Rothesay
Royal Scotsman
Royal Ulsterman
St Kilda
Scylla
Shakespeare
Sheffield
Sheppey
Sirius
Stalker
Stella Carina
Stornoway
Tango
Tartar
Tetcott
Thruster
Troubridge
Tumult
Tyrian
Uganda
Ulster Monarch

Ulster Queen
Unicorn
Valiant
Visenda
Warspite
Whaddon
Wheatland
MLs: *238, 273, 280, 283, 336, 554, 555, 556, 557, 559, 560, 561, 562, 564, 566.*
HDMLs: *1242, 1246, 1247, 1253, 1254, 1258, 1270, 1271, 1297, 1301.*
BYMSs: *11, 14, 24, 209.*
MMSs: *5, 133, 134.*
MSMLSs: *121, 126, 134, 135.*
FAA Squadrons: *807, 808, 809, 810, 820, 834, 878, 879, 880, 886, 887, 888, 893, 894, 897, 899.*

## AEGEAN 1943−4

7 September−28 November 1943 and 1944
Ajax
Aldenham
Argonaut
Attacker
Aurora
Beaufort
Belvoir
Beves
Bicester
Black Prince
Boksburg
Blencathra
Brecon
Bruiser
Caledon
Calpe
Carlisle
Catterick
Cleveland
Clinton
Colombo
Croome
Dido
Dulverton
Easton
Echo
Eclipse
Emperor

Exmoor
Farndale
Faulknor
Fury
Gribb
Hambledon
Haydon
Hedgehog
Hursley
Hunter
Hurworth
Intrepid
Jervis
Kelvin
Khedive
Kimberley
Lamerton
Langlaate
Larne
Ledbury
Liddesdale
Marne
Meteor
Musketeer
Orion
Panther
Pathfinder
Penelope
Penn
Petard
Phoebe
Prince David
Protea
Pursuer
Rinaldo
Rockwood
Rorqual
Royalist
Saksern
Saxifrage
Searcher
Seraph
Severn
Shakespeare
Sibyl
Sickle
Simoon
Sirius
Southern Maid
Sportsman
Stalker
Teazer

*Termagant*
*Terpsichore*
*Tetcott*
*Thruster*
*Torbay*
*Treern*
*Trespasser*
*Trooper*
*Troubridge*
*Tumult*
*Tuscan*
*Tyrian*
*Ulster Queen*
*Ultimatum*
*Ultor*
*Unrivalled*
*Unruly*
*Unsparing*
*Unswerving*
*Vampire*
*Vigorous*
*Virtue*
*Vivid*
*Vox*
*Whaddon*
*Wilton*
*Zetland*
FAA Squadrons: 800, 807, 809,
879, 881, 899.

## NORTH CAPE 1943
26 December
*Belfast*
*Duke of York*
*Jamaica*
*Matchless*
*Musketeer*
*Norfolk*
*Opportune*
*Savage*
*Scorpion*
*Sheffield*
*Saumarez*
*Virago*

## ADRIATIC 1944
*Aldenham*
*Aphis*
*Atherstone*
*Avon Vale*
*Belvoir*
*Bicester*

*Blackmore*
*Blean*
*Brocklesby*
*Cleveland*
*Colombo*
*Delhi*
*Eggesford*
*Grenville*
*Janus*
*Jervis*
*Kimberley*
*Lamerton*
*Lauderdale*
*Ledbury*
*Loyal*
*Quantock*
*Scarab*
*Teazer*
*Tenacious*
*Termagant*
*Terpsichore*
*Tetcott*
*Troubridge*
*Tumult*
*Tuscan*
*Tyrian*
*Ulster*
*Undine*
*Urchin*
*Whaddon*
*Wheatland*
*Wilton*
*Zetland*

## ANZIO 1944
22–31 January
*Albacore*
*Barmond*
*Barndale*
*Beaufort*
*Boxer*
*Bruiser*
*Bude*
*Bulolo*
*Cadmus*
*Cava*
*Circe*
*Crete*
*Delhi*
*Dido*
*Espiègle*
*Faulknor*

Glengyle
Grenville
Hornpipe
Inglefield
Janus
Jervis
Kempenfelt
Laforey
Loyal
Mauritius
Orion
Palomares
Penelope
Prinses Beatrix
Rinaldo
Rothesay
Royal Ulsterman
St Kilda
Sheppey
Spartan
Tetcott
Thruster
Two-step
Ulster Queen
Ultor
Urchin
Waterwitch
MLs: 134, 295, 307, 338, 443,
462, 554, 555, 558, 565, 567,
569, 575, 581.

## NORMANDY 1944
6 June – 3 July
Abelia
Adventure
Affleck
Ajax
Albatross
Alberni
Albrighton
Albury
Algonquin
Apollo
Ardrossan
Arethusa
Argonaut
Aristocrat
Ameria
Ashanti
Aylmer
Azalea
Bachaquero

Baddeck
Balfour
Balsam
Bangor
Beagle
Beaumaris
Belfast
Bellona
Bentley
Bickerton
Blackpool
Black Prince
Blackwood
Blairmore
Blankney
Bleasdale
Blencathra
Bligh
Bluebell
Boadicea
Bootle
Borage
Boston
Braithwaite
Bridlington
Bridport
Brigadier
Brissendon
Britomart
Bulolo
Burdock
Buttercup
Calgary
Cam
Camellia
Campanula
Campbell
Camrose
Cape Breton
Capel
Capetown
Caraquet
Catherine
Cato
Cattistock
Celandine
Ceres
Charlock
Chaudière
Chelmer
Clarkia
Clematis

| | |
|---|---|
| Clover | Gleaner |
| Cockatrice | Glenearn |
| Cooke | Glenroy |
| Cotswold | Goatfell |
| Cottesmore | Goathland |
| Cowichan | Godetia |
| Crane | Golden Eagle |
| Dacres | Goodson |
| Dahlia | Gore |
| Dakins | Gorgon |
| Danae | Gozo |
| Despatch | Grecian |
| Deveron | Grenville |
| Diadem | Grey Fox |
| Dianella | Grey Goose |
| Dianthus | Grey Owl |
| Domett | Grey Seal |
| Dominica | Grey Shark |
| Dornoch | Grey Wolf |
| Douwe Aukes | Grou |
| Drumheller | Guysborough |
| Duckworth | Haida |
| Duff | Halcyon |
| Duke of Wellington | Halsted |
| Dunbar | Hambledon |
| Eastbourne | Hargood |
| Eglinton | Harrier |
| Elgin | Hart |
| Emerald | Havelock |
| Emperor | Hawkins |
| Enterprise | Heather |
| Erebus | Hilary |
| Eskimo | Hind |
| Essington | Holmes |
| Fame | Honeysuckle |
| Fancy | Hotham |
| Faulknor | Hotspur |
| Fernie | Hound |
| Forester | Huron |
| Fort William | Hussar |
| Fort York | Hydra |
| Fraserburgh | Icarus |
| Friendship | Ilfracombe |
| Frobisher | Impulsive |
| Fury | Inconstant |
| Garlies | Inglis |
| Garth | Invicta |
| Gatineau | Isis |
| Gazelle | Jason |
| Gentian | Javelin |
| Geranium | Jervis |
| Glasgow | Keats |

Kellett
Kelvin
Kempenfelt
Kenora
Keppel
Kingcup
Kingsmill
Kitchener
Kite
Kootenay
Lapwing
Largs
Lark
Larne
Lavender
Lawford
Lawson
Lennox
Lightfoot
Lindsay
Llandudno
Loch Fade
Loch Killin
Lochy
Locust
Londonderry
Loosestrife
Louisburg
Loyalty
Lunenburg
Lydd
Lyme Regis
Mackay
Magpie
Malpeque
Matane
Mauritius
Mayflower
Melbreak
Melita
Mendip
Meon
Meynell
Middleton
Mignonette
Milltown
Mimico
Minas
Misoa
Montrose
Moorsom
Moosejaw

Mounsey
Mourne
Narborough
Narcissus
Nasturtium
Nelson
Nith
Northway
Obedient
Offa
Onslaught
Onslow
Onyx
Opportune
Orchis
Orestes
Oribi
Orion
Orwell
Ottawa
Outremont
Oxlip
Pangbourne
Parrboro
Pelican
Pelorus
Pennywort
Persian
Petunia
Pickle
Pincher
Pink
Pique
Plover
Plucky
Poole
Poppy
Port Arthur
Port Colborne
Postillion
Potentilla
Prescott
Primrose
Prince Baudouin
Prince Charles
Prince David
Prince Leopold
Prins Albert
Prinses Astrid
Prinses Josephine Charlotte
Pursuer
Pytchley

Qu'Appelle
Qualicum
Queen Emma
Quorn
Ramillies
Rattlesnake
Ready
Recruit
Redpole
Regina
Restigouche
Retalick
Rhododendron
Rifleman
Rimouski
Riou
Roberts
Rochester
Rodney
Romney
Ross
Rowley
Royal Ulsterman
Rupert
Ryde
Rye
St Helier
St John
St Laurent
Salamander
Saltash
Sandown
Saskatchewan
Saumarez
Savage
Scarborough
Scawfell
Scorpion
Scott
Scourge
Scylla
Seagull
Seaham
Selkirk
Serapis
Seymour
Shippigan
Sidmouth
Sioux
Sirius
Skeena
Southdown

Southern Prince
Speedwell
Spragge
Starling
Starwort
Statice
Stayner
Steadfast
Stevenstone
Stockham
Stork
Stormont
Strule
Summerside
Sunflower
Sutton
Swansea
Sweetbriar
Swift
Tadoussac
Talybont
Tanatside
Tartar
Tasajera
Tavy
Teme
Tenby
Thames Queen
Thornborough
Torrington
Tracker
Trentonian
Trollope
Tyler
Ulster Monarch
Undaunted
Undine
Urania
Urchin
Ursa
Vanquisher
Venus
Vegreville
Versatile
Verulam
Vervain
Vesper
Vestal
Vidette
Vigilant
Vimy
Virago

*Vivacious*
*Volunteer*
*Waldegrave*
*Walker*
*Wallflower*
*Walpole*
*Wanderer*
*Warspite*
*Wasaga*
*Waskesiu*
*Watchman*
*Waveney*
*Wedgeport*
*Wensleydale*
*Westcott*
*Whimbrel*
*Whippingham*
*Whitaker*
*Whitehall*
*Whitehaven*
*Whitshed*
*Wild Goose*
*Windsor*
*Woodstock*
*Worthing*
*Wren*
*Wrestler*
*X20*
*X23*
FAA Squadrons: 808, 885, 886, 897.
Note: For reasons of space limitations, names of the following have been omitted: Small Craft and Auxiliaries comprising: A/S trawlers, other trawlers, surveying vessels, Danlayers, Mulberries, Pluto ships and Blockships.

In the following entries, the figures in brackets denote the number of vessels:
MTB flotillas: 1st (8), 5th (7), 13th (8), 14th (12), 21st (7), 22nd (7), 29th (8), 35th (10), 51st (7), 52nd (9), 53rd (7), 55th (12), 59th (8), 63rd (8), 64th (7), 65th (19).
MLs: 1st (8), 2nd (9), 4th (4), 5th (12), 7th (4), 10th (10), 11th (13), 13th (8), 14th (13), 15th (6), 19th (4), 20th (14), 21st (9), 23rd (8), 33rd (7), 50th (5), 51st (4), 103rd (8), 150th (9), 151st (9).
MGBs: 1st (6).
MMSs: 101st, 102nd, 104th, 115th, 132nd, 143rd, all of them comprising ten boats, and 205th (11).
BYMSs: 150th, 159th, 165th and 167th all comprising 10 vessels.
SGBs: 1st (6).

## SABANG 1944
25 July
*Ceylon*
*Cumberland*
*Gambia*
*Illustrious*
*Kenya*
*Nigeria*
*Phoebe*
*Quality*
*Queen Elizabeth*
*Quickmatch*
*Quilliam*
*Racehorse*
*Raider*
*Rapid*
*Relentless*
*Renown*
*Rocket*
*Roebuck*
*Rotherham*
*Tantalus*
*Templar*
*Victorious*
FAA Squadrons: 831, 1830, 1833, 1834, 1836, 1837, 1838.

## SOUTH FRANCE 1944
15–27 August
*Ailsa Craig*
*Ajax*
*Aldenham*
*Antares*
*Antwerp*
*Aphis*
*Arcturus*
*Argonaut*

Aries
Atherstone
Attacker
Aubretia
Aurora
Bardolf
Barford
Barholm
Barmond
Beaufort
Belvoir
Bicester
Black Prince
Blackmore
Borealis
Brave
Brecon
Brixham
Bruiser
Bude
Caledon
Calm
Calpe
Catterick
Cleveland
Clinton
Colombo
Columbine
Crowlin
Delhi
Dido
Eastway
Eggesford
Emperor
Farndale
Foula
Haydon
Highway
Hunter
Keren
Khedive
Kintyre
Larne
Lauderdale
Liddesdale
Lookout
Mewstone
Nebb
Oakley
Octavia
Orion
Polruan

Prince Baudouin
Prince David
Prince Henry
Prins Albert
Prinses Beatrix
Product
Pursuer
Ramillies
Rhyl
Rinaldo
Rosario
Rothesay
Royalist
Satsa
Scarab
Searcher
Sirius
Skokolm
Spanker
Stalker
Stormcloud
Stornoway
Stuart Prince
Teazer
Tenacious
Termagant
Terpsichore
Thruster
Troubridge
Tumult
Tuscan
Tyrian
Ulster Queen
Welfare
Whaddon
Zetland
FAA Squadrons: 800, 807, 809,
879, 881, 882, 899.
MLs: 273, 299, 336, 337, 338,
451, 456, 458, 461, 462, 463,
469, 471, 555, 556, 557, 559,
560, 562, 563, 564, 567, 576,
581.
BYMSs: 2009, 2022, 2026, 2027,
2171, 2172.

## LEYTE GULF 1944
20−27 October
Ariadne
Arunta
Australia
Gascoyne

*Shropshire*
*Warramunga*

**WALCHEREN 1944**
*1 November*
*Erebus*
*Kingsmill*
*Roberts*
*Warspite*
*ML 146*
*ML 902*
In addition there were about 180 landing craft of various classes.

**MALAYA 1942−5**
*Emperor*
*Jupiter*
*Saumarez*
*Scythian*
*Seascout*
*Selene*
*Sturdy*
*Subtle*
*Taciturn*
*Tally Ho*
*Taurus*
*Telemachus*
*Thorough*
*Thule*
*Tiptoe*
*Tradewind*
*Trenchant*
*Trespasser*
*Trump*
*Tudor*
*Venus*
*Verulam*
*Vigilant*
*Virago*
FAA Squadron: 851

**NEW GUINEA 1942−4**
*1942*
*Warrego*

*1942−4*
*Arunta*
*Australia*
*Ballarat*
*Bendigo*
*Broome*

*Colac*
*Deloraine*
*Katoomba*
*Latrobe*
*Lithgow*
*Shropshire*
*Stuart*
*Swan*
*Whyalla*

*1943*
*Ararat*

*1943−4*
*Benalla*
*Bunbury*
*Bundaburg*
*Echuca*
*Gladstone*
*Glenelg*
*Kapunda*
*Pirie*
*Reserve*
*Shepparton*
*Stawell*
*Vendetta*
*Wagga*
*Warramunga*

*1944*
*Cootamunda*
*Cowra*
*Gascoyne*
*Geelong*
*Goneburn*
*Gympie*
*Hawkesbury*
*Kiama*
*Mildura*
*Parkes*
*Rockhampton*
*Stahan*
*Townsville*

**PACIFIC 1942−5**

*1942*
*Armidale*
*Deloraine*
*Kalgoorlie*
*Voyager*
*Warrnambool*

1942–5
Arunta

1945
Barco
Burdekin
Colac
Diamantina
Dubbo
Gascoyne
Hawkesbury
Hobart
Kiama
Lachlan
Latrobe
Lithgow
Shropshire
Stawell
Warramunga
Warrego

**BURMA 1944–5**
October 1944–April 1945
May–August 1945

1944–5
Ameer
Barpeta
Barracuda
Cauvery
Eskimo
Flamingo
Haitan
Jumna
Kathiawar
Kedah
Kenya
Kistna
Konkan
Llanstephan Castle
Napier
Narbada
Nepal
Newcastle
Nguva
Nigeria
Norman
Nubian
Paladin
Pathfinder
Phoebe
Queen Elizabeth

Raider
Rapid
Redpole
Rocket
Roebuck
Shoreham
Spey
Teviot
White Bear
FAA Squadron: 815.

1945
Agra
Bann
Bengal
Bihar
Bombay
Ceylon
Chameleon
Cumberland
Cyclone
Deveron
Emperor
Empress
Glenroy
Godavari
Halladale
Hunter
Jed
Khedive
Khyber
Kumaon
Lahore
Largs
Lulworth
Nith
Orissa
Pamela
Patna
Penn
Persimmon
Pickle
Pincher
Plucky
Poona
Prins Albert
Punjab
Racehorse
Rajputana
Recruit
Redoubt
Rifleman

Rohilkhand
Rotherham
Royalist
Sandray
Saumarez
Scaravay
Shah
Shiel
Silvio
Stalker
Suffolk
Sussex
Sutlej
Taff
Tartar
Test
Trent
Una
Venus
Verulam
Vestal
Vigilant
Virago
Virginia
Waveney
FAA Squadrons: 800, 804, 807, 808, 809, 851, 896, 1700.

## LINGAYEN GULF 1945
5−9 January
Arunta
Australia
Gascoyne
Warramunga
Warrego

## PALEMBANG 1945
24 January
Illustrious
Indefatigable
Indomitable
Victorious
FAA Squadrons: 820, 849, 854, 857, 887, 894, 1770, 1830, 1833, 1834, 1836, 1839, 1844.

## OKINAWA 1945
26 March−25 May
Achilles
Argonaut
Avon
Ballarat

Bendigo
Black Prince
Cairns
Chaser
Crane
Euryalus
Findhorn
Formidable
Gambia
Grenville
Howe
Illustrious
Indefatigable
Indomitable
Kempenfelt
King George V
Napier
Nepal
Nizam
Norman
Parret
Pheasant
Quadrant
Quality
Queensborough
Quiberon
Quickmatch
Quilliam
Ruler
Slinger
Speaker
Striker
Swiftsure
Tenacious
Termagant
Troubridge
Uganda
Ulster
Undaunted
Undine
Unicorn
Urania
Urchin
Ursa
Victorious
Wager
Wessex
Whelp
Whimbrel
Whirlwind
Whyalla
Woodcock

FAA Squadrons: 820, 848, 849,
854, 857, 885, 887, 894, 1770,
1830, 1833, 1834, 1836, 1839,
1840, 1841, 1842, 1844, 1845.

## JAPAN 1945
16 July–11 August
*Formidable*
*Implacable*
*Indefatigable*
*Victorious*
FAA Squadrons: 801, 820, 828,
848, 849, 880, 887, 1771, 1772,
1834, 1836, 1841, 1842.

## ATLANTIC 1939–45
*Abelia*
*Aberdeen*
*Acanthus*
*Acasta*
*Achates*
*Active*
*Activity*
*Acute*
*Affleck*
*Agassiz*
*Ailsa Craig*
*Aire*
*Alaunia*
*Albatross*
*Alberni*
*Alca*
*Alcantara*
*Aldenham*
*Algoma*
*Alisma*
*Allington Castle*
*Alnwick Castle*
*Alynbank*
*Amaranthus*
*Amazon*
*Amberley Castle*
*Ambuscade*
*America*
*Amethyst*
*Amherst*
*Anchusa*
*Anemone*
*Angle*
*Anguilla*
*Annan*
*Annapolis*

*Antares*
*Antelope*
*Anthony*
*Antigonish*
*Antigua*
*Antwerp*
*Aquamarine*
*Arab*
*Arabis*
*Arawa*
*Arbiter*
*Arbutus*
*Archer*
*Arctic Explorer*
*Arctic Pioneer*
*Arctic Ranger*
*Arcturus*
*Ardent*
*Argus*
*Ariguani*
*Armeria*
*Arnprior*
*Arran*
*Arrow*
*Arrowhead*
*Arsenal*
*Arvida*
*Asbestos*
*Ascania*
*Ascension*
*Ashanti*
*Asphodel*
*Assinboine*
*Aster*
*Asturias*
*Atherstone*
*Atholl*
*Atmah*
*Attacker*
*Aubretia*
*Auckland*
*Audacity*
*Aurania*
*Auricula*
*Ausonia*
*Avon*
*Avon Vale*
*Awe*
*Aylmer*
*Ayrshire*
*Azalea*
*Bachaquero*

Baddeck
Badsworth
Baffin
Bahamas
Balfour
Ballinderry
Balsam
Banborough Castle
Banff
Barberry
Barcliff
Barle
Barnwell
Barrie
Barthorpe
Bartizan
Bath
Battleford
Battler
Bayfield
Bayntun
Bazely
Beacon Hill
Beagle
Beauharnois
Beaumaris
Beaver
Bedouin
Begonia
Belleville
Belmont
Bellwort
Bentinck
Bentley
Bergamot
Berkeley Castle
Berkshire
Bermuda
Berry
Berwick
Betony
Beverley
Bickerton
Bideford
Birdlip
Biter
Bittersweet
Blackfly
Black Swan
Blackmore
Blackwood
Blairmore

Blankney
Bleasdale
Bligh
Bluebell
Boadicea
Bombadier
Borage
Border Cities
Boreas
Boston
Bowmanville
Bradford
Braithwaite
Brandon
Brantford
Brecon
Breda
Bredon
Bridgewater
Brilliant
Brimnes
Brissendon
Broadwater
Broadway
Brocklesby
Brockville
Broke
Bruiser
Bryony
Buckingham
Buctouche
Bude
Bugloss
Bulldog
Bullen
Bulolo
Burdock
Burges
Burke
Burlington
Burnham
Burra
Burwell
Bush
Bushwood
Bute
Butser
Buttercup
Buttermere
Buxton
Byard
Byron

Cachalot
Caicos
Cairo
Calder
Caldwell
Calendula
Calgary
California
Cam
Camellia
Camito
Campania
Campanula
Campbell
Campbeltown
Campeador V
Campion
Camrose
Candytuft
Canso
Canton
Cap-de-la-Madelaine
Cape Argona
Cape Breton
Cape Clear
Cape Comorin
Cape Mariato
Cape Palliser
Cape Portland
Cape Warwick
Capel
Capilano
Caradoc
Carisbrook Castle
Caraquet
Carlplace
Carnarvon Castle
Carnation
Carnoustie
Carthage
Castleton
Cathay
Catherine
Cato
Cauvery
Cava
Cavina
Cayman
Celandine
Celia
Ceres
Chambly

Chamois
Chance
Chanticleer
Charlestown
Charlock
Charlottetown
Charybdis
Chaser
Chaudière
Chebogue
Chedabucto
Chelmer
Chelsea
Cheshire
Chesterfield
Chicoutimi
Chilliwack
Chitral
Churchill
Cilicia
Clare
Clarkia
Clayoquot
Clematis
Clevela
Cleveland
Clinton
Clover
Coaticook
Cobalt
Cobourg
Coldstreamer
Coll
Collingwood
Colombo
Coltsfoot
Columbia
Columbine
Combatant
Comorin
Conn
Conqueror
Convolvulus
Cooke
Copinsay
Copper Cliff
Coreopsis
Corfu
Corinthian
Cosby
Cossack
Cotillion

Cotton
Coventry
Coventry City
Cowdray
Cowichan
Cowslip
Crane
Crabstoun
Crispin
Crocus
Croome
Cubitt
Cuckmere
Culver
Cumbrae
Curaçoa
Cutty Sark
Cyclamen
Cygnet
Dacres
Dahlia
Dainty
Daneman
Dangay
Dart
Dasher
Dauntless
Dauphin
Davy
Dawson
Deane
Decoy
Delhi
Delphinium
Deptford
Derby County
Derbyshire
Derwent
Despatch
Deveron
Devon City
Dianella
Dianthus
Digby
Dittany
Dochet
Domett
Dominica
Dorade II
Dornoch
Dorothy Gray
Dorsetshire

Douglas
Dovey
Drumheller
Drummondville
Drury
Duckworth
Dumbarton Castle
Duncan
Duncton
Dundas
Dundee
Denedin
Dunkery
Dunnottar Castle
Dunvegan
Dunvegan Castle
Dunver
Earl Kitchener
East View
Ebor Wyke
Echo
Eclipse
Eday
Edinburgh
Edmunston
Effingham
Eglantine
Eglinton
Egret
Ekins
Electra
Ellesmere
Elm
Emeral
Emperor
Empress
Enchantress
Encounter
Engadine
Enterprise
Erebus
Erica
Erin
Eriskay
Erne
Erraid
Escapade
Escort
Esk
Esperance Bay
Esquimalt
Essington

Ettrick
Evadne
Evenlode
Exe
Exmoor
Exmouth
Eyebright
Fairfax
Fal
Fame
Fandango
Fantôme
Farndale
Faulknor
Fearless
Fencer
Fennel
Fergus
Fetlar
Fidelity
Findhorn
Firedrake
Fishguard
Fitzroy
Flatholm
Fleetwood
Fleur de Lys
Flint
Flint Castle
Foley
Folkestone
Foresight
Forest Hill
Forester
Fort Francis
Fort William
Fort York
Fortune
Fowey
Foxhound
Foxtrot
Fraser
Fredericton
Freesia
Friendship
Fritillary
Frontenac
Fury
Fusilier
Gallant
Galt
Gananoque

Gardenia
Gardiner
Garland
Garlies
Gateshead
Gatineau
Gavotte
Gazelle
Genista
Gentian
Georgetown
Georgian
Geranium
Ghurka
Giffard
Gipsy
Glace Bay
Gladiolus
Gleaner
Glenarm
Glowworm
Gloxinia
Goathland
Godavari
Goderich
Godetia
Goodall
Goodson
Gore
Gorleston
Gorgon
Gossamer
Gould
Gozo
Grafton
Granby
Grandmère
Great Admiral
Grecian
Grenade
Grenadier
Grenville
Greyhound
Griffin
Grindall
Grou
Grove
Gruinard
Guardsman
Guelph
Guysborough
Haarlem

Hadleigh Castle
Halifax
Hallowell
Hamilton
Hamlet
Hardy
Hargood
Hart
Hartland
Harvester
Hascosay
Hastings
Hasty
Havant
Havelock
Havock
Hawkesbury
Hazard
Hazel
Heartsease
Heather
Helmsdale
Heliotrope
Hepatica
Hereward
Hermes
Heron
Herschell
Hertfordshire
Hespeler
Hesperus
Heythrop
Hibiscus
Highlander
Hilary
Hollyhock
Holmes
Homeguard
Honesty
Honeysuckle
Hornpipe
Hoste
Hostile
Hotspur
Huddersfield Town
Hugh Walpole
Humberstone
Hunter
Huntsville
Hurricane
Hurst Castle
Hurworth

Husky
Hussar
Hyderabad
Hydrangea
Hyperion
Ibis
Icarus
Ilex
Ilfracombe
Imogen
Imperial
Imperialist
Impulsive
Inchkeith
Inchmarnock
Inconstant
Indian Star
Inglefield
Inglis
Ingonish
Inkpen
Inman
Intrepid
Inver
Iroquois
Isis
Itchen
Ithuriel
Ivanhoe
Jacinth
Jackal
Jaguar
Janus
Jaseur
Jasmine
Jason
Jasper
Javelin
Jed
Jervis Bay
Joliette
Jonquière
Jonquil
Juliet
Jumna
Juno
Kale
Kamloops
Kamsack
Kampuskasing
Keats
Keith

Kelly
Kelvin
Kempenfelt
Kempthorne
Kenilworth Castle
Kenogami
Kenora
Kent
Kentville
Kenya
Keppel
Kerrera
Khyber
Kilbirnie
Kilbride
Killegray
Kilmarnock
Kilmartin
Kilmington
Kilmore
Kimelford
Kincardine
King George V
King Sol
Kingcup
Kingston
Kingston Agate
Kingston Amber
Kingston Beryl
Kingston Chrysolite
Kipling
Kirkella
Kistna
Kitchener
Kite
Kiwi
Knaresborough Castle
Kokanee
Konkan
Kootenay
La Hulloise
La Malbaie
La Malouine
Lacencia
Lachine
Lachute
Laconia
Lady Beryl
Lady Elsa
Lady Hogarth
Lady Lilian
Lady Madeleine

Lady Shirley
Laforey
Lagan
Lamerton
Lanark
Lancaster
Lancer
Landguard
Largs
Larkspur
Lasalle
Lauderdale
Launceston Castle
Lauzon
Lavender
Lawson
Leamington
Leaside
Leda
Leeds Castle
Leeds United
Legion
Leith
Lethbridge
Letitia
Levis
Leyland
Liddesdale
Lightfoot
Linaria
Lincoln
Lincoln City
Lindsay
Lively
Lobelia
Loch Achray
Loch Craggie
Loch Eck
Loch Fada
Loch Fyne
Loch Glendu
Loch Insh
Loch Killin
Loch More
Loch Oskaig
Loch Quoich
Loch Ruthven
Loch Scavaig
Loch Shin
Loch Tulla
Lockeport
London

Londonderry
Long Branch
Longueil
Loosestrife
Lord Hotham
Lord Middletown
Lord Nuffield
Lord Stanhope
Loring
Lossie
Lotus
Louis
Louisburg
Lowestoft
Ludlow
Lulworth
Lunenburg
ML170
ML172
ML175
MMS80
MMS81
MMS303
MMS1066
Macbeth
Mackay
Magnolia
Magpie
Mahone
Malaya
Malcolm
Malines
Mallow
Maloja
Malpeque
Man-o-War
Manners
Mansfield
Maori
Maplin
Margaree
Marguerite
Marigold
Maron
Marsdale
Martin
Matane
Matapedia
Mauritius
Mayflower
Mazurka
Meadowsweet

Medicine Hat
Melbreak
Melita
Melville
Menestheus
Meon
Merceditta
Merrittonia
Meteor
Middlesex
Middleton
Midland
Mignonette
Mildenhall
Milford
Milltown
Milne
Mimico
Mimosa
Minas
Minna
Miscou
Moa
Moncton
Monkshood
Monnow
Montbretia
Montclare
Montgomery
Montreal
Montrose
Mooltan
Moorsman
Moorsom
Moosejaw
Morden
Moreton Bay
Morpeth Castle
Morris Dance
Mounsey
Mourn
Moyola
Mulgrave
Musketeer
Myosotis
Myrmidon
Nab Wyke
Nairana
Nanaimo
Napanee
Narborough
Narcissus

Narwhal
Nasturtium
Nene
Neptune
Ness
Nestor
New Glasgow
New Waterford
New Westminster
New York City
Newark
Newmarket
Newport
Niagara
Nigella
Niger
Nigeria
Nipigon
Noranda
Norfolk
Norsyd
North Bay
Northern Dawn
Northern Foam
Northern Gem
Northern Gift
Northern Pride
Northern Reward
Northern Sky
Northern Spray
Northern Sun
Northern Wave
Norwich City
Notts County
Nyasaland
Oakham Castle
Oakville
Oasis
Obdurate
Obedient
Odzani
Offa
Onslaught
Onslow
Ophelia
Opportune
Orangeville
Orchis
Orduna
Orfasy
Oribi
Orient Star
Orillia

Orion
Orissa
Orwell
Oshawa
Ottawa
Otway
Outremont
Owen Sound
Oxford Castle
Oxlip
Oxna
PC74
Palomares
Panther
Papua
Parrett
Parrsboro
Parry Sound
Pasley
Pathfinder
Patroller
Paynter
Peacock
Pegasus
Pelican
Pelorus
Penetang
Penn
Pennywort
Pentland Firth
Penstemon
Penzance
Peony
Perim
Periwinkle
Perth
Peterborough
Peterhead
Petronella
Petunia
Pevensey Castle
Pheasant
Philante
Picotee
Pict
Pictou
Pimpernel
Pincher
Pink
Pirouette
Plym
Polruan

Polyanthus
Poppy
Porcher
Porchester Castle
Porpoise
Port Arthur
Port Colborne
Port Hope
Portage
Portsdown
Postillion
Potentilla
Poundmaker
Pozarica
Premier
Prescott
Pretoria Castle
Primrose
Primula
Prince David
Prince Robert
Prince Rupert
Prodigal
Prompt
Prospect
Protea
Puffin
Puncher
Punjabi
Pursuer
Pylades
Qu'Appelle
Quadrille
Qualicum
Quantock
Queen
Queen Emma
Quentin
Quesnel
Quiberon
Quickmatch
Quinte
Racehorse
Rajah
Rajputana (AMC)
Rajputana (M/s)
Ramillies
Ramsey
Ranee
Ranpura
Rapid
Ravager

Reading
Reaper
Recruit
Reculver
Red Deer
Redmill
Redoubt
Redpole
Redshank
Regina
Registan
Reighton Wyke
Reindeer
Renown
Repulse
Resolution
Restigouche
Retalick
Retriever
Revenge
Rhododendron
Richmond
Rimouski
Ringdove
Ripley
Rivière du Loup
Rochester
Rockliffe
Rockingham
Rockrose
Rockwood
Rodney
Rorqual
Rosaura
Rose
Rosemary
Rosthern
Rother
Rowley
Roxborough
Royal Marine
Royal Mount
Royal Scotsman
Royal Sovereign
Ruler
Runnymede
Rupert
Rushen Castle
Rutherford
Rye
Sabina
Sable

Sabre
Sackville
Sagitta
Saguenay
St Albans
St Apollo
St Boniface
St Cathan
St Catherines
St Clair
St Croix
St Elstan
St Francis
St John
St Kenan
St Kilda
St Lambert
St Laurent
St Loman
St Mary's
St Nectan
St Pierre
St Stephen
St Thomas
St Wistan
St Zeno
Sainte Thérèse
Saladin
Salisbury
Salopian
Salvia
Samphire
Sanda
Sandwich
Saon
Sapper
Sarawak
Sardonyx
Sarnia
Saskatchewan
Saskatoon
Saulte Sainte Marie
Saxifrage
Scarba
Scarborough
Sceptre
Scimitar
Scottish
Scylla
Scythian
Sea Cliff
Sea Rover

Seadog
Seaford
Seaham
Seal
Sealyham
Seanymph
Searcher
Seascout
Selkirk
Sennen
Setter
Severn
Seychelles
Shakespeare
Shalimar
Sharpshooter
Shawinigan
Shediac
Sheffield
Sheldrake
Sherbrooke
Sherwood
Shiant
Shiel
Shikari
Shippigan
Shropshire
Sidon
Sikh
Sioux
Skagi
Skate
Skeena
Skomer
Smilax
Smiter
Smith's Falls
Snakefly
Snapper
Snowberry
Snowdrop
Snowflake
Somaliland
Sorel
Southern Flower
Southern Gem
Southern Isle
Southern Pride
Southern Prince
Southern Sea
Southern Shore
Spark

Spartan
Speaker
Spearhead
Speedwell
Spey
Sphene
Spikenard
Spirea
Sportsman
Sposa
Staffa
Stafnes
Stalker
Stanley
Starling
Starwort
Statice
Steadfast
Stella Capella
Stella Carina
Stella Pegasi
Stellarton
Stoic
Stoke City
Stonecrop
Stonetown
Stora
Stork
Storm
Stormont
Stratford
Strathadam
Strathella
Strathroy
Striker
Stroma
Strongbow
Strule
Stuart Prince
Stubborn
Sturdy
Stygian
Sudbury
Summerside
Sunflower
Supreme
Surf
Surprise
Sussexvale
Swale
Swansea
Sweetbriar

Swift Current
Sybil
Symbol
Taciturn
Tadoussac
Tamarisk
Tanatside
Tango
Tantivy
Tarantella
Tattoo
Taurus
Tavy
Tay
Tedworth
Tees
Test
Texada
Thalassa
Thane
The Pas
Thetford Mines
Thirlmere
Thorlock
Thornborough
Thrasher
Three Rivers
Thule
Thunder
Thyme
Tillsonburg
Timmins
Tintagel Castle
Tiree
Tobago
Torbay
Torrington
Tortola
Totland
Tourmaline
Towey
Tracker
Trail
Transcona
Trent
Trentonian
Trident
Trillium
Tritellia
Trondra
Trouncer
Truant

Truculent
Trumpeter
Truro
Tui
Tumult
Tunsberg Castle
Turcoman
Tweed
Tyler
Tyrian
Ullswater
Ulster Queen
Ultimatum
Ultor
Uganda
Ungava
Universal
Unruly
Unsparing
Unst
Unswerving
Untiring
Upstart
Usk
Valentine
Valleyfield
Vancouver
Vanessa
Vanoc
Vanquisher
Vansittart
Varanga
Vascama
Vegreville
Veleta
Velox
Venetia
Vengeful
Venomous
Verbena
Verity
Veronica
Versatile
Vervain
Vesper
Vetch
Veteran
Victoriaville
Victrix
Vidette
Ville de Québec
Vimy

Vindex
Violet
Viscount
Visenda
Visigoth
Viva II
Vivacious
Viviana
Vizalma
Voltaire
Volunteer
Voracious
Vortigern
Vulcan
Wakeful
Walker
Wallaceburg
Wallflower
Walney
Walpole
Wanderer
Warspite
Warwick
Wasaga
Waskesiu
Watchman
Waveney
Wear
Wedgeport
Wellard
Wellington
Wells
Wensleydale
Wentworth
Wessex
West York
Westcott
Westmount
Weston
Wetaskiwin
Weyburn
Whimbrel
Whirlwind
Whitaker
Whitby
Whitehall
Whitehaven
Whitehorn
Whitethroat
Whitshed
Wild Goose
Wild Swan

Wildflower
William Scoresby
Willowherb
Winchelsea
Winchester
Windermere
Windflower
Windsor
Windrush
Winnipeg
Wishart
Wisteria
Witch
Witherington
Wivern
Wolborough
Wolfe
Wolsey
Wolverine
Woodcock
Woodpecker
Woodruff
Woodstock
Woolston
Worcester
Worcestershire
Worthing
Wren
Wrestler
Yes Tor
York
York City
Yorkshireman
Zanzibar
Zetland
Zinnia
Zulu
FAA Squadrons: 700, 802, 804, 807, 808, 810, 811, 813, 814, 816, 818, 819, 820, 825, 833, 834, 835, 836, 837, 838, 840, 846, 860, 881, 882, 892, 896, 898, 1832.

## ENGLISH CHANNEL
### 1939–45
Abelia
Acacia
Acanthus
Affleck
Albrighton
Algoma

Alisma
Amarose
Ambroise Paré
Anchusa
Anthony
Aristocrat
Armana
Armeria
Ashanti
Assinboine
Atalanta
Athabaskan
Atherstone
Avon Vale
Azalea
Bachaquero
Baddeck
Balfour
Balsam
Bangor
Barrie
Bay
Beagle
Ben Urie
Berkeley
Berkshire
Bickerton
Bideford
Bilsdean
Birch
Blackpool
Black Prince
Blackthorn
Blackwood
Bleasdale
Blencathra
Bligh
Blyth
Borage
Boreas
Boston
Bradford
Brazen
Brecon
Brilliant
Brissenden
Brocklesby
Bude
Bulldog
Burdock
Burges
Burke

| | |
|---|---|
| Byron | Dornoch |
| Calgary | Drumheller |
| Calpe | Duckworth |
| Cambridgeshire | Duff |
| Campanula | Eastbourne |
| Campbell | Easton |
| Camrose | Egilsay |
| Canalside | Eglinton |
| Cape Comorin | Ekins |
| Capel | Elgin |
| Capstone | Ellesmere |
| Caton Wyke | Ennerdale |
| Cattistock | Ensay |
| Celandine | Erebus |
| Charles Henri | Eskdale |
| Charybdis | Eskimo |
| Chelmer | Essington |
| Chiddingfold | Felixstowe |
| Clarkia | Fernie |
| Clematis | Fidelity |
| Cleveland | Fir |
| Clyne Castle | Fitzroy |
| Commander Evans | Fleetwood |
| Conn | Fluellen |
| Conqueror | Forester |
| Convolvulus | Ganilly |
| Cooke | Garth |
| Corinthian | Gaston Rivière |
| Coriolanus | Gentian |
| Cornelian | Geranium |
| Cosby | Glaisdale |
| Cotswold | Gloxinia |
| Cottesmore | Goathland |
| Cowdray | Godetia |
| Crane | Good Hope |
| Cranstoun | Goodson |
| Curzon | Grenville |
| Cyclamen | Grey Fox |
| Daffodil | Grey Goose |
| Dahlia | Grey Owl |
| Dakins | Grey Seal |
| Daneman | Grey Shark |
| Deane | Grey Wolf |
| Delphinium | Griffin |
| Deodar | Grimsby Town |
| Deptford | Grimstead |
| Deveron | Gweal |
| Dianella | Haida |
| Dianthus | Halstead |
| Domett | Hambledon |
| Dominica | Hart |
| Doon | Hartland |

Hatsuse
Havelock
Heather
Herschell
Hesperus
Holmes
Honeysuckle
Horatio
Hornbeam
Huron
Hyderabad
Hydrangea
Icarus
Ideshire
Ijuin
Ilfracombe
Impulsive
Inchgower
Inconstant
Iris
Istria
Jackal
Jasper
Javelin
Juliet
Kalan
Keppel
Kingcup
Kingsmill
Kingston Andalusite
Kingston Chrysoberyl
Kitchener
Kittiwake
Kootenay
Labuan
Lark
Lavender
Leeds United
Leith
Lerwick
Limbourne
Lincolnshire
Lindsay
Lioness
Loch Achanalt
Loch Alvie
Loch Fada
Loch Fyne
Loch Killin
Loch Ruthven
Locust
Londonderry

Longa
Loosestrife
Lord Essendon
Lord Hailsham
Lord Howe
Lord Plender
Lord Snowden
Lord Stanhope
Lord Stonehaven
Lord Wakefield
Louisburg
Lundy
Lunenburg
Mackay
Malaya
Malcolm
Mangrove
Manor
Mayflower
Melbreak
Mendip
Meon
Meynell
Middleton
Mignonette
Milford Duchess
Mimico
Montrose
Moosejaw
Morris Dance
Mourne
Mousa
Myosotis
Narbada
Narbrough
Nasturtium
Ness
Newport
Night Hawk
Northward Ho
Notre Dame de France
Ocean View
Offa
Olive
Olvina
Ommering
Orchis
Ottawa
P511
PC74
Pangbourne
Parrsboro

| | |
|---|---|
| Patti | Rutherford |
| Pearl | St Albans |
| Pelican | St Helena |
| Penylan | St John |
| Perim | St Kilda |
| Peterhead | Saladin |
| Petunia | Sasebo |
| Pine | Scalpay |
| Pink | Scarborough |
| Pointer | Scarron |
| Poppy | Scimitar |
| Port Arthur | Shakespeare |
| Port Colborne | Shippigan |
| Prescott | Skate |
| Primrose | Snowberry |
| Prince Charles | Spragge |
| Prince Leopold | Staffa |
| Prince Robert | Star of India |
| Princess Iris | Starwort |
| Prins Albert | Stata |
| Prospect | Statice |
| Puckeridge | Stayner |
| Puffin | Stevenstone |
| Pytchley | Stockham |
| Quadrille | Stonecrop |
| Qualicum | Stormont |
| Quickmatch | Stratagem |
| Quorn | Stronsay |
| Radnor Castle | Sulist |
| Reboundo | Summerside |
| Redmill | Sunflower |
| Redwood | Sussexvale |
| Regina | Sutton |
| Retalick | Swansea |
| Revenge | Swansea Castle |
| Rhododendron | Swordfish |
| Rhyl | Talybont |
| Righto | Tanatside |
| Rimouski | Tartar |
| Rocket | Tavy |
| Rockwood | Thornborough |
| Rodney | Torbay |
| Romsey | Torrington |
| Rosevean | Towy |
| Rothesay | Trentonian |
| Rousay | Trollope |
| Rowan | Tyler |
| Rowley | Tynedale |
| Royal Eagle | Ullswater |
| Ruby | Ulster |
| Rupert | Ulster Monarch |
| Ruskholm | United Boys |

394

Unseen
Vanity
Vanoc
Vanquisher
Vatersay
Versatile
Vesper
Victrix
Vidette
Ville de Québec
Vimy
Vivacious
Volunteer
Waldegrave
Walker
Walpole
Wanderer
Warspite
Watchman
Waterfly
Wedgeport
Wensleydale
Westcott
Westminster
Weston
Whalsey
Whimbrel
Whitaker
Whitehall
Whitshed
Wild Goose
Winchester
Windsor
Witherington
Wolsey
Woodcock
Woodstock
Worcester
Wrestler
Zanzibar
MLs: 163, 291, 1231
MGBs: 608, 615.
MTBs: 15, 17, 22, 31, 32, 49, 52, 55, 56, 69, 84, 86, 95, 229, 236.
SGBs: 6, 9.
FAA Squadrons: 811, 812, 819, 825, 841.

## NORTH SEA 1939−45

Acanthus
Acute
Adonis

Aigon
Ailsa Craig
Alarm
Alberni
Albrighton
Ampulla
Angle
Annan
Aquilla
Arab
Ardrossan
Arrow
Ascension
Aster
Atherstone
Atmah
Ayrshire
Baluchistan
Bassett
Bayntun
Begonia
Berkeley
Berkshire
Betony
Black Swan
Blean
Bleasdale
Blencathra
Blyth
Bonito
Borage
Bournemouth Queen
Bressay
Braithwaite
Bridgewater
Broadway
Broke
Brontes
Burges
Bute
Byron
Cadmus
Caistor Castle
Calgary
Camellia
Campbell
Camrose
Cape Comorin
Cape Palliser
Cape Portland
Cape Sable
Carnatic

Castlenau
Castleton
Cattistock
Charlestown
Charlock
Chelmer
Cleveland
Clover
Coll
Congre
Conn
Conqueror
Copper Cliff
Corinthian
Cosby
Cotillion
Cotswold
Cottesmore
Coverley
Cranstoun
Cubitt
Culver
Curaçoa
Curzon
Daffodil
Dahlia
Dakins
Damsay
Daniel Clowden
Davy
Deane
Doon
Dudgeon
Dunavon
Dunbar
Duncton
Dunkery
Easton
Ebor Wyke
Eglinton
Ekins
Else Rykens
Eroican
Erebus
Escort
Estrella D'Alva
Estrella Do Norte
Evelyn Rose
Exmoor
Farndale
Fencer
Fernie

Filla
Fitzroy
Flamingo
Flores
Fortune
Foxtrot
Garth
Gavotte
Ghurka
Gleaner
Goatfell
Goathland
Godetia
Goldcock
Goodwin
Gossamer
Graph
Grayling
Greenfly
Grenadier
Guillemot
Gunner
H49
Halsted
Hambledon
Haydon
Holderness
Holmes
Hornbeam
Hornpipe
Hyderabad
Hydra
Icarus
Imogen
Indian Star
Inglefield
Invercauld
Jason
Jasper
Jura
Kashmir
Kellett
Kenilworth Castle
Kennet
Killegray
Kingcup
Kings Grey
Kingston
Kingston Agate
Kingston Amber
Kingston Olivina
Kintyre

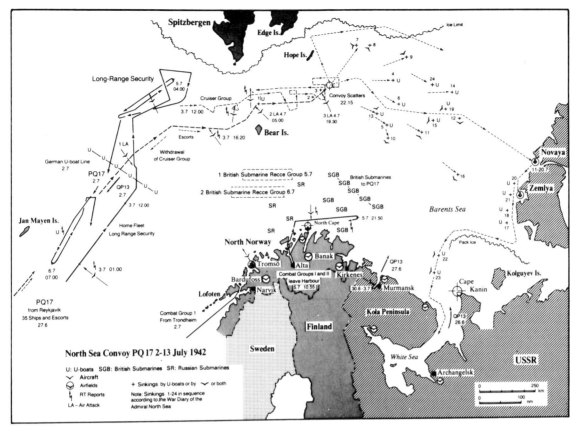

RUSSIAN CONVOYS (PQ 17)

Kittiwake
Lacerta
Lady Estella
Lady Madeleine
Lancaster
Lapwing
Lark
Lauderdale
Leeds
Leicester City
Lewes
Liddesdale
Limbourne
Lincoln
Loch Dunvegan
Lock Eck
Londonderry
Loosestrife
Lord Austin
Lord Howe
Lord Plender
Lowestoft
Ludlow

Lydd
Lynton
Macbeth
Mackay
Magnolia
Malcolm
Mallard
Mallow
Man-o-War
Maron
Mazurka
Melbreak
Mendip
Meynell
Middleton
Mignonette
Millet
Minster
Minuet
Mona's Isle
Monnow
Montrose
Moorsom
Narwhal

Neil Mackay
Nene
Newark
Northern Foam
Northern Sun
Oakley
Ocean Brine
Ogano
Olive
Onyx
Ophelia
Orchis
Oresay
Orkney
Othello
P247
Pearl
Pennywort
Pentland Firth
Peterhead
Phrontis
Pink
Pintail
Pirouette
Pitstruan
Polka
Polo Norte
Poppy
Port Colborne
Portsdown
Potentilla
Preston North End
Primrose
Prince Charles
Puffin
Pytchley
Quadrille
Qualicum
Quantock
Quorn
Rattlesnake
Rayon
Redmill
Regardo
Reighton Wyke
Restigouche
Retako
Retalick
Retriever
Rinaldo
Ringwood
Riou

Rosalind
Ross
Rousay
Rowena
Ruskholm
Rupert
Rutherford
St Albans
St Elstan
St John
St Kilda
St Mary's
Sainte Thérèse
Salmon
Saltarelo
Sapphire
Scalpay
Scarborough
Sealion
Selkirk
Seymour
Shark
Shearwater
Sheldon
Sheldrake
Sheppey
Sherwood
Shippigan
Sir Galahad
Sir Geraint
Snowflake
Sorel
Southdown
Southern Gem
Spearfish
Speedy
Spirea
Spurs
Staffa
Starwort
Stayner
Stella
Stella Canopus
Stella Polaris
Stella Rigel
Stevenstone
Stoke City
Stork
Stornoway
Sturgeon
Sturton
Sunfish

Sunflower
Surface
Switha
Sword Dance
Tadoussac
Talybont
Tango
Tarantella
Tartan
Thames Queen
Thetford Mines
Thirlmere
Thornborough
Thyme
Tirce
Torrington
Trident
Tumby
Turquoise
Typhoon
Ursula
Valorous
Valse
Vanity
Vascama
Vega
Veleta
Verdun
Verity
Versatile
Vesper
Veteran
Viceroy
Vimiera
Vimy
Violet
Visenda
Vivacious
Vivien
Vizalma
Volunteer
Vortigern
Wakeful
Wallace
Wallflower
Walpole
Wedgeport
Wellard
Wells
Wensleydale
Westminster
Weston

Westray
Whaddon
Whiting
Whitshed
Widgeon
Wilton
Winchelsea
Winchester
Windsor
Witch
Wivern
Wolfhound
Wolsey
Wolves
Woolston
Worcester
Worcestershire
Worthing
Urge
Yes Tor
FAA Squadrons: 803, 811, 812, 826.
MGBs: 17, 20, 21, 38, 39, 59, 61, 64, 67, 74, 75, 86, 87, 89, 111, 112.
MTBs: 32, 34, 69, 70, 88, 93, 224, 230, 233, 234, 241, 617, 622, 624, 628.

## BISCAY 1940−5

Abdiel
Albrighton
Archer
Ashanti
Assinboine
Bellona
Berry
Bideford
Borage
Brissendon
Cachalot
Calgary
Charybdis
Chaudière
Conqueror
Crane
Dahlia
Diadem
Dominica
Duckworth
Edmunston

Egret
Enterprise
Essington
Glasgow
Godetia
Graph
Haida
Hastings
Havelock
Hurricane
Iroquois
Kite
Kootenay
Landguard
Loch Killin
Louis
Mauritius
Monkshood
Nene
Onslow
Ottawa
Pimpernel
Qu'Appelle
Restigouche
Rockingham
Saskatchewan
Saxifrage
Sceptre
Scylla
Seanymph
Sheffield
Skeena
Snowberry
Starling
Stubborn
Tally Ho
Tanatside
Tartar
Thunderbolt
Tuna
Tweed
Unbeaten
Unique
Ursa
Victorious
Vimy
Viscount
Volunteer
Warspite
Warwick
Waveney
Wear

Wild Goose
Woodpecker
Wren
FAA Squadron: 817

## MEDITERRANEAN 1940−5
Abercrombie
Ajax
Alynbank
Aphis
Argonaut
Ark Royal
Atherstone
Aubretia
Aurora
Barham
Beaufort
Bicester
Blackfly
Blankney
Blencathra
Bluebell
Brecon
Calcutta
Caledon
Calpe
Capetown
Clyde
Cockchafer
Coventry
Croome
Cuckmere
Dainty
Decoy
Deptford
Diamond
Dido
Dulverton
Duncan
Eagle
Easton
Enchantress
Encounter
Erebus
Eridge
Euryalus
Exmoor
Farndale
Faulknor
Fearless
Firedrake
Fleetwood

| | |
|---|---|
| Foresight | Ladybird |
| Formidable | Laforey |
| Foxhound | Lamerton |
| Fury | Lance |
| Galatea | Largs |
| Gallant | Lauderdale |
| Garland | Legion |
| Ghurka | Liddesdale |
| Glenearn | Lively |
| Glengyle | Liverpool |
| Gloucester | Lookout |
| Gloxinia | Lotus |
| Gnat | Loyal |
| Grenville | Malaya |
| Greyhound | Marigold |
| Griffin | Mauritius |
| Haarlem | Mendip |
| Hambledon | Meteor |
| Hasty | Misoa |
| Havock | Mohawk |
| Hereward | Mull |
| Hermione | Naiad |
| Hero | Nelson |
| Hobart | Neptune |
| Holcombe | Newfoundland |
| Hotspur | Nubian |
| Hursley | Offa |
| Hurworth | Orion |
| Hyacinth | Osiris |
| Hyperion | P31 |
| Ilex | P33 |
| Illustrious | P34 |
| Imperial | P35 |
| Inglefield | P37 |
| Isis | P42 |
| Islay | P46 |
| Jackal | P228 |
| Jade | P247 |
| Jaguar | Pakenham |
| Janus | Paladin |
| Javelin | Pandora |
| Jersey | Panther |
| Jervis | Parthian |
| Juno | Penelope |
| Jupiter | Penn |
| Kandahar | Petard |
| Kashmir | Phoebe |
| Kelly | Poppy |
| Kelvin | Porpoise |
| Kent | Port Arthur |
| Kilmarnock | Prinses Beatrix |
| Kipling | Protea |

Proteus
Quail
Queenborough
Queen Emma
Quentin
Quiberon
Quilliam
Raider
Ramillies
Regent
Regina
Renown
Restigouche
Roberts
Rodney
Rorqual
Rover
Royal Ulsterman
Rysa
Safari
Sahib (P212)
Saltarelo
Saracen (P247)
Saxifrage
Scarab
Seraph
Shakespeare
Sheffield
Shoreham
Sickle
Sikh
Simoon
Sirius
Southern Isle
Southern Maid
Southern Sea
Spartan
Splendid (P228)
Sportsman
Starwort
Stuart
Sydney
Tactician
Taku
Talisman
Tartar
Taurus
Tetrarch
Teazer
Tenacious
Termagant
Terror

Tetcott
Thorn
Thrasher
Thunderbolt
Tigris
Torbay
Triad
Trident
Triton
Triumph
Trooper
Troubridge
Truant
Tumult
Turbulent
Tyrian
Uganda
Ulster
Ultimatum (P34)
Ultor
Umbra (P35)
Unbeaten
Unbending (P37)
Undine
Unique
United
Universal
Unrivalled
Unseen
Unshaken
Untiring
Upholder
Upright
Uproar
Upstart
Urchin
Urge
Ursula
Utmost
Valiant
Vendetta
Vetch
Ville de Québec
Voyager
Warspite
Whaddon
Wilton
Wishart
Woolongong
Wrestler
Wryneck
York

Zetland
Zulu
MTBs: *311, 633, 634, 635, 637, 639, 656*
FAA Squadrons: 700, 767, 800, 803, 806, 810, 812, 813, 815, 816, 818, 819, 820, 821, 824, 826, 828, 829, 830.

## MALTA CONVOYS 1941–2

*Ajax*
*Amazon*
*Antelope*
*Arethusa*
*Ark Royal*
*Argus*
*Arrow*
*Avon Vale*
*Ashanti*
*Aurora*
*Badsworth*
*Beaufort*
*Bedouin*
*Beverley*
*Bicester*
*Blankney*
*Bonaventure*
*Boston*
*Bramham*
*Breconshire*
*Cachalot*
*Cairo*
*Calcutta*
*Carlisle*
*Charybdis*
*Cleopatra*
*Clyde*
*Coltsfoot*
*Cossack*
*Dainty*
*Decoy*
*Defence*
*Derwent*
*Diamond*
*Dido*
*Dulverton*
*Duncan*
*Eagle*
*Echo*
*Edinburgh*
*Encounter*
*Eridge*

*Escapade*
*Eskimo*
*Euryalus*
*Farndale*
*Faulknor*
*Fearless*
*Firedrake*
*Fleur de Lys*
*Foresight*
*Forester*
*Fortune*
*Foxhound*
*Furious*
*Fury*
*Gallant*
*Geranium*
*Ghurka*
*Gloucester*
*Gloxinia*
*Greyhound*
*Griffin*
*Hasty*
*Havock*
*Hebe*
*Hereward*
*Hermione*
*Hero*
*Heythrop*
*Hurworth*
*Hyacinth*
*Hythe*
*Icarus*
*Ilex*
*Illustrious*
*Indomitable*
*Inglefield*
*Intrepid*
*Ithuriel*
*Jaguar*
*Janus*
*Jervis*
*Jonquil*
*Juno*
*Kandahar*
*Kelvin*
*Kenya*
*Keppel*
*Kimberley*
*Kingston*
*Kipling*
*Laforey*
*Lance*

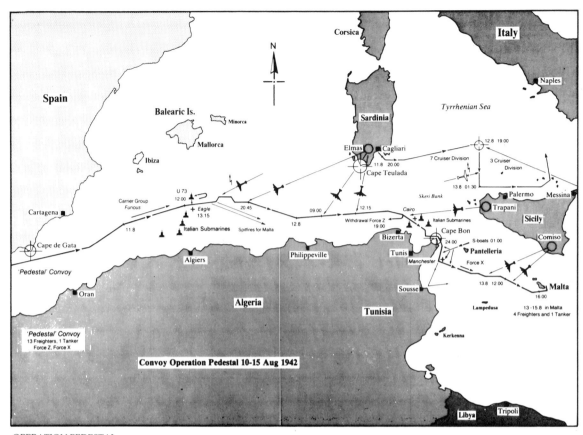

OPERATION PEDESTAL

Ledbury
Legion
Lightning
Lively
Liverpool
Lookout
Malaya
Malcolm
Manchester
Manxman
Maori
Marne
Matchless
Mohawk
Naiad
Nelson
Neptune
Nestor
Nigeria
Nizam
Nubian
Olympus
Onslow
Oribi

Orion
Osiris
Otus
P31
P32
P34
P36
P42
P43
P44
P211
P222
Pandora
Parthian
Partridge
Pathfinder
Penelope
Penn
Peony
Perth
Phoebe
Porpoise
Prince of Wales
Proteus
Quentin

Renown
Rodney
Rorqual
Rye
Salvia
Sheffield
Sikh
Sirius
Somali
Southampton
Southwold
Speedy
Spirea
Talisman
Tartar
Thunderbolt
Triumph
Trusty
Unbeaten
Unique
Upholder
Upright
Urge
Ursula
Utmost
Valiant
Vansittart
Venomous
Victorious
Vidette
Warspite
Welshman
Westcott
Wilton
Wishart
Wolverine
Wrestler
York
Zetland
Zulu
MLs: *121, 134, 135, 168, 459, 462.*
FAA Squadrons: 800, 801, 806, 807, 808, 809, 812, 813, 816, 820, 824, 825, 827, 831, 832, 884, 885.

## ARCTIC 1941–5
Acanthus
Achates
Active
Activity

Airedale
Algonquin
Allington Castle
Alnwick Castle
Alynbank
Amazon
Ambuscade
Angle
Anguilla
Anson
Arab
Argonaut
Argus
Ashanti
Athabaskan
Avenger
Ayrshire
Badsworth
Bahamas
Bamborough Castle
Bazely
Beagle
Bedouin
Belfast
Bellona
Belvoir
Bentinck
Bergamot
Bermuda
Berwick
Beverley
Bickerton
Blackfly
Black Prince
Blankney
Bluebell
Boadicea
Borage
Bramble
Bramham
Brissendon
Britomart
Broke
Bryony
Bulldog
Burdock
Bute
Byron
Caesar
Cambrian
Camellia
Campania

Campanula
Campbell
Cape Argona
Cape Breton
Cape Mariato
Cape Palliser
Caprice
Cassandra
Cavalier
Celia
Charlock
Chaser
Chiltern
Cockatrice
Conn
Cotton
Cowdray
Cumberland
Curaçoa
Cygnet
Daneman
Dasher
Deane
Denbigh Castle
Devonshire
Diadem
Dianella
Dido
Douglas
Dragon
Drury
Duckworth
Duke of York
Duncton
Echo
Eclipse
Edinburgh
Eglantine
Electra
Elm
Escapade
Eskdale
Eskimo
Essington
Farndale
Farnham Castle
Faulknor
Fencer
Fitzroy
Foresight
Forester
Fury

Garland
Glasgow
Gleaner
Goodall
Graph
Grou
Grove
Haida
Halcyon
Hamlet
Hardy
Hazard
Heather
Hebe
Honeysuckle
Hound
Howe
Hugh Walpole
Huron
Hussar
Hyderabad
Hydra
Icarus
Impulsive
Inconstant
Indian Star
Inglefield
Intrepid
Iroquois
Jamaica
Jason
Javelin
Kent
Kenya
Keppel
King George V
King Sol
Kite
La Malouine
Lady Madeleine
Lamerton
Lancaster
Lancaster Castle
Lapwing
Lark
Leamington
Leda
Ledbury
Liverpool
Loch Alvie
Loch Dunvegan
Loch Insh

Loch Shin
London
Lookout
Lord Austin
Lord Middleton
Lotus
Louis
Loyalty
Macbeth
Mackay
Magpie
Mahratta
Majesty
Malcolm
Manchester
Marne
Martin
Matabele
Matane
Matchless
Mermaid
Meteor
Meynell
Middleton
Milne
Monnow
Montrose
Mounsey
Musketeer
Myngs
Nairana
Nene
Newmarket
Newport
Niger
Nigeria
Norfolk
Northern Gem
Northern Pride
Northern Spray
Northern Wave
Notts County
Nubian
Oakley
Obdurate
Obedient
Offa
Onslaught
Onslow
Onyx
Ophelia
Opportune

Orestes
Oribi
Orwell
Outremont
Oxlip
P45
P54
P212
P221
P247
P614
P615
Palomares
Pasley
Paynter
Peacock
Poppy
Port Colborne
Pozarica
Premier
Punjabi
Pytchley
Quadrant
Queen
Queenborough
Raider
Rattlesnake
Ready
Redmill
Renown
Retriever
Rhododendron
Richmond
Rodney
Rupert
St Albans
St Elstan
St John
St Kehan
St Pierre
Saladin
Salamander
Sardonyx
Saumarez
Savage
Saxifrage
Scimitar
Scorpion
Scourge
Scylla
Seadog
Seagull

Sealion
Seanymph
Seawolf
Serapis
Sharpshooter
Sheffield
Shropshire
Shusa
Silja
Sioux
Sirius
Skate
Snowflake
Somali
Somaliland
Speedwell
Speedy
Starling
Starwort
Stella Capella
Stormont
Striker
Strule
Sturgeon
Suffolk
Sulla
Sumba
Sweetbriar
Swift
Tango
Tartar
Taurus
Tavy
Termagant
Tigris
Torbay
Tortola
Tracker
Tribune
Trident
Trinidad
Truculent
Trumpeter
Tuna
Tunsberg Castle
Ulster Queen
Ulysses
Unique
Unruly
Ursula
Venomous
Venus

Verdun
Verulam
Victorious
Vigilant
Vindex
Virago
Vivacious
Viviana
Vizalma
Volage
Volunteer
Walker
Wallflower
Wanderer
Waskesiu
Westwater
Watchman
Wells
Westcott
Wheatland
Whimbrel
Whitehall
Wild Goose
Wilton
Windsor
Woolston
Worcester
Wren
Wrestler
Zambesi
Zealous
Zebra
Zephyr
Zest
Zodiac
FAA Squadrons: 802, 809, 811, 813, 816, 819, 822, 824, 825, 832, 833, 835, 842, 846, 853, 856, 882, 883, 893, 1832.


## KOREA 1950–3

Alacrity
Alert
Amethyst
Anzac
Athabaskan
Bataan
Belfast
Birmingham
Black Swan
Cardigan Bay

Cayuga
Ceylon
Charity
Cockade
Comus
Concord
Condamine
Consort
Constance
Cossack
Crane
Crusader
Culgoa
Glory
Haida
Hart
Hawea
Huron
Iroquois
Jamaica
Kaniere
Kenya
Modeste
Morecambe Bay
Mounts Bay
Murchison
Newcastle
Nootka
Ocean
Opossum
Putaki
St Bride's Bay
Shoalhaven
Sioux
Sparrow
Sydney
Taupo
Telemachus
Theseus
Tobruk
Triumph
Tutira
Tyne
Unicorn
Warramunga
Whitesand Bay
RFAs: *Wave Premier*
*Wave Prince*

Wave Sovereign
Brown Ranger
Green Ranger
Wave Baron
Wave Chief
Wave Knight
Wave Laird
FAA Squadrons: 800, 801, 802,
804, 805, 807, 808, 810, 812,
817, 821, 825, 827, 898

## VIETNAM 1964−75[11]

Brisbane
Hobart
Perth
Vendetta
FAA Squadron: 723

## FALKLAND ISLANDS 1982

Active
Alacrity
Ambuscade
Andromeda
Antelope
Antrim
Ardent
Argonaut
Arrow
Avenger
Brilliant
Bristol
Broadsword
Cardiff
Conqueror
Cordella
Courageous
Coventry
Dumbarton Castle
Endurance
Exeter
Farnella
Fearless
Glamorgan
Glasgow
Hecla
Herald
Hermes
Hydra

---

11  Dates for the Vietnam War are not easy to assign, but in 1964 American aircraft first bombed the North, and 1975 saw the fall of Saigon.

Intrepid
Invincible
Junella
Leeds Castle
Minerva
Northella
Onyx
Penelope
Pict
Plymouth
Sheffield
Spartan
Splendid
Valiant
Yarmouth
RFAs: *Appleleaf*
Bayleaf
Blue Rover
Brambleleaf
Engadine
Fort Austin

Fort Grange
Olmeda
Olna
Pearleaf
Plumleaf
Regent
Resource
Sir Bedivere
Sir Galahad
Sir Geraint
Sir Lancelot
Sir Percivale
Sir Tristram
Stromness
Tidepool
Tidespring
Typhoon
FAA Squadrons: 737, 800, 801, 809, 815, 820, 824, 825, 826, 829, 845, 846, 847, 848, 899.

# B

## SINGLE-SHIP ACTIONS

| Ship | Battle Honour |
|------|---------------|
| *Revenge* | Azores 1591 |
| *Princess* | North Sea 1667 |
| *Mary Rose* | The Seven Algerines 1669 |
| *Adventure* | *Golden Horse* 1681 |
| *Calabash* | *Golden Horse* 1681 |
| *Kingfisher* | Sardinia 1681 |
| *Adventure* | *Two Lions* 1681 |
| *Centurion* | *N.S. de Covadonga* 1743 |
| *Portland* | *Auguste* 1746 |
| *Nottingham* | *Magnanime* 1748 |
| *Portland* | *Magnanime* 1748 |
| *Antelope* | *Aquilon* 1757 |
| *Southampton* | *Émeraude* 1757 |
| *Monmouth* | *Foudroyant* 1758 |
| *Revenge* | *Orphée* 1758 |
| *Dorsetshire* | *Raisonnable* 1758 |
| *Vestal* | *Bellone* 1759 |
| *Unicorn* | *Vestale* 1761 |
| *Thunderer* | *Achille* 1761 |
| *Thetis* | *Bouffone* 1761 |
| *Bellona* | *Courageux* 1761 |
| *Alert* | *Lexington* 1777 |
| *Pearl* | *Santa Monica* 1779 |
| *Serapis* | *Bonhomme Richard* 1779 |
| *Countess of Scarborough* | *Pallas* 1779 |
| *Foudroyant* | *Pégase* 1782 |
| *Nymphe* | *Cléopâtre* 1793 |
| *Crescent* | *Réunion* 1793 |
| *Romney* | *Sibylle* 1794 |
| *Artois* | *Révolutionnaire* 1794 |
| *Blanche* | *Pique* 1795 |
| *Lively* | *Tourterelle* 1795 |
| *Astraea* | *Gloire* 1795 |
| *Thetis* | *Prévoyante* 1795 |
| *Hussar* | *Raison* 1795 |
| *Dido* | *Minerve* 1795 |
| *Lowestoffe* | *Minerve* 1795 |
| *Indefatigable* | *Virginie* 1796 |
| *Santa Margarita* | *Tamise* 1796 |
| *Unicorn* | *Tribune* 1796 |
| *Dryad* | *Proserpine* 1796 |
| *Terpsichore* | *Mahonesa* 1796 |
| *Indefatigable* | *Droits de l'Homme* 1797 |
| *Amazon* | *Droits de l'Homme* 1797 |
| *St Fiorenzo* | *Résistance* 1797 |
| *Nymphe* | *Constance* 1797 |
| *Phoebe* | *Néréide* 1797 |
| *Mars* | *Hercule* 1798 |
| *Lion* | *Santa Dorotea* 1798 |
| *Fisgard* | *Immortalité* 1798 |
| *Sibylle* | *Forte* 1799 |
| *Telegraph* | *Hirondelle* 1799 |
| *Surprise* | *Hermione* 1799 |
| *Peterel* | *Ligurienne* 1800 |
| *Penelope* | *Guillaume Tell* 1800 |
| *Lion* | *Guillaume Tell* 1800 |
| *Foudroyant* | *Guillaume Tell* 1800 |
| *Vincejo* | *Guillaume Tell* 1800 |
| *Dart* | *Désirée* 1800 |
| *Seine* | *Vengeance* 1800 |
| *Phaeton* | *San Josef* 1800 |
| *Phoebe* | *Africaine* 1801 |
| *Speedy* | *Gamo* 1801 |
| *Beaver* | *Athalante* 1804 |
| *Scorpion* | *Athalante* 1804 |
| *Acheron* | Cape Tenez 1805 |
| *Arrow* | Cape Tenez 1805 |

| | | | |
|---|---|---|---|
| St Fiorenzo | Psyche 1805 | Eurotas | Clorinde 1814 |
| Phoenix | Didon 1805 | Hebrus | Étoile 1814 |
| London | Marengo 1806 | Phoebe | Essex 1814 |
| Amazon | Belle Poule 1806 | Cherub | Essex Junior 1814 |
| Comus | Frederickscoarn 1807 | Endymion | President 1814 |
| Sappho | Admiral Jawl 1808 | Columbine | Kua Kam 1849 |
| St Fiorenzo | Piémontaise 1808 | Fury | Kua Kam 1849 |
| Virginie | Gelderland 1808 | Phlegethon | Kua Kam 1849 |
| Seahorse | Bandere Zaffer 1808 | Shannon | Lucknow 1857–8 |
| Comet | Sylphe 1808 | Pearl | Amorha 1858 |
| Centaur | Sevolod 1808 | Carmania | Cap Trafalgar 1914 |
| Implacable | Sevolod 1808 | Sydney | Emden 1914 |
| Amethyst | Thétis 1808 | Mersey | Königsberg 1915 |
| Onyx | Manly 1809 | Severn | Königsberg 1915 |
| Amethyst | Niemen 1809 | Achilles | Leopard 1917 |
| Bonne Citoyenne | Furieuse 1809 | Dundee | Leopard 1917 |
| Diana | Zefier 1809 | Broke | Dover 1917 |
| Scorpion | Oreste 1810 | Swift | Dover 1917 |
| Thistle | Havik 1810 | Glowworm | Admiral Hipper 1940 |
| Sylvia | Echo 1810 | Acasta | Scharnhorst 1940 |
| Victorious | Rivoli 1812 | Ardent | Scharnhorst 1940 |
| Weazel | Mercure 1812 | Jervis Bay | Admiral Scheer 1940 |
| Northumberland | Groix Island 1812 | Sydney | Kormoran 1941 |
| Growler | Groix Island 1812 | Perth | Sunda Strait 1942 |
| Weazel | Boscaline Bay 1813 | Bengal | Hokoku Maru 1942 |
| Shannon | Chesapeake 1813 | X6 | Tirpitz 1943 |
| Pelican | Argus 1813 | X7 | Tirpitz 1943 |
| Royalist | Weser 1813 | XE1 | Takao 1945 |
| Scylla | Weser 1913 | XE3 | Takao 1945 |

# BOAT SERVICE ACTIONS

| Ship | Battle Honour |
|---|---|
| Lively | Mutine 1797 |
| Minerve | Mutine 1797 |
| Amethyst | Cerbère 1800 |
| Impétueux | Cerbère 1800 |
| Viper | Cerbère 1800 |
| Beaulieu | Chevrette 1801 |
| Doris | Chevrette 1801 |
| Robust | Chevrette 1801 |
| Uranie | Chevrette 1801 |
| Ville de Paris | Chevrette 1801 |
| Centaur | Curieux 1804 |
| Galatea | Lynx 1807 |

# C

## FLEET AIR ARM SQUADRONS

Fleet Air Arm Battle Honours which have been promulgated do not not cover events prior to World War II. This is not to say that naval aviators and their squadrons have not been engaged in battle prior to that period: indeed, a naval aircraft sank a U-boat in 1917. It is all to do with nomenclature. The Fleet Air Arm's title was originally the Royal Flying Corps, Naval Wing. It then became the Royal Naval Air Service. In 1918 it lost its identity and became merged into the Royal Air Force. It was not until 1937 that the Fleet Air Arm regained its independence and new title. It is from this date that its battle honours have been awarded.

Until now the accepted source for naval battle honours has been Oliver Warner's *Battle Honours of the Royal Navy*[12] but his account proved wanting in many respects. Consequently I have resorted to the primary source at the Admiralty Library, and the following compilation can be regarded as the definitive listing. In some instances Warner allowed awards which were not substantiated by the Library: these have been deleted.

I am grateful for the assistance of J. D. Brown, of the Ministry of Defence, Historical Branch.

12 Published by George Phillip & Son Ltd, 1956.

**700 Squadron**
River Plate 1939
Norway 1940
Spartivento 1940
Atlantic 1940−1
Matapan 1941
Mediterranean 1942−3
North Africa 1942−3

**701 Squadron**
Norway 1940

**723 Squadron**
Vietnam 1967−71

**737 Squadron**
Falkland Islands 1982

**767 Squadron**
Mediterranean 1940

**800 Squadron**
Norway 1940
Mediterranean 1940−1
Spartivento 1940
*Bismarck* Action 1941
Malta Convoys 1941−2
Diego Suarez 1942
North Africa 1942
Aegean 1943−4
South France 1944
Burma 1944−5
Korea 1950
Falkland Islands 1982

**801 Squadron**
Norway 1940−1
Dunkirk 1940
Malta Convoys 1942
Japan 1945
Korea 1952−3
Falkland Islands 1982

**802 Squadron**
Norway 1940
Atlantic 1941
Arctic 1942
Korea 1952

**803 Squadron**
North Sea 1939
Norway 1940
Libya 1940−1
Matapan 1941
Mediterranean 1941

**804 Squadron**
Norway 1940−4
Atlantic 1941

North Africa 1942
Burma 1945
Korea 1951−2

**805 Squadron**
Crete 1941
Libya 1941−2
Korea 1951−2

**806 Squadron**
Norway 1940
Dunkirk 1940
Mediterranean 1940−1
Libya 1940−1
Matapan 1941
Diego Suarez 1942
Malta Convoys 1942

**807 Squadron**
Atlantic 1940
Malta Convoys 1941−2
North Africa 1942−3
Sicily 1943
Salerno 1943
South France 1944
Agean 1944
Burma 1945
Korea 1950−3

**808 Squadron**
Spartivento 1940
*Bismarck* Action 1941
Malta Convoys 1941
Atlantic 1943
Salerno 1943
Normandy 1944
Burma 1945
Korea 1951−2

**809 Squadron**
Arctic 1941
Malta Convoys 1942
North Africa 1942
Salerno 1943
Aegean 1944
South France 1944
Burma 1945
Falkland Islands 1982

**810 Squadron**
Norway 1940
Mediterranean 1940−1
Spartivento 1940
*Bismarck* Action 1941
Atlantic 1941
Diego Suarez 1942
Salerno 1943
Korea 1950−3

**811 Squadron**
English Channel 1942
North Sea 1942
Atlantic 1943−4
Arctic 1944

**812 Squadron**
North Sea 1940
English Channel 1940−2
Mediterranean 1941
Malta Convoys 1941
Korea 1951−2

**813 Squadron**
Calabria 1940
Mediterranean 1940−1
Taranto 1940
Libya 1940−1
Malta Convoys 1942
Atlantic 1944
Arctic 1944−5

**814 Squadron**
Atlantic 1940

**815 Squadron**
Mediterranean 1940−1
Taranto 1940
Libya 1940−1
Matapan 1941
Burma 1944
Falkland Islands 1982

**816 Squadron**
Norway 1940
Malta Convoys 1941
Mediterranean 1941
Atlantic 1943
Arctic 1944

**817 Squadron**
Norway 1941
North Africa 1942
Biscay 1942
Sicily 1943
Korea 1951−2

**818 Squadron**
Norway 1940
Spartivento 1940
Mediterranean 1940−1
*Bismarck* Action 1941
Atlantic 1941

**819 Squadron**
Libya 1940
Taranto 1940
Mediterranean 1940−1
English Channel 1942

Atlantic 1943−4
Arctic 1944

**820 Squadron**
Norway 1940−4
Spartivento 1940
Mediterranean 1940
*Bismarck* Action 1941
Atlantic 1941
Malta Convoys 1941
North Africa 1942−3
Salerno 1943
Sicily 1943
Palembang 1945
Okinawa 1945
Japan 1945
Falkland Islands 1982

**821 Squadron**
Norway 1940
Libya 1942
Mediterranean 1942−3
Korea 1952−3

**822 Squadron**
North Africa 1942−3
Arctic 1943

**823 Squadron**
Norway 1940

**824 Squadron**
Calabria 1940
Mediterranean 1940
Taranto 1940
Libya 1940−1
Malta Convoys 1942
Arctic 1944
Falkland Islands 1944

**825 Squadron**
Dunkirk 1940
English Channel 1940−2
Norway 1940
*Bismarck* Action 1941
Malta Convoys 1941
Arctic 1942−5
Atlantic 1944
Korea 1952
Falkland Islands 1982

**826 Squadron**
Dunkirk 1940
North Sea 1940−4
Matapan 1941
Mediterranean 1941−3
Libya 1941−2
Falkland Islands 1982

**827 Squadron**
Diego Suarez 1942
Malta Convoys 1942
Norway 1944
Korea 1950

**828 Squadron**
Mediterranean 1941−3
Norway 1944
Japan 1945

**829 Squadron**
Matapan 1941
Mediterranean 1941
Diego Suarez 1942
Norway 1944
Falkland Islands 1982

**830 Squadron**
Mediterranean 1940−2
Norway 1944

**831 Squadron**
Diego Suarez 1942
Malta Convoys 1942
Norway 1944
Sabang 1944

**832 Squadron**
Arctic 1942
Malta Convoys 1942
North Africa 1942

**833 Squadron**
North Africa 1942
Arctic 1944
Atlantic 1944

**834 Squadron**
Atlantic 1942
Salerno 1943

**835 Squadron**
Atlantic 1943−4
Arctic 1944−5

**836 Squadron**
Atlantic 1943−5

**837 Squadron**
Atlantic 1942−3

**838 Squadron**
Atlantic 1943

**840 Squadron**
Atlantic 1943

**841 Squadron**
English Channel 1943
Norway 1944

**842 Squadron**
Norway 1944
Arctic 1944

**845 Squadron**
Falkland Islands 1982

**846 Squadron**
Atlantic 1944
Norway 1944−5
Arctic 1944−5
Falkland Islands 1982

**847 Squadron**
Falkland Islands 1982

**848 Squadron**
Okinawa 1945
Japan 1945
Falkland Islands 1982

**849 Squadron**
Palembang 1945
Okinawa 1945
Japan 1945

**851 Squadron**
Malaya 1945
Burma 1945

**852 Squadron**
Norway 1944

**Squadron 853**
Arctic 1944−5
Norway 1945

**854 Squadron**
Palembang 1945
Okinawa 1945

**856 Squadron**
Norway 1944−5
Arctic 1945

**857 Squadron**
Palembang 1945
Okinawa 1945

**860 Squadron**
Atlantic 1944−5

**878 Squadron**
Salerno 1943

**879 Squadron**
Salerno 1943

**880 Squadron**
Diego Suarez 1942
North Africa 1942

Sicily 1943
Salerno 1943
Norway 1944
Japan 1945

**881 Squadron**
Diego Suarez 1942
Norway 1944
Aegean 1944
South France 1944
Atlantic 1944

**882 Squadron**
Diego Suarez 1942
North Africa 1942
Atlantic 1943–4
South France 1944
Norway 1944–5
Arctic 1945

**883 Squadron**
Arctic 1942
North Africa 1942

**884 Squadron**
Malta Convoys 1942
North Africa 1942

**885 Squadron**
Malta Convoys 1942
North Africa 1942–3
Sicily 1943
Normandy 1944
Okinawa 1945

**886 Squadron**
Salerno 1943
Normandy 1944

**887 Squadron**
Salerno 1943
Norway 1944
Palembang 1845
Okinawa 1945
Japan 1945

**888 Squadron**
North Africa 1942–3
Sicily 1943
Salerno 1943

**891 Squadron**
North Africa 1942

**892 Squadron**
Atlantic 1943

**893 Squadron**
North Africa 1942–3
Sicily 1943
Salerno 1943
Arctic 1943

**894 Squadron**
Salerno 1943
Norway 1944
Palembang 1945
Okinawa 1945

**896 Squadron**
Atlantic 1944
Norway 1944
Burma 1945

**897 Squadron**
Salerno 1943
Normandy 1944

**898 Squadron**
Norway 1944
Atlantic 1944
Korea 1952–3

**899 Squadron**
Sicily 1943
Salerno 1943
South France 1944
Aegean 1944
Falkland Islands 1982

**1700 Squadron**
Burma 1945

**1770 Squadron**
Norway 1944
Palembang 1945
Okinawa 1945

**1771 Squadron**
Norway 1944
Japan 1945

**1772 Squadron**
Japan 1945

**1830 Squadron**
Sabang 1944
Palembang 1945
Okinawa 1945

**1832 Squadron**
Atlantic 1944
Norway 1944
Arctic 1944

**1833 Squadron**
Sabang 1944
Palembang 1945
Okinawa 1945

**1834 Squadron**
Norway 1944
Sabang 1944
Palembang 1945
Okinawa 1945
Japan 1945

**1836 Squadron**
Norway 1944
Sabang 1944
Palembang 1945
Okinawa 1945
Japan 1945

**1837 Squadron**
Sabang 1944

**1838 Squadron**
Sabang 1944

**1839 Squadron**
Palembang 1945
Okinawa 1945

**1840 Squadron**
Norway 1944
Okinawa 1945

**1841 Squadron**
Norway 1944
Okinawa 1945
Japan 1945

**1842 Squadron**
Norway 1944
Okinawa 1945
Japan 1945

**1844 Squadron**
Palembang 1945
Okinawa 1945

**1845 Squadron**
Okinawa 1945

# D

## NAVAL HONOURS WON BY ARMY REGIMENTS

**A Naval Crown superscribes the following awards:**

*The Queen's Royal Regiment*   1st June 1794 (Glorious First of June)

*The Worcestershire Regiment*   1st June 1794 (Glorious First of June)

*The Welch Regiment*   12th April 1782 (The Saintes)
14th February 1797 (St Vincent)

*The Royal Berkshire Regiment*   2nd April 1801 (Copenhagen)

*The Rifle Brigade*   2nd April 1801 (Copenhagen)

# E

## ROYAL MARINES

*The Royal Marines*   Gibraltar (Capture of the Rock 24 July 1704)

The Royal Marines have taken part in every major campaign and fleet action since 1704. This is symbolized by their emblazoned colours bearing 'The Globe surrounded by a Laurel wreath.'

# SECTION 5
# NAVAL CHRONOLOGY
# 1660-1987

# NAVAL CHRONOLOGY

## 1660

**1 Jan:** Samuel Pepys began his *Diary*.
**25 May:** Charles II landed at Dover from Holland: The Restoration.
**29 June:** Pepys appointed Clerk of the Acts.

## 1663

George Byng (later Viscount Torrington) born.

## 1664

**28 Oct:** Charles II sanctioned formation of the Duke of York and Albany's Maritime Regiment of Foot (or King's Regiment) for service afloat: forerunners of the Royal Marines.

## 1665

Second Dutch War began and lasted till 1667.
The Plague in Europe and England.
**20 May:** Admiral Jacob Wassenaer attacked an English convoy off the Dogger Bank and precipitated the Battle of Lowestoft where the Duke of York's fleet defeated Wassenaer's.
**18 Aug:** Navy Yard at Sheerness was established.

## 1666

**1−4 June:** The Four Days' Battle. Duke of Albemarle fought Admiral De Ruyter. Death of Admiral Myngs.
**25 July:** Battle of Orfordness. Prince Rupert and Duke of Albemarle defeated Admiral De Ruyter. Also known as the St James's Day Fight.
**9 Aug:** Captain Sir Robert Holmes's Bonfire in Terschelling Roads.
**2 Sept:** Fire of London started.

## 1667

**June:** Admirals De Ruyter and Van Ghent invaded the Thames and Medway: they burned English ships and captured and towed away to Holland the flagship *Royal Charles*, blockaded London, caused panic and captured Sheerness.
**20 May:** Battle of Nevis.
**2 July:** Dutch landed a force at Felixstowe.
**31 July:** Dutch war ended.
**8 Oct:** British captured Surinam.

## 1669

**31 May:** Pepys closed his *Diary*.

## 1670

**3 Jan:** George Monck, Duke of Albemarle, died.

## 1671

**8 May:** Vice Admiral Sir Edward Spragge fought the Battle of Bugia.

## 1672

Third Dutch War began and lasted till 1674.
**12 March:** Captain Sir Robert Holmes fought Dutch Smyrna fleet off Isle of Wight.
**28 May:** Battle of Solebay. Duke of York fought Admiral De Ruyter. Earl of Sandwich drowned.

## 1673

Dutch agreed to strike colours to English ships in English waters.
**March:** Test Act excluded Roman Catholics from holding public office.

**28 May:** Battle of Schooneveld I fought between Prince Rupert and Admiral De Ruyter.
**4 June:** Schooneveld II was a continuation of the first battle.
**11 Aug:** Battle of the Texel. Prince Rupert and De Ruyter fought the last battle of the Third Dutch War.

## 1675

**10 Aug:** Royal Observatory founded at Greenwich.

## 1676

Commodore Sir John Narborough's squadron destroyed four Algerine men-of-war off Tripoli. Thomas Mathews born.

## 1677

**18 Dec:** Exams for qualifying lieutenants introduced.

## 1679

Pepys resigned secretaryship of the Admiralty and was sent to the Tower.

## 1682

**29 Nov:** Prince Rupert died.

## 1683

**Nov:** Purser officially reimbursed by making 'savings' — by cheating seamen of their rations. Originally Bursar, then Purser, later Pusser and in 1956 Supply Officer.

## 1684

Pepys reappointed Secretary of the Admiralty.
**12 Nov:** Edward Vernon born.

## 1685

**February:** Death of Charles II.

## 1688

William of Orange landed at Torbay.

## 1689

**Feb:** Pepys resigned as Secretary of the Admiralty. Office of Lord High Admiral of England effectively removed from James II by appointing Lords Commissioners.
**1 May:** Admiral Arthur Herbert fought Battle of Bantry Bay.
**29 July:** Relief of Londonderry.

## 1690

**30 June:** Admiral Arthur Herbert fought Battle of Beachy Head.

## 1692

**19 May:** Battle of Barfleur and Battle of La Hogue which followed won glory for Admiral Sir Edward Russell and Vice Admiral Sir George Rooke.

## 1693

**17 June:** Disaster of the Smyrna Convoy and the Battle of Lagos. Vice Admiral Sir George Rooke and Rear Admiral van der Goes fought Admiral Comte de Tourville.

## 1694

**25 Oct:** Royal Hospital Greenwich founded by William and Mary's Royal Charter. The foundation stone was laid 30 June 1696 by Sir Christopher Wren and John Evelyn.

## 1697

**23 April:** George Anson (later first Baron) born.

## 1702

**19 Aug:** Battle of Santa Marta: Vice Admiral John Benbow fought Captain M. Du Casse. Captains Kirby and Ware executed for cowardice.
**12 Oct:** Battle of Vigo Bay: victory for Admiral Sir George Rooke.

## 1703

**26 May:** Samuel Pepys died.
**26 Nov:** Great storm destroyed Eddystone lighthouse, thirteen warships and a total of 1,500 seamen drowned.

## 1704

French assented to striking colours to English ships in English waters.
John Byng (later executed) born.
**24 July:** British capture Gibraltar.
**13 Aug:** Battle of Malaga, near Marbella. Admiral Sir George Rooke fought one of the bloodiest sea battles against Comte de Tourville.

## 1705

**10 Mar:** Relief of besieged Gibraltar by Vice Admiral Sir John Leake following his victory at the Battle of Marbella.
**June:** Royal Hospital Greenwich opened.

## 1706

28 July: Bombardment and storming of Alicante by Vice Admiral Sir John Leake and Earl of Peterborough.
George Pocock born.

## 1707

22 Oct: *Association* and other ships lost on the Scilly Isles: Admiral Sir Clowdisley Shovel killed.

## 1708

11 March: The Cruiser and Convoy Act allocated prize money to captors at the Crown's expense: a great incentive for captains and their crews.
28 May: Commodore Charles Wager fought Battle of Cartagena.

## 1711

19 Aug: Edward Boscawen born.
Marriott Arbuthnot born.

## 1714

Hyde Parker born (d.1782)

## 1718

31 July: Battle of Cape Passero, Sicily. Admiral Sir George Byng defeated Vice Admiral Don Antonio de Gasteneta.
Richard Kempenfelt born.

## 1719

13 Feb: George Brydges Rodney (later 1st Baron) born.
6 Oct: Capitulation of Vigo.

## 1721

Peter Parker born (d.1811)
12 Dec: Alexander Selkirk, master's mate of *Weymouth*, died: he was Defoe's inspiration for Robinson Crusoe.

## 1723

John Byron (Foul Weather Jack) born.
Hugh Palliser born.

## 1724

12 Dec: Samuel Hood (later Viscount Hood) born.

## 1725

24 April: Augustus Keppel (later first Viscount) born. Thomas Graves born.

## 1726

19 Mar: Richard Howe (later first Earl) born.
14 Oct: Charles Middleton (later first Baron Barham) born.
Alexander Hood (later Viscount Bridport) born.

## 1730

Naval manning estimates 10,000.
Royal approval given to *Regulations for Naval Service*, the forerunner of QR and AI.

## 1731

1 July: Adam Duncan (later first Viscount) born.

## 1735

John Jervis (later first Earl St Vincent) born.

## 1739

Vice Admiral Edward Vernon captures Porto Bello with six of the line, result of a quarrel with Walpole.
1 Aug: Vernon first used the signal "Take, sink, burn or destroy'.
Hyde Parker born (d. 1807)

## 1740

1 Aug: First performance of *Rule Britannia!*
21 Aug: Vernon ordered watering of seamen's rum.

## 1742

23 Mar: Victualling yard on Tower Hill was transferred to Deptford by Order in Council. Deptford was responsible for the blending of the Navy's rum.

## 1744

9 Jan: Battle of Toulon ashore.
11 Feb: Battle of Toulon at sea. Fought by Admiral Thomas Mathews: inconclusive. Both Mathews and Lestock subsequently court martialled.
25 Feb: William Cornwallis born.

## 1745

Naval manning estimates 40,000.
16 June: Capture of Louisburg and Cape Breton Island by Commodore P. Warren.
Robert Calder born.

## 1746

7 Jan: George Keith Elphinstone (later 1st Viscount Keith) born.
25 June: Battle of Fort St David near Madras: Commodore Edward Peyton.

## 1747

**3 May:** Battle of Cape Finisterre I: Rear Admiral George Anson defeated the French.
**3 June:** Captains who were not to be employed again when automatically promoted to flag rank became 'Superannuated'. Rear Admirals: nicknamed the Yellow Squadron.
**14 Oct:** Rear Admiral Hawke defeated French squadron and convoy 200 miles off Ushant: Finisterre II.

## 1748

**9 Feb:** John Thomas Duckworth born.
**8 Mar:** Capture of Port Louis, Haiti by Rear Admiral Charles Knowles.
**13 April:** Admiralty order instructing officers to wear uniform clothing.
**26 Sept:** Cuthbert Collingwood (later first Baron Collingwood) born.
**1 Oct:** Battle of Havana: Knowles later court-martialled.

## 1751

Admiral Anson became First Lord of the Admiralty for the next ten years.
John Campbell Orde born.

## 1754

William Bligh born.

## 1755

**April:** Fifty independent companies of Royal Marines were raised and grouped into three Grand Divisions at Chatham, Portsmouth and Plymouth.

## 1756

Seven Years' War began. Calcutta was captured by Vice Admiral Charles Watson.
**20 May:** Admiral the Hon. John Byng fought Battle of Minorca.
**27 June:** Surrender of Minorca.
**28 Dec:** Trial of Byng began: it lasted 29 days.
James Gambier (later first Baron) born.

## 1757

Thomas Foley born.
**11 Mar:** James Saumarez born.
**14 Mar:** Admiral John Byng was executed at midday on his quarter-deck.
**19 April:** Edward Pellew (later Viscount Exmouth) born.
**21 Oct:** Battle of Cap François.

## 1758

Alexander F. Inglis Cochrane born. Israel Pellew born.
**4 April:** Battle of Ile d'Aix: victory for Admiral Sir Edward Hawke.
**29 April:** Battle of Cuddalore I: Vice Admiral Sir George Pocock.
**6 June:** Destruction of shipping at St Malo by Commodore Richard Howe.
**26 July:** Admiral Edward Boscawen captured Louisburg and Cape Breton Island.
**3 Aug:** Battle of Negapatam I: Vice Admiral Sir George Pocock.
**8 Aug:** Commodore Richard Howe destroyed Cherbourg.
**29 Sept:** Horatio Nelson (later first Viscount) born.

## 1759

**23 July:** Keel of *Victory* laid.
**18 Aug:** Admiral Edward Boscawen defeated French at Battle of Lagos Bay II.
**10 Sept:** Battle of Pondicherry: Vice Admiral Sir George Pocock.
**13 Sept:** Capture of Quebec achieved by brilliant navigation of Vice Admiral Sir Charles Saunders.
**20 Nov:** Battle of Quiberon Bay: Admiral Sir Edward Hawke won significant victory over Admiral the Comte de Conflans.

## 1760

The following future admirals were born during this year: Benjamin Hallowell; Thomas Louis; Richard John Strachan; Thomas Troubridge (d. 1807).

## 1762

Britain declared war on Spain.
Home Riggs Popham born.
**19 Jan:** Harrison's fourth chronometer passed First Board of Longitude Test at Jamaica.
**16 Feb:** British capture of Martinique by Rear Admiral Rodney.
**13 Aug:** Capture of Havana by Admiral Sir George Pocock.
**6 Oct:** Capture of Manila by British.
**27 Nov:** Samuel Hood (later Sir Samuel) born.

## 1763

At the Peace of Paris marking the end of the war France ceded to Britain: Canada, Nova Scotia, Cape Breton and all land east of the Mississippi.

## 1764

**13 May:** Harrison's fourth chronometer tested in *Tartar*.
**21 June:** William Sidney Smith born.

## 1765

Thomas Francis Fremantle born.
**7 May:** HMS *Victory* launched.
**19 May:** Gosport victualling yard established.

## 1767

Admiral Hawke appointed First Lord of the Admiralty till 1771.

## 1768

James Cook's first great voyage of discovery, till 1775. Edward Berry born.

## 1769

James Cook explored New Zealand coasts.
Thomas Masterman Hardy born.

## 1770

Spanish troops expelled British sailors from Falkland Islands, but the islands were soon restored to Britain.
**27 April:** Edward Codrington born. Henry Blackwood was also born this year.
**6 May:** James Cook discovered Port Jackson, later to become Sydney.

## 1771

Earl of Sandwich became First Lord of the Admiralty, till 1781.
**12 July:** James Cook (*Endeavour*) returned from first voyage of exploration.

## 1772

James Cook set out on second voyage of exploration, till 1775.
George Cockburn born. He later burnt the White House.

## 1773

**17 Jan:** James Cook made first crossing of the Antarctic Circle.
**22 April:** All captains entitled to half pay.
**11 Oct:** First Battle of Lake Champlain.

## 1774

Francis Beaufort — of the Scale — born.

## 1775

Naval manning estimates 18,000.
American War of Independence 1775–83.
**30 July:** Return of Commander James Cook (*Resolution*) from second great voyage of exploration

in the Pacific.
**14 Dec:** Thomas Cochrane (later tenth Earl of Dundonald) born.

## 1776

James Cook's third great voyage of discovery (*Resolution* and *Discovery*), till 1780.
Philip Bowes Vere Broke born.

## 1777

James Cook discovered Christmas Islands.
John Ross born.

## 1778

War with France.
**27 July;** the drawn Battle of Ushant I. Admiral Augustus Keppel fought Vice Admiral D'Orvilliers. Keppel and Palliser subsequently court-martialled.
**16 Oct:** Capture of Pondicherry after close blockade by Commodore Sir Edward Vernon.
**15 Dec:** Battle of St Lucia. Rear Admiral Samuel Barrington fought Admiral the Comte D'Estaing.
**30 Dec:** Capture of St Lucia.

## 1779

War with Spain.
Siege of Gibraltar: 1779–82.
**14 Feb:** Captain James Cook murdered by natives at Hawaii.
**11 June:** Nelson promoted Post Captain.
**6 July:** Battle of Grenada. Vice Admiral John Byron fought Admiral the Comte D'Estaing.
**July:** Fruit juice ordered as remedy for scurvy.
**23 Sept:** Battle of Flamborough Head: Captain Pearson fought John Paul Jones.
**18 Dec:** Rear Admiral Hyde Parker scored victory at Fort Royal, Martinique.

## 1780

Britain declared war on Holland.
**16 Jan:** Moonlight battle of Cape St Vincent: Admiral Sir George Rodney (*Sandwich*) won excellent victory against Spanish squadron and convoy.
**20 Mar:** Captain William Cornwallis fought French off Monte Christi, Haiti.
**11 May:** Capitulation of Charleston, S. Carolina to Vice Admiral Arbuthnot.
**20 June:** Cornwallis fought second Battle of Monte Christi.
William Hoste born.

## 1781

**3 Feb:** Admiral Sir George Rodney captured St Eustatius, W. Indies.
**16 Mar:** Rear Admiral Arbuthnot beat French Captain Des Touches at Battle of Chesapeake I.
**16 April:** Battle of Porto Praya under Commodore George Johnstone.
**29 April:** Battle of Martinique. Rodney and Samuel Hood fought French Admiral de Grasse.
**5 Aug:** Vice Admiral Hyde Parker fought Rear Admiral J. Zoutman east of Dogger Bank.
**5 September:** Battle of Chesapeake II. Rear Admiral Thomas Graves (*London*) fought French Admiral de Grasse.
**12 Nov:** Capture of Negapatam by Vice Admiral Sir Edward Hughes.
**1 Dec:** William Parker born.
**12 Dec:** Battle of Ushant II. Rear Admiral Richard Kempenfelt defeated the French.

## 1782

**25 Jan:** Rear Admiral Samuel Hood won Battle of St Kitts.
**17 Feb:** Battle of Sadras, first of five battles fought between Vice Admiral Sir Edward Hughes and Commodore Suffren.
**9 April:** Battle of Dominica II, Rear Admiral Samuel Hood under Admiral Rodney.
**12 April:** Battle of Providien, second of the Hughes/Suffren encounters.
**12 April:** Battle of the Saintes, Rodney's great victory over the French off Dominica.
**6 July:** Negapatam II, the third encounter between Hughes and Suffren.
**Aug:** Sinking of the *Royal George* at Spithead. Rear Admiral Kempenfelt drowned.
**3 Sept:** Trincomalee: fourth battle between Hughes and Suffren.
**11 Oct:** Relief of Gibraltar by Lord Howe.

## 1783

Naval manning estimates 110,000.
**20 June:** Cuddalore II, fifth battle between Hughes and Suffren.
Treaty of Versailles ended the war. Britain recognized independence of America and received Dominica, Grenada, St Vincent, St Kitts, Nevis, Montserrat and Gambia.

## 1786

Separate residence for First Lord added to the Admiralty.
Navy Board occupied Somerset House, till 1832.
Charles Napier born.

## 1787

Captain Bligh's voyage to the Pacific, till 1789.
**13 May:** first convoy with convicts sailed from Portsmouth to Botany Bay.

## 1788

**26 January:** Founding of Australia. Marines from First Fleet hoisted flag at Sydney Cove, Port Jackson.

## 1789

**28 April:** Mutiny in the *Bounty*. Bligh began his epic boat voyage.
**14 June:** He arrived at Kupang, Timor, after 3,618-mile voyage in an open boat.

## 1790

Naval manning estimates 20,000.
French navy mutinies at Toulon and Brest.
William Edward Parry born.

## 1791

Captain Bligh began his voyage to the Pacific in *Providence*. It lasted till 1793.
Robert Napier (he developed steam engines) born. He died in 1876.

## 1792

Court martial of the Bligh mutineers.
Merchant navy comprises 10,633 ships and 87,569 men.

## 1793

French Revolutionary War began, and lasted till 1802.
**Aug:** Toulon surrendered to the Mediterranean Fleet under Vice Admiral Lord (Samuel) Hood. Britain captured Tobago.
**11 Sept:** Horatio Nelson met Lady Emma Hamilton.
**18 Dec:** Evacuation of Toulon, the French recapturing the port.

## 1794

**2 Feb:** Mutiny in *Culloden*.
**17 Mar:** Vice Admiral Sir John Jervis's action at Fort Royal, Martinique. On 22 March the whole island was captured.
**1 June:** Admiral Earl Howe won a great victory at The Glorious First of June.
**August:** Nelson in *Agamemnon* helped capture Calvi and Bastia. Corsica surrendered after a 37-day siege. Nelson lost an eye.

## 1795

**March:** Action off Genoa between Vice Admiral William Hotham and Rear Admiral Pierre Martin, whose fleet escaped from Toulon.
**1 May:** Able Seaman Provo Wallis signed on, and died as Admiral of the Fleet 15 February 1892.
**17 June:** Cornwallis's Retreat, or Battle of Belle Isle.
**23 June:** Battle of Ile de Groix under Admiral Lord Bridport.
**13 July:** Battle of Hyères: Admiral William Hotham.
**16 July:** Shutter telegraph started on Admiralty roof capable of sending signal to Portsmouth in 15 minutes.
**12 Aug:** Hydrographer's Department established.
**16 Sept:** Vice Admiral Sir George Keith Elphinstone captured Cape of Good Hope.

## 1796

Spain declared war on Britain.
Admiral Jervis evacuated Corsica and the British fleet left the Mediterranean for its base at Gibraltar.
Rear Admiral Sir Cloberry Christian gained Guadaloupe and St Lucia from France and Demerara from Spain.

## 1797

**14 Feb:** Admiral Sir John Jervis scored a great victory at Cape St Vincent. Nelson gave courageous support.
**22 Feb:** French force landed at Fishguard Bay but surrendered two days later.
Britain gained Trinidad from Spain.
**5 May:** Second mutiny at Spithead. A week later, mutiny at the Nore.
**8 May:** Sailor's Bill passed improving conditions of service.
**30 June:** Parker, Nore Mutiny leader, hanged.
**3 July:** Bombardment of Cadiz.
**25 July:** Nelson lost his right arm during unsuccessful assault on Santa Cruz, Tenerife.
**11 Oct:** Battle of Camperdown, a great victory for Admiral Adam Duncan.

## 1798

**14 May:** Sea fencibles formed by Order in Council.
**28 May:** Lord St Vincent introduced first sick bay in Mediterranean fleet.
**July:** Napoleon Bonaparte evaded Nelson's squadron in the Mediterranean, and his invasion force captured Alexandria.
**1 August:** Battle of the Nile, or Aboukir Bay. Rear Admiral Sir Horatio Nelson won a dramatic victory over the French Vice Admiral Brueys.
**12 Oct:** Battle of Donegal, under Commodore Sir John Warren.
**10 Nov:** Capture of Minorca by Commodore John Duckworth.

## 1799

**20 May:** Siege of Acre raised after brilliant defence by Captain Sir Sidney Smith.
**28 Aug:** Admiral Viscount Duncan received surrender of Dutch fleet at the Texel.
**9 Oct:** *Lutine* wrecked off Holland: bell salved and hung in Lloyds.

## 1800

Merchant navy comprises 12,198 ships and 105,037 men.
**5 Sept:** Capitulation of Malta.

## 1801

**2 April:** Battle of Copenhagen. Nelson's famous victory and blind eye incident.
**6 July:** Battle of Algeciras. Rear Admiral Sir James Saumarez fought Spanish squadron, and on 12 July fought again in the Gut of Gibraltar.
**2 Sept:** Alexandria capitulated to Admiral Lord Keith.

## 1802

War ended with Peace of Amiens, by which Britain kept Ceylon and Trinidad but returned other colonies to France, Spain and the Netherlands.
**29 April;** King George III gave new style of *Royal* Marines in recognition 'for meritorious service'.

## 1803

Napoleonic War began and lasted till 1815.
Joseph Whitworth born. He was an armaments engineer and died 1887.
**16 May:** Britain declared war on France.
**June:** British forces captured St Lucia and Tobago.

## 1804

Napoleon formed a base camp for invasion of England at Boulogne.
**5 May:** Commodore Samuel Hood captured Surinam. He also captured and fortified Diamond Rock.
**5 Dec:** Rank of Sub-Lieutenant established by Order in Council.

## 1805

Robert Fitzroy born.
John Penn born: he developed marine engines and died 1878.
Naval manning estimates 120,000.
Year of Trafalgar: Villeneuve's escape from Toulon, voyage to the West Indies to assemble a fleet.
**22 July:** Vice Admiral Sir Robert Calder fought Villeneuve off Finisterre.

**21 Oct:** Battle of Trafalgar and Nelson's greatest victory, and his death.
**4 Nov:** Captain Sir Richard Strachan's Battle of Cape Ortegal — capturing survivors of the Battle of Trafalgar.

## 1806

Purser, surgeon and chaplain achieved quarterdeck rank.

Britain declared coastline from Elbe to Ems in a state of blockade in retaliation for Napoleon's Continental System. An Order in Council forbade neutrals to trade between ports from which British ships were excluded by the Berlin Decree of 21 November, declaring the British Isles in a state of blockade.
**8 Jan:** Nelson's body taken from Greenwich to Whitehall.
**9 Jan:** Nelson's funeral in St Paul's Cathedral.
**10 Jan:** Cape Town capitulated to Maj.-General Sir David Baird and Commodore Sir Home Riggs-Popham *(Diadem)*.
**1 Feb:** King George III required Naval Academy at Portsmouth to be renamed Royal Naval College.
**6 Feb:** Battle of San Domingo under Vice Admiral Sir John Duckworth.
**27 June:** Commodore Sir Home Riggs-Popham captured Buenos Aires.
**27 Nov:** Rear Admiral Sir Edward Pellew destroyed Dutch squadron at Batavia.

## 1807

3 Feb: British captured Montevideo with a naval brigade.
**19 Feb:** Vice Admiral Sir John Duckworth forced the Dardanelles.
**5 July:** Withdrawal of British ships from the Rio de la Plata.
**2 Sept:** Bombardment of Copenhagen by Admiral James Gambier.
**7 Sept:** Gambier accepted surrender of Danish fleet. British tightened blockade of North German coast. Order in Council (November) and Milan Decree (December) increased pressure on neutrals not to trade with Britain. Smuggling flourished because Europe could not dispense with manufactured goods and produce from the colonies. The Continental System harmed Europe more than it did Britain. Practical extinction of neutral shipping allowed Britain to capture the trade: she benefited, and on the whole the system increased rather than diminished the commercial prosperity of England.[1]

## 1808

**20 Sept:** Order in Council gave Masters status of Lieutenants. Marked change in emphasis in naval policy. Until now the Navy had been employed principally in capturing French, Spanish and Dutch islands and in securing the Mediterranean. This policy of 'filching sugar islands' was exchanged for military intervention on a large scale in Europe. Thus Wellington in his Peninsula campaign came to enjoy support from the Navy such as he never experienced before, right up to 1814.

## 1809

**24 Feb:** Capture of Martinique by Rear Admiral Sir Alexander Cochrane.
**11 April:** Captain Lord Cochrane's fireships attack French squadron at Battle of Basque and Aix Roads under Lord Gambier.
**11 Aug:** Britain sent 40,000 men to attack Antwerp, landing at Walcheren and besieging Flushing. The campaign failed and the troops were evacuated.

## 1810

Naval manning estimates 145,000.
**5 Feb:** Capture of Guadaloupe: Admiral Sir Alex Cochrane.
**17 Feb:** Capture of Amboina, Moluccas.
**3 Dec:** Capture of Ile de France (Mauritius) by British.
**6 Dec:** Ceylon retaken for the third and last time from France.

## 1811

**13 Mar:** Battle of Lissa, Captain William Hoste's frigate action in the Adriatic.
**20 May:** Battle of Tamatave, Madagascar.
**18 Sept:** Reduction of Java by Rear Admiral Robert Stopford.

## 1812

War with America (1812 – 14)
**June:** The Continental System brought to an end. It materially contributed to the overthrow of Napoleon.[2]
Naval War of 1812 included:
**June:** HMS *Shannon* captured *Chesapeake* off Boston.
**Aug:** US frigate *Constitution* took HM frigate *Guerrière*.
**Oct:** US frigate *Wasp* took HM brig *Frolic*. She was subsequently retaken and *Wasp* captured.
**Oct:** US frigate *United States* took HM frigate *Macedonia*.
**Dec:** US frigate *Constitution* took HM frigate *Java*.

---

1 *Revolutionary Europe*, Morse Stephen, p.351.

2 'The most stupendous proof of Napoleon's incapacity as a stateman.' *Modern Europe*, Lodge.

## 1813

**10 Sept:** British Lake Squadron defeated by American Squadron on Lake Erie.

## 1814

Navy List published monthly, then quarterly.
**18 April:** Capture of Genoa.
**28 April:** Napoleon surrendered to Captain Usher of *Undaunted* for passage to Elba.
**11 Sept:** second Battle of Lake Champlain. British defeated in Plattsburgh Bay.
Two Admirals named Hood died in the same year, to add to the confusion of names and ranks. Viscount Bridport (Admiral Alexander Hood) died 12 May. Vice Admiral Sir Samuel Hood died 24 December.

## 1815

Naval manning estimates 90,000.
Naval estimates: £4,992,653.
Congress of Vienna: Great Britain received Malta, Heligoland, the protectorate of the Ionian Isles — and thus the command of the Mediterranean, the mouth of the Elbe and the Adriatic. Her colonial empire was extended by the acquisition of Mauritius, Tobago and St Lucia from France, Trinidad from Spain and Ceylon and the Cape of Good Hope from Holland.
**7 Aug:** Napoleon sailed from Plymouth to St Helena aboard HMS *Northumberland*.

## 1816

Naval estimates: £3,758,220.
**Aug:** Admiral Edward Pellew bombarded Algiers.

## 1817

Naval estimates: £3,758,220.
**12 Oct:** *Trincomalee* launched. Exists still in Portsmouth as the *Foudroyant*.

## 1818

Naval estimates: £4,367,604.
Commander John Ross's expedition left to discover the NW Passage.

## 1819

Naval estimates: £4,483,794.
John Barrow entered the Barrow Strait in North Arctic.

## 1820

Naval estimates: £4,435,650.
Manning estimates 23,000.
Lieutenant Perry's first expedition sailed to the Arctic.

## 1821

Lieutenant Edward Perry's second expedition sailed, and lasted till 1823.
Greek War of Independence till 1829.

## 1822

Establishment of HM Coastguard.

## 1823

31 Dec: Dock was renamed Devonport.

## 1824

Perry's third expedition sailed.
First Burmese War lasting till 1826.
**11 May:** Capture of Rangoon.

## 1825

Rum ration halved.
Naval estimates: £5,983,126.
Manning estimates 29,000.

## 1826

**19 Jan:** Irrawaddy operations: steam vessel employed for first time in military operations.

## 1827

**20 Oct:** Battle of Navarino — last major sea fight of the sailing navy. Vice Admiral Sir Edward Codrington destroyed the Turco-Egyptian fleet.
Invention of the ship's screw.
Duke of Clarence appointed the last Lord High Admiral till Queen Elizabeth II assumed the title.

## 1830

Naval estimates: £5,708,751.
Manning estimates 30,000.
HMS *Excellent*, the gunnery school, was founded.

## 1831

**24 Aug:** Royal Navy Long Service and Good Conduct medal introduced.
**27 Dec:** *Beagle* sailed with Charles Darwin on five-year voyage of exploration and circumnavigation.

## 1832

George Tryon born.

## 1834

Formal abolition of slavery in the British Empire. Efforts of Wilberforce had virtually secured abolition of the slave trade in the Dominions in 1807. It still flourished elsewhere, notably under Spain and Portugal and under the US flag till 1865.

## 1835

Naval estimates: £4,245,723.
Manning estimates 26,500.

## 1836

Naval pay office abolished and incorporated with the Army's into the Paymaster General's Office.

## 1837

Accession of Queen Victoria.
**30 Mar:**  RN College Portsmouth closed.
**19 July:**  Engine-room branch established by Order in Council.

## 1838

Brunel's ss *Great Eastern* crossed the Atlantic.
**8 July:**  RNC re-established at Portsmouth by Order in Council under command of HMS *Execllent* until 1905.

## 1839

Anglo-Chinese Opium War, lasting till 1842.
**19 Jan:**  Capture of Aden.
**3 Feb:**  Capture of Karachi.

## 1840

Naval estimates: £5,824,074.
Manning estimates 39,665.
Screw propeller introduced into the Royal Navy.
Dame Agnes Weston born: she founded seamen's homes. She lived till 1918.
**10 Sept:**  Start of operations against Mehemet Ali, lasting till 10 Dec. Bombardment of Beirut.
**4 Nov:**  Capture of Acre by Admiral Sir Robert Stopford.

## 1841

John Arbuthnot Fisher born (later Lord Fisher of Kilverstone).
  James Ross discovered Antarctic continent in first of three yearly expeditions. He named volcanoes *Erebus* and *Terror* (after the monitors) and claimed Victoria Land for the Crown.
  First Chinese War 1841–2: capture of Chinese forts, Canton river. Hong Kong formally occupied by Commodore Sir James Bremer.
**25 May:**  Capture of forts guarding Canton.
**26 Aug:**  Capture of Amoy, China, by Rear Admiral Sir William Parker.

## 1842

**4 Mar:**  Arthur Knyvet Wilson born.
**15 Mar:**  Defeat of Chinese at heights of Segaon.
**21 July:**  Capture of Chinkiang by Sir William Parker.

## 1843

William James Lloyd Warton born.
**22 June:**  Purchase of *Dwarf,* first screw vessel in the Royal Navy.

## 1844

Word 'port' formally replaced 'larboard'.

## 1845

Naval estimates: £6,936,192.
Manning estimates 40,000.
**May:**  *Rattler* v. *Alecto* duel established superiority of screw over paddle for propulsion.
Sir John Franklin's last expedition sails in *Erebus* and *Terror.*
New Zealand War 1845 – 7.

## 1846

**10 Feb:**  Charles William de la Poor Beresford born.
**12 Sept:**  Sir John Franklin's expedition frozen in.

## 1847

**27 Feb:**  Senior engineers became commissioned officers.
**3 April:**  Terms enforced on Chinese at Canton.
**29 April:**  Canned meat added to ships' victualling stores.
**11 June:**  Sir John Franklin died.
**31 Dec:**  Electric telegraph introduced: made semaphore tower at the Admiralty obsolete.

## 1848

**22 April:**  Captain Crozier, in command after Franklin's death, abandoned ship and began to walk: all perished. *Erebus* and *Terror* abandoned in Arctic ice.
Admiralty commissioned first screw frigates *Dauntless* and *Arrogant.*

## 1849

The *San Josef* (112), captured by Nelson, broken up.
Good-conduct badges and pay reviews proposed by Captain Milne adopted by the Admiralty.

## 1850

Naval estimates: £5,849,423.
Manning estimates 39,000.
Rum ration halved — again.

Don Pacifico affair in Greece. Mediterranean fleet sent to Athens.
**June:** First screw ship of the line launched: a three-decker, 91 guns.

## 1851

The Navy sacked and captured Lagos, West Africa, the heart of the slave-trading traffic.

## 1852

Second Burmese War, till 1853.
Commander Inglefield discovers the Polar Sea.
First screw-propelled warship *Agamemnon* completed for the Admiralty.
**26 Feb:** Loss of troopship *Birkenhead* (ex *Vulcan*) off Point Danger, Simons Bay, South Africa.
**5 April:** Pursers designated Paymasters by Order in Council.
In Burma, Rangoon, Prome and Pegu are captured by naval forces.

## 1853

Naval estimates: £6,235,493.
Percy Moreton Scott born.
Queen reviews the fleet at Spithead.
Naval coast volunteers introduced.
**8 April:** *Malacca* launched at Moulmein, Burma: first warship fitted with HP steam engine at 60 psi.
**22 Oct:** French and British fleets passed Dardanelles, precipitating war between Russia and Turkey.
Naval Volunteer Act allowed recall of pensioners.

## 1854

Crimean War began, and lasted till 1856.
Naval estimates: £7,487,948.
Bombardment of Odessa, Bomarsund and Sevastopol.
Admiral Sir Charles Napier led squadron of fifteen steam-ships — first of its kind — to the Baltic.
**24 May:** Prince Louis of Battenberg born (later first Marquess of Milford Haven).
**21 Oct:** Admiral Sir Thomas Byam died aged eighty-nine. He had been on retired list forty-five years and had never hoisted his flag. First occasion when the senior admiral was not automatically promoted.

## 1855

Naval estimates: £8,646,675.
Manning estimates 70,000.
Queen reviewed Baltic Fleet at Spithead.
W.G. Armstrong produced a new gun to fire shells, not balls.
Capture of Canton and bombardment of Sveaborg.
**30 Jan:** RM designated a Light Corps and became RM Artillery and RM Light Infantry until 1923 – the Blue and Red Marines. Several bombardments of

Sevastopol, and its capture in September. Helsinki bombarded.

## 1856

Naval estimates £12,148,641.
Second Anglo-Chinese War.
First VC awarded to the Navy's Lieutenant Lucas.
**March:** Peace signed in Russia.
**29 Jan:** VC instituted by Royal Warrant, to be worn on a blue ribbon by naval recipients.

## 1857

Naval estimates £10,951,510.
Indian Mutiny.
New-design large frigate *Ariadne* announced.
**30 Jan:** Uniforms introduced for POs, seamen and boys. Three rows of white tape decided upon for seamen's collars.
**17 Nov:** Relief of the Residency, Lucknow, by *Shannon's* naval brigade.

## 1858

Naval estimates £8,821,371.
The Honourable East India Company taken over by the Crown.
**16 Mar:** *Shannon's* naval brigade at the capture of Lucknow.
**May:** Anglo-French squadron under Rear Admiral Sir Michael Seymour captured the Taku Forts. Tientsin also occupied.
**Nov:** Armstrong rifled breech-loading gun adopted.

## 1859

Naval estimates: £12,802,200.
Establishment of RNR by Royal Navy Reserves (Volunteers) Act.
Pei-Ho forts subdued.
*Britannia* became cadet training ship.
Frederick Charles Doveton Sturdee born.
**5 Dec:** John Rushworth Jellicoe (later first Earl) born.

## 1860

Naval estimates: £12,802,200.
Manning estimates 84,100.
Second New Zealand War, lasting till 1864.
French build first plated frigate, the *Gloire*.
**13 July:** Last man to be hanged at the yardarm — Private Dallinger RM — for attempted murder.
Taku forts captured again: Admiral Sir James Hope.

## 1861

Royal Commission recommended Board of Admiralty.
HMS *Warrior*, first all-iron warship, joined the fleet.
**16 April:** Master's Mates restyled Sub-Lieutenants.
Captains' insignia increased to four stripes.

**8 May:** Board of Admiralty accepted Controller's submission that all ships be armoured: effectively the official end of wooden walls.
**6 Aug:** Naval Discipline Act passed. First edition of QR and AI published.

## 1862

These three admirals were born this year: John Michael de Robeck; Hugh Evan-Thomas and Charles Edward Madden.
**21 Mar:** Royal Marines formally divided into two corps, RM (Artillery) and RM (Light Infantry), until 1923.

## 1863

Twin or double screwed vessels introduced into the Navy.
Navy comprises 1,014 ships of all classes, including 85 line-of-battle ships, 69 frigates and 30 screw corvettes.
Mr E.J. Read appointed Chief Constructor of the Navy.
Reginald Hugh Spencer Bacon and John Franklin Parry were born.

## 1864

Formal construction of the Whitehead torpedo: it was to revolutionize naval strategy and tactics.
Royal School of Naval Architecture was established in South Kensington.
Rosslyn Erskine Wemyss (known as 'Rosie' even to King George V) born.
**5 Aug:** The White Ensign was allotted to the RN, the Blue to the RNR and the Red to the MN.

## 1865

Formal end of slavery in the USA.
Naval estimates: £10,392,224.
Manning estimates 69,000.
Henry Francis Oliver (influential Admiral of the Fleet of WWI) born.
**6 Feb:** *Hector* fitted with first armour-piercing steel shot.

## 1866

**27 Jan:** Electric firing cartridges introduced.
**28 Feb:** Grape shot declared obsolete in RN.
**6 Mar:** First ship built as a ram introduced, the *Pallas*.
**Aug:** New Naval Discipline Act passed.

## 1867

Grand naval review at Spithead, thirty years after Queen's accession.

**2 Feb:** Writer rating introduced.
**26 June:** Navigating officers replace Masters in the RN.
**1 Sept:** Launch of *Cerebus*, first ship to dispense with sail, and to have fore-and-aft guns.

## 1868

First armour-clad turret ship, the *Monarch*, launched. Also the first ship to have 12" guns.
47 armoured vessels afloat now, with 598 guns.
**28 Mar:** ERAs established.
**25 April:** Last wooden capital ship, *Repulse*, launched: also the last major ship launched at Woolwich.

## 1869

Opening of the Suez Canal.
Last ship to be built at Deptford, HMS *Druid*.
Satisfactory trial trip of the Reserve Squadron.
**24 June:** Moustaches only banned and beards permitted in RN. Only full sets allowed.

## 1870

Naval estimates: £9,250,530.
Manning estimates 63,000.
Flogging suspended in peacetime.
HMS *Captain* capsized in storm with heavy loss of life.
**10 May:** Reginald Yorke Tyrwhitt born, as was Horace Wood and William Reginald Hall in this same year.
**1 Sept:** Successful first firing of a Whitehead torpedo.

## 1871

**17 Jan:** David Beatty born.
**11 June:** Walter Harvey Cowan born.
**12 July:** HMS *Devastation* launched, a revolutionary new battleship.
**15 Sept:** Herbert William Richmond born.

## 1872

Steam corvette *Challenger* set off on 3½-year expedition.
Murray Frazer Sueter born.
**4 Oct:** Roger John Brownlow Keyes (later first Baron Keyes of Zeebrugge) born.

## 1873

Slave market in Zanzibar abolished.
Shah of Persia attended Spithead Review of the Fleet.
Completion of the last wooden ships — 'Amethyst' class corvettes.
RNC Greenwich established by Order in Council.

**5 Aug:** RN Artillery Volunteers formed.
**17 Sept:** Alfred Ernle Montague Chatfield born.

## 1874

Naval Brigade defeated the Ashantis.

## 1875

Naval estimates: £10,784,644.
Manning estimates 60,000.
Sir George Nares's expedition in the *Alert* and *Discovery* set out.
**19 Jan:** *Nassau* and *Rifleman* capture Fort Mozambique, Mombasa.
**26 Mar:** William Wordsworth Fisher born.
**7 April:** *Alexandra*, first iron-clad to be launched by member of the Royal Family. This was also the first to have the accompaniment of a religious ceremony, and the first to serve as a flagship all her days.
**1 Sept:** *Vanguard* rammed and sunk by *Iron Duke* in Irish Sea – the first capital ship to be lost by collision.
**Nov:** Disraeli bought controlling influence in the Suez Canal.

## 1876

HMS *Inflexible* with 18″ armour and 81-ton guns launched.
**29 Jan:** Admiralty decided to found Engineering College.
**26 April:** *Vernon* established in 1872 as a torpedo school, became an independent command from *Excellent*.

## 1877

First time torpedo used in action when *Shah* and *Amethyst* attacked the Peruvian *Huascar*.
**23 Jan:** Naval Intelligence Department established.
**28 Aug:** Alfred Dudley Pickman Rogers Pound born.

## 1878

Construction of *Devastation*, the most powerful iron-clad ever built. First turret ship to be completed without any masts: 10,886 tons, 38 ton turrets, 8,000 HP.
**13 Feb:** Vice Admiral Phipps Hornby took Mediterranean squadron through the Dardanelles to Constantinople.
Two admirals were born this year: Roger Backhouse and Frederick Charles Dreyer.

## 1879

Even wartime flogging no longer allowed.
Rifled muzzle-loading 38-ton gun in *Thunderer* burst, killing crew and precipitating return to breech-loading.

**7 May:** Lieutenants of 8 years seniority awarded half stripes.

## 1880

Naval estimates: £10,492,935.
Manning estimates 58,000.
Edward Ratcliffe Garth Russell Evans born.

## 1881

First Boer War.
**Feb:** Naval brigade included in defeat at battle of Majuba Hill.
HMS *Inflexible* completed, with 16″ guns MLR.
**1 Mar:** RN medical school opened at Haslar.
Three distinguished admirals were born this year: Alfred Francis Blakeney Carpenter, Charles Morton Forbes and William Milbourne James.

## 1882

Bombardment of Alexandria by Admiral Sir Frederick Seymour.
Battle of Tel-el-Kebir.
**18 Mar:** *Edinburgh* launched: first RN ship to carry breech-loading guns.
**17 July:** James Fownes Somerville born.

## 1883

**7 Jan:** Andrew Browne Cunningham born. Also born this year: Martin Eric Dunbar Nasmith, Bertram Home Ramsay and on 29 Nov Max Horton.
**Mar:** *Agamemnon* and *Ajax* completed: last battleships to be fitted with rifled muzzle-loading guns, and the first to have a specific secondary armament.
**23 Aug:** Royal Corps of Naval Constructors established by Order in Council.

## 1884

African slave trade formally abolished.
Naval brigade fought at battle of Tamaai, Sudan.
**17 Oct:** Sick Berth branch formed by Order in Council.

## 1885

Naval estimates: £13,090,440. Manning estimates 58,334.
Death of Gordon in Khartoum. Conquest of Burma lasting till 1886.
Naval flotilla operations on the Nile.
**7 Mar:** John Cronyn Tovey (later 1st Baron of Langton Matravers).
**1 April:** Naval Nursing Service formed: QARNNS in 1902.
John Henry Dacres Cunningham born.

## 1886

Naval estimates: £13,650,626.
Gordon Campbell born.

## 1887

Golden Jubilee of Queen Victoria. She reviewed the fleet at Spithead. There was a Colonial Conference.
Naval estimates: £13,162,249.

## 1888

Naval estimates: £13,776,572.
**5 Feb:** Bruce Austin Fraser born.
**22 Nov:** Charles Forbes born.

## 1889

Naval estimates: £14,361,810.
Naval Defence Act passed.
Kaiser Wilhelm II made Admiral of the Fleet in the RN by his grandmother, Queen Victoria.
**16 Mar:** *Calliope* survived destructive Samoan hurricane to become drillship of Tyne RNVR 1907, and FO Tyne in WW II.

## 1890

Naval estimates £14,557,856. Manning estimates 68,800.

## 1891

Naval estimates: £15,210,620.
**26 Feb:** Launch of *Royal Sovereign:* first ship to carry all main armament on weather deck and secondary in casemates: first to exceed 12,000 tons and to have steel armour.
**1 May:** Gunnery School at Whale Island commissioned as HMS *Excellent.*

## 1892

Naval estimates: £15,266,811.
**1 April:** RN Artillery Volunteers disbanded.

## 1893

Naval estimates: £15,267,674.
Loss of HMS *Victoria* (Vice Admiral Sir George Tryon) in collision with *Camperdown* (Rear Admiral A.H. Markham) off Tripoli.
**Dec:** *Havoc,* first British destroyer (TBD) commissioned.

## 1894

Naval estimates: £18,371,713.
Philip Vian born.

## 1895

Naval estimates: £19,613,821. Manning estimates 88,850.
HMS *Vernon* shifted to Porchester Creek.

## 1896

Naval estimates: £22,774,318.
**20 Aug:** *Defiance* made first RN wireless transmission.

## 1897

Queen Victoria's Diamond Jubilee. Spithead Review of the Fleet.
Naval estimates: £22,770,473.
**18 Feb:** Benin, Nigeria, captured.

## 1898

Naval estimates: £24,773,822.
Nile flotilla in action at Battle of Omdurman.
**8 April:** Lieutenant David Beatty led rocket party at battle of Atbara, Sudan.

## 1899

Naval estimates: £27,578,039.
Naval brigades engaged in battle of Colenso in December.

## 1900

Naval estimates: £28,553,222. Manning estimates 114,880.
RN started experimenting with oil fuel.
*Powerful's* naval brigade engaged at Ladysmith.
First use of wireless to co-ordinate naval action at Lourenço Marques, Mozambique.
**10 June:** Pekin threated in Boxer Rebellion.
**17 June:** Taku forts captured.
**14 Aug:** Pekin Legation relieved.
Louis Francis Albert Victor Nicholas Mountbatten (later Earl Mountbatten of Burma) born. Charles Lambe also born this year.

## 1901

Death of Queen Victoria.
First British submarine launched to the design of John Holland.
**7 May:** Commissioning of first turbine-driven TBD, *Viper.*

## 1902

Naval estimates: £32,376,717.
Anglo-Japanese Alliance.
**6 Mar:** Queen Alexandra Royal Naval Nursing Service constituted by Order in Council.

## 1903

Naval estimates: £35,836,841.
**30 April:** RNB Chatham commissioned as HMS *Pembroke*.
**22 July:** Opening of RM School of Music.
**4 August:** King Edward VII opened RNC Osborne (closed 1921). RNVR instituted.

## 1904

Naval estimates: £38,327,838.
Admiral Fisher became First Sea Lord.
Russo-Japanese War. Japanese victory at Tshushima.

## 1905

Manning estimates 129,000.

## 1906

HMS *Dreadnought* launched. She made all other ships obsolete. First major ship driven by turbines; she carried 10−12″ guns. She was built in one year and a day.
HMS *Iphigenia* converted to become RN's first minelayer.

## 1907

*Indomitable, Inflexible* and *Invincible* were launched; they were cruiser versions of *Dreadnought*. They made all armoured cruisers obsolete.

## 1908

**16 May:** *D1*, the first British diesel submarine, launched at Barrow.
**25 June:** *Indomitable*, the first battlecruiser, commissioned.

## 1909

**July:** The Navy visited the Thames; large ships anchored off Southend. Other ships visited as far as Tower Bridge.

## 1910

Manning estimates 131,000.
Captain Robert Falcon Scott's expedition to the South Pole in *Discovery*.
**18 Feb:** Bunga-Bunga hoax on *Dreadnought*.
**4 May:** Establishment of the Royal Canadian Navy.

## 1911

Improved super-dreadnought designed, the *Iron Duke*.
HMS *Thunderer*, last warship to be built in London at the Thames Ironworks.

**22 Mar:** RFA Service established by Order in Council.

## 1912

13.5″ guns replace 12″ in 'Orion' class ships.
Prince Louis of Battenberg appointed First Sea Lord.
**10 Jan:** First British aircraft launched from a warship — *Africa* — at anchor: and first British aircraft to take off from a ship at sea, HMS *Hibernia*.
**17 Jan:** Captain Scott reached South Pole.
**30 Mar:** Scott and his party died in the Antarctic.
**14 Mar:** RFC with Naval Wing constituted by Royal Warrant.
**21 Oct:** *Queen Elizabeth* laid down. First oil-fuelled capital ship. First armed with 15″ guns, and the first to exceed 24 knots.

## 1913

**22 Jan:** Battleship for Brazil launched at Vickers Yard, Elswick. Sold to Turkey, but the Admiralty confiscated her into RN service as *Agincourt*: three nationalities in a year! She carried largest number of heavy guns of any warship afloat. Last ship in the RN to carry 12″ guns. Her seven turrets were named after the days of the week.
**21 Aug:** Michael Le Fanu born.

## 1914

Naval estimates: £53,573,261. Manning estimates 151,000. Kiel Canal opened.
Naval Review at Spithead.
Lieutenants of 8 years seniority restyled Lieutenant Commanders.
**1 July:** RNAS formed from RFC Naval Wing.
**2 Aug:** First Lord (Winston Churchill) and First Sea Lord (Prince Louis of Battenberg) mobilize the RN.
**4 Aug:** World War I starts and lasts till 11 November 1918.
**28 Aug:** Battle of Heligoland Bight.
**1 Nov:** Defeat at Coronel of Vice Admiral Sir Christopher Cradock by Vice Admiral Graf von Spee.
**3 Nov:** Coast near Gorleston, Norfolk bombarded.
**5 Nov:** Rear Admiral Troubridge court-martialled.
**8 Dec:** Battle of Falklands: Vice Admiral Sir Doveton Sturdee defeated Vice Admiral Graf von Spee.

## 1915

Engineering officers become part of the military branch, with executive curls on their stripes.
**24 Jan:** Action off the Dogger Bank.
**3 Feb:** Repulse of Turkish attack on Suez Canal.
**19 Feb:** Anglo-French bombardment of outer forts of Dardanelles begins.
**5 Mar:** Bombardment of Smyrna forts.
**14 Mar:** Last survivor of Graf Spee's squadron located and scuttled.
**15 Mar:** ms *Blonde* first merchant ship to be attacked

by German aircraft.

**18 Mar:** Maiden flight of non-rigid naval airship *SS No.1* at Kingsnorth on Medway.

**23 April:** Sub-Lieutenant Rupert Brooke buried on Scyros.

Blockship operation at Ostend and Zeebrugge by Roger Keyes.

**1 May:** Landing at Gallipoli. *Majestic* sank in seven minutes, 27 May.

**6 Aug:** Suvla landings.

**12 Aug:** First enemy ship sunk by torpedo from British seaplane.

**Dec:** Evacuation from Anzac and Suvla beachheads.

## 1916

**8 Jan:** Evacuation of Gallipoli peninsula completed.

**16 Feb:** War Office assumed responsibility from Admiralty for AA defence of UK.

**18 Feb:** Conquest of Cameroons complete.

**1 April:** East coast attacked by German ships. Zeppelin *L15* the first to be brought down by gunfire.

**14 April:** RNAS bomb Constantinople and Adrianople.

**14 April:** German battlecruiser raid on Lowestoft and Yarmouth.

**31 May/1 June:** Battle of Jutland.

**5 June:** HMS *Hampshire* sunk and Lord Kitchener drowned.

Anti-Submarine Division of the Admiralty set up.

## 1917

**16 Jan:** The Zimmermann Telegram — decoded by NID — helped bring USA into the war. 'We propose to begin on 1st February unrestricted submarine warfare' (Berlin to Washington).

**23 Jan:** Harwich Force fought German 6DF off the Schouwen light-vessel.

**1 Feb:** Unrestricted submarine warfare began.

**25 Feb:** German warships raid Margate and Westgate, while in March German destroyers raided the Dover Straits and later Ramsgate and Broadstairs.

April merchant shipping losses peaked at 423 ships of 849,000 tons.

**April:** *Swift* and *Broke* destroyer action.

**14 May:** Post of First Sea Lord and CNS combined.

**5 June:** First experiments with ASDIC at Harwich.

**7 June:** Construction of *Zubian* completed.[3]

**17 Nov:** Light cruiser action off Heligoland Bight.

**28 Nov:** WRNS instituted.

## 1918

**14 Jan:** German raid on Yarmouth and the next month in the Dover Straits on the barrage, while a U-boat shelled Dover.

**7 Mar:** Start of naval operations against Murmansk and Archangel.

**1 April:** Amalgamation of RFC and RNAS as the RAF.

**3 April:** Seven British submarines destroyed at Helsingfors to evade capture.

**5 April:** British and Japanese marines landed at Vladivostok.

**12 April:** Grand Fleet base moved from Scapa to Rosyth.

**10 May:** Blockship operation (HMS *Vindictive*) at Ostend.

**1 Aug:** Allied Expeditionary Force captured Archangel.

**11 Nov:** Armistice Day.

**21 Nov:** German High Seas Fleet surrendered off May Island and arrived at Rosyth on way to Scapa Flow for internment.

## 1919

Jellicoe visited Dominion governments regarding naval defence of the Empire. The Treaty of Versailles officially ended WWI, 1919.

Naval net expenditure: £334,091,000. Average numbers borne 381,311.[4]

**21 June:** German High Seas Fleet scuttled: 11 battleships, 5 battlecruisers, 5 cruisers, 22 destroyers were sunk; 3 cruisers and 18 destroyers were beached.

## 1920

Naval net expenditure: £154,084,000. Average number borne 176,987. First assembly of the new League of Nations.

## 1921

Naval net expenditure: £92,505,000. Average numbers borne 124,009.

**Nov:** Washington Disarmament Conference began and lasted till February 1922. Treaties for limiting naval armaments and for prohibiting submarine attacks on merchant ships received assent of USA, Great Britain, France and Japan.

## 1922

Naval net expenditure: £75,896,000. Average numbers borne 127,180. *Victory* moved into No.2

---

3 Two badly damaged ships were cannibalized: *Zulu* and *Nubian*.

4 Naval estimates and manning estimates are replaced here by new titles with more relevant definition.

Dry Dock, Portsmouth, the oldest dry dock in the world. HM Coastguard reconstituted.

**13 October:** Supply Branch established by Order in Council.

**28 Dec:** *Nelson* and *Rodney* laid down. Only British ships to mount 16″ guns and main armament in triple turrets. Nicknamed The Cherrytrees (because they were cut down by the Washington Naval Treaty).

Mussolini came to power.

## 1923

RMA (blue) and RMLI (Red) amalgamated to form the Royal Marines by Order in Council. Ranks of 'Gunner' and 'Private' become Marine. Eastney Barracks established for Portsmouth Division. Naval net expenditure: £57,492,000. Average numbers borne 107,782.

## 1924

Shipborne element of the RAF recognized as the Fleet Air Arm.

Naval net expenditure: £54,064,000. Average numbers borne 99,107.

## 1925

Naval net expenditure: £55,694,000. Average numbers borne 99,453.

## 1926

Naval net expenditure: £60,005,000. Average numbers borne 100,284. Stalin came to power. Germany joined the League of Nations.

## 1927

Naval net expenditure: £57,143,000. Average numbers borne 100,791.

## 1928

Naval net expenditure: £58,123,000. Average numbers borne 101,916.

**4 April:** Court martial of Captain K.G.B. Dewar of *Royal Oak.*

**26 April:** First Admiralty order for pom-pom guns.

## 1929

Naval net expenditure: £57,139,000. Average numbers borne 100,680.

## 1930

Naval net expenditure: £55,988,000. Average numbers borne 99,300.

**22 Jan:** London Naval Conference on naval armaments opened; concluded 22 April. Great Britain, USA, France, Italy and Japan participated.

## 1931

Naval net expenditure: £52,274,000. Average numbers borne 94,921. Japan occupied Manchuria in defiance of League of Nations.

**12 September:** Mutiny at Invergordon over naval pay cuts.

## 1933

Roosevelt became President. Hitler came into power. Germany and Japan left the League of Nations.

## 1934

Naval net expenditure: £53,444,000. Average numbers borne 89,863.

**20 July:** National Maritime Museum Bill received Royal Assent.

## 1935

Naval net expenditure: £56,616,000. Average numbers borne 91,351.

Anglo-German Naval Agreement. Abyssinian War began, and lasted till 1936.

**23 Jan:** *Hood* collided with *Renown.*

**14 Oct:** Radio Direction Finding (RDF) development at HM Signal School, Portsmouth.

## 1936

Naval net expenditure: £64,888,000. Average numbers borne 94,259.

London Naval Treaty defined the relative strengths of fleets of the Powers, Britain, USA and France. The Spanish Civil War started, and lasted till 1939.

## 1937

Naval net expenditure: £80,976,000. Average numbers borne 99,886.

**27 April:** National Maritime Museum opened by King George V.

Chinese War with Japan began.

## 1938

Naval net expenditure: £78,259,000. Average numbers borne 107,040.

Germany annexed Austria. Munich Crisis and Agreement.

**15 August:** *Sheffield* fitted with first RN radar.

## 1939

Naval net expenditure: £96,396,000. Average numbers borne 118,167.

**15 Mar:** Germany occupied Prague.

**7 April:** Italy annexed Albania.
**12 April:** WRNS formed.
**1 May:** Painted Hall at Greenwich opened as Mess of the RNC.
**1 June:** *Thetis* foundered in Liverpool Bay on acceptance trials.
**1 Sept:** Start of World War II with invasion of Poland by Germany. Lasted till 1945.
**3 Sept:** Britain and France declared war on Germany.
**Sept/Oct:** Dover barrage of 6,000 mines laid.
**14 Oct:** *Royal Oak* sunk in Scapa Flow by *U-47*.
**13 Dec:** Battle of the river Plate. Later *Admiral Graf Spee* was scuttled.

## 1940

**1940−43:** Malta convoys.
**15 Feb:** Germany announced that all British merchant ships would be treated as warships.
**16 Feb:** *Altmark* prisoners released by *Cossack*.
**28 Feb:** Launch of *KGV*: first ship to carry 14" guns since 1915: two have quadruple mountings and are designed to carry aircraft.
Naval net expenditure £99,429,000.
**8 April:** Start of Norwegian campaign. 10 April, First Battle of Narvik. German *Königsberg* sunk by Skuas — first major warship sunk by air in WW II.
**13 April:** Second Battle of Narvik.
**26 May:** Evacuation of BEF from Dunkirk: Operation Dynamo.
**8 June:** *Glorious*, *Acasta* and *Ardent* sunk by *Scharnhorst* and *Gneisenau* off Norway.
**10 June:** Italy entered war against the Allies.
**3 July:** Attack on French ships at Mers-el-Kebir (Oran) by Force H.
**19 July:** Battle of Cape Spada in Mediterranean.
**28 Aug:** First German acoustic mines dropped.
**5 Sept:** USN transfer 50 US destroyers and 10 escorts to RN for lease of bases in West Indies.
**23 Sept:** Abortive attack on Dakar by Vice Admiral John Cunningham.
**11 Nov:** Attack on Italian Fleet at Taranto by Fleet Air Arm.
**27 Nov:** Battle of Spartivento.

## 1941

**January:** Operation Excess convoy to Malta.
**7 Feb:** Western Approaches command shifted from Plymouth to Liverpool.
**9 Feb:** Bombardment of Genoa by Force H.
**March:** Lofoten Island Raid. Convoy HX112 and sinking of *U-99* and *U-100*. *York* sunk by Italian explosive motorboat in Sudo Bay.
**28 Mar:** Battle of Cape Matapan.
**April:** Operation Demon — evacuation from Greece. Captain Mack's DF14 destroyed Italian convoy off Sfax. Bombardment of Tripoli.
**May:** *Hood* sunk by *Bismarck*. Pusuit of *Bismarck*, and her sinking on 27th.
**Sept:** Operation Halberd — Malta convoy.

**13 Nov:** *Ark Royal* torpedoed and sunk in Mediterranean.
**19 Nov:** HMAS *Sydney* v. *Kormoran* off Western Australia.
**Nov:** *Barham* sunk by torpedoes from *U-331* off Sidi Barani.
**Dec:** 242-day siege of Tobruk raised.
**7 Dec:** Japan attacks Shanghai, Hong Kong, Singapore, Malaya and US bases from Philippines to Pearl Harbour in Hawaii.
**10 Dec:** Force Z disaster: *Prince of Wales* and *Repulse* sunk.
**17 Dec:** first Battle of Sirte.
**25 Dec:** Hong Kong capitulated to Japanese forces.

## 1942

**12 Feb:** Channel dash by *Scharnhorst* and *Gneisenau*.
**15 Feb:** Singapore capitulates to Japan.
**Feb 25:** Formation of Royal New Zealand Navy.
**27 Feb:** Battle of the Java Sea.
**28 Feb:** Battle of the Sunda Strait.
**22 March:** second Battle of Sirte.
**28 March:** attack on St Nazaire by Commander R.E.D. Ryder VC.
**9 April:** Attack on Colombo by Japanese aircraft. *Hermes* sunk off Trincomalee.
**15 April:** GC awarded to Malta.
**4−8 May:** Battle of the Coral Sea.
**5 May:** Capture of Diego Suarez, Madagascar.
**21 July:** Operation Substance — Malta convoy.
**August:** Operation Pedestal — Malta convoy.
**9 August:** Battle of Savo Island.
**11 August:** Loss of HMS *Eagle* in Mediterranean, sunk by *U-73* south of Majorca.
**19 August:** Raid on Dieppe, Captain Hughes-Hallett commanding.
**2 Oct:** *Curaçoa* lost in collision with RMS *Queen Mary* in Atlantic.
**8 Nov:** Operation Torch: landings in North Africa.
**31 Dec:** Convoy JW51B and the Battle of the Barents Sea.

## 1943

**12 Mar:** *Bayntum* fitted with early Hedgehog A/S weapon.
**15 Mar:** RN X-craft launched.
**30 April:** Landing of 'The Man Who Never Was' (Major Martin RM) on Spanish coast by HMS *Seraph*.
**22 May:** Doenitz recalled all U-boats from Atlantic.
**11 June:** Surrender of Pantellaria.
**10 July:** Operation Husky — landings in Sicily.
**8 Sept:** Italy surrendered and signed armistice.
**9 Sept:** Salerno landings: Operation Avalanche.
**11 Sept:** Surrendered Italian battle fleet arrived at Malta.
**23 Sept:** Midget submarines attacked *Tirpitz* in Altenfjord.
**26 Dec:** Sinking of the *Scharnhorst* in the Battle of North Cape.

## 1944

**11 Jan:** *Tally Ho* sank Japanese cruiser *Kuma* in Malacca Strait.
**22 Jan:** Anzio landings — Operation Shingle.
**20 Mar:** *Graph* (ex-*U-570*) wrecked on west coast of Islay: salvaged but scrapped 1947.
**3 April:** Operation Tungsten, FAA attack on *Tirpitz* in Altenfjord.
**19 April:** Strike against Sabang by East Indies fleet.
**17 May:** Strike against Sourabaya by East Indies fleet.
**6 June:** Normandy Landings — Operation Neptune.
**9 July:** Captain F.J. Walker CB, DSO*** died: greatest U-boat killer.
**25 July:** Strike against Sabang by East Indies fleet.
**15 Aug:** Allied landings in S. France.
**15 Oct:** Reoccupation of Athens.
**26 Oct:** Accountant Branch restyled Supply and Secretariat Branch — the prefix Paymaster being abolished.
**1 Nov:** RMs assault Walcheren Island.

## 1945

**16 Jan:** *Porpoise* sunk by Japanese aircraft in Malacca Strait: the 76th and last RN submarine sunk in WW II.
**January:** Assaults on islands off Arakan, Burma and air strikes against Palembang by Rear Admiral Sir Philip Vian.
**March:** Operation Iceberg: Task Force 57 (Vice Admiral Sir Bernard Rawlings in *KGV*) of BPF attack on Sakishima Gunto: flew 5,335 sorties.
**9 April:** *Admiral Scheer* sunk by RAF at Kiel.
**Jan to April:** Force 63 (Vice Admiral H.T.C. Walker) bombards Sabang, Padang and Nicobars following assault on Myebon and RM commandos battle of Hill 170.
**2 May:** Operation Dracula, the assault on Rangoon.
**8 May:** VE, Day the end of war in Europe.
**16 May:** Sinking of the *Haguro*.
**15 June:** Air strike at Truk in Carolines.
**29–30 June:** *KGV* last British battleship to use her guns on the enemy in the bombardment of Honshu, Japan.
**6 Aug:** First atomic bomb exploded over Hiroshima.
**9 Aug:** second one exploded over Nagasaki.
**15 August:** Japan surrenders. VJ Day. WWII ended.
**2 September:** Japanese signed surrender aboard USS *Missouri*.
**3 December:** First jet aircraft landed on deck of HMS *Ocean*.

## 1946

**1 July:** First nuclear air-burst explosion over unmanned fleet at Bikini atoll.
**10 Oct:** Formation of Torpedo and Anti-Submarine Branch.
**22 Oct:** The Corfu Incident.

## 1947

HMS *Royal Arthur*, first PO training school, commissioned at Corsham.
**23 April:** *Warspite* ran aground in Prussia Cove, Cornwall, on way to breakers.

## 1948

**17 March:** Brussels Treaty (Belgium, France, Luxembourg, Netherlands, UK) signed; later widened into North Atlantic Alliance.

## 1949

**1 Feb:** WRNS became permanent and integral part of the Naval Service but not subject to the Naval Discipline Act.
**4 April:** North Atlantic Treaty signed and NATO set up.
**30 July:** HMS *Amethyst* ran gauntlet of Chinese Communist guns along Yangstze to rejoin the fleet on 31 July.
**2 Dec:** *Implacable* (ex *Duguay-Trouin*, captured 4 Nov 1805) scuttled off the Owers; she was the oldest warship still afloat.

## 1950

**11 Jan:** HM Sub *Truculent* sunk after collision in Thames Estuary.
**22 Mar:** RM establishment at Chatham closed and replaced by HMS *Serious* training establishment for Supply and Secretarial Branch.
Korean War 1950 – 3.
**20 June:** first engagement of RN ships in Korean waters.
**2 July:** start of United Nations operations in Korea.
**15 Sept:** invasion of Inchon.
**30 Nov:** battle of Chosin Reservoir, Korea.

## 1951

**5 Jan:** Evacuation of Inchon completed. Ships engaged were Gun Fire Support Group comprising cruisers *Kenya* and *Ceylon*, RAN destroyers *Warramunga* and *Bataan*, USS *Rochester* and RNethN *Evertsen*.
Evacuation totalled 68,913 personnel, 1,404 vehicles, 62,144 tons of stores.
**17 April:** HM Sub *Affray* lost in the Channel.
**31 July:** *Vidal* launched: first RN ship designed as a surveying vessel and first with cafeteria messing.
**22 Oct:** Greece and Turkey joined NATO.

## 1952

RNR and RNVR adopted straight stripes with R in the curl.
WRNVR formed.
**12 Jan:** Royal Naval Minewatching Service instituted.

**30 Jan:** First Allied Supreme Commander of NATO appointed.
**21 Feb:** Admiral Sir Arthur Power appointed first NATO C-in-C Channel.

## 1953

**20 Mar:** First time troops lifted into action by naval helicopters: RN Sikorskis in Malaya.
**27 July:** Armistice signed for end of Korean War.

## 1954

Introduction of mirror deck-landing gear for aircraft carriers.

## 1955

**5 May:** West Germany joined NATO.

## 1956

**1 May:** White cap-covers to be worn all year round, not removed 30 Sept.
**31 October:** Suez Campaign: British and French intervened in Israeli-Egyptian war.

## 1957

**10 Mar:** Air Branch of RNVR disbanded after only ten years.
**5 April:** Central Drafting Authority set up at *Centurion*, Haslemere.

## 1958

RN Supply School *Ceres* moved to Chatham.
**1 Sept:** Fishery dispute with Iceland.
**1 Nov:** RNR and RNVR combined to form new RNR.

## 1959

Manning estimates 1959−60: 106,000.
Economies wrought changes throughout the world's navies.
**3 Mar:** HM Dock Yard at Malta privatized.
**7 Sept:** East Indies Station closed.
**28 Nov:** Dock Yard at Hong Kong closed.

## 1960

Manning estimates 1960−1: 102,000.
HMS *Bulwark* commissioned as first Commando Carrier.

**15 June:** First operational Guided Missile ship, *Devonshire*, launched.[5]
**21 October:** First RN nuclear-powered submarine, *Dreadnought*, launched. She was the RN's first true submarine as opposed to submersible.[6]

## 1961

Naval estimates 1961−2: £406,073,400. Manning estimates: 100,000.
More economies: 31 Mar: the closure of the Nore Command, and three months later that of Deptford's Royal Victoria Yard.

## 1962

Naval estimates 1962−3: £422,273,000. Manning estimates: 100,000.
**5 Nov:** RNXS — Royal Naval Auxiliary Service formed from the Mine Watching Service.
**Dec:** Borneo Rebellion. Lasted till 1966. RN and RM units engaged.

## 1963

Naval estimates 1963−4: £439,951,600. Manning estimates: 100,000.
**8 Feb:** First experimental touch-and-go landing by VTO P1127 aboard *Ark Royal* at Portland. Admiral of the Fleet Cunningham of Hyndhope died this year.
**May:** Four Polaris submarines (SSBN) ordered.

## 1964

Naval estimates 1964−5: £487,690,000. Manning estimates: 103,000.
**26 Mar:** Last meeting of the Board of Admiralty.
**31 Mar:** Queen Elizabeth II appointed Lord High Admiral when the Board of Admiralty formally became the Admiralty Board of the new Defence Council.

## 1965

Naval estimates 1965−6: £589,040,000. Manning estimates: 104,000.
**30 Jan:** Sir Winston Churchill's State funeral.

## 1966

Naval estimates 1966−7: £597,129,000. Manning estimates: 103,000.
**25 Feb:** MCD Branch formed (Mine Warfare and Clearance Diver).
**27 Mar:** Beria Patrol formed off Mozambique as a

---

5 International designation DDG.

6 International designation for submarines: nuclear-powered and armed with ballistic missiles = SSBN: the B and N standing for ballistic and nuclear. Nuclear-propelled and armed with conventional torpedoes = SSN. Attack submarine = SSK.

result of Rhodesia's UDI (Unilateral Declaration of Independence). The Patrol lasted nine years.
**15 Sept:** HMS *Resolution*, the Navy's first SSBN, launched.

## 1967

Naval estimates 1967−8: £648,043,500. Manning estimates: 100,000.
**Nov:** Vickers laid the keel of HMS *Sheffield*, the first Type 42 DDG.

## 1968

Naval estimates 1968−9: £668,715,000. Manning estimates: 100,000.
NATO Standing Naval Force Atlantic formed (STANAVFORLANT).
**15 Feb:** *Resolution* fired the first British Polaris missile while submerged 30 miles off Cape Kennedy.
**8 Dec:** Closure of the boys' training establishment *St Vincent* at Gosport.

## 1969

Naval estimates 1969−70: £642,043,600. Manning estimates: 95,500.
Merchant service: 4,020 ships; 21,920,980 tons gross.
**1 July:** C-in-C Plymouth (Admiral Sir John Frewen) became the first C-in-C Naval Home Command: CINCNAVHOME.
**6 Nov:** First Type 21 frigate, *Amazon*, laid down.

## 1970

Naval estimates 1970−1: £659,378,500. Manning estimates: 89,000.
Merchant service: 3,858 ships; 23,843,799 tons gross.
**2 June:** Tactical school opened at Woolwich, HMS *Dryad*.
**10 June:** *Sheffield* launched by HM the Queen.
**30 July:** Last issue of rum.

## 1971

Naval estimates 1971−2: £690,000,000. Manning estimates: 87,000.
Merchant service: 3,822 ships; 25,824,820 tons gross.
Naval pay computerized.
**30 Mar:** First Fleet CPOs appointed by Warrant.

## 1972

Naval estimates 1972−3: £700,000,000.[7] Manning estimates: 83,000.
Merchant service: 3,785 ships; 27,334,695 tons gross.
**18 Jan:** First plastic (GRP: glass-reinforced plastic) warship, the minelayer HMS *Wilton*, launched.

## 1973

Manning estimates: 84,000.
Merchant service: 3,700 ships; 28,624,875 tons gross.
**4 May:** NATO Naval Force Channel inaugurated at Ostend.
**15 May:** Second fishing dispute with Iceland. Lasted till November.

## 1974

Manning estimates: 81,000.
Merchant service: 3,628 ships; 30,159,543 tons gross.
**Dec:** Malta became a republic.

## 1975

Manning estimates: 77,100.
Operations Branch formed.
**April:** Generalissimo Chiang Kai-shek died aged eighty-seven. Saigon fell and the Communists renamed it Ho Chi Minh City.
**May:** USN launched USS *Nimitz*, 95,000-ton nuclear-powered carrier.
**June:** Reopening of Suez Canal after 8 years' closure.
Referendum on Britain staying in the Common Market. Beira patrol withdrawn after nine years.
**Sept:** Permanent British naval presence at Singapore ended after a century and a half.
**Nov:** three frigates sent to Iceland waters for fishery protection service.

## 1976

Manning estimates: 76,200.
Merchant ships: 3,622; 33,157,422 tons gross.
**Mar:** Field Marshal Montgomery died aged eighty-eight.
**April:** Harold Wilson resigned as prime minister. Succeeded by James Callaghan, onetime RNVR officer.
**June:** Britain and Iceland conclude six-month agreement ending the 'Cod War'.

## 1977

Manning estimates: 78,100.
Merchant ships: 3,549: 32,923,308 tons gross.
**Jan:** Jimmy Carter sworn in as President in USA.
*Superb* commissioned: first of new class SSN. Three Type 42 destroyers completed: six more on order. Seven Type 21 frigates completed.
**3 May:** HM the Queen launched the through-deck cruiser *Invincible* at Barrow.
**7 June:** Queen's Silver Jubilee.
**28 June:** Jubilee Review of the Fleet by HM the Queen as Lord High Admiral.

---

7   Hereafter the Naval Estimates are not truly comparable with previous years. See *Statement on the Defence Estimates 1973*, Cmd 5231 and subsequent years, HMSO.

**13 July:** WRNS became subject to Naval Discipline Act.
**30 Oct:** HMS *Dreadnought* (SSN) refused permission to transit through Suez Canal.

## 1978

Manning estimates: 75,400.
Merchant ships: 3,549: 32,923,308 tons gross.
**13 Nov:** First deck landing by a Sea Harrier on *Hermes*.
**21 Dec:** *Ark Royal* paid off. Last fixed-wing aircraft carrier.
Her squadrons of Phantoms and Buccaneers transferred to RAF.

## 1979

Manning estimates: 72,600.
*Illustrious* launched and new *Ark Royal* laid down.
Boeing jet foil purchased. *Broadsword* commissioned, with three more Type 22 building and two more ordered.
**17 Jan:** Shah of Persia went into exile. Ayatollah Khomeini assumed power in Iran.
**19 Feb:** First appointment of WRNS officer as First Lieutenant of RN establishment, *Mercury*.
**29 Mar:** Airey Neave, Shadow Secretary for Northern Ireland, killed by car bomb.
**31 Mar:** RN withdrew from Malta at midnight.
**4 May:** Margaret Thatcher became first British woman prime minister.

## 1980

Manning estimates: 71,900. Naval Air Branch Reserve formed: 80 ex-FAA officers.
Merchant ships: 3,211; 27,951,342 tons gross.
**15 July:** announced replacement of 'Resolution' class SSBN would be four or five submarines armed with Trident I missiles to commission early 1990s.
Later decision taken to acquire Trident D5 missiles each with 13 MIRV warheads.

## 1981

Manning estimates: 74,300.
Merchant ships: 3,181; 27,135,156 tons gross.
**2 June:** *Ark Royal* launched by the Queen Mother at Wallsend.
**17 July:** First 'stretched' Type 22 frigate, HMS *Boxer*, launched. Announced that only two new carriers were to be retained in service.
**October:** SSNs undertake final testing Harpoon (50-mile range) anti-ship missile before entering service in 1982.
**17 Oct:** Commandant General RM, Lieut.-General Sir Stuert Pringle, severely wounded by car bomb attack.

## 1982

Manning estimates: 74,200.
Merchant ships: 2,975; 25,419,427 tons gross.
**March – June:** Falkland Islands War.
**2 April:** Argentine invades Falklands.
**5 April:** *Hermes* and *Invincible* set sail with Task Force under Rear Admiral J.F. Woodward. Lord Carrington resigns as Defence Secretary.
**22 April:** SAS and SBS men land in South Georgia. Argentine submarine *Santa Fe* crippled.
**2 May:** cruiser *General Belgrano* sunk by SSN *Conqueror* with 2 wire Tigerfish torpedoes.
**4 May:** *Sheffield* hit by air-launched Exocet. Sinks six days later.
**21 May:** 3 RM Brigade land at San Carlos. *Ardent* hit, and sinks next day.
**23 May:** *Antelope* lost to bomb damage.
**25 May:** *Coventry* and *Atlantic Conveyor* sunk.
**8 June:** LSLs *Sir Galahad* and *Sir Tristram* sunk. *Plymouth* damaged.
**11 June:** *Glamorgan* hit.
**14 June:** Argentine forces surrender.
**1 July:** Confirmed closure of Chatham Dock Yard

## 1983

Gibraltar Dock Yard to close after 177 years of British control.
Merchant ships: 2,826; 22,505,265 tons gross.

## 1984

Manning estimates: 71,100.
Russians set an endurance record in space with *Salyut-7*: 238 days.
**March:** beginning of year-long miners' strike.
**6 Sept:** China and Britain agreed terms on the future of Hong Kong after 1997, when it will no longer be a British colony.
**12 Oct:** Bomb attempt on British cabinet at Grand Hotel, Brighton.

## 1985

Manning estimates: 66,900.
**30 Apr:** Facsimile of seventeenth-century sailing-ship *Godspeed* sailed from Isle of Dogs on re-creation of 6,000-mile voyage in 1606 to colonize Jamestown, Virginia.
**4 Sept:** Wreck of *Titanic* on seabed off Newfoundland photographed by remote control.
**11 Nov:** Queen Mother attended commissioning ceremony of *Ark Royal* at Portsmouth.

## 1986

Manning estimates: 68,200.
Merchant ships: 2,468: 15,874,062 tons gross.
Westland Helicopter scandal; Defence Secretary of State Michael Heseltine resigned.
US F1-11 aircraft strike against Libyan targets from

UK bases.

**28 Jan:** US space shuttle *Challenger* explodes shortly after take-off from Cape Canaveral.

**31 Mar:** *Discovery* returns to Dundee after fifty-one years alongside in London.

**8 April:** frigate *Coventry*, replacing loss at Falklands, launched in secret to beat a strike by the shipworkers.

**26 April:** Chernobyl nuclear disaster near Kiev.

**May:** Admiral of the Fleet Hill-Norton Committee Report conflicts with Defence Scientific Advisory Committee re short/fat hull and long/thin hull design of warships.

*Upholder*, first non-nuclear submarine launched since

1963: first Trident submarine — *Vanguard* — ordered.

## 1987

Merchant ships: 2,378; 14,343,512 tons gross. It was announced that less than 100 years ago British ship yeards produced 80 per cent of the world's merchant shipping tonnage; by 1947 this figure was 50 per cent. By 1960 it had dropped to 14 per cent, and by 1987 it would probably fall below 2 per cent. By March 1987 the total shipbuilding work-force will be 5,500, compared with 34,000 only ten years ago.